CHARTER POLITICS

CHARTER POLITICS

Rainer Knopff
F.L. Morton

Department of Political Science
University of Calgary

Nelson Canada

© Nelson Canada,
A Division of Thomson Canada Limited, 1992
1120 Birchmount Road
Scarborough, Ontario
M1K 5G4

To show your appreciation for the time and effort that the authors and publisher have invested in this book, please choose **not** to photocopy it. Choose instead to add it to your own personal library. The investment will be well worth it.

Canadian Cataloguing in Publication Data
Knopff, Rainer, 1948–
    Charter politics

Includes bibliographical references and index.
ISBN 0–17–603514–1

1. Canada. Canadian Charter of Rights and
Freedoms. 2. Canada – Constitutional law –
Interpretation and construction. 3. Civil rights –
Canada. I. Morton, F.L. (Frederick Lee), 1949 –
II. Title.

KE4381.5.K56 1992 342.71' 085 C91–095527–1
KF4483.C519K56 1992

Acquisitions Editor Dave Ward
Supervisory Editor Wayne Herrington
Art Director Bruce Bond
Cover Design Tracy Walker
Text Design John Robb

Printed and bound in Canada
  3 4   WC   95 94

CONTENTS

COPYRIGHT ACKNOWLEDGMENTS

John Agresto, *The Supreme Court and Constitutional Democracy.* Ithaca, N.Y.: Cornell University Press, 1984.

Stephen Bindman, "Door opens: Supreme Court lets groups intervene in cases," *Ottawa Citizen,* March 9, 1991.

Robert Bork, *The Tempting of America: The Political Seduction of the Law.* New York: Free Press, 1990.

A. Alan Borovoy, *When Freedoms Collide: The Case for our Civil Liberties.* Toronto: Lester & Orpen Dennys.

Alan C. Cairns, "The Embedded State," in Keith Banting, ed., *State and Society: Canada in Comparative Perspective.* Toronto: University of Toronto Press, 1986.

_____, "The Judicial Committee and Its Critics," *Canadian Journal of Political Science* 4:3 (1971).

Government of Canada, *The Constitution Act, 1982.*

Lord Haldane, "The Work of the Empire of the Judicial Committee of the Privy Council," *Cambridge Law Journal* 1 (1923).

Donald Horowitz, *The Courts and Social Policy.* Washington: The Brookings Institution, 1977.

Gad Horowitz, "Creative Politics, Mosaics and Identity," *Canadian Dimension* 3 (1965).

Rainer Knopff, *Human Rights and Social Technology: The New War on Discrimination.* Ottawa: Carleton University Press, 1989.

Michael Mandel, *The Charter of Rights and the Legalization of Politics in Canada.* Toronto: Wall and Thompson, 1989.

Sir Robert Menzies, *Central Power in the Australian Commonwealth.* London: Cassell, 1967.

Patrick Monahan, *Politics and the Constitution: The Charter, Federalism and the Supreme Court of Canada.* Toronto: Thomson Professional Publishing Canada: Carswell/Richard De Boo Publishers, 1987.

Richard Morgan, *Disabling America: The Rights Industry in Our Time* New York: Basic Books, 1984.

T.C. Pocklington, "Some Drawbacks of the Politics of Constitutional Rights," *Constitutional Forum* 2:2 (1991).

Peter H. Russell, "On Standing Up For Notwithstanding," 30 *Alberta Law Review* (1991).

_____, "The effect of a Charter of Rights on the policy-making role of Canadian courts," *Canadian Public Administration* 25:1 (1982).

Richard Simeon, "Meech Lake and Shifting Conceptions of Canadian Federalism," *Canadian Public Policy* 14: supplement (1988).

Goldwin Smith, *Canada and the Canadian Question.* Toronto: University of Toronto Press, 1971.

Alexis de Tocqueville, *Democracy in America,* ed. J.P. Mayer, trans. George Lawrence. Garden City, N.Y.: Anchor, 1969. Reprinted by permission of HarperCollins.

James W. Tuttleton, "Authority in English Studies," *Academic Questions* 2:4 (1989).

Reg Whitaker, "Democracy and the Canadian Constitution," in Keith Banting and Richard Simeon, eds., *And No One Cheered: Federalism, Democracy and the Constitution Act.* Toronto: Methuen, 1983.

Christopher Wolfe, *The Rise of Modern Judicial Review: From Constitutional Interpretation to Judge-Made Law.* New York: Basic Books, 1986.

Some of the authors' previous work has been adapted for use in this book. We gratefully acknowledge permission to incorporate material from the following publications:

Rainer Knopff, "The Charter of Rights and National Integration," in Roger Gibbins, Keith Archer, and Stan Drabek, eds., *Canadian Political Life: An Alberta Perspective.* Dubuque: Kendall/Hunt, 1990.

_____, "Parliament vs. The Courts: Making Sense of the Bill of Rights Debate," *Legislative Studies* 3:2 (1988).

Rainer Knopff and **F.L. Morton**, "Nation Building and the Charter," in Alan Cairns and Cynthia Williams, eds., *Constitutionalism, Citizenship and Society in Canada.* Toronto: University of Toronto Press, 1985.

F.L. Morton, "The Political Impact of the Charter of Rights, 1982–1989," in M.O. Dickerson et al., eds., *Introductory Readings in Government and Politics,* 3rd ed. Toronto: Nelson Canada, 1991.

_____, "Morgentaler v. The Queen: A Political Analysis," in Ian

Gentles, ed., *A Time to Choose Life: Women, Abortion and Human Rights*. Toronto: Stoddart, 1990.

_____, "The Political Impact of the Canadian Charter of Rights and Freedoms," *Canadian Journal of Political Science* 20:1 (1987).

F.L. Morton and **Rainer Knopff,** "Permanence and Change in a Written Constitution: The 'Living Tree' Doctrine and the Charter of Rights," *Supreme Court Law Review* (2nd) 1 (1990).

PREFACE

This book explores the growing interrelationship between law and politics fostered in contemporary Canada by the Charter of Rights and Freedoms. We are especially concerned to bring to light the political dimensions of legal argument and debate. Jurisprudential controversy about the scope and meaning of the Charter's various provisions—and, indeed, about the proper spirit in which to approach this interpretive task—is itself an increasingly important form of politics in Canada. It is a rather strange kind of politics, however, employing the language and techniques of the courtroom rather than the more familiar methods of the politician on the hustings. To most students of politics (who tend to lack legal training) the controversies animating "Charter politics" will thus appear arcane, technical, and difficult to follow—in short, rather dry and lifeless stuff. Certainly we have never met the beginning student who would rank a Supreme Court Charter decision very high on his or her list of bedtime reading! Appearances can be deceiving, however. We like to think of the off-putting surface of much Charter controversy as a clever disguise thrown up by lawyers and judges to keep a good game to themselves. In fact, plenty of political life and excitement can be found beneath the legalistic surface; we hope to guide the reader into the depths of the inner world.

The road to this inner world is neither straight nor easy. Not only is Charter politics covered by a legalistic veil, but its deeper reaches are rather labyrinthian. There is really no escaping the complexities of its arguments; they must be met and mastered. Thus this is not the kind of introduction that, in the name of greater accessibility, shies away from the inherent subtleties and difficulties of its subject. Our aim is not so much to simplify Charter controversies as to permit the reader, by stages, to enter fully into them. We do so, especially in Part Two (the heart of the book), by gradually unfolding an ongoing dialogue between advocates of modern, activist judicial review and what we dub the "Charter sceptic." Throughout the book, moreover, we have tried to contribute to the literature as well as synthesizing it for pedagogical purposes. Indeed, we will count the book a success if it holds the interest of experienced scholars as they teach it to their students.

We are keenly aware that we have been active contributors to the dialogue we here attempt to introduce. Like just about everyone else writing in this area, we are not just scholarly observers of, but also active participants in, Charter politics. Nevertheless, we have striven mainly to articulate the debates rather than our own side in them. Our own views will be clear enough, and we have not refrained from criticizing arguments we consider weak or contradictory. Still, we hope we have fairly articulated the views of those who disagree with us. They, and our readers generally, must judge.

We gratefully acknowledge the following friends and colleagues for their valuable advice on portions of the manuscript: Janet Ajzenstat, Carl Baar, Ian Brodie, Thomas Flanagan, Roger Gibbins, Meg Kinnear, Leslie Pal, and Peter Russell. Christian Jaekl, Christopher Manfredi, and William Mathie assessed an earlier version of the book for Nelson Canada. Their detailed and comprehensive reports were models of helpful criticism and laid the foundation for major improvements. At Nelson, David Ward kept us on track with just the right blend of gentle prodding and good-humoured patience, and Wayne Herrington expertly guided the copyediting and production process.

Much of the structural logic of the book was worked out while Knopff held a four-month research fellowship at the Australian National University in 1988. That sojourn "down under" is also the source of the occasional Australian comparisons appearing in these pages. Brian Galligan and John Uhr of the A.N.U. gave generously of their time, expertise, and friendship.

Thanks also to Clifford Orwin for inviting Knopff to participate in a 1989 University of Toronto conference commemorating the 150th anniversary of the publication of the second volume of Alexis de Tocqueville's *Democracy in America*. Chapter Nine of this book, which is based on the paper Knopff prepared for the conference—and which benefited from the conference discussion—would not otherwise have been written.

Some of the research reported in this book was funded by the Social Sciences and Humanities Research Council of Canada (grant no. 410-91-1396). Among other things, this grant allowed us to retain the research assistance of Cindy Peters, who collected materials, checked facts, tracked down references, and helped with the index. Her work was invaluable. We are also grateful to Dominique Fournier for completing the index.

The authors' division of labour was as follows: Knopff, who conceived and designed the book, wrote Chapters One, Three through Nine, and Eleven. Morton contributed Chapter Ten, and co-authored Chapters Two, Twelve, and Thirteen.

CHAPTER ONE

Introduction

The title of this book indicates its premise: that the Canadian Charter of Rights and Freedoms is as much a political as a legal document. It is the occasion not just for new kinds of lawsuits, but also for a new form of constitutional politics. Indeed, lawsuits are an integral part of "Charter politics." In "Charterland"[1] law and politics are virtually indistinguishable, with jurisprudential debates about the proper approach to legal interpretation becoming politically charged, and political controversies being cast in the technicalities and abstractions of legalese.

Canadians have always enjoyed (or suffered) legalized politics, of course. Canada had a written constitution long before the Charter's advent, and constitutional law, as the most political of laws, always generates the most legalized politics. Still, the degree and scope of legalized politics occasioned by the Charter far surpasses what we had become accustomed to under the constitutional law of federalism. In a myriad of ways, the Charter of Rights and Freedoms has truly transformed the Canadian political landscape since its enactment in 1982.

This introduction to Charter politics is divided into three parts. Part One, consisting of two chapters, provides the necessary background information and context for the more substantive analysis in Parts Two and Three; it sets the stage as it were. Thus Chapter Two provides both a brief account of how the Charter came to be and an overview of its impact on public affairs since its enactment. The process of Charter-making was the first chapter in the story of Charter politics and set some of its enduring themes. The post-1982 story strikingly reveals the extent to which the Charter has become enmeshed in virtually all aspects of our public life. Taken together, the two sections of Chapter Two provide a schematic tour through Charterland from its imaginative conception to the present.

One cannot go very far in the study of Charter politics without understanding the legal rhetoric that constitutes its form. Charter politicians speak a technical language of legal categories, involving the elaboration of a complex structure of legal formulae. These formulae are then used to convey and resolve real-life conflicts. The legal rhetoric of Charter politics grows out of the attempt to specify the practical meaning of the Charter's various provisions. This interpretive enterprise has two main components.

First, interpreters (whether or not they wear judicial robes) must give concrete meaning to the often general and ambiguous language of Charter provisions. They must ask whether the Charter covers or protects the kind of interest or activity at issue. Does its guarantee of freedom of expression, for instance, extend to obscene publications, or does freedom of religion encompass killing deer for use in religious ceremonies?[2] Second, if a law constrains a protected interest or activity, thus infringing a right, interpreters must ask whether it is nevertheless saved by section 1 of the Charter, which permits "such reasonable limits" on protected rights "as can be demonstrably justified in a free and democratic society." Section 1 saves only reasonable limits that are "prescribed by law," however, so this second stage of analysis does not occur when the Charter is used to challenge the discretionary authority of administrative or executive officials. When the officials are law enforcement authorities who act unconstitutionally in acquiring evidence for legal proceedings, a different second question must be asked: Should the tainted evidence be excluded from the proceedings? Section 24(2) of the Charter requires such evidence to be excluded if, "having regard to all the circumstances," its admission "would bring the administration of justice into disrepute." An examination of section 1 and the exclusionary rule in relation to the Charter's substantive rights embraces many of the issues lying at the heart of Charter rhetoric and provides a good introduction to the interpretive structure of the Charter. In undertaking this examination, Chapter Three illustrates the degree of choice or discretion involved at virtually every point in the interpretive enterprise. It is this judicial discretion that makes constitutional interpretation as much a political as a legal phenomenon. Power is the ability to make publicly influential choices, and politics gravitates to the arenas where such choices are made. The Charter has substantially enhanced the status of the courtroom as a political arena.

Having thus "introduced" the Charter, we proceed in Part Two (Chapters Four through Nine) to disentangle the various "dimensions of Charter politics." One of these concerns the Charter's contribution to Canada's symbolic politics. A country's constitution is an important depository of political symbols, and the Charter has shifted the balance of Canada's symbolic resources, consolidating the identities and enhancing the status of certain political interests at the expense of others. Whereas the pre-1982 constitution focused on governments and their interrelations, giving constitutional pride of place to the politics of regionalism and intergovernmental relations, the Charter gives individuals and certain groups—most prominently women, natives, racial and ethnic groups, and official-language minorities—a direct stake in the regime's symbolic order quite independent of their membership in the geographic communities of Canadian federalism. The Charter, in short, emphasizes either what all Canadians have in common as individuals, or group identities and interests that transcend provincial boundaries. In both respects, it promotes a national sense of community (or communities) at the expense of provincial identities—as, indeed, its founders intended.[3] The resulting tension between what Alan Cairns has called the "governments' constitution" of federalism and the new, Charter-based "citizens' constitution" has become a fertile source of constitutional politics, as shown most dramatically by the controversy over the Meech Lake Accord between 1987 and 1990.[4] Meech Lake was an attempt by government-led provincial communities to regain some of the constitutional status they had lost to the Charter. In the words of Richard Simeon, Meech Lake "represent[ed] something of a provincialist revenge against the nationalizing thrust of [the Charter]."[5] The politics of symbolic status transcends the tension between the governments' and citizens' constitution, however, and is evident in more than the politics of formal constitutional amendment; it is also a distinctive feature of the day-to-day Charter politics conducted in the courtroom. Treating the Charter as a source of, and arena for, this symbolic politics of status, Chapter Four summarizes and builds upon the work of such Canadian political scientists as Cairns and Simeon, whose imaginative insights are drawn from contemporary neo-institutionalist approaches to the study of politics. This neo-institutionalism escapes narrow legal debates to set the Charter in the wider context of Canadian constitutional politics.

In addition to altering the symbolic framework of Canadian public life, the Charter has changed the institutional structure in and through which politics is conducted. In conferring important new political powers on judges, it has made the courtroom a more pervasive and visible arena of politics and imposed the form of legal disputation on more of our public life. By the same token, it has focused attention on the judges themselves as political actors. The Charter has, in brief, "legalized politics" and opened the way to a "politicization of the judiciary."[6]

Certainly this lesson has not been lost on Canadian interest groups, many of whom have diverted some of their lobbying energies from governments to the courts, trying to gain in court what they have been unable to win in the arena of representative democracy. To persuade judges that their policy preferences are required by the constitution, such groups involve themselves in relevant cases, either by providing their favoured litigant with funds and a lawyer, or by requesting intervener status. Perhaps the best example of such interest-group activity is the Legal Education and Action Fund (LEAF), a feminist organization that systematically uses Charter litigation to promote feminist policy objectives.

The extent to which the hopes of such interest groups are fulfilled—i.e., the extent to which the Charter proves to be a useful lever for new policy departures—depends decisively on how the country's judges (especially Supreme Court judges) approach their task. A judiciary inclined to give the benefit of the doubt to other policy-makers, presuming constitutionality whenever possible, will affect the polity quite differently from one that approaches the deeds of the other branches of government in a suspicious frame of mind, ready to detect and remedy constitutional imperfections. Judicial "self-restraint," as the former posture is known, limits judicial influence on public policy, and discourages political interests from pursuing their agendas in court. The latter, "activist" posture, by contrast, enhances the policy influence of judges and attracts interest groups to the courtroom door. Thus far the courts have adopted a significantly more activist approach to the Charter than they did to the quasi-constitutional Canadian Bill of Rights (a statutory instrument protecting rights against infringement by the federal government). For example, although the Bill of Rights did not keep Dr. Henry Morgentaler out of jail in 1975 for committing illegal abortions,[7] in 1988 he managed to have Canada's abortion law struck down for infringing the Charter.[8]

The clashing perspectives of judicial activism and restraint are closely related to two conflicting jurisprudential orientations known as interpretivism and noninterpretivism. Interpretivism holds that judges should be guided in their reading of otherwise ambiguous constitutional language by either the original intent of its framers or well-established traditional meanings. Noninterpretivism, as the name suggests, takes the opposite view. Noninterpretivists insist that constitutions must grow and develop to accommodate a changing society, and that this growth should be impeded by neither original intent (which they think can rarely be unambiguously specified in any case) nor tradition narrowly defined. To allow the past to weigh down the present, they often argue, is illegitimately to permit dead generations to rule living ones.

The Supreme Court of Canada's restrained approach to the 1960 Bill of Rights was based on a distinctly interpretivist view of appropriate judicial reasoning. For example, the Court decided that the federal Lord's Day Act, a Sunday-closing statute, did not violate the Bill. From the Bill's declaration that its enumerated rights and freedoms "have existed and shall continue to exist" in Canada, the Court concluded that it protected only rights and freedoms as they were understood up to the Bill's enactment. Since the pre-existing religious freedom had co-existed with the Lord's Day Act, it followed that the two were compatible.[9] Not surprisingly civil libertarians tended to deride this "frozen-concepts" reading of the Bill of Rights and urge the adoption of a more flexible "living-tree" (i.e., noninterpretivist) approach.

Clearly the debate between interpretivism and noninterpretivism, however technical and legalistic it may at first appear, is of immense political significance. It affects the extent to which the courts can be used to achieve new policy departures—after all, a court limited to enforcing original or traditional understandings may impede novel policies but is unlikely to generate them—and is thus intensely interesting to political partisans who expect either to gain or lose from judicial policy-making. So heated has the partisan division between restrained interpretivists and noninterpretivist activists become in the United States that it has led to a very colourful (many would say unsavoury) politicization of judicial appointments. The most prominent recent example is the highly charged battle over President Reagan's nomination of Robert Bork, a leading exponent of interpretivism, to the Supreme Court in 1987. In the event, an overtly political campaign by Bork's noninterpretivist opponents succeeded in preventing his confirmation by the U.S. Senate. We have not reached this point in Canada, and there are reasons for believing that our appointment process is unlikely to become so sharply politicized. Nevertheless, we certainly have our own version of the controversy. This "politics of interpretation" is the subject of Chapter Five.

Activist jurisprudence is controversial insofar as it involves appointed judges overriding the policy decisions of elected representatives. Those who defend judicial review under the Charter insist that it is a necessary adjunct of the protection of fundamental rights. The majoritarianism of democracy, they argue, is not the only principle worthy of respect. Rather, majority rule should often give way to individual and minority rights. Too important to be left to democratic political processes, rights are understood as "trumps" that can override those processes. As such, their protection must be entrusted to an institution insulated from the majoritarian whims and passions that need to be trumped. That institution is the judiciary. In enforcing constitutional rights, moreover, judges are simply enforcing the fundamental law, not imposing their own policy choices. Judicial review, in short, respects the traditional separation of powers between the judiciary and the more democratically accountable branches of government.

Charter sceptics, on the other hand, insist that judicial review is rarely, if ever, a matter of enforcing law-like rights against majority will. What judges typically enforce is *their* reading of ambiguously worded provisions. Charter provisions, in this view, are generally open to alternative interpretations, one of which would almost always preserve the democratically adopted policy. When such policies are trumped in the name of the Charter, they are trumped not by the Charter, but by judges, and the result is the vindication not of rights, but of sore losers in the democratic process. The only law involved is the law judges *make.* Sceptics, in short, often claim that Charter jurisprudence embroils judges in formulating rather than implementing fundamental legal policy. This is considered illegitimate in part because it facilitates (nay forces) judicial trespass on the political domain, thus infringing the appropriate separation of powers between the two realms.

Clearly both defenders and critics of the Charter appeal to separation-of-powers theory as a criterion of judgment. Participants in this aspect of the debate share the assumption that judges should stick to the law and avoid politics. They differ only about which kind of activity Charter jurisprudence usually entails. Chapter Six explores this separation-of-powers dimension of Charter politics.

Chapter Seven reviews a related debate. According to some observers (known as "legal realists") the very distinction between law and politics is untenable and it is thus foolish to expect judges to stay out of politics. Legal interpretation, they argue, is inherently and inescapably political; simply put, one cannot interpret law without at the same time making it. Legal realism need not mean, however, that there is no appropriate separation of powers between the judiciary and the other branches of government, though it does exclude basing this separation on a law–politics distinction. According to an alternative view of the separation of powers, the peculiar preserve of the judiciary is to adjudicate concrete disputes between individuals or between individuals and the state. If judges make law through the interpretation of ambiguous legal language, they do so only because they must often interpret the law in order to settle the disputes before them. If someone charged with driving without a seat-belt alleges that mandatory seat-belt laws infringe the section 7 right "to life, liberty and security of the person and the right not to be deprived thereof except in accordance with the principles of fundamental justice," the judge has no choice but to decide the merits of that claim. The plain wording of section 7 provides no immediate answer, and any answer given by the judge will thus make new law in an important sense. Judicial policy-making will be particularly evident if the judge upholds the claim and refuses to apply the law. But if judicial lawmaking is an unavoidable corollary of adjudication, why should its impact not be confined to the immediate adjudicative context? In our example, the judge who finds the seat-belt law unconstitutional should certainly free the accused, but why should other policy-makers accept this finding as gospel for their own purposes? For example, why should prosecutors not continue to charge offenders in other courts and before other judges, at least until the highest relevant appeal court has imposed a uniform decision binding on all trial judges? This proposal sounds heretical to modern ears, but it has a respectable lineage. It was the view, for example, of Abraham Lincoln, who insisted that while judicial decisions bound the litigants in the immediate case, the constitutional reasoning used to reach those decisions was not binding more generally in the realms of other policy-makers. For Lincoln, the separation of powers was violated not by judicial lawmaking, but by the extension of this lawmaking beyond the adjudicative context. We find such views strange today only because we have increasingly come to understand the judiciary as the only legitimate oracle of the constitution. Other public officials, we tend to think, play a subordinate role at best in the authoritative interpretation of constitutional law, and must always defer to the oracular pronouncements of even the most minor judge, at least until some higher judge rules otherwise. Although the oracular view is rapidly becoming the dominant view, Chapter Seven shows that echoes of the narrower adjudicative perspective persist and continue to affect Charter politics.

Concluding that the Charter draws the courts out of the judicial into the political domain need not lead one to reject its legitimacy. Politicians with robes on can be defended as part of a system of explicitly *political* checks and balances, pitting different kinds of policy-makers against each other in a kind of moderating institutional tug of war. Whether activist judicial policy-making is a desirable addition to such a system of checks and balances depends in part on whether one thinks the existing system needs improvement. If one concludes that it does, one must also ask whether judicial review constitutes the best available improvement, or whether reform of the legislative process (through, for example, a more effective bicameralism or a relaxing of party discipline) might prove a better alternative. The answer to this question depends in turn on how one assesses the relative strengths and weaknesses of the courts as policy-making institutions. The *legitimacy* of the judiciary's more activist involvement in the policy-making process, in short, depends on its *capacity* to do the job. These questions, the subject of Chapter Eight, form an important part of Charter politics.

In Chapter Nine we turn from institutional questions bearing on the legitimacy of judicial review to more partisan-political or ideological questions. Whether one likes the Charter will depend in part on whether one thinks judicial power is likely to further one's political agenda. Certainly partisans of both the left and right have asked whether judicial power is more apt to be progressive or conservative and have come to varying conclusions about the desirability and legitimacy of judicial review depending on their answers. Chapter Nine explores the conflicting answers to this question.

It is all well and good to carve Charter politics up into its various "dimensions"—indeed, it is necessary in order to become fully aware of all that is at stake in concrete Charter controversies—but there is in the end no substitute for studying particular episodes of Charter politics as a whole. We intend Parts One and Two of this book to equip students with the information and analytical perspectives required to undertake their own assessments of the politics of Charterland, but we would be remiss if we did not illustrate such "holistic" analysis through some case studies of our own. This is the main purpose of Part Three. In Chapters Ten through Twelve we attempt to convey a more complete picture of Charter politics as it actually presents itself, through the detailed study of three issues that have been, or are being, litigated before the courts. Taken together, we believe these case studies illustrate most of the important dimensions of Charter politics.

Many issues could have been selected for treatment in Part Three, and we freely confess to choosing those that have most closely occupied our recent attention both as students of and participants in Charter politics. Thus Chapter Ten looks at the abortion litigation in the *Morgentaler, Borowski,* and *Daigle* cases, a subject that has been one of Morton's scholarly preoccupations for several years.

The next two chapters study litigation for which both authors were employed to develop expert evidence and testimony. Chapter Eleven studies an issue raised under the Charter's section 3 right to vote: Does legislation preventing prisoners from voting infringe this right, and if so is the legislation nevertheless a "reasonable limit" on that right under section 1? When a prisoner challenged Manitoba's disqualification in 1986, Morton was hired by the provincial government to assist in the development of evidence. Since then, Knopff has made written submissions and/or given oral testimony in several cases challenging the federal disqualification.

Section 3 also figures in Chapter Twelve, which examines challenges to the geographical apportionment of legislative constituencies in several Canadian jurisdictions on the grounds that existing constituencies vary too much in population size to sufficiently approximate the principle of "equal voting power" (or "one person, one vote"), which the claimants believe is entailed in the right to vote. One of the jurisdictions whose legislation has been challenged is Alberta, whose government hired both authors to pre-pare relevant evidence.

We hope that the intimate knowledge afforded by participation in the reapportionment and prisoners'-voting-rights cases improves our case stud-ies of these issues, though readers should also be on guard against possi-ble bias. We certainly have strong views on these issues, as we do on vir-tually every issue discussed in this book. Though we do not try to hide our views, we have tried to be fair to all sides of the debates we analyze.

The book ends with a short discussion—a "note" rather than a full-blown chapter—taking up the claim that the Charter is likely to exercise a centralizing influence on Canadian politics. As Chapters Two and Four make plain, the expectation that the Charter would exert such an influence was common ground among both its proponents and opponents during the period of Charter-making. What can we say about the accuracy of this claim after several years of Charter jurisprudence? Not a case study of a single litigated issue like Chapters Ten through Twelve, this note explores a persistent theme of Charter politics that cuts across many substantive Charter issues. It addresses one of the first and most enduring questions raised about the Charter, a question no introduction to Charter politics can afford to ignore. Using the conceptual tools developed in Part Two, this final note refines our understanding of the potential contribution of judicial review to national integration, and assesses the available evidence bearing on its actual effect in this regard.

PART ONE

Introducing the Charter

CHAPTER TWO

The Development and Impact of the Charter

■ THE ROAD TO THE CHARTER

A constitutional charter of rights had always been high on the agenda of the government of Pierre Elliott Trudeau.[1] Indeed, Trudeau began to argue explicitly in favour of the constitutional entrenchment of rights while he was justice minister in the government of Lester Pearson.[2] Trudeau's own government made several attempts to achieve a constitutional charter of rights in the 1970s, but without success. It came closest in 1971 at the first ministers' meeting on the constitution held in Victoria. Among other things, the so-called "Victoria Charter" would have incorporated three categories of rights into the constitution.[3] First, both levels of government would have been forbidden to infringe "freedom of thought, conscience and religion; freedom of opinion and expression; and freedom of peaceful assembly and association," roughly the "Fundamental Freedoms" covered by section 2 of the 1982 Charter. Second, the Victoria Charter guaranteed universal suffrage and free elections; gave citizens the right to vote or stand for office without discrimination because of "national origin, colour, religion or sex"; imposed a five-year limit on the life of Parliament and the legislatures, except when two-thirds of an assembly's members agreed to extend that limit in an emergency; and required annual legislative sessions. A similar set of "Democratic Rights" is found in sections 3 to 5 of the current Charter of Rights. Third, the Victoria document guaranteed the right to use and receive services in both English and French in several areas of public life. All of these language rights applied at the federal level; at the provincial level some were of general application, while others applied only to specified provinces. Language rights, of course, had always been a preoccupation of Trudeau, and they occupy a pre-eminent place in the 1982 Charter.

The Victoria Charter seemed close to securing the agreement of all eleven first ministers. However, Quebec's premier, Robert Bourassa, was unwilling to commit his government at the conference. To accommodate him, the premiers agreed that each government would have eleven days in which to make a final decision. In response to vigorous opposition mounted by Quebec nationalists, Bourassa backed away from the Charter well before the eleven-day waiting period expired, and this attempt at constitutional amendment was thus abandoned.[4]

The Trudeau government's next major attempt at constitutional reform came in 1978, when it introduced proposals setting out a three-year agenda of constitutional change encompassing, most prominently, Senate reform; changes to the constitutional status of the Supreme Court, and to the manner of appointing its judges; and a charter of rights and freedoms. In addition to the categories of rights contained in the Victoria Charter, the 1978 proposal included the entrenchment of a number of "legal," "nondiscrimination," and "mobility" rights. This was, in short, a much more comprehensive charter, more closely resembling the one Canada finally adopted in 1982. These proposals generated a flurry of constitutional activity and debate, but like the Victoria Charter, they did not succeed.[5]

A contributing factor to the demise of the 1978 proposals was the electoral defeat the Liberals suffered in 1979 at the hands of the Progressive Conservatives under Joe Clark. Shortly thereafter Trudeau announced his resignation as Liberal leader. After eleven years as prime minister it seemed that Trudeau's political career had ended, and with it perhaps his dream of a constitutional charter of rights. Both Trudeau and his dream were given a new lease on life, however, when to almost everyone's surprise Clark's minority government was defeated on a crucial budget vote on December 13, 1979. Not having had time to replace Trudeau, the Liberal Party prevailed on him to withdraw his resignation and lead them in another election. The Liberals won that contest, in February 1980, and Trudeau's political resurrection was complete. Instead of bringing the Trudeau era to a close, the Conservative government of 1979 merely interrupted it for a brief interval. Trudeau would remain as prime minister until 1984, when he turned over the reins to the ill-fated John Turner, whose prime ministership gave way almost immediately to that of the Conservative Brian Mulroney.

Trudeau's political resurrection coincided with a referendum on sovereignty-association in Quebec. In the 1976 provincial election campaign, René Lévesque and his separatist Parti Québécois had promised they would not lead the province out of Confederation until Quebeckers had a chance to vote on the desirability of doing so in a referendum. The PQ won that election, and made good on its referendum promise toward the end of its mandate, in 1980, just as Trudeau, Lévesque's arch rival, was rising like a phoenix out of the ashes. Trudeau, who had made his intellectual reputation and built his political career on his vehement hostility to cultural nationalism in general and Quebec nationalism in particular,[6] relished the opportunity to do battle in the referendum campaign, and could now do so not just as a concerned private citizen, but as the Prime Minister of Canada. In the event, Trudeau campaigned on the somewhat ambiguous promise that if sovereignty-association was voted down, his government would work for a "renewed federalism."

When the referendum question was defeated, Trudeau, true to his word, convened a meeting of the provincial premiers to set the agenda for constitutional reform. This meeting agreed to a list of priority items, including reform of the federal–provincial distribution of powers, restructuring of the Supreme Court and Senate, a charter of rights, and a new, entirely domestic amending formula to end the remaining role of the British Parliament in Canadian constitutional change. (The old amending procedure, which required British legislation, would have to be used one last time in order to bring the new formula into effect, but once the latter was in place the constitution would effectively have been "patriated.") After a committee of ministers worked on proposals in these areas, the first ministers met to discuss them in September 1980. They were unable to reach agreement.[7]

The attempt to secure intergovernmental agreement was consistent with a widespread assumption that, as a matter of constitutional convention, amendments of such significance could be made only with the consent of the provinces, and this was generally assumed to mean unanimous consent.[8] The fate of the Victoria Charter, for example, was arguably based on this assumption. When the September first ministers' meeting failed to produce consensus, however, Ottawa quickly showed that it would not be bound by this assumption. Trudeau announced on October 2 that his government would proceed unilaterally with a package of amendments reflecting its own priorities, in particular a "patriated" amending formula and a charter of rights.[9] Parliament would ask Britain to pass this "patriation" package without provincial consent. Ottawa claimed that the convention of provincial consent did not exist, or that if it did, it was merely a *convention* with no legal force—that as a matter of strict law Ottawa was entitled to proceed unilaterally.[10]

The government referred the October proposals for study to a Special Joint Committee of the Senate and House of Commons, which received 1208 submissions and heard 104 witnesses.[11] After the committee reported in February 1981, the government prepared a revised version of its amendment package, based partly on the joint committee's recommendations. Resolutions requesting the British Parliament to enact the amendments were passed by both the House of Commons and the Senate in April. The package was not actually transmitted to Britain, however, because by this time three provincial governments—Manitoba, Quebec, and Newfoundland—had resorted to the courts to stop the federal government, and Ottawa agreed to await the outcome of this challenge to its unilateralism before proceeding.

The three provinces that went to court were supported by all of the other provinces except for Ontario and New Brunswick. Known as the "gang of eight," the opposing provinces were naturally hostile to the idea that major amendments affecting their interests could be passed without their consent, but they also had serious misgivings about the substance of the proposals, and especially about the Charter. In Quebec, of course, no constitutional change short of sovereignty-association was likely to meet the approval of the more radical *indépendantistes* in the Parti Québécois, but Ottawa's proposal did not satisfy even more moderate Québécois. Far from augmenting the jurisdictions of the provincial government, the Trudeau proposals threatened to diminish them. In particular, the proposed Charter contained "language rights" explicitly designed to invalidate important parts of Bill 101, the act establishing French as Quebec's official language. The educational provisions of Bill 101, for example, required all children to attend French-language schools unless one of their parents had been educated in English *in Quebec*. The Trudeau Charter, by contrast, gave official-language minorities in each province the right to educate their children in the minority language if the parents had been educated in that language *in Canada*.[12] Under Bill 101 an English family moving to Quebec from, say, Saskatchewan had no right to educate its children in English. The proposed Charter would give it this right, and would invalidate the more restrictive provisions of a law adopted by the Quebec legislature. Nationalistic policies designed to preserve the "visage linguistique" of the province by restricting the use of English signs were also open to challenge under the Charter's guarantee of "freedom of expression."[13] Although it was justified as a part of the constitutional reform promised as a reward for defeating the independence referendum, the Charter was seen by many Québécois, and by sympathetic English-Canadian observers, as a betrayal of that promise. It was certainly not what "renewed federalism" meant to many of those who heard Trudeau use that phrase in the referendum debate.

The other dissenting provinces also worried that the Charter would diminish their jurisdictional discretion by imposing national standards where provinces had previously been free to vary. Thus the "gang of eight" mounted a strong and sustained opposition to Trudeau's patriation package.

Provincial hostility to the Charter was matched by its popularity among the Canadian public at large, and particularly among a number of interest groups who stood to gain constitutional recognition for themselves and, they hoped, for their policy preferences. As long as Ottawa was trying to bring the provinces onside it was willing to water down the Charter by defining rights narrowly, thus risking the ire of Charter enthusiasts. When it adopted the strategy of unilateralism, on the other hand, the government began to cultivate the support of a variety of constituencies interested in a strong Charter. The joint committee's hearings in late 1980 and early 1981 provided a convenient forum for many of these groups, and Ottawa responded by accepting several amendments they proposed. Instead of narrowing the scope of the Charter to placate the provinces, it expanded it in accordance with the recommendations of these constituencies.[14]

It was at this point that the "gang of eight" launched its legal challenge, choosing the three provincial courts where it thought it stood the best chance of winning. In the event, the Manitoba and Quebec courts were divided on the issue, with the majority of judges in each case favouring the federal argument that provincial consent was not a constitutional requirement. The Newfoundland court, by contrast, unanimously came to the opposite conclusion. These decisions were appealed to the Supreme Court of Canada, and in the spring of 1981, in response to a Conservative filibuster in the House of Commons, the government agreed to await and abide by the result of this appeal.[15]

The Supreme Court handed down its decision in this momentous case on September 28, 1981. In a decision that has been described as "bold statecraft, but questionable jurisprudence,"[16] it gave each side half a loaf. All of the judges drew a stark distinction between constitutional law and convention, deciding that convention was a purely political matter that could not be enforced by a court of law. A majority of the court then found that in strict law the federal government was entitled to proceed unilaterally. A different majority, however, despite their conclusion that convention was not enforceable in court, nevertheless opined that a convention of "substantial provincial consent" did exist (hence the "questionable jurisprudence"), adding that conventions are often constitutionally more important that strict law.

This decision dramatically transformed the strategic context and effectively forced both sides back to the bargaining table (hence the "bold statecraft"). While it was constitutional for Ottawa to pursue its unilateral strategy in a strict legal sense, it was unconstitutional in a broader and perhaps more important sense, and the Trudeau government would not lightly risk the charge of acting unconstitutionally. On the other hand, the provinces knew that the Charter was publicly popular and that if they were seen to be overly obstructionist Ottawa would eventually be able to rely on the simple legality of unilateralism. In the short term, at least, the Supreme Court decision had given both sides new and powerful reasons for compromise

And compromise they did. As we will discuss in greater detail in Chapter Four, Ottawa agreed to an amending formula that was more favourable to the provinces in return for provincial agreement to the Charter. The provinces did not allow the Charter to pass unaltered, however. They left their mark on it especially by insisting on the addition of section 33, the legislative override. Section 33 allows legislatures to pass legislation containing an express declaration that "the Act or a provision thereof shall operate notwithstanding a provision included in section 2 or sections 7 to 15" of the Charter. Such a "notwithstanding" (or "*non-obstante*") clause immunizes the legislation from judicial review under the Charter for renewable five-year periods.

The compromise package, known as the "Constitution Act, 1982," was proclaimed on April 17, 1982. The Charter of Rights and Freedoms comprises the first 34 sections of this act. The remaining sections (35 to 60) deal with aboriginal rights; the principle of equalization; the new amending procedure; enhanced provincial jurisdiction over nonrenewable natural resources; and general matters such as the primacy of the constitution over all other laws, the equal status of English and French versions of constitutional documents, and the commencement of various parts of the act.

■ THE POLITICAL IMPACT OF THE CHARTER

How has the Charter affected Canadian public life since 1982 and how is it likely to affect it in the future? This question underlies much of the rest of the book. It is useful, however, to begin with a sense of what has happened thus far. The rest of this chapter provides a brief and selective overview of the Charter's political impact during its first decade.

Increased Judicial Activism

One of the simplest measures of the Charter's impact is to compare the pre- and post-Charter decisions of the Supreme Court of Canada in civil liberties cases. The outcome of these decisions can be interpreted as tending toward judicial self-restraint or judicial activism. Judicial activism refers to the disposition to interpret rights broadly and to enforce them vigorously. Activist judges display "a readiness to veto the policies of other branches of government on constitutional grounds,"[17] usually by striking down statutes or excluding evidence in criminal cases. Self-restraint, by contrast, "connotes a judicial predisposition to find room within the constitution for the policies of democratically accountable decision makers."[18] Cumulatively, the outcome of these decisions shape the relationship of the courts to the legislative and executive branches of government. An activist court uses the power of judicial review to intervene and to influence the making and enforcement of laws. A self-restrained court tends to avoid such intervention.

The most striking comparison in this respect is between Charter cases since 1982 and previous civil liberties cases arising under the Canadian Bill of Rights. The latter instrument, enacted by the Diefenbaker government in 1960, was narrower in scope than the Charter because it applied only to matters within federal jurisdiction. More important, it was an ordinary statute, not a constitutional document. Although it was sometimes described as being "quasi-constitutional," Canadian judges proved reluctant to use an instrument of less than full constitutional status to invalidate federal legislation. Only once between its enactment and the coming into effect of the Charter, in the 1970 *Drybones* case,[19] did the Supreme Court use the Bill of Rights to invalidate a law.[20]

This did not mean that only Drybones won a case under the Bill of Rights. If a law clearly violates rights, judges can vindicate the latter only by striking the law down, as they did in *Drybones*. If, on the other hand, a law is open to competing interpretations, courts can adopt the interpretation that does not entail infringing rights. This is sometimes called "interpretive avoidance" because it "avoids" a clash between legislation and rights by "interpreting" the former to conform to the latter. Judgments based on this technique may overrule the interpretation relied upon by administrative officials without invalidating the law itself. Occasionally rights claimants would win Bill of Rights cases on this basis.[21] But even if one adds to *Drybones* the victories based on interpretive avoidance, the overall success rate in Bill of Rights cases is only 15 percent. The relatively low probability of bringing a successful Bill of Rights challenge to federal policy seems to have discouraged would-be litigants, for between 1960 and 1982 the Supreme Court heard only thirty-four such cases.

The contrasting experience under the Charter could not be more marked. By November 1989, just over seven years after it came into effect, the Supreme Court had decided its first one hundred Charter cases. In thirty-five cases the rights claimant won; in sixty-one cases the Crown won; and there were four cases with no clear winner. This success ratio of 35 percent is over twice the 15 percent (five out of thirty-four) achieved under the 1960 Bill of Rights in its first twenty-two years, perhaps accounting for the greater willingness of litigants to raise Charter issues and pursue them to the highest court in the land. During this period the Supreme Court invalidated portions of nineteen statutes, compared to the single instance of judicial nullification under the Bill of Rights.[22] The Court also overruled several of its own Bill of Rights decisions in order to rule in favour of Charter litigants in similar cases.[23] The great volume of cases, their higher success rate, the larger number of nullifications, and the overruling of pre-Charter precedents are all indicators of a new era of judicial activism ushered in by the Charter.

Public Policy Impact

Court decisions have had a considerable impact on public policy in Canada. The area most affected has been the Criminal Code and criminal law enforcement. Three out of every four Charter cases deal with legal rights, and they account for seventy-four of the Supreme Court's first one hundred Charter decisions. The Supreme Court has given a broad interpretation to the legal rights enumerated in sections 7 to 14 of the Charter, in effect creating a new code of acceptable police conduct. For example, the Supreme Court's interpretation of the section 10(b) right to counsel has had a major impact on policing. It has been interpreted to require police immediately to inform those they detain or arrest of their right to the assistance of counsel and their right not to speak until such assistance is procured.[24] Police have been told that they cannot persist in questioning a suspect who has requested a lawyer,[25] nor use tricks such as placing undercover agents in jail cells.[26] If suspects are too intoxicated to understand the gravity of the right to counsel, police must cease questioning until they sober up.[27] If an arrested person wants a lawyer but cannot afford one, the Court has said that section 10(b) requires the police to inform him or her of the availability of legal aid.[28] The cumulative effect of these decisions is to decrease the likelihood of voluntary confessions or incriminating statements, since the first thing lawyers tend to tell a client is to say nothing to the police.

The Court's activist interpretation of the section 8 right against unreasonable search or seizure has also had a significant effect on law enforcement practices. The Court ruled that section 8 does not permit the continued use of writs of assistance[29] and creates a presumption of invalidity against all warrantless searches.[30] In *Hunter* v. *Southam*[31] the Supreme Court laid down strict new rules for obtaining a valid search warrant. An acceptable search warrant must be issued by a judge or someone "capable of acting judicially," that is, impartially. In particular, a warrant may not be issued by an administrator who also fulfils enforcement or investigatory functions. A valid search warrant can only be issued on grounds of "probable cause," not merely "possible cause." Finally, a warrant must specify the details of the search it authorizes: who is to do the searching, when, where, and for what. In sum, the Court has used section 8 to significantly tighten up the requirements for valid search-and-seizure practices.

In a sharp reversal of pre-Charter practice, the Court has often excluded evidence from a trial if the police do not follow any of the new rules outlined above, regardless of how important or reliable the evidence may be.[32] The Court's use of the section 24(2) "exclusionary rule" has thus forced the Crown to abandon many criminal cases for lack of admissible evidence.

The Court's legal-rights decisions are significant not just because they have reversed a number of pre-Charter precedents. Some actually favour the accused more than comparable American decisions. A recent study found this to be so in Canadian cases affecting waiver of the right to counsel, roadside detention for breathalyzer tests, police lineups, and involuntary blood samples.[33] The net effect of the Court's activism in this area has thus been to enhance substantially the procedural defences of those accused of crimes, a result applauded by civil libertarians and defence lawyers. The cost has been a proportional decrease in the efficiency of law enforcement and crime control, a trend that worries others.

While criminal procedure has been the object of the Court's most extensive de facto efforts at law reform, it has thus far escaped public notice. American experience shows that such judicial reform of the criminal law process can become an issue of partisan political conflict. Beginning with Richard Nixon's 1968 presidential campaign, the Republican

Party has criticized "liberal" judges for being "soft on criminals." Republican presidents have successfully exploited the "law and order" issue in the appointment of federal judges.

As a result of Republican appointments, the U.S. Supreme Court is now backing away from some of its earlier "pro-defendant" precedents. For example, in 1990 the U.S. Court decided that the use of incriminating statements gathered by undercover police informers placed in jail cells did not violate the accused's right against self-incrimination or right to counsel. Ironically, the same month the Canadian Supreme Court reached the opposite conclusion in a similar case.[34] Only time will tell whether a Canadian political party will follow the lead of United States Republicans in making Supreme Court decisions the basis of a law-and-order campaign.

One of the most politically significant Charter decisions to date is the 1988 *Morgentaler* decision.[35] In this case the Court invalidated the law making abortion a criminal offence except when a therapeutic abortion committee (TAC) concluded that the life or health of the mother was at risk. The law was struck down mainly because of procedural defects. The Court left open the possibility of a substantially similar law with an improved procedural framework. Nevertheless, the immediate effect of the decision was to create a policy vacuum in a highly charged area. The government struggled for more than two years to fill this vacuum by framing a new abortion policy. In June 1990, after several failed attempts, the House of Commons in a free vote adopted Bill C-43, a compromise measure that left abortion in the Criminal Code but allowed therapeutic abortions when pregnancy threatened the life or health of the mother. Had it become law, Bill C-43 would have abolished the old requirement of committee approvals, leaving the "threat to health" issue to be determined by a woman and her doctor. Bill C-43 did not become law, however; in February 1991 it was defeated in a free vote in the Senate, and Canada thus remains in the situation created by *Morgentaler:* no criminal law regulation of abortion at all.

A lesser-known Charter case, but one with a major policy impact, was the 1985 *Singh* decision.[36] Under the law challenged in this case, a person applying for refugee status, accompanied by legal counsel, was first examined under oath by an immigration officer. A sworn transcript of this examination was then sent to a committee for a decision. The claimant did not appear before this committee. If the committee rejected the refugee claim, the claimant could appeal, and an appeal board would meet if it thought the claimant had a "reasonable" chance of succeeding. The claimant (and his or her lawyer) had the right to attend and to participate in this appeal. In short, the old refugee determination process was neither auto-cratic nor cursory. Indeed, it had been praised by the United Nations as a worthy model for other Commonwealth and European nations, many of which do not even allow appeals in their refugee determination pro-cesses.[37]

Why then did the Supreme Court strike the law down? The Court found that the refugee determination process violated the right to a fair hearing because the committee making the initial determination did not provide an oral hearing to the refugee claimant. This, declared Justice Wil-son, resulted in an "inadequate opportunity" for the claimant "to state his case and know the case he has to meet."[38] Many might contest Justice Wilson's interpretation of the procedure. The initial interview is certainly an "oral hearing" of sorts, and a full oral hearing was provided for if the appeal request was allowed. These facts notwithstanding, Justice Wilson found the procedure so unfair as to violate the "principles of fundamental justice."

The fallback position of the government was that even if the refugee determination procedure did restrict the full right to a fair hearing, it was "demonstrably justified" as a "reasonable limitation" under section 1 of the Charter. The reasonableness of Canada's practice was supported by noting the United Nations' approval and its favourable comparison of Canada to other Western nations. In addition, the government told the Court that there was already a high volume of refugee cases and that requiring an oral hearing for each one "would constitute an unreasonable burden on the Board's resources."[39]

These arguments did not impress Justice Wilson. "Utilitarian consider-ations" and "administrative convenience," she declared, cannot justify infringing the principles of fundamental justice. "Even if the cost of com-pliance with fundamental justice is a factor to which the courts would give considerable weight," she concluded, "I am not satisfied ... that this cost would be so prohibitive as to constitute a justification within the meaning of s. 1."[40]

In view of subsequent events, Justice Wilson's casual dismissal of cost as a mere "administrative convenience" seems questionable. *Singh* is a classic example of the unintended (and sometimes costly) consequences of judicial policy reform. The government's initial response was simply to hire more personnel to conduct oral hearings. But this bandaid approach did little to address the growing backlog of refugee claimants. In addition to the seven litigants in the *Singh* case, the Court's decision affected 13 000 other refugee claimants and 7000 unexecuted deportation orders.[41] Realizing that the government could not possibly cope with this backlog, illegal immigrants already in Canada (encouraged by their lawyers and activist immigrant support groups) also began applying for refugee status in order to buy time, thus further clogging the system. Within eighteen months of the *Singh* decision, Canada faced a mini-crisis in its immigration policy: a backlog of over 20 000 refugee claimants that was growing daily.[42]

The Mulroney government responded in 1986 by declaring a general "amnesty" and introducing Bill C-55, a new refugee determination process. The amnesty was intended to clear the decks, and allowed 15 000 waiting claimants to acquire landed immigrant status, regardless of the validity of their claims to be refugees.[43] Under Bill C-55, all claimants who arrived in Canada before January 1, 1989, received a hearing before a two-member tribunal, either of whom could pass the claimant on to a full hearing before two other officials. The program was originally to cost $100 million, take two years to complete, and result in the deportation of about 20 000 applicants. By November 1989, the program had fallen nine months behind schedule, with 124 000 pending cases, and the tab almost doubled. As we write, the Commons Immigration Committee is considering recommending yet another general amnesty, this time for 45 000 claimants.[44]

The Charter has also significantly affected the area of Sunday-closing legislation. Directly overruling its own 1962 Bill of Rights precedent, the Supreme Court ruled in *Big M Drug Mart*[45] that the federal Lord's Day Act violated the freedom-of-religion provision of the Charter. Two years later, in its *Edwards Books* decision, the Court upheld an Ontario Sunday-closing statute enacted for the explicitly secular purpose of a common day of rest.[46] A majority of the Court found that although the law's "effect" was to violate the freedom of religion of some Saturday-sabbatarian shopkeepers, it was nevertheless justified as a "reasonable limit" under section 1.

Despite the fact that its law was upheld, the Ontario government repealed the Sunday-closing provisions of its Retail Business Holidays Act, and substituted a "local option" for municipalities.[47] In Alberta the Lougheed government was reluctant to deal with what it regarded as an emotional, no-win issue, and also left the problem to municipalities to handle on a local option basis.[48] Critics say that while the local option policy sounds good in theory, it does not work in practice. When one community forces its merchants to close while a neighbouring community allows its retail stores to remain open, the retailers in the first community lose potential sales. Research suggests that the resulting economic pressure creates a "domino effect" that forces all municipalities to open, especially in urban corridors such as Oshawa–Toronto–Hamilton and Edmonton–Red Deer–Calgary. The result has been increasingly wide-open Sunday shopping in both provinces.[49]

The Charter has also affected Canadian elections. The Canada Elections Act placed strict limitations on independent "political action committee" (PAC) expenditures in federal elections. Just prior to the 1984 national elections, the National Citizens' Coalition, a conservative public interest group, successfully challenged these provisions as violating the Charter's freedom-of-expression provision in *National Citizens' Coalition* v. *Canada (A.-G.)*.[50] Because it was handed down on the eve of the 1984 elections, Ottawa did not appeal this Alberta Court of Queen's Bench decision. While the demise of the anti-PAC clause had little effect in the 1984 elections, the subsequently elected Conservative government never acted to plug the loophole created by the decision. When the November 1988 elections turned into a one-issue referendum on the Mulroney free trade agreement with the United States, the absence of any legal restrictions on non-party spending allowed pro–free trade groups to spend millions of dollars on political advertising in the closing weeks of the campaign. This advertising blitz helped to reverse an eleventh-hour surge of anti–free trade sentiment and to re-elect Prime Minister Mulroney and his Tories. Thus a 1984 Court of Queen's Bench interpretation of the Charter right to freedom of expression may have determined the fate of the 1988 free trade agreement, one of the most important decisions ever made by Canadians.

The Charter is also affecting the electoral system by calling into question existing constituency boundaries. In 1989 the British Columbia Supreme Court declared that province's system of electoral districting to be in violation of the Charter's section 3 "right to vote."[51] The Court said section 3 must be interpreted as guaranteeing a "meaningful" right to vote, and that the unequal numbers of voters in British Columbia's electoral districts violated this principle. The Court did not embrace a strict "one person, one vote rule," but said that the population of an electoral district cannot vary by more than 25 percent from the provincial average.

The British Columbia decision triggered a wave of "one person, one vote" cases across the country. Dissatisfied urban voters in Alberta, Saskatchewan, and the Northwest Territories went to the courts to challenge electoral districts with unequal regulations. In 1991 the Saskatchewan Court of Appeal struck down the province's electoral distribution law even though it complied with the 25 percent rule approved in British Columbia. While the Supreme Court subsequently overturned this decision, it did rule that the section 3 right to vote includes a "right to fair and effective representation."[52] As explained in Chapter Twelve, this ruling is certain to encourage further litigation.

The British Columbia government also suffered a serious reversal in the field of health policy. In 1985 the government decided to act on what it regarded as an intolerable undersupply of doctors in rural areas and a corresponding oversupply in the urban lower mainland. It formulated a policy that denied new doctors in the province a billing number for the province's public health-insurance system unless they first worked a specified number of years in designated rural areas. Without such a billing number a doctor could hardly practise, so the intended effect of the policy was to force new doctors into the countryside for at least the first several years of their professional careers. Instead, a group of disgruntled younger doctors went to court and successfully challenged the new policy as a violation of their section 7 right to "liberty."[53] The B.C. government was denied leave to appeal by the Supreme Court.

Interest Groups and the Charter

The Charter may have its most enduring impact on the political process through the creation of a new forum for interest-group activity. Historically Canadian interest groups have concentrated their lobbying activities at the cabinet and senior levels of the bureaucracy. Unlike their American counterparts, they avoided lobbying parliamentary committees and rarely used litigation as a political tactic. This pattern of Canadian interest-group activity is explained by the "closed" character of the Canadian policy-making process. Unlike the American congressional system, Canada's parliamentary system offered little opportunity to influence public policy in either parliamentary committees or the courts. In our tradition of "cabinet government," party discipline negates legislative independence and thus any real power of parliamentary committees. The tradition of parliamentary supremacy relegated the courts to a secondary political role and a more legalistic exercise of the judicial function. Interest groups accordingly concentrated their efforts at the executive level of the policy process. The adoption of the Charter of Rights has changed their strategy by creating a new access point in the decision-making process. Interest groups that fail to achieve their policy objectives through the traditional political party and bureaucratic channels can now turn to the courts.

The federal government gave a crucial boost to interest-group use of Charter litigation when it launched the Court Challenges Program in September 1985. The government allocated $9 million over five years to fund litigation arising under the equality-rights, language-rights, and multiculturalism provisions of the Charter. Applications for financial support are screened according to the criteria of "setting of social justice priorities ... legal merit ... [and] consequences for a number of people"[54]; in other words, funded litigation should have maximum policy impact. Selected cases are eligible for $35 thousand at each stage of the litigation process: trial, provincial appeal court, and the Supreme Court of Canada. During its first five-year mandate, the Court Challenges Program funded 150 equality-rights cases and fifty language-rights cases. In 1990 Parliament renewed the Court Challenges Program for another five years with funding in excess of $13 million.

An early and highly publicized example of interest-group use of the Charter was the *Operation Dismantle* case.[55] This coalition of peace and antinuclear groups challenged the testing of the American cruise missile in Canadian territory as a violation of the rights to "life" and "security of the person" protected by section 7 of the Charter. While ultimately unsuccessful in stopping the cruise, the litigation achieved considerable publicity for the peace movement. Such publicity and the legitimacy it can confer was probably the realistic objective of Operation Dismantle all along, and in this sense the case was a victory of sorts.

The National Citizens' Coalition's challenge to the Canada Election Act (discussed above) is one of the most successful instances of interest-group use of the Charter. At the time of the decision, all three national parties were on record as supporting the restrictions on nonparty spending during elections. The NCC could not have successfully challenged this policy through any forum other than the courts.

Other examples of interest-group success can be found in the area of minority-language rights. English groups within Quebec and francophones outside of Quebec have both used section 23 of the Charter to gain more favourable education policies from their respective provincial governments. We have seen that Quebec nationalists worried that the Charter would undo important aspects of Bill 101, known as the "Charter of the French Language." These fears were soon borne out. As soon as the Charter was adopted, the Quebec Protestant School Board, with the help of the federal government's Court Challenges Program, attacked the education provisions of Bill 101 in Quebec, which severely restricted access to

English-language education. The Supreme Court found this policy to be an unconstitutional violation of section 23.[56] In the 1990 *Mahé* case, which was also funded by the Court Challenges Program, the Supreme Court ruled that section 23 entitled francophones in Edmonton not just to separate French-language schools, but also to administrative control over instruction, curriculum, and buildings.[57] The impact of the *Mahé* decision will extend far beyond Alberta, as it will constitute a precedent for similar section 23 suits pending in most other English-speaking provinces.

The most publicized instances of interest-group use of the Charter have been the pro- and anti-abortion challenges to Canada's abortion law. Pro-abortion groups spent over half a million dollars in legal fees to finance Dr. Henry Morgentaler's successful challenge.[58] Anti-abortion groups spent almost as much to support the Charter challenge of Joe Borowski.[59] Borowski argued that the existing law was too permissive and violated the unborn child's right to life, as protected by section 7 of the Charter, the same section that Morgentaler's pro-abortion lobby invoked to combat any restrictions on abortion. Unfortunately for Borowski, his case arrived at the Supreme Court just nine months after the Court had struck down the abortion law in *Morgentaler*. The Court ruled that because there was no longer an abortion law to challenge, Borowski's case had become "moot," and declined to answer the question of the rights of the unborn under the Charter.[60]

Canadian feminists have mounted the best organized interest-group use of the Charter. Feminists gained a headstart on other interest groups by successfully lobbying Parliament for favourable wording of the section 15 equality-rights provisions while the Charter was still in draft stage. Soon after, the Canadian Advisory Council on the Status of Women (CACSW) commissioned a study concluding that with the Charter's enactment "we find ourselves at the opportune moment to stress litigation as a vehicle for social change."[61] The study recommended the creation of a single, nationwide legal action fund to coordinate and pay for a policy of systematic litigation of strategic test cases. On April 13, 1985, only days before the equality-rights section of the Charter came into effect, the Women's Legal and Education Action Fund (LEAF) was launched. Its purpose is "to assist women with important test cases and to ensure that equality rights litigation for women is undertaken in a planned, responsible, and expert manner."[62]

Since its inception LEAF has raised more than a quarter of a million dollars from private sources and has received a $1 million grant from the government of Ontario. It has also received funding from the federal government's Court Challenges Program. LEAF has participated in numerous Charter cases both as a litigant and as an intervener. It intervened successfully in both the *Borowski* and *Daigle*[63] abortion cases. LEAF has also enjoyed success in cases involving a boys-only hockey league in Ontario,[64] the use of original surnames by married women,[65] and the eligibility of natural fathers for "maternity" leave.[66] Perhaps LEAF's most important achievement came in the Supreme Court's first major equality-rights decision, *Andrews,* in which the Court adopted an interpretation of section 15 that favours "disadvantaged groups," precisely what LEAF had argued for.[67] More than any other interest group, Canadian feminists have done their homework and are poised to use Charter litigation to advance their policy objectives

The Charter and Governmental Behaviour

Canadian governments have been actively involved in Charter politics. In addition to defending the constitutionality of their statutes and the conduct of their officials, some governments have participated in Charter politics through the devices of the section 33 legislative override and the reference procedure.

Use of the legislative override has been quite limited except for Quebec, which is generally seen as a unique case. As indicated above, Quebec was the only province that did not consent to the constitutional amendments of 1982. The separatist government of Premier René Lévesque viewed the Constitution Act, 1982, as a massive and unconstitutional intrusion into the political autonomy of Quebec.[68] To manifest his government's objection, Lévesque passed Bill 62—an "omnibus" legislative override act—only weeks after the Charter took effect. Bill 62 retroactively inserted the "notwithstanding" clause into every existing Quebec statute.[69] In addition, each new Quebec statute was enacted with a "notwithstanding" provision.

While the symbolic effect of Quebec's rejection of the Charter has important repercussions for Canadian unity, it has not had much practical effect on the freedoms of the people of Quebec. In the first place, important parts of the Charter continued to apply in Quebec despite the blanket override. For example, since the legislative override cannot be applied to language rights, Quebec's anti-English language policies have still been subject to Charter attacks, some successful. Second, Quebec has its own Bill of Rights, which applies even where a section 33 override has preempted the analogous Charter provisions. The provincial bill is in many respects broader in coverage than the Charter, and a statute violating the Charter would almost certainly violate the Quebec Bill of Rights as well.

Outside Quebec there has been only one instance of a government using the legislative override. In January 1986, the Conservative premier of Saskatchewan, Grant Devine, attached a notwithstanding clause to Bill 144, a back-to-work bill aimed at striking provincial employees. The Devine government feared that the statute might be successfully challenged as a violation of the freedom-of-association clause of the Charter, and sought to pre-empt such a challenge through the use of section 33.[70] This action was widely criticized by labour and civil liberties groups across the country as setting a dangerous precedent that could undermine the Charter; and there was speculation that Devine decided to use the override to bolster his leadership image in preparation for the upcoming provincial election.[71] One local columnist suggested that Devine's "union bashing" was calculated to consolidate the Conservatives' control of Saskatchewan's rural ridings.[72] If this was indeed the premier's strategy, it worked to perfection nine months later. In the October 1986 elections, the Conservatives swept all but one rural riding while losing all but one urban seat, to hang on to a majority. The use of section 33 was a nonissue in the rural areas, while in the more heavily unionized cities, especially Regina, it was one of several factors contributing to the perception of the Devine Conservatives as anti-labour. The Saskatchewan case suggests that if the legislative override is used in a politically astute fashion, it will not necessarily harm a government, and may even help.

The reference procedure also allows Canadian governments to initiate rather than react to Charter issues. References allow governments to pose legal questions directly to appeal courts (the Supreme Court for Ottawa and provincial courts of appeal for the provinces) without having to wait for the issue to arrive there in the course of ordinary litigation.[73] Since its inception in 1875, critics have claimed that constitutional references tend to be abused for political purposes. Governments have sought to avoid responsibility for politically controversial issues by collapsing the policy issue (Is it good?) into a constitutional issue (Is it legal?), and then referring the latter to the courts.[74] The reference thus becomes a convenient device for politicians who wish to avoid "political hot potatoes" or "no-win issues" by passing them on to the courts. This form of "issue avoidance" may be used for different tactical purposes. It can be used to confer constitutional legitimacy on a policy initiative favoured by the government party but heavily criticized by the opposition or the public. Alternatively, a government can try to delegitimate a policy it opposes by referring it to the relevant court and hoping for a negative answer.[75] In both instances the judicial decision may not "solve" the controversy, but if the avoidance tactic works, it becomes an additional political resource for the government to use in its larger political strategy.

Issue avoidance was successfully practised by the Saskatchewan government in a 1985 Charter reference. The Progressive Conservatives had ousted the New Democratic government in the 1982 provincial elections. An important part of the Conservative election strategy was an appeal to the anti-abortion vote, a predominantly rural, Catholic vote that historically had supported the populist policies of the New Democrats.[76] Once in office, the Devine government was quickly pressured by its new allies to deliver on its election promises. When the Cabinet was slow to respond, a newly elected backbencher, Gay Caswell, introduced a private member's bill that would have reduced access to abortion services in the province.[77] Caswell claimed her bill had support of Cabinet, but neither the premier nor any other senior cabinet members would publicly endorse it on the floor of the legislature. Sensing a sharp division on the issue in the government caucus, the New Democrats taunted the Devine government to act on the bill.[78]

The government escaped this dilemma through the reference procedure. Just hours before the Caswell Bill was supposed to receive its third and final reading, Attorney General Gary Lane, a suspected opponent of the bill, announced that the government would delay the vote and instead refer the bill to the courts for a determination of its constitutionality. The government's hopes were realized when the Saskatchewan Court of Appeal subsequently found the Caswell Bill unconstitutional.[79] With an automatic appeal to the Supreme Court of Canada, the bill was sent to the judicial deep-freeze until well after the upcoming provincial elections. In the October 1986 elections, Caswell lost her seat in the NDP sweep in Saskatoon, perhaps to the relief of Conservative pragmatists such as Lane.

The reference procedure was successfully used by the Tory government of Bill Davis in Ontario for the opposite purpose: to confer legitimacy on a government policy initiative that faced potential opposition from within the governing caucus. Ontario has the largest French-speaking population outside of Quebec, but has historically restricted French-language education services. After 1982, the Davis government saw that its existing Education Act was certain to run afoul of the new minority-language-education section of the Charter. Davis was prepared to amend the act to conform with the Charter, but feared a political backlash from the latent but still strong antifrancophone sentiment in the province, especially in his own party. His solution was to refer the Ontario Education Act to the provincial Court of Appeal. When, as anticipated, the Court ruled that the act violated the Charter, the government was able to introduce amendments significantly extending French-language education services.[80] Naysayers were simply told that this is what the constitution now requires. The telltale sign of the government's strategy was its decision not to appeal its "loss" to the Supreme Court. In effect the government had received what it wanted: the added legitimacy of a judicial stamp of approval for its policy initiative.[81]

The Davis government did not fare nearly so well in its next venture into Charterland. In June 1984, in a reversal of longstanding Conservative Party policy, and without any prior discussions with his Cabinet, Premier Davis announced his intention to provide full public funding for Grades 10 to 12 in the separate Catholic school system in Ontario. This represented a major extension of the existing, constitutionally mandated policy of funding the separate Catholic schools through Grade 10, the level at which they were funded at the time of Confederation.[82] While neither of the opposition parties opposed Davis's proposal, it was widely criticized by the public and in the press. The funding extension was subsequently challenged in court by the Metropolitan Toronto School Board and the Ontario Secondary Schools Teachers' Federation, who estimated that by 1990 the new policy would cost the public school system 130 000 students and 8000 jobs. Any extension of funding for Catholic schools beyond Grade 10, it was argued, would discriminate against non-Catholics, violating the section 15 equality-rights clause of the Charter.

Premier Davis unexpectedly resigned as Conservative leader later in the year, and his successor, Frank Miller, inherited the troublesome issue. When Miller called an election in the spring of 1985, the three party leaders tacitly agreed not to exploit the issue. This "conspiracy of silence" was vehemently criticized by the Toronto *Globe and Mail,* whose editorials proclaimed the Catholic-funding extension the "biggest unofficial issue" of the campaign.[83] The high point of the issue—and the low point of the campaign—occurred when the Anglican archbishop of Toronto, Lewis Garnsworthy, called a press conference to denounce the funding extension and compared former premier Davis's political tactics to those of Adolf Hitler.[84] On May 2, election day, the Conservatives lost control of the Ontario legislature for the first time in forty-two years. There was much speculation that discontent within the party over the separate-school-funding issue cost them the election.

The new Liberal premier, David Peterson, was anxious not to fall into the same trap as Davis and Miller on the school-funding issue, yet he led a party that was historically committed to equal funding for Catholic schools. His predicament was exacerbated by the fact that he headed a minority government and was dependent upon the continued support of the New Democrats. Once again the reference procedure proved to be the way out of a political dilemma. Peterson announced that he would refer the issue of possible discrimination against non-Catholics to the Ontario Court of Appeal, and abide by its decision. If he "lost" Peterson could tell equal-funding supporters that he had tried. If he "won" he could tell equal-funding opponents that their constitutional objections had been found invalid. In the end, a sharply divided Court of Appeal upheld the school-funding legislation by a vote of three to two. Peterson was presumably not worried when opponents asked the Supreme Court to hear the case again on appeal.[85] By resorting to the reference to collapse the policy issue into the legal issue, he achieved an apparent "no-lose" situation.

These political dramas demonstrate how the legislative override and the reference procedure provide Canadian governments with interesting political options in the game of Charter politics. In particular, there seems to be a trend of "issue avoidance" by elected political leaders through the reference procedure. The abortion-access, French-language-education, and Catholic-school-funding controversies suggest that the increasing political role of the courts under the Charter may come not only because judges arrogate to themselves a policy-making function, but also because politicians abdicate this responsibility.

∎ CONCLUSION

The foregoing only samples the ways in which the Charter has affected Canadian public life. We have not yet addressed the Charter's influence on the conduct of symbolic politics, or its impact on the federal system. These are subjects we explore at length in subsequent chapters. Enough has been said, however, to show how thoroughly the Charter has become embroiled in the everyday conduct of Canadian politics and policy-making. Certainly neither interest groups nor governments have been slow to discern the political advantages to be gained from Charter litigation. Ordinary individuals, of course, may also launch cases having a profound effect on public policy, as the *Singh* case shows. Cumulatively, these cases represent a substantial "legalization" or "judicialization" of politics. The significance of this revolution, and whether it is legitimate or desirable, are questions taken up in Part Two of this book. First, however, we need a more precise understanding of the Charter's interpretive structure.

CHAPTER THREE

The Charter Two Step

We have investigated the historical origins of the Charter and sampled its impact on our public life since it came into effect in 1982. The introductory foundation for what follows in Parts Two and Three of this book is not yet completely in place, however. Before untangling the "dimensions of Charter politics" in Part Two or proceeding to the case studies in Part Three, we need to familiarize ourselves with the actual content and structure of the Charter, and with the interpretive framework established by the Supreme Court to deal with Charter litigation. The legal rules and categories of interpretation constitute the rhetorical form of our newest mode of public debate and policy-making. Without a grounding in its form one cannot hope to penetrate the substance of Charter politics.

This chapter focuses on what is perhaps the key feature of the Supreme Court's interpretive approach: a two-stage procedure that we dub the "Charter Two Step." The first step involves defining the scope of the right in question. The second step, which occurs if the right is violated, takes two forms: (1) if the right is violated by a law, the court must determine whether the law should nevertheless stand as the kind of "reasonable limit" that can be "demonstrably justified in a free and democratic society"; (2) if law enforcement officials violate a Charter right in the course of acquiring evidence of illegality, the second step is to determine whether the evidence should be excluded from the trial. Our examination of these two versions of the Two Step by no means exhausts what can be said about the interpretive enterprise, but it does illustrate its most important structural feature. It also suffices to demonstrate the amount of decision-making leeway involved in Charter interpretation. This interpretive room is an obvious source of Charter politics, for conflicting political interests will naturally favour quite different readings of the Charter, and will often work hard to induce judges to adopt their preferred interpretation. Interpretive leeway also poses one of the central questions dividing Charterphiles and Charter sceptics (whose ongoing dialogue occupies our attention in much of Part Two): Is there any reason to believe that judges will make the "correct" or at least better choices between interpretive alternatives, or do judicial choices simply second-guess the equally legitimate choices of the other branches of government?

▮ THE CHARTER AT A GLANCE

The Charter contains both provisions setting out substantive rights and freedoms and provisions spelling out how those substantive guarantees should be interpreted, applied, and enforced. Following a brief preamble recognizing "the supremacy of God and the rule of law," section 1, the first interpretive section, states that the Charter "guarantees the rights and freedoms set out in it subject only to such reasonable limits prescribed by law as can be demonstrably justified in a free and democratic society"; this is the foundation of the first version of the Two Step. The Charter then moves through seven categories of substantive provisions: Fundamental Freedoms (section 2), Democratic Rights (sections 3 through 5), Mobility Rights (section 6), Legal Rights (sections 7 through 14), Equality Rights (section 15), Official Languages (sections 16 through 22), and Minority Language Educational Rights (section 23). Following these substantive sections is section 24, entitled "Enforcement," which in subsection 1 authorizes "anyone" whose Charter rights are infringed "to apply to a court of competent jurisdiction to obtain such remedy as the court considers appropriate and just in the circumstances." Subsection 24(2) requires courts hearing such cases to exclude evidence "obtained in a manner that infringed or denied any rights or freedoms guaranteed by this Charter," if the judge concludes that "having regard to all the circumstances, the admission of it in the proceedings would bring the administration of justice into disrepute." This is known as the "exclusionary rule," and gives rise to the second version of the Two Step. The Charter concludes with a number of interpretation, application, and limitation sections. These specify, for example, that the substantive rights are "guaranteed equally to male and female persons," "notwithstanding anything in this Charter" (section 28); that they shall be interpreted in a manner consistent with aboriginal rights (section 25) and the "preservation and enhancement" of our "multicultural heritage" (section 27); "that the equality rights in section 15 come into effect three years after the rest of the Charter (section 32(2)); that the Charter applies to Canadian legislatures and governments, including the Yukon and Northwest Territories (sections 30 and 32(1)), and thus not to purely private violations of rights; and, of course, that legislation may be expressly declared to operate "notwithstanding" sections 2 and 7 to 15 of the Charter for renewable five-year periods (section 33).

Section 52 of the Constitution Act, 1982, declares the Charter, along with the rest of Canada's documentary constitution, to be "the supreme law of Canada," and states that "any law that is inconsistent with the provisions of the Constitution is, to the extent of the inconsistency, of no force or effect." Section 52 is usually understood as explicitly authorizing the judicial invalidation of unconstitutional legislation. How do judges carry out the task of judicial review?

■ THE TWO (AND SOMETIMES THREE) STEP

When faced with a Charter case, the courts first ask the rights claimant to demonstrate that a Charter right has indeed been violated. This involves determining the meaning and scope of the right, to see whether it covers the situation of the claimant. For example, if the claimant is charged with distributing obscene material, or soliciting for the purposes of prostitution, the court must decide whether these activities come within the meaning of "expression" in the section 2(b) guarantee of "freedom of expression." If they do not—if obscenity and soliciting are not protected forms of "expression"—then the prohibitory laws applying to these activities do not violate the right and the case is at an end. If the activities do come within the meaning of the right, on the other hand, then the government prohibitions are *prima facie* unconstitutional, unless they can be "demonstrably justified" under section 1 as "reasonable limits" in a "free and democratic society." While the onus for establishing a rights violation lies with the claimant, the onus for defending the violation under section 1 falls upon the government. If the government succeeds in persuading the court that its policy is indeed "demonstrably justified," the law stands and the claimant loses. If the court remains unpersuaded, the law is declared of "no force or effect" under section 52 of the Constitution Act, and the claimant succeeds.

Section 1 can save a policy that otherwise violates Charter rights only if the violation is "prescribed by law." But not all violations stem from laws. Suppose the evidence required to convict someone of breaking a perfectly constitutional law is found illegally, during a warrantless search of the suspect's home. This would constitute a violation of the section 8 guarantee against unreasonable searches and seizures, but this violation would not be "prescribed by law," and it would not, therefore, be eligible for section 1 justification. This situation brings into play the second version of the Charter Two Step. Having determined that the evidence was acquired through the violation of a Charter right, the court is required under section 24(2) to determine whether admitting it would bring the administration of justice into disrepute. If it would, the evidence must be excluded, and perhaps the offender would go free, however guilty he or she may be. However, section 24 explicitly leaves open the possibility of admitting constitutionally tainted evidence if the court concludes that, having regard to all the circumstances, no disrepute would result. Deciding which of these routes to take is the second part of the Charter Two Step when a rights violation results from administrative action rather than being "prescribed by law." Of course, constitutionally tainted evidence in a judicial proceeding may also result from administrative procedures that are "prescribed by law." In that case, section 24(2) becomes the final stage of a Charter Three Step: (1) finding that the law violates a right; (2) finding that this violation is not saved by section 1; and (3) determining whether the evidence resulting from this violation should be excluded. We shall examine section 1 and section 24(2) in turn.

▋ REASONABLE LIMITS

There is widespread agreement that few if any rights are absolute, that it is sometimes reasonable to limit them. For example, no one should be able to rely on freedom of expression to justify shouting "fire" in a crowded theatre, or on freedom of religion to justify human sacrifice. Laws prohibiting libel and polygamy are perhaps more controversial examples of limits on these two rights, but these laws receive sufficient support to maintain them as important parts of our legal system. The legitimacy of such limits on rights is explicitly provided for in section 1 of the Charter.

Earlier proposals for an entrenched bill of rights contained similar qualifications. For example, the Victoria Charter's guarantee of freedom of conscience, religion, thought and expression, and peaceful assembly and association was limited by the following provision:

> Nothing in this part shall be construed as preventing such limitations on the exercise of the fundamental freedoms as are reasonably justifiable in a democratic society in the interests of public safety, order, health or morals, of national security, or of the rights and freedoms of others, whether imposed by the Parliament of Canada or the Legislature of a Province, within the limits of their respective legislative powers, or by the construction or application of any law.[1]

In a similar vein, but much more succinctly, a very early draft of section 1 of the Charter stated simply that the guaranteed rights were "subject only to such reasonable limits as are generally accepted in a free and democratic society."[2] Worded in this way, the limitations clause was clearly designed to promote judicial deference to the policy decisions of the more openly political branches of government.

In the federal government's October 1980 draft of the Charter, section 1 read as follows:

> The Canadian Charter of Rights and Freedoms guarantees the rights and freedoms set out in it subject only to such reasonable limits as are generally accepted in a free and democratic society with a parliamentary system of government.[3]

The judicial deference implied by this wording was too much for many rights enthusiasts, who complained bitterly that it would eviscerate the Charter. If Canadian legislatures adopted a policy limiting rights, they asked, might that in itself be sufficient to demonstrate that the policy was "generally accepted in a free and democratic society with a parliamentary system of government," and that it was therefore "reasonable"? If so, the courts could never strike down a law, in which case what was the point of having a Charter?

These criticisms eventually led to the current wording, which replaces "generally accepted" with "demonstrably justified," drops the reference to a parliamentary system of government, and adds the requirement that limits can be justified only if they are "prescribed by law." As Peter Hogg remarks, "each of these [three] changes tends to narrow the limitation clause, and by indirection to broaden the guarantees."[4] The words "demonstrably justified," for example, mean that legislation violating Charter rights can be saved by section 1 only by clearing a hurdle much higher than that erected by the phrase "generally accepted." They also place the burden in establishing a section 1 defence squarely on the government. Under the "generally acceptable" standard, in other words, the mere fact that a democratically elected legislature had adopted the policy might have created a presumption in its favour, which would have to be rebutted by those seeking its invalidation. The fact that something is "generally accepted" does not "demonstrably justify" it, however, and thus no presumption in favour of a policy is created by the simple fact of its enactment. The party challenging a law must demonstrate that rights have indeed been violated, but once this is accomplished the onus shifts to the government to show that the violation is "demonstrably justified."

A violation must be justified, moreover, by the standards of "free and democratic" societies simply, not just those with parliamentary systems of government. This forces the courts to consider the experience of such nonparliamentary regimes as the United States.[5] It casts a wider comparative net, and to the extent that comparative analysis is relevant to a section 1 defence, it suggests that if any free and democratic society manages to do without a particular limitation, it is not "demonstrably justified," even if it has been "generally accepted" in Canada or other parliamentary democracies.

Finally, only those violations of Charter rights that are "prescribed by law" are eligible for justification under section 1. This excludes policies embedded in administrative practice, rather than in explicit legislation. Nor will vague enabling legislation suffice to make a policy eligible for section 1 justification. For example, if a censorship law is so vague that it lays down no clear guidelines of what is to be censored, then the actual standards used by the law's administrators are *their* standards, not the law's.[6] Not being "prescribed by law," they cannot avail themselves of a section 1 defence, even if they are otherwise "demonstrably justified in a free and democratic society."

Section 1 has no explicit counterpart in the United States Bill of Rights. Since Americans agree that rights must be subject to reasonable limits, their judges have had to find other ways of establishing those limits. A characteristic response has been to impose definitional limits on the literal wording of the protected rights. The technique is a familiar one in legal interpretation. We can all agree, for example, that a bylaw stating "no vehicles in the park" should not be read to apply to tricycles, even if they fall under the strict dictionary definition of "vehicle." A sensible judge will throw out a charge brought against a 5-year-old tricyclist by an overzealous and literalist police officer on the grounds that, whatever the dictionary says, the *legal* meaning of "vehicle" in this case includes cars and motorcycles but not tricycles. In a similar fashion, American judges have found that obscenity or libel simply do not form part of the "speech" or "press" protected by the first amendment to the constitution. Once it has been determined that a particular expression is obscene or libellous, a law limiting or prohibiting it violates no constitutional right.

Such definitional limitations of constitutional language need not in themselves settle the immediate policy issues involved. In the case of obscenity, for example, the American constitutional rule excluding it from first amendment protection leaves room for disagreement in determining whether a particular expression is in fact obscene. Such disagreement has been rampant among American judges.[7] In an important sense, therefore, the practical scope of freedom for obscene expression has been determined less by the constitutional rule than by the shifting definitions of what counts as obscene. Thus for several years the constitutional rule that obscenity did not deserve first amendment protection was vitiated by the Supreme Court's reluctance to find anything obscene. The constitutional rule remained symbolically important, however, and provided the basis for some return of censorship as the Supreme Court acquired a majority with a broader practical definition of obscenity.[8]

In addition to defining rights narrowly, so that certain activities and interests are entirely excluded from their scope, American courts have also rank ordered activities and interests that are covered. For example, the fourteenth amendment to the U.S. constitution says that no state shall "deny to any person within its jurisdiction the equal protection of the laws." This can be read as a very broad prohibition of governmental discrimination. But virtually all legislation discriminates. Criminal law, for example, discriminates against criminals; progressive tax laws discriminate against the better off[9]; and minimum-age qualifications for voting, drinking, or driving discriminate against the young. Surely the equal protection clause of the fourteenth amendment does not prohibit all such laws. The U.S. Supreme Court could have avoided this problem simply by placing definitional limits on the applicability of the equal protection clause—by, for example, interpreting it to prohibit only discrimination based on race or ethnicity. The Court did not take this route, however. Instead, leaving intact the provision's literal application to all forms of discrimination, it created a rank ordering of kinds of discrimination, subject to varying degrees of judicial scrutiny. At one end were classifications based on race or national origin, which were subject to a "strict scrutiny" that was virtually impossible to survive. This level of scrutiny, it has been said, is "strict in theory but fatal in fact."[10] At the other end were most other kinds of classifications, which were subject to "minimal scrutiny." Technically these kinds of legislative classifications were covered by the equal protection clause, but they would survive judicial scrutiny relatively easily. If strict scrutiny was almost always fatal, minimal scrutiny virtually never led to the invalidation of a law. In a sense, then, the difference between excluding an interest or activity from the coverage of a constitutional right by definition and giving it a low ranking is more formal than real: if an interest is covered but its legislative limitation is always justified, it might as well have been definitionally excluded.

For a time, strict and minimal scrutiny were the only two classifications, but the U.S. Court eventually added a third, including most prominently sex, which was subject to "intermediate scrutiny." Such classifications would be more difficult to justify than those subject to minimal scrutiny, but also more difficult to invalidate than those subject to strict scrutiny.[11] This "intermediate" category obviously increases judicial discretion. Because the kinds of discrimination it covers are neither automatically sustained nor automatically invalidated, their fate will depend on variable circumstances, as judges perceive them in each case.

Both definitional exclusion and rank ordering may be called "internal" limitations on constitutional language, in the sense that they are located within the substantive provision itself. They are contrasted with "external" limitations, such as section 1 of the Canadian Charter.[12] Where external limitations are available, it is not necessary to define the protected rights narrowly or to rank order the interests they cover. In Canada, for example, the section 2 guarantee of freedom of expression can be read broadly and literally to include obscenity or libel, so that laws restricting these forms of expression are *prima facie* violations of the Charter, and those laws can nevertheless be upheld as "demonstrably justified" under section 1. Similarly, instead of rank ordering the equality rights provided by section 15, one can rank order limitations on those rights under section 1.[13]

Some judges and commentators contend that the latter is the correct approach to the Charter, that the judicial development of internal limits to Charter rights should be avoided in favour of an exclusive reliance on section 1 for any necessary limits. David Beatty provides the most intransigent development of this view. Given the existence of section 1, Beatty argues, internal limits are unnecessary and Charter rights should therefore be given the widest interpretation possible. He concedes that "occasionally, certain interests or activities might not fall within the protection of one of the rights and freedoms entrenched in the Charter," but insists that "most laws could be shown to impact adversely on some aspect of the constitutional freedom and/or equality of those they affected" because "all law coerces and puts some constraint on the freedom of some people to govern their lives by their own lights." "The result," he concludes, "would be that most, if not all, Canadian law would be subject to being evaluated against" the standards of section 1.[14] This means that interpretation of the scope of substantive Charter rights—in terms of what interests they cover or which of the covered interests take precedence over others—is largely irrelevant. For Beatty, the process of judicial review properly understood has "relatively little to do with defining which interests and activities are protected by the rights and freedoms which the Charter guarantees" because virtually all interests and activities are covered. "Justification, not interpretation," he insists, "is what the Charter and judicial review is mostly about. Section 1, not the substantive sections in which the rights and freedoms are entrenched, is where all of the action takes place."[15]

Although the Supreme Court of Canada has sometimes employed Beatty's preferred approach, it has not done so consistently. Much to Beatty's dismay, the Court has persisted in defining internal limits for Charter rights. For example, a majority of the Supreme Court decided that labour strikes were not among the kinds of activities covered by the section 2 right to "freedom of association."[16] Because there is no constitutional right to strike, there is no need for governments to justify limitations on the freedom to strike under the "external" standards of section 1.

Even such judges as Justice Wilson who appear to accept Beatty's vision and usually act in accordance with it sometimes resort to internal limitations. This happened in *R. v. Jones*,[17] a case raising questions of religious freedom. Pastor Larry Jones of Calgary, who operated an alternative Christian school, refused to apply to provincial authorities for certification and accreditation, as Alberta's School Act required. Jones claimed that his educational mission came from God, not the State, and that while the secular authorities were free to visit and inspect his school and certify it if they wished, he could not apply to them for permission to carry out his God-given responsibility without compromising his religious beliefs. There is no reason to question the sincerity of Pastor Jones's beliefs, or the fact that they would have been compromised by complying with the legal requirements, but Justice Wilson nevertheless concluded that the limitation of his religious freedom, if any, was too trivial to count as a violation of section 2 of the Charter.[18] In other words, she built into the definition of religious freedom a threshold of the importance or significance of a violation. Legally, infringements too trivial to pass the threshold were not infringements at all. Again, this meant that there was no need to assess Alberta's law under the standards of section 1.

Other judges in *Jones* preferred to rely on external limits, reaching the same result by finding that Jones's Charter right to religious freedom had indeed been violated, but that the violation was "demonstrably justified" under section 1.[19] This shows that in particular cases the result of the internal and external approaches may be the same, and one is thus led to wonder why judges and commentators debate the relative merits of the two approaches so vigorously. In fact, there are substantial differences, even when, as in *Jones,* both approaches lead to the same bottom-line decision. For one thing, the rhetorical significance is quite different. Where the law is saved by a definitional or internal limit on the right, no constitutional violation has occurred. Saving a law under the external standards of section 1, by contrast, implies that rights have been violated, but that the violation is justified by other considerations. The different symbolism associated with the two approaches is bound to have political consequences and thus attracts the interest of political partisans. (We shall have much more to say about the symbolic dimensions of Charter politics in the next chapter.)

Equally important is the fact that internal limitations reduce the scope for judicial review by excluding entire areas of activity from the effective control of Charter rights, either by definitionally excluding them or by considering them so unimportant that government interference is almost always justified. This has the effect of exempting laws regulating these areas from the necessity of justifying themselves under section 1. Peter Russell uses the example of freedom of association to make this point. "If this freedom were interpreted widely enough to encompass business organizations and their essential economic activities," he writes, "then virtually every regulation of business would be deemed to encroach on a constitutional right and could be saved only by government lawyers persuading judges that the regulation was a reasonable and justifiable limit under section 1." This interpretation would mean an endless stream of cases in which virtually the only question would be the judicial reconsideration of the government's conclusion as to the reasonableness of the law. "If on the other hand," Russell continues, freedom of association "were construed more narrowly to exclude the essential economic activities of business corporations, then the opportunities for judicial review would be considerably reduced."[20] This difference is obviously important in the debate between Charterphiles, who want to expand the opportunities for judicial review, and Charter sceptics, who want to restrict them.

In fact, even friends of judicial review have argued against an overreliance on the external limitations of section 1. Thus Paul Bender, an American observer who enthusiastically welcomed the advent of the Canadian Charter, argued that "it is a serious mistake to assume that the Charter has constitutionalized all concerns about legislation and governmental practices that may affect individual or commercial interests, thus requiring courts, in every case ... to ask whether there is a constitutionally adequate justification for the challenged rules or activities."[21] Bender worried that if virtually all policy *prima facie* violated the Charter (as Beatty has suggested), the necessity of justifying most of it would lead to "extremely weak and deferential standards" of section 1 justification. It is because he wanted Charter violations to be relatively difficult to justify under section 1 that he counselled the definitional exclusion from Charter protection of those activities and interests whose limitation is more easily justified.[22] Bender, in short, supported definitional limits in the name of increased judicial activism in areas that remain within the ambit of Charter protection.

Nor is the controversy exhausted by the question of how much room for section 1 consideration should be left by the process of defining Charter rights. One must still ask what guidelines should cover section 1 analysis when it is brought into play by a finding that Charter rights have been infringed. In the 1986 case of *R. v. Oakes*,[23] the Supreme Court of Canada set out a two-stage procedure for applying section 1. If the government wishes to defend a law that violates Charter rights, it bears the burden of demonstrating first that the violation is justified by a "pressing and substantial" objective, and second that the legislative means are "proportional" to that objective. The "proportionality test" is itself divided into three components: first, the legislative means must not be arbitrary—that is, they must be "rationally connected" to the law's purpose inasmuch as they actually achieve it. This is commonly known as the "rational connection" test. Second, the legislative means must impair the relevant Charter right (or rights) as little as possible. This second component of "proportionality" is often called the "minimal impairment" or "least drastic means" test. Since it implies a comparative assessment of different ways of achieving the same policy purpose, it is also referred to as the "alternative means" principle. Third, what the legislative means cost in lost rights must be proportional to their benefits in general welfare—that is, "the more severe the deleterious effects, the more [pressing and substantial] the objective must be," or as Ian Greene puts it, "the cure cannot be allowed to be more harmful than the disease."[24]

Oakes is a judicial attempt to give more precise meaning to the general wording of section 1. In closing off some interpretive doors, however, it opens others. *Oakes* is itself open to interpretation; it does not apply itself in an automatic manner. Judges can and do disagree about whether the means chosen by a legislature to achieve its purpose are arbitrary, whether their infringement of Charter rights is minimal, or whether the benefits achieved are worth the cost.

A significant variation in interpretive approaches is possible. If they were so inclined judges could use the various components of the *Oakes* test, in combination with a generous definition of substantive rights, to make it very difficult for legislation to achieve section 1 justification. If a stringent application of *Oakes* is combined with the notion that Charter rights should be read very broadly, with few internal limitations, a very activist jurisprudence—that is, a judicial willingness to strike down legislation—would result. If rights are interpreted broadly, in other words, they will be easy to violate, and if the *Oakes* test is applied stringently, those violations will be difficult to justify. The very presence of section 1 makes it plausible to argue that the substantive rights should be read broadly—the required limits, after all, can be justified under section 1 and need not be imposed through definitional restriction[25]—and the relatively strict wording of section 1, as embellished by the *Oakes* test, could erect a high standard of justification. Ironically, although section 1 had its origin in the desire to promote judicial deference to political judgments, it has the potential of supporting judicial activism instead.[26] The extent to which it should be taken in this direction is an important issue in Charter politics. We can safely predict that it will not be taken to the logical extreme, however, because, as Bender suggests, judges will not place themselves in the absurd position of finding virtually all policies in *prima facie* violation of the Charter *and* making all of them very difficult to justify under section 1.

It is not surprising, then, to find that the Supreme Court has not fully exploited the activist potential of section 1. For example, the Court seems to have decided that the standard established by *Oakes* for assessing legislative objectives is "too stringent for application in all cases."[27] Instead of asking whether the purpose is "pressing and substantial," Justice McIntyre argued in 1989, the Court's first question should sometimes be "whether the limitation represents a legitimate exercise of the legislative power for the attainment of a desirable social objective which would warrant overriding constitutionally protected rights."[28] Speaking for a unanimous panel of seven judges in *Rocket* v. *Royal College of Dental Surgeons of Ontario,* a 1990 freedom-of-expression case, Justice McLachlin dropped any reference to the "pressing and substantial" standard, arguing simply that the legislative objective "must be of sufficient importance to warrant overriding a constitutionally protected right."[29] The stricter formulation of the *Oakes* case has certainly not been abandoned, but it is no longer applied in all cases. Of course, this imposes yet another choice on judges—they must now determine which standard is best suited to a particular law—and thus provides another access point for Charter politics.

Although it has symbolic importance, we should not overemphasize the practical significance of the Court's dilution of the "pressing and substantial" standard. For reasons we shall explore in Chapter Six, the courts will rarely invalidate legislation because its objective is not important enough, even if the standard of importance is "pressing and substantial." If legislation cannot be justified under section 1, it will almost always be because the means are not proportional to the ends, not because the ends themselves have been directly called into question under the first branch of the *Oakes* test. Substituting "desirable" or "sufficiently important" for "pressing and substantial" can be understood as a way of making the almost inevitable judicial blessing of legislative purpose rhetorically more palatable.

The Court has also softened the minimal impairment branch of the *Oakes* test, apparently better to accommodate the diversities of federalism.[30] *Oakes* addressed the constitutionality of a federal statute, and thus did not raise the question of different provincial statutes using a variety of means to pursue the same objective. Taken literally, the minimal impairment test suggests that if provincial legislation addressing a common policy concern varied in the degree to which it infringed Charter rights, the province with "minimal impairment" would set the constitutional standard for all the others. The very existence of its less intrusive legislation would show that the other provinces had not met the minimal impairment standard, and that their legislation was unconstitutional. Such an approach would certainly confirm the worry, expressed by provincial critics of the Charter during the period leading up to its enactment, that the Charter would go too far in imposing national standards in provincial areas of jurisdiction, thus substantially reducing the policy-making authority of provincial governments. To avoid this result, the majority of the Supreme Court, in *Edwards Books* (a 1986 case addressing the constitutionality of a provincial Sunday-closing law), modified the *Oakes* rule that a law should impair Charter rights "as little as possible," substituting the phrase "as little as is *reasonably* possible."[31] The legislative limit, added Chief Justice Dickson, could be sustained if it was "one that was *reasonable* for the legislature to impose."[32] This looser formulation enabled the Court to uphold Ontario's Sunday-closing law despite the fact that, in certain respects, it restricted religious freedom more than the laws of other provinces. The looser formulation, of course, also expands judicial discretion. What is "reasonable" in the circumstances is not nearly as obvious as the "least drastic means."

The Court's reluctance fully to embrace the activist potential of section 1 is also apparent in its adoption of an American-style rank ordering of the interests and activities covered by certain rights. We have seen that the Court sometimes places definitional limits on the scope of Charter rights. Nevertheless, its general tendency has been to give the protected rights a "large and liberal" interpretation, so that a great many interests and activities are covered. On the other hand, the Court has begun to attribute varying degrees of constitutional importance to the covered interests for purposes of applying section 1. Protected interests and activities are distinguished by their proximity to the "core" values underlying a right. The more distant or "peripheral" they are in relation to the core, the easier it will be to justify legislative limits under section 1.

In *Cotroni,* for example, the Court decided that although extradition violated the Charter's section 6 mobility rights, it "lies at the outer edges of the core values sought to be protected by that provision."[33] The core consisted of such matters as exile or banishment. Because extradition lay at the periphery of the range of interests covered by section 6, it was more easily justified under section 1.

The Court's freedom-of-expression cases provide another good example of rank ordering. In these cases the Court has placed almost no definitional limits on the kinds of expression protected by section 2(b). As long as a meaning of some kind is being conveyed, and as long as that meaning is not communicated in a violent form (e.g., a political assassination), it comes within the Charter's protection. Thus commercial advertising,[34] soliciting for the purposes of prostitution,[35] and the promotion of hatred[36] have all been deemed protected forms of expression. On the other hand, the Court has made it clear that not all laws limiting protected expression will be subject to equally searching scrutiny under section 1. Again, it depends on how closely the regulated or prohibited expression approaches to the values lying at the core of section 2. These the Court defines as "seeking truth"[37] in the "marketplace of ideas,"[38] participation "in the political process,"[39] and the individual achievement of "spiritual or artistic self-fulfillment."[40] The courts will not readily permit section 1 to be used to justify limits on expression closely linked to these ends. On the other hand, the Court considers purely commercial expression, such as advertising, to be sufficiently distant from the core that "restrictions on expression of this kind might be easier to justify than other infringements."[41] According to Justice Dickson, for example, "it can hardly be said that communications regarding an economic transaction of sex for money lie at, or even near, the core of the guarantee of freedom of expression,"[42] a perception that clearly influenced his decision to uphold the Criminal Code prohibitions of soliciting in the *Prostitution Reference*. Similarly, in his majority opinion in *Keegstra,* a 1990 challenge to a federal law prohibiting the promotion of hatred of identifiable groups, Justice Dickson concluded that hate-mongering "is of limited importance when measured against free-expression values."[43] Because it is "a category of expression which strays some distance from the spirit of s. 2(b)," he wrote, its limitation is "easier to justify" under section 1.[44] Needless to say, there is bound to be controversy about where on the continuum from "core" to "periphery" a protected interest falls. Because the answer to this question strongly influences the outcome of a Charter challenge, it is likely to become a significant focus of Charter politics.

Charter claimants who do not succeed in securing "core" status for their favoured interest will obviously not be pleased. Nevertheless, they should not succumb to total despair. While governments will certainly find it easier to justify legislative limits on interests and activities ranked low on the scale of constitutional importance, they cannot assume that such limits will always pass constitutional muster. The Court has been careful not to turn its rank ordering into a de facto form of definitional exclusion. Such a transformation of rank ordering into definitional exclusion would occur if the low ranking of specified kinds of interests led to complete judicial deference to legislative judgments about limits on those interests. In the United States just this kind of deference is entailed in the minimal scrutiny given to legislative limits on certain less important interests. As we have seen, interests subject to minimal scrutiny can be limited virtually at will by legislatures, with no real threat of judicial invalidation. Although they technically fall within the protection of constitutional provisions, interests receiving such a low ranking turn out to be practically indistinguishable from those that have been definitionally excluded from constitutional protection. The Supreme Court of Canada has explicitly rejected the categorical application of minimal scrutiny to limits on certain kinds of protected interests and activities.[45] Once again we find judicial discretion preserved. Not even a finding that an interest claiming protection lies far from the Charter's "core" puts an end to Charter politics.

■ THE EXCLUSIONARY RULE

When legislation infringes a Charter right, the second part of the Two Step involves determining whether the violation is nevertheless "demonstrably justified" as a "reasonable limit" in a "free and democratic society." When evidence relevant to a legal proceeding is obtained through the violation of a right, the second step (or third, if the violation is "prescribed by law") is to determine whether to exclude the evidence under section 24(2).

Although the section 24(2) "exclusionary rule" is new in Canada's legal system, the exclusion of evidence is not. Canadian courts have always excluded evidence obtained in a manner that undermined its reliability. A confession extracted by torture, for example, has dubious probative value and would have been excluded as readily before 1982 as after. Prior to the Charter, however, Canadian courts tended to admit improperly obtained evidence that was relevant and reliable.[46] Section 24(2) thus effects a dramatic change in Canadian criminal procedure. It tells judges that they "shall" exclude evidence "obtained in a manner" that infringes Charter rights if they believe its admission "would bring the administration of justice into disrepute." This means that perfectly reliable evidence may be excluded, and that offenders who would previously have been convicted may now go unpunished. The extent of the change, of course, depends on what kinds of evidence judges think would bring the administration of justice into disrepute. The more reluctant judges are to assume that the admission of tainted evidence will cause disrepute, the smaller the impact on the traditional approach. Here again we encounter no small measure of judicial discretion. Very early in the Charter's history, the Supreme Court showed little reluctance to exclude evidence, and thus set in motion a significant transformation of the legal system.

The contrast between *Hogan* v. *The Queen* (1975) and *R.* v. *Manninen* (1987)[47] illustrates the change judges have wrought in the name of section 24(2). The police spotted Hogan driving erratically in 1972 and pulled him over. Observing signs of alcohol consumption, they took Hogan to the police station and asked him to submit to a breathalyzer test. Hogan was accompanied by his girlfriend and asked her to call his lawyer. The lawyer arrived at the station before the test was administered, and hearing his voice in the next room, Hogan asked to see him. The police refused, informing Hogan that he had to take the test first, and that if he did not he would be charged with the alternative crime of refusing a breathalyzer. Hogan blew and was found to have an illegal blood-alcohol level. The Court concluded that the evidence was admissible despite the fact that the police officers had infringed the 1960 Canadian Bill of Rights in refusing to let Hogan see his lawyer.

Violation of the Charter's section 10(b) right to counsel had a markedly different effect on the admissibility of evidence in Manninen's case. When the police arrested Manninen in 1982 on suspicion of robbery, they twice "read him his rights," indicating that he had "the right to retain and instruct counsel without delay" and was "not obliged to say anything." After the first reading Manninen made a "flippant remark" to the effect that "it sounds like an American T.V. programme."[48] After the second reading, Manninen responded: "Prove it. I ain't saying anything until I see my lawyer. I want to see my lawyer." Then followed this exchange between the officer and Manninen:

> Q. What is your full name?
> A. Ronald Charles Manninen.
> Q. Where is your address?
> A. Ain't got one.
> Q. Where is the knife that you had along with this (showing respondent the CO2 gun found in the car) when you ripped off the Mac's Milk on Wilson Avenue?
> A. He's lying. When I was in the store I only had the gun. The knife was in the tool box in the car.[49]

Manninen had clearly expressed his desire to see his lawyer before answering further questions, but the police continued questioning him nonetheless, beginning with two rather innocuous, "record keeping" questions, followed by a question designed to elicit a confession. The ruse worked easily, perhaps to the officer's surprise. In any case, the Supreme Court found that the continued questioning of Manninen after he had asked to contact a lawyer violated his section 10(b) right to counsel. The Court then considered whether or not to exclude the evidence. Prior to the Charter, Manninen's statement would certainly have been admitted, even by a court that disapproved of the way in which the police obtained it. But no longer. Although it had no doubt that the statement was reliable, clearly establishing Manninen's guilt in the commission of a serious offence,[50] the Supreme Court decided that the violation of Manninen's right to counsel justified excluding the statement.

No doubt there was other evidence pointing to Manninen's guilt, and his statement may not have been as crucial to his conviction as the breathalyzer evidence was in Hogan's case. This should not obscure the novel judicial thinking represented by *Manninen,* however. The same thinking has led the Court to exclude even evidence absolutely central to a conviction. In *Therens,*[51] for example, the Court excluded breathalyzer evidence because the police had infringed the accused's right to counsel, even though the violation was much less blatant than it was in *Hogan.* (We shall discuss *Therens* in greater detail in Chapter Eight.) Clearly judges have used their discretion under section 24(2) to work a minor revolution in Canadian criminal process. Should judges use their discretionary authority under fairly vague and indeterminate constitutional language to undertake such dramatic policy reforms? This question lies at the heart of Charter politics.

There are two main justifications for excluding constitutionally tainted evidence from trials even if its reliability is not in question: one may wish to exclude such evidence either to deter police misbehaviour or to avoid bringing the administration of justice into disrepute. The second justification is explicitly written into section 24(2) of the Charter. The United States constitution contains no analogous provision explicitly providing for the exclusion of tainted evidence, and the American rule is thus a judicially created remedy. When the U.S. Supreme Court created this remedy it grounded it in part on the first justification—that is, in excluding tainted evidence the Court hoped to deter police misbehaviour by depriving officers of the "reward" of conviction.[52] In Canada judges have occasionally flirted with the "deterrence" rationale for excluding evidence,[53] but on the whole the Supreme Court has emphasized the role explicitly stated in section 24(2), namely to maintain the good reputation of the judicial system. Evidence should be excluded, in other words, if admitting it would bring the administration of justice into disrepute, even if such exclusion does not deter police misbehaviour.[54] But, of course, admitting tainted evidence does not always bring the administration of justice into disrepute. Indeed, in some circumstances exclusion may cause greater damage to the reputation of the system, as when someone who is obviously guilty of a serious crime goes free because the police made minor technical mistakes in obtaining crucial evidence. This is why section 24(2) requires evidence to be excluded only if the court is satisfied that, "*having regard to all the circumstances,* the admission of it in the proceedings would bring the administration of justice into disrepute."[55]

But how does one know when disrepute is most likely to occur? Answering this question appears to require judges to determine how the general public is likely to react to the admission or exclusion of evidence in the circumstances of a particular case. How are judges, who are carefully insulated from the effects of public opinion, to arrive at such a judgment? Dale Gibson has suggested that the Court pay some attention to public opinion polls,[56] but the Supreme Court has rejected this as an impractical and unjudicial proposal, which concedes too much to unreflective public passion. Instead, it has directed judges to imaginatively place themselves in the shoes of the "reasonable person."[57] The potential for disagreement and controversy is obvious.

The Supreme Court has articulated several criteria that judicial surrogates for the hypothetical "reasonable person" should take into account in deciding whether to exclude or admit constitutionally tainted evidence. First they must ask whether admitting the evidence would undermine the fairness of the trial.[58] An unfair trial would certainly bring the administration of justice into disrepute, and evidence contributing to unfairness should thus generally be excluded. Abstractly considered, this view would occasion little dissent. Everything depends, of course, on what kind of evidence is found to render a trial unfair. It is here that controversy is bound to arise.

To aid in determining when unfair trials would result, the Court has distinguished between two kinds of evidence. "Real" evidence exists whether or not rights were infringed in obtaining it. The existence of a "smoking gun" bearing the suspect's fingerprints, for example, is not affected by the fact that it was found in the course of an illegal search. "Evidence emanating from the accused," on the other hand, might not exist at all had constitutional rights been respected.[59] Thus Manninen's incriminating statement might never have been made had the police ceased all questioning until a lawyer arrived to help stiffen his resolve to remain silent. In the Court's view evidence of this kind, which would not exist but for the constitutional violations involved in obtaining it, almost always renders the trial unfair and thus should be excluded. It undermines the principle of a fair trial by negating one of its central components: the right against self-incrimination. On the other hand, "real" evidence, which exists despite the constitutional violation, will rarely render the trial unfair and is thus more likely to be admitted.[60]

Again, the Court's abstract claim that the right against self-incrimination is essential to a fair trial would likely garner widespread support. But, as *Manninen* shows, the Court is actually protecting neither the right to refuse to take the stand in one's own defence at one's trial, nor the right not to incriminate oneself in the course of testifying against someone else—rights that are clearly protected by sections 11(c) and 13 of the Charter—but the right not to incriminate oneself in the process of pre-trial investigation. In the Court's view, the trial is rendered unfair not only by nonspontaneous self-incrimination at the trial itself, but also by similar pre-trial self-incrimination. The right clearly protected in the context of a trial is interpretively pushed back into the pre-trial context, to which it does not as obviously apply. Indeed, despite the more questionable status of a pre-trial right to silence, the Court understands the main purpose of the section 10(b) right to counsel to be to guarantee this right.[61] This is apt to be more controversial. The public, in short, might well be more likely to concede Manninen's right to remain silent during the trial than to agree that his self-incriminating pre-trial statement should be excluded from the trial. Placing the onus on the prosecution to prove guilt beyond a reasonable doubt without the opportunity to cross-examine the accused at trial is one thing. Requiring the prosecution to rely almost exclusively on "real" rather than "statement" evidence in proving its case—which is surely the likely effect of interpreting the right to counsel as the guarantee of pre-trial silence—is quite another and probably more controversial thing. Certainly in the United States, as we noted in the previous chapter, a similar judicially created barrier to eliciting and using pre-trial statements has contributed to a backlash against what is seen as the "coddling of criminals" by liberal judges.

In fact, the Canadian Supreme Court used its interpretive discretion to extend even greater protection to criminal suspects than has its American counterpart. While verbal statements such as Manninen's are the most obvious examples of "evidence emanating from the accused," the Court's use of this broad phrasing made it easy subsequently to bring other kinds of evidence under the same rule. Use of the "emanating-from-the-accused" formulation, in other words, introduced new interpretive possibilities, which the Court was not slow to exploit. The Court soon declared that evidence "emanating from the accused" in the context of a Charter violation includes not only statements, but any evidence "that could not have been obtained but for the participation of the accused in the construction of the evidence for the purposes of the trial,"[62] such as breathalyzer certificates[63] or identification resulting from participation in a lineup.[64] In such circumstances, too, the accused must be informed of the right to retain counsel and given the opportunity to exercise that right.

In the United States, by contrast, although the right to counsel is also seen as guaranteeing a pre-trial right against self-incrimination, the latter right applies only to self-incrimination in the form of statements elicited during custodial interrogation. Thus American police "are not required to warn suspects [about their right to counsel] before they are placed in pre-indictment line-ups, before hand-writing samples are obtained, or before blood samples are taken." Such evidence, gained in the absence of legal counsel, does not violate the right against self-incrimination as the U.S. Court understands it, and is thus admissible in legal proceedings.[65] By contrast, all of these situations would appear to fall under the broader emanating-from-the-accused test adopted by the Canadian Court, and the resulting evidence would thus be excluded.[66] If the American exclusionary rule has occasioned what Peter Russell calls "court bashing,"[67] its broader applicability in Canada certainly does nothing to diminish the prospects of a similar backlash. Whether such a backlash becomes part of Canada's Charter politics remains to be seen, but the potential is there.

Whether or not to exclude evidence also depends on a set of factors having to do with the seriousness of the Charter violation. The less serious the violation, the more likely it is that the evidence will be admitted. The seriousness of a Charter violation is affected by a number of factors, including whether "it was committed in good faith, whether it was inadvertent or of a merely technical nature, whether it was motivated by urgency or to prevent the loss of evidence, and whether the evidence could have been obtained without a Charter violation."[68]

Urgency and preventing the loss of evidence are self-explanatory. The other two factors are well illustrated by *R. v. Duarte*.[69] This case provides an example of a "good faith" violation that was not necessary to obtain the evidence. Duarte was charged with conspiring to import a narcotic on the basis of statements he made to a "wired" undercover policeman. The Criminal Code required the police to obtain a judicial warrant for most kinds of electronic surveillance, but exempted the kind of "participant surveillance" that occurred in *Duarte*. Participant surveillance takes place when one of the participants in a conversation (in this case the undercover police officer) secretly records statements voluntarily made by another participant. This is distinguished from such circumstances as a telephone wiretap, in which the police are "third parties" whose presence is unknown to the suspect. Under the law, telephone wiretaps required a judicial warrant, but placing a "wire" on an undercover officer did not. The majority of the Court found warrantless participant surveillance to be an unreasonable search and seizure in violation of section 8 of the Charter, and thus subjected such surveillance to the general requirement of judicial authorization. Nevertheless, Justice La Forest, writing for the majority, concluded that "[t]he police officers acted entirely in good faith. They were acting in accordance with what they had good reason to believe was the law—as it had been for many years before the advent of the Charter."[70] Had they been aware of the constitutional requirement the Court would set, moreover, they could easily have gotten the required warrant and obtained the evidence legally. Summing up his view, Justice La Forest wrote that "the Charter breach stemmed from an entirely reasonable misunderstanding of the law by the police officers who would otherwise have obtained the necessary evidence to convict the accused in any event."[71] For this reason, the illegally acquired evidence was admitted. *Duarte* shows that the Court will sometimes admit even statement evidence, which might not exist in the absence of the Charter violation, and which the Court believes usually undermines the fairness of the trial. Real evidence obtained through a "good faith" violation is all the more likely to be admitted.

If the Charter violation is not overly serious, the judge must also consider the importance of the evidence to the trial. If the evidence is not particularly central, it might be excluded even if the Charter violation through which it was obtained is not terribly serious. On the other hand, "the administration of justice may be brought into disrepute by excluding evidence essential to substantiate the charge where the breach of the Charter was trivial."[72] By the same token, the judge must consider the seriousness of the charge against the accused. The more serious the alleged offence, the more likely it is that the administration of justice will be brought into disrepute by the exclusion of essential evidence, especially if the Charter violation was trivial. In other words, major criminals should not go free on the basis of mere technicalities.[73] On the other hand, even evidence essential to substantiating a serious charge should be excluded if it would result in an unfair trial. Indeed, "[i]f any relevance is to be given to the seriousness of the offence in the context of the fairness of the trial, it operates in the opposite sense: the more serious the offence, the more damaging to the system's repute would be an unfair trial." Thus, while the seriousness of the charge weighs in favour of admitting essential "real" evidence, it counts against admitting evidence "that could not have been obtained but for the participation of the accused in [its] construction."[74] In other words, even serious criminals may go free if reliable statement evidence essential to their conviction was obtained in violation of a Charter right (usually the right to counsel). If Manninen's incriminating statement were the only evidence against him, he would go free, however reliable the court might think the statement was. He would go free because, in the Court's view, admitting the statement would bring the administration of justice into disrepute in the eyes of the "reasonable person." One might be forgiven for suspecting that many Canadians (probably a majority) would not be "reasonable" by this standard. Again, the potential for Charter politics is obvious.

■ JUDICIAL DISCRETION AND CHARTER POLITICS

Charter politics arises because judges have the power to make important choices between alternative readings of what the Charter requires, choices that can significantly influence political symbolism and public policy. Political partisans are drawn to the courtroom because they understand that judges have great discretion in placing the considerable moral weight of the Charter on one side or another of a political controversy.

Judicial discretion is evident at every stage of the interpretive exercise. In the first part of the Charter Two Step, judges must give concrete meaning to the general language of most substantive Charter rights, thus determining which interests receive what degree of constitutional protection. As we shall see in the next chapter, the symbolic stakes in this allocation of constitutional status are high and constitute an important dimension of Charter politics.

A protected interest may not always be able to make its claim stick, however, depending on its position in the hierarchy of constitutional status and the weight of competing considerations. If the latter are sufficiently weighty, the courts may conclude, in the second part of the Two Step, that the rights limitation complained of is "demonstrably justified" as a "reasonable limit in a free and democratic society." This decision itself is highly discretionary. It involves several judgments, none of which is completely automatic. Judges must ask whether the purpose of a challenged law is sufficiently important to justify some infringement of the Charter, and if so whether the infringement under consideration is proportional to the purpose—i.e., whether the legislative means actually achieve the purpose without significantly more restriction of rights than plausibly available alternatives, and without costing more in lost rights than the legislative benefit is worth. Each question is replete with opportunities for disagreement, and the answers, with their policy ramifications, are thus often in doubt. The same is true of the second version of the Two Step, in which the second step concerns the admission or exclusion of constitutionally tainted evidence.

The consequence of judicial discretion is Charter politics: the public debate about the interpretive choices posed both by the Charter itself and by previous judicial glosses on its language. This debate is carried out in the courtroom by litigants and interest groups who place contending arguments before the judges, and outside the courtroom in a burgeoning "advocacy" literature designed to influence judicial choices.

Not surprisingly, the controversies of Charter politics are not so much settled by the judges as replicated among them. Like any other collective body faced with making discretionary policy choices, the members of a court are likely over time to divide into contending factions. And so it has been with Canada's Supreme Court. A study of the Court's first one hundred Charter cases found that, after an initial "honeymoon" period when most decisions were unanimous, the Court divided into distinguishable voting blocs who exercised their discretionary choice in predictably different ways.[75] An "activist" wing, led by Justice Wilson, tended to define rights broadly, which frequently impelled it to find violations of the Charter. Coming to the second part of the Two Step, this group was least likely to justify laws as "reasonable limits" under section 1 and most likely to exclude evidence under section 24(2). At the other end of the continuum was an alliance of self-restrained judges, led by Justice McIntyre, which was more inclined to place restrictive definitional limits on Charter rights, and when it did find a violation, to accept section 1 defences or admit improperly acquired evidence. We refer to Justices Wilson and McIntyre as "leaders" because they were most consistent in their respective activism and restraint. The "parties" they led, however, were somewhat loose and fluid alliances rather than the disciplined parties of Parliament. Voting across "party lines" is much more common on the Court than in the House of Commons. Still, Justice Lamer and to a lesser extent Justice Dickson were fairly reliable allies of Justice Wilson. Similarly, Justices L'Heureux-Dubé and La Forest were most likely to vote with McIntyre.

The point is that the outcome of a case might well be affected by the composition of the panel of judges hearing it. Unlike the U.S Supreme Court, which always sits as a full court of nine judges, Canada's Supreme Court often hears cases in panels of seven, and occasionally even in panels of five judges. The relative significance of either of the voting blocs might thus shift from case to case. To take only the most extreme example, a

Charter claimant is more likely to succeed before a panel including the activist wing and excluding its restrained counterpart than before a panel with the opposite composition.[76]

In courts as in other public decision-making bodies, in other words, the discretionary choices made are affected partly by *who* makes them. Just as the choices emanating from Parliament will differ depending on the relative strengths of the contending legislative parties, so the choices made by appeal courts will depend in part on the relative strengths of the parties of judicial activism and restraint. We should thus not be surprised to find the attempt to influence the composition of major appeal courts emerging as an important component of Charter politics.

Certainly a politics of judicial appointment has become well established in the United States, where it has long been recognized that it makes a very great difference whether the Supreme Court is dominated by the kind of judge represented by William O. Douglas (a member of the Court from 1968 to 1986), who supported civil liberties claims over 90 percent of the time, or William Rehnquist (the present Chief Justice), who rejects over 80 percent of such claims.[77] As we shall see in Chapter Five, the politics of appointment is most intense when a new appointee might tip the existing balance between the activist and restrained wings of the Court. In that chapter we shall also explain why a similar politics of appointment has not yet arisen in Canada, and why, in fact, it is less likely to arise. This does not mean, however, that the attempt to influence the kind of judge making choices under the Charter is absent from Charter politics. If the direct attempt to influence particular appointments turns out not to be a viable alternative for interest groups, it might still be possible to "re-educate" sitting judges to one's way of thinking. Thus Canadian feminist organizations have persuaded the Canadian Judicial Centre to hold special education seminars designed to sensitize existing judges to feminist perspectives on a variety of legal issues. Not surprisingly, antifeminist groups have challenged this privileged access to judges. Presumably they would like to see it ended, or expanded to provide them with similar "educational" opportunities. It remains to be seen whether this post-appointment attempt to influence judicial choices becomes an established part of Charter politics.

The concern with *who* gets to make the choices posed by the Charter is obviously not limited to judges' views on a range of substantive policy questions, such as abortion or censorship, but extends to the more general jurisprudential principles that influence the activist or restrained dispositions of judges. The contending approaches are examined in Chapters Five and Six. A closely related question concerns how much respect and finality should be accorded to judicial opinions; this question is taken up in Chapters Seven and Eight. The overt form of much of the debate about these questions is highly legalistic, but the underlying political reality is not lost on most of the participants. Nor should it be lost on the student of Canadian politics.

PART TWO

The Dimensions of Charter Politics

CHAPTER FOUR

Political Symbols and the Politics of Status

■ POLITICAL SCIENCE AND THE STUDY OF CONSTITUTIONAL LAW

Although constitutional politics has long been a Canadian preoccupation, the systematic study of constitutional law and judicial decisions has only recently regained prominence among Canadian political scientists. We say "regained" because constitutional law was a central component of the emergent discipline of Canadian political science in the late 19th and early 20th centuries. As Peter Russell has observed, up to about the 1920s the term "political science" in Canada "was primarily a rubric for a cluster of subjects comprised of political philosophy, economics, constitutional history and constitutional law."[1] There was less disciplinary separation in those days, and much of the constitutional literature was written by lawyers and judges. Although this work was sometimes animated by philosophical concerns,[2] the typical account of legal provisions and judicial decisions was descriptive and historical, with little attempt at political or critical analysis. The scope of the field expanded somewhat in the 1930s when the Judicial Committee of the Privy Council (JCPC), Canada's final court of appeal until 1949, invalidated much of the regulatory and social welfare legislation proposed by the Bennett government to deal with the Depression. The JCPC, continuing its by then well-established tradition, gave a very decentralist reading to the federal distribution of powers in the British North America (BNA) Act (now the Constitution Act, 1867), finding that important parts of the Bennett "New Deal" fell within provincial jurisdiction. This aroused the indignation of many nationalist and centralist commentators, who insisted that this provincialist interpretation was out of step with both the needs of the country and an accurate reading of the BNA Act. The latter they understood as embodying the centralist aspirations of Sir John A. Macdonald, one of the most prominent architects of Confederation and the country's prime minister during most of its first twenty-five years. The result was a burst of critical analysis of the JCPC's jurisprudence, but this did not produce a lasting interest in the courts and

63

constitutional law among political scientists. As the disciplines of law and political science increasingly separated from each other, political scientists were happy to leave legal matters to the lawyers, especially as judicial review of federalism seemed to decline in importance in the postwar period.[3] With the rise of "cooperative federalism" in the 1950s and 1960s, the nature and balance of jurisdictional powers became less a matter of constitutional definition than one of intergovernmental negotiation of fiscal and monetary policy. "The courts are retiring, or being retired, from their posts as the supervisors of the [federal] balance," said J.A. Corry in 1958.[4] "The lawyers are moving out and the economists are moving in," agreed Frank Scott in 1961.[5]

The same decline of federalism jurisprudence was occurring in the United States, but there the courts had developed a new activist role under the Bill of Rights. In 1954 and 1955 the U.S. Supreme Court handed down politically explosive decisions invalidating the officially segregated school systems of the southern states and ordering desegregation to proceed with "all deliberate speed."[6] These cases were followed by court orders to bus students between school districts in order to achieve racial balance in the schools,[7] even in northern jurisdictions where there had been no history of legally mandated educational segregation.[8] Needless to say, the busing decisions were equally explosive. In other controversial decisions the U.S. Supreme Court invalidated school prayers[9] and flag salutes,[10] told the states that they could not prohibit abortion during the first six months of pregnancy,[11] established a rule for the exclusion of illegally obtained evidence that was so strict it allowed the obviously guilty to go free on mere technicalities,[12] and required constituencies of close to equal numerical size in order to approximate the principle of "one person, one vote."[13] So controversial were many of these decisions that they, and the Court itself, became major issues in party platforms and election campaigns. Clearly no student of American politics could afford to ignore constitutional law and the courts, and their study flourished within American political science.

In Canada, the vacuum left by the declining political significance of federalism jurisprudence was not filled by a similar rights-based jurisprudence. Canada had no constitutional bill of rights, although a small minority of Supreme Court judges had occasionally tried to argue that one was implied in the preamble and parliamentary structure of the BNA Act.[14] It is true that the Court handed down a few civil libertarian decisions during the 1950s, all involving Quebec policies, but it based them either on the federal distribution of powers, striking down the challenged laws because they were beyond provincial jurisdiction, or on common law rules of statutory interpretation.[15] Civil libertarians would have preferred a more overtly rights-based jurisprudence and were disturbed by the fact that powers denied to the provinces were by that very fact available to the federal government. In any case, the Court did not sustain a civil libertarianism based on the BNA Act into the 1960s and 1970s.[16]

During much of the postwar period there had been considerable interest in adding a bill of rights to the constitution.[17] Until 1982, however, the idea always aroused sufficient opposition to prevent it from coming to fruition. The most its advocates could achieve was the enactment in 1960 of the Canadian Bill of Rights (often called the Diefenbaker Bill of Rights because it was one of Prime Minister Diefenbaker's favoured projects and was enacted by his government). As we pointed out in Chapter Two, this was a simple statute of the federal government and applied only in areas of federal jurisdiction. Lacking constitutional status, moreover, the Bill was treated very cautiously by Canadian judges. The Supreme Court used it only once to override a federal law between 1960 and 1982.[18]

If the declining significance of federalism jurisprudence in Canada during the 1950s and 1960s was not accompanied by a sustained growth in politically controversial rights-based judicial activism such as the United States experienced, the courts and judicial decision-making were not therefore irrelevant to the political and policy-making process. Their influence took less visible or dramatic forms, such as developing the common law, shaping the practical meaning of ambiguously worded statutes, and setting sentencing policy within the very wide limits imposed by the Criminal Code.[19] But Canadian political scientists paid little attention to these phenomena, perhaps because they were too dazzled by the grander scale of judicial power in the United States to notice the other ways in which judges influence public policy. In the words of Peter Russell, one of the few Canadian political scientists who did study judicial power during this period, "the development of Canadian political science from the mid-1930s until well into the 1960s was marked by a general withdrawal of interest in legal phenomena."[20]

Today interest in these phenomena among students of Canadian politics has not only been rekindled, but is blossoming as never before. There are at least three reasons for this. First, the predicted demise of the judicial review of federalism did not occur. Whereas the U.S. Supreme Court came close to making its withdrawal from the area of federalism official in 1985,[21] the Canadian Court experienced a resurgence of federalism jurisprudence. After 1975, in the midst of the conflictual and litigious atmosphere of the "Trudeau era," the number of federalism cases rose dramatically,[22] so much so that our Supreme Court was probably more active in the area of federalism than the comparable court of any other federal country.[23] Second, and more important, since 1982 the Canadian Supreme Court has had available to it an entrenched Charter of Rights and Freedoms, and is clearly using it more aggressively than it had used the statutory 1960 Bill of Rights. Indeed, with active roles in both rights and federalism jurisprudence the political significance of the Canadian courts now rests on a broader constitutional base than that of their American counterparts.

The third factor is a development in the intellectual rather than the political realm. The increased salience of judicial review has coincided with the development of a scholarly "neo-institutionalism" that rejects earlier tendencies to see legal categories and institutions as merely the superstructural reflections of more fundamental subpolitical realities. For some time the old emphasis on law and institutions had lost its pre-eminence to a paradigm that sought to explain how societal forces influenced political institutions and outcomes. Recently the institutionalist perspective has re-emerged in a new form.[24] Without reverting to a simplistic institutional determinism, this neo-institutionalism revives the view that society is as much shaped by institutions as the other way around.[25] Because it sees law not just as the outcome of more fundamental forces, but as an independent variable in political life, this neo-institutionalism is bound to pay closer attention to legal phenomena than the society-based explanatory approaches that preceded it.

As employed by Canadian political scientists, this neo-institutionalist approach has been particularly sensitive to the interrelationships between constitutional law and political identities, and to the political significance of the symbolic and legal resources provided by constitutional law. It has shed light especially on the relationships and tensions between Charter politics and the traditional constitutional politics of federalism. This chapter summarizes and builds upon what neo-institutionalism has taught us about Charter politics.

■ NEO-INSTITUTIONALISM AND THE DIALECTIC OF STATE AND SOCIETY

Alan Cairns is the Canadian scholar who has most explicitly drawn out the implications of neo-institutionalism for this country's constitutional politics. The body of Cairns's work over time can be seen as a sustained critique of two opposing determinisms. First is a legal determinism that assumes that behaviour actually follows legal categories, and that the most important scholarly task is thus meticulously to describe the relevant law. When those who hold this view are politically active, they assume that the problems concerning them are due to bad laws, and that legal reform must top the political agenda. This perspective is reflected in those nationalist critics of the JCPC who thought that the centralist regime they preferred would have been achieved if only the nefarious British law lords had interpreted the BNA Act in the "proper" Macdonaldian fashion, that blame for the decentralist fragmentation they deplored was appropriately laid on the constitutional law fashioned by a small group of foreign judges.

Much of Cairns's earlier work is devoted to undermining this legal determinism. "It is impossible to believe," he wrote in a famous piece on the JCPC, "that a few elderly men in London deciding two or three constitutional cases a year precipitated, sustained, and caused the development of Canada in a federalist direction the country would otherwise not have taken."[26] In fact, the Macdonaldian BNA Act was better understood as an unrealistic attempt to graft a centralist constitution on a decentralized society that would not and could not accept it. Far from creating decentralism, the JCPC simply brought the constitution into line with a decentralist reality that drew its vitality from a variety of nonlegal factors, and that was successfully placing its stamp on the country's constitutional structure quite independently of anything the JCPC did.[27] For example,

> the powers of reservation and disallowance were not eroded by the stupidity or malevolence of British judges but by concrete Canadian political facts. The failure to employ section 94 of the BNA Act to render uniform the laws relating to property and civil rights in the common law provinces was not due to the prejudice of Lords Watson and Haldane, but to the utopian nature of the assumptions which inspired it, and the consequent failure of Canadians to exploit its centralizing possibilities.[28]

"It is evident," Cairns concludes, "that on occasion the provinces found an ally in the Privy Council, and that on balance they were aided in their struggles with the Federal government." But "to attribute more than this to the Privy Council strains credulity."[29]

This rejection of legal determinism was not peculiar to Cairns. In this respect he was part of the much larger tendency to focus on the "societal" determinants of political behaviour. If taken too far, however, this tendency could slip over into the mirror image of legal determinism, namely, sociological determinism. This is the second determinism opposed by Cairns. The critique of sociological determinism is already evident in his early work,[30] but it becomes a sustained theme with his 1977 presidential address to the Canadian Political Science Association, "The Governments and Societies of Canadian Federalism."[31]

As applied to federalism, sociological determinism was expressed in W.S. Livingston's 1956 assertion that "federalism is a function not of constitutions but of societies."[32] This determinism was associated with the view that federalism should decline as the forces of modern technology and industrialism made societies more alike. Federal constitutions might survive for a time, but they would increasingly become quaint anachronisms. In Canada this analysis seemed to be confirmed by the convergence of homogenizing industrialism, wartime and postwar centralism, and the declining judicial supervision of federalism during the 1950s and 1960s.

As so often happens, however, events upset theory. Far from withering away, nationalism in Quebec seemed actually to increase as Quebec society became more like that of English-speaking North America. Regionalism and provincialism in the rest of Canada, particularly in the West, burgeoned in the 1970s. Cooperative federalism, which worked out pragmatic agreements without paying too much attention to legal niceties, gave way to a suspicious constitutional litigiousness, accounting in part for the post-1975 surge in federalism jurisprudence. Obviously federalism and intergovernmental conflict were quite compatible with the increasing homogenization of society.

Cairns explains the continuing vitality of federalism in terms of the independent influence of the federal constitution and the governments it establishes. In the era of the modern interventionist state, he argues, the national and provincial identities that sustain federalism are not dependent on subpolitical diversities rooted in such factors as history, culture, and economics; they are sustained by the sheer prominence of the two levels of government in the lives of their citizens. The programs and policies of the modern state touch on virtually every aspect of our lives, carrying out many social functions that used to be the preserve of family, church, and other purely voluntary social networks. And as we increasingly "relate to one another through the state,"[33] as we live more and more of our daily lives responding to the incentives and coercions of state policies, our very identities become politicized. In the modern age, Cairns argues, identities are more political than religious or economic.[34] They are not necessarily unified and monolithic, however. The same modern state that induces politicized identities is itself fragmented, divided not only among levels of government, but also by a multiplicity of government departments and quasi-independent agencies and corporations. This "multiple, scattered and diffuse"[35] state generates a confusing and often contradictory web of policies, and the resulting state–society interdependencies are similarly fragmented. Although the modern state generates politicized identities, those identities are as fragmented as the state itself. In Canada they are fragmented most obviously by the federal division of the state.

In the modern era, in short, the divided identities that sustain federalism are generated in part by federalism itself. The "coexisting interventionist governments" arising out of the federal constitution, says Cairns, "do not so much reflect underlying national and provincial communities, but continuously recreate them and enhance their practical significance for the citizenry."[36] "As a by-product of its routine interventionist activity," he continues, the federal state "divid[es] and combin[es] us at the same time as the more traditional bases of community are attenuated by modern conditions."[37] But the federal state itself owes its very existence to the federal constitution. Thus Livingston's dictum should be reversed: "federalism, at least in the Canadian case, is a function not of societies but of the constitution, and more importantly of the governments that work the constitution."[38]

This emphasis on the constitution and the state as more than dependent variables did not mean that Cairns had changed his mind and was returning to the old legal and institutional determinism he had earlier dismissed. In his mature reflections he rejects the view that either state or society can determine the other. This is because state and society are no longer distinct entities to be understood in the relation of independent and dependent variables.[39] In an earlier, simpler era society may have generated superstructural legalities, as the underlying reality of regionalism generated and sustained a federal constitution despite the preferences of Macdonald.[40] But once a federal constitution was in place, it drew in its wake a politics of "province building" that rivalled the politics of "nation building," especially as the state at both levels became increasingly active and interventionist, politicizing society and binding citizens to it in spreading but fragmented webs of interdependence. In our time, therefore, it is no longer appropriate to think in terms of either an independent society determining the activities of the state or a fully autonomous state free to shape and mould society. Rather, "the state, in confronting society, confronts its own past, and the society that seeks to influence the state directs its efforts to transforming the multiple linkages that interpenetrate and affect almost every facet of its functioning."[41] State and society, in short, are engaged in an ongoing dialectic of mutual influence. Cairns refers to the modern interpenetration of state and society as the "embedded state."

■ THE ROLE OF CONSTITUTIONAL LAW

Although Cairns sees ultimate determining power in neither state nor society, he clearly accords more explanatory power to the institutions and structures of the state than do the previously dominant society-based paradigms. To a considerable extent modern politicized identities reflect the fragmented structures of the state. Since constitutional law, especially the law of federalism, influences these structures in important ways, it must be given its proper weight in any explanation. The governments that work the constitution may be more important than the constitution itself, but this does not mean that the constitution is insignificant.

The constitutional law of federalism is important because it establishes the two levels of government and grants them their powers. The ability of each level to undertake policies important in the lives of its citizens, and thus to politicize their identities, depends in part on how much policy-making power it is accorded by the constitution. It depends on it only in part because nothing requires governments to make full use of their powers or, if they do, to use them effectively. Before the 1960s "Quiet Revolution" in Quebec, for example, the government of Maurice Duplessis, imbued by an antistatist ideology, adopted a decidedly noninterventionist stance, leaving education and social welfare to the church, and steering clear of economic regulation. Similarly, during and immediately after World War II the normal distribution of powers between the two levels of government was virtually suspended in favour of consolidated federal power. Thus ideology and externally generated circumstances may induce governments to let their jurisdictional powers lie unused.

On the other hand, governments of an interventionist bent can often find ways to surmount apparent constitutional obstacles to the pursuit of their objectives. As Peter Russell points out, "sometimes when a law is found *ultra vires,* government is able to achieve pretty much the same policy objective through a better drafted law or using some other constitutional power."[42] His example is Saskatchewan's attempt in the mid-1970s to appropriate all of the windfall profits accruing to oil companies because of the sudden, OPEC-induced rise in the international price of oil. When the Supreme Court ruled that raising the royalties it charged by the amount of the price rise was a constitutionally prohibited form of "indirect" taxation, Saskatchewan simply re-enacted the policy in the form of a "direct" oil-well income tax. Similarly, although the JCPC found that the federal government could not enact anticombines legislation under its trade and commerce power, it upheld the policy when it was cast in the form of criminal law legislation. Governments can also get around the constitutional division of powers by delegating administrative powers to each other, as they have in designing constitutional marketing-board legislation. The federal government can also use its "spending power" to gain significant influence in areas of provincial jurisdiction, such as medical insurance and higher education.[43] Thus Russell concludes that "the level of a government's activity in a given field of policy depends less on its constitutional resources than on its will to use the resources it has."[44] Patrick Monahan is even more dismissive of the ability of constitutional constraints actually to determine governmental behaviour in the area of federalism. "It is *always* possible," he writes, "to do indirectly what you cannot do directly."[45]

None of this means that constitutional law can be ignored as unimportant. Constitutional constraints may have little determining power, but neo-institutionalism teaches us to look for influence rather than ultimate causal determination. Russell indicates two ways in which the constitutional law of federalism significantly shapes policy and politics. First, although constitutional barriers may not exclude a government completely from a policy field in which it is keenly interested, "they will certainly influence the choice of instruments available to government in any given field."[46] And the available policy instruments may not be the most effective. For example, although the federal government had enacted anticombines legislation in the permissible form of criminal law (rather than in the impermissible form of trade and commerce legislation), this subjected prosecutions to all the rigours of a criminal trial, which made it more difficult to enforce.[47] Such constitutional barriers to the most effective policy instruments may affect the politicization of identities in a federal system. The generation of politicized national or provincial identities depends on the active presence of governments in the lives of their citizens. If the choice of policy instruments imposed by constitutional law weakens the effective presence of a level of government, it also weakens the politicized identity associated with that level, thus affecting the balance between the federal and provincial spheres.

Second, the constitutional distribution of powers influences the natural and ongoing competition between the two levels of government by establishing the legal resources they can bring to the bargaining table. "From this perspective," says Russell, "constitutional power should be viewed as a political resource just as popularity or a good international economic climate are resources for democratic politicians."[48] It is only one resource among many, of course, and thus rarely determines the outcome of federal–provincial battles, but it is not a negligible resource.

Perhaps the best example is the "Patriation" case,[49] which significantly altered the symbolic context for the contestants in the battle over patriating an amended constitution.[50] When this decision was handed down, Ottawa could no longer pretend that its proposal to patriate unilaterally was constitutional. By deciding that "substantial provincial consent" was an important constitutional convention, the Court provided the eight dissenting provinces with very useful legal ammunition. What the Court gave the provinces with one hand, however, it withdrew with the other when it conceded that however unconstitutional unilateral patriation might be in the conventional sense, it was perfectly constitutional in the strict legal sense. In the short term, Ottawa was unlikely to proceed in a manner that was conventionally unconstitutional, but given the popularity of the Charter, it might eventually have exploited its purely legal power to do so if the provinces continued their intransigent obstruction for too long. Both sides clearly had new reasons to rekindle the process of negotiation, and most observers agree that the Supreme Court's judgment was an important factor in promoting the ultimate settlement. It was only one factor, however. By giving the disputants new reasons to compromise it invited them back to the bargaining table, but it could not guarantee that the invitation would be accepted and that compromise would result.

The politics of offshore mineral resources provide another striking example of how the law affects political struggles without necessarily determining them. Although judicial decisions have conferred exclusive jurisdiction over such resources on the federal government, provincialist resistance has been strong enough to prevent federal politicians from exercising the degree of control to which they are legally entitled. Instead, they have agreed to share revenue and regulatory control with the affected provinces. On the other hand, Ottawa's bargaining strength in negotiating the terms of this sharing was greatly enhanced by the fact that it enjoyed full legal control.[51] No doubt the balance between the two levels of government in this policy field would have been quite different had the legal resources been on the side of the provincial governments. Again we find that the significance of the two levels of government for the lives of Canadians is substantially affected, though clearly not determined, by constitutional law.

■ THE CHARTER AND NATIONAL UNITY

The federal distribution of powers is not the only way in which constitutional law affects the balance between the national and provincial communities and their governments. The Charter of Rights also plays an important role. Although many Canadians take the Charter at face value as a device for the better protection of rights and freedoms, it was seen very differently by the two levels of government during the debate about its addition to the constitution. The Trudeau government had long been interested in a constitutionally entrenched bill of rights because of its potential for enhancing national unity. For Trudeau, the forces of provincialism, especially as expressed in Quebec separatism and Western alienation, had grown so powerful that they threatened the sense of national community on which the legitimacy of the federal government rested. Trudeau clearly understood how the federal constitution itself contributed to the growth of regional discontent and thus sought constitutional solutions for what he considered constitutional ills. As Cairns put it: "The enhanced capacity of provincial governments to penetrate and mould their societies generate[d] a counter tendency for the federal government to attempt to preserve and foster a Canada-wide community."[52] The Charter was a central part of the Trudeau government's strategy to achieve this end. Whereas the federal constitution fostered provincial identities, encouraging people to think of themselves in terms of their membership in politicized provincial societies, Trudeau hoped the Charter would emphasize what all Canadian citizens shared in common: a set of rights and freedoms beyond the reach of governments. In symbolic terms a constitutional charter would oppose a national community of rights bearers to the provincialized identities of federalism.

The constitutional entrenchment of a charter of rights had always been part of Trudeau's nationalizing agenda. Trudeau had entered federal politics in order to oppose what he considered to be excessively decentralist opinions, especially in Quebec. He wished to restore the federal balance against arguments that "had magnified provincial autonomy into an absolute, and were reducing federal power to nothing."[53] His government's response to the perceived threat was twofold. First it was prepared to contemplate some institutional changes, especially Senate reform, that might make the central institutions of government more regionally responsive and hence regionally legitimate. However, Trudeau was never entirely comfortable with the inarticulate premise of such reform, namely, that the national interest is found primarily in the accommodation of regional interests. In the words of Jennifer Smith, this way of achieving national unity "risks an identifiable national discourse by promoting a self-consciously regional one. It unavoidably promotes while it accepts and placates regionalism, in which case the remedy exacerbates, not cures, the political ill."[54] The Trudeau government was resolutely opposed to the idea of Canada as nothing more than a "community of communities"; it always held that there was a national community transcending the regions that was properly represented by the central government. Thus, in addition to reforming the central institutions of government (indeed, in preference to this strategy), Trudeau sought ways to articulate and strengthen the national identity. The Charter of Rights was part of this second nation-building strategy.

An earlier example of this second strategy was the Official Languages Act, enacted by the Trudeau government in 1969, which was designed to defuse provincialist tendencies in Quebec, not by restructuring the institutions of the central government, but by ensuring that more government employees spoke French and that government services were more widely available in French. Thus did Ottawa attempt to undermine the claim of Quebec nationalists that Quebec is the only real homeland of francophones in North America and that only the government of Quebec can represent them. The policy of the Official Languages Act was subsequently enshrined in sections 16 to 20 of the Charter. These sections also reiterate the guarantees of section 133 of the BNA Act regarding the use of English and French in Parliament and the courts. Both kinds of guarantees are also entrenched for New Brunswick. In addition, section 23 of the Charter guarantees the rights of the French or English linguistic minority in any province to have their children educated in the minority language where numbers warrant. That Trudeau refused to permit these rights to be governed by the section 33 legislative override is an indication of their relative importance in his mind.

Ironically, the policy designed to lessen alienation in Quebec exacerbated it in the West. One of the reasons for this was a tendency to associate bilingualism with biculturalism, a link that was made by the Royal Commission on Bilingualism and Biculturalism in the 1960s. According to this argument, language is the primary vehicle of culture, which is in turn a way of life, a way of "being, thinking and feeling."[55] Other ethnic groups interpreted this to mean that official bilingualism entailed official biculturalism and that those adhering to other cultures had thus been consigned to the status of second-class citizens.[56] In fact, the Trudeau government never accepted this link between bilingualism and biculturalism. Arguing that official languages, in addition to being vehicles of culture, can serve a culturally neutral, utilitarian function of communication among citizens of different cultures, the government insisted on the compatibility of bilingualism and *multi*culturalism.[57] As early as 1971, just three years after Trudeau became prime minister and two years after the enactment of the Official Languages Act, multiculturalism became official government policy.[58] Multiculturalism, too, is now constitutionally recognized in the Charter, in section 27, which enjoins the courts to interpret the Charter "in a manner consistent with the preservation and enhancement of the multicultural heritage of Canadians."

Constitutionally entrenching the policies of bilingualism and multiculturalism in the Charter of Rights and Freedoms was clearly intended to enhance their symbolic status as central attributes of Canadian citizenship and components of the Canadian identity, and thus to improve their nation-building potential. This national-unity function of the Charter, however, was not meant to be limited to the fact that these two policies were embedded in it. The document as a whole, it was hoped, would serve to strengthen a nonregionalized Canadian identity by encouraging citizens to perceive themselves as bearers of rights that know no local boundaries.

Considered as a whole, the Charter was expected to achieve this purpose by emphasizing the constitutional primacy of the people rather than of governments. The British North America Act emphasizes governments and has very little to say about relationships between government per se and the people.[59] According to Reg Whitaker, this constitutional emphasis on governments, inasmuch as it obscured the more fundamental sovereignty of the people, robbed the country of one of the most potent sources of national identification and thus of national unity:

> Even a federation—perhaps *especially* a federation—needs some mass attachment of an emotional or sentimental nature to the national level. A functioning federal state must strike some stable balance between regional, provincial or subcultural identities, and an identity of citizens *qua* citizens with their national state. The recognition of the principle of the sovereignty of the people is a way of encouraging such attachment over more limited identities.[60]

In 1978 the Liberal government made the same argument. "The renewal of the Federation," it declared, "must confirm the pre-eminence of citizens over institutions." This elevation of the stature of citizens, it continued, would be achieved by a constitutional charter that would "guarantee their rights and freedoms and ensure that these rights and freedoms are inalienable."[61] A charter, in other words, would ensure that the constitution was at long last concerned "at least as much with relationships between citizens and the state" as it was with relationships between governments. Sovereignty of the people would thus be emphasized.

A charter of rights emphasizes the sovereignty of the people because the idea of rights entails the notion that government exists to serve the people. This connotation of the term "rights" may be traced to the "state of nature" teaching with which it was originally associated. According to that doctrine, rights are pre-political goods, the protection of which is the primary reason that people consent to government. Although the idea of a state of nature is no longer in vogue, the perception of rights as inherent in human beings as such, rather than as grants from a government to its citizens, retains its vigour, as does the corollary that government exists to protect rights. It is because of the vitality of these connotations that Trudeau, soon after he became prime minister, was able to defend the idea of a charter by declaring that "government should not be an end in itself, but instead a means of promoting the well-being of the people." He made this statement in the context of explaining why a charter should precede such questions as the reform of the federal division of powers on the agenda of constitutional reform. "In the process of constitutional review," he said, "we should ... look to the needs of people before we look to the needs of government."[62] The same thinking was evident in his description of the Charter during the debates of 1980–81 as a "people's package" that did not change the relative strengths of governments, but gave power to the people against governments as such.[63]

The Charter's symbolic contribution to a sense of national citizenship is not limited to its emphasis on popular sovereignty. More concretely, a public discourse based on the language of rights, which the Charter clearly promotes, has nationalizing implications. On the one hand, it is beyond question that rights are not absolute, especially in relation to each other—a truth that is recognized in the "reasonable limits" section of the Charter. On the other hand, the term "rights" implies universality. Within their proper ("reasonable") boundaries, "human" rights are something to which every human being is entitled. This is why when certain social benefits are described as rights, the notion of making them available only on the basis of testable need or only to the "worthy poor" becomes suspect. This universalist connotation of the term "rights" formed part of the Trudeau government's claim that the Charter ought to apply to both levels of government, and was the basis of its opposition to a "notwithstanding" provision. If something was a "right" worthy of inclusion in the Charter, the government argued, it ought to be available to all Canadians regardless of geographical location.

The Charter might also be expected to refashion identities by enhancing the policy-making power of a national institution of government: the Supreme Court. The Charter does not transfer policy-making power directly from provincial legislatures to the federal Parliament, but it does transfer such power to the court system, which is hierarchically unified under the supervision of the Supreme Court. Where Charter rights are implicated, policy decisions otherwise within provincial jurisdiction, and thus subject to provincial variation, will be significantly constrained by court decisions of country-wide application.[64] In the modern politicized state, the significance of provincial governments in the lives of their citizens will lose some ground, not directly to the overtly political branches of the federal government, but to a national institution nonetheless. Politicized citizens, accustomed to looking to state institutions for the satisfaction of their needs and desires, will find themselves looking more to the court system, and thus less to provincial governments, than they used to. A growth of national identities is the result predicted by Cairns's neo-institutionalism.

This way of understanding the political significance of the Charter explains why its enthusiastic promotion by the federal government was matched by provincial suspicion. Indeed, as we have seen, eight of the ten provincial governments maintained a vigorous opposition to entrenchment of the Charter almost until the last minute. All but Quebec finally agreed, but not because they had become Charter enthusiasts. As the price of agreement, these provinces insisted that section 33, the legislative override, be added to the Charter, thus preserving a degree of legislative supremacy in policy areas touching on certain Charter rights.

▋ THE GOVERNMENTS' CONSTITUTION VS. THE CITIZENS' CONSTITUTION

The Charter is important not only for its contribution to the traditional form of constitutional politics in Canada—the politics of federalism—but also because it has set in motion a new kind of constitutional politics. Prior to 1982 the only political entities that enjoyed constitutional recognition were the governments of Canadian federalism, and constitutional politics was a battle over their relative legal status. Individuals or social groups were constitutionally relevant only as members of politicized national and provincial communities whose relative prestige and power depended in part on the success of their governments in the struggle over legal resources. The Charter emerged out of this intergovernmental struggle, but its enactment gave individuals and nongovernmental groups constitutional status in their own right. The constitution was no longer just about the structure of governments and their relations to each other; it now gave prominence to the relations between people and the state as such, regardless of the state's federal division. Individuals and groups could now employ the resources of constitutional law in asserting their claims against the state just as governments had always used such resources in their claims against each other. For these reasons Cairns sees the Charter as the foundation for a new "citizens' constitution," which he juxtaposes to the old "governments' constitution" of federalism.[65] The latter, he says, "is of concern primarily to the governments whose affairs it regulates." If the last quoted remark is meant to suggest that the federal constitution is of little concern to citizens, it is an exaggeration—the status of the Quebec state, for example, is surely a matter of importance to citizens of Quebec—but Cairns's distinction does capture the relative importance of governments and citizens in the day-to-day conduct of two kinds of constitutional politics.

It is worth pausing to note that Cairns's labels are not without difficulty. Cairns recognizes that the term "citizens' constitution" is technically a misnomer because many Charter rights apply not just to citizens, but to "everyone," "any person," or "every individual." Nevertheless, he employs the term because he is concerned to explore "the impact of the Charter on the conceptions and practice of citizenship."[66] He is concerned, in short, with how the Charter has changed the patterns of citizen participation in Canada's constitutional politics.

Those who remain sceptical about the value of the Charter's contribution to our public life might object to its depiction as the "citizens' constitution" for another reason. The term connotes increased citizen participation, and who could be against that? But, as subsequent chapters will show in detail, sceptics insist that the Charter's main beneficiaries are special interest groups, who invoke it to persuade appointed judges to reverse the decisions of democratically elected representatives. The sceptics see these groups turning to an undemocratic institution to seek victories they are unable to win in the normal process of democratic participation. Sceptics, in short, see the Charter not as a "citizens'" constitution, but as the constitution of special interests. Since these special interests promote the transfer of power from legislatures to courts, sceptics might be happier to describe the Charter as the constitutional foundation for a "court party" in Canadian politics. By "court party" we do not mean a party like the Liberals or the NDP. The court party, as some Charter sceptics perceive it, is more like a social movement. It embraces a constellation of interests, which, like the "court party" of old, prefers the policy-making power of the less obviously democratic governmental institutions. Historically the "court party" rallied around the "court" of the king (the executive branch) in opposition to the power of democratic legislatures. Today the new court party's undemocratic vehicle is the judiciary. The modern court party includes not only the kinds of "citizen" interest groups discussed by Cairns, but also important elements within state bureaucracies, law schools, the broader intellectual community, and the media.

Despite its ambiguous and contentious character, the term "citizens' constitution" has become well established in the literature, and especially in this chapter we shall follow Cairns in using it. When elaborating the sceptical viewpoint, however, we sometimes refer to the "court party" to designate the interests that most strongly favour the enhanced judicial power generated by the Charter.

For Cairns, the Charter gives citizens a direct stake in constitutional law and encourages them to think of themselves as constitutional actors.[67] In a sense this is true for all individual citizens—and generally for resident noncitizens as well—who become significant constitutional actors whenever they go to court to seek redress for perceived violations of Charter rights. However, the Charter, especially in sections 15 to 29, also gives special recognition to a variety of group identities and interests. Women receive explicit recognition in section 15, which guarantees a variety of "equality rights" "without discrimination because of sex," and section 28, which guarantees all Charter rights equally to male and female persons, "notwithstanding anything in this Charter." Racial and ethnic groups are covered by some of the explicitly prohibited grounds of discrimination in section 15 (race, national or ethnic origin, colour, religion) and by section 27, which requires the Charter to "be interpreted in a manner consistent with the preservation and enhancement of the multicultural heritage of Canadians." Section 15 also gives explicit recognition to age-based groups and the mentally and physically handicapped. Eight full sections (16 through 23) deal with the rights of official-language minorities. Section 29 ensures that the Charter will not undermine the existing rights of denominational schools. Finally, sections 25 and 35 "recognize and affirm" aboriginal and treaty rights and guarantee that they will not be undermined by other Charter rights.[68]

The "citizens' constitution," in short, is only in part the constitution of all citizens considered as individuals. In addition to their status as discrete individuals sharing in a common humanity, the members of any polity are divided into groups by an almost endless variety of nonuniversal characteristics, including occupation, income, class, sex, sexual orientation, language, educational attainment, race, religion, place of residence, ethnicity, physical size, health, and intelligence. Many of these are politically relevant, but only some of them enjoy constitutional status. Moreover, the relative status of groups recognized by the Charter is beset by ambiguity and fluidity, much as the relative status of federal and provincial governments within the federal system is never fixed. Thus the citizens' constitution can be understood as an arena for competitive "status building" in much the same way that the constitution of federalism provides the background for the rival phenomena of nation building and province building. The two kinds of constitutional politics, of course, remain in continuing tension with each other.

■ THE POLITICS OF STATUS

The prominence of certain "Charter groups" is due in part to their own efforts during the process of Charter-making. Although the Charter was the project of the Trudeau government, a variety of groups, especially women and aboriginals, perceived the opportunity to enhance their own status and to acquire valuable legal resources by having their identities explicitly enshrined in Charter provisions. They thus lobbied hard to secure the most favourable Charter wording possible.[69]

Cairns understands this aspect of the politics of Charter-making as another manifestation of modern politicized society. In this era of active governments, the successful pursuit of individual and group goals increasingly depends on the ability to negotiate the labyrinth of public policy. More and more time must be devoted to calculating how best to fulfil state-imposed obligations, avoid those that are particularly burdensome, or turn public policy to personal advantage. As Cairns puts it, "political calculation is diffused to realms of society and economy for which it was historically irrelevant"[70]:

> The accounting profession, dispensing helpful advice to minimize financial obligations to the state, rides the crest of a wave. For accountants, April is the month of shortened nights and profitable days as the deadline for filing income tax approaches. Political advisers become executive assistants to corporation presidents. Faculties of Commerce and Business Administration increasingly employ political scientists and devote major attention to business interactions with the state. A late December flurry of marriages to take advantage of the tax system reveals the interaction of private planning and state planning in the most intimate areas of our existence. The sale of registered retirement savings plans (RRSPs) greatly increases in January and February in response to tax considerations. We now operate in terms of many state calendars indifferent to the movements of the solar system.[71]

Our political calculating is directed not only to co-opting or evading existing state policies (Cairns uses the growing underground market as the most dramatic example of evasion), but also to changing those policies— to modifying or dismantling policies that burden us, or to extracting new benefits from the state. Self-conscious and organized groups are particularly apt to make such demands on the state, and their success depends in part on the groups' public visibility and status. Status is achieved most dramatically through explicit recognition as a constitutional category. Constitutional status gives a group official public status of the highest order, and groups who enjoy it have an advantage in pressing their claims against government over groups who do not. As Richard Simeon observes, "constitutional recognition has become the essential mark of status and acceptance for a multitude of groups."[72] The groups who played a major role in the process of Charter-making were clearly attempting to negotiate this kind of favoured status:

> The opening up of the constitutional issue, and the self-interested bargaining that it unleashed and revealed, were especially pointed lessons of what citizens and groups had been learning since the Depression: that the state is more than an umpire, and that it is not exclusively an instrument that involves our better selves playing civic roles and making disinterested contributions to the public weal. Rather, it is intimately involved in what William Goode reminds us is the ubiquitous societal process of constant renegotiation of the status of members of society.[73]

Although virtually all significant political entities have come to see constitutional status as a good thing, its value is diluted the more widely it is dispersed. Politics is the competitive struggle between competing interests and visions, and those enjoying constitutional status can deploy it in gaining an advantage over their competitors. If too many rivals enjoy an equal constitutional status, this advantage disappears. Simply put, the wide dispersion of constitutional status cheapens its value. Like all other resources, the value of legal resources is a function of their relative scarcity. Thus some constitutional politics takes the form of existing members of the constitutional club attempting to protect the value of their resource by resisting the admission of new members, especially competing members. Those who are already members of the club will also fight among themselves for relative advantage, claiming that there is a hierarchy of constitutionally recognized interests, with their own at or near the top.

A dramatic example of this is the ongoing struggle between the governments' constitution and the citizens' constitution. Of course, not all members of the old constitutional club were opposed to changing the rules and admitting new members. The Charter, as we have seen, was desired by the federal government as a way of diminishing the strength of its provincial rivals and promoting the sense of national community. More-over, Ottawa treated many of the groups lobbying for Charter status as allies in its battle to overcome provincial opposition. Many of the prov-inces, on the other hand, strongly resisted the admission to the constitu-tional club of new members who defined themselves and their agendas in nonfederal terms. Newcomers of this kind challenged the prominence of provincial communities and their governments in Canadian politics. The old governments' constitution had served the provinces well and they wished to maintain its exclusivity.

We have seen that the provincial defenders of the governments' con-stitution fought a successful rearguard action in forcing the addition of a legislative override to the Charter. This override was not their only signif-icant victory. The package of constitutional reforms proposed by the Trudeau government in 1980–81 was designed not only to enact the Char-ter, but also to "patriate" the constitution. Before 1982 the judicially enforceable part of the Canadian constitution, the BNA Act, remained a British statute, and could be amended in many important respects only by the British Parliament. Patriating the constitution, bringing it home as it were, required the adoption of an entirely Canadian amending formula. Advocates of the governments' and citizens' constitutions fought not only about the Charter, but also about the amending formula, and in this case the victory fell to the governments' constitution, with the citizens' consti-tution fighting the rearguard actions.

The federal government had lobbied for a formula emphasizing the role of regions and people, rather than provincial governments, in enact-ing constitutional amendments. Amendments would require the consent of each of the major regions of the country, and in the West and the Atlantic provinces this meant approval by the legislatures of only two of the prov-inces in those regions. Ontario and Quebec would each have to consent, but because of their status as major regions rather than provinces. At one point, Ottawa's proposals further emphasized regions at the expense of provinces by insisting that the required two western and Atlantic provinces contain at least 50 percent of the population of their respective regions.

Although these proposals emphasized regions, they still permitted the expression of regional consent through the voice of the provincial legisla-tures. Ottawa's suggestions went even further, however, and proposed that the regions otherwise stipulated by the formula could also express their consent through referenda initiated by the federal Parliament. This alterna-tive formula, while maintaining the importance of regions, eliminated pro-vincial governments from the amending process altogether.

Not surprisingly the provinces opposed these proposals as vigorously as they did the Charter. When they finally agreed to the Charter, the price they exacted included not only the section 33 legislative override, but also a much more provincialist and government-oriented amending formula. Originating in Alberta, and supported by the so-called "gang of eight" provinces that opposed Ottawa's patriation initiative, this formula required the consent of two-thirds of the provincial legislatures and permitted provinces to opt out of amendments reducing provincial powers. The idea of involving the people directly through referenda was dropped. The only remnant of Ottawa's emphasis on citizens was a requirement that the consenting provinces represent at least 50 percent of the Canadian population.

If the Charter was intended to symbolize a nonprovincialized Canadian identity, the amending formula did precisely the opposite. From Garth Stevenson's critical perspective, the formula implies "that there is no Canadian nation, but merely an arrangement of convenience among sovereign provinces.... In the last analysis, the compact theory, that malignant legacy of Canadian history, triumphed over democracy, freedom and national unity."[74] Or, as Cairns put it:

> Either the Alberta amending formula and no Charter, or the federal amending formula and a strong Charter lacking a *non-obstante* clause would have been internally consistent in their basic assumptions about the nature of community in Canada. The constitutional settlement which combines a nationalizing Charter and a provincializing amending formula is a contradiction posing as a compromise.[75]

In addition, a second, even more governmentalist amending formula—one requiring the unanimous consent of Ottawa and all the provinces—was adopted for selected subject matters. Under this "unanimity" formula, each government has a veto over the specified kinds of amendments.

The conflict between the two constitutional orientations was sharply displayed in the 1987–90 Meech Lake debate. When the federal Conservatives led by Brian Mulroney and the Quebec Liberals under Robert Bourassa came to power in 1984 and 1985 respectively, the conditions were set for an attempt to heal the wound caused by Quebec's refusal to consent to the 1982 patriation package. With the old implacable foes of Trudeau and Lévesque off the political stage, the eleven governments of Canada attempted to bring Quebec "back into the constitutional family."[76]

In a purely legal sense, of course, Quebec was "in" or subject to the constitution, because only "substantial," not unanimous, provincial consent was required to validate the 1982 amendments, and the agreement of the other nine provinces was sufficiently "substantial."[77] The legitimacy of constitutional provisions is as much a political as a legal matter, however, and the 1982 amendments lacked political legitimacy in Quebec, as shown by the fact that the province immediately enacted a blanket use of the section 33 override to exempt all existing Quebec legislation. It was in this political sense that Quebec needed to be brought back into the constitution. The efforts to do so culminated in a meeting of the eleven first ministers at Meech Lake, Quebec, on April 30, 1987. At this meeting the rudiments of the "Meech Lake Accord" were hammered out, and after some discussion and refinement, all of the first ministers signed it in Ottawa in early June.

The Meech Lake Accord responded to five requirements established by the Bourassa government in June 1985 as minimal conditions for Quebec's consent to the Constitution Act. "These were: constitutional recognition of Quebec as a 'distinct society,' a constitutionally secured provincial role in immigration, a provincial role in Supreme Court appointments, limitations on the federal power to spend in areas of provincial jurisdiction, and an assured veto for Quebec in any future constitutional amendments."[78] The last four requirements were met by institutionalizing them not only for Quebec, but also for all the other provinces, thus satisfying the desire of many of the latter to maintain the principle of provincial equality. Thus the accord would have given all provinces (1) the right to negotiate with the federal government constitutionally entrenched agreements "relating to immigration"; (2) the right to provide a list of potential Supreme Court appointees from which Ottawa would select a candidate it considered "acceptable"; (3) the right to opt out of national shared-cost programs with "reasonable compensation" from Ottawa as long as the province had a comparable program of its own that was "compatible with the national objectives" of the shared-cost program; and (4) a veto over a broader range of constitutional amendments, achieved by expanding the list of matters requiring unanimous provincial consent. The accord also went beyond Quebec's five conditions and responded to the concerns of other provinces by providing for annual first ministers' conferences on the constitution to discuss, among other things, Senate reform. In the meantime, all provinces were to have a nominating role for Senate appointments similar to that applying to Supreme Court appointments.

The major exception to provincial equality—the main concession to "special status" for Quebec—concerned the recognition of Quebec as a distinct society. Even here, however, the relevant provision began by underlining the importance of both English and French to Canada as a whole, and thus the equality of all governments in relation to this "dualism." Section 1.2 of the accord recognized "the existence of French-speaking Canadians, centred in Quebec but also present elsewhere in Canada, and English-speaking Canadians, concentrated outside Quebec but also present in Quebec" as "fundamental characteristics of Canada," and affirmed the role of Parliament and the provincial legislatures to "preserve" these characteristics. Responding more directly to Quebec's demand, this section eventually asserted "the recognition that Quebec constitutes within Canada a distinct society," and affirmed the role of its "legislature and Government" to "preserve *and promote*" this "distinct identity."[79]

If the entrenchment of the Charter in 1982 is seen as a victory for the citizens' constitution, the governments' constitution (especially insofar as it favoured *provincial* governments) would clearly have regained much lost ground through adoption of the Meech Lake Accord. Both in its substantive provisions and in the process through which it was developed, the accord was a provincializing document.[80] Substantively it expanded the powers of provincial governments, and underlined their symbolic and practical importance as major players in the game of constitutional politics. Procedurally, Meech highlighted the continuing prominence of intergovernmental negotiation, mainly by the eleven first ministers, in the crucial matter of constitutional amendments. The victory secured in 1981 by the provincial governments in the struggle over the amending formula was fully exploited in the development of the accord. The document was produced by the first ministers meeting behind closed doors and was presented as a "seamless web," an unalterable *fait accompli,* on a take-it-or-leave-it basis.

None of this sat very well with the nongovernmental players that had been dealt into the constitutional game by the Charter. Groups that had been encouraged by the Charter to see themselves as constitutionally significant now found themselves shut out of the crucial process of constitutional amendment, and they actively resented the fact. Symbolically, amendment by first ministers suggested that governments remained the dominant constitutional actors, and that the constitutional status of other groups was decisively subordinate, always at the mercy of the government-controlled amendment process. For a variety of "Charter groups," the danger in governmental ascendancy was evident in the Meech Lake

Accord itself. Through this accord, the governments would have enhanced both the symbolic and practical aspects of "their" constitution, thereby diminishing the relative status of the citizens' constitution and the identities it nourishes.

These conflicts between the governments' and citizens' constitutions are parallelled by similar struggles within each of the camps. Federal and provincial governments continue to jostle for mutual advantage in the interpretation of the constitutional distribution of powers. Similarly, within the ambit of the citizens' constitution, conflicts arise over the relative status of the various interests recognized by the Charter.

A good example of the latter occurred in the 1980–81 debates about section 15, the "equality rights" section of the Charter. When the Trudeau government first introduced its draft Charter, section 15 prohibited public discrimination "because of race, national or ethnic origin, colour, religion, age or sex."[81] Feminist groups worried about the inclusion of age in the list of prohibited grounds of discrimination. Legal distinctions based on age, they thought, were more often reasonable and acceptable than distinctions based on race, ethnicity, or religion, and thus more likely to be upheld by the courts. The presence of age, in other words, would require judges to develop a hierarchy of prohibited grounds, giving some greater importance than others. Feminists worried that once the idea of a hierarchical ranking was introduced, sex might end up being relegated to a lower rank than such categories as race. If age were excluded, it would be easier to resist the idea of hierarchy and maintain that all the prohibited grounds enjoyed equal status, thereby assimilating sex to the stringent standards of judicial review one could expect in cases of racial discrimination.

Thus the Advisory Council on the Status of Women proposed that age be excluded from the list of explicitly prohibited grounds of discrimination. As a compensation, however, it also proposed a more open-ended wording for section 15 under which it would be possible to challenge forms of discrimination other than those in the explicitly enumerated list. Thus complaints of discrimination on the basis of age could still be brought under the open-ended wording. Indeed, complaints based on a host of other grounds would now be possible. It was clearly anticipated, however, that the explicitly listed grounds, including sex, would enjoy a favoured status as compared to unlisted grounds. A hierarchy would still exist, but only between listed and unlisted grounds, not among the listed grounds, which would share equally the benefits of first place.

Although they were remarkably successful in influencing the wording of the Charter in other respects, feminists failed to exclude age from the list of prohibited grounds. Once a social category has a foothold on constitutional terrain, it is difficult to dislodge. Indeed, the desire of other social groups to gain admittance to the section 15 club overcame the desire of feminists to restrict its membership: as a result of vigorous lobbying mental and physical disability were added to the listed grounds. Like age, disability is likely to attract more relaxed judicial assessment than some of the other categories, thus reinforcing the idea of a hierarchy among listed grounds. On the other hand, the proposal to open up the wording of section 15 was accepted, so that it now guarantees equality rights "without discrimination and, in particular, without discrimination" based on the specified grounds.[82]

Another example of the struggle for status within the citizens' constitution was raised by Meech Lake. The accord did not just express the interests of the governments' constitution in its battle with the citizens' constitution as a whole; in important respects, its provisions would have readjusted the relative status of competing interests within the citizens' constitution. At the broadest level the interests at stake were, on the one hand, those who see Canada in "dualistic" terms as the political expression of two founding nations, British and French, and on the other hand, the increasing number of Canadians that do not trace their political lineage back to Wolfe and Montcalm on the Plains of Abraham.[83] The latter, often referred to as "third-force" Canadians, resent any implication that, in terms of constitutional status, they are second-class citizens.

The 1982 Charter struck a balance between Trudeau's concept of dualism[84] and the concerns of third-force Canadians, a balance that was threatened by Meech Lake. On the one hand, dualism was constitutionally entrenched in the establishment of English and French as the official languages of Canada, and in the provision of linguistic educational rights to the English minority in Quebec and the French minority elsewhere. On the other hand, section 27 says that the Charter "shall be interpreted in a manner consistent with the preservation and enhancement of the multicultural heritage of Canadians." In short, the balance between *bi*lingualism and *multi*culturalism established at the statutory level early in Trudeau's prime ministership was duplicated at the constitutional level in the Charter. Meech Lake would have tilted the balance in favour of dualism by recognizing it as "a fundamental characteristic of Canada," a status not accorded to multiculturalism. As Cairns points out, third-force Canadians considered this as "a rebuff, as the latest indication that the multicultural components of Canadian society are not to enjoy equivalent constitutional status with founding peoples."[85] In recognizing Quebec as a distinct society, and in giving its government the role not only of "preserving" but also of "promoting" this distinctiveness, the accord also suggested that the French majority in Quebec had gained significant ground on the English minority, which had received constitutional recognition and protection in 1982.[86]

Other Charter groups also resisted the distinct society clause. Feminists, for example (mainly those outside of Quebec),[87] worried that it might justify a less stringent interpretation in Quebec of Charter rights to sexual equality. And aboriginals wondered why, if historical primacy was the basis for recognizing the English–French dualism as a "fundamental characteristic" of Canada, they were not given similar recognition, or indeed, why they were not deemed worthy of constitutional recognition as a "distinct society."[88]

Although the constitutional status of aboriginals and third-force Canadians was diminished relative to the founding nations, the Meech Lake Accord did state that the Charter sections of most concern to them—sections 25 of the Charter, 35 of the Constitution Act, 1982, and 91(24) of the BNA Act for aboriginals; section 27 for the multicultural groups—were not affected by the interpretive guidelines relating to dualism and "distinct society." No such guarantee was offered to women with respect to sections 15 and 28. This led women to see the accord as placing them lower on the constitutional totem pole than aboriginals and third-force Canadians, a bit of constitutional symbolism that fuelled their opposition to the accord.[89]

The Meech Lake Accord was never adopted, although it came very close to succeeding. It was a far-reaching package of amendments, some of which fell under the 1982 general amending procedure requiring the consent of the federal Parliament and the legislatures of seven provinces having at least 50 percent of the national population. The general formula stipulated that this degree of consent had to be achieved within three years of the resolution initiating the proposal. Other parts of the accord were subject to the alternative "unanimity" formula. Unlike the general formula, however, there was no time limit on acquiring the unanimous consent required by the alternative procedure. All of the governments proceeded on the assumption that to pass the package as a whole the requirements of both amending formulae had to be met simultaneously, which could be done only by combining the most stringent aspects of each. This meant that the package had to achieve unanimous consent within three years.[90] When the deadline arrived on June 23, 1990, the accord died. Manitoba had not passed it, and Newfoundland, which had given but then rescinded its consent, had not repassed it. The opposition of groups who had a stake in the citizens' constitution had much to do with the accord's ultimate failure.

■ CONFLICTING VISIONS

No doubt the governments and interest groups who compete for status in the arena of constitutional politics, as well as individual citizens who make constitutional claims in court, do so in part out of simple self-interest. But their claims are justified, explicitly or implicitly, in the name of particular conceptions of the just or good regime. Constitutional politics is as much the conflict between competing visions of justice as between the groups and individuals whose interests are served by these visions. The struggle over the relative status of groups overlaps and parallels a struggle over the relative status of justifying visions.

The conflict between federal and provincial governments, for example, reflects the opposition between what Richard Simeon calls "nation-centred" and "province-centred" visions of the country:

> The first vision stresses the primacy of the national political community over the provincial communities. Confederation was an act of nation-building, creating a new national community; and the federal government, the only institution which represented all Canadians, was the natural instrument of that community. This model also rejects the equation of the interests of provinces with the interests of provincial governments. The federal government represents regional interests, in areas of federal jurisdiction; it has the larger role of fostering a national interest which transcends those of provinces.
>
> The province-centred view challenges this national majoritarianism and its implication of the ultimate superiority of the federal government. It emphasizes a bottom up view; Canada is a collection of provincial political communities equally as legitimate as the national community. Provincial governments are the primary political expression of these communities, not only for matters constitutionally within provincial jurisdiction, but also for national issues. Hence there are 11 equal governments in Canada; there is no nat-

ural federal superiority. At the limit, this model adopts the "compact" view of Confederation, seeing the federal government as the creation of the provinces.[91]

These conflicting visions lie behind the particularities of the constitutional politics of federalism, and also affect the conflict between the governments' constitution of federalism and the citizens' constitution represented by the Charter.

Closely related to nation-centred and province-centred visions of Canadian federalism is the broad conflict between liberal individualism and a group-oriented vision of politics. Liberal individualism holds that, for public purposes at least, people should be conceived and treated as discrete individuals, with little regard to any group-identifying traits they might possess, such as region of residence, occupation, social and economic class, religion, race, ethnicity, or sex. This individualistic outlook has always been in tension with a vision that accords primacy to groups. The latter takes many forms, depending on which group identities are seen as worthy of public recognition. Federalism, for example, is a way of constitutionally recognizing that, for some purposes at least, groups defined by their geographic location take primacy over the collection of discrete individuals composing the national population. This is most evident when the provinces or states in a federal system are given greater political representation in the central legislature than is justified by the individualistic formula of representation by population. "Rep. by pop." is a simple matter of counting heads (the heads of discrete and equal individuals) and apportioning political representation accordingly. In the Senates of both the United States and Australia (and in the reformed Senate desired by some Canadians) the states enjoy (and the Canadian provinces would enjoy) equal representation regardless of population differences.

The tension between individualism and regionalism is evident even in the composition of the Canadian House of Commons. Although "rep. by pop." was a leading principle in constituting that legislative chamber at Confederation, it has been significantly limited by regional considerations.[92] In 1915, for example, a "senatorial clause" was added to the BNA Act, guaranteeing that no province should have fewer MPs than senators. Its practical effect was to guarantee that Prince Edward Island's representation in the House of Commons would not be less than four, even though its population no longer justified it. In 1951, responding to relative population declines in Nova Scotia, Saskatchewan, and Manitoba, a new amendment stipulated that no province could lose more than 15 percent of the seats it had held under the previous adjustment. In 1974 yet another attempt was made "to ensure no further loss of seats by slow-growth provinces."[93] However, the 1974 reforms would have caused overly rapid growth of the House of Commons and were thus abandoned a decade later, to be replaced by a "grandfather clause" guaranteeing each province's 1976 allocation of seats as a minimum.[94] The result is that six provinces have a total of twelve more seats than they are entitled to by their population. It was projected that by 1991 these figures would grow to seven provinces and seventeen seats.[95] John Courtney has described these reforms as providing "special protection of a non-population kind ... to two-thirds of the provinces." Courtney concludes that Parliament has "never accepted the principle of 'rep. by pop.' as applying to the distribution of Commons seats among the various provinces."[96]

At the provincial level, the same tension is played out in electoral distribution schemes that attempt to give relatively equal representation to urban and rural interests, rather than just to equal collections of discrete individuals. Until 1990, for example, Alberta's Electoral Act established forty-two urban and forty-one rural ridings, despite the fact that two-thirds of the province's people live in urban districts.

As we saw in Chapter Two, the use of region rather than simple population to apportion constituencies has been challenged on the grounds that giving the votes of individuals in small ridings much more weight than their counterparts in large ridings robs the latter of a "meaningful" right to vote under section 3 of the Charter. In this case the Charter is being used to promote liberal individualism at the expense of a vision that accords substantial weight to regional groups. As we shall see, the Charter can also be used for the opposite purpose.

Liberal individualism is also in tension with socialist visions, which emphasize social classes over individuals. Unlike region, however, class distinctions play little role in Canada's formal constitution. Indeed, the federal constitution has been seen by some socialists as an impediment to the emergence of a vigorous politics of class in Canada. In this view, the enemy is not only liberal individualism, but also a constitution that privileges the wrong kind of group identity. In 1965, for example, Gad Horowitz deplored the way in which the ethnic and regional conflicts characteristic of Canadian federalism (and promoted by the federal constitution) submerged a more "creative" class-based politics:

> There is a real dilemma here, a truly vicious circle. The ethnic and regional conflicts must be dealt with. They cannot be ignored. We cannot move towards a more creative politics simply by exhorting people to think in terms of left-right rather than unity-discord. But since we are constantly dealing with the national unity question, the left-right polarization is constantly being suppressed; and since it is always being suppressed, regional and ethnic divisions just keep on rolling along.[97]

Horowitz, and before him John Porter,[98] hoped that Canada's national-unity obsession might eventually be cured by the emergence of a left–right, class-based polarization that would cut across regional cleavages and submerge them, just as the latter had for so long submerged the former. This strategy for achieving national unity is akin to the strategy implicit in the Charter, but also quite different in its emphasis on social class over individual rights.

The hopes of Porter and Horowitz have not been realized. Far from growing in strength, class has declined significantly since the 1960s as an explicit factor in the politics not only of Canada, but of other Western democracies, particularly the other Anglo-American regimes.[99] This decline has not been accompanied by a corresponding decline of group-oriented visions, however. The gap left by "class dealignment" has been filled by a vision that emphasizes group identities based on race, ethnicity, and sex. Natives, "visible" and ethnic minorities, and women's groups have moved to the centre of the political stage, and placed their issues and concerns at or near the top of the public agenda.[100] The leadership of these groups increasingly rejects such individualistic notions as formal "equality of opportunity" regardless of race, ethnicity, or sex, and insists that special benefits be provided to groups defined by these characteristics in order to achieve "equality of result." Those in favour of the latter approach call it "affirmative action" or "equity"; those who oppose it call it "reverse discrimination." This clash pits liberal-individualist against group-oriented visions of equality. Unlike social and economic classes, these groups have a solid constitutional foothold in the Charter, and they actively promote the adoption of group-oriented interpretations of relevant Charter sections. The Charter can certainly be used to further the individualistic vision—as in the case of the electoral apportionment challenges—but the Charter groups being considered here prefer to use it for the opposite purpose. The Charter is clearly a battleground for competing visions of justice.

More detailed philosophic visions are also at work in many Charter cases. For example, courtroom battles arising under the Charter sometimes pit libertarians, who accept John Stuart Mill's proposition that the state should never interfere with individual liberty unless direct, tangible harm is being done to others,[101] against moralists, who believe that the necessary moral foundations of a free society require constant public support.[102] This debate underlies such Charter controversies as whether the censorship of obscenity violates freedom of expression or whether denying the political franchise to imprisoned criminals violates the democratic right to vote. On the question of obscenity, libertarians also find themselves clashing with feminists who see censorship as essential, not to maintain traditional morality, but to effect a revolutionary transformation of society by controlling the socialization of its members. Other revolutionary feminists believe that censorship is merely treating the symptoms rather than the causes of the ills they wish to eradicate, and thus find themselves in alliance with libertarians.[103]

The examples could be multiplied, but the point is clear: just as the particularities of federal–provincial politics are illuminated by the more general visions underlying them, so Charter politics must be understood as reflecting deeper theoretical visions. Charter politics is often about which of a set of conflicting visions will achieve the symbolic backing of constitutional status.

▮ THE POLITICS OF STATUS AND VISION IN COURT

The politics of status and vision is most dramatic and visible in disputes over formal legal amendment, such as the 1980–81 debate about patriation and the Charter, and the 1987–90 debate about Meech Lake. But formal legal change, especially at the constitutional level, is difficult and relatively rare. Amendment controversies are important occasions for symbolic politics, but they rarely lead to a conclusion or resolution—the failure of Meech Lake in 1990 represents the norm to which the success of patriation in 1982 is an exception. Real symbolic gains or losses are more likely to occur in an incremental fashion through judicial interpretation. The courtroom is therefore an important arena in which to conduct the politics of status and vision. Neo-institutionalism has been described as "bringing the state back in" as a central variable in the study of politics. Within this general orientation one of the most urgent tasks is to bring the courts back in as an important component of state activity, and thus as a significant locus for political activity.[104]

Courts, especially appellate courts, are politically significant because the constitutional reasons they give to justify the outcome of a particular dispute shape the law at stake, with consequences extending well beyond the immediate case. The actual litigants may be more concerned with the bottom-line result, but there are broader constitutional constituencies who care little about the litigants and much about how the justifying reasons shape the order of symbolic resources. Thus, when Mark Andrews, a non-citizen, argued that his "equality rights" under section 15 of the Charter were violated by a British Columbia law limiting membership in the bar to Canadian citizens,[105] two members of the section 15 club (women and the handicapped) sought and received intervener status in the case, not because they were concerned about the fate of the litigant, but because they wished to ensure that the Supreme Court's first major pronouncement on "their" section of the Charter provided the symbolic ammunition they needed for their causes.[106] In particular, they wished to preserve the favoured status they enjoyed by virtue of being explicitly mentioned in section 15. The problem was the open-ended nature of section 15. Since citizenship is not one of the listed categories, Andrews was required to claim a constitutional violation under the open-ended part of the section. The established Charter groups were very concerned to prevent their own favoured status from being diluted by an interpretation of the open-ended aspect of section 15 that would admit too many newcomers to their company.[107] They were also concerned that section 15 be interpreted to reflect the vision of equality as requiring the achievement of equal results.[108]

In studying courtroom politics, one must pay attention to the way in which political interests are constrained to make their case in terms of legal categories that may have little to do with their actual goals. For example, it is hard to imagine that a large corporation has a religious conscience that can be infringed by Sunday-closing laws. Its interest in opposing these laws is likely to be rooted in economic rather than religious concerns, but if it wishes to use the courtroom to achieve its ends, it must work with the available legal categories. Thus a secular dispute involving the complex and different interests of labour, consumers, large and small retailers, and mall owners is fought in court as a dispute turning on the question of religious freedom.[109] Thus do legal categories shape political argument. By forcing nonconstitutionalized interests to clothe themselves in the garb of constitutionalized interests, moreover, courtroom politics further strengthens the status of the latter. In this case, the status of religious interests was enhanced by secular interests that could not appear in court in their own name.

The open-endedness of section 15 provides another example of constitutionally favoured interests assimilating concerns that could have been differently presented. Some of the explicitly listed groups have opposed an interpretation of this open-endedness that would allow too many unlisted groups to make equality claims in their own right. On the other hand, they have argued in favour of a "systemic" interpretation of the discrimination prohibited by section 15. According to this interpretation, the listed groups should be able to challenge not only classifications based directly on their defining characteristic (e.g., no women in the RCMP), but also classifications that indirectly burden a listed group (e.g., no small people in the RCMP). Under a generous interpretation of the open-endedness of section 15, small people (including both men and women) could make a claim of unreasonable discrimination in their own right against a minimum-size employment policy in the RCMP, thus gaining a bit of symbolic purchase in the constitution for an unlisted group. Under the systemic interpretation favoured by Charter groups, the same claim can be made, with the same immediate effect—i.e., small men will also benefit from a successful "women's" challenge to size restrictions—but in symbolic terms this approach further entrenches the status of women as favoured Charter Canadians.[110]

Not only do legal categories force some interests to pursue their goals in a distorted manner, but sometimes the short-term concern of winning the particular case can lead interests to contribute to the building of a constitutional symbolism that runs counter to their broader political agendas. The 1976 *Anti-Inflation Reference,* for example, asked whether federal anti-inflation legislation, which intruded on matters normally within provincial jurisdiction, could be sustained under the BNA Act's "Peace, Order and Good Government" clause if inflation could be shown to be a matter of "national concern" (which it clearly was) or only if it amounted to an "emergency" (which was more contentious). The legislation could only be defeated if the Court was persuaded to adopt the emergency test and then find that no emergency existed. In their zeal to defeat the law, the labour unions involved in the case argued in favour of the restrictive "emergency" interpretation of the federal power. Given labour's long-term interest in stronger federal power, this position was rather anomalous. In pursuing a short-term goal in court, the unions had to argue a position that would deplete the constitutional resources the NDP would prefer to have should it ever form a government in Ottawa.[111]

This emphasis on the symbolic utility of judicial decisions means that one must pay close attention to how judges justify the ultimate result. There is sometimes a tendency among social scientists to eschew doctrinal analysis; the parsing of decisions entailed in such analysis seems too dry and legalistic, too much the domain of legal academics—far better and more exciting to concentrate on the bottom-line result (who wins and loses) and study the actual impact of a decision on the real world. Yet the wins and losses inherent in judicial decisions involve not just the immediate litigants, but the broader interests contending over the regime's symbolic order. These symbolic wins and losses, and their impact, cannot be studied without some lawyer-like doctrinal analysis. Political activists certainly parse the cases; if political scientists are truly interested in the politics of constitutional law they must follow suit. The politics of interpretation, moreover, is concerned not only with how the results of particular cases are justified, but with the broader constitutional theories that inform and shape the process of judicial justification. These theories are the subject of the next chapter.

CHAPTER FIVE

The Politics of Interpretation

The role of the courts in allocating symbolic status among competing visions of justice and the groups whose interests are served by these visions does not exhaust their political significance under the Charter. The courts are important not just because they provide a forum for symbolic politics, but also because they have a direct impact on public policy whenever they invalidate an existing policy, legitimate one by upholding it, or impose a new one. The extent to which this occurs, of course, depends on how judges approach the task of legal interpretation. The Canadian Bill of Rights, for example, had little impact because the Supreme Court exercised great self-restraint in applying its provisions to the policies of the federal government. The political impact of the Charter thus depends on whether judges undertake their interpretive task in an activist or restrained frame of mind, and on the theories of constitutional interpretation they employ. This chapter reviews the leading judicial approaches to constitutional interpretation.

■ ACTIVISM VS. RESTRAINT

The practical impact of the Charter depends significantly on the balance between judicial "activism" and judicial "self-restraint" in the courts. To repeat the definition we provided in Chapter One, judicial activism refers to the disposition to interpret rights broadly and to enforce them vigorously against the other branches of government, usually by striking down statutes or excluding evidence in criminal cases. Judicial self-restraint, by contrast, "connotes a judicial predisposition to find room within the constitution for the policies of democratically accountable decision makers."[1] The political and policy impact of the Charter obviously depends on the degree of activism exhibited by the Canadian judiciary, and especially by the Supreme Court.

In assessing how activist or restrained a court is, one must look not only at the bottom-line outcome of its cases, but also at the judicial reasoning employed in these cases. As we have seen, the reasoning used to

justify a decision often has symbolic implications transcending the immediate outcome of the case. The Supreme Court's 1988 *Morgentaler* decision
provides a convenient illustration.[2] Dr. Henry Morgentaler, Canada's leading pro-abortion activist, was prosecuted for carrying out illegal abortions,
and defended himself partly by claiming that the law was unconstitutional.
By a margin of five to two, the Court agreed, ruling that the abortion law
violated section 7 of the Charter. But the five-judge majority divided three
different ways on why the law was invalid. Only Justice Wilson explicitly
declared a constitutional right to abortion, although she conceded a legitimate state interest in protecting the life of the unborn child at some point.
The other four judges who ruled against the law did so because it violated
the *procedural fairness* required by section 7, not because that section
guaranteed any independent right to abortion. These four disagreed
among themselves on just how serious even the procedural violations
were. Two, Dickson and Lamer, said that the requirements of the current
law—such as approval by a therapeutic abortion committee (TAC)—were
inherently unfair and would have to be scrapped. The other two judges,
Beetz and Estey, defined the procedural problems much more narrowly
and thus as remediable. While certain requirements *as currently written*—
such as the TAC approval—created unfair delays and burdens, a revised
version of the TAC might be acceptable. Specifically, Beetz and Estey ruled
that in principle there was no legal problem with the existing law's
requirement that abortions be permitted only when the continuation of a
pregnancy "would threaten the life or health of the mother," or with its
requirement that the issue of life or health be judged by an independent
and impartial third party such as the TAC.

Although all three of these opinions lead to the same activist result—
striking down the law—they differ greatly in their limitation of legislative
discretion. Justice Wilson's opinion is clearly the most activist in that it
would force the most radical reforms in the law. Although she acknowledged a legitimate state interest in protecting the fetus, her opinion would
preclude any prohibition of abortion early in the pregnancy. The Beetz-
Estey opinion, on the other hand, would permit Parliament to re-enact the
essence of the existing policy, while cleaning up some of the procedural
problems. The Dickson-Lamer opinion falls somewhere in the middle.
Since none of these opinions commanded the support of a majority of the
Court (or even a majority of the majority), the question of the overall activism or restraint of the decision was left unresolved. It was anyone's guess
what kind of new law might pass constitutional muster.

Under the Charter, judicial activism takes the form of defining a right broadly enough to cover the challenged policy, and then finding that the policy is not justified under section 1. At the other pole, the most dramatic versions of judicial restraint take the form of placing internal limits on the relevant rights, so that the interests or activities regulated by the challenged policy receive no Charter protection. The two dissenters in *Morgentaler,* Justices McIntyre and Le Dain, exercised this kind of restraint in finding that abortion was simply not covered by section 7. The Court majority did the same thing when it excluded labour strikes from the ambit of the section 2(d) guarantee of freedom of association.[3] In between these two poles are judgments defining Charter rights broadly enough to bring them into conflict with the challenged policy, but justifying the policy under section 1. In the right-to-strike cases, for example, Justice Dickson rejected the majority's definitional limit on section 2(d), finding that the section did encompass labour strikes, but upheld legislative limits on that right under section 1. Such judgments combine elements of judicial activism and restraint. As far as the particular case is concerned, the bottom line is indistinguishable from that achieved by definitional exclusion—the rights claimant loses and the challenged legislation is upheld—and in that sense the judgment represents judicial restraint. By defining rights broadly, however, such judgments open the door to continuing section 1 jurisprudence in the future. Even if the Charter violation at issue in the particular case is "demonstrably justified," other limitations of the same right may not be. Simply by expanding the number of laws that might need to be assessed under section 1, such judgments expand the opportunities for future judicial activism. At the very least, they encourage more judicial review. In this sense, such intermediate judgments exhibit more judicial activism than do judgments relying on definitional exclusion, which exempts entire categories of laws from the necessity of justifying themselves as "reasonable limits ... demonstrably justified in a free and democratic society."

Judicial activism and restraint should not be confused with political liberalism and conservatism.[4] In the United States the Warren Court's 1954 desegregation decision, *Brown* v. *Board of Education*,[5] launched a spate of activist decisions favouring the liberal political agenda, and its jurisprudence has led many to associate judicial activism with liberalism. Thus recent decades have seen liberals supporting activism while conservatives preached judicial restraint. In Canada it was partly a wistful longing by liberals for the kind of liberal activism displayed by the Warren Court that fuelled the drive for a constitutional Charter of Rights. But this association between judicial activism and political liberalism is rooted in historical forgetfulness rather than in the nature of things. In both Canada and the United States judicial activism during the 1930s was a conservative force, resulting in the invalidation of the early attempts to establish the welfare state. At that time the political affiliation of supporters and opponents of judicial activism was the mirror image of what it is now. The conservatives of that day, whose policy outlook was reflected in judicial decisions, sang the praises of judicial activism, while the liberals were then apostles of judicial restraint. There is obviously an element of political opportunism in the praise and blame heaped on judicial activism.

Judicial activism comes in both negative and positive forms. Negative activism invalidates the policy initiatives of the other branches of government. Such negative vetoes often have positive policy implications, of course. In saying what was wrong with Canada's abortion law, for example, all of the judges who voted to strike it down provided implicit standards that a constitutionally valid policy would have to meet. To be sure, the guidance provided by the Court was thoroughly confused by the multitude of opinions, and a unanimous opinion would have provided a better example of the positive implications of simple invalidation. But that is really beside the point. Even if the Court had spoken with a single voice, Parliament would not have been required to act upon the positive standards implicit in striking down the law. It was perfectly free to let the matter lie where the Supreme Court left it: with no law at all—which, indeed, is precisely what pro-abortion activists wanted. At bottom, negative activism remains a statement of what the government may *not* do, with no legal requirement that it undertake positive action of any kind. Having found a law invalid, courts who practise negative activism will refuse to enforce it, but beyond that they leave it to the legislature to take whatever steps it deems appropriate to comply with the ruling, including no steps at all.

When judges engage in positive activism, by contrast, they tell other policy-makers not only what they may *not* do, but also what they *must* do. Courts that engage in positive activism display a willingness to issue affirmative remedies or "structural injunctions" to enforce constitutional rights. Until recently negative activism was the norm and a judicial finding of invalidity rarely entailed ordering the government to take any specific steps to remedy the situation. Again, the Warren Court represents a new point of departure. Under its guidance American courts began issuing "structural injunctions" to force governments to adopt specific policies. The process began not long after *Brown* v. *Board,* when the Supreme Court decided that the equal protection clause of the fourteenth amendment required not only an end to the practice of legally forcing children into racially segregated schools, but also the statistical integration of the schools. The racial mix of each school was to reflect the proportions of the races in the school district as a whole. Given the fact of racially concentrated neighbourhoods, such integration could not be achieved by giving all children, whatever their race, the free choice to attend their neighbourhood schools[6]; it could only be achieved by busing children back and forth between neighbourhoods, a positive remedy the courts soon imposed on school boards.[7] Armed with this precedent, American courts began to order positive remedies in many other areas of social policy. Donald Horowitz supplies a partial list:

> In the past few years, courts have laid down elaborate standards for food handling, hospital operations, recreation facilities, inmate employment and education, sanitation, and laundry, painting, lighting, plumbing, and renovation in some prisons; they have ordered other prisons closed. Courts have established equally comprehensive programs of care and treatment for the mentally ill confined in hospitals. They have ordered the equalization of school expenditures on teachers' salaries, established hearing procedures for public school discipline cases, decided that bilingual education must be provided for Mexican-American children....[8]

Although we have not come quite so far in Canada, the Federal Court of Appeal recently upheld a trial judge who ordered the government to pay out additional benefits to a group of persons not included in the Unemployment Insurance Act. The UI Act allowed adoptive parents to choose which spouse would stay home to care for a newly adopted baby. With natural parents, only the mother could qualify for "maternity" benefits. A natural father challenged this distinction as an unjust discrimination against natural parents and won. Rather than simply declaring the entire benefit section invalid, leaving it to the government to decide how to remedy the problem, the Federal Court "amended" the UI Act by extending the benefits to natural fathers as well. Indeed, the Court went much further in this respect than might have been expected. Instead of ordering that the existing "maternity" benefits be split between natural mothers and fathers according to their own choice—thus equalizing the situations of adoptive and natural parents—the Court responded to feminist arguments that the existing benefits of natural mothers should not be reduced in any way and *added* to them an optional "paternity" benefit. Assuming that no more than 5 percent of natural fathers availed themselves of this option, it was estimated that expenditures would rise by up to $50 million. If all fathers took advantage of the policy, the additional cost would be over $1 billion.[9] The Crown appealed on the grounds that judges do not have the authority to order spending not authorized by Parliament, but the Appeal Court upheld the decision.[10]

The courts have also ordered positive remedies in the area of language rights. The Supreme Court has interpreted the section 23 right to minority-language education facilities to include the right to "management and control" of these facilities as well. The Court said that section 23 was "remedial in purpose" and placed "positive obligations" on governments. The Court assumed for itself the power to tell governments the specifics of these "obligations," including the power to order governments to create entirely new school boards to govern the minority schools.[11] Judgments of this kind are still the exception rather than the rule in Canada, but they show that positive activism has become part of the arsenal of Canadian courts.

Sometimes courts order positive remedies because they believe them to be necessary to give effect to a negative invalidation, not because they think the positive remedies are constitutionally required in themselves. A 1988 case involving prisoners' voting rights illustrates the point. In *Badger* v. *A.-G. Canada*, Justice Hirschfield of the Manitoba Court of Queen's Bench addressed the constitutionality of the law making "every person undergoing punishment as an inmate in any penal institution for the commission of any offence" ineligible to vote in federal elections.[12] Justice Hirschfield found that this law infringed the section 3 right of "every citizen of Canada" to "vote in an election of members of the House of Commons," and that it was not saved by section 1. For prisoners actually to vote, however, it was not enough simply to strike the law down; positive steps had to be taken by the chief electoral officer to enable them to exercise their right—for example, by enumerating them and providing them with mail-in ballots or special in-prison polling stations. Justice Hirschfield thus imposed on the electoral officials the positive duty to make appropriate arrangements.[13] He did so, however, not because he thought that prisoners had an unqualified right to vote, but because he considered this particular disqualification to be too broad to pass the proportionality component of the *Oakes* test. For example, he objected to the fact that "a minimal infraction of a regulatory statute which is penalized by a few days' imprisonment may result in the effective loss for four years or more of the right to vote."[14] Justice Hirschfield clearly stated that a more carefully tailored law, limiting the prisoner disqualification to those convicted of more serious offences, would pass constitutional muster.

> Had the words "penal institution" been defined to mean only a Federal penitentiary, and had "any offence" been defined to mean an indictable offence, the result which I am about to announce would have been radically different. In my view the proportionality test referred to in *Oakes* would then have been weighted in favour of disqualification.[15]

Thus, in Hirschfield's view, the right to vote of many prisoners, including Badger (who was serving time in a federal penitentiary for the commission of an indictable offence), could be "reasonably" limited by appropriate legislation. Clearly he did not believe that the positive steps he imposed to enable such prisoners to vote in the upcoming elections were constitutionally required in themselves. As with the *Morgentaler* decision, the legislature was free to respond to this judgment with new, more carefully crafted legislation. In the meantime, however, no valid legislative limits existed and all prisoners enjoyed at least a temporary right to vote, which required positive remedies to implement. Justice Hirschfield's decision combines moderate versions of both negative and positive activism. Considered in itself, his invalidation of the law displays negative activism, though of a relatively moderate variety because his reasoning would permit legislative re-enactment of the essence of the policy. As regards remedies, on the other hand, Justice Hirschfield clearly engages in positive activism, though again of a moderate sort because the full range of positive duties he imposes is not constitutionally required in itself, and can be supplanted by appropriate legislation.

Other judges considering the same issue have found Hirschfield's approach to be far too activist for their taste. His decision was ultimately overturned by the Manitoba Court of Appeal, for example.[16] A more striking contrast is provided by a decision made about two years earlier by Justice Scollin, also of the Manitoba Court of Queen's Bench, in a case concerning the similar provincial disenfranchisement of prisoners.[17] (This case had also been brought by Badger, along with two other inmates of the Stony Mountain Penitentiary.) Whereas the Court of Appeal disagreed with Hirschfield altogether, finding the federal legislation to be constitutionally valid, Scollin found the provincial law to be unconstitutional, but took a much more restrained view of the remedies a judge could legitimately impose. The contrast between Hirschfield and Scollin in their approach to the question of remedies further refines our understanding of the varieties and degrees of judicial activism and restraint.

Anticipating Hirschfield's reasoning, Justice Scollin invalidated the Manitoba law mainly because of its unnecessary scope. He, too, assumed that a more carefully tailored law, presumably limiting the prisoner disqualification to those convicted of more serious offences, would pass constitutional muster. And he implied that a valid law could legitimately disqualify the petitioners in this case, who were "serving jail terms of nine, five and seven years respectively for grave breaches of the criminal law."[18] Unlike Justice Hirschfield, however, Scollin did not consider it appropriate to order the immediate enfranchisement of all criminals, including those who could be legitimately disqualified (and who the existing legislation obviously intended to disqualify), because the law unconstitutionally disenfranchised too many offenders. In his view, a judicial remedy of such scope would not only be disproportionate to the constitutional violation, but would pre-empt the legislative prerogative of designing public policy. As the Manitoba Court of Appeal subsequently put it, Hirschfield's ruling entailed "an absolute right to vote for all inmates even though Hirschfield, J. realized that there could be good and logical reasons to disenfranchise those in federal penitentiaries. The task of enfranchising all or certain prisoners should be left to the elected members of Parliament."[19] On similar grounds, Justice Scollin refused "to order that the name of any convicted prisoner be placed on the [provincial] voters' list" or "to order that any other steps be taken to enable any convicted prisoner in this province to participate in this election."[20] In arriving at this conclusion, Justice Scollin also took into account the fact that the litigation had been brought with an election looming on the horizon.

> I am, of course, compelled to declare that s. 31(d) of the Election Act is invalid. However, having struck down a long-standing election law only a few days before the election itself and in circumstances where all rights of appeal cannot properly be exercised, I have decided that the legislators who are about to be elected must have an opportunity to decide what, if any, limits society should place on the otherwise unfettered right of imprisoned felons to influence the shape of the society from which they have been temporarily barred.... Until the legislators have had a reasonable opportunity to decide on their course of action in this significant civic

matter, it is neither just nor appropriate that the votes of the qualified and registered electors should now be diluted as a result of these applications. Moreover, the declaration, already made, that an integral part of the electoral structure is invalid leaves the whole system crippled or distorted and lacking properly framed rules to deal with such basic issues as the residence of prisoners for the purpose of voting. The court has no business trying to hack a path through this administrative jungle.[21]

Justice Scollin concluded that "the only remedy to which the applicants are entitled is the declaration that the impugned law is invalid."[22] As compared with Hirschfield's decision, Justice Scollin's is characterized by a combination of moderately reasoned negative activism and remedial restraint.

In a sense, the differences between Hirschfield and Scollin might appear to be overstated. At bottom, both seem to envisage a more moderate, middle-of-the-road law, which disenfranchises those in prison for the commission of more serious crimes rather than indiscriminately disqualifying all inmates of penal institutions regardless of the nature of their offence or the length of their incarceration. Both judges tell the relevant legislature that although *this* law goes too far, a more carefully drafted law would find favour in their eyes. Justice Scollin appears to think that declaring the *law* to be invalid without immediately reforming existing *practice* will suffice to nudge the legislature in the desired direction. Justice Hirschfield's "over reform" of existing practice—"over reform" because it extends the effective right to vote far more widely than he thinks the legislature is required to extend it—might be expected to achieve the same end. Indeed, might one not expect Justice Hirschfield's sword to bring legislators to their senses more quickly and effectively than Justice Scollin's scalpel?

Perhaps not. If the desirable objective is the moderate middle on a scale of policy restrictiveness, as both Scollin and Hirschfield seem to imply, it may be easier to achieve by moving from a more restrictive than from a less restrictive status quo. It may be easier, in other words, to ameliorate overly restrictive legislation than to reintroduce more moderate restrictions after judges have given effect to the least restrictive policy on the continuum. The aftermath of the *Morgentaler* case, as we shall see in Chapter Ten, provides some support for this hypothesis. Here it suffices to note that all attempts to reintroduce even the kind of criminal restrictions on abortion clearly permitted by *Morgentaler* have failed and show no sign of succeeding anytime soon. *Morgentaler* has given practical effect to much more of the pro-abortion agenda than is warranted by either the decision or public opinion. One can summarize these reflections by suggesting that the most common tools available to activist judges in their attempts to reform policy are often too crude to achieve the desired ends. Remedying policy excess by creating a new policy less restrictive than required by the constitution may turn out to have been unintended overkill. What the judge may see as temporary policy radicalism, spurring legislators on to moderating action, may turn out to be more permanent than anyone anticipated. If so, then the difference between the activisms of Justices Scollin and Hirschfield takes on new significance.

Ironically, even decisions that clearly uphold a challenged policy can sometimes help to undermine that policy. Or, more accurately, the process of judicial review can weaken a policy to such an extent that the bottom-line validation of the policy is not sufficient to revive it. The process itself, in other words, can have an activist bent—it can have the same result as an activist decision, even when the actual decision is restrained. Constance Robinson uses the *Edwards Books* case to illustrate this point. In *Edwards Books* the Supreme Court upheld Ontario's Sunday-closing legislation. But Robinson points out that during the lengthy period of litigation, from initial trial to Supreme Court decision, constitutional uncertainty made the law very difficult to enforce. Some retailers, such as Paul Magder, a Toronto furrier and party to the *Edwards Books* litigation, repeatedly and publicly flouted the law, simply accumulating charges and fines while awaiting the Supreme Court's determination. "By the time the Supreme Court handed down its decision on 18 December 1986, there were 285 outstanding charges against him."[23] Magder was not an isolated example; as the litigation proceeded, there was a dramatic rise in the number of violations.[24] Thus Robinson argues that the judicial process weakened the authority and enforceability of the law even though the official outcome of that process was a judgment upholding the law. Enforceability, moreover, is often easier to maintain than to re-establish once it has been weakened.

The difficulty in re-establishing enforceability was exacerbated by the fact that *Edwards Books* did not put an end to constitutional uncertainty. Magder, for example, was back in court almost immediately arguing that the law infringed the Charter's section 15 prohibition of discrimination on the grounds of religion, an issue not decided in *Edwards Books*. By July 1987, a provincial court judge had ruled in his favour, prompting the attorney general to appeal.[25]

The Ontario government responded to this uncertainty, and to the damaged authority of its legislation, by announcing that it would abandon province-wide legislation and hand the whole question over to the municipalities.[26] The litigation process itself, independently of its outcome, probably contributed to this result. As Michael Mandel observes, "despite the loss in *Edwards Books*, the very existence of the Charter has given [the cause of Sunday shopping] a seemingly inexhaustible litigation platform."[27] Thus *Edwards Books* "resolved nothing for the government," in effect forcing it "to go right back into court to defend the law against new litigation and ... to face the lobbyists and the press all over again."[28] Mandel did not find it surprising that the government responded by abdicating to the municipalities.

■ THE "LIVING TREE": INTERPRETIVISM VS. NONINTERPRETIVISM

Judges differ not only in their dispositions to be activist or restrained, but also in their theories of legitimate constitutional interpretation. Conflicting theories spring up especially around the question of the proper scope and limits of constitutional flexibility. Everyone agrees that constitutions are intended to endure for long periods of time and must therefore be flexible enough to accommodate a changing society. This, indeed, is why constitutional provisions are usually drafted in language sufficiently open-ended (or "open-textured," to use the term employed by legal theorists) to meet the unforeseeable needs of the future without constant formal amendment. In Canada this truism is often expressed through the image of the constitution as a "living tree" that grows and develops over time. Since the point is precisely to achieve flexibility without formal amendment, it is usually assumed that the tree's growth should be tended by judicial gardeners. Virtually everyone agrees, in short, that it is an important function of judicial review periodically to update the constitution. However, this general agreement hides a profound disagreement about what kind of updating is appropriate and legitimate. Two conflicting versions of the "living-tree" imagery are possible.

The first and narrower kind of judicial updating applies existing and well-established understandings of rights to new and unforeseen facts. For example, when the framers of the U.S. constitution prohibited unreasonable search and seizure, they knew nothing of modern electronic surveillance. When the American Supreme Court extended the right against unreasonable search and seizure to electronic eavesdropping in 1967, this represented a logical extension of its meaning, not the creation of a new right.[29] In Canada the Supreme Court made the same point in a case concerning video surveillance. The Charter's section 8 right to be secure against unreasonable search and seizure, argued Justice La Forest, was "meant to keep pace with technological development, and, accordingly, to ensure that we are ever protected against unauthorized intrusions upon our privacy by the agents of the state, whatever technical form the means of invasion may take."[30] Similarly, when the Canadian framers provided in section 133 of the BNA Act that the "Acts of the Parliament of Canada and of the Legislature of Quebec shall be printed and published in both" French and English and that either language may be used in the "courts" of those two jurisdictions, they were unfamiliar with the modern administrative state; nevertheless, when the Canadian Supreme Court decided in 1979 that "Acts" included regulations and that "court" included administrative tribunals, it could plausibly argue that it was merely extending "original intent."[31] Bringing new facts under the control of existing rights does not fundamentally change the latter.

The second and broader kind of judicial updating involves attributing such new meaning to a traditional right that it substantially changes (and even reverses) the application of the right. For example, freedom-of-religion provisions might originally be understood to prohibit the public preference of one religious sect over others, but to permit the preference of religion as such to irreligion. This understanding of religious freedom would allow such practices as nondiscriminatory public aid to religiously based private schools. At a later time, the courts might give freedom of religion a broader meaning that would prohibit such aid. This in fact is just what happened in the United States.[32] If the living-tree metaphor embraces this kind of updating, it involves changing the rights to suit new understandings. Instead of applying established rights to new facts, this approach subjects old facts to new, judicially created rights, usually with negative implications for established policy. Following our example, it would mean prohibiting aid to religious schools where it had previously been allowed, thus making unconstitutional what had previously been accepted as constitutional.[33]

These conflicting approaches to the issue of constitutional flexibility have been labelled, rather inelegantly, "interpretivism" and "noninterpretivism." Interpretivists strive to remain true to the original understanding of constitutional provisions, while conceding the need to work out the implications of that understanding for new circumstances. For interpretivists, the constitution is certainly a "living tree" that grows and changes in response to changing contextual circumstances, much as a real tree flexibly strives for the sun in a changing environment, but not one that can transform itself into another species, as if an oak could become a poplar.

Noninterpretivists, by contrast, deny that judicial updating can or should be limited by the established understanding of constitutional provisions. They are particularly hostile to the notion of original understanding, which they insist is often too obscure to provide much guidance. More fundamentally, they argue that courts must be free to ignore original or traditional understandings even when they are perfectly clear. To be limited by old understandings is to be shackled to the past, to allow long-dead generations to govern living ones.[34] Noninterpretivists do not believe that our evolving conceptions of justice should be hampered in this way. Noninterpretivism was starkly represented by Chief Justice Earl Warren's tendency impatiently to dismiss legal technicalities and appeals to precedent with the question: "But is it right, is it good?"[35] For noninterpretivists, in short, judicial gardeners must not only assist the living constitutional tree to reach the maturity of its species, but must sometimes help it mutate into the new species called for by our evolving sense of justice. Or, to vary the metaphor, while interpretivists strive to keep the times in tune with the constitution, noninterpretivists want to keep the constitution in tune with the times.

It might be argued that this debate between interpretivists and noninterpretivists has little application to judicial enforcement of the Canadian Charter because the latter is so new. Unlike the U.S. Bill of Rights, the Canadian Charter is not the product of past generations, whose handiwork might have to be judicially revised to give effect to the fundamental values of the present. When this book appears it will be just ten years old. Not only does this appear to make noninterpretivism unnecessary, but it suggests that it is unlikely to arise. As members of the same generation that produced the Charter, the judges who apply it are likely to give effect to its original understanding rather than changing it. If their decisions reflect new rights, it is because the Charter rights themselves are new, not because they have been transformed by judicial decision.

But this view is too simple. In the first place, as we shall see, the original understanding of even recently adopted constitutional provisions is controversial, as is the desirability of judicial fidelity to such understanding if it can be discovered. The Canadian Supreme Court has already interpreted at least one Charter right (section 7) more broadly than its own reading of original understanding warranted, and it did so quite consciously on the basis of a noninterpretivist rejection of original understanding as a weighty judicial consideration. We shall return to this point below.

Perhaps more important, many of the rights in the Charter are in fact not new. Freedom of religion and expression, the right to be presumed innocent until proven guilty, the right against self-incrimination—these and many other Charter rights have a long lineage in liberal democracies, including Canada. They have long been given effect by the Canadian legal system according to established understandings about their proper scope and limits. What is new about these rights in Canada is not their existence as fundamental principles of the regime, but their constitutional entrenchment. Unless the framers of the Charter clearly intended to change the content or meaning of these rights in the course of entrenching them, judicial decisions that make such changes can be considered noninterpretivist in character. They can be seen as transforming the traditional understanding of the proper scope and limits of a right without warrant in the original understanding of the constitutional provision they rely upon. In this view, such decisions use vague constitutional language, which is usually quite compatible with the right as traditionally understood, to create a new right. The legitimacy of doing so is as much a matter of debate among Canadian judges and commentators as it is among their American counterparts.

An example will help to clarify the point. In *Dubois* v. *The Queen*,[36] the Supreme Court considered the scope of section 13 of the Charter, which gives "a witness who testifies in any proceedings ... the right not to have any incriminating evidence so given used to incriminate that witness in any other proceedings, except in a prosecution for perjury or for the giving of contradictory evidence." Dubois had been tried for second-degree murder, and had given evidence in his own defence. He did not have to do so. It is a long-established right in Canada not to have to testify in one's own trial, and this right is now entrenched in section 11 of the Charter. Nevertheless, one is free to testify if one believes it would help one's case. Dubois took this route, admitting that he had killed the victim, but arguing that his action was justified by circumstances. The jury was not persuaded and convicted him. As it turned out, however, the judge had misdirected the jury on the proper interpretation of the law, and an appeal court ordered a new trial. At his second trial, Dubois exercised his right not to take the stand or to call any evidence. The prosecutor responded by reading into evidence the self-incriminating testimony Dubois had given at the first trial. Dubois claimed this violated section 13 of the Charter by using his former testimony to incriminate him in "other proceedings."

Prior to the Charter the right against self-incrimination received a degree of legislative protection, but not to the extent of excluding from a second trial incriminating evidence given by the accused at the first trial. What the prosecutor had done would have been perfectly legal prior to 1982. Had the Charter changed anything? It all depends on whether the second trial of the same accused on the same charge comes within the meaning of "other proceedings" in section 13. The majority of the Court decided that it did, and that the old practice of admitting first-trial testimony of an accused into evidence at the second trial would have to be discontinued. Justice McIntyre dissented. For McIntyre, there was nothing in the language of section 13 that required treating Dubois's second trial as "another proceeding." If an accomplice had testified against Dubois, and had then been charged himself, the latter trial would clearly fall within the meaning of "other proceedings." But it was perfectly plausible, McIntyre thought, to treat the second trial of the same accused on the same charge as simply a different stage of the same proceeding, much like the preliminary hearing or an appeal, in which case section 13 would not transform the existing practice. For McIntyre, this was the better approach. In his view, the majority had adopted "an interpretation of s. 13 not dictated by its language, involving an abandonment of long-accepted and sound principles of evidence."[37] Those long-accepted principles, of course, had been based on the traditional understanding of the proper scope of the right against self-incrimination. For McIntyre, the majority had created a new right that the constitutional language did not require. In this case, as in many others, he clearly adopted an interpretivist posture in opposition to the noninterpretivist action of his colleagues. In short, the newness of the Charter does not absolve Canadians from thinking through the debate between interpretivism and noninterpretivism.

It would be wrong to assume that the new (or newly understood) rights developed by noninterpretivist jurisprudence will always yield "liberal" or "progressive" decisions. Prior to 1937, for example, the U.S. Supreme Court used a highly noninterpretive reading of the due process clause of the fourteenth amendment to build a conservative blockade of social welfare policies being developed by state legislatures. The "due process" clause prevents state governments from depriving "any person of life, liberty and property, without due process of law." It is widely agreed that this wording was intended to mean just what it says: that a state could regulate property, for example, as long as the *process* it used to do so was "due" or fair. The clause, in short, was designed to provide a purely procedural protection: as long as the "process" was "due," the "substance" of the legislation could not be impugned, however much it might limit the goods of life, liberty, or property. Yet the Supreme Court, undeterred by the resulting oxymoron, read the clause as if it had said "substantive due process." This meant that some legislation could violate the clause because its substance was unjust, even if its procedures were unimpeachable. This was clearly the noninterpretivist creation of a new right. The "substantive" standards of justice read into the due process clause were those of laissez-faire capitalism, which the Court used to overturn such social welfare policies as maximum-hour[38] and minimum-wage legislation.[39] This was noninterpretivism harnessed to a conservative political agenda.

A similar phenomenon occurred in Canada during roughly the same period, when the JCPC, following a line of decentralizing precedents established earlier, invalidated the Canadian version of the "New Deal."[40] The JCPC insisted it was simply applying traditional rules of statutory interpretation to the BNA Act, and there is some debate about the extent to which this claim is justified,[41] but most observers agree that at least a certain degree of constitutional rewriting was necessary for the Court to reach its decentralist result. They find support for this in the admission of Lord Haldane, who wrote many of the JCPC's decisions during the 1920s, that his court had been engaged in statesmanship rather than simple application of the law. Praising his predecessor, Lord Watson, Haldane stated that

> ... as the result of a long series of decisions, Lord W: son put clothing upon the bones of the Constitution, and so covered them over with living flesh that the Constitution of Canada took a *new* form. The provinces were recognized as of equal authority co-ordinate with the Dominion, and a long series of decisions were given by him which solved many problems and produced a new contentment in Canada with the Constitution they had got in 1867. It is difficult to say what the extent of the debt was that Canada owes to Lord Watson....[42]

Again we see noninterpretivism used for conservative ends.

It must be said, however, that in recent decades noninterpretivism has generally been associated with the liberal or progressive end of the political spectrum. Since 1937, for example, the American Supreme Court has abandoned all notions of economic substantive due process, and has given legislatures free rein in economic regulation.[43] The demise of *economic* substantive due process, however, has not entailed the demise of substantive due process altogether. The Court has continued its practice of reading new substantive rights into the due process clause, only now they are the rights of social privacy rather than economic privacy. Among other things, the Court decided in the famous 1973 case *Roe* v. *Wade* that this "right to privacy" gives women a relatively free choice in the matter of abortion during the first six months of pregnancy, and that state legislation limiting this "substantive" right violates the "due process" clause, even if the legislation displays no procedural defects.[44] Previous generations had never suspected that such a constitutional right to abortion existed. For many observers, this is a new right created by noninterpretivist judges. This time, however, noninterpretivism was placed in the service of the liberal political agenda.

■ TRADITIONAL VS. MODERN JUDICIAL REVIEW

In fact, the judicial majority in *Roe* would deny that they had created a *new* right. John Hart Ely defines noninterpretivism as the view that courts should "enforce norms that cannot be discovered within the four corners of the [constitutional] document,"[45] but few judges ever admit that they are straying from the text. For example, when the U.S. Supreme Court first discovered a general "right to privacy" in the 1965 case of *Griswold* v. *Connecticut*,[46] it did so by extrapolating from several constitutional provisions that clearly do protect aspects of privacy. In protecting freedom of speech and of religion, for example, the first amendment creates a "zone of privacy." Such "zones of privacy" are also established by the third amendment's ban on quartering soldiers in private homes, the fourth amendment's prohibition of unreasonable search and seizures, and the fifth amendment's guarantee of the freedom from self-incrimination. The Court concluded that "emanating" from the "penumbras" (shadows) of these rights, was a more general right to privacy, which it lodged in the "due process" clause. In other words, it decided that since certain kinds of privacy were explicitly protected by the constitution, the protection of privacy in general must be implicit in that document. A few years later in *Roe* the Court concluded that this general right to privacy included the freedom to decide whether or not to have an abortion.

In basing the general right to privacy on more explicit and particular provisions, the Court was clearly suggesting that this was not a newly *created* but a newly *discovered* right, that it had been there all the time, lurking in the shadows of other provisions and waiting to be found by the light of modern progressive consciousness. In form at least, the Court can even be understood to be appealing to the interpretivist standard of original understanding: it argued that a number of constitutional provisions clearly show that the framers were concerned with the protection of privacy, and that following through the implications of that concern is merely to fulfil their intentions. This shows that the opposition between interpretivism and noninterpretivism as we have presented it thus far is misleading. It is not really a dispute between those who accept and those who reject the constitutional text and its original or traditional understanding as crucial guides to constitutional interpretation. As Ronald Dworkin notes, "almost any constitutional theory relies on some conception of an original intention or understanding."[47] The real dispute concerns the appropriate level of generality or abstraction at which to state the original understanding, with interpretivists preferring more particular or concrete intentions, and noninterpretivists insisting on greater levels of abstraction. Thus in the dispute about the right to privacy, interpretivists insist that the constitution protects only those concrete manifestations of privacy that the framers explicitly wrote into the text, while noninterpretivists contend that the particular provisions are merely concrete illustrations of a more general or abstract concern with privacy, and that the abstract principle is just as important constitutionally as its concrete examples.

Since both interpretivists and noninterpretivists engage in textual interpretation, including the search for some form of original understanding, it might be better to use Christopher Wolfe's labels of "traditional" and "modern" judicial review. Traditionalism is what we have thus far called interpretivism. Its essential assumption, says Wolfe, "was the intelligibility of a broad Constitution whose principles were 'substantial' [i.e., concrete] enough to provide determinative guidance in distinguishing constitutional powers and rights. The Constitution was broad or general, but—at least, for the most part—it was not merely 'vague' or 'ambiguous.'"[48] Modern judicial review, by contrast, assumes that the constitution is composed of vague principles stated at a high level of generality, which judges must adapt to changing circumstances and needs. This is what we have called noninterpretivism.

Ironically the roots of "modern" judicial review in the United States extend far into the past. Modern review is exemplified most clearly by the judicially developed doctrine of substantive due process, which Wolfe traces to pre–Civil War cases, and which, as we have seen, flourished in its laissez-faire version during the early decades of this century. Although these economic-substantive-due-process cases reflect the practice of modern review, the theoretical justifications of this jurisprudential approach were developed mainly by progressive opponents of the Supreme Court's laissez-faire decisions. Although they could have criticized these cases on traditionalist grounds, as departures from the constitution as originally understood, "legal thinkers such as Oliver Wendell Holmes, historians such as J. Allen Smith and Charles Beard, and political scientists such as Woodrow Wilson generally accepted the argument that identified the founders and the Constitution with laissez-faire policy."[49] To overcome this constitutional orientation, they were forced to oppose the idea of original understanding and to develop theoretical justifications for doing so:

> Rather than attack the [laissez-faire] Court on the grounds that its judicial review was a departure from the Constitution, many of them sought to detach the Constitution from the founders and their supposed economic dogmas. This sundering of the Constitution and framers was accomplished by elevating the Constitution's meaning to a level of high generality and then arguing that application of this vague set of principles had to be "adapted" to the circumstances of each new era: the framers' views were fine for their day but now new circumstances unforeseen by them required new views. The influence of late-nineteenth-century Darwinian or evolutionary thought supported this conception of a thoroughly elasticized Constitution.[50]

Modern judicial review, argues Wolfe, did not come fully into its own until Supreme Court justices unabashedly embraced this perspective after the Court crisis of 1937. "Holmes's disciples," he writes, "became dominant on the Court after 1937 through a series of Franklin Roosevelt appointments, and they firmly committed the Supreme Court to modern judicial review."[51] Wolfe thus defines the earlier development of substantive due process as a "transitional period" between eras of self-conscious traditionalism and modernism.[52]

Wolfe distinguishes the transitional and modern periods not only by the degree of self-consciousness with which the judges justified their practice of modern judicial review, but more importantly by the way in which modern review was harnessed to judicial restraint in the former period and judicial activism in the latter. The theory of a highly elasticized constitution was developed during the transitional period in order to make it easier for judges to *uphold*, not invalidate, controversial social welfare legislation:

The chief concern of Holmes and other advocates of the notion of judicial legislation in constitutional cases was to make it possible to uphold legislative acts that were inconsistent with the "Constitution" (as the Court majority interpreted it). The meaning of the Constitution was to be "adapted" precisely to make possible the legislation the Court majority had been striking down—different forms of economic regulation. Again, ironically, the assertion of a broad new understanding of judicial power had all the appearance of a power much more deferential to legislatures, much more limited.[53]

After 1937, by contrast, the modern theory of judicial review has been used primarily to expand rights limiting legislative power rather than removing such limits. Judges practising modern judicial review during the modern era tend to develop new rights that they use to invalidate the policies of the other branches of government. In a sense they are doing precisely what the theory of modern review was developed to overcome.[54]

The same pattern is evident in Canada. The notion of the constitution as a "living tree" to be judicially adapted to the changing needs of society was originally used mainly to justify a flexible approach to the federal–provincial distribution of powers in order to accommodate new legislative initiatives that the courts had been resisting. It provided the theoretical justification for the practice of judicial restraint. Under the Charter of Rights, by contrast, the same "living-tree" analogy is used to defend the judicial creation of new rights, which is to say the activist imposition of new limits on government.[55]

One of the most "modern" features of contemporary noninterpretivism is its association with a recently popular theory of literary interpretation known as deconstructionism. Followers of this school deny that writing flows from the attempt to apprehend and express truth. This may be what authors think they are doing, but they are mistaken. They are mistaken because there is no truth independent of historical and social context. "Truth" and "knowledge" are really expressions of the writer's underlying "will to power." Thus written texts must be understood as the rationalizations of the dominating power (or the desire for such power) of the racial, sexual, or class interests unconsciously represented by the author. To understand a text, one should not so much pay attention to its surface appearances as "deconstruct" that surface to reveal the unconscious power interests lying beneath.[56]

This deconstructive theory supports a view of literary interpretation very much like the legal noninterpretivism of modern judicial review. To the extent that a text might convey truth known to its author, the attempt to read it as intended by the author makes sense. If texts express only a "will to power," on the other hand, there is little reason to defer to authorial intention. Indeed, there is no reason why those whose interests differ from the author's should not exploit the indeterminacy of language to pour their own meaning into the text:

> If language is merely rhetorical rather than representational or expressive, if there is no connection between language and reality, then the reader is freed from trying to discover what the text means. He is delivered from the illusion that the text has any inherent meaning at all. For meaning is not inherent in the text and does not have reference to an extralinguistic world out there, but is rather created by the reader as rhetorical formulation imposed on the text. Every reading is therefore a misreading having no particular exegetical authority.[57]

As Stanley Fish, a leading proponent of this approach to literary criticism, has put it, interpretations "give texts their shape, *making them* rather than, as it is usually assumed, arising from them."[58] In fact, new readers (or new generations of readers), given their very different and rationally unbridgeable social situations, cannot help *remaking* texts to suit their needs and interests rather than the author's. As Richard Rorty puts it, an interpreter is one who "simply beats the text into a shape which will serve his own purpose."[59] In effect, the reading of texts, especially those that have acquired an aura of "greatness," becomes an act of political "occupation," a way of turning their mythical "authority" to new and different political purposes.[60] It should not surprise us that proponents of modern, noninterpretivist jurisprudence should find inspiration in this literary deconstructionism. Allan Bloom correctly notes that "deconstructionism has colored the public discussions about 'original intent' as the guide for judges' interpretation of the Constitution...."[61] A revealing indication of the alliance between literary and legal deconstructionists is the fact that Stanley Fish professes both literature and law at Duke University.[62]

Wolfe's labels of "traditional," transitional," and "modern" have allowed us to refine our understanding of the two major approaches to constitutional interpretation. Unlike interpretivism and noninterpretivism they more easily focus attention on the main issue—the level of generality at which constitutional principles are cast—without the confusing implication that only one side in the debate is engaged in interpretation. By emphasizing the historical dimension of the debate, moreover, Wolfe's labels highlight the ironic fact that the modern theory now used to justify the judicial imposition of new limits on government was originally developed to remove such limits and encourage a posture of judicial deference. They also readily accommodate the inspiration noninterpretivism now draws from deconstructionist literary theory. The traditional–modern continuum, in short, has certain advantages over the interpretivism–noninterpretivism dichotomy.

Wolfe's terminology also suffers some comparative disadvantages, however. As he himself recognizes, "modern" judicial review has a long history, and "traditional" review continues to attract its defenders, both on and off the bench. Although the relative prominence of these approaches has changed over time, they seem in some respects to be perennial adversaries on the jurisprudential battlefield rather than belonging to distinct historical periods. Moreover, given the prevalence of "progressive" assumptions about historical change, the use of the labels "traditional" and "modern" might subtly prejudice the issue in favour of the latter. We believe the debate, which is worth considering on its own merits, should not be obscured by this assumption. Finally, the terminology of interpretivism and noninterpretivism is now so well established in the literature that it seems imprudent to muddy the waters with new labels. Thus, although we shall use Wolfe's labels for greater clarity in certain contexts, we shall follow established practice in referring mainly to interpretive and noninterpretive jurisprudence. The lessons of Wolfe's analysis should be incorporated into our understanding of these terms, however.

■ ABSTRACT VS. CONCRETE INTENT: THE EXAMPLE OF RONALD DWORKIN

The two jurisprudential approaches we have been discussing are most obviously distinguished by the levels of generality they attribute to constitutional principles.[63] This distinction can be clarified by a revealing example provided by Dworkin. He claims that it would be legitimate for the American Supreme Court to find that capital punishment violates the eighth amendment's ban on "cruel and unusual punishments."[64] The difficulty such an argument must overcome stems from several constitutional provisions that explicitly assume the legitimacy of capital punishment. The fifth amendment, for example, states that "no person shall be held to answer for a capital, or otherwise infamous crime, unless on a presentment or indictment of a Grand Jury…; nor shall any person be subject for the same offence to be twice put in jeopardy of life or limb;… nor be deprived of life, liberty, or property, without due process of law…." As Robert Bork observes, this amendment "three times assumes the availability of the death penalty."[65] Moreover, as we have already seen, the fifth amendment's assumption that one may be "deprived of life" in accordance with the "due process of law" was repeated in the due process clause of the fourteenth amendment. One might conclude from this that capital punishment was clearly permitted by the constitution as originally understood, and that to find it unconstitutional now, the Court would have to create a new right. Dworkin draws no such conclusion. Indeed, he explicitly opposes those who "believe that the Court ought to make a fresh determination of whether the death penalty is cruel." Such people "say that ideas of cruelty change over time," and that the Court's proper response is to "change what the Constitution enacted," but Dworkin considers this mode of argument to be "vulnerable." Like interpretivists, he thinks judicial review can only be justified if judges are applying the actual constitution, not writing a new one.[66] But how can a constitution that explicitly concedes the legitimacy of capital punishment end up prohibiting it unless the judges illegitimately rewrite it? The answer lies in Dworkin's reliance upon the abstract rather than the concrete intention embodied in the constitution.

Dworkin often uses the labels of "concept" and "conception" to discuss the differences between abstract and concrete intentions. To illustrate this distinction Dworkin poses as a father telling his children to act fairly.[67] In issuing such a command, the paternal Dworkin undoubtedly has in mind specific examples of what it means to act both fairly and unfairly, and may use these examples to help the children understand how to act. But these examples will not settle all issues for the children. In the first place, unforeseen situations not covered by the examples are bound to arise, and because Dworkin will not always be around, the children will have to decide for themselves what their father's ideas imply for those situations. Second, Dworkin stands "ready to admit that some particular act I had thought was fair when I spoke was in fact unfair, or vice versa, if one of my children is able to convince me of that later."[68] In acting contrary to his father's original examples, the child in this situation would not be disobeying his instructions because Dworkin is there to amend the list of examples. But Dworkin does not consider this to be a fundamental change in instructions. "I should want to say," he argues, "that my instructions covered the case he cited, not that I had changed my instructions. I might say that I meant the family to be guided by the *concept* of fairness, not by any specific *conception* of fairness I might have had in mind."[69]

Indeed, a child who abandons his father's *conception* of fairness lives up to the latter's instruction to abide by the *concept* even when the father is no longer around to be persuaded. This is required by Dworkin's argument because the father is meant to stand for long-dead constitutional framers and the child for today's judges. Like the father ordering fairness, the framers ordered subsequent generations not to impose cruel and unusual punishments. Like the father, however, they were commanding adherence to the *concept* of cruel and unusual, not to the particular *conception* of it they held. In effect, they were commanding future generations to think for themselves about the true meaning of "cruel and unusual," to apply "fresh moral insight"[70] when it became available. Thus today's judges can reject the "fathers'" examples of what is cruel and unusual, and the conceptions on which those examples are based, just as Dworkin's child can reject his father's conception of fairness—and both can do so without departing from the original understanding, which related only to concepts, not to conceptions. To be specific, the framers' conception of what is cruel and unusual is revealed by their evident assumption, clearly embodied in the constitutional text, that capital punishment is not per se cruel; but the present generation can best live up to the framers' concept, and thus their deepest intention, by ignoring this conception and substituting the new one called for by "fresh moral insight." Capital punishment can become constitutionally impermissible, despite the framers' contrary assumption, without departing from original intent. As in the case of the general right to privacy, this hypothetical example leads to significant constitutional change within the context of a formal appeal to the interpretive standard of original understanding.

Dworkin's argument is ingenious, but it does not persuade many interpretivists. For the latter, the "concepts" Dworkin identifies with original understanding are so general as to be virtually meaningless. Every sane person is in favour of fairness, and no father worthy of the name would command his children to act unfairly. Similarly, no sane constitution-maker would order the imposition of cruel and unusual punishments. If "fathers," both natural and constitutional, intend to lay down standards only at this level of generality, they would be commanding only what no one disputes, in which case their commands would be entirely superfluous. What really matters, from this perspective, is precisely the conceptions Dworkin dismisses as irrelevant to original intent. The "concept" of fairness is a highly general standard, for example, whereas a "conception" of fairness is a more specific theory of why a particular act is either fair or unfair.[71] On a conservative conception of fairness a particular act might be considered fair, while a liberal or progressive conception of fairness would lead one to conclude that the same act was unfair. When he issued his fatherly command, Dworkin might have held a conservative conception of fairness, while his child eventually came to hold a liberal conception. For Dworkin, the difference between conservative and liberal conceptions of fairness is less important in determining original intent than the fact that both speak the language of fairness. For an interpretivist, on the other hand, the common language is meaningless, and the important point in determining original intent is precisely to discover the founding *conception,* not the concept. From this perspective, constitutions are intended to govern the future, which they cannot do if the principles they lay down are so general that almost any meaning can be poured into them.

Thus, for the sceptical interpretivist, Dworkin is doing precisely what he says should not be done, namely, defending the right of judges to "change what the Constitution enacted." The argument is subtle, but those of an interpretivist bent see it as little more than an ingenious smokescreen designed to deflect attention from what is really going on, namely, the judicial creation of a new right. Again, although Dworkin retains the form of an appeal to original understanding in his argument about capital punishment, an interpretivist would insist he has actually turned that understanding inside out. Far from developing the intrinsic implications of the original understanding of cruelty, he is reading a new understanding into the constitution, one that makes unconstitutional what had long been considered constitutional. Similarly, interpretivists maintain that the weakness of the argument in favour of a general right to privacy is evident in its "penumbral" or "shadowy" nature. They find it more plausible to assume that the framers intended only to protect certain aspects of privacy, not privacy as such; that neither they nor subsequent generations ever thought that by protecting against unreasonable search and seizure or the quartering of soldiers in private homes the constitution was guaranteeing a right to abortion. For interpretivists, in short, a new right had emerged through the process of noninterpretivist creation, just as it had in the case of economic substantive due process. Interpretivists also like to point out that the "fresh moral insight" leading to such constitutional revolutions comes not from democratic majorities who, evidently retaining the defective understanding of the framers, insist on maintaining capital punishment or restrictions on abortion, but from intellectuals such as Dworkin and the judges he hopes to enlist in his cause.[72]

Interpretivist proponents of adherence to a more specific and narrow version of original understanding also point out that nothing prevents legislatures from abandoning the practice of capital punishment or enacting more liberal abortion laws. Although the constitution as originally understood permits the death penalty and restrictions on abortion, it does not require them. Whether to impose the death penalty in the kinds of cases for which the framers considered it legitimate, or what degree of choice to permit in the matter of abortion, were questions left up to the political process, which was not prevented from moving in the direction desired by modern progressives. Nothing prevents legislatures from imposing new limitations on themselves beyond those imposed by the constitution; constitutional rewriting is not necessary.[73] Indeed, if the people feel so strongly about a new right that they wish constitutionally to entrench it rather than leaving it to ordinary legislation, they are free to do so through the process of constitutional amendment.

Interpretivists, in other words, are perfectly prepared to concede Dworkin's claim that future generations should be free to add to or extend the rights entrenched in the constitution. They simply insist that this must not be done by judges. The interpretivist sceptic sees the noninterpretivist creation of new rights by judges as necessary only when the people and their representatives do not desire these rights, and when the original constitution does not require them. In this view, noninterpretive jurisprudence is simply a way for minorities to achieve through the judicial process, in the name of nonexistent constitutional rights, what they could not achieve in the political arena.[74] Far from avoiding rule by dead majorities, noninterpretivism overcomes rule by living ones.[75] This kind of thinking underlies the sceptical depiction of Canada's Charter of Rights as the "court party's constitution" rather than the "citizens' constitution."

The interpretivist preference for specific over general versions of original intent should not be overstated. It does not mean that the constitution is frozen in time, applying only to situations known to or foreseen by the framers, as former Justice William Brennan of the U.S. Supreme Court apparently thinks:

> In its most doctrinaire incarnation [the theory of original intent] demands that Justices discern exactly what the Framers thought about the question under consideration and simply follow that

intention in resolving the case before them. It is a view that feigns self-effacing deference to the specific judgments of those who forged our original social compact. But in truth it is little more than arrogance cloaked as humility. It is arrogant to pretend that from our vantage we can gauge accurately the intent of the Framers on application of principle to specific, contemporary questions.[76]

For most interpretivists, this is an extreme caricature, and thus a serious misrepresentation, of their position. For example, Robert Bork, a leading proponent of interpretivism in the United States, agrees that "the view described by Justice Brennan is arrogant, or would be, if anybody took such a position." According to Bork, however, "Justice Brennan demolished a position no one holds, one that is not only indefensible but undefended."[77] For Bork, interpretivism was more fairly and accurately described by another of its critics, John Hart Ely:

> What distinguishes interpretivism from its opposite is its insistence that the work of the political branches is to be invalidated only in accord with an inference whose starting point, whose underlying premise, is fairly discoverable in the Constitution. *That the complete inference will not be found there—because the situation is not likely to have been foreseen—is generally common ground.*[78]

Interpretivists, in other words, concede that the constitution must be applied by judges to situations unforeseen by the framers. The principles of unreasonable search and seizure, for example, must be applied to modern techniques of electronic surveillance. As we have already noted, virtually everyone agrees that constitutions must be flexible enough to accommodate the future. Interpretivists insist, however, that judges must limit themselves to working out the implications of old principles (in the form of Dworkin's concrete conceptions, not his abstract concepts) for new circumstances, that they must never reform or change the principles themselves to create new rights.

Nor do interpretivists claim that it will always be easy to determine what is implied by old principles for new circumstances. Judges acting in good faith might well come to divergent conclusions. The point is that judges must endeavour *in good faith* to reason from premises "fairly discoverable in the Constitution." Interpretivists do not believe this can be said of the judicial creation of "substantive due process" in either its conservative or liberal versions, or of the effort to find capital punishment unconstitutional despite the plain words of the text. For interpretivists, constitutional flexibility is a good thing, but not flexibility of this kind or to this degree.

■ THE CONUNDRUM OF BROWN V. BOARD OF EDUCATION

In the United States much of the debate between interpretivism and non-interpretivism has focused on *Brown* v. *Board of Education,* the case that finally desegregated the schools. As Bork observes:

> The end of state-mandated segregation was the greatest moral triumph constitutional law had ever produced. It is not surprising that academic lawyers were unwilling to give it up; it *had* to be right. Thus, *Brown* has become the high ground of constitutional theory. Theorists of all persuasions seek to capture it, because any theory that seeks acceptance must, as a matter of psychological fact, if not of logical necessity, account for the result in *Brown*.[79]

There is evidence that, while the framers of the fourteenth amendment wished to protect the newly freed slaves and to promote their equality, they did not think this required desegregated schools.[80] In its decision, the Supreme Court tried to fudge this uncomfortable fact by arguing that the historical record was too inconclusive to discover a clear intent regarding segregation, but few observers find these efforts convincing. The Court obviously thought that it could reach the desired result in *Brown* only by departing from original intent. Many noninterpretivists agree, and use that fact to defend creative jurisprudence. In this view noninterpretivism is justified because it was the only way to overcome what virtually everyone now agrees was a profound injustice. Because it was justified in that case, moreover, it is justified as a general approach to constitutional interpretation, applicable in other contexts. *Brown,* in other words, has become a trump card for the noninterpretivist side of the debate.

In responding to this contention, interpretivists concede the justice of the result in *Brown.* They also admit that a judicial decision was necessary to break the political logjam concerning segregation. The states that engaged in the practice were not about to dismantle it, and Congress would not act because its positions of power, being based on seniority, had come to be dominated by what was then the one-party Democratic South, whose representatives were elected virtually for life. Nor do interpretivists deny that the framers of the fourteenth amendment assumed the continuation of segregation. Nevertheless, critics of noninterpretivism insist that "a perfectly good interpretivist opinion could be written for *Brown*,"[81] that "the result in *Brown* is consistent with, indeed is compelled by, the original understanding of the fourteenth amendment's equal protection clause."[82] How is this possible?

For interpretivists, the result in *Brown* should have been justified by the unambiguous fact that the equal protection clause of the fourteenth amendment was originally understood by all concerned to promote the equality of blacks. It is true that these same framers also assumed that equality was compatible with segregation, but the clause enacts *equality*, not segregation. "Segregation is not mentioned in the clause, nor do the debates suggest that the clause was enacting segregation."[83] The framers' assumption that segregation was compatible with equality does not make segregation the primary purpose of the equal protection clause. For interpretivists, experience between the drafting of the fourteenth amendment and 1954, when *Brown* was decided, had shown conclusively that the primary purpose of equality was undermined by continuing segregation. This meant not that the courts should depart from original understanding, but that they were forced to choose between different aspects of it, in particular between its primary and secondary aspects:

> By 1954, when *Brown* came up for decision, it had been apparent for some time that segregation rarely if ever produced equality. Quite aside from any question of psychology, the physical facilities provided for blacks were not as good as those provided for whites. That had been demonstrated in a long series of cases. The Supreme Court was faced with a situation in which the courts would have to go on forever entertaining litigation about primary schools, secondary schools, colleges, washrooms, golf courses, swimming pools, drinking fountains, and the endless variety of facilities that were segregated, or else the separate-but-equal doctrine would have to be abandoned. Endless litigation, aside from the burden on the courts, also would never produce the equality the Constitution promised. The Court's realistic choice, therefore, was either to abandon the quest for equality by allowing segregation or to forbid segregation in order to achieve equality. There was no third choice.

Either choice would violate one aspect of the original understanding, but there was no possibility of avoiding that. Since equality and segregation were mutually inconsistent, though the ratifiers did not understand that, both could not be honored. When that is seen, it is obvious the Court must choose equality and prohibit state-imposed segregation. The purpose that brought the fourteenth amendment into being was equality before the law, and equality, not separation, was written into the text.[84]

This kind of reasoning might look a little like Dworkin's appeal to general concepts in order to overcome the inconvenience of more particular conceptions. If one can appeal to one part of the framers' perspective (equality) to overcome another part of their perspective (segregation), why can't one appeal to their ban on cruel and unusual punishments to overcome their assumption of the legitimacy of capital punishment? Part of the interpretivist answer might be that the status of the death penalty in relation to the idea of cruel and unusual punishment was closer to the framers' central concerns than was segregation, as shown by the fact that the death penalty is explicitly and repeatedly embodied in the constitutional text while segregation clearly is not.

What of the general right to privacy the Court discovered emanating from the penumbras of the constitution? Could this not be justified as an extrapolation from founding intent just as the interpretivists propose to extrapolate desegregation? Interpretivists respond to this kind of claim by arguing that desegregation relates to the very clear and specific intent to promote equality for blacks, whereas the right to privacy requires searching the penumbras of specific rights for very general emanations. In the words of Richard Morgan, an interpretivist version of *Brown* would rest on the fact that

> while the framers of the Fourteenth Amendment ... were able to conceive of trivial state imposed separations based on race, almost a century of experiences made clear that such state discriminations substantially undercut *the specific (not the general) and manifest (not underlying)* purposes of the equal protection clause. Just as in the Fourth Amendment context interpretivism can justify substitution of "zones of privacy" for physical premises in order to preserve the purposes of the framers against the potential of electronic surveillance which they could not have foreseen, so "separate but equal" could have been jettisoned.[85]

No doubt there is room for more discussion and further refinements in this debate about *Brown,* but enough has been said to underscore Bork's point: both sides do indeed want to occupy "the high ground of constitutional theory" by appropriating "the greatest moral triumph constitutional law had ever produced." Important as this competition over *Brown* is, however, it is not necessarily decisive. Even if the noninterpretivists are right in their claim that the result in *Brown* could be reached only by abandoning original intent, this would not impel most interpretivists into the noninterpretivist camp. The problem, as interpretivists see it, lies in extending the principle of constitutional revisionism beyond the confines of the desegregation issue. If original understanding had to be abandoned to achieve justice in *Brown,* that fact is used by noninterpretivists to make justice, rather than original understanding, the interpretive touchstone in other contexts. But the situations are usually not comparable. In the case of segregation it can plausibly be said that the will of a national majority was being frustrated by a sectional minority (white southerners) whose representatives wielded disproportionate influence in Congress, and that noninterpretivist jurisprudence (if, indeed, that was what was required) aided democratic majoritarianism. Aiding majoritarianism is not usually the effect of noninterpretivist judicial review, however, especially in the modern era. Nowadays it typically involves creating a new right in order to invalidate majority preferences. Both the right to an abortion and Dworkin's proposed invalidation of capital punishment are good examples. If noninterpretivist review was necessary to achieve *Brown,* it could be said to reflect a new consensus about justice that differed from that of the framers, and that, owing to unusual circumstances, could not be implemented through the normal legislative process. In most other contexts, noninterpretivist review imposes a new vision of justice on a majority not yet ready to reject the framers' vision. This majority, moreover, is usually free to adopt the new vision legislatively if it wants to. The view of justice that displaces original understanding is that of a minority. Thus Bork concludes that even if *Brown* could only be achieved by noninterpretivist jurisprudence (which he does not concede), "that would not affect the legitimacy of the philosophy [of original understanding]":

> Constitutional philosophy is a theory of what renders a judge's power to override democratic choice legitimate. It is no answer to say that we like the results, no matter how divorced from the intentions of the lawgivers, for that is to say that we prefer an authoritarian regime with which we agree to a democracy with which we do not.[86]

■ THE CANADIAN DEBATE

Although this jurisprudential debate is more highly developed in the United States, it has not been absent from Canadian discussions. Our examination of *Dubois* above shows that it has become a part of judicial debate about the Charter. In fact, however, this debate has important historical precedents. The JCPC's invalidation of much of the "Bennett New Deal" gave rise to this country's first major debate over jurisprudential interpretivism and noninterpretivism, though these modern terms were not used.[87]

According to one side in the JCPC controversy, a court's proper role in constitutional interpretation was to give effect to the founding intention. This "originalist" argument was used both by those who liked and those who disliked the JCPC's decentralist leanings. The Court's defenders argued that it had indeed discovered and implemented the original intent, while its critics insisted that original intent had been betrayed. Another set of arguments was based on the noninterpretivist claim that rather than implementing original intent, the proper judicial task was to keep the constitution in tune with the times. Again, this position was employed both to defend and criticize the JCPC's jurisprudence. The critics claimed that, whatever the original constitutional intention may have been, the country *needed* a strong central government and the JCPC had fallen down in its task in neglecting to supply that need. Noninterpretivist defenders, on the other hand, argued that the JCPC had engaged in valuable statesmanship by adjusting a centralized constitutional text to better suit the decentralist reality of the country. Perhaps the best distillation of this view was Pierre Trudeau's remark that, had it not been for the JCPC, a separate Quebec would long ago have been a reality rather than a threat.[88] Although these positions are analytically distinct, they were often confused in practice. Critics of the JCPC, for example, appealed to both a Macdonaldian original intent and the objective needs of the country, as rhetorical convenience dictated. Nevertheless, the general outlines of what we are calling jurisprudential interpretivism and noninterpretivism, as well as the tension between them, are clearly visible.

The debate between interpretivism and noninterpretivism has emerged once again, and has grown in importance, with the advent of the Charter.[89] In the Supreme Court's first Charter case, *Law Society of Upper Canada* v. *Skapinker,*[90] Justice Estey expressed the noninterpretivist viewpoint when he refused to ground the Court's new mandate for judicial review on founding intention.[91] In another early case, the *B.C. Motor*

Vehicles Reference, Justice Lamer (later to become Canada's Chief Justice) gave further support to noninterpretivism, warning that judicial fidelity to "original understanding" would "freeze" the meaning of the Charter and make it incapable of "growth, development, and adjustment to changing social needs."[92] The case concerned the Charter's guarantee in section 7 that "everyone has the right to life, liberty and security of the person and the right not to be deprived thereof except in accordance with the principles of fundamental justice." The issue was whether "the principles of fundamental justice" were substantive or purely procedural, whether, in other words, "life, liberty and security" could be deprived as long as the deprivations were procedurally fair, or whether "fundamental justice" meant that certain deprivations of those rights were prohibited even if the standards of procedural fairness were met. Original intent may often be difficult to discover, but less so in this case. Many observers agree that the "fundamental justice" clause was designed to be a procedural, not a substantive provision. Indeed, it was chosen as an alternative to the traditional "due process" phrasing because of the "substantive" interpretation given to the latter in the United States. The drafters of the Charter hoped to avoid the incorporation of American "substantive due process" by choosing a different wording.[93] Yet a scant three years after the Charter's enactment, Justice Lamer concluded that "growth, development, and adjustment to changing social needs" were in order, and that original intent must be set aside.

Where original intent specific to the drafting of the Charter is murky, traditional understandings of Charter rights may nevertheless be embodied in existing practice. The Court has given ample indication that such traditional understandings limit judicial creativity no more than specific original intent. The *Dubois* case, discussed above, is one example. Another is *Big M Drug Mart,* in which the Court invalidated the federal Lord's Day Act.[94] When this same act had been challenged about twenty years earlier under the Diefenbaker Bill of Rights, the Supreme Court had upheld it because it did not infringe religious freedom as that right had come to be understood in Canada. The Court relied on section 1 of the Bill, which "recognized and declared that in Canada there *have existed and shall continue to exist*" the specified rights and freedoms. Since religious freedom "had existed" in conjunction with the Lord's Day Act, it followed that the latter did not infringe the former, and that both could "continue to exist" together.[95] This became known (and reviled) among civil libertarians as the "frozen-concepts" approach, which they generally contrasted with their preferred "living-tree" approach. As Lamer's comments in *B.C. Motor Vehi-*

cles show, the Court has abandoned "frozen concepts" in favour of the "living tree" even in the case of relatively specific original intent. In striking down the Lord's Day Act in *Big M Drug Mart,* it did the same thing with the "traditional" understandings embodied in existing practice.

The disavowal of founding intention or traditional understanding does not mean that the Court altogether rejects the idea of a guiding purpose underlying Charter provisions. Indeed, the cornerstone of Charter jurisprudence, launched by Chief Justice Dickson in several early cases, is "purposive analysis."[96] Underlying the broad language of each Charter right is a purpose, or a set of interests and activities it is meant to protect, and in applying the right judges must identify and be guided by that purpose. The purpose of a Charter right must be sought not in the explicit intentions of the constitution-makers, however, but in the evolving traditions and principles of our liberal democratic society—the *evolving* traditions, it must be emphasized, not the existing traditions as embodied in existing practice. Indeed, as cases like *Big M Drug Mart* show, the point of purposive analysis is often to overcome existing traditions. In Dworkian terms, purposive analysis generally means the selective abstraction of highly general concepts from the tradition of liberal democracy in order to transform actual practice. This purposive approach, in short, provides ample scope for noninterpretivist judicial creativity. It also leaves room for judicial disagreement. As Peter Russell puts it: "The history and philosophy of liberal democracy do not exactly form an open book containing clear definitions of the activities and interests which are not be interfered with by government."[97] And, indeed, although all of the judges appear to accept the purposive approach, such disagreement has become quite common.

Judicial disagreement had not yet emerged in *B.C. Motor Vehicles,* in which Justice Lamer spoke for a unanimous panel of seven judges, suggesting that perhaps the entire Court was adopting a noninterpretivist posture. Indeed, the Court was unanimous in most of the cases decided during its first year of Charter jurisprudence. But this consensus was soon to break down, in part because judges began to split along the interpretivist–noninterpretivist divide. The interpretivist side of the Court displayed its proclivities most dramatically in cases asking the judges to find a right to strike and a right to abortion in, respectively, the section 2(d) right to "freedom of association" and the section 7 right to "life, liberty and security of the person." In the *Alberta Labour Reference* Justices La Forest, Beetz, and Le Dain criticized the discovery by Justices Dickson and Wilson of an "implied right" to strike in the "freedom of association" provision.[98] The clearest criticism of the noninterpretivist "living-tree" approach, however, came, not surprisingly, from the pen of Justice McIntyre. While conceding that "a liberal and not overly legalistic approach should be taken to constitutional interpretation," McIntyre stressed that "the Charter should not be regarded as an empty vessel to be filled with whatever meaning we might wish from time to time."[99] He made the point even more clearly in his stinging dissent in *Morgentaler*, when he declared that "the courts must confine themselves to such democratic values as are clearly found and expressed in the Charter, and refrain from imposing or creating other values not so based."[100] To find a right to abortion in section 7, as Justice Wilson did, especially when the evidence clearly indicated that the framers intended to leave this controversial matter to the political arena, was just such an imposition.

McIntyre's interpretivism placed him on the side of judicial restraint in these two cases, as it had in *Dubois* and other cases, while his more noninterpretivist colleagues reached activist conclusions. This is not surprising. Interpretivism is not intrinsically hostile to judicial activism, but it opposes the other branches of government only in the name of rights as traditionally understood, and such rights are less likely to be infringed. New, judicially created rights are almost always "needed" to overcome policies consistent with traditional rights and not opposed (sometimes even actively desired) by democratic majorities. The judicial creation of new rights, in other words, is necessary mainly when legislatures refuse to impose those rights on themselves, something they are always perfectly free to do. Thus noninterpretivist jurisprudence (at least as it is typically practised in the modern era) will generally be associated with judicial activism, while interpretivist jurisprudence is likely to be found on the side of judicial restraint.

Stated differently, interpretivism tends toward judicial restraint because it leads to more narrowly defined rights—rights with more internal limits. In the Canadian context, an interpretivist approach would mean that less legislation would have to be defended as "demonstrably justifiable" under section 1. To turn the coin over, noninterpretive judicial review, by defining rights more broadly than tradition or original intent would warrant, subjects more legislation to the process of section 1 justification. The direction of influence between section 1 and noninterpretive judicial review might also run in the other direction, however. That is, the very existence of section 1 can be seen as a stimulus to the broad definition of rights characteristic of noninterpretive judicial review. Section 1, to recapitulate our earlier discussion, seems to make it unnecessary to define rights narrowly. In the extreme represented by David Beatty, rights would be defined so broadly that virtually all legislation would *prima facie* violate the Charter. Beatty's approach, of course, would constitute the ultimate in the noninterpretivist creation of new rights—rights far transcending any concept of original or traditional understanding.

While this triumph of noninterpretivism would clearly open the door to much greater judicial activism than the interpretivist approach represented by Justice McIntyre, it would not guarantee it. After all, legislation that violates the new rights of noninterpretivist jurisprudence *can* be saved by section 1. As indicated above, there is a possible middle ground between activist definition of Charter rights, and restrained application of those rights under section 1. It is worth repeating, however, that despite the bottom-line similarity between such decisions and those based on McIntyre-style interpretivism, the former are more activist at their core. They imply much more frequent resort to the justificatory standards of section 1, which may prove to be relatively difficult to meet.

■ THE POLITICS OF INTERPRETATION AND THE POLITICIZATION OF THE JUDICIARY

These debates over the proper judicial approaches to constitutional interpretation may seem somewhat abstract and far removed from the substantive issues arising under the Charter, but they are crucial in the battle over legal resources discussed in the previous chapter. Those who can gain the legal resources they desire only through the judicial creation of new rights are bound to be advocates of noninterpretivist judicial review. This is especially the case when groups seek constitutional resources to force policy concessions that legislative majorities are unwilling to grant—for example, the complete freedom to choose whether or not to abort a fetus. If such policies are not clearly required by the constitutional text, or by the original or traditional understandings of its provisions, they can be achieved only through noninterpretivist judicial review. Similarly, those who resist such judicially imposed policies, either because they don't like them, or because they wish to maintain the integrity of the democratic process, will tend to line up on the side of interpretivist principles. Thus the debate between interpretivism and noninterpretivism is not a matter of abstract legal theory that can safely be left to legal theorists. The political stakes are high, as most politically involved people in the United States have long understood, and as Canadians are increasingly coming to appreciate.

The political salience of the debate between interpretivism and non-interpretivism is dramatically displayed in the United States by the intense political battles often fought over the appointment of judges of one or the other persuasion. A leading example is President Roosevelt's scheme to overcome the Court's hostility to social welfare policies by expanding the size of the Court and filling the new positions with judges more sympathetic to the New Deal. The initial public reaction to this "court-packing" scheme was hostile and Roosevelt abandoned it, but it may have played some role in the Court's decision in 1937 to stop resisting the welfare state. One of the members of the five-judge majority that had been striking down welfare policies, Justice Roberts, changed his vote, thus creating a five-judge majority in favour of upholding such policies. Because the New Deal had widespread public support, which might eventually have been translated into support for a court-packing scheme to overcome continuing judicial obstructionism, Justice Roberts's reversal has become known as the "switch in time that saved nine."

More recently, it has been conservative Republicans who have been upset with the Court and who have tried to influence its work through a politics of appointment. With the exception of Jimmy Carter's presidency from 1976 to 1980, the Republican Party has controlled the White House since 1968, and beginning with Richard Nixon, Republican presidents have attempted to reverse the controversial, left-leaning decisions of the Warren Court by appointing what Nixon referred to as "strict constructionist" judges, or in Ronald Reagan's words, judges who believe their task is "to interpret rather than rewrite the Constitution the Founding Fathers crafted with such care and precision"[101]—in other words, interpretivist judges. For conservative politicians, the Warren Court had plainly rewritten the constitution, illegitimately entrenching liberal policy on matters that were intended to be left to the political process, and thus pre-empting the policy agenda that conservative politicians were elected to pursue. Thus it was imperative to appoint interpretivist judges in order to return the constitution to its original meaning. In the same vein, liberal politicians, whose political agenda had been furthered by noninterpretivist court decisions, resisted this appointment policy.

The fact that both the president and the Senate play an important role in the U.S. appointment process (the former "nominates" and the latter "confirms"), together with the fact that the two institutions were often controlled by different parties, provided the basis for a highly partisan politics of appointment. The potential for an explosive confrontation between a Republican president and a Democratic Senate grew as the Republican appointment strategy threatened to succeed in replacing a noninterpretivist with an interpretivist majority on the Supreme Court. The opportunity to tip the balance came in 1987, when Justice Lewis Powell announced his retirement. When President Reagan nominated Robert Bork, one of America's most prominent exponents of fidelity to original understanding, to fill the vacancy, a group of liberal Democrats in the Senate, led by Senator Edward Kennedy, immediately launched a vigorous campaign of opposition. This campaign quickly spilled out of the Senate chamber and became a public *cause célèbre*, ultimately leading to the defeat of Bork's nomination.

Such a "politicization of the judiciary" has not occurred in Canada, and does not loom large on the horizon. In part this may reflect the continuing vitality in Canada of the legalistic view that judges simply apply the law rather than make political decisions, a view we will consider at length in the next chapter. It also reflects the fact that, thus far, the Canadian Supreme Court has been somewhat more restrained than the American Court in cases turning on issues of intense public controversy.

The rudiments of this "moderate activism" can be seen even in *B.C. Motor Vehicles*, where Justice Lamer tempered his rejection of a purely procedural reading of "fundamental justice" with the assurance that the substantive reading adopted by the Court would be employed only in cases turning on "the basic tenets of our legal system," and would not be extended to the "realm of general public policy."[102] In other words, substantive principles of "fundamental justice" would be applied primarily in assessing the constitutionality of the criminal justice system, "the inherent domain of the judiciary."[103]

Even in the latter realm, the Court has been cautious in addressing substantive questions when it was possible to dispose of a highly controversial issue on procedural grounds. Again, *Morgentaler* is the best example. In *Roe* the U.S. Supreme Court essentially read a right to abortion on demand during much of the pregnancy into the due process clause of the fourteenth amendment. In *Morgentaler*, by contrast, Canada's abortion law was struck down largely on procedural grounds. Justice Wilson argued that the Court should address the substantive question of whether section 7 contained a right to abortion because, if such a right existed, purely procedural improvements on the existing policy of restricting abortion would not suffice. In other words, Parliament might respond to the Court's procedural guidelines, only to find in a subsequent case that its efforts were wasted because the substance of the law was unconstitutional.[104] As a matter of abstract logic, this makes sense. But, perhaps with the example of *Roe* in mind, the rest of the Court's majority declined Wilson's invitation. By deciding on procedural grounds, the majority's reasoning favoured neither side in the very heated public controversy about whether there is, or should be, a right to abortion. As a consequence, the Canadian Court avoided becoming a central issue in this volatile partisan controversy.

In the United States, where the Supreme Court itself decided the crux of the controversy, embedding the preferences of one side in constitutional law, the Supreme Court building has become the focus of semi-annual demonstrations by both pro- and anti-abortion activists. Both sides have come to believe that on this issue "the primary political branch of government, to which they must address their petitions, is the Supreme Court."[105] In such circumstances it is hardly surprising that judges, and their conflicting theories of constitutional interpretation, should themselves become the subject of political controversy, and that the appointment process should become highly politicized. When appointed judges take it upon themselves to decide the most politically contentious issues, political partisans will compete to influence them politically, or to control their positions for political purposes, as they do with all other politically influential positions. *Morgentaler* was the Canadian Supreme Court's major opportunity to pronounce on the substantive merits of such an issue. It refused to do so and thus avoided (or perhaps delayed) the politicization that has plagued its American counterpart.

It would be wrong, however, to leave the impression that no politicization of the judiciary has occurred in Canada. We noted in Chapter Three that attempts to exercise partisan influence over the judiciary are already underway in Canada, taking the form not of an overt American-style politics of appointment, but of an attempt, pioneered by Canadian feminists, to "educate" sitting judges. Still, this tactic is not nearly as dramatic as the kind of appointment politics aroused by the Bork nomination. Nor is post-appointment education likely to be as attractive if judges begin to take more open stands on highly divisive moral issues: it is obviously easier to educate judges who have not already publicly committed themselves.[106] Given a heightened policy polarization among sitting judges, and thus fewer opportunities for "educational" conversion, interest groups may find it necessary to seek more direct influence over appointments.

Even if the Canadian Supreme Court were to take sides more clearly on the major public issues of the day, however, a full-blown politics of judicial selection might not emerge. It is possible that partisan battles over control of the Court will take the form of struggles over the use of section 33, rather than overtly political struggles over appointment. It might not be necessary to influence the interpretive choices of judges through politicized appointment, in other words, if one can simply use a legislative override to reverse their decisions. As Peter Russell observes, section 33 "affords political leaders disgruntled with judicial decisions a more civilized remedy than court-bashing or court-packing."[107] Section 33 would only be a partial substitute for the politicization of appointment, however, because it applies only to sections 2 and 7 to 15 of the Charter. Controversial decisions based on other sections are not subject to the override.

In sum, the politics of interpretation is more muted in Canada, and has not led to the dramatic politicization of the judiciary that characterizes the United States. Politicization is not absent, however. It has clearly emerged among the judges themselves, as well as among interest groups who hope to benefit from a particular interpretive posture. If the politics of interpretation becomes more dramatically public, it may do so in part in the guise of controversies about the uses of section 33 rather than in the form of an openly politicized appointment process, though some increase in the latter cannot be discounted, if only because section 33 does not reach all judicial decisions.

CHAPTER SIX

Legalism and the Separation of Powers

The political influence of courts under entrenched constitutional law, and especially under constitutional bills of rights, raises questions of democratic legitimacy. Why should appointed judges be given such influence over the authoritative symbols and policy outputs of a democratic state? In countries that do not have a constitutional bill of rights (e.g., Great Britain and Australia), this question plays an important role in debates about the desirability of acquiring one; in countries that already have such a bill or charter (e.g., Canada and the United States), the legitimacy question takes the form of a debate about how activist or restrained judges should be in reviewing the decisions of the other branches of government. As we have seen, this debate between proponents of activism and restraint is in turn related to the debate about interpretivism and noninterpretivism, or traditional and modern approaches to judicial review.

The legitimacy debate turns in part on a central concept of modern constitutional theory: the "separation of powers." According to separation-of-powers theory, the legislative, executive, and judicial functions of government are distinct and should be carried out by separate and independent institutions. The separation of powers is most fully institutionalized in the United States, where the constitution not only establishes an independent judiciary, but also uses separate elections and fixed and staggered terms to make the executive independent of the legislature. In parliamentary systems, by contrast, the executive and legislative branches are not so clearly distinguished. Although the political executive or "cabinet" (or simply the "government") is conceptually distinct from the legislature and performs executive functions not accorded to the legislature, members of the cabinet are also members of the legislature. Elected as legislative representatives of localized constituencies along with all other parliamentarians, they take on their additional executive responsibilities because they are prominent members of the winning party. Furthermore, the political fate (and hence the political interests) of the cabinet and its partisan supporters in the legislature are closely linked by the convention of "responsible government," which permits a "government" to remain in power only so long as it enjoys the support of the majority of elected members. In the United States, by contrast, Congress and the presidency are often controlled by different parties, and conflict between them does not lead to "dissolution" and new elections.

The tradition of institutional separation between the judiciary and the other branches of government, however, is just as strong in parliamentary as in American-style systems.[1] Indeed, the idea that judges should be made completely independent of political pressure and influence is if anything stronger in the British parliamentary tradition than it is in the United States. An important separation-of-powers issue in parliamentary systems thus concerns the relationship between the "political" and "judicial" realms. This is an *issue*, rather than an automatic division of responsibilities, because the distinction between legal and political questions is often controversial. Such controversy lies at the heart of the legitimacy debate: Are Charter rights really legal entities suitable for judicial resolution, or do they pose political questions most appropriately settled by Parliament? Is judicial review of the Charter best understood as constitutional law or courtroom politics? This chapter reviews the debate about these questions.

■ THE LEGALISTIC CHARTER

The most common defence of the legitimacy of judicial review takes the form of denying that judges are engaged in courtroom politics rather than constitutional law. According to this legalistic view, when judges override the decisions of the political branches of government, they are not making policy, but merely enforcing the law of the constitution. Our judges themselves never tire of repeating that they are simply securing "the full benefit of the Charter's protection," not second-guessing political judgments about the wisdom of public policies.[2] To be sure, activist judicial decisions embody policy orientations different from those adopted by legislators or executive officials, but these overriding policies, it is argued, are not "made" by judges—they were adopted by the political process of constitutional amendment and are embodied in the country's fundamental law. In *B.C. Motor Vehicles,* for example, Justice Lamer responded as follows to the claim that the Charter had established a "judicial 'super-legislature' beyond the reach of Parliament, the provincial legislatures and the electorate":

This is an argument which was heard countless times prior to the entrenchment of the Charter but which has in truth, for better or for worse, been settled by the very coming into force of the Constitution Act, 1982. It ought not to be forgotten that the historic decision to entrench the Charter in our Constitution was taken not by the courts but by the elected representatives of the people of Canada. It was those representatives who extended the scope of constitutional adjudication and entrusted the courts with this new and onerous responsibility. Adjudication under the Charter must be approached free of any lingering doubts as to its legitimacy.[3]

In other words, when ordinary democratic majorities violate the constitution, they are departing from policies established as fundamental law by the extraordinary majorities required by the process of constitutional amendment. In overriding such policies, judges are not intruding on the democratic process; they are simply applying the most fundamental democratic consensus against the more ephemeral and transient will of ordinary legislative majorities. They are performing the traditional judicial task of applying the law, not the political task of making law.

What is the distinction between law and politics embodied in this argument? In common parlance, the term "politics" evokes images of disagreement and controversy, while "law" suggests the provisional settlement of political controversy. Politicians argue about the good or just policy, but such debates are "settled" when, according to prescribed rules, one side "wins" and enacts its policy preferences into law. The controversy may remain open in principle, but the emergence of a law indicates that it is closed in practice. The matter is officially settled, and the law must be obeyed, at least until the balance of political forces shifts enough to repeal or amend it. Until it is formally changed, citizens should be able to rely on its even-handed application by officials not involved in the political controversy about its desirability.

If law in general "settles" political issues, "entrenched" constitutional law settles the most fundamental issues concerning the overall organization and character of the regime. Moreover, it settles these issues in a more fundamental way than other kinds of law. Ordinary legislation can be enacted by simple legislative majorities, and can be repealed and amended in the same way. The enactment or amendment of constitutional law requires a much higher level of agreement.

It is because the level of agreement required for amendment is so difficult to achieve that we refer to constitutional law as "entrenched." Entrenchment suggests that the most fundamental and long-term commitments of the regime are at stake, commitments reflecting a relatively permanent degree of social consensus rather than just the will of a temporary legislative majority. The issues "settled" by constitutional law, in short, are not only more fundamental, but more thoroughly settled.

To the extent that it represents a settled consensus, constitutional law is beyond ordinary political disputation in ways that ordinary law is not. A law representing nothing more than the will of a temporary majority may well remain the subject of legitimate political controversy. Such a law "settles" issues only in the sense of being legally binding until it is changed, and nothing prevents a new majority from changing it. A consensus about the most important matters, on the other hand, will not give rise to ordinary political partisanship precisely because it is a *consensus*. It embodies the widespread agreement about fundamentals within which ordinary political debate about less important questions takes place. It sets the nonpartisan horizon or boundaries for normal partisan politics.

This understanding of constitutional law coincides almost perfectly with the common understanding of rights, and rights thus appear to be especially suitable candidates for constitutional entrenchment. The language of rights is inherently legalistic, connoting settled questions that are beyond legitimate political partisanship. The original terminology was one of "natural rights" reflecting the permanent necessities of an unchanging human nature, and thus establishing the ends and limits for government. Legitimate partisanship was limited to the question of how best to protect and secure universal natural rights; the rights themselves were beyond question—they set the boundaries of politics rather than forming its substance. Just as ordinary laws set limits on the legitimate activities of citizens (including lawmakers in their capacity of citizens), so there was a "higher law" of "natural rights" governing the activity of government itself.

These connotations of the language of rights persist even though the use of nature as a standard for political life has gone out of fashion, taking with it the idea of natural rights. Nowadays rights are likely to be described as "values," a term that grew out of the rejection of natural standards. Originally an economic term expressing the relativity of demand and supply, "value" was transformed by Nietzsche and Weber to signify a more general moral relativity.[4] This relativism introduces an ambiguity into the understanding of rights as the nonpartisan horizon for politics. Values are deep-seated preferences that are not rooted in nature and that may vary with time, place, and even person. Indeed, the language of values is typically used to convey the legitimacy of pluralism and variety. Values, in short, are matters of legitimate disagreement and, one presumes, legitimate political partisanship. In a sense, the language of values expresses dissatisfaction with the intolerant universalism of the language of rights. Thus if rights are values, it is hard to see why they should not be the subject of legitimate political partisanship.

Nevertheless, we persist in wanting to place some values beyond politics, and when we do so we resort to the older language of rights, conjuring up the aura of solidity it acquired from its original grounding in nature. The values that become rights are the regime's most "fundamental" values, which, like their natural-rights predecessors, represent the settled consensus within which decent and moderate partisanship can take place, and which must themselves be beyond politics in order for such moderate partisanship to emerge. Unlike natural rights, fundamental values can vary from one society to another, and even within a particular society, though, being fundamental, the latter kind of change takes a very long time. At any particular point, however, a society will have some values that are so fundamental they may be described as rights. As the law-like "horizon" of politics, such rights are clearly "constitutional" and would seem to belong in the regime's entrenched constitutional law. This perspective has been especially prevalent in justifications of a judicially enforceable charter of rights in Canada. As Andrew Petter and Allan Hutchinson observe, all such justifications, despite very great differences in other respects, rest on "the notion that Charter rights reflect some form of social consensus, whether grounded in conventional norms, community relations or an evolving tradition."[5]

Because they represent settled issues, rights are law-like entities, and because they settle issues of the highest order it seems appropriate to include them in the regime's highest order of law. Thus we arrive at the conclusion that rights should be entrenched in the formal constitution, and the corollary that, like other forms of law, they belong to the judicial rather than the political realm.

This legalistic defence of judicially enforceable constitutional rights must overcome an obvious objection. In the most dramatic cases, judicial enforcement of the constitution involves invalidating ordinary laws passed by democratically elected legislatures. If constitutional rights represent a widespread and long-term consensus about the most fundamental things, how could democratic majorities in favour of conflicting legislation arise?

Wouldn't the emergence of legislation infringing entrenched rights show that those rights no longer reflected the kind of consensus justifying their entrenchment, that they had become the object of political controversy rather than the agreed-upon horizon of politics? If there really were an agreed-upon horizon of politics, in other words, how could legislative majorities come to disagree with it? And if disagreement shows that no constitutional consensus exists, why is judicial review anything more than appointed judges imposing their political will on that of democratic majorities?

The answer to this objection begins with the observation that while constitutional law represents settled issues, it does not settle all issues that arise for judicial resolution in a direct or immediate way. As we saw in the previous chapter, partisans of both interpretivism and noninterpretivism agree that constitutional language is typically cast in broad and general terms precisely to accommodate the unforeseen circumstances of an unpredictable future. Thus constitutional law must be understood as settling only basic principles, not the details of particular cases, though interpretivists and noninterpretivists disagree about the level of abstraction or generality at which these settled principles are best understood. Whatever the appropriate level of abstraction, the meaning of the principles for particular circumstances is often unclear and controversial, and from the legalistic perspective judges are better equipped than legislatures to discern the correct, or at least the better, answer. Thus, rather than indicating the breakdown of consensus about the fundamental principles settled by constitutional law, judicial invalidation of legislation is a matter of correcting legislative mistakes in reasoning from the general consensus to its practical implications.

But why should we assume that judges are better than legislators at working out the implications of agreed-upon principles? In answering this question, defenders of judicial review often resort to a well-known tension between principle and interest. In our personal lives we have all been tempted by interest or passion to contravene cherished principles. Succumbing to these temptations does not necessarily mean that we have abandoned our principles. It is more likely that we block those principles from our minds, ignoring the tension between them and our actions, or that we twist and distort the meaning and practical corollaries of our principles in order to make them compatible with our self-interested actions. When we are forced to face the conflict between our principles and our temptations, we often experience shame and refrain from the interested action, or resolve not to repeat it.

Public life involves a similar tension between principle and interest, and defenders of judicial review associate judges with the former and politicians with the latter.[6] Courts are said to be institutionally distanced from public passions, and judges are professionally trained to give priority to arguments from principle. Politicians, on the other hand, tend to be more sensitive to public passions than to principle, and are institutionally inclined to sacrifice the latter to the former. However, the political sacrifice of principle to interest does not mean democratic majorities and the politicians who represent them have abandoned their principles. Like the individual who succumbs to temptation, they simply need to be shown how their passions have led them to ignore or distort the public consensus about principles. The best way to do this is to embody the fundamental principles of the community in constitutional law, and allow judges, in interpreting this law, to act as the conscience of the community.

This justification apparently resolves the question of democratic legitimacy. If constitutional law does represent a fundamental value consensus, it cannot be undemocratic to remind the people of what this consensus requires when they have been blinded by interest or passion. If the people really disagree with the judges—if, that is, their fundamental value commitments have changed—then they can formally amend the constitution. Since amendment requires extraordinary majorities, it would indicate that a fundamental value change had occurred. If formal amendment turns out to be impossible, the judges must assume that there hasn't been a sufficient value change to warrant abandoning the original commitments. "Until the public will is translated into ... constitutional amendment," argues Barry Strayer, "the courts must follow the last formal expression of [that] will." Strayer concludes that, "in theory at least," judicial review "is not a matter of judges imposing their will in conflict with the popular will; it is a matter of judges forcibly reminding the public and its elected representatives that some immediately attractive goal is in conflict with more pervasive and durable norms previously accepted by this society."[7]

■ THE POLITICAL CHARTER

This legalistic defence of the legitimacy of judicial review has not gone unchallenged. Many observers, from all parts of the political spectrum, maintain that in important respects judges "make" the constitutional law they apply—that the constitution is often what the judges say it is—and that the Charter must thus be understood as transferring significant political power to the courts.

Peter Russell begins his version of this critique with a distinction between the "core" and the "periphery" of Charter rights. Russell observes that "those parts of the Charter which deal with what might be termed universal rights and freedoms (as opposed to rights and freedoms based on the particular circumstances of Canadian history) are related to core values or ideals of all contemporary liberal democracies: political freedom, religious toleration, due process of law and social equality."[8] These principles were once the subject of serious political controversy between the early proponents of liberal democracy and their theocratic and aristocratic opponents. As late as 1877, for example, Wilfrid Laurier, who would later become Prime Minister of Canada, had to defend the principles of political and religious freedom in Quebec against the charge of heresy.[9] And in the United States a civil war was necessary in the mid-19th century to settle the issue of slavery. Such battles were decisively won by the liberal democrats, however, and today the "central core" of liberal principles arouses no serious opposition. No one recommends a return to the days when the state would officially impose civil disabilities on individuals simply because of their religious beliefs. And, although it was later in developing, there is now a similarly "wide-spread acceptance of the ideal that each person should be treated as an individual on his or her merits and not penalized or denied opportunities by the state because of gender, skin colour, ethnic background or other distinguishing characteristics of birth."[10]

These core principles of liberal democratic regimes resemble Dworkin's abstract "concepts." At this level the Charter does indeed represent a consensus about settled questions. Charter sceptics point out, however, that these questions are so well settled that they do not arise as partisan issues and thus as matters for judicial review. At this level of fundamental consensus, in short, judicial review is unnecessary.

Let us suppose, however, that judicial review of such fundamental issues did become necessary, that old-fashioned theocrats, aristocrats, or racists gained control of public policy. Their policies would clearly be unconstitutional, and perhaps our judges would have the courage to say so, but surely no one could plausibly describe such judicial pronouncements as "reminding the public and its elected representatives that some immediately attractive goal is in conflict with more pervasive and durable norms previously accepted by this society." Conflicts of this sort do not arise because interest clouds perception of what is required by agreed-upon norms; they arise because those norms are themselves in question. If such fundamental issues became matters of judicial review under the Charter, the consensus about liberal principles that allegedly justifies judicial review would no longer exist.

More to the point, it is unlikely that judges exercising the power of judicial review would be able to settle issues of such fundamental importance. When the U.S. Supreme Court decided that it was unconstitutional for Congress to prohibit slavery in the federal territories,[11] the liberal opponents of that "peculiar institution" did not acquiesce, but precipitated a civil war. When the Judicial Committee of the Privy Council decided in 1874 that Joseph Guibord, who had been excommunicated by the Quebec Catholic Church because of his political liberalism, had a right to be buried in consecrated ground, the attempt to do so precipitated a riot in Montreal, and the burial was successfully carried out only on a second attempt with the aid of police and nearly 1000 militia. Guibord was buried in concrete to prevent the easy removal of his remains, but it was all for nought, because the next day the bishop deconsecrated his grave.[12] Both of these cases represented clear-cut conflicts between liberalism and its most obvious enemies, conflicts so fundamental they could not be settled by judicial decision. There was no more fundamental value consensus transcending the conflict to which judges could appeal in attempting to achieve a resolution.

The same would be true in the hypothetical situation proposed by Alan Borovoy, legal counsel to the Canadian Civil Liberties Association, in his argument against an entrenched Charter of Rights. Borovoy asks us to consider a legislative majority simply outlawing "all other political parties together with democratic elections and freedom of speech...." He concedes that "[t]he prospects of such a disaster give redress to the courts an alluring appeal," but thinks that "the hope for judicial rectification in such a situation would be more academic than real."

> If we ever faced so overwhelming an assault on the democratic processes, I can't imagine that the courts would be able to do anything about it. Indeed, it is likely that they would be abolished along with the other components of the democratic system. My argument against giving the courts such constitutional power presupposes the general operation of political democracy. If such were not the case, the courts would not likely be helpful in any event.[13]

In sum, at the core level of Charter rights the common-sense distinction between principle and interest is superfluous because requirements of the core are too clear to be violated out of interest by those who accept them. Their violation, if it did occur, would represent a conflict of fundamental principles rather than a conflict between interest and agreed-upon principle. Judges, moreover, cannot realistically be expected to resolve such fundamental conflicts.

In fact, the kinds of questions most likely to arise for judicial review under the Charter do not concern such basic challenges to the "central core" of liberal democratic principles. The bulk of Charter jurisprudence turns on questions encountered "as we move out from the central core of these values" toward the periphery.[14] In these outer reaches we find not a settled consensus, but deep dissensus. Those who agree about the core often disagree profoundly about how to implement it in practice. For example, virtually everyone would agree with the principle of religious freedom. But those who participate in this antitheocratic consensus cannot agree whether the principle requires exemptions from otherwise valid laws for religious dissidents, or whether such exemptions would violate the principle by reinvigorating the theocratic principle that only God's laws (as one understands them) are worthy of respect and obedience. Does it infringe freedom of religion, for instance, to apply hunting laws to Indians who kill a deer out of season in order to use the meat in a religious ceremony?[15] Or do provincial Sunday-closing laws, which are enacted for the purely secular purpose of promoting a common day of rest and recreation, violate the religious freedom of Saturday-sabbatarian retailers, who must close two days a week (once for religious and once for legal reasons) while their Sunday-sabbatarian or nonreligious competitors close for only one day?[16] These are not uncontroversial questions. Similarly, virtually everyone defends the principle of equality, but does this principle require the formally equal treatment of all individuals even if this leads to unequal results, or does it mandate the differential treatment of unequals in order to achieve equal results? Those who are united in their opposition to the aristocratic praise of inequality divide on this important but secondary question depending on whether they subscribe to liberal-individualist or group-oriented visions of political life.

The wording of the Charter is a tolerably clear expression of the regime's core principles, but with respect to these secondary issues it is ambiguous and indeterminate. Section 2(a), for example, simply guarantees to "everyone" the "freedom of conscience and religion." Surely this five-word phrase does not settle the debate about religiously based exemptions in any obvious way. Both sides in this debate, as in the debates about equality, are able to enlist the same Charter wording in support of their cause.

The indeterminacy of Charter wording is apparent even in provisions that at first glance appear quite clear and specific. For example, section 13 of the Charter protects trial "witnesses" from having self-incriminating testimony used against them in "other proceedings." In some respects, this wording conveys an unambiguous meaning to every reader. It tells us, for example, that an accomplice who testifies against the accused need not worry that his testimony will be used against him if he himself is placed on trial. But the meaning of section 13 is not this clear for all the situations in which its protections might be invoked, as was clearly demonstrated by the case of *Dubois* v. *The Queen*.[17] Recall that Dubois claimed that his second trial on the same charge was "another proceeding" in which his first-trial testimony could not be used to incriminate him. But as Justice McIntyre's dissent in this case shows, this conclusion is not inescapable. Granting immunity to witnesses against the accused might be unsavoury, but we can all understand the trade-off underlying such a policy: to speak plainly, it is sometimes necessary to cooperate with one crook to catch another. And in any case, even if we oppose this trade-off, it is fairly clearly required by the language of section 13: there can be no doubt that if the witness against the accused were put on trial it would not be the same proceeding. On the other hand, protecting an accused against the incriminating effect of his own prior testimony if he is lucky enough to get a second trial—especially if the flaws in the first trial have no bearing on the validity or reliability of the testimony—is more difficult to understand and is thus much more controversial. Nor is this controversy obviously settled by the language of section 13: it is not at all obvious that "other proceedings" includes a second trial of the same person on the same charge.

We may now return to the justification of judicial review as the triumph of principle over interest. As we have seen, this theory is superfluous with respect to the core principles embodied in Charter wording. If it has any utility, it must be with respect to the secondary questions that actually arise for judicial determination, questions that divide inhabitants of a more fundamental consensus, and that are not settled in any obvious way by the Charter's wording. With respect to such questions, the principle-interest theory, if it has any validity, implies that correct answers can be deduced as logical corollaries of agreed-upon primary principles, and that controversy reflects the distorting effect of interest or passion. Since judges are more likely than politicians to reason logically, their opinions about these matters must be given priority. How well does this view stand up?

Consider the question of religiously based exemptions from otherwise valid secular laws. In both Canada and the United States, the courts have decided that religious freedom requires such exemptions unless they would seriously undermine a compelling purpose of the law.[18] That they might weaken a merely convenient law is insufficient justification for denying exemptions. If we accept the principle-interest theory, it follows that these decisions represent the logically reasoned implications of the agreed-upon principle of religious freedom, and that those who would deny exemptions have been blinded by passion and interest.

But if this is true, John Locke, universally recognized as one of the philosophic founders of the modern principle of religious freedom, was somehow blinded by passion to the true implications of his own theory. For Locke was clearly against religiously based exemptions to secular laws. In his *Letter Concerning Toleration* he maintained that whatever was lawful in ordinary life was also lawful in the exercise of religion. Thus, if the legislature generally permitted people to drink wine or slaughter animals, it could not prohibit these same activities when they formed part of a religious observance. By the same token, however, Locke argued that whatever was prohibited "in the ordinary course of life" was similarly prohibited in the exercise of religion, provided that "the law is not made about a religious but a political matter."[19] In short, no exemptions.

Judges are certainly entitled to disagree with Locke about the questions of exemptions, but it seems absurd to assume that they must be right because they are more resistant to the distorting effects of interest and passion than a "mere" philosopher. It seems more sensible to understand the debate about religious exemptions as a conflict between competing principles of justice at a lower level of abstraction, not as a conflict between principle and interest. In Dworkin's terms it is a conflict of competing "conceptions" of a more abstract and agreed-upon "concept." No doubt when legislatures refuse to grant religiously based exemptions from otherwise valid laws, they are responding in part to considerations of interest and convenience, but they also have the reasoned arguments of Locke on their side. If interest plays a role, it is not that it has distorted an accurate perception of an agreed-upon principle, but that it happens to coincide with one side in a conflict of principles.

The same is true of the conflict between theories of formal equality of opportunity and substantive equality of result. "While women's rights groups invoke substantive equality to support special programs for women, men's rights groups invoke formal equality to attack special programs for women."[20] Again, self-interest clearly plays a role in which of these conflicting principles is supported by the respective groups, but this does not make it any less a matter of conflicting principles. After all, while self-interest is powerful, it is not all powerful: there are men who support special programs for women *on principle,* just as there are women who insist on formal equality of opportunity, also *on principle.* When judges disagree with legislatures about the relative merit of these conflicting principles, it is not a simple matter of reason prevailing over passion.

In addition to conflicting interpretations of any particular right, the Charter poses conflicts between rights—for instance, the well-known tension between liberty and equality. With regard to pornography, for example, libertarians use the Charter's freedom-of-expression guarantee to argue against censorship, while some women's groups insist that censorship is required by the Charter's equality-rights section. Again, the Charter does not resolve such issues in any obvious way, and in deciding them judges are making a political choice between competing conceptions or visions of justice, rather than applying agreed-upon principles against the distorting effects of interest or passion. Judicial review, in short, is best understood not as the application of settled principles, but as the judicial exercise of political choice under the guise of law.

This conclusion might be blunted to the extent that the interpretivist standard of original understanding is a plausible one. It might be the case that language that, considered in itself, can be read to suit either side in a battle of conflicting principles was originally understood as entrenching the position of one of the contenders. Perhaps the religious-freedom clauses of the American first amendment, for example, were originally understood as embodying the Lockean view that there is no fundamental right to religiously based exemptions from otherwise valid secular laws. Judges would then be obligated to accept that understanding, at least until formal amendment changed it, and in doing so they would be acting upon what was politically settled by others, rather than making political choices of their own. They would resist all attempts to impose a policy of exemptions upon legislatures unwilling to enact them, though, of course, nothing would prevent legislatures from providing for such exemptions as a matter of privilege if they chose to do so. Despite the open-textured language of the first amendment, such judicial review would be a matter of applying law rather than engaging in politics. If, on the other hand, noninterpretivists are right in their claim that original understanding is too elusive to serve as a reliable guide to the meaning of open-textured language, it is difficult to avoid the conclusion that judicial review is courtroom politics rather than constitutional law. Many Charter sceptics do in fact believe that original intent is often no clearer than the constitutional language itself.

If judicial review is indeed the kind of courtroom politics alleged by the sceptics, then it cannot be defended as reminding temporary majorities of the corollaries entailed by a more durable societal consensus. Rather, activist review, especially of the noninterpretivist variety, would generally be a matter of judicially supported minorities prevailing politically over legislative majorities.

The difficulty of constitutional amendment also takes on a new significance in this sceptical view. Instead of protecting a fundamental societal consensus against temporary passions, it would really operate to immunize new policy departures imposed by minorities from change by democratic majorities. What John Agresto says of the American amending procedure seems generally applicable:

> The Constitution was made difficult to amend in order to prevent precipitous changes and to deflect innovations not widely supported throughout the country. But the difficulty of amendment was not meant to protect a political or judicial decision that itself might be a radical departure, or unsupported by a wide constituency, from reversal. In simple terms, the amending process was meant to ensure that every major political change would have deep and wide support; it cannot be turned into an argument in support of policies made and protected by the smallest of national minorities.[21]

Or, as Paul Weiler has put it, to permit only formal amendment to override judicial interpretations of the constitution "means that a tiny minority could hold the nation in a constitutional vise from which, as the American people have found, it might take even a war to break loose."[22] This leads Weiler to favour the section 33 legislative override, which permits ordinary legislative majorities to reverse unpopular judicial decisions. We shall return to this point in Chapter Eight.

■ POLITICAL JURISPRUDENCE AND SECTION 1 OF THE CHARTER

For Charter sceptics the political and policy-making dimensions of judicial review are evident not only in the interpretation of indeterminate rights, but even more dramatically in the balancing required by section 1 of the Charter. As we have seen, section 1 "guarantees the rights and freedoms set out in [the Charter] subject only to such reasonable limits prescribed by law as can be demonstrably justified in a free and democratic society." Thus, in addition to choosing between competing interpretations of Charter rights, judges must ask whether a law infringing a right is nevertheless "reasonable" and "demonstrably justified" in a free and democratic society. However fundamental Charter rights may be, in other words, they are not absolute. The extent to which they will be protected in any particular case depends on the balance between them and competing considerations, particularly considerations of general welfare. Section 1 requires judges to strike this balance.

But, as Patrick Monahan points out, "this process of 'interest balancing' seems just another way of asking the fundamental legislative question: 'is this worth what it costs?'"[23] In enacting the impugned legislation, the legislature has presumably already concluded that the benefits in general welfare are worth the costs in Charter rights. "Section 1 of the Charter appears to invite the Court to assess and to second-guess the 'wisdom' of the balance struck by the legislature." Interest balancing, says Monahan, is the "quintessentially legislative task,"[24] and section 1 hands it over to the courts.

The potential for this quintessentially political task of "interest balancing" under section 1 is enhanced to the extent that judges resist placing internal or definitional limits on Charter rights. We have seen that in the presence of the explicit limitations of section 1 judges are free to give substantive rights very broad and literal definitions, thus greatly expanding the range of potential Charter violations. This is so because the inevitable limitations can be taken care of later, when the section 1 issue is reached. If internal limits are built into Charter rights, then certain interests and activities are excluded from Charter protection by definition. The decision to impose a definitional limit, of course, is itself politically controversial, but once it is taken it reduces the scope for politically controversial judicial review by reducing the number of Charter violations that must be assessed under section 1.

From Monahan's perspective, the test for applying section 1 established by the Court in *Oakes* must be understood as an attempt to cast a veil of legalism over the unavoidably political business of section 1 analysis. To recapitulate, under *Oakes* the government bears the onus of demonstrating first that the violation is justified by a "pressing and substantial" objective, and second that the legislative means are "proportional" to that objective. Proportional means, moreover, cannot be arbitrary, must impair the right as little as possible, and must provide benefits in general welfare that outweigh their costs in lost rights. In fact, the Court almost always concedes that the purpose of the impugned law is sufficiently compelling to justify some violation of Charter rights; if it chooses to strike the law down, it does so because it has failed some aspect of the proportional means test. This can surely be understood as part of an attempt to deflect the charge that section 1 jurisprudence involves second-guessing the political judgments of legislatures.[25] Disagreeing with the legislature about the importance of a policy objective is obviously a political disagreement. It is far less confrontational to say to a legislature, "we agree with what you are trying to do—indeed, your objective is sufficiently compelling to justify some violation of rights—but you have violated those rights more than necessary." This suggests that the major defect in the legislation is the failure of careful draftsmanship, that a more carefully crafted version of the law would be acceptable. And since putting a policy objective into its most effective legal form seems a quintessentially lawyerly task—while choosing between alternative objectives is an obviously political one—emphasizing the proportional means test places section 1 jurisprudence squarely into the realm of law, not politics.

Or does it? Patrick Monahan claims that the alleged focus on means rather than ends is a charade, that the Court cannot avoid assessing the importance of legislative objectives, however much it may deny that it is doing so. This is so especially when the Court invalidates a law under the first prong of the proportionality test, because it is arbitrary or irrational in light of the law's purpose. To illustrate his point, Monahan borrows from John Hart Ely the example of a law making a new and much safer (but also more expensive) braking system mandatory for all trucks except those carrying seafood.[26] It is obvious that an important purpose of the law is to promote safety. That objective would no doubt have been promoted even more thoroughly if the legislature had required the new technology in all vehicles; but it exempted trucks involved in the seafood industry as well as all cars. Viewed from the perspective of safety, the exemption of cars makes some sense. Being lighter than trucks, they are easier to stop and the increase in safety gained by the new brakes would be proportionally less. Since the brakes are expensive, the legislature obviously concluded that the safety benefits were not worth the additional cost, especially since, in the case of cars, those costs would be borne more often by individuals than by companies. The loss in safety benefits is perhaps regrettable, but limiting the mandatory use of the new system to heavy vehicles makes some sense *in light of safety itself*. This cannot be said of the exemption for trucks carrying seafood. Given the legislative purpose of safety, this exemption seems completely arbitrary or irrational. If it were assessed under the guidelines of the *Oakes* test for section 1, it would fail the first part of the proportionality test.

Monahan argues that although such a judgment seems to be about the irrational fit between ends and means, it really entails a veiled disagreement with the legislature about ends. The exemption for trucks in the seafood industry is not irrational in light of the legislative purpose because the law clearly has more than one purpose:

> [T]here is nothing mysterious about the inclusion of such a distinction in a statute. The purpose of the distinction is obviously to give a preference to the owners of trucks in the seafood business. The exemption will save these truckers the cost of installing the new brake and, presumably, grant them an advantage over their competitors. It is apparent that the law had two purposes, rather than one. The first purpose was to increase traffic safety by requiring most trucks to install new brakes. The second purpose was to ensure that these gains in traffic safety did not come at the expense of increasing the costs of truckers transporting seafood.[27]

Finding the seafood exemption to be irrational in light of one of the law's purposes while ignoring the purpose it obviously promotes may look like a disagreement about the means chosen to achieve agreed-upon ends, but is actually a dispute about ends. As Monahan puts it, "the claim of irrationality is really little more than a judgment that one of these purposes—the goal of preferring seafood truckers—is unacceptable. The court simply ignores the impugned purpose, and then concludes that the legislation does not further the goals which remain."[28]

Monahan's example speaks mainly to the use of the first part of the proportional means test. In fact, however, the courts rarely invalidate legislation under section 1 because it is arbitrary or irrational in light of the purpose they have attributed to the law. Much more frequently they concede that the means chosen by the legislature are indeed rational, in the sense that they actually do tend to achieve the law's compelling purpose, but that alternative means are available that would achieve the purpose equally well with less infringement of Charter rights. This use of the second branch of the proportionality test—the "minimal impairment" or "alternative means" principle—seems less open to the charge that the judges have ignored important legislative purposes. The minimal impairment test assumes that the legislative means under consideration do serve a legislative purpose (indeed, a compelling legislative purpose), but that in reaching into its policy toolkit the legislature has chosen a "sledgehammer to achieve [its] social objectives where a more precision instrument would have done the trick."[29] David Beatty defends section 1 against the charge of political second-guessing on these grounds. Indeed, he argues that far from compromising democracy, judicial review based on the principle of alternative means enhances it.

Beatty agrees that the courts should not question the purpose of legislation,[30] and he does not recommend easy use of the arbitrariness or rationality standard embodied in the first prong of the proportionality test.[31] Nor does he believe the courts will, or should, rely very much on the third prong of proportionality: if legislation is invalidated under the alternative means principle, he suggests, there is no need to proceed to this third stage; and if legislation is upheld because it achieves a compelling purpose with minimal impairment of Charter rights, the courts should not lightly question the legislature's judgment that the benefits in general welfare outweigh the necessary cost in rights.[32] The reader will recall that for Beatty "section 1, not the substantive sections in which the rights and freedoms are entrenched, is where all of the action takes place." It turns out that in fact he wants most of the action to take place under the "alternative means" component of the proportionality test. The great virtue of this test, he argues, is that it shows proper judicial deference to legislative objectives and to the overall balance legislators have chosen to strike between rights and other compelling considerations. Under this approach legislators remain free to set their own policy agendas, and judges merely assist them in discovering the least oppressive means for achieving their ends. The focus is not on whether legislators are doing the right thing, but on how they have chosen to do it, not in the sense of asking whether particular means are completely arbitrary (which Beatty might concede is a veiled way of disagreeing about purposes), but in the sense of asking whether the means are better or worse than available alternatives. This approach, argues Beatty, is not undemocratic. Indeed, it enhances democracy by forcing legislators to take into account as many interests as possible (i.e., all those interests who resist the law's coercion) and to tailor the law to infringe freedoms as little as possible. This is why Beatty so staunchly resists the idea of placing internal limits on Charter rights. With respect to *Jones,* for example, he is prepared to concede for the sake of argument that the violation of religious freedom was trivial, but insists that this is the wrong question: "Wilson and her colleagues," he complains, "never considered whether, even if it was 'trivial,' the restriction on [Pastor Jones's] religious freedom was necessary at all; whether Alberta's law could meet the principle of alternative means."[33]

But can judicial reliance on the minimal impairment test really avoid Monahan's problem of second-guessing legislative purpose? The Supreme Court opinions in the 1990 "prostitution" reference suggest not.[34] Although prostitution itself is not illegal, the legislation at issue in this case makes it a criminal offence to communicate or attempt to communicate "in a public place or in any place open to public view … for the purpose of engaging in prostitution or of obtaining the sexual services of a prostitute."[35] "Public place" is further defined as "any place to which the public have access as of right or by invitation, express or implied, and any motor vehicle located in a public place or in any place open to public view."[36] All of the participating judges agreed that this law infringed the Charter's guarantee of "freedom of expression." In proceeding to section 1 analysis, moreover, all agreed that the law had the requisite "compelling purpose" and that the means chosen to achieve the purpose met the rational connection component of the proportionality test—i.e., the means were not arbitrary; they actually achieved the purpose. Disagreement emerged, however, on the question of alternative means. Was the legislative purpose achieved with "minimal impairment" of freedom of expression? In separate opinions, Justice Dickson (writing for Justices La Forest and Sopinka) and Justice Lamer found that the minimal impairment test was satisfied and upheld the legislation. Justice Wilson (joined by Justice L'Heureux-Dubé) dissented on this point. As it turned out, however, this disagreement about minimal impairment or alternative means was really a disagreement about legislative ends.

Justice Wilson argued that the impugned provision "constitutes a more serious impairment of the individual's freedom than the avowed legislative objective would warrant."[37] The legislative objective, in her view, was to control the "social nuisance" stemming from soliciting. This nuisance included not just "the interference by prostitutes and their customers of the citizens' use of public places," but also the "secondary effects" of "all night noise, traffic congestion, trespass, reduced property values and other adverse consequences."[38] However, the legislation catches activities that "need not result in [these] kinds of problems."[39] For example, the broad definition of "public place" means that "the prohibition is not confined to places where there will necessarily be lots of people to be offended or inconvenienced by it. The prohibited communication may be taking place in a secluded area of a park where there is no one to see or hear it."[40] For Justice Wilson, "such a broad prohibition as to the locale of the communication would seem to go far beyond a genuine concern over the nuisance caused by street solicitation in Canada's major centres of population. It enables the police to arrest citizens who are disturbing no one solely because they are engaged in communicative acts concerning something not prohibited by the Code."[41] To achieve its purpose, the legislation need not have been phrased so broadly, and thus fails the minimal impairment test.

Justice Dickson agreed that "the means used to attain the objective of the legislation may well be broader than would be appropriate were actual street nuisance the only focus."[42] He disagreed with Justice Wilson not because she wrongly analyzed the relationship of means to the ends she attributed to the legislation, but because she attributed the wrong ends. Dickson believes the legislation was intended to remedy more than mere "street nuisance," though he concedes that the latter is part of its purpose. For Dickson, the legislature's concern with "nuisance" is broader than Justice Wilson was prepared to concede:

> It is argued that the legislation is over-broad because it is not confined to places where there will necessarily be many people, or, in fact, any people, who will be offended by the activity. The objective of this provision, however, is not restricted to the control of actual disturbances or nuisances. It is broader, in the sense that it is directed at controlling, in general, the nuisance-related problems ... that stem from street soliciting. Much street soliciting occurs in specified areas where the congregation of prostitutes and their customers amounts to a nuisance. In effect, the legislation discourages prostitutes and customers from concentrating their activities in any particular location. While it is the cumulative impact of individual transactions concentrated in a public area that effectively produces the social nuisance at which the legislation in part aims, Parliament can only act by focusing on individual transactions. The notion of nuisance in connection with street soliciting extends beyond inter-

> ference with the individual citizen to interference with the public at
> large, that is with the environment represented by streets, public
> places and neighboring premises.[43]

Because the legislative objective extends beyond "actual street nuisance"
to "the general curtailment of visible solicitation for the purpose of prostitution," Dickson finds that the legislative means are "not unduly intrusive."[44]

Justice Lamer took an even broader view of legislative purpose. For
Lamer, the legislation was designed to constrain "an activity that is degrad-
ing to the individual dignity of the prostitute and which is a vehicle for
pimps and customers to exploit the disadvantaged position of women in
our society."[45] Legislative means that Justice Wilson considered more
intrusive than necessary to limit overtly public nuisance were for Lamer
admirably suited to "minimizing the public exposure of this degradation
especially to young runaways who seek refuge in the streets of major
urban centres, and to those who are exposed to prostitution as a result of
the location of their homes and schools in areas frequented by prostitutes
and who may be initially attracted to the 'glamorous' lifestyle as it is
described to them by pimps."[46]

Clearly the stand taken in this case on the question of minimal impairment or alternative means depended on the kind of purpose attributed to
the legislation. The broader the purpose, the easier it was to find that the
legislation passed this component of the proportionality test. Not only was
the debate about alternative means not separate from the question of purpose, but the two were virtually indistinguishable. At least in this case, a
focus on alternative means did not escape the problem Monahan attributes
to the arbitrariness standard. Justice Wilson could not conclude that the
legislation was unconstitutional under the minimal impairment test without
choosing a more narrow reading of legislative purpose than necessary.
Plausible broader readings existed, as shown by the fact that other judges
adopted them. The legislative means Justice Wilson found broader than
necessary to achieve the more limited purpose were well suited to achieve
the broader purpose. Had Justice Wilson prevailed, the sceptic would conclude that she did so not by focusing on alternative means, but by second-
guessing the more obviously political question of legislative purpose.

Deciding whether legislation achieves its purpose while minimally
impairing Charter rights, in other words, may depend on a prior choice
between competing possible legislative purposes. If so, then Beatty is

wrong in thinking that the minimal impairment test, unlike the arbitrariness standard, leaves legislatures free to set their own policy agendas and focuses only on the means chosen to pursue those agendas.

Even if Beatty were right on this point, he would be unlikely to persuade all Charter sceptics that reliance on the principle of alternative means would keep the courts out of politics. Beatty appears to assume that the central political questions concern the objectives of policy and the balance to be struck between competing interests, and that the question of the best (or least intrusive) means is a purely technical question, so that when judges disagree with the legislative choice of alternative means, they are not second-guessing political judgments. But this is open to question. One will often be able to discover less intrusive means to achieve any particular legislative purpose, but it may be that the less intrusive means are also less efficient or more costly. The new procedures for dealing with refugee claims that followed on the *Singh* case, for example, have increased costs in the order of $200 million.[47] In weighing the benefits to be achieved by a law against its costs in rights, legislators will generally take the relative cost effectiveness of available means into account. Less cost to the public purse, after all, is arguably a significant aspect of the general welfare. In choosing means that are somewhat more intrusive than necessary, legislators may well be making a political judgment about the proper balance to be struck between lost "rights" and the efficient and cost-effective achievement of the law's compelling purpose. In forcing a less intrusive but more costly alternative on the legislature, the sceptic will insist, judges are clearly second-guessing an important political judgment.

The language of rights is, of course, hostile to the notion of countervailing costs.[48] And considering any particular policy in isolation, it may seem plausible to argue that rights should "trump" considerations of mere efficiency and cost, that the greater protection of rights is worth the extra cost or lost efficiency. But it is a mistake to consider policies in isolation. Each policy is part of the immensely large and interrelated web of public policy as a whole, and extra costs imposed in one policy area may well be met by depriving another area, perhaps to the detriment of needy beneficiaries. Indeed, greater protection of rights in one area might well lead to less protection in another. In imposing more costly alternative means in a particular policy area, then, judges may force a readjustment of overall priorities.[49] Legislators who have established one set of priorities may be compelled by judges to adopt another. Surely, our sceptic will suggest, this involves second-guessing political decisions. The setting of overall policy priorities within a confines of existing budgetary resources is, after all, a central, perhaps *the* central, task of the political branches of government. Of course, it is usually possible for legislatures to increase benefits in one area without diminishing them (in absolute terms) in other areas simply by increasing taxation. But this too would be a readjustment of the previous political decision not to raise taxes. (And at some point, of course, the tax pie is limited.) In short, the principle of alternative means may have other virtues, but the Charter sceptic will insist that it does not avoid judicial meddling in essentially political matters.

Let us summarize the sceptical view of the Charter. The Charter is a rich source of controversies about the "true" meaning of ambiguously worded provisions and the correct balance both among the various rights and freedoms and between these rights and competing considerations of general welfare. Do women have a right to abortion as part of their section 7 right to liberty and security, or does the right to life guaranteed by the same section extend to the fetus? If both rights exist, how are their conflicting demands to be balanced? Does cruise-missile testing violate the right to life and security, or might it actually contribute to security by strengthening deterrence? Is the promotion of hatred protected by the section 2 guarantee of freedom of expression, or is its prohibition required by the section 15 equality rights? Is commercial speech (e.g., a storefront sign) protected by section 2? Does section 15 require the government to stack "parental" leave benefits for purposes of child*caring* on top of existing maternity-leave benefits associated with child*bearing*? If the legislative answers to any of these questions differ from the answers judges "discover" in the constitution, can the former nevertheless be "demonstrably justified" as "reasonable limits" in a "free and democratic society"? These and many similar questions were matters of partisan controversy before the Charter, and sceptics do not believe the relevant sections have settled them either as a matter of wording or as the logical deduction from agreed-upon principles.

The language of the Charter does indeed embody a law-like consensus about core values, but this consensus is so solid and widespread that there will be little need for judges to enforce it against conflicting policies. As one moves out from this core, however—as one shifts to the issues that actually arise under the Charter—one finds that they are not settled in any obvious way by the Charter's language. With respect to these issues, the Charter's wording is vague and indeterminate. Conflicting interpretations are possible, and in choosing among them judges are not applying a settled consensus against the distorting effect of interest, but making a political choice between contending principles. Indeed, some commentators argue that Charter provisions are so indeterminate that they "resemble blank slates on which the judiciary can scrawl the imagery of their choice,"[50] or "empty sacks that cannot stand up on their own until they have been filled [by judges] with political content,"[51] or "limp balloons which the constitution makers handed to the judiciary" and into which "the judges must now decide how much air to blow."[52] Such imagery does not seem to take seriously the possibility that original understanding has much to do with the content of the sacks or the amount of air blown into the balloons. Judicial discretion seems very great. Moreover, having scrawled their imagery, or filled their sacks, or inflated their balloons, judges must then perform the "quintessentially legislative task" of balancing the resulting rights against the competing considerations of general welfare—balances that are no more deducible from a societal value consensus than is the meaning of the rights themselves. Far from applying constitutional law, in other words, judges make it up as they go along. The constitution is what the judges say it is, which is to say that we are ruled not by a constitution, but by judges. For the critics of legalism, in short, judicial review of the Charter is better understood as courtroom politics than as constitutional law. They often argue on separation-of-powers grounds that such questions should be left to the political branches of government. For the same reason they tend to be strong defenders of the section 33 override.

■ ENTRENCHMENT DEBATES AND JUDICIAL DISAGREEMENTS

The separation-of-powers debate occurs whenever the question of entrenching rights in a written constitution is addressed. During the Canadian entrenchment debate, for example, Trudeau and his allies insisted that the Charter was necessary for the adequate protection of individual rights, which they clearly saw as legal entities. Critics, such as Saskatchewan Premier Alan Blakeney and political scientist Donald Smiley, on the other hand, understood the Charter mainly as a transfer of policy-making power from the political branches of government to the courts.[53]

The same debate also exists in Australia, where, in fact, the sceptics have thus far carried the day. A small number of rights are protected by the original Australian constitution, but they are limited in scope and apply only to the federal government. There have been several attempts to enact a more comprehensive bill of rights. To date, all of these have been defeated, at least in part because of a sceptical regard for legalism.

For example, opponents of a 1988 proposal to amend the constitutional guarantee of freedom of religion and extend it to the states[54] frequently wondered why the courts should be given the power to second-guess political judgments about such things as public prayer, religious education and practices in public schools, and public aid to private religious schools.[55] They obviously did not consider these to be matters of fundamental right, but political matters that are properly decided by the political institutions. Nor were their worries calmed by pointing out that the High Court's decisions on the existing religious-freedom provision were very restrained and had not challenged such policies. The opposition response was that the constitution "is what the judges say it is" and that experience shows that judges frequently change their minds.[56] The point was not whether judges would use their power sensibly, but why they should be given the power at all when political questions (not fundamental rights) were at stake. The fact that judges change their minds, moreover, was itself evidence that their decisions usurp the political function. "The reality," said an opposition senator, "is that what the judges think at any time about what these broad guarantees mean will change according to changes in the judges and changes in community values."[57] But if the meaning of the guarantees can shift with changing values, why should one favour judicial as opposed to legislative judgments concerning the meaning and requirements of the changing values. The senator concluded that "nothing can be found in the precedents in terms of High Court consideration of existing so-called guarantees that would lead one to believe that its consideration of these matters is superior to that of democratic politicians."[58]

Where a bill of rights or charter exists, the clash between legalism and its critics is played out among the judges who enforce it. Judges who are prepared to override policies on the basis of constitutional rights—or even seriously to consider the possibility—frequently assert that they are simply applying legal standards, while their dissenting colleagues insist that they are actually, and illegitimately, second-guessing the legislative judgment about the wisdom of the policy.

Such judicial controversies have long plagued American Bill of Rights jurisprudence, and have more recently emerged in the interpretation of the Canadian Charter of Rights. In its first series of cases under the Charter, the Supreme Court of Canada took pains to distance itself from the restrained approach it had taken to the Canadian Bill of Rights. In one after another of these early Charter cases, we find stirring announcements of the dawning of a new age of civil libertarian activism. At the same time, however, the Court displayed what Patrick Monahan has called "an overwhelming concern ... to ensure that this civil libertarian stance does not result in the collapse of the distinction between law and politics."[59] The separation of powers was to be maintained at all cost. Since Monahan wrote, however, the apparent consensus about the compatibility of judicial activism and legalism has evaporated.[60] Increasingly we find some of the judges accusing their more activist colleagues of illegitimately trespassing on the political realm.

A revealing example is the 1986 *Edwards Books* case, the first case in which this disagreement emerged. The issue was whether Ontario's Sunday-closing legislation infringed the religious freedom of Saturday sabbatarians, such as Jews and Seventh Day Adventists. The question was raised by the act's so-called "Saturday exemption," which permitted small stores to open on Sundays if they had closed the preceding Saturday, but which denied this opportunity to conscientious Saturday sabbatarians whose establishments exceeded the specified size limit. The latter would have to close for both days. A majority of the Court found that the competitive disadvantage suffered by such retailers violated their freedom of religion, but that the act, including the size limit on the "Saturday exemption," was nevertheless saved by section 1 of the Charter. The separation-of-powers issue emerged most clearly in a disagreement between Chief Justice Dickson and Justice La Forest about this section 1 question.

Justice Dickson found the purpose of the legislation to be sufficiently compelling to justify some limitation of Charter rights. He regarded as "self-evident"

> the desirability of enabling parents to have regular days off from work in common with their child's day off from school, and a day off enjoyed by most other family and community members.... I am satisfied that the Act is aimed at a pressing and substantial concern.[61]

Dickson did not mean, however, that the legislature could ignore the plight of Saturday sabbatarians altogether. For Justice Dickson, the constitution required some attempt to accommodate the religious conscience of those who found it burdensome to abide by the law. In short, some form of exemption was required. On the other hand, the legislature was justified in limiting the exemption to the extent necessary to maintain the integrity of the legislation—i.e., to prevent the exemption from undermining the "compelling and substantial" end that the legislation was designed to secure. The question was whether the Ontario legislature had chosen means to achieve this end that violated the constitutional right to freedom of religion as little as possible. Answering this question involved comparing the "Saturday exemption" to possible alternatives.

Justice La Forest objected to this judicial comparison of alternative legislative schemes. He took the sceptics' view that many substantive constitutional questions are not questions of rights versus nonrights, but questions about how to distribute the benefits and burdens of competing rights, that limiting the opportunities of some is often to expand the opportunities of others, and that these are matters about which reasonable people can disagree. "[A]ttempts to protect the rights of one group," said La Forest, "will inevitably impose burdens on the rights of other groups. There is no perfect scenario in which the rights of all can be equally protected."[62] As an example, he referred to the fact that just as Sunday-closing imposes disadvantages on retailers who observe a Saturday sabbath, so an exemption for such retailers may impose similar burdens on their Sunday-observing employees. "How," asked Justice La Forest, "is a court able to second-guess the legislature on such issues?"[63] He added that employers faced with this problem "might seek to avoid infringing other people's religious beliefs by hiring only their co-religionists but this, too, is a result a legislature might not wish to encourage."[64] Thus, while he personally favoured exemptions, Justice La Forest was "of the view that the nature of the choices and compromises that must be made in relation to Sunday closing are essentially legislative in nature. In the absence of unreasonableness or discrimination, courts are simply not in a position to substitute their judgment for that of the legislature."[65]

Justice La Forest opposed not only the judicial weighing of alternative accommodations, but also the constitutional requirement of accommodation itself because the latter inevitably led to the former. If an exemption was required, the courts would inevitably be called on to second-guess legislatures on the appropriateness of particular exemptions. Having upheld Ontario's scheme, for example, the courts would have to determine whether Quebec's narrower exemption, "limited as it is to establishments that are operated by no more than three persons at any one time (and then subject to Ministerial approval and conditions), is sufficient to pass constitutional muster."[66] This would be inappropriate, said Justice La Forest, because "what may work effectively in one province (or in a part of it) may simply not work in another without unduly interfering with the legislative scheme. And a compromise adopted at a particular time may not be possible at another."[67] In other words, everything depended on various and changing circumstances, which the courts were not well equipped to judge and monitor.

Justice Dickson concluded his review of alternatives by emphasizing "that it is not the role of this Court to devise legislation that is constitutionally valid, or to pass on the validity of schemes which are not directly before it, or to consider what legislation might be the most desirable. The discussion of alternative legislative schemes that I have undertaken is directed to one end only, that is, to address the issue whether the existing scheme meets the requirements of the second limb of the test for the application of s. 1 of the Charter as set down in *Oakes*."[68] He thus rejected Justice La Forest's contention that such evaluation of alternative exemptions is inevitably to second-guess the legislature on the question of "what legislation might be the most desirable." The debate between legalism and its critics is quite evident in this exchange.

▮ FEDERALISM

The difference between the conflicting answers to the separation-of-powers question is especially significant in the context of federal countries like Canada and Australia. In both countries, those who oppose bills of rights often invoke a "states' rights" argument, claiming that such a bill is really a way of limiting traditional state or provincial jurisdiction and imposing uniformity where variation would otherwise have been possible. Bill of rights enthusiasts, on the other hand, argue that all governments are limited alike in the name of the fundamental rights of the people, and wonder why states should want the power to infringe rights. The latter argument makes eminent sense if one thinks constitutional rights really protect the fundamental societal consensus about the proper bounds of politics. On this understanding, federal variation on the kinds of questions covered by a bill of rights would entail a territorially based departure from the fundamental consensus, and would contribute to a regime crisis, perhaps along separatist lines. If, on the other hand, the questions raised by a bill of rights are legitimate political questions about which reasonable differences are possible, then there is no good reason why such differences should not emerge among the provinces in matters within their jurisdiction. In this view, a nationally applicable bill of rights would indeed be an untoward incursion into provincial jurisdiction because it transfers ultimate political power from federally divided legislatures to a single, unitary institution, the final (and national) appellate court, whose decisions would bind all of the states.

The clash between these two perspectives on the relationship between federalism and rights has been a significant theme in Canadian constitutional debate both before and since the adoption of the Charter. Prior to the Charter, such provincial premiers as Saskatchewan's Alan Blakeney argued against the judicial imposition of national standards under the proposed Charter in matters otherwise within provincial jurisdiction.[69] This argument clearly entailed the claim that the Charter transferred policy-making power from legislatures to the courts, especially from provincial legislatures to the national Supreme Court. Such arguments had little influence, however. Canadians seemed generally to accept the federal government's claim that the Charter transferred power from governments as such to the people, not from provincial to national decision-makers. This implied that the Supreme Court, in interpreting and applying the Charter, was not engaged in courtroom politics, but was applying legal standards.

The same two perspectives were at work in the debate about the Meech Lake Accord. The issue was raised especially by the clause recognizing Quebec as a "distinct society" within Canada, and giving the government of Quebec the power not only to "preserve" but also to "promote" this distinctiveness. Among other controversies, Meech Lake raised questions concerning the effect of the distinct society provision on the Charter. The separation-of-powers issue was implicit in this issue.

As a potential interpretive qualification on the Charter's application in Quebec, the distinct society clause raised the possibility of legitimate territorial variation in rights, which meant either that the rights in question were not the fundamental rights of Canadian society (that they were in fact secondary questions about which reasonable disagreements were possible), or that there was no Canadian consensus about the boundaries of politics transcending the country's "two nations." In either case, the distinct society clause suggested that there were no common rights setting the limits to partisanship, including regional partisanship, throughout the country. This implication was strongly resisted by the "Charter groups," groups like the feminist lobby, who take a proprietary interest in certain sections of the Charter, which they see as resources to pursue their policy aspirations on a national level. Such groups have little interest in the traditional Canadian preoccupation with regionalism and federal–provincial relations, and positively fear this preoccupation when it distracts attention from, or even directly threatens, their policy agenda. Such groups tend to insist that Charter rights are fundamental throughout Canada and regard the possibility of regional variation as anathema. Thus feminists opposed the distinct society clause because they feared the distinctiveness of Quebec might entail sexist policies that would otherwise be unconstitutional by virtue of the Charter's equality rights.

■ LEGAL REALISM

Before leaving the subject of this chapter, we need to clear up a potential misconception. It would be wrong to leave the impression that critics of legalism believe that only *constitutional* law involves judges in the political task of lawmaking, that in other areas judges simply apply the law. In fact, most critics of legalism accept the premises of legal realism, which insists that judges cannot avoid making law, that all judging is political. They point out, for example, that judges must choose between alternative interpretations not only of constitutional law, but also of ordinary statutes, which also contain ambiguous or "open textured" language. All interpretation, in other words, involves lawmaking, and if the separation of powers means that judges should avoid this political task, it is a naive account of reality. Put more bluntly, to base the separation of powers between legislators and judges on a distinction between making and applying the law is to base it on a distinction without a difference. Understood in this way, the separation of powers simply does not exist.

If one accepts this perspective, the legitimacy of constitutional judicial review cannot be impugned simply by indicating its political and policy-making dimensions. Indeed, the "realist" critique of the law–politics distinction might even be used to defend judicial policy-making under the Charter. If all judging is unavoidably political, in other words, one might argue that there is nothing new and objectionable in the policy-making dimensions of constitutional jurisprudence.[70] A moment's reflection, however, reveals the weakness in such a defence. Simply put, judicial policy-making at this level cannot be as easily undone as other kinds of judicial policy-making. In principle at least, an ordinary legislative majority can override the judicial interpretation of a law simply by spelling out its policy preference more clearly in a new version of the law. In Chapter Four we pointed out that judges also exercise a significant policy influence through their development of the common law and in establishing sentencing policies. Here, too, legislatures can intervene by replacing the common law with legislation or by reducing the sentencing discretion in criminal offences. Judicial interpretations of constitutional law, on the other hand, are much more difficult to overcome. Unless judges change their minds, their decisions can be reversed only through the very cumbersome process of constitutional amendment, or through their gradual replacement, upon death or retirement, by judges of a different policy persuasion. For all intents and purposes, judicial policy-making at the constitutional level is exceedingly resistant to the opposition of ordinary democratic majorities. In short, the realist conclusion that judicial policy-making is unavoidable cannot be used to rescue judicial review of constitutional documents from the problem of democratic legitimacy. On the other hand, legal realists who challenge the legitimacy of constitutional judicial review must do so for reasons other than its transgression of the distinction between law and politics. Nevertheless, the law–politics distinction remains an important part of everyday political discourse, and the separation-of-powers debate as we have thus far characterized it continues to play an important role in the legitimacy debate.

At this point another misconception is likely. It is easy to assume that if one adopts the realist posture and rejects the law–politics distinction, one must also reject the idea of a separation of powers between the judiciary and the other branches of government, in which case, whatever the unsophisticated might think, the legitimacy debate should be grounded on some other principle. In fact, the separation of powers need not depend on the law–politics distinction. It is possible to ground the legitimacy debate on an alternative understanding of the proper distinction between appropriate judicial and legislative roles. The next chapter explores this alternative.

CHAPTER SEVEN

The Oracular Courtroom

The realist conclusion that all judicial interpretation is political, that there is no neat distinction between law and politics, need not lead one to abandon the idea of a separation of powers. It may be naive to think judges are simply engaged in applying rather than making law, but there are other ways of understanding what is distinctive about the judicial function. Indeed, "applying" or "enforcing" the law seems a more appropriate way of labelling the executive function. Of course, executive officials also have to interpret the laws they apply, which means that they too "legislate" by choosing between alternative interpretations. Still, common sense tells us that there are significant differences between the activities of legislators, executive officials, and judges, even though those differences are not captured by the distinction between making and applying the law. How else can the distinction be formulated, and with what implications for the legitimacy of judicial policy-making? This chapter articulates an alternative, and traditional, understanding of the separation of powers, and spells out its implications for the practice of judicial review. It also shows how this traditional understanding is steadily losing ground to the legalistic perspective described in the previous chapter.

The legalistic view holds that judges are the best expositors of legal meaning because they are more likely to reason correctly from agreed-upon principles than are more politically responsive officials, who are apt to be misled by interest and passion. Judges, in short, are the best oracles of what the law actually requires. The correct legal meaning may not be immediately obvious, but it exists and judges are best equipped to divine it. Judges thus "apply" the law, properly understood; they do not "make" it. Because only they can accurately discover the inner meaning of ambiguous constitutional provisions, moreover, their legal divinations must be binding on the other branches of government. This "oracular" view of the judicial function contrasts with a more traditional view, according to which the primary judicial task is to adjudicate concrete disputes. This is not an either-or distinction. With some exceptions (such as reference cases, which we discuss below) courts generally adjudicate concrete disputes, and in the course of doing so they cannot avoid pronouncing on the meaning of the relevant law, including constitutional law. The distinction between the adjudicative and oracular perspectives turns on which of these functions is primary and which is relegated to a subordinate position.

Important practical consequences flow from how one strikes the balance. The view that adjudication is primary places important restrictions on the scope and significance of judicial review. Placing the judiciary's oracular function in first place, by contrast, liberates judicial review from these constraints, significantly enhancing its reach and power. In Chapter Five we explored Christopher Wolfe's distinction between traditional and modern judicial review. We should now add that noninterpretivism—the idea that judges should keep the constitution in tune with the times by reading new conceptions into highly general concepts—does not exhaust what is new in modern judicial review. The movement from traditional to modern judicial review is also characterized by the ascendancy of the oracular over the adjudicative perspective. Modern judicial review gains much of its potency through combining the primacy of the oracular function with a noninterpretivist view of what that function entails.

▮ THE ADJUDICATIVE COURTROOM

The distinctive judicial function has traditionally been described as adjudicating disputes rather than applying law. If we go to a courtroom and watch judges at work, we will see them deciding such matters as which of two divorcing spouses gets custody of the children, whether or not one of the parties to a contractual agreement has failed to perform required duties, whether the prosecution in a criminal case has proved guilt beyond a reasonable doubt, or whether someone who is clearly guilty of breaking a law should go unpunished because the law itself is unconstitutional. These are concrete disputes between individuals or between individuals and the state, and courts exist primarily to determine the winners and losers in these disputes.

Judges do not adjudicate any and all disputes, however. If the members of a family cannot agree whether to take their next winter vacation in Florida or Hawaii, they cannot go to court and ask a judge to decide for them. Judges adjudicate only disputes raising questions of *legal* right or wrong. The litigants in a case cannot implore the court to grant them victory because they deserve it on moral, aesthetic, or utilitarian grounds;

they must persuade the judge that they have a *legal* right to win. There is no such legal right to win a family dispute about where to take a vacation, but someone is entitled to a legal victory in a contractual dispute or a criminal case. Yet the dispute about who is legally right often turns on the interpretation of an ambiguous law—including, sometimes, constitutional law—and such interpretation, as we have seen, involves lawmaking. Thus to say that adjudication is the distinguishing judicial function does not mean that judges can avoid lawmaking, including constitutional lawmaking.

Although they cannot avoid it, interpretive lawmaking is not, in this view, the primary function of judges, but an unavoidable corollary of adjudication—just as it is an inescapable corollary of the executive function of government (no more than judges, can cabinet ministers, civil servants, or police forces avoid interpreting, and thus "making," the laws they "apply"). At the level of constitutional law even legislatures engage in interpretation to determine whether their agendas conform to constitutional standards. Legal interpretation, in other words, is a proper function of each branch of government, not the distinctive preserve of one of them; it spans the separation of powers rather than defining it.[1]

On this account of the separation of powers, each branch of government has a legitimate role in interpreting the constitution as a necessary part of carrying out its own distinct functions. Legislatures must determine constitutional meaning in order to enact valid statutes, executive officials in order to conduct valid enforcement activities, and judges in order to determine who is legally entitled to win a dispute turning on constitutional issues. Unlike the legalism described above—which assumes that judicial interpretations are always more accurate and thus to be given priority over the interpretations of the other branches—this perspective sees the interpretive authority of each branch as equally legitimate and authoritative *within its own proper sphere of influence.* No branch need abandon its constitutional judgments in favour of the judgments of another branch as a matter of the latter's inevitable institutional superiority. The constitutional interpretations of judges, in other words, have final and conclusive authority only in determining the cases before them, and need not supplant the contrary judgments of the other branches in the conduct of their legitimate activities. Constitutional law, in other words, is what the judges say it is only in their courtrooms and for the purpose of settling the disputes before them; in other contexts, and for other purposes, it is what the legislators or executive officials say it is. The latter also have the responsibility to uphold—and thus to interpret—the constitution.

Sanford Levinson aptly calls this dispersal of interpretive authority the "protestant" approach to constitutional interpretation. Like religious Protestantism, it rejects the idea of a single, final (and infallible) interpreter of foundational texts, preferring to share the interpretive task among the "priesthood of all believers." The "catholic" approach to constitutional interpretation, by contrast, is "papalist" inasmuch as it makes authoritative interpretation the exclusive preserve of a single hierarchical institution. The "papal" institution in the constitutional realm—in our terms the chief constitutional oracle—is the Supreme Court.[2]

In the United States the conflict between these two approaches dates back at least to *Marbury* v. *Madison,* the 1803 case in which Chief Justice John Marshall claimed the power to invalidate national legislation.[3] In support of this power Marshall pointed out that judges were constitutionally required to swear an oath promising to support the constitution. How could they enforce unconstitutional laws, he asked, without becoming "knowing instruments for violating what they swear to support"?[4] The classic "protestant" critique of Marshall's reasoning was penned twenty-two years later in *Eakin* v. *Raub* by Justice Gibson of the Pennsylvania Supreme Court:

> The oath to support the constitution is not peculiar to judges, but is taken indiscriminately by every officer of the government and is designed rather as a test of the political principles of the man, than to bind the officer in the discharge of his duties: otherwise, it were difficult to determine what operation it is to have in the case of a recorder of deeds, for instance, who, in the execution of his office has nothing to do with the constitution.[5]

Among others, members of Congress and the president also swear the oath and thus share with the judiciary the responsibility of upholding the constitution. For their part, judges fulfil their oath best by remaining within their traditional adjudicative sphere. There they can certainly employ their understanding of the constitution—by using it as a guide to statutory interpretation, for example—but for Gibson the attempt completely to invalidate legislation transcends the legitimate judicial function. Indeed, judges violate their oaths more seriously by invalidating legislation they consider unconstitutional than by giving it effect, for "the oath was more probably designed to secure the powers of each of the different branches from being usurped by any of the rest; for instance, to prevent the house of representatives from erecting itself into a court of judicature, or the supreme court from attempting to control the legislature...."[6] Justice Gibson clearly thought the constitutional views of each branch should prevail within its proper sphere of authority. In particular, the constitution did not direct the judge "to stray from the path of his ordinary business, to search for violations of duty in the business of others...."[7]

Although Gibson's opinion clearly represents constitutional protestantism, it would be wrong to exaggerate the papalism or oracularism of his target: John Marshall's opinion in *Marbury*. Marshall's opinion "gave practical effect to" Alexander Hamilton's defence of judicial review in *Federalist* No. 78, and neither argument provides clear support for the modern oracular court.[8]

The explicit theme of *Federalist* No. 78 is judicial independence. Having "no influence over either the sword or the purse," the judiciary, according to Hamilton, is both the "least dangerous" and the "weakest" of the branches of government. Thus the judiciary must be given the means to defend itself from the incursions of its more powerful cousins. On these grounds Hamilton defends the constitutional proposal to grant tenure to judges "during good behaviour"—i.e., in most cases for life. The independence secured by life tenure, continues Hamilton, is particularly important "in a limited constitution" to enable courts to declare void unconstitutional acts by the other branches. Thus begins the defence of judicial review that Marshall adopts in *Marbury*.[9]

It should be noted, however, that Hamilton defends the judicial invalidation of only "acts contrary to the manifest tenor of the Constitution." His only example is the passage of bills of attainder or *ex post facto* laws, which are clearly and explicitly prohibited by the constitution.[10] In *Marbury* Marshall adds two further examples. The first is a state duty on exportable goods contrary to the clear constitutional declaration that "no tax or duty shall be laid on articles exported from any state." Supposing a duty of this kind is imposed, asks Marshall, "ought judgment to be rendered in such a case? Ought the judges to close their eyes on the constitution, and only see the law?" Marshall's second addition to Hamilton's example concerns a law permitting conviction for treason on the basis of either an out-of-court confession or the testimony of one witness, contrary to the constitutional requirement of confession in open court or the testimony of two witnesses to the same overt act.[11] The examples of "acts contrary to the manifest tenor of the Constitution" are few, and they all illustrate relatively clear and uncontroversial violations, involving little interpretive ambiguity. In short, both Hamilton and Marshall defend the invalidation only of legislation that clearly violates specific constitutional provisions, "and in *Federalist* No. 81, [Hamilton] considered judicial actions to the contrary 'usurpations on the authority of the legislature' and grounds for impeachment."[12] Neither man appears to contemplate more than occasional and limited judicial review.

Nor should we forget that judicial review comes to light in *The Federalist* during a discussion of how a weak judiciary might defend itself against the depredations of the more powerful branches of government. *Marbury* itself shows how judicial review might serve this purpose. The case arose because James Madison, the Secretary of State in the newly ensconced administration of Thomas Jefferson, refused to give Marbury a commission appointing him to a judgeship. The commission had been signed, sealed, but not delivered by John Marshall, President Adams's Secretary of State, during the final, hectic, "lame duck" days of the outgoing Federalist administration. (Marshall did not forget to pick up his own commission appointing him to the Supreme Court.) When Marbury went directly to the Supreme Court, requesting a writ of *mandamus* ordering Madison to deliver his commission, Marshall was faced with a dilemma. Jefferson and Madison (not implausibly) considered the flurry of eleventh-hour judicial appointments to be a retreat of their defeated opponents to the bench, from which they were likely to obstruct the elected government whenever possible. The new administration was in no mood to obey a *mandamus,* especially one issued by Marshall, who was himself a hated Federalist and the leading example of the cowardly escape to the bench. Indeed, Jefferson let it be known that his government would impeach Marshall should he issue the *mandamus.* Not only would this have deprived Marshall of his new job, but it would have severely damaged the status and authority of the Supreme Court, which as a fledgling institution was much more vulnerable than it is today. Backing down in the face of the administration's threat, however, would not have done the Court much good either. Marshall's brilliant escape from this dilemma was to find that Marbury was indeed entitled to his commission, but to refuse to issue the *mandamus* because the legislation enabling litigants to seek this writ directly from the Supreme Court was an invalid addition to the original (i.e., trial-level as opposed to appellate) jurisdiction given the Court by the constitution. This first invalidation of congressional legislation, in other words, was used to avoid a head-on clash between the Court and the executive that the former was bound to lose. Indeed, the judicial invalidation turned a likely defeat into victory, for it enabled Marshall to claim increased status and authority for his Court even as he retreated on the immediate issue of the *mandamus*.

In sum, both *Federalist* No. 78 and *Marbury* defend a fairly limited and circumscribed form of judicial review, confined mainly to overruling relatively "clear mistakes" by the other branches. In both cases, moreover, "judicial review emerges as a judicial defence against legislative and executive encroachments on the status and authority of courts, not as a broad power to review the other branches' actions with respect to their own responsibilities."[13] At the very least, the arguments of *Federalist* No. 78 and *Marbury* are too ambiguous to provide support for the much broader interpretation of judicial power that emerged after *Brown* v. *Board of Education*.[14] In short, although Hamilton and Marshall are not as radically protestant as Judge Gibson, neither do their arguments fall within the radically papalist or oracular view of the Court characteristic of our own time. Their views remain compatible with an essentially adjudicative courtroom.

Those who take an oracular view of the Court differ somewhat about the leeway that ought to be given to contrary constitutional opinions when the Court finds legislation to be constitutional. In particular, is it appropriate for elected officials to resist a policy on the grounds of constitutional scruple even though the Supreme Court has declared it constitutional? A classic example of such political resistance to a judicial finding of constitutionality is President Andrew Jackson's veto of legislation renewing the charter of the Second Bank of the United States. Jackson vetoed the legislation because he considered it to be unconstitutional, despite the fact that John Marshall had found in *McCulloch* v. *Maryland*[15] that Congress had the constitutional authority to charter a national bank.[16]

Although many constitutional papalists would concede the legitimacy of actions such as Jackson's, not all do. Thus Daniel Webster, Jackson's contemporary, deplored the bank veto, arguing that the Supreme Court's *McCulloch* decision was "final, and from [it] there is no appeal."[17] A more modern example of this extreme papalism occurred in 1984, when the mayor of Minneapolis vetoed an ordinance restricting the distribution of sexually explicit though nonpornographic material because, in his view, it violated the first amendment. The mayor's veto drew an angry letter from Professor Laurence Tribe of Harvard. Tribe was "prepared to assume that [the mayor] acted from a good faith assessment of [his] constitutional duty," but could not accept "the role [he] chose to play *in interposing himself so pre-emptively* between those who believe their rights are violated by anti-female pornography, and the courts—which *alone* can fairly decide whether this proposed protection of those alleged rights can be reconciled with the transcendent importance of free speech in an open society."[18] As Levinson remarks: "One cannot imagine a stronger articulation of what I have been terming the 'catholic' view of institutional supremacy."[19]

Proponents of constitutional oracularism are much more united about the exclusivity of a judicial invalidation. What the Court kills, they agree, must not be resurrected by the political branches. This view was denied by Abraham Lincoln, one of the most thoughtful exponents of constitutional protestantism and the adjudicative courtroom. Unlike Justice Gibson, Lincoln conceded the power of the Court to invalidate laws, but he clearly attempted to limit the impact of such invalidation to the actual case before the Court.

Lincoln was forced to address the question when he was confronted with the U.S. Supreme Court's decision in the infamous *Dred Scott* case.[20] Dred Scott, a slave, claimed he had gained his freedom when his master took him into a federal territory where slavery was prohibited. The Supreme Court disagreed, deciding that neither Congress nor the territorial legislatures could prohibit slavery, because the secure possession of property in slaves was a constitutional right. Dred Scott, accordingly, remained a slave. Moreover, if the Court's reasoning determined the wider political issue, the prohibition of slavery in new territories was no longer constitutionally permissible.

Although Lincoln disagreed with the judgment in *Dred Scott,* he did not try to interfere with the immediate result of the case. The separation of powers meant that the courts must have final authority over the outcome of the concrete cases before them.[21] Neither the legislature nor the executive had the right to turn courtroom winners into losers and vice versa. Thus, although he considered the judges to have been seriously mistaken, Lincoln concluded nothing could be done for Dred Scott. "In so far as [the Supreme Court] decided in favor of Dred Scott's master and against Dred Scott and his family," he said, "I do not propose to disturb or resist the decision."[22] The constitutional reasons given by the Court to justify their resolution of Dred Scott's case were another matter altogether. Lincoln was not about to accept, and act upon, a constitutional right to slavery merely on the say so of nine judges. The judges had a right to their opinion, and the decision based on that opinion was binding on the litigants, and on the other branches of government in the sense that they must not interfere with that concrete result, but the authority of judicial opinion extended no further. In particular, the reasons used by the judges to determine the outcome of the concrete case were not binding on the legislative and executive branches of government. Judicial opinions could determine the outcome of particular cases, but were not entitled to determine the overall policy of the country.[23] As Chief Executive, Lincoln insisted on his right to disagree with the constitutional judgments of the Court and to act, in his executive capacity, on the basis of his own, contrary judgment.[24] Similarly, he argued that legislators were free to vote for the prohibition of slavery in new territories despite the *Dred Scott* decision.[25] Indeed, Lincoln maintained in his first inaugural address that "if the policy of the Government upon vital questions affecting the whole people is to be irrevocably fixed by decisions of the Supreme Court, the instant they are made in ordinary litigation between parties in personal actions, the people will have ceased to be their own rulers, having to that extent practically resigned their Government into the hands of that eminent tribunal."[26]

This version of the separation of powers, according to which the function of constitutional interpretation is shared among the branches of government, does not mean that the constitutional judgments of each branch can be hermetically sealed within its own sphere of competence, with no spill-over effects. To take only the most obvious example, the enforcement of a criminal law requires the cooperation of the courts and can be undermined by judges who refuse to find violators guilty because they conclude the relevant law is unconstitutional. If enough judges act on this view, or if all of them are required to do so by a binding decision of the Supreme Court, the law becomes a dead letter, however much the legislative and executive branches may believe it is constitutional.

This does not mean that there are no practical differences between the oracular and adjudicative versions of the separation of powers. Under the oracular approach constitutional interpretation is the exclusive preserve of judges, whose opinions must be accepted as authoritative by everyone else. At the extreme, this perspective leads governments to suspend their enforcement of a law on the say so of a single trial-level judge. In 1989, for example, a lower court judge in Alberta refused to penalize someone who had obviously violated the province's mandatory seat-belt legislation because, in the judge's opinion, that law infringed the accused's section 7 "right to life, liberty and security of the person and the right not to be deprived thereof except in accordance with the principles of fundamental justice."[27] The government immediately announced that it was ceasing all prosecutions, pending appeal.[28] As it turned out, the Court of Appeal eventually overruled the original decision and the enforcement of the law was restored.[29] What was significant, however, was the government's assumption that a single judge in a single case could suspend the law's operation and that only other judges could restore it. The government and its policies were assumed to be entirely at the mercy of judicial opinions.

Under the adjudicative approach, enforcement officials would have continued to prosecute offenders in other courts, before other judges. Surely some, perhaps most, of these judges would have taken the position eventually adopted by the Court of Appeal. In their courts, the law would have remained enforceable, and culprits would have been found guilty. Only if many trial-level judges agreed that the seat-belt legislation was unconstitutional, or if higher courts imposed such a conclusion on them, would the law expire. In the meantime, enforcement could continue. To be sure, the law's effectiveness would be weakened, but only in some courts and before some judges. This alternative to legalism is reflected in Alexis de Tocqueville's discussion of judicial review in the United States of the mid-19th century. When a judge finds a law unconstitutional, said Tocqueville, "the law thus censured is not abolished; its moral force is diminished, but its physical effect is not suspended. It is only gradually, under repeated judicial blows, that it finally succumbs."[30]

The difference between oracular legalism and the adjudicative approach to the separation of powers is even more evident in the case of nonprohibitory laws, whose day-to-day administration does not require the cooperation of the courts. In such cases, the constitutional opinions of judges do not have the same ability to prevail gradually over the contrary judgments of other branches. Consider a policy of maternity benefits for women with no comparable paternity benefits for men. A court might find this to be unconstitutionally discriminatory and declare it to be of "no force or effect" under section 52 of the Constitution Act, 1982, but aside from repeating this declaration, what could it do if the government continued to apply the policy? In such cases courts can voice their opinions about constitutionality, but their cooperation is not an integral part of the distribution of benefits, and they cannot make their constitutional opinion stick by withholding that cooperation.

This difficulty is most pronounced when judicial opinions not only require governments to abandon existing policies, but also require them to undertake new ones. Equality between men and women in parental-leave benefits, for example, could be achieved by abolishing existing maternity benefits (thereby saving money), dividing those benefits between mothers and fathers (thereby maintaining current expenditures), or adding a new paternity benefit fund to the existing maternity benefits (thereby increasing expenditures). Feminists, not wanting a reduction in existing benefits for women, have argued that the constitution requires the third, and most expensive alternative. If the courts agree, as the Federal Court has tentatively done,[31] how can they force an unwilling government to make the required expenditures?

In short, judicial opinions about the kind of social benefits required by the constitution can prevail only because the other branches are persuaded by them, or because they act on the legalistic assumption that constitutional interpretation is the preserve of judges, whose opinions are binding on everyone else. Under the adjudicative version of the separation of powers, unpersuaded governments would be free to disregard such judicial opinions and continue acting on their own views of constitutional requirements.

∎ THE ORACULAR COURTROOM

Of the two views of the separation of powers, oracular legalism is becoming increasingly dominant. It is widely assumed that constitutional interpretation is a matter for judges alone, and that their opinions are binding on the other branches of government in their policy-making activities. Certainly governments are increasingly taking this view, as shown by the Alberta government's response to a single judge's decision in the seat-belt case.

Section 33 of the Charter, to be sure, embodies a scepticism of judicial finality in matters of constitutional interpretation, but with the exception of Quebec (and, in one case, Saskatchewan), governments have been reluctant to use it to override judicial decisions. No doubt they do not want to be seen to be violating rights. But this perception itself attests to the strength of oracular legalism—it assumes that section 33 can be used only to override rights as defined by judges rather than to express an alternative interpretation of those rights. It assumes, in other words, that Charter rights are what the judges say they are. Interestingly, this legalistic view of the legislative override is supported by the very wording of section 33, which allows legislatures to enact statutes "notwithstanding" specified sections of the Charter. This clearly suggests that the legislation will be allowed to stand *despite* its violation of Charter rights. It is surely eloquent testimony to the power of legalism that the Charter provision most obviously embodying nonlegalistic scepticism of judicial power was phrased in legalistic language. The form and content of section 33 are mutually contradictory, and the former symbolically undermines the latter!

The oracular version of the separation of powers has also become dominant among judges. Former Chief Justice Dickson, for example, described the Charter not as adding to the legal background against which judges resolve concrete disputes, but as giving the courts responsibility for the "elucidation and resolution of some of the values most fundamental to the Canadian way of life."[32]

Judges have always been tempted by the view that they are the best and most authoritative interpreters of constitutional law, of course, but in the past they also subscribed to a good many implications of the adjudicative alternative. For example, the view that judicial interpretation of the law is an unavoidable by-product of dispute resolution rather than the judiciary's central function was embodied in traditional rules of "standing." According to these rules judges would grant standing to raise an issue of legal interpretation in court only to someone embroiled in a concrete dispute turning on the law in question. One could not, for example, challenge a censorship law in court simply because one did not like it. Such public-spirited opposition to a public policy was a purely political matter and belonged in the political arena. The courtroom was not to be turned into a substitute for electoral politics. Only if one was being prosecuted for violating the law did one have standing to raise the matter of its constitutionality. Not only was the defendant in such a case embroiled in the kind of concrete dispute with the state that judges are required to adjudicate, but the court could not settle the dispute without ruling on the defendant's claim that the law is unconstitutional. If it was upheld on appeal to the Supreme Court, a ruling of unconstitutionality arising out of such a case might be no different in its political effect than if the case had been brought merely by a concerned citizen, but its legitimacy would be less open to question. As Tocqueville put it, in commenting on the 19th-century practice of judicial review in the United States:

> The American judge is dragged in spite of himself onto the political field. He only pronounces on the law because he has to judge a case, and he cannot refuse to decide the case. The political question he has to decide is linked to the litigants' interests, and to refuse to deal with it would be a denial of justice.[33]

The same defence of judicial review is not available in cases brought by concerned citizens, who could just as easily, and more appropriately, lobby their political representatives, join parties or interest groups, and vote in elections. Accordingly, judges in the past refused to grant standing to would-be litigants of this ilk.

The corollary of this strict view of standing is that some constitutional issues could never arise in court. In Tocqueville's words, judicial review "under this system cannot cover all laws without exception, for there are some laws which can never give rise to that sort of clearly formulated argument called a lawsuit."[34] A traditional example is tax laws. One could not challenge a tax because one thought some of the monies raised were being spent for unconstitutional purposes.

Under a strict view of standing, the anti-abortion crusade waged in the courts by Joe Borowski, Canada's leading pro-life spokesman, would have been impossible. Borowski's legal position was quite different from that of Dr. Henry Morgentaler, his chief rival in Canada's courtroom battles about abortion. Both Morgentaler and Borowski challenged the constitutionality of section 251 of the Criminal Code, but for opposite reasons, with Morgentaler criticizing its prohibitive elements and Borowski taking aim at its permissive exemptions. Morgentaler had clear standing to raise the constitutional issue because he was already in court being prosecuted for illegally performing abortions outside of approved hospitals and without the authorization of a TAC. He challenged the law's constitutionality as part of his legal defence. But what stake, other than that of a concerned citizen, did Borowski have in the application of the law's permissive side that would entitle him to challenge it in court? Indeed, it is difficult to know who would have such a stake. Clearly neither the doctor performing the abortion nor the woman taking advantage of the law's permissive exception is likely to challenge it. The fetus has the clearest interest, but is obviously in no position to press its claims in court. The person who could most plausibly bring a legal action under traditional rules of standing is a father who wishes his child to live. Certainly Borowski would have had no standing.

Borowski first raised the question of standing before the Charter came into effect, when his challenge to the legislation was based on the Canadian Bill of Rights. He took his arguments all the way to the Supreme Court. In that court, the traditional view of standing was summarized in a dissenting judgment by Chief Justice Laskin:

I start with the proposition that, as a general rule, it is not open to a person, simply because he is a citizen and a taxpayer or is either the one or the other, to invoke the jurisdiction of a competent Court to obtain a ruling on the interpretation or application of legislation or on its validity, when that person is not either directly affected by the legislation or is not threatened by sanctions for an alleged violation of the legislation. Mere distaste has never been a ground upon which to seek the assistance of a Court. Unless the legislation itself provides for a challenge to its meaning or application or validity by any citizen or taxpayer, the prevailing policy is that a challenger must show some special interest in the operation of the legislation beyond the general interest that is common to all members of the relevant society. This is especially true of the criminal law. For example, however passionately a person may believe that it is wrong to provide for compulsory breathalyzer tests or wrong to make mere possession of marijuana an offence against the criminal law, the Courts are not open to such a believer, not himself or herself charged or even threatened with a charge, to seek a declaration against the enforcement of such criminal laws.[35]

Laskin derived this policy from the traditional adjudicative function of the courts. "They are," he said, "dispute-resolving tribunals, established to determine contested rights or claims between or against persons or to determine their penal or criminal liability when charged with offences prosecuted by agents of the Crown." Where a concrete dispute of this sort does not exist, courts should not "answer questions in the abstract merely to satisfy a person's curiosity or perhaps his or her obsessiveness with a perceived injustice in the existing law."[36]

Borowski's case was certainly brought to satisfy his "obsessiveness with a perceived injustice" in the abortion law. Nevertheless, the majority of the Court granted him standing. Writing for this majority, Justice Martland clearly rejected the traditional view expressed by Tocqueville, that some laws could escape judicial review because no one would ever have standing to litigate them. Martland maintained that

to establish status as a plaintiff in a suit seeking a declaration that legislation is invalid, if there is a serious issue as to its invalidity, a person need only to show that he is affected by it directly or that he

has a genuine interest as a citizen in the validity of the legislation
*and that there is no other reasonable and effective manner in which
the issue may be brought before the Court.* [37]

As noted above, the putative father might come closer to the traditional
rules of standing than Borowski. But Martland considered "the possibility
of the husband bringing proceedings to attack the legislation [to be] illusory."[38] Given the definite time limits on pregnancy and the much longer
time it takes most cases to wend their way through the court system, "the
abortion would have occurred, or a child would have been born long
before the case had been finally terminated."[39] Thus there was really no
way of bringing the issue before the court that was more "reasonable and
effective" than a suit by a genuinely interested citizen, such as Borowski.

In this formulation the traditional relationship between the dispute-
resolving function of the courts and their authority to assess the constitutionality of legislation is reversed. No longer is the judicial assessment of
constitutionality a necessary corollary of the primary function of resolving
concrete disputes; it is now the *primary* function. All laws must be open to
judicial scrutiny for constitutional imperfections, and if one cannot imagine
a concrete dispute that would provide for such scrutiny in the traditional
manner, then one must dispense with the requirement for concrete disputes.

So powerful is this modern view of the judiciary's essential function
that it was accepted even in Justice Laskin's dissenting opinion in
Borowski. Laskin cites with approval several exceptions that have developed in the traditional rules. For example, municipal taxpayers should be
able to challenge allegedly illegal municipal expenditures because "unless
a taxpayer action was permitted the illegality would go unchallenged and
unchallengeable."[40] Similarly, Laskin approves of relaxing the rules of
standing in the case of declaratory or directory statutes. This situation
arose in the case of *Thorson* v. *A.G. Canada*,[41] in which a taxpayer challenged the validity of the federal Official Languages Act. Unlike regulatory
or penal laws, this act "created no offences and imposed no penalties." It
simply declared the principle of two official languages and directed certain
government actions to implement those principles. No one was likely to
be found guilty and punished by a court for violating this act. Thus,
"unless a citizen or taxpayer action was permitted to question its validity,
there would be no way in which its validity could be tested unless the federal Attorney General did so through a reference."[42] It was unlikely, how-

ever, that the government would refer to the courts the question of the validity of legislation it strongly supported, and in fact a request for such a reference had been turned down. In short, Laskin agreed with the majority that if "there is no other reasonable and effective manner in which the issue may be brought before the Court," the rules of standing should be jettisoned, and lawsuits brought by litigants with no greater stake than "genuine interest as a citizen" should be allowed. He disagreed with the majority mainly in concluding that a challenge to the abortion law's permissive provisions could be brought more reasonably and effectively, which is to say more concretely, by persons having a more direct interest than Borowski. Laskin had in mind doctors, hospitals, and husbands. He acknowledged that doctors and hospitals might also have difficulty meeting the traditional rules of standing if they wished to challenge the exculpatory aspects of the law, but he insisted that "at worst" theirs was a "more compelling and immediate interest than that asserted by" Borowski.[43] At bottom, however, Laskin, too, was willing to subordinate the judiciary's adjudicative function to the idea that all constitutional questions must be given their day in court, whether or not they can be brought there by litigants engaged in a concrete dispute. As Kenneth Swan observes, *Borowski* caps a series of cases in which the Supreme Court provided "what is undoubtedly the greatest degree of popular access to the courts found anywhere in the Anglo-American legal system."[44]

Another feature of the traditional adjudicative view of the courts, one closely related to the matter of standing, is the doctrine of mootness. A case is moot if the concrete dispute involved no longer exists by the time a court is called upon to resolve it.[45] A case may become moot for many reasons. One of the parties to the litigation may die, for example. This happened in the case of *R. v. Mercure,* which involved Father Mercure's challenge to the constitutional validity of a speeding ticket issued in Saskatchewan that was printed only in English.[46] Father Mercure died before the litigation had run its course, and his legal dispute thus no longer existed—it had become moot. The Supreme Court's first Charter case, *Skapinker,*[47] was technically moot for another reason. Skapinker had challenged an Ontario law requiring all members of the bar to be Canadian citizens. By the time the case had reached the Supreme Court, however, Skapinker had in fact become a citizen and been admitted to the bar. He thus no longer had a concrete stake in challenging the law. Another avenue to mootness is illustrated by Borowski's case. Having gained standing to challenge the permissive aspects of Canada's abortion law, Borowski finally arrived in the Supreme Court only to find that Morgentaler had preceded him and had succeeded in having the law struck down. With no law left to challenge, Borowski's legal journey ended in a moot case.

From the traditional adjudicative perspective, moot cases raise merely "hypothetical or abstract" questions, which courts should refuse to answer because their decisions would not resolve a live controversy directly affecting the rights of the litigants. As in the case of standing, however, this view has given way to a much more flexible approach. Courts still decline to decide cases on the grounds of mootness, but insist that they have a discretion to entertain such cases in appropriate circumstances. Thus, although the Supreme Court refused to answer the substantive questions in Borowski's appeal because it had become moot, it heard and decided the cases brought by Skapinker and Mercure. In *Borowski* the Court gave several reasons for exercising its discretion to decide moot cases. The most important one, in the present context, is "to ensure that an important question which might independently evade review be heard by the court."[48] The Court used the example of cases challenging the validity of an interlocutory injunction prohibiting strike action, pointing out that the strike will almost always be settled, and the case rendered moot, by the time it reached the Supreme Court for ultimate resolution. Thus, "if the point was ever to be tested, it almost had to be in a case that was moot."[49] Again, we see the strength and influence of the view that all constitutional issues must have their day in court. True, the Court is sensitive to the possibility that "pronouncing judgments in the absence of a dispute affecting the rights of the parties may be viewed as intruding into the role of the legislative branch."[50] In other words, it fully understands the traditional view that the courts are adjudicative institutions, whose lawmaking activities are legitimate only to the extent that they are the unavoidable by-product of settling concrete disputes. Nevertheless, the Court rejects the logical implication of this view, the implication articulated by Tocqueville, that some constitutional issues might thus never come up for judicial resolution.[51] The contemporary judiciary sees itself as the ultimate expositor of constitutional meaning and evidently cannot abide any restrictions on that function stemming from its traditional adjudicative role.

Oracular legalism is also evident in the increasing tendency of courts to decide legal issues not directly raised by the facts of the cases before them,[52] a practice frowned upon by adjudicative traditionalists. For example, the Supreme Court found that the federal Lord's Day Act violated religious freedom in a case brought by Big M Drug Mart, a corporation that, as the Court admitted, was an abstract legal entity that "cannot be said to have a conscience or hold a religious belief."[53] The Court allowed Big M to raise the question of religious freedom, and invalidated the law on that basis, despite the fact that Big M had no religious conscience to violate. In effect, Big M was permitted to raise the issue on behalf of hypothetical third parties not actually before the Court. The Court obviously decided the question simply because it was an important constitutional question, not because it was forced to decide it by the concrete facts of the actual case.[54]

An even more dramatic example of judicial straying from the facts of the case occurred in *R. v. Edward Dewey Smith*.[55] On returning from a trip to Bolivia, Smith was caught attempting to smuggle illegal drugs into Canada. At trial he pleaded guilty to importing a narcotic contrary to section 5(1) of the Narcotic Control Act and was sentenced to eight years in prison. In appealing the sentence, Smith claimed that the law violated the Charter's ban on cruel and unusual punishments because it imposed a mandatory minimum sentence of seven years for importing narcotics. This meant that a judge would be required to impose a seven-year sentence on "a young person, who while driving back into Canada from a winter break in the U.S.A., is caught with only one, indeed, let's postulate, his or her first 'joint of grass.'"[56] The majority of the Court agreed that such a sentence would indeed be cruel and unusual and thus invalidated the seven-year minimum sentence.

In fact, however, Smith was not returning with a single "joint of grass." He entered Canada with an amount of pure cocaine which, after dilution, was estimated to have a street value of between $126 and $168 thousand.[57] Justice McIntyre expressed the traditional adjudicative view when he stated in his dissenting opinion that "there is an air of unreality about this appeal because the question of cruel and unusual punishment, under s. 12 of the Charter, does not appear to arise on the facts of the case."[58] McIntyre pointed out that Smith was sentenced to eight years by a trial judge who believed the seven-year minimum was unconstitutional, and that all but one of the judges on the Court of Appeal affirmed the sentence, with the dissenting judge preferring a sentence of five years. All of the judges "who have considered the case," said McIntyre, "are unanimously of the view that a long sentence of imprisonment is appropriate and no one has suggested that the appellant has been sentenced to cruel and unusual punishment."[59] The appellant admitted as much when he based his case not on his own situation, but on "a hypothetical 'first time importer of a single marijuana cigarette.'" "In effect," concluded McIntyre, "the appellant is stating that while the law is not unconstitutional in its application to him, it may be unconstitutional in its application to a third party and, therefore, should be declared of no force or effect."[60] McIntyre did not consider this a "sound approach" to applying the Charter.

Deciding issues not raised by the facts of the immediate case may be incompatible with the traditional adjudicative view of the judicial function, but is quite congenial to the legal mind more broadly conceived. Lawyers are prone to what has been called "every last case" reasoning.[61] When lawyers draw up a will, for example, they strive to anticipate and provide for every possible contingency, even those that seem highly remote or just barely imaginable to the ordinary person. Lawyers, in short, insist on dotting all the i's and crossing all the t's. In constitutional cases, this way of thinking tempts judges (who are, of course, lawyers) to imagine how a law *might* be applied in hypothetical extreme circumstances, rather than focusing on how it has actually been applied in the case before them. The norms of the adjudicative courtroom militate against this temptation, but these norms have been seriously weakened if not entirely abandoned. In today's oracular courtroom the lawyer's tendency to "every last case" reasoning is given free rein.

As do the changing rules of standing and mootness, the increasing tendency of appellate courts to stray from the facts of their cases shows how strongly judges have come to see settling important questions of legal interpretation as their primary function rather than as the inevitable corollary of adjudicating concrete disputes. In the words of Michael Mandel, cases such as *Big M* and *Smith* show "how far the courts have strayed from their role as *judges* with the advent of the Charter." They demonstrate that the case is often "merely a *pretext* to review the law on grounds that have nothing to do with parties in court."[62] Or, as Donald Horowitz says of similar American developments, "the individual case and its peculiar facts have on occasion become mere vehicles for an exposition of more general policy problems. Consequently, somewhat less care can be devoted by lawyers and judges alike, to the appropriateness of particular plaintiffs and to the details of their grievances." For Horowitz, "the increasing subordination of the individual case in judicial policy-making" signifies "the expansion of judicial responsibility more nearly to overlap the responsibilities of other governmental institutions."[63]

Taken together, these developments have eroded the distinction between ordinary court cases and reference cases. In Canada both levels of government have given themselves the power to "refer" abstract or hypothetical questions to the courts in the absence of a traditional dispute conforming to the rules of standing. Governments can use this device to refer legislation to the courts for an assessment of its constitutionality when no private litigant has challenged it, or when such a challenge is unlikely because of the difficulties posed by the traditional rules of standing or mootness. Reference cases can also be used to determine the constitutional validity of *proposed* legislation, which has not even been passed, something that would be impossible under the adjudicative model. Each level of government can even refer the question of the validity of legislation passed or proposed by the other level. A good example of this is the "Patriation" case, in which three of the dissenting provinces launched reference cases questioning the validity of Ottawa's proposal to patriate the constitution unilaterally.

In the United States the constitution does not permit governments to refer hypothetical questions to the courts. Under article 3 of the U.S. constitution the "judicial power" is limited to the consideration of "cases" and "controversies." This wording has been interpreted as constitutionally limiting the courts to the traditional judicial function of resolving concrete disputes. Canadian-style reference cases violate the U.S. "case and controversy" requirement.[64] Similar considerations were raised about the Canadian constitution in a 1912 JCPC case.[65] In objecting to the federal government's legislation establishing its right to refer questions to the Supreme Court, the provinces argued that section 101 of the BNA Act, under which the Supreme Court was established, authorizes only the creation of a "court," which by its very nature must be limited to judicial tasks. Answering abstract questions outside of the context of ordinary litigation was not one of those tasks. The JCPC showed some sympathy with this view, confessing that "no one who has experience of judicial duties can doubt that, if an Act of this kind were abused, manifold evils might follow, including undeserved suspicion of the course of justice and much embarrassment and anxiety to the judges themselves."[66] Nevertheless, their lordships considered this a judgment about the wisdom of the law, not its legality. In strict law, they concluded, there was nothing to prevent Ottawa from saddling the courts with reference cases.

From the traditional adjudicative perspective, the answering of abstract hypothetical questions is not a judicial function, and there are strong hints that even in upholding reference cases the JCPC took this view. The JCPC saw no legal bar to the addition of these nonjudicial functions to the tasks required of courts as long as they remained courts in their core functions, but it did not seriously challenge the traditional view that these new functions were indeed nonjudicial. Thus reference cases can be seen as a distinct exception to the true judicial function of deciding concrete "cases" and "controversies." With the growth of the oracular courtroom, however, the exception appears to have swallowed the rule. Cases brought by private litigants such as Borowski, Smith, and Big M Drug Mart are much less like the concrete disputes contemplated by the adjudicative model, and much more like reference cases. In both instances the courts are asked to answer questions not raised by a concrete dispute of the traditional sort. In the oracular courtroom cases brought by private litigants are often little more than "private references."[67]

■ THE ORACLE'S DISCRETION

The view that judges are the authoritative and final expositors of constitutional meaning leads naturally to the idea that the rights guaranteed by the Charter would be meaningless without judicial protection. This idea was eloquently expressed by Chief Justice Dickson in *B.C. Government Employees' Union* v. *British Columbia*.[68] The union was engaged in a legal strike against the government, and was picketing the Vancouver courthouse. The Chief Justice of British Columbia encountered the picket line on his way to work and, "without benefit of a complainant,"[69] immediately issued an injunction against the picketing. When the union's appeal reached the Supreme Court, Chief Justice Dickson rejected it, arguing that the picketing interfered with "that which alone makes it in fact possible to benefit" from Charter rights, "that is, access to a court." "Of what value," he asked, "are the rights and freedoms guaranteed by the Charter if a person is denied or delayed access to a court of competent jurisdiction in order to vindicate them?" He concluded that without unhindered access "the Charter protections would become merely illusory, the entire Charter undermined."[70] Thus, although the injunction violated the union's freedom of expression, it was clearly justified by section 1. In a concurring judgment, Justice McIntyre went even further, denying that there was any violation of Charter rights to be justified under section 1. "What is in issue here," he wrote, "is the question of whether any person or group may have a Charter right to engage deliberately in conduct calculated to abridge the Charter rights of others. In my view, no such right can exist and resort to s. 1 ... was therefore unnecessary."[71]

This case is an example of judicial deference to government action. The government action at issue, however, was a judicial injunction. Thus the Supreme Court judges were deferring only to one of their own, and they did so in the name of the idea that Charter rights would be entirely illusory without judicial enforcement. What they were deferring to, in effect, was the principle and practice of judicial intervention. This might be said to be judicial restraint in the service of judicial activism.

The idea that the Charter would be illusory without its judicial guardians is obviously entailed in the high opinion of the judiciary as the only true oracle of the constitution. In this view the judiciary is the institutional embodiment of the constitution; judicial pronouncements *are* the constitution—or, to use a well-known formula, "the constitution is what the judges say it is."[72] As Edward S. Corwin once put it: "The juristic conception of judicial review [what we are calling the oracular view] invokes a miracle. It supposes a kind of transubstantiation whereby the Court's opinion of its Constitution ... becomes the very body and blood of the Constitution."[73] But if the judiciary is truly the "body and blood" of the constitutional deity, it follows that it must control the political branches of government. The syllogism leading to this conclusion is quite simple: government is subject to the constitution; in practical terms the courts *are* the constitution; ergo government is subject to the courts. The reverse is also true: government must not be permitted to control the courts, for given the identity between courts and the constitution, this would place government above the constitution. The constitution/court must rule government, not the other way around. It also follows that the judiciary cannot be considered a branch of government, for this would be to concede that judicial review involves little more than one branch of government exercising *political* power over the others. Indeed, it would entail the *political* supervision of the elected branches by the most undemocratic branch of government. Thus Justice McIntyre declares in *Dolphin Delivery* (1986) that while it "is probably acceptable" for political scientists "to treat the courts as one of the three fundamental branches of Government," they do not come within the legal definition of "government" in section 32 of the Charter, which "applies" the Charter to Canadian legislatures and "governments."[74] The courts that apply the Charter, in other words, are not subject to the Charter in the same sense as the political branches of government. How could they be, since the courts and the Charter are one?[75]

From the perspective of the Charter sceptic all of this is merely the mystical way in which judges enhance their own discretionary power at the expense of the discretion of other officials. *B.C. Motor Vehicles,*[76] for example, enhanced the discretionary power of judges at the expense of prosecutors. The law at issue made driving without a licence an "absolute liability" offence. This meant that one could be convicted and punished (in this case, even jailed) for the offence even if one was unaware that one's licence had been suspended. The Supreme Court found that this violation of "liberty" infringed the principles of "fundamental justice" enshrined in section 7 of the Charter. Punishment involving a potential jail sentence, it argued, could not meet the standards of fundamental justice unless the offender exhibited *mens rea* (a "guilty mind").

In the abstract, it is difficult to quarrel with this decision. Who would advocate jailing someone who was completely unaware that he or she was driving with a suspended licence? But, as Michael Mandel observes:

> The number of cases where people without valid licenses have no reason to suspect that their licenses are suspended, or some other good excuse for driving while it is suspended, must be few indeed. The decision itself was on a reference and did not actually involve any such real person. Whether the rare genuine case will be worth all the phony ones lawyers will now be hired to argue in court is dubious.[77]

For Mandel, the *B.C. Motor Vehicles Reference* represents the excesses of every-last-case reasoning. More to the present point, Mandel insists that where there are legitimate excuses, police and prosecutors generally exercise their discretion not to pursue the case. "However tough the laws appear in themselves, they are invariably softened in application on grounds which do not seem to differ much from the judicial ones."[78] The main consequence of the case is to shift this discretionary power from prosecutorial officials to judges. It "merely means judges have the final say. They can overrule police or prosecutorial unwillingness to accept a defence."[79]

Mandel sees the same tendency at work in *R. v. Vaillancourt*.[80] This case challenged a provision in the Criminal Code that defined even an accidental killing as "murder" if death was caused during the commission of certain other specified offences, such as robbery, when the accused was carrying a lethal weapon. The main effect of this provision was to bring the accused within the more severe penalty structure applying to murder. Since the abolition of the death penalty, this meant that someone in possession of a weapon who accidentally caused death during the commission of a specified offence might be subject to longer imprisonment. The Court struck this provision down because the majority thought it violated "fundamental justice" to label as a murderer someone who did not exhibit the degree of *mens rea* normally required for that offence. The Court did not question the policy of more severe punishments for robbers who cause death, however accidentally, during the commission of their crime; it merely objected to achieving this policy by bringing the offender within the definition of murder. As Justice McIntyre put it in his dissent:

> The principal complaint in this case is not that the accused should not have been convicted of a serious crime deserving of severe punishment, but simply that Parliament should not have chosen to call that crime murder.[81]

Vaillancourt was guilty, and should be punished severely—perhaps just as severely as if he had been convicted of murder—but this punishment must be imposed for the crime of manslaughter.

In one sense, one is inclined to agree with McIntyre, and see the difference as a rather silly dispute about the proper label for the crime. After all, if the same punishment results, what difference does the label make? But in fact the label does make an important difference, not so much for the culprit and his punishment as for the judges who impose it. As Mandel puts it:

> The main difference between murder and manslaughter is judicial discretion. The practical effect of this decision is again to loosen one of the few formal constraints on judges. Where a murder conviction binds the judge to an automatic life sentence, with release only under authority of the parole board, in manslaughter and almost all other cases, the Court is free to do what it wants. The net effect of the decision then is to increase (however slightly) the realm of judicial decision making at the expense of Parliament and prosecutorial authorities.[82]

The invalidation in *Smith* of the mandatory minimum sentence for importing drugs increased judicial discretion in the same way. Here, too, the legislature had placed limits on the sentencing discretion of judges, only to find its own discretion limited by the judges instead. On the other hand, where legislation enhances judicial discretion by allowing judges to exceed normal *maximum* penalties, the Court has found no violations of fundamental justice. Thus in *Lyons*[83] it upheld legislation allowing judges to impose "indeterminate" detention on a "dangerous offender," regardless of the penalties provided for the offence actually committed.[84]

For Mandel, these cases show how exalted is the place of the judiciary in its own eyes:

> [These] cases ensure that the final determination of important questions of criminal liability and punishment are gathered into the hands of the judiciary and not transferred to bureaucratic administration. Everything must pass through the exalted and sanctified forum of the courtroom for judicial approval unfettered by externally imposed constraints.[85]

"Exalted and sanctified"—exactly the right words to describe an "oracle." It is not surprising that an institution with an oracular self-image would come to see itself as the only effective guarantor of Charter rights.

For Charter sceptics, of course, the idea that Charter rights would be illusory without the power of judicial review is sheer hubris. Such sceptics often point out that Canada's record on human rights prior to the Charter, or the records of such countries as Britain, Australia, and New Zealand, was (or is) reasonably good, or at least no worse than the record of the United States, and markedly better than some regimes with constitutionally entrenched rights. Sceptics buttress this point with the kinds of arguments outlined in the previous chapter, particularly the claim that judicial decisions under the Charter do not so much protect agreed-upon rights as transfer power to decide issues of reasonable disagreement from the political branches of government to the courts.

■ INTERVENERS AND INTEREST GROUPS

The oracular courtroom is open to litigants who have little more stake in the outcome of their case than concerned citizens generally; it decides moot cases when it considers the issues posed by them to be sufficiently important; and its pronouncements are considered binding not just on the litigants, but on the polity as a whole. All of these departures from the adjudicative perspective stem from the view that the judiciary's primary function is to elucidate and resolve our most fundamental values as a people, not the more humble task of settling concrete disputes. It follows that the courtroom should be accessible not only to public interest litigants, but also to public interest interveners. After all, our judicial oracles do not work unaided. Although they have been substantially liberated from the restrictions of the adjudicative model, they continue to work within some of its more important forms. In particular, judges depend on the adversaries before them to help clarify the nature and significance of the interpretive alternatives. But the parties are understandably concerned primarily with their immediate interests, and are unlikely to address the concerns of the wider range of interests having a stake in the outcome. They cannot be expected to explore and assess the full range of interpretive alternatives. When judicial pronouncements were considered binding mainly on the litigants or on lower courts deciding similar cases, this limitation was not a major drawback. As judicial decisions came to be seen as establishing generally binding constitutional policy, on the other hand, the limited perspective of the litigants came to be seen as far too narrow. If many interests other than the immediate parties are likely to be affected by the consequences of the judicial decision, surely arguments flowing from these interests should be heard and considered by the judges. As Swan puts it, if the central judicial task is "the elucidation and resolution" of our most fundamental values, "one would have thought that our judges would have welcomed all the help they could get."[86] The most logical way of getting such help is to grant access to additional parties, or interveners. In fact, during its early experience with the Charter, the Supreme Court was so overwhelmed by its new responsibilities that it tried to lighten its load by severely restricting access to interveners, who complained vociferously.[87] More recently, however, it has followed through on the oracular implications of its very liberal policy on standing by adopting a similarly liberal approach to intervention. Thus, while the Court allowed interventions in only one case in 1982, since 1987 "interventions have been allowed in about a dozen cases a year by as many as 30 groups."[88]

Intervening in cases brought by others is one of the main avenues through which interest groups can use the courtroom to pursue their policy agendas. Litigation groups such as LEAF also fund and provide legal assistance to litigants whose positions they favour. This strategy is not entirely satisfactory, however. Inevitably cases will be brought by litigants inviting the courts to adopt legal interpretations opposed, or tangential, to the interest group's concerns. Where the interests and arguments of the litigants do not coincide with those of the interest group,[89] intervener status provides the latter with the only realistic way of placing its arguments before the court. Such interest-group involvement in the judicial process is, of course, elicited by the oracular view of the judiciary's function, and indeed, interest groups who hope to gain from courtroom politics have a stake in promoting the oracular view. There would be little point in using court cases as vehicles for policy reform if the constitutional reasons given to support the court's decision were not seen as generally binding outside the context of the particular case.

■ CONCLUSION

Judges adjudicate concrete disputes and interpret law. Both tasks are integral to the judicial function—indeed, they are inextricably bound up with each other—and neither can be avoided. The proper relationship between these two aspects of the judicial function is contentious, however. According to one view, the primary function of courts, the function that distinguishes them from the other branches of government, is to settle concrete disputes. In performing this function courts cannot avoid choosing between alternative readings of the laws implicated in their cases. In other words, courts cannot avoid sharing in the political function of lawmaking. In this view, however, the judicial lawmaking power is carefully circumscribed by its adjudicative context. Judges must make law only to resolve the factual dispute between the actual litigants. The law they make, moreover, has final authority only for those litigants. Outside the context of the case, the judicial reading of law has persuasive power only; it is not the final and authoritative reading for all purposes and in all contexts. The law is what the judges say it is for the litigants, but not necessarily for everyone else. The other branches of government have an equal authority to determine the meaning of the law for their own purposes. Legal interpretation, in short, is the shared responsibility of all branches of government—with each branch having the final word in certain situations and for certain purposes—not the defining characteristic of only one branch. In this view the separation of powers is violated not by judicial lawmaking, which is unavoidable, but by judicial lawmaking outside the adjudicative context.

This traditional view of the proper judicial role has been largely displaced by one in which judges are the final and authoritative expositors of legal meaning for all circumstances and in all contexts. This means that all legal issues must be able to find their way to court whether or not they can come there in the form of a concrete dispute, and that the legal meanings chosen by judges to decide a case become binding law for the entire country, not just the litigants. In particular, judicial opinions are binding on the other branches of government in their own areas of responsibility. This obviously enhances the political power of judges, especially by extending the scope and significance of the symbolic and legal resources provided by their decisions. It also raises problems of democratic legitimacy not inherent in the adjudicative view of the judicial role. No one will challenge the legitimacy of appointed and politically independent judges settling concrete disputes, and the lawmaking incident to that function is likely to be accepted as long as it is seen as the unavoidable corollary of the primary adjudicative function, and is closely circumscribed by the adjudicative context. When the relationship between the two judicial functions is reversed, however, with the concrete case becoming a mere pretext for the authoritative declaration of what the law requires in circumstances extending well beyond the confines of the case, the problem of democratic legitimacy looms much larger.

Defenders of the expanded judicial role often respond to this problem of legitimacy by insisting that, far from making law, judges simply apply it, especially by rationally discovering the logical implications of agreed-upon legal principles in situations where more politically sensitive institutions are likely to be distracted by interest and passion. As we have seen, however, this defence is highly contentious, and satisfies few sceptics. The latter believe that judicial review, especially when liberated from the adjudicative context, is irretrievably political, and that all attempts to insist upon its legal *bona fides* are little more than rhetorical evasions. They often conclude, at least in part on separation-of-powers grounds, that modern judicial review is illegitimate, that it involves judges leaving their proper realm and trespassing on political ground belonging to the other branches of government.

But the separation of powers is only one side of liberal democratic institutional theory; the other is expressed in the phrase "checks and balances." Can one concede that modern judicial review is inescapably political, that it infringes the separation of powers, and nevertheless defend its legitimacy as part of a healthy system of checks and balances? We turn to this question in Chapter Eight.

CHAPTER EIGHT

Checks and Balances

The debate about the legitimacy of judicial review turns not only on sep-aration-of-powers theory, but also on the related concept of checks and balances. The idea of "checks and balances" depends on, but is not iden-tical with, the "separation of powers." It depends on it to the extent that the separate institutions are intended to check each other; it departs from it because enabling them effectively to check each other often involves giv-ing the different institutions a share in each other's powers, thus infringing the strict model of separation. The convention of responsible government can be understood in this way: by mixing executive and legislative power it gives each branch a measure of influence over the other. The cabinet is disciplined by the necessity of maintaining majority support, but its parti-san supporters are similarly disciplined by the prospect of facing the elec-torate sooner than necessary (and in the electorally unattractive context of party disunity) should they withdraw their support. In the United States the most common examples of checks and balances are the presidential veto, which gives the political executive a prominent legislative role, and the senatorial confirmation of treaties and major presidential appointments, which gives the legislative branch a share of executive power. Further-more, the system of checks and balances is not exhausted by relations between the branches, as shown by the common practice, known as "bicameralism," of dividing legislatures into two houses or chambers.

An important purpose of "checks and balances" is to promote rela-tively deliberate, balanced, and moderate policy outcomes by ensuring that different institutional perspectives are effectively brought to bear on public affairs. One justification of judicially enforced rights is that they remedy the absence of effective checks and balances within and among the other branches of government. In parliamentary systems the argument concerns the ability of Parliament to check either the executive or willful majorities; since Parliament is (or has become) inadequate to the task, it is suggested, the courts must be brought in to fill the gap.

Grounding an argument in favour of a constitutional bill of rights on the principle of checks and balances does not depend on characterizing rights as legal entities. Because checks and balances operate as much by mixing as by separating the conceptually distinct governmental functions, the transfer of *political* power to a *legal* institution can be understood to serve a function similar to the mixing of legislative and executive powers in the presidential veto of American constitutionalism. Indeed, the similarities between judicial review and the presidential veto are revealing. Both are vetoes rather than powers to legislate directly, but they necessarily entail the power of positive suggestion. Of course, courts do not engage in the equivalent of the throne speech or the American "state of the union" address. Unlike the executive branch, in other words, they do not encroach on the legislative realm to the extent of mounting an explicit and comprehensive legislative program. But neither can their "nays" be adequately understood in purely negative terms. In striking down a policy, they are often telling the political branches to pursue perfectly legitimate ends in other and "better" ways. For example, in *Morgentaler* the Canadian Supreme Court found that the government could legitimately balance the interests of the fetus against the freedom of women to control their own bodies, but struck down the existing attempt to balance these concerns because the law was inequitably administered.[1] The government remained free to prohibit nontherapeutic abortions, but it had to find a better administrative formula.

The positive suggestions contained in judicial vetoes amount to a legislative program of sorts. Furthermore, while a judicial veto can often be circumvented, or even overridden,[2] this may be no easier and perhaps more difficult than the American Congress overriding a presidential veto. It thus behooves the other branches to heed the positive program inherent in the veto.

■ JUDICIAL VS. POLITICAL CHECKS

Opposition to a bill of rights can be based on the perceived adequacy of the system of checks and balances within the political branches. This argument was made by some of the American founders during the constitutional ratification debates. For example, Thomas McKean, a Federalist supporter of the constitution from Pennsylvania, argued that a bill of rights "is an unnecessary instrument, for in fact the whole plan of government is nothing more than a bill of rights."[3] He had in mind such things as representative government (referred to in the *Federalist Papers* as part of the "new science of politics"), limited grants of power to the central government, and the system of checks and balances.

Similarly, opponents of constitutionally entrenched rights in parliamentary systems frequently claim that rights are best protected by the system of responsible government, not by the courts. For example, the Australian jurist Sir Owen Dixon once told an American audience that his country's founders had "conscientiously studied" the American Bill of Rights, but that "the study fired no one with enthusiasm for the principle." He added that Australians remained "impenitent" in their "steadfast faith in responsible government and in plenary legislative powers distributed, but not controlled."[4] Elaborating on this statement, former Australian prime minister Menzies wrote:

> With us, a Minister is not just a nominee of the head of the Government. He is and must be a Member of Parliament, elected as such, and answerable to Members of Parliament at every sitting. He is appointed by a Prime Minister similarly elected and open to regular question. Should a Minister do something which is thought to violate fundamental human freedom he can be promptly brought to account in Parliament. If his Government supports him, the Government may be attacked, and if necessary defeated. And if that, as it normally would, leads to a new General Election, the people will express their judgment at the polling booths.
>
> In short, responsible government in a democracy is regarded by us as the ultimate guarantee of justice and individual rights.[5]

For Dixon and Menzies, the checks and balances of responsible parliamentary government provided sufficient protection for rights, and there was thus no reason to abandon the British tradition of parliamentary supremacy in favour of the American system of judicial supremacy.

Bill of rights enthusiasts in parliamentary systems reject this defence of responsible government as outmoded and naive. In their view, the checks and balances of parliamentary government are much overrated. They argue that if these checks and balances ever existed, they have been completely undermined by the modern reality of disciplined parties. We know, for example, that while Robert Menzies correctly articulates the theory of responsible government—that ministers can be called to account and controlled by their caucus—the reality is quite different. The caucus often fears the electoral consequences of party disunity more than ministers fear the loss of caucus support, thus giving the executive effective control. Bringing the executive within the legislature and making it depend on the support of a majority of legislators was historically intended to solve the problem of executive tyranny. Ironically, it is argued, the lines of control have been reversed: in the context of modern democratic politics, interdependence led to disciplined parties through which the executive could turn the tables and control the house.

Nor do bill of rights enthusiasts think more effective control of the executive would solve the problem. Along with executive tyranny, after all, we need to worry about the tyranny of the majority. It is sometimes suggested that the tradition of parliamentary constitutionalism, as opposed to its American offshoot, paid too much attention to the problem of executive tyranny and not enough to that of majority tyranny. Commenting on the difference between Americans and the English, for example, Lord Bryce remarked on the "curious ... way in which usage and tradition mould a nation's mind."

> Parliament was for so long a time the protector of Englishmen against an arbitrary executive that they did not form the habit of taking precautions against the abuse of the powers of the Legislature; and their struggles for fuller freedom took the form of making Parliament a more popular and representative body, not that of restricting its authority.[6]

Even if the house controlled the executive, in other words, that would only solve the problem of executive tyranny by increasing the scope for majority tyranny.

Many of the early theorists of liberal democracy hoped to counteract the danger of tyrannical majorities through the device of representation. Representation was seen not simply as a way of broadening the scope of democracy, but also as a way of moderating it. For such theorists, representation was supposed to filter, elevate, and moderate public opinion, rather than simply mirroring it in its unrefined and often passionate state. Representation was a way of protecting the people from themselves as well as from the executive. Indeed, as discerning an observer as John Stuart Mill noted in the 19th century that it would be the executive, not the legislature, that would occupy public attention and become the institutional vehicle of majoritarian democracy. It is to the executive, he argued, that the people's "hopes and fears ... are directed, and by it ... the benefits, and the terrors and prestige of government, are mainly represented to the public eye." The executive "wields the immediate power and is in direct contact with the public."[7] In checking the executive, then, Parliament also checks democracy.

However, we have seen that modern party discipline makes it difficult for representatives at large to control the executive, and this is true whether the latter is understood as a vehicle for minority or majority tyranny. The image of Parliament as a truly deliberative institution, bringing together the representatives of diverse constituencies and interests in a moderating debate that would issue in decent policy is said to founder on the same rock. The same party discipline that permits executive dominance, it is alleged, also stifles the genuine deliberation through which popular views might be elevated and moderated. The increasingly plebiscitary style of modern democratic politics, moreover, lends weight to Mill's contention that the chief political executive is often the direct bearer of public opinion, rather than its natural opponent. Thus the dangers of executive power and majority tyranny are brought together in a new and fearsome alliance, for which Parliament is a tool rather than a check. From this perspective it follows that effective checks on power must be sought elsewhere—particularly in a judicially enforceable bill of rights.

But is the plight of checks and balances in parliamentary systems really as bad as this account suggests? We have not yet investigated the contribution of bicameralism to the system of parliamentary checks and balances. Might an effective upper house support a claim, much like the one made by Dixon and Menzies, that Parliament enjoys sufficient checks and balances, so that the addition of constitutionally based judicial checks remains unnecessary?

This is not an abstract question. It formed an important theme in the 1988 Australian debate about whether to expand the constitutional protection of rights. In this debate, the defence of parliamentary supremacy against judicial supremacy focused on the Senate and, not surprisingly, was institutionally located *in* the Senate. Opposition senators conceded that checks and balances were lacking in the lower house, but insisted that this criticism did not apply to Parliament as a whole because it did not apply to the Senate. The Senate, they argued, is not only independent and powerful, but also a genuinely *parliamentary* (which is to say representative and deliberative) institution, much better suited to the task of protecting rights than the courts. For example, when opposition Senator Chaney doubted that the High Court's consideration of issues raised by constitutionally entrenched rights "is superior to that of democratic politicians," he had in mind mainly democratic politicians in the Senate. It was in the Senate that true parliamentary deliberation could take place. "To the extent that there is a genuine legislative element in this Parliament," he said, "it is in this place. It is in this place because there are some degrees of insulation from the power of executive government."[8]

Other senators similarly linked their opposition to a bill of rights (and hence their support for continued parliamentary supremacy) to the Senate. Thus Senator Harradine approvingly quoted Sir Stanley Burbury, former Chief Justice of Tasmania:

> I would prefer the democratic control of legislation through the political sanction of the ballot box *and a strong second Chamber of Parliament* to handing over a substantial measure of control of legislation to a judicial tribunal of a few men—eminent in their profession though they may be. Judges are but men and are as subject to subtle corruption by the exercise of great power as other men.[9]

Even more explicitly, Senator Sheil remarked that "the Senate is the watchdog for the people and the States to see that they are not robbed of any of their rights or freedoms. It is the people's insurance or safety valve. It is the House of review for all legislation."[10]

Interestingly, although there was much debate about the reason for the Senate's character, there was significant bipartisan agreement that it did indeed have a special character. Senator Tate, for example, the Labor justice minister responsible for leading bill of rights supporters in the upper house, agreed that the Senate "does have a deliberative aspect to it which does not immediately characterize the House of Representatives."[11]

One reason for the perception of the Senate as a more deliberative legislative institution was expressed in Senator Chaney's remark that it had come to enjoy a degree "of insulation from the power of executive government." In other words, the executive, which was institutionally located in the lower house, could not enforce complete party discipline on senators. For reasons too complicated to explore here, it had become virtually impossible by the late 1970s for either of the two major parties to achieve majority dominance of the Senate. Since the disciplined coherence of these parties could no longer control the outcome of Senate debates, the status of party discipline in that chamber declined somewhat. It would be wrong to suggest that discipline broke down altogether in the Senate—indeed, it remained very powerful—but senators no longer experienced to quite the same extent the iron grip in which party discipline held members of the lower house.

Although the proposed extensions of constitutionally protected rights at stake in this Australian debate were relatively modest by the standards of the Canadian Charter or the American Bill of Rights, they were soundly defeated in amendment referenda held in 1988. There is no way of knowing what role the Senate argument played in this defeat. The point here is simply to note that some of the leading players in the debate saw it at least in part as a trade-off between two kinds of checks and balances. These players opposed constitutional rights because they preferred senatorial to judicial checks.

In Canada such a debate is scarcely possible. Although our appointed Senate is theoretically the virtual equal of the House of Commons, and although it occasionally uses its great powers in dramatic public fashion, almost everyone agrees that it lacks democratic legitimacy. For this reason, the Senate usually plays a rather insignificant role in Canada's political life. The Senate may be useful in cleaning up the legislative drafting that emerges from the House of Commons, but it does not often occupy a visible and substantial place in an overtly political system of checks and balances, as do the American and Australian upper houses. Whenever the Canadian Senate does take a more prominent political position, the legitimacy of doing so is always very much in question. It is interesting to speculate, however, on what might happen should the always-lurking possibility of Senate reform end in an elected Senate with significant power. If a reformed Canadian Senate was less subject to the strict party discipline obtaining in the House of Commons, could we expect a Canadian version of the Australian debate about the relative merits of bicameral and judicial checks?

Such a debate could also emerge from reform of the House of Commons and the unicameral provincial legislatures. A more effective bicameralism is not, after all, the only way to reinvigorate the system of checks and balances within the Canadian legislative arena. Roger Gibbins has argued that, whatever its intrinsic merits or defects, a reformed Senate of the Triple E (equal, elected, and effective) variety is highly unlikely in the foreseeable future, and that Canadians would be well advised to consider reforming the House of Commons instead. Gibbins has in mind reforms that would decrease executive dominance and thereby weaken party discipline. He envisages more autonomous and "more generously resourced" legislators operating "a more open and influential committee system." In other words, Gibbins wants to restore the kind of balance between the executive and the legislative branches in the House of Commons that predated disciplined parties and that still informs our official mythologies.[12] This balance might be enhanced by weakening the cabinet's authority to treat defeat of its legislative proposals as "nonconfidence" motions requiring the resignation of the government and usually precipitating new elections. A constitutional amendment setting election dates at specified intervals would do the trick. So would the development of new conventions making it difficult for governments to regard most legislative defeats as expressing nonconfidence. Of course, reforms along these lines would "Americanize" our political structures by more clearly separating the executive and legislative branches, and might be opposed by Canadians on that account. But as Gibbins points out, Canada has already embraced an American-style "presidential" politics. Both electorally and in political decision-making we have increasingly emphasized the predominant role of first ministers. Adopting the presidential side of the American political experience without also embracing some version of its countervailing legislative checks, Gibbins thinks, might prove to be unwise:

> [W]e are moving towards a presidential system without at the same time reaping one of the principal advantages of a presidential system, and that is the existence of a relatively autonomous and robust legislative process. Whereas in the United States a presidential system coexists with a vital legislative branch, in Canada the presidentialization of politics has had the effect of strangling rather than strengthening the legislative process.[13]

We have suggested that the "strangled" system of checks and balances between Canadian executives and legislatures has strengthened the claim for judicial checks. In Christopher Manfredi's words, the argument in favour of judicially enforceable constitutional rights is bolstered in Canada by the fact that our "legislative process lacks the formal and informal institutional checks on the majority's will found in the United States,"[14] or, we might add, in Australia. Does it follow that effective reform of either or both legislative chambers would weaken support for judicial checks? Perhaps, though it is unlikely that an improved system of legislative checks and balances in Canada would revive the kind of outright opposition to entrenched constitutional rights that a powerful Senate helped to sustain in Australia. The Charter is too well embedded in at least the English-Canadian psyche for that. In Canada an effective system of legislative checks and balances would more likely be used to encourage judicial restraint than to fuel a movement to repeal the Charter altogether. Alternatively, the increased public legitimacy of legislative institutions might sustain a more active use of section 33 of the Charter to check judicial activism. It might, in short, support the notion that it is just as legitimate for legislatures to check courts as it is for courts to check legislatures. We shall return to this point below.

The presence of effective alternatives to judicial power in the system of checks and balances may affect debates about the desirability of constitutional rights or about the relative merits of judicial activism and restraint, but it need not determine the outcome of such debates. In Australia, for example, Senator Tate's agreement about the importance and power of the Senate did not lead him to abandon support for constitutionally entrenched rights. This shows that although the case for the Senate as a truly parliamentary institution helps to establish an effective argument against a bill of rights, it is not sufficient. One might well support both. For example, although the American founders argued that a bill of rights was not really necessary, they did not strenuously oppose it either. Thomas Keane was quoted earlier as representing the view of many of the American founders that it was "unnecessary" to add a bill of rights to a constitution that was itself a bill of rights. However, he also said that such an addition "can do no harm."[15] After all, if checks and balances are a good thing, one might wish to improve a reasonably good system by providing increased scope for judicial review. The desirability of a constitutional bill of rights, then, depends not just on the presence or absence of an otherwise adequate system of checks and balances, but also on whether increased judicial power will improve the system or at least "do no harm."

■ SOBER SECOND THOUGHT?

Judicial review of constitutionally entrenched rights can be understood to improve the system of checks and balances by providing the opportunity for "sober second thought." It is often pointed out that judges exercising judicial review can defy the popular will only temporarily. In both Canada and the United States, for example, activist courts resisted the regulatory and social welfare legislation developed to deal with the Great Depression. This judicial obstruction of the emerging welfare state was eventually overcome, however, and has not been repeated. More recently there was a similar confrontation between the legislative and judicial branches in France after the election of the socialist government of François Mitterrand.

Initially, the French Constitutional Council struck down almost half of the collectivist, interventionist reforms of the new government, but within a few years most of the impugned legislation had been successfully re-enacted in somewhat modified form.[16] As Robert Dahl observed in the American context, "the fact is that the policy views dominant on the Court are never long out of line with the policy views dominant among the law-making majorities of the United States. Consequently it would be most unrealistic to suppose that the Court would, for more than a few years at most, stand against any major alternatives sought by a lawmaking major-ity."[17] Thus judicial review can at best exercise a delaying influence on the development of new policy. But delaying democratic majorities without ultimately stopping them can be seen as part of a healthy system of checks and balances. By providing time for sober second thought, delay ensures that only "the cool and deliberate sense of the community"[18] will prevail in the policy arena and that the temporary delusions and passions that generate oppressive policies will have time to dissipate. In this sense judi-cial review of constitutionally entrenched rights can be seen as a positive addition to the system of checks and balances.

Critics will respond that such a defence of judicial review does not take into account the modern reality of positive judicial activism. As we have seen, judicial review is no longer simply a matter of invalidating and hence delaying (however temporarily) the policies of the other branches of government. Increasingly judges are telling other policy-makers not only what they may not do, but also what they must do. Still, the bulk of judicial activism, especially in Canada, remains of the negative variety pre-supposed by the "sober-second-thought" defence. It is thus worth explor-ing this defence in its own terms.

Attractive as the delaying argument is, it makes practical sense only if the political system places few other brakes on popular will. If there are already plenty of other opportunities for "sober second thought," adding yet another one might do more harm than good. By delaying policy already moderated by an otherwise healthy system of checks and bal-ances, in other words, the courts will more often than not delay beneficial rather than oppressive legislation. In the United States, for example, it is difficult to argue that nonjudicial checks and balances are in short supply. It follows, as John Agresto has argued, that

> merely on the basis of statistical probability, an institution that voided legislation that had survived the rigors of the internal legis-lative scheme that the Founders developed would rarely be voiding

"tyrannical" legislation. All too often what the Court would nullify would be the concerted opinion of the democracy filtered through various chambers and modes of election and refined by time and compromise. Such legislation may well be so compromised as to fall short of being *effective,* but it will only rarely be oppressive or despotic. The odds are, in other words, against an easy equation of an active court with liberty or social justice. At the level of national legislation, a Court whose primary mission is to check legislation will only on the rarest occasions be checking illiberal or oppressive enactments. It is more likely to find itself hindering compromised, benign, fair, and often long-overdue legislation.[19]

It is true, of course, that the U.S. Supreme Court played a leading role in dismantling racial segregation, but only after it had first given segregation its blessing for over sixty years. And for every progressive case there are several illiberal ones. In Agresto's words, a list of the Supreme Court's civil liberties cases "would be heavily weighted not with cases in which the Court deferred to the illiberality of the more political branches but with cases in which the Court, invoking the name of either the Constitution or of liberty, itself voided liberating and progressive as well as necessary legislation."[20] A particularly dramatic example is the repeated attempts by Congress to restrict the use of child labour after 1916. Twice the Court struck down the legislation, relenting only in 1941. The Court had ensured twenty-five years of "sober second thought," but this can hardly be seen as a victory of human rights over oppressive democratic majorities. Contrary to Dahl, moreover, there is little consolation in the fact that the Court finally gave in:

> [I]f the Court always does fall in line with the popular will after holding up legislation for a time (twenty-five years, for example, in the case of all child labor laws), the power of judicial review hardly seems worth the bother. If the argument contained in such scholarship is to be believed, the Court's function seems to be to take national legislation (which is itself often too little too late), prevent its effectuation for some time, and then relent.[21]

Might the delaying function of judicial review make more sense in a system with fewer other checks and balances, such as Canada's parliamentary system? Is Paul Weiler right in thinking that "the case for external judicial review of the political process is stronger in the context of a parliamentary government"?[22] Perhaps, though one must wonder whether our political structure is really so deficient in this respect. After all, although Canada's pre-Charter record on issues of rights and liberties is far from spotless, it is on the whole no worse (and in some respects better) than that of the United States with its more elaborate system of checks and balances, including its long history of judicial review of constitutionally entrenched rights.

Moreover, even if our system needs additional delaying mechanisms, this would not in itself make the case for activist *judicial* review. As suggested above, we might wish to explore more adequate checks and balances in the legislative arena instead. Whether judicial review is either a desirable alternative to legislative checks and balances or a useful addition to them depends in part on an evaluation of the policy-making capacity of courts.

■ INSTITUTIONAL CAPACITY

Whether judicial policy-making is beneficial or at least "will do no harm" turns on whether courts have the institutional capacity effectively to carry out a significant policy-making role. The modern oracular court sets policy on a grand scale, but it still does so in the context of an institution designed to adjudicate particular cases. Adjudicative norms may have been weakened, but many essentials of the adjudicative context remain in place. Accordingly, sceptics argue that institutional mechanisms designed for the adjudication of individual disputes are ill-equipped to make general policy for the "run of cases."

One difficulty stems from the judicial system's greater ability to elicit the "historical" or "adjudicative facts" involving the particular situations of the litigants than the "legislative" or "social facts" required for wise policy-making. Donald Horowitz defines "historical" facts as "the events that have transpired between the parties to a lawsuit."[23] These facts answer the questions of who did (or said) what to whom under what circumstances. Did the accused really pull the gun out of malevolence toward the victim, for example, or was he acting in self-defence? The adjudicative process was designed to determine the answers to such questions, which are essential to settling the concrete dispute between the litigants. A process designed to elicit historical facts, however, turns out to be rather ill-suited to acquiring social or legislative facts, which Horowitz defines as "the recurrent patterns of behavior on which policy must be based."[24] Unlike an adjudicator, in other words, policy-makers are concerned less with what happened in a particular set of circumstances than with what is likely to happen in most circumstances.

The relative inability of the judicial process to elicit social facts is illustrated by the adoption of a strict "exclusionary rule" by the U.S. Supreme Court. We saw in Chapter Three that the U.S. Supreme Court created the exclusionary remedy in part to deter police misbehaviour. This assumes, however, that police are more interested in conviction (a "reward" exclusion deprives them of) than in harassing and generally making life difficult for criminals. The latter can often be achieved most effectively by officers who have little regard for procedural niceties. In the absence of a concern with conviction, the extra-legal behaviour of such officers will be unaffected by an exclusionary rule.[25] The Court fashioned the exclusionary rule in a single case, without any way of ascertaining whether its behavioural assumption was correct.

But why should this matter? Surely some police officers will be interested in conviction and will be deterred by exclusion. Why should this additional weapon be eschewed? Here another weakness of the courts' focus on individual cases comes into play. Because they take cases one at a time, courts also tend to take the issues raised in discrete isolation.[26] Thus the question whether to exclude evidence flowing from the violation of a right is likely to be treated separately from the question of what qualifies as a relevant violation of a right. If, in answer to the latter question, the courts interpret even the mildest police pressure as violating a constitutional right and thus as requiring exclusion, as the U.S. Supreme Court did,[27] the exclusionary rule may ironically contribute to the decline of interest in conviction on the part of the police, thereby undermining a major justification for exclusion.[28] The left hand often doesn't know what the right hand is doing. No doubt, this is a problem for all policy-making institutions; it is exacerbated in the judicial arena, however, by the focus on individual cases.

Another kind of social-fact difficulty is raised by the Canadian approach to the exclusion of evidence under section 24(2) of the Charter. The Canadian Supreme Court has emphasized the role of section 24(2) in maintaining the good reputation of the judicial system rather than deterring police misbehaviour. But deciding what will bring the administration of justice into disrepute is surely a social-fact question involving some assessment of likely public reaction. Instead of relying on polls our judges have adopted the strategy of giving voice to the deliberate conclusions of a hypothetical "reasonable person." But it turns out that reasonable people, and their judicial surrogates, can disagree intensely about such matters.

R. v. *Therens* provides a case in point.[29] Nine days after the Charter came into effect in 1982, Paul Mathew Therens ran his car off the street and into a tree in Moose Jaw, Saskatchewan. Suspecting that Therens was drunk, Constable Measner, the attending officer, took him to the police station for a breathalyzer test. The test confirmed that Therens had been driving with more than the legal limit of alcohol in his blood. Therens was obviously guilty of a criminal offence, and would have been convicted but for the fact that the officer failed to inform him of his right to counsel as required by section 10(b) of the Charter. When Therens's case reached the Supreme Court, the judges agreed that the breathalyzer evidence had been obtained in violation of his right to counsel, but disagreed about whether the evidence should be excluded under section 24(2). The majority saw the officer's failure to observe the requirements of section 10(b) as a "flagrant" violation, which would "clearly 'bring the administration of justice into disrepute.'"[30] Two dissenting judges, Le Dain and McIntyre, came to the opposite conclusion. For Le Dain, the circumstances of the case did not warrant exclusion because the officer had acted in good faith with no way of knowing that he was violating a Charter right. Several years earlier, in *Chromiak* v. *The Queen,*[31] the Supreme Court had interpreted section 2(c) of the Diefenbaker Bill of Rights, which, like section 10(b) of the Charter, provided a right to counsel upon "arrest or detention."[32] *Chromiak* established that requiring a suspect to provide a breath sample did not constitute arrest or detention, which meant that the right to counsel did not apply in such situations. In *Therens* the Court had obviously changed its mind and overruled *Chromiak*. Henceforth demands for breathalyzer evidence would be considered a "detention." But when Constable Measner dealt with Therens on April 24, 1982, he could not have known that such a reversal was in the offing. Constable Measner had acted in good faith on established and Court-approved practice. After *Therens* police officers would know the new rules and it would be entirely appropriate to exclude breathalyzer evidence obtained in violation of the right to counsel. Given the very different circumstances obtaining in April 1982, however, Justice Le Dain concluded that the evidence should be admitted. Justice McIntyre added that the admission of constitutionally tainted evidence was not the only way of undermining the reputation of the justice system. In the circumstances of this case, he insisted, the administration of justice was more likely to be brought into disrepute by *excluding* the evidence.

Justices Le Dain and McIntyre were in the minority in this case and the police officer's good-faith behaviour did not therefore protect the cause of law enforcement against the exclusionary rule. Despite his obvious guilt, Therens had successfully relied on the Charter to evade punishment. He would not have fared as well in the United States. The Supreme Court of that country has unanimously held that roadside traffic stops do not entail the kind of coercive, police-dominated environment in which the right to counsel is essential. Thus the requirement to inform people of their right to counsel (the famous *Miranda* warning[33]) does not extend to those detained and questioned in such circumstances. Suspects taken to a police station must be given the *Miranda* warning, but only if police intend to elicit statements, not "if they intend to obtain only a breath sample."[34] In the United States, Therens's right to be informed of the right to counsel would not have been violated, and his breathalyzer evidence would not have been excluded.[35]

Although the majority of the *Therens* Court did not accept Justice Le Dain's suggestion that the good-faith action of Constable Measner should tip the balance in favour of admitting the evidence, the Canadian Supreme Court does not always accord such a hostile reception to good-faith behaviour on the part of the police. The case of *R. v. Duarte*[36] provides a revealing contrast to *Therens* in this respect. The reader will recall from Chapter Three that the majority of the Court in *Duarte* found warrantless participant surveillance to violate the section 8 prohibition of unreasonable search and seizure. Nevertheless, the evidence was admitted because "the Charter breach stemmed from an entirely reasonable misunderstanding of the law by the police officers who would otherwise have obtained the necessary evidence to convict the accused in any event." The same, of course, could have been said of *Therens:* had he known it was required, Constable Measner could easily have informed Therens of his right to counsel, and it is doubtful that Therens's exercise of that right would have prevented him from "blowing" and thus providing the required evidence. Whereas such considerations persuaded only a minority in *Therens,* they convinced the majority in *Duarte* to admit the tainted evidence. Thus Duarte languished in jail while Therens went free.

If judges stand in for "reasonable people" in determining when the administration of justice will be brought into disrepute, one can only conclude that reasonable disagreements about this question are entirely possible. The majority–minority breakdown among judges, moreover, need not reflect the corresponding breakdown in the broader community. When a group of researchers from the University of Toronto, Stanford University, and Berkeley surveyed Canadian public opinion on the exclusionary issue, using a factual example based on *Therens*,[37] they found that a substantial majority of the Canadian public supported the position favoured by the American Court and the judicial minority in *Therens*. Only among senior lawyers (an elite minority) was a majority in favour of excluding the evidence.[38] The broader public overwhelmingly supported admitting the evidence and finding the culprit guilty.[39] Unless we are prepared to consign the public majority (along with Justices Le Dain and McIntyre, and the entire U.S. Supreme Court) to the ranks of *un*reasonable people, reserving the label of "reasonable" mainly for the legal elite, we must conclude that Justice McIntyre was right in thinking that excluding the evidence was more likely to bring the administration of justice into disrepute. Judges obviously have difficulty in acquiring accurate social-fact evidence even in areas, such as the exclusion of evidence, that lie squarely within the traditional judicial domain.

The social-fact difficulties posed for judicial policy-making in areas outside their traditional domain are illustrated by *Edwards Books,* the Ontario Sunday-closing case discussed in Chapter Six. Recall Justice La Forest's contention that comparing policy alternatives to determine whether the violation of a right was a reasonable limit under section 1 of the Charter involved "second-guessing" the policy judgments of the legislature. La Forest's objection to the alleged second-guessing was based not just on the illegitimacy of violating the separation of powers, but also on the perceived incapacity of the courts to make adequate policy because of their tendency to lack adequate "social fact" information. Looking at Dickson's evaluation of alternatives from La Forest's perspective will illustrate the point.

Among others, Justice Dickson considered the alternative of providing an exemption to all non-Sunday sabbatarians, regardless of the size of their establishments. This is the kind of exemption found in the Sunday-closing legislation of New Brunswick. Said Justice Dickson:

> Such an exemption has advantages and disadvantages relative to subs. 3(4) of the Ontario Act. From the perspective of the Saturday-observing consumer the New Brunswick exemption is more beneficial than Ontario's in including within its ambit large stores with

> more than 7 employees or 5,000 square feet of floor space, but less
> beneficial in the restriction of its availability to retailers with a spec-
> ified religious or conscientious belief.[40]

Dickson was "unable to say whether one scheme results in a greater
availability of Sunday shopping services to the Jewish or Seventh Day
Adventist consumer than the other," although he noted that according to
evidence from the 1961 census the vast majority of retail outlets were small
enough to take advantage of the Ontario size limits. Even if the proportion
of large stores had doubled in the meantime, he observed, "a very substantial variety of products, including speciality products such as Kosher
foods, [would] be available to Sunday shoppers."[41] Thus Ontario's
approach was sustained because it did not compare unfavourably to that
of New Brunswick.

Perhaps so, but doesn't this approach underline La Forest's contention
that everything depends on the circumstances, which courts are rarely in a
position adequately to evaluate? Dickson's argument implies that the validity of Ontario's exemption depends on the extent to which its size limitation does not unduly prohibit Sunday shopping for kosher products. This
means that if most stores, especially kosher stores, were larger than the
limit, Ontario's exemption might become unconstitutional, and that something like New Brunswick's religiously oriented exemption would have to
be substituted for it. Yet the very nature of the evidence available in this
case—twenty-six-year-old census figures (which apparently tell one nothing about the size of kosher stores)—reveals the weakness of the courts in
making such judgments.

Dickson also preferred Ontario's religiously neutral exemption to New
Brunswick's explicitly religious exemption because the latter requires
"state-conducted inquiries into religious beliefs"—i.e., sincerity tests. Given
the legitimate purpose of a single common day of rest, any exemption
must be structured so that it doesn't overwhelm that purpose, turning a
single day into two or more days. Ontario's law does this by limiting its
exemption to small stores. Explicitly religious exemptions must do so by
requiring proof of the sincerity of religious belief, in order to prevent the
nonreligious from inventing religious excuses for violating the law if shopping on Sunday should prove more profitable than on Saturday. "The striking advantage of the Ontario Act," said Justice Dickson, "is that it makes
available an exemption to the small and mid-size retailer without the indig-
nity of having to submit to such an inquiry."[42] Justice Dickson conceded
that exemptions requiring a sincerity test will sometimes be unavoid-

able[43]—e.g., where a religiously neutral size limitation will not make enough kosher shopping available—but he argued they "should be avoided wherever reasonably possible, since they expose an individual's most personal and private beliefs to public airing and testing in a judicial or quasi-judicial setting."[44]

While Justice Dickson's views on this point are attractive, it is not as obvious as he would have us think that Ontario's religiously neutral exemption for small stores achieves his constitutional requirement of maximal accommodation for religious interests without undermining the purpose of a common day of rest. "In terms of intrusion on religion," replied Justice La Forest, "there can be no difference ... between the owner of a large or small establishment. Indeed, the owner of the larger establishment is likely to suffer a greater economic loss than the owner of the smaller one."[45] Such considerations led Justice Wilson, in dissent, to prefer the New Brunswick–style religious exemption, and thus to strike down the size limitation in the Ontario act. For La Forest, these considerations further underlined his conviction that this is not a matter for judicial resolution, that everything depends on the circumstances. It would depend, for example, on how many Saturday sabbatarians inhabited a province, and on the size of establishments operated by Saturday-observing retailers or catering to Saturday-observing consumers. If there were too many Saturday-observing retailers to ensure the "substantial and compelling" purpose of a predominantly common day of rest, a size limitation might be the answer. If, on the other hand, the stores operated by and catering to Saturday observers were generally very large, so that a neutral size limitation that would capture them would also apply to too many other establishments to guarantee a common day, a religious exemption limited by a sincerity test would be preferable, provided that those who could legitimately take advantage of it were not too numerous. Perhaps neither scheme could ensure the desired common day of rest, in which case, in La Forest's view, the legislature would be free to enact legislation with no accommodation for non-Sunday sabbatarians.

Justice La Forest would rather leave such matters to legislative judgment because legislatures have better access to the kinds of information necessary for sound policy judgment. In this case, for example, the Court obviously lacked adequate evidence about the size of the Saturday-sabbatarian religious community or about the number and size of Saturday-observing retail establishments serving that community. Nor did the Court have any way of acquiring the required evidence. Legislatures can secure social-fact evidence by holding committee hearings, commissioning studies, or appointing task forces or royal commissions. Courts, by contrast, are largely passive institutions, acting only when called upon to do so by litigants, and relying mainly on the evidence placed before them by those litigants. But private litigants may not always have either the inclination or the resources to bring all of the relevant social-fact evidence into court. Granting easy access to interveners may alleviate this problem somewhat, but if, for whatever reason, the resulting evidence turns out to be inadequate, the ability of courts actively to seek out the missing information is severely limited.

The passive nature of the courts also curtails their ability to monitor and modify the results of their policy-making endeavours. The other branches of government can more easily track the progress of a policy initiative, determining whether it is having the intended effect or is being undermined by unintended consequences. On the basis of such evaluation, these branches can make periodic policy adjustments. The ability of judges to engage in this kind of policy assessment and modification depends decisively on whether litigants bring appropriate issues and evidence before them. And even if the right cases are forthcoming, the judiciary's ability to change policy direction is hampered by its reluctance to be seen violating *stare decisis* (the rule of precedent) too often.

Another policy-making difficulty raised by judicial passivity is expressed in the old adage that "hard cases make bad law." Because courts must passively respond to whatever cases litigants choose to bring, "judicial decision becomes a chance occurrence, with no guarantee that the litigants are representative of the universe of problems their case purports to present. In fact," says Horowitz, "the guarantees are all the other way. As a matter of litigation strategy, plaintiffs' lawyers are likely to bring not the most representative case but the most extreme case of discrimination, of fraud, of violation of statute, of abuse of discretion, and so on."[46] Thus the case that invites significant judicial policy-making will more often than not be unrepresentative of the class of cases to which the policy will apply. Faced with a "hard" but unrepresentative case, the lawyer's tendency to "every-last-case reasoning"[47] (i.e., closing all foreseeable loopholes) may lead to undesirable or ineffective outcomes in cases that would otherwise have been "easy." For example, "a white criminal caught in the act in California may go free because of legal procedures created when an innocent black was railroaded to jail by an all-white jury in Mississippi."[48] As Horowitz puts it: "Courts see the tip of the iceberg as well as the bottom of the barrel. The law they make may be law for the worst case or for the best, but it is not necessarily law for the mean or modal case."[49]

Sometimes every-last-case reasoning inclines judges to prevent the atypical abuse of power by undermining or abolishing the power itself. Indeed, we have seen that judges sometimes invalidate a law on the basis of a hypothetical extreme case that is not actually before them, such as the hypothetical person entering Canada with his or her "first joint" relied on by the majority in *Smith*. Imaginary hard cases may also make bad law.

An example is the judicial invalidation of vagrancy laws in the United States because they were allegedly too vague to satisfy the constitution's "due process" requirement. Now, clarity is indeed a legal virtue, because in order for laws to be effective (indeed, in order for the rule of law even to exist) those subject to the law must know what is expected of them. On the other hand, as Richard Morgan observes, "there is a great difference in language and law between clarity and specificity":

> Clarity is always required, but specificity, while desirable, is not always possible or necessary. There are large areas of human misbehavior that can only be addressed by the legislature in general terms. "Reckless driving" and "driving to endanger" are familiar examples, as are "cruelty to animals" and "neglect of children." In each case the ordinary usages of language and the common experience of a culture provide perfectly clear notice of a range of behavior that is criminalized.[50]

While the "core" meaning of the behaviour prohibited by such laws is tolerably clear, the outer limits are not. Such clear but imprecise laws obviously involve a discretionary enforcement power that may be abused. Overzealous enforcement may extend to cases that are very far from the recognized core and that were probably never intended to be covered. The possibility of the abuse of discretion, however, does not necessarily mean that the law is so vague as to violate due process. Furthermore, it is the traditional and unquestioned function of the courts gradually to specify the limits of discretion on a case-by-case basis. They can invalidate particular applications of the law as being beyond jurisdiction without affecting the legitimacy of the law itself and, indeed, without recourse to constitutional rights. Where a constitutional right to due process exists, they have the corresponding option of finding the law unconstitutionally vague "as applied" rather than "on its face." The latter course was sometimes taken by American appellate courts in vagrancy cases.[51] It is possible, in other

words, for judges to leave an imprecise power intact and restrict themselves to remedying or compensating the particular abuse. But constitutional rights pose a strong temptation to take the broader route.

The broader route was taken by the U.S. Supreme Court in vagrancy
cases. The Court chose not to invalidate abuses of discretion, but to prevent the very possibility of abuse by finding the law unconstitutionally
vague on its face. Furthermore, the Court did this not in a case that clearly
fell outside the core meaning of "vagrancy," but because such cases were
possible.[52] The consequence was to make it more difficult for police to
engage in traditional, preventative "order maintenance," such as questioning suspicious characters, moving them along, and "breaking up youth
gatherings which are becoming annoying to merchants and passersby."[53]
These activities depend on such age-old offences as vagrancy and loiter-
ing, and when these no longer exist police are limited to passive patrol
(usually in vehicles), intervening only after a more serious infraction has
occurred. Thus, on the basis of hypothetical abuse, the Supreme Court
contributed to a major and highly contentious change in police behaviour.
No doubt the John Stuart Mill of *On Liberty* would have approved. But *On
Liberty* is not the universally acknowledged bible of liberalism. Should the
courts pre-empt the political resolution of such longstanding debate within
the liberal tradition?

If courts sometimes err in implementing policy designed for hypothetical extremes not actually before them, they can also make the opposite
mistake—i.e., designing policy for the wide range of cases when actually
faced by an extreme one. The latter difficulty is well illustrated by *Askov,* a
1990 Supreme Court case raising the question whether an administratively
caused twenty-three-month delay between committal and trial violated the
Charter's section 11(b) right "to be tried within a reasonable time."[54] The
Court had before it the affidavit of Professor Carl Baar, reporting the results
of his research into comparative trial delays. Baar's data showed that the
judicial district of Peel, out of which *Askov* arose, was by far the slowest in
the country and "generally substantially slower than the slowest United
States jurisdiction."[55] Furthermore, the delay in *Askov* itself, which
occurred in 1986, was longer than 90 percent of the cases completed in
Peel in the following year. As the Court put it, "this case ... represents one
of the worst from the point of view of delay in the worst district not only
in Canada, but so far as the studies indicate, anywhere north of the Rio
Grande."[56] Not surprisingly, the Court found the *Askov* delay in violation
of section 11(b) of the Charter.

A less oracular court might have been satisfied to invalidate the extreme delay actually presented by the case. This would have gotten Askov off the hook and, by virtue of the rule of precedent, would have invalidated similar delays of equal or greater length. The claim that shorter delays might also be unconstitutional would have been left to future cases turning on appropriate facts. Instead, the Supreme Court attempted immediately to devise a more general standard for all cases. A delay "in the range of some six to eight months between committal and trial," it declared, "might be deemed to be the outside limit of what is reasonable."[57] The Court arrived at this figure by "doubling the longest waiting period" recently experienced in the Montreal area (a region the Court obviously considered an appropriate comparison to Peel, which borders Toronto). If similarly "busy metropolitan districts" in Quebec rarely exceeded half the time limit the Court was establishing, surely Peel could meet that limit. And if Peel, the country's slowest district, could meet the standard, so could every other district. The Court obviously thought it was setting a fairly generous standard.

The Court was wrong! In Ontario 43 640 charges were stayed, dismissed, or withdrawn on the basis of *Askov* by mid-1991.[58] These included at least one charge of manslaughter,[59] 817 "extreme assault" offences (e.g., assault with a weapon, assault on a police officer, or assault causing bodily harm), 290 sexual assault charges, 402 lesser sex offences, and 11 623 charges of impaired driving.[60] This "staggering impact," as Justice Arbour of the Ontario Court of Appeal subsequently put it[61] (or "draconian result," as Ontario Chief Justice Dubin called it),[62] was hardly anticipated by the Supreme Court. Its six-to-eight-month standard, which apparently suited the Quebec situation, turned out to be highly problematic in Ontario. Indeed, Justice Dubin wrote that the "staying of so many charges has had a serious impact on the administration of justice in this province and, I fear, has eroded the public's confidence in the administration of justice."[63]

The problem stemmed from the predictable difficulties courts experience in acquiring and processing social facts. Although the Court clearly wanted to compare trial delays in Canada's two largest urban areas, the fact is that it was presented with no evidence upon which to ground such a comparison. Baar's affidavit explicitly excluded Quebec data because the institutional and procedural context of trials in that province differed sufficiently from the rest of Canada to make direct comparisons difficult. Indeed, neither counsel in *Askov* had presented data from Quebec. Where, then, did the Court get its Quebec data? It acquired it on its own initiative.

Someone at the Supreme Court contacted the Quebec courts, who supplied the data for Montreal-area trials. The Supreme Court, in short, used data that had not been tested or commented on at either trial or appeal, and that turned out not to be comparable. Nor had the question of the potential effect of a six-to-eight-month standard been directly addressed in the oral presentations to the Court. Had the matter come up, someone would no doubt have directed the judges to Table 1 of Exhibit E of Baar's affidavit, which indicated that such a time ceiling could have threatened almost 25 percent of the district court cases disposed of in Toronto in 1987. Similar evidence was available in the sworn affidavit of Ontario's deputy attorney general.[64] Had they considered the evidence actually before them,[65] rather than making their own unsystematic inquiries, the judges could have predicted the "staggering impact" that subsequent events made plain. More to the point, had the Court decided only the extreme case actually before it, refraining from the temptation to set more general policy for all cases, a problem of such dimensions would not have arisen: Baar's data indicated that less than 10 percent of cases disposed of in Peel in 1987 might have been jeopardized by a twenty-three-month ceiling on administrative delays from committal to trial.

Askov has prompted some concerted judicial backpedalling. The Ontario Court of Appeal, for example, has taken great pains to deny what almost everyone had previously assumed: that *Askov* imposed a six-to-eight-month ceiling.[66] According to that Court, Justice Arbour's "staggering impact" and Justice Dubin's "draconian result" were not required by *Askov*, but were based on a widespread misunderstanding of its reasoning. Properly understood, the Ontario Court argued, *Askov* mandated a more nuanced consideration of individual circumstances, and did not impose an inflexible ceiling on the permissible delay from committal to trial.[67] Whether the Ontario Court of Appeal is engaged in clarifying its superior's reasoning or in creatively correcting its errors, a somewhat embarrassed Supreme Court is certain to be grateful for its efforts. Indeed, Justice Cory, who wrote the lead opinion in *Askov*, has publicly complained that crown counsel did not tell the Court how many cases might be affected by its decision, and maintains that the judges never intended such an extensive impact, indeed, that they were "shocked" by it.[68] This "virtually unprecedented" attempt by a judge to engage in "off-the-bench reinterpretation of what [a judgment] really meant"[69] indicates that the Supreme Court would welcome the opportunity to "clarify" its ruling, perhaps along the lines suggested by the Ontario Court of Appeal. Indeed, Justice Cory's public comments may have simply underscored what had already become apparent to those closely involved in the criminal justice process. Thus Ontario's attorney general, Howard Hampton, reports "hearing rumours for some time that some members of the Supreme Court of Canada were shocked and did not feel comfortable with what was happening."[70] If the Court is angling for another opportunity to address the issue, it is likely to get its wish. "We've been pressing to get another case on before the Supreme Court to give them a second chance," said Hampton.[71] Whatever the ultimate outcome, *Askov* will stand for some time as a monument to the policy-making difficulties judges sometimes face when they stray beyond the facts of the immediate case.

Judicial policy-making under a regime of constitutionalized rights may also distort the inevitable trade-offs involved in policy choices. Goods that are constitutionalized are called rights and competing goods that are not constitutionalized are called costs. (Sometimes, of course, the competing goods in a trade-off are both constitutionalized, as when one finds constitutional rights to both "fair" and "speedy" trials.[72]) Since costs are virtually by definition accorded a lower status than rights, they may be unduly depreciated or even ignored. Rights, after all, are "trumps."[73]

For example, "due process" and "crime control" are desirable ways of promoting aspects of personal security: effective crime control protects the security of the potential victim of criminal activity, and due process prevents innocent parties from being caught in the web of overzealous crime control. Clearly they are competing principles—the more due process the less crime control—and the policy task is to establish an acceptable balance. But constitutional due process clauses protect only one side of the security equation. Furthermore, as courts concentrate on strengthening the "right" of due process, often in response to "hard cases," that right may come to serve more as a protection of the obviously guilty than of the probably innocent, with significant costs for the crime-control side of the equation. If experience in the United States is any guide, not only will punishment of the guilty be much delayed or even foregone, leaving them free to continue their criminal activities, but the legal system will become so bogged down with the procedural requirements of due process in a few cases that it will be unable to respond adequately to the whole body of cases calling for its attention.[74] In the United States much litigation came to turn on the interpretation and elaboration of the ever growing procedural law itself, not on the substantive question of guilt and innocence. Thomas Sowell observes that "premeditated murderers, witnessed in the act, were able to continue appeals for more than a decade without even *claiming* to be innocent, but merely challenging legal procedure."[75] The time spent in such activity is obviously not available for other cases. Plea bargaining and other ways of frustrating the rule of law and effective crime control are the obvious result.[76] Such developments have been taken further in the United States than elsewhere, but other countries have been travelling the same road.[77] It is possible to travel this road through ordinary legislation, of course, but it is more likely to be travelled (and to be travelled further) when the process of making the necessary trade-offs is freighted with the language of constitutional rights versus costs.

■ MODERATION OR POLARIZATION?

Whether or not judicial policy-making "will do no harm" as part of a system of checks and balances also depends on whether it in fact contributes to the moderation of political debate and policy that checks and balances are supposed to achieve. Some argue that the courtroom context, combined with the language of rights, tends to do the opposite, that it encourages confrontations of "black and white," subordinating the shades of grey in between—in short, that it contributes to polarization rather than moderation. If so, judicial power would undermine the purpose of checks and balances rather than contribute to them.

Peter Russell, for example, argues that

> transferring the policy-making focus from the legislative to the judicial arena ... represents a further flight from politics, a deepening disillusionment with the procedures of representative government by discussion as a means of resolving fundamental questions of political justice. The attempt to settle differences in our society on issues such as obscenity, Sunday closing, abortion, the rights of the elderly and the benefits available to the disabled through the judicial process entails the danger, however the courts resolve these issues, of transforming these matters into technical legal questions and of making the answers to those questions hinge on the outcome of a contest between legal adversaries rather than on a political process more likely to yield a social consensus.[78]

Russell clearly sees moderating compromise as more likely to emerge from the political process of representative government than from the adversarial courtroom.

T.C. Pocklington also argues that the "politics of constitutional rights ... are inimical to important political practices such as negotiation, persuasion, bargaining and compromise." For Pocklington, the culprit is the uncompromising rhetoric of rights:

> Rights are "things" which, like a sports car or pneumonia, people either have or lack. They are not things, "like speed afoot or sensitivity to the feelings of others," that people possess in greater or lesser degree. As a result, disputes about rights tend to become very intransigent, and inhospitable to reasoned argument. I claim that homosexuals should have constitutionally entrenched equality rights; you deny it. Where do we go from here? Into a shouting match? From a rights perspective, crucial questions tend not to get asked, let alone answered, much less answered in a way that appeals to rational argument and pertinent evidence rather than sheer assertion.[79]

If the language of rights undermines negotiation, persuasion, bargaining, and compromise, so does the courtroom setting in which the politics of rights is often conducted. For one thing, judges must "justify their decisions by reference to reason," which "may mean that adjudication is not appropriate for those problems best resolved by a process of negotiation." After all, "compromise outcomes are often not defensible by resort to reason."[80] Because of its greater tendency to "stand on principle," the judicial process is more likely to polarize than to moderate political conflicts.

The very form of litigation exacerbates this tendency. As Russell suggests, the courtroom is an inherently "adversarial" place. It pits two main parties against each other in a carefully structured, black-and-white form of combat. The issues are narrowed, simplified, and framed as polar opposites, so that, in classic zero-sum fashion, what one side wins the other loses. The courtroom setting is inherently biased in favour of polarization and against bargaining and compromise.

Not only does the courtroom present issues in a starkly polarized way, but it may exaggerate the intensity with which the opposing positions are actually held:

Dependent as it is on an uncompromisingly partisan presentation, the adversary process is not conducive to the ordering of preferences. It compels the litigants to argue favorable positions with a vigor that may be out of proportion to their actual preferences and that may therefore mislead the judge; in any case, their preferences may have little support in the wider social group the litigants ostensibly represent. In ascertaining the configuration and intensity of public preferences, the judge is, for the most part, left to roam at large.[81]

The distortion of real preferences is exacerbated by the necessity, discussed in Chapter Four, to frame issues in terms of available legal categories, which may not match the real-life concerns underlying the litigation. Thus the predominantly secular concerns underlying the Sunday-shopping controversy become subordinated to publicly less pressing issues of religious freedom.

The tendency of judicial review to distort and polarize public issues is well illustrated by the politics of abortion. Abortion is, of course, an intensely controversial issue almost everywhere, but citizens of Canada and the United States might be surprised at the very different nature of the debate and policy outcomes in many other Western countries. Although there has been widespread liberalization of abortion laws in recent decades, most Western regimes retain more regulation in favour of the fetus than either the United States (since *Roe*)[82] or Canada (since *Morgentaler*). Moreover, abortion in other countries is usually discussed as part of a wider debate on family policy. Often liberalized access to abortion is balanced by policies designed to discourage its use as simply a convenient method of birth control, to encourage other ways of dealing with unwanted pregnancies, and generally to affirm publicly the human value of fetal life and express disapproval of too readily aborting such life. In other words, there is often a policy compromise of sorts.[83] This surely has something to do with the fact that outside of Canada and the United States "no country [in the industrialized world] speaks of a 'right to an abortion.'"[84] Moreover, "almost every one of them has dealt with the problem of abortion through a legislative process of compromise and consensus building."[85] Indeed, on the basis of a comparative study of abortion politics in twenty countries Harvard Law Professor Mary Ann Glendon argues that "when the legislative process is allowed to operate, *political compromise is not only possible but typical*":

These compromises, reached in the usual democratic way, are not entirely satisfactory to everyone. They distinguish between early and late abortions by drawing a line that is difficult to defend on rational grounds, and they weigh the competing interests in a way that is apt to be distasteful to pro-life and pro-choice activists alike. But the European countries have been able to live relatively peacefully with these laws without experiencing the violence born of complete frustration and without foreclosing re-examination and renegotiating of the issues.[86]

In Canada and the United States, by contrast, the debate about abortion

is severely constrained by Supreme Court decisions which define access to abortion as a fundamental constitutional right. There is a legislative vacuum, as pro- and anti-abortion forces paralyse politicians with threats to challenge any and every law before the courts.

The abortion question is rarely if ever discussed in connection with social policies that might help women and families with dependent children cope with unwanted pregnancies. The issue is debated in constitutional terms, as a battle of women's against fetal rights.[87]

This more narrowly focused, black-and-white version of abortion politics, moreover, is at odds with the reality of public opinion, which provides more support for the middle-ground compromise solutions that have emerged from the legislative processes of Europe than for either of the extremes that dominate the judicial arena.[88]

In short, the overly simplified and polarized nature of debate in Canada and the United States is explained in part by the central role of the courts in the policy-making process of the two countries. As Glendon has written about the United States, the judicialization of politics has "shut down the legislative process of bargaining, education, and persuasion on the abortion issue."[89] The same seems increasingly true of Canada. If the politics of abortion is a reliable guide, judicial review of constitutional rights is more apt to undermine than to serve the moderating purpose of a system of checks and balances.

■ ORACULAR FINALITY VS. LEGISLATIVE REVIEW OF JUDICIAL REVIEW

In the previous chapter we reviewed a "protestant" reading of the separation of powers, according to which the judicial determination of the dispute between the actual litigants cannot be set aside by the other branches, but the broader constitutional reasoning on which the decision rests need not be accorded a similar finality. The drawbacks of judicial policy-making discussed above provide additional reasons against according overriding status and reverence to the broader policy implications of judicial opinions.

In fact, the entire checks-and-balances perspective outlined in this chapter militates against the assumption of judicial finality in constitutional interpretation. As noted, to view the courts as part of an institutional system of checks and balances, one need not deny the *political* dimension of their work. Checks and balances, after all, are designed to pit different *political* perspectives, grounded in different institutional structures, against each other in the hope of securing more moderate, consensus-based policy outcomes. Logically, there is no place in this perspective for the oracular claim that judicial pronouncements on matters of general policy are final and authoritative because judges, and only judges, can accurately give voice to the constitution. If constitutional law is usually contestable, and if disagreements among the governmental branches about its correct interpretation are generally reasonable disagreements among equally legitimate interpreters, then there is no basis for the claim of judicial finality. The courts' lack of policy-making capacity and their tendency to promote polarization rather than moderation only strengthen this conclusion.

Denying judicial pronouncements the status of oracular finality, however, does not necessarily mean restricting them to the narrow adjudicative role outlined in Chapter Seven. From a checks-and-balances perspective there may be advantages in factoring the judicial perspective on general policy into the overall policy equation, *as long as everyone understands that it is only one contributing factor, not the controlling factor.* The weakness of the courts in the making of general policy is due largely to their partial and incomplete perspective—a perspective emphasizing the often unrepresentative individual case rather than the run of cases good policy-making must take into account. Yet, however incomplete the judicial perspective may be, it is not likely to arise in the other branches, which have their own institutional biases. The judicial perspective may thus round out the process of deliberating about public policy. After all, if it is wrong to make general policy in light mainly of the unrepresentative individual case, it is equally wrong to ignore the unforeseen exception. Judicial review can benefit the ongoing process of policy development by bringing unanticipated problems to light.

In addition, judicial opinions take the form of reasoning from fundamental principles. We have seen that policy-making can suffer from too much unmitigated reason, because the compromises necessary to much good policy may often be difficult to justify by the standards of strict principle. Still, reason and principle should be consulted. To be sure, those inhabiting the other branches of government also engage in principled reasoning, but in the case of appellate judges such reasoning is their main public contribution to the policy process. Judges may not always do the job well, but this is no reason for rejecting their efforts out of hand. At their best, judicial opinions can illuminate and clarify fundamental principles, or at least raise the level of debate about those principles.

In sum, judges can make valuable contributions to the policy-making process, as long as their pronouncements are seen as precisely that: contributions, not legalistic trumps. Upon reconsideration, the objections to judicial policy-making outlined in the previous sections should more properly be seen as objections to oracular judicial finality than to judicial involvement in the policy process altogether.

Thus even some critics of oracular finality conclude that it would be a shame to limit the impact of judicial reasoning to the strict adjudicative function of justifying the resolution of concrete disputes. It seems particularly senseless to limit a country's highest court of appeal to a strictly adjudicative function. Litigants appearing before the Supreme Court have already had their cases considered by a trial court and at least one appeal court. They have had their day(s) in court, and their disputes have been settled. Yet another level of appeal seems redundant unless it serves some function other than providing the immediate litigants with another opportunity to continue their dispute.[90] Simple institutional economy, in other words, suggests that the Supreme Court should be seen not as an additional level of appeal for strictly adjudicative purposes, but as a mechanism for resolving interpretive issues of national importance—issues raised by the immediate litigation but of significance to the polity as a whole rather than just to the litigants. Thus John Agresto, an emphatic critic of what we call "oracular finality," affirms that the U.S. Supreme Court "exists to do more than merely decide cases; its grandest function is to think and reason with the polity on the best application of our highest principles to our common, present, and pressing concerns."[91] For Agresto, however, the emphasis is on thinking and reasoning *with* rather than *for* the polity. Supreme Court judges can make an important contribution to the overall policy debate, but their pronouncements must not be treated as the legalistic last word that authoritatively ends debate. Judicial pronouncements that bear on general policy must, in this view, be integrated into a *political* system of checks and balances that recognizes both their strengths and weaknesses (especially the difficulties the adjudicative context presents for the making of general policy); they must not be permitted to occupy the mythical realm of legalism above and beyond, and thus presiding over, the political fray. Judicial opinions, in short, should be granted a respectful hearing, but not the status of oracular finality.

Even overtly noninterpretive activism is acceptable to Agresto as long as the courts can be integrated into the checks-and-balances perspective. He does not consider judicial restraint a solution to the problems of judicial policy-making because it merely reduces the occasions for judicial intervention without guaranteeing the wisdom of those interventions that even restrained judges are impelled to make. One would still be left with the problem of what to do about judicial mistakes, although that problem might arise less often.[92] More to the point, Agresto believes it is unrealistic to expect much judicial restraint in any case:

> One need not have a Hobbesian view of man as constantly searching for greater power to see that in human affairs—especially at the highest level of political life, where not merely interests but vital principles of right and justice are at stake—the call for self-restraint is always destined to be a vain request. The vigorous demand for self-restraint in scholarly literature, in judicial opinions, and in careful judicial selection ... seems to have had minimal effect.[93]

For Agresto, it would be more effective (and closer to the original design and general spirit of American constitutionalism) to bring the courts within the overall system of checks and balances. "[W]hat we need," he says, "is a theoretical and practical base on which to oversee the [Supreme] Court as the Court itself oversees Congress and the president. That, in essence, is what the principle of checks and balances demands."[94] Such a system would allow the polity to benefit from the contributions of activist judges without suffering as much from their mistakes.

Agresto reviews a number of ways "by which, in a system of checks and balances, the power of judicial review can be kept from devolving into the practice of judicial finality."[95] He regrets, however, that the most obvious and best solution is not available in the United States:

> In many ways the perfect constitutional solution to the problem of interpretive finality and judicial imperialism would have been for the judiciary to possess the same legislative relationship to Congress as that which governs the executive. Just as Congress, by special majority, can override a presidential veto, a similar process could from the outset have been established to review judicial objections. To have subjected judicial "vetoes" to the same process of review as that to which the Constitution subjects presidential vetoes would have been the most unobjectionable method of combining the benefit of active judicial reasoning and scrutiny with final democratic oversight. It would have been the perfect balancing of the principle of constitutionalism with active popular sovereignty.[96]

Agresto is here outlining what Peter Russell has called "the legislative review of judicial review," a phrase Russell used to describe the Charter's section 33 legislative override.[97] At least with respect to matters falling under sections 2 and 7 to 15 of the Charter, section 33 provides Canada with the checks-and-balances mechanism Agresto would like to see in the United States.

Russell has most cogently summarized the virtues of a legislative override.[98] Pointing out that all constitutional democracies find ways of reversing unpalatable judicial decisions, he assesses the relative strengths and weaknesses of the available alternatives. Formal amendment is, of course, the most obvious alternative. "But in most constitutional democracies (and most certainly in Canada), amending the constitution is an extraordinarily difficult process which may leave decision making power in the hands of a small group of people who are indifferent to or beneficiaries of the injustice resulting from a judicial decision."[99] Here the reader will recall Weiler's contention that if formal amendment were the only way of reversing judicial decisions, "a tiny minority could hold the nation in a constitutional vise."[100] In fact, however, amendment is far from the only avenue open to opponents of judicial pronouncements. "The more usual method of reversing the constitutional decisions of the courts, at least in the United States, is to change or threaten to change the composition of the judicial bodies most influential in interpreting the constitution." Referring to these "more usual" methods as "court packing" and "court bashing," Russell observes that they involve "the application of raw majoritarian power to the judicial branch," and thus "seem less appropriate devices than legislative debate and discussion for challenging judicial decisions on issues pertaining to fundamental rights. The legislative override," he concludes, "has the merit, when properly used, of applying reasoned discussion in a publicly accountable forum to the great issues of justice and public well-being associated with contested judicial decisions."[101]

Russell, in short, sees in section 33 the foundation of an interinstitutional dialogue, in which courts and legislatures issue reasoned responses to each other's initiatives, thereby improving the quality of both public deliberation and its policy outcomes. This, of course, is precisely the central purpose of any system of checks and balances. Indeed, Russell is quite clear about his checks-and-balances orientation:

> Both courts and legislatures are capable of being unreasonable and, in their different ways, self-interested. By providing a legislative counterweight to judicial power the Canadian Charter establishes a prudent system of checks and balances which recognizes the fallibility of both courts and legislatures and gives closure to the decisions of neither. A legislature's decision to use the override, it must be remembered, is not ultimate. It is good for only five years. After five years it can be reviewed but not without re-opening the issue for public debate and discussion.[102]

Paul Weiler has made a similar point. Like Agresto, Weiler believes a section 33–style override would improve even the American system of government, precisely because it would bring judicial review within the general framework of checks and balances, thus making it part of a moderating dialogue rather than a polarizing trump on such dialogue. Says Weiler: "Any measure that could be navigated through all the branches of the national legislative process, each reflecting a variety of constituencies and points of view, might well be considered a more sensible approach to the problem than would a verdict from a bare majority of five on the Court."[103]

Note that Weiler refers to "more sensible" approaches rather than to the "best" policies. The moderation achieved by the more complex checks-and-balances approach advocated by Russell and Weiler need not always yield what might abstractly be considered the "best" policy outcomes. Certainly Russell does not defend the legislative override because it guarantees "that we will arrive at the right answers to the questions of political and social justice raised by the Charter." Nor does he do so because it ensures "that the will of the majority prevails."[104] Russell values the override, rather, because it secures a role for democratic participation in the formulation of public policy. For Russell, it is a central purpose of public institutions in a democracy to permit citizens, acting through their elected representatives, to participate in the deliberation about and resolution of important public issues. The fact of participation itself is an important "process value," quite apart from whether that process yields "the right answers" to substantive policy questions.[105] Thus, while judicial decisions can enrich public deliberation, they should not be allowed to supplant it. Judges have much to offer, but giving them "the last word, the definitive say, on issues of social and political justice is to exclude citizens from participation in the essential activity of a political community."[106]

In order to meet Russell's criterion of enriching public deliberation, however, it is essential that "reasoned debate in the legislature" be the basis of any section 33 override. Russell believes this condition was undermined by the Supreme Court's decision in *Ford*, which upheld Quebec's blanket use of section 33 and decided that "in using the override legislatures are not even required to name the rights or freedoms which are to be restricted." To Russell, this suggests that legislatures "are free to use the override without discussion and deliberation," thus undermining its primary purpose, which is precisely to promote such discussion.[107] Russell sees this as a weakness in judicial interpretation, however, not in the idea of an override as such. To overcome this problem he recommends a constitutional amendment requiring legislatures "to identify the specific legislative provision which in its judgment needs protection or the right or freedom which in its view should not be given priority over the rights and interests to be secured by its legislation."[108] Russell and Weiler have also proposed amending section 33 to

> require that any use of the override be subject to two enactments, one before and one after an election. This would ensure a cooling off period and time for second thoughts. What is even more important, it would also ensure broad citizen involvement in the resolution of rights issues thus contributing to the fundamental process value of the override.[109]

The major obstacle to achieving Russell's interinstitutional dialogue, of course, lies less in any imperfections in the existing section 33 than in the perspective of oracular legalism. To the extent that judicial pronouncements are seen as the very embodiment of the constitution, rather than as debatable interpretations of it, the use of section 33 will be seen as illegitimate. As noted in the previous chapter, the strength of this assumption is shown by the fact that the very wording of section 33 relies on it. Its strength is also shown by the extent to which leading politicians have succumbed to it. Prime Minister Mulroney, for example, has called section 33 "that major flaw of [the constitutional settlement of] 1981, which reduces your individual rights and mine," and has suggested that as long as it exists the Charter is "not worth the paper it is written on."[110] On the judicial side, the strength of the assumption is revealed by the reluctance of judges to admit the political character of the enterprise of judicial review. We have seen that even as conservative a judge as Justice McIntyre was impelled to resist the political scientist's inclination "to treat the courts as one of the three fundamental branches of Government," and to insist that they do not come within the legal definition of "government" for constitutional purposes.[111]

There are some signs, however, that the judicial reluctance to admit the political dimensions of constitutional review may be diminishing somewhat. Consider the following remarks made by Justice Sopinka in an interview with a newspaper reporter:

> When you are deciding a Charter case, the court is in a sense legislating. I think it took a little while for it to sink in that when the court is dealing with Charter cases, they're not dealing with the law as we used to deal with it. Now, when the court is asked to strike down a statute, it is often dealing with the types of decisions that were made previously by elected representatives....[112]

Sopinka is here acknowledging what Justice Frankfurter of the U.S. Supreme Court insisted upon long ago. "People have been taught to believe," said Frankfurter, "that when the Supreme Court speaks it is not they who speak but the Constitution, whereas, of course, in so many vital cases, it is *they* who speak and not the Constitution."[113] Those who would like to see section 33 become the cornerstone of an explicitly political, checks-and-balances approach to the Charter can only hope that more

Canadian judges will follow Justice Sopinka in openly recognizing the quasi-legislative character of judicial review, and that the nonlegalistic premises of such statements will penetrate the public mind.

Integrating the courts in a system of checks and balances is forestalled not only by the strength of oracular legalism, but also by the weakness of Canada's legislative institutions. As indicated earlier, the perceived lack of adequate checks and balances within our legislative institutions is one of the reasons for turning to judicial review. It may also strengthen the inclination to accord unwarranted finality to judicial decisions and unnecessarily to depreciate the "legislative review of judicial review." According to Roger Gibbins, the lack of checks and balances within and among the political branches robs them of the public legitimacy that might sustain the active use of the section 33 override. This context of legislative illegitimacy, in short, provides fertile ground for the growth of the doctrine of oracular judicial finality. An effective challenge to that doctrine in the name of a more subtle and comprehensive theory of checks and balances depends on revitalizing and thus relegitimating the legislative process. Thus Gibbins believes that legislative institutions must be reformed before we can expect them to act as an effective "counterweight for the courts":

> There is a need … to return some balance to the political system by strengthening legislative institutions. At the very least, we will need some legislative strength to counter-balance the courts when the day comes, as it will, that the courts take the Charter beyond the bounds of public acceptability. Just as the Charter and the courts now serve as a check on the legislatures, so too must the legislatures serve as a check on the courts, as both sections 1 and 33 of the 1982 Constitution Act imply. If they are to do so, however, their public image and legitimacy must be enhanced.[114]

■ CONCLUSION

One can defend judicial review as part of a healthy system of political checks and balances *and* maintain the legalistic perspective of oracular finality only at the cost of self-contradiction. To concede that judges may legitimately interfere with the powers of the more openly political branches of government, in other words, logically entails the corollary that the other branches may similarly interfere with the judicial power. Reciprocal involvement of governmental branches in each other's powers, across the strictly logical divisions of separation-of-powers theory, is after all what checks and balances are all about. Checks-and-balances theory begins with the assumption that each branch has both distinctive strengths and weaknesses in the overall policy-making process, and that better (if not always the "best") policy is promoted by bringing together the partial perspectives of all the branches. This logically precludes the notion that any one branch gets the final word. The idea of *judicial* finality, moreover, seems particularly suspect in a democratic age. And when one considers how ill-suited adjudicative institutions are to some of the central policy-making tasks, the case against judicial finality seems complete.

It is possible to reject judicial finality, however, without rejecting judicial review. Indeed, the less the judiciary is granted the status of authoritative oracle, the easier it is to accept even noninterpretive judicial activism. The policy opinions of a judiciary fully integrated into an overtly political system of checks and balances can be seen as partial but valuable contributions to the wider policy debate—contributions to be respected (because of the distinctive strengths of the judicial perspective), but not venerated (because of the inherent defects of this same perspective); contributions that, upon consideration, can be accepted or rejected by the other branches with equal legitimacy.

The possibility of such an openly acknowledged and publicly legitimate system of checks and balances, however, depends not only on a realistic assessment of the strengths and weakness of adjudicative policy-making, but also on the availability of healthy legislatures and executives. It must be conceded that the attractions of oracular legalism are enhanced by the widespread disillusionment with the more openly political branches of government. Reflection on the judiciary as part of a system of checks and balances thus points to more comprehensive (and comparative) institutional diagnosis and prescription.[115] A healthy system of checks and balances obviously requires careful attention to all of its parts. While this broader analysis comes to light as we near the boundaries of our present subject, it nevertheless lies beyond them.

CHAPTER NINE

Ideology

How questions about the desirability of activist judicial review are answered depends not only on considerations arising out of the interrelated theories of separation of powers and checks and balances, but also on more overtly political calculations about the way judges are most likely to exercise their power. Other things being equal, partisans of the political left and right will favour or oppose the Charter depending on whether they think the new power it confers on judges is likely to promote their political agendas. Those on the political left and right divide both between and among themselves on this question. There are those at both ends of the political spectrum, for example, who believe that activist judicial review is most likely to further leftist political causes. Naturally those who share this view will favour the Charter if they are on the left and oppose it if they are on the right. Others, again spanning the ideological divide, argue that judicial power is inherently conservative, either because judges are typically drawn from conservative segments of society, or because the legal mind, into which all lawyers and judges are socialized regardless of their class origin, is unavoidably conservative. The latter contention is common to such "conservative"[1] thinkers as the 19th-century diagnostician of American democracy Alexis de Tocqueville and an influential group of leftist legal scholars writing in Canada today. Not surprisingly, this shared opinion led Tocqueville to favour judicial enforcement of written constitutions while it leads his modern counterparts on the left to oppose it.

Is judicial enforcement of constitutional law a progressive or conservative practice? This chapter reviews the debate about that question. We organize our discussion around one of the central divisions between left and right: the clash between the principles of formal equality of opportunity and substantive equality of result. Certainly this issue is of immense significance to both Tocqueville and the contemporary left. Our discussion begins with Tocqueville's 19th-century reflections because they take us most directly to the heart of the matter.

■ TOCQUEVILLE'S "CONSERVATIVE" DEFENCE OF LEGALIZED POLITICS

Among students of constitutional law Tocqueville is famous for observing that, because of judicial review of the constitution,[2] "there is hardly a political question in the United States which does not sooner or later turn into a judicial one."[3] Tocqueville saw this not just as a matter of political questions going to court, but as the source of a more general legalization of public life. As a consequence of the judicialization of politics, he said, "the language of everyday party-political controversy has to be borrowed from legal phraseology and conceptions."[4]

Naturally this legalization of political discourse gives lawyers a leading role in public life, a role that, as an ambitious elite,[5] they are more than willing to play. Nor is their high status undermined by a democratic people's traditional suspicion of the influential few. As democracy excludes "the rich, the noble, and the prince" from political authority, Tocqueville argues, "the lawyers ... step into their full rights, for they are then the only men both enlightened and skillful, but not of the people, whom the people can choose."[6] Of the potential ruling elites, in short, lawyers have a special interest in favouring democracy, the regime in which they can truly come into their own. Thus lawyers are important not only because they take political questions to court, but also because they are democracy's natural elite and are likely to dominate most public institutions.[7]

If Tocqueville is right, lawyers, as democracy's natural political elite, would "apply their legal habits and turn of mind to the conduct of affairs" even without judicial review of a written constitution. On the other hand, the legalization of public life is certainly extended by an entrenched constitution.[8] And the wider the ambit of the constitution, the greater its contribution to judicialized (hence legalized) politics. Whether one looks on judicial review with favour thus depends on one's assessment of the pros and cons of legalized politics. Tocqueville thought its advantages outweighed its disadvantages.

Tocqueville liked judicial review because by enhancing the public influence of lawyers and the legal mind it strengthened what he considered to be one of the most salutary restraints on democratic excesses. His discussion of the influence of lawyers forms the bulk of a chapter entitled "What Tempers the Tyranny of the Majority in the United States," indicating that he considered legalized politics as an antidote to the most dangerous inclination of democracy. Tocqueville says he is aware of the "inherent defects of the legal mind," but he immediately goes on to express doubt that "a republic can hope to survive unless the lawyers' influence over its affairs grows in proportion to the power of the people."[9] The prominence of lawyers benefits the regime because it mixes the legal mind with the democratic mind, supplying the latter's defects.[10] Their training gives lawyers "habits of order, something of a taste for formalities, and an instinctive love for a regular concatenation of ideas," all of which make them "naturally strongly opposed to the revolutionary spirit and to the ill-considered passions of democracy."[11]

The lawyers' "taste for formalities" turns out to be especially important. To understand why, we must appreciate the political significance of the democratic dislike of formalities. Tocqueville explains that "looking to results without getting entangled in the means toward them and looking through forms to the basis of things" are among the "principal characteristics of ... the American [read 'democratic'] philosophical method."[12] This stems from the fact that in the atomized individualism of an explicitly egalitarian regime no one defers to recognized intellectual superiors—because among more or less similar individuals no one stands out[13]—and all are thus thrown back on their "individual effort and judgment."[14]

> Being accustomed to rely on the witness of their own eyes, they like to see the object before them very clearly. They therefore free it, as far as they can, from its wrappings and move anything in the way and anything that hides their view of it, so as to get the closest view they can in broad daylight. *This turn of mind soon leads them to a scorn of forms, which they take as useless, hampering veils put between them and truth.*[15]

This aspect of democracy's "philosophic method" undermines the ceremonial formalities of religious worship[16] and the stylistic formalities of literature[17] that characterize aristocratic ages. The taste "for the tangible and real and [the] contempt for tradition and formalities" also accounts for the democratic emphasis on a result-oriented applied science to the neglect of theoretical studies.[18]

Tocqueville devotes considerable space to exploring the pros and cons for intellectual life of this dimension of the democratic mind, and to suggesting remedies for its deficiencies. He is obviously concerned with the detrimental impact of the regime on intellectual life. An admirer of Pascal, who was capable of sacrificing everything to his intellectual quest, Tocqueville wonders rather pessimistically whether democracies are capable of producing such thinkers.[19] But his concerns also run in the other direction: he is worried not just about how the regime affects the mind, but also about how the mind affects the regime. In particular, he worries that the central characteristics of the democratic mind will fuel the tendencies to democratic despotism. It is in this context that we must understand his praise of the legalization of politics. Lawyers are not only an intellectual elite whose tastes run counter to the intellectual deficiencies of the democratic mind; they are also a political elite who can benefit democracies *politically* by making nondemocratic intellectual tastes, especially the taste for formalities, publicly influential.

The political problem to which legal formalism provides an antidote is identified early in the book as a struggle between two ways of pursuing equality:

> There is indeed a manly and legitimate passion for equality which rouses in all men a desire to be strong and respected. This passion tends to elevate the little man to the rank of the great. But the human heart also nourishes a debased taste for equality, which leads the weak to want to drag the strong down to their level and which induces men to prefer equality in servitude to inequality in freedom. It is not that peoples with a democratic social state naturally scorn freedom; on the contrary, they have an instinctive taste for it. But freedom is not the chief and continual object of their desires; it is equality for which they feel an eternal love; they rush on freedom with quick and sudden impulses, but if they miss their mark they resign themselves to their disappointment; but nothing will satisfy them without equality, and they would rather die than lose it.[20]

Reformulated in terms of modern debates, this is obviously the aforementioned distinction between formal equality of opportunity and equality of result. Clearly the desire to elevate the little to the level of the great cannot be a desire to achieve substantive equality of result. Tocqueville does not believe that capacities for achievement are equally distributed and that those with "little" capacity can actually achieve "greatly." The differences between the little and the great will always be with us. Elevating the former to the level of the latter, then, must mean treating those who are "little" through the accidents of birth and circumstance as *formally* equal— as entitled to an equal vote in the political sphere and to the opportunity to rise socially and economically if their capacities are greater than their current station. It might even mean public policy designed to relieve them from such truly crushing circumstances as would undermine the ability of even real talent to make its presence felt.[21] Thus understood, the "welfare state" does indeed pursue equality of result, but only as much of it "as 'equality of opportunity' requires."[22] The emphasis is still on a formal equality of opportunity that gives scope to unequal faculties and is expected to issue in substantive inequality. Tocqueville's "debased" taste for equality, on the other hand, seems to be a taste for equality of result simply and for its own sake, which, given the fact of unequal capacities, can only be achieved by restricting the liberty that allows the talented to flourish and dragging them down to the level of the mediocre.

Tocqueville does not appear confident about the fate of what he calls the "manly passion for equality" in democratic societies. The passion for equal opportunity is really a passion for equal liberty, and although democrats love liberty, they love equality more. Certainly the democratic mind, as Tocqueville describes it, would seem to fuel the passion for equal results more than the passion for equal liberty. After all, why shouldn't the democratic hostility to formality extend to formal equality of opportunity? Can we who live in the late 20th century doubt that it has done so?

Tocqueville's characteristic prescription for the ills of democracy is to promote some legacy or analogue of aristocratic traits to supply democratic deficiencies. For example, he argues that religion, which he thinks cannot be generated by democracies, should be preserved by them as the most precious legacy of aristocratic ages.[23] Similarly, Tocqueville encourages the study of pure science and the classics to counteract the more utilitarian tendencies of modern education.[24] He recommends the legalization of public life for the same reason. "Hidden at the bottom of a lawyer's soul," he tells us, "one finds some of the tastes and habits of an aristocracy."[25] In particular, lawyers acquire through their professional studies an aristocracy's "preference for order and its natural love of formalities." In the British common law world, moreover, the emphasis on precedent gives lawyers "a taste and respect for what is old" to combine with their "liking for regularity and legality."[26] Tocqueville adds that, like aristocrats, lawyers "conceive a great distaste for the behavior of the multitude and secretly scorn the government of the people."[27] This does not, however, make lawyers the natural enemies of democracy. For, as we have already noted, although "their tastes naturally draw lawyers toward the aristocracy and the prince, their interest as naturally pulls them toward the people."[28] Thus, instead of trying to overthrow democracy, lawyers prefer to play a prominent role within it, guiding it "along lines to which it is not inclined by methods foreign to it."[29] They are able to do so because they keep their scorn "secret," and because the people, knowing the interest lawyers have in democracy, trust them. In fact "the legal body is the only aristocratic element which can unforcedly mingle with elements natural to democracy and combine with them on comfortable and lasting terms."[30] Thus the aristocratic influence exercised by lawyers in the United States is much more subtle than a balance between opposing classes who recognize each other as natural opponents. Tocqueville sums it up as follows:

> [L]awyers constitute a power which is little dreaded and hardly noticed; it has no banner of its own; it adapts itself flexibly to the exigencies of the moment and lets itself be carried along unresistingly by every movement of the body social; but it enwraps the whole of society, penetrating each component class and constantly working in secret upon its unconscious patient, till in the end it has molded it to its desire.[31]

This subtle legalization of democratic life, says Tocqueville, is the strongest barrier "against the faults of democracy."[32] Chief among these faults is the tendency of "the weak to want to drag the strong down to their level" and "to prefer equality in servitude to inequality in freedom." In short, one would expect the legal mind, with its aristocratic taste for formalities, to support the regime of formal equality and resist the pursuit of equal results. Since "the courts are the most obvious organs through which the legal body influences democracy,"[33] this beneficial impact is strengthened when public life is judicialized through a written constitution.

■ LEFTIST ACTIVISM

Tocqueville clearly saw judicial review as a conservative influence, one that would restrain and check the democratic mind. Until relatively recently this seemed a fairly accurate description of the actual practice of judicial review, and Tocqueville's opponents on the left, while disliking what he liked, would have agreed with his account of the conservatism of judges. We have seen, for example, that in both Canada and the United States judges in the 1930s threw significant obstacles in the way of the emerging welfare state, to the universal horror of progressive intellectuals. The same happened more recently in France. Despite the Declaration of the Rights of Man in 1789 there was no judicial enforcement of rights until the 1970s. Indeed, the practice remained very modest until the 1980s, when the Constitutional Council, almost all of whose judges had been appointed by the previous Conservative government, began striking down the economic initiatives of the newly elected Socialist-Communist coalition government. The response of Socialist deputies reflected the deep distrust of the French left for the judiciary. "We represent the people," said a typical deputy, "*they* represent the majority of an earlier time."[34] In Britain, too, despite the lack of a power of judicial review, the left saw the courts as exercising creative powers of common law and statutory interpretation to impede progressive policy. For the British left, "the courts with their class bias stood as a fortress for privilege."[35] According to J.A.G. Griffith, senior British judges form part of that country's political oligarchy and thus naturally "show themselves alert to protect the social order from threats to its stability or to the existing distribution of political and economic power."[36]

In North America, however, the left's suspicion of judicial power has clearly diminished. The Warren Court's liberal reform program in the 1950s and 1960s was the catalyst of change. Nowadays most North American defenders of activist judicial review situate themselves to the left of centre on the political spectrum.

Left-leaning defences of judicial review in North America, moreover, often come from the pens of lawyers. Certainly it is difficult to recognize Tocqueville's tradition-oriented lawyer in the legal intellectuals who produce most of the literature on the Canadian Charter. Much of this literature sees the Charter not as a defender of traditional rights, but as an instrument for the creation of new rights. Rather than looking to a bygone golden era for solutions to today's problems, these writers see the past, with its legacy of sexism, ageism, mistreatment of aboriginals, and so on, as the problem. They typically portray the Charter as a prescription for curing this unending list of social ills, with the courts administering the medicine. One need hardly add that in this respect left-leaning lawyers in Canada have followed the lead of their American counterparts.[37]

In fact, Tocqueville predicted this. He was careful not to claim "that *all* lawyers will ever, or that most of them will *always,* prove supporters of order and enemies of change." "An elite body," he tells us,

> can never satisfy all the ambitions of all its members; if talents and
> ambitions are always more numerous than places, there are bound
> to be many who cannot rise quickly enough by making use of the
> body's privileges and who seek fast promotion by attacking them.[38]

Thus, just as nobles have led most democratic revolutions, so "under all free governments, of whatever sort, one finds lawyers in the leading ranks of all the parties."[39] One should not be surprised, therefore, to find lawyers spearheading the party of equal results in democratic countries. Nevertheless, although he seemed to have foreseen such legal defectors to the party of equal results, Tocqueville thought they would always be a minority and that the profession as a whole would maintain its essentially conservative characteristics. He wrote that when lawyers hold "that high rank in society which is naturally their due," as they do in democracies, "their temper will be eminently conservative and will prove antidemocratic."[40]

Today it is surely possible to doubt the validity of this assessment. Indeed, it sometimes seems as though there is a bipartisan agreement that Tocqueville was wrong. Those on the political right regret and many of those on the left welcome an apparent transformation of both the legal mind and legal institutions. Far from counteracting the result-oriented tendencies of the democratic mind, the legal mind seems to have been infected by democratic tendencies. A striking example of this is the capitulation of traditional formalism to the forces of legal realism. Legal realism is itself a manifestation of the democratic tendency to uncover formalities, revealing the substance beneath. Peering beneath the formal surface, its most extreme proponents "reveal" that judges read their policy preferences into the law rather than applying it, from which it follows that the important thing about a judicial decision is not to get the law right, but to read the "correct" policy preference into its indeterminate language.

The opportunity for judges to "do the right thing," moreover, has expanded as policy-making judges have relaxed the rules of standing and mootness, which limited judicial review to concrete cases and controversies involving allegations of injured private interests. This, too, is an example of restrictive legal formalities giving way to the result-oriented democratic mind. It is increasingly difficult to accept Tocqueville's description of the judge being "dragged in spite of himself onto the political field," pronouncing on the law only because he must in order to judge a matter of private interest he cannot justly refuse to decide.[41] Nowadays the adjudicative "case and controversy" limitations have given way to the oracular determination that no constitutional question can be kept out of court. It is worth repeating what the Supreme Court of Canada said about the rights guaranteed by the Charter in *B.C. Government Employees Union:* "that which alone makes it in fact possible to benefit from such guarantees [is] access to a court."[42] Tocqueville could no longer write that judicial review was limited by the fact that some laws "can never give rise to that sort of clearly formulated argument called a lawsuit."[43]

Nor could Tocqueville maintain his assumption that judicial review is a *negative* power, limited to striking down laws. We have seen that positive judicial activism, which entails telling governments what they must do, has been added to negative activism in the judicial arsenal. Judicial review is no longer just a matter of invalidating laws that infringe private rights; it is now possible for judges to order the more openly political branches of government to take positive (or "affirmative") action. The ability to require substantive redistribution is, of course, essential if the courts are to become an important vehicle for the achievement of equal results.

Such changes have been a source of hope and comfort for legal intellectuals on the result-oriented left. Had Tocqueville been right about the inherent conservatism of the legal mind, they would have had to train their critical guns on their own profession, and especially on any inclination to rely on the courts as a transformatory institution. Instead, many lawyers on the left have embraced judicial activism as a preferred mechanism for achieving their political agenda. Instead of being the breakaway minority from a predominantly conservative profession, as Tocqueville predicted, these lawyers live in the hope, even the expectation, of completing what appears to be an already well-advanced transformation of the profession in their own image.

■ WHY EGALITARIAN DEMOCRATS FAVOUR THE UNDEMOCRATIC ELITISM OF JUDICIAL REVIEW

There is an apparent irony in the attraction activist judicial review holds for the left. After all, the left's overt goals are greater equality and more effective democracy. "Elitism" is a very bad word in its lexicon. Does the left not contradict itself by using the most elitist and undemocratic branch of government to achieve its ends? In fact, the left's affinity for judicial review can be understood as logically entailed by its deepest assumptions about the nature of things. According to Thomas Sowell, judicial activism is the appropriate corollary of the left's "unconstrained" vision of human "nature." By the same token, Sowell associates judicial restraint with a more conservative, "constrained" vision of human nature.[44]

The constrained vision holds that human nature, including its less attractive aspects, is basically fixed and unchangeable. Human beings are neither perfect nor perfectible, and this fact places inescapable "constraints" on human aspiration and action. Thus Adam Smith took it as a given that individuals would always be more concerned with their immediate interests than with the fate of unknown others. A "man of humanity in Europe," he argued, would certainly take note if an earthquake were to swallow up all of China; indeed, such a disaster would deeply sadden him and cause him to reflect "upon the precariousness of human life, and the vanity of all the labours of man, which could thus be annihilated in a moment." Yet "when all this fine philosophy was over, when all these humane sentiments had been once fairly expressed, he would pursue his business or his pleasure, take his repose or his diversion, with the same ease and tranquility as if no such accident had happened."

> The most frivolous disaster which could befall himself would occasion a more real disturbance. If he was to lose his little finger tomorrow, he would not sleep to-night; but, provided he never saw them, he would snore with the most profound security over the ruin of a hundred million of his brethren....[45]

Smith did not see this human trait as a "moral defect" to be overcome, but accepted it as a fact of life to be squarely confronted. "The fundamental moral and social challenge," observes Sowell, "was to make the best of the possibilities which existed within that constraint, rather than dissipate energies in an attempt to change human nature—an attempt that Smith treated as both vain and pointless."[46] Thus Smith did not believe that moral behaviour toward others could reliably be achieved by overcoming innate selfishness. For him, the more realistic course was to structure a system of incentives that would harness selfishness itself in the service of morality. Preaching to people that honesty is simply right and good for its own sake, for example, is less apt to be effective than making it likely that honesty will be the "best policy." Smith's "was not an atomistic theory that individual self-interests added up to the interest of society."

> On the contrary, the functioning of the economy and society required each individual to do things for other people; it was simply *the motivation* behind these acts—whether moral or eco-

nomic—which was ultimately self-centered. In both his moral and his economic analyses, Smith relied on incentives rather than dispositions to get the job done.[47]

For the unconstrained vision, by contrast, the kind of self-centred egoism Smith took for granted is not understood as a permanent feature of the human condition. William Godwin, for example, conceded that "men are capable ... of preferring an inferior interest of their own to a superior interest of others,"[48] but insisted that "this preference arises from a combination of circumstances and is not the necessary and invariable law of our nature." For Godwin, it was entirely possible for people to be moral in a higher sense, to benefit others directly and intentionally, because it was the right thing to do, not because it would indirectly redound to their own benefit. According to Godwin's "unconstrained" view of human nature "man was capable of directly feeling other people's needs as more important than his own, and therefore of consistently acting impartially, even when his own interests or those of his family were involved."[49] "If a thousand men are to be benefitted," he wrote, "I ought to recollect that I am only an atom in the comparison, and to reason accordingly."[50] People as they actually existed, of course, did not often attain this higher morality—indeed, their actual behaviour more often corresponded to Smith's descriptions than to Godwin's hopes. Nevertheless, not only was it possible to overcome selfishness, but the fulfilment of human happiness ultimately depended on it. It was not nature, but the social system, that stood in the way of Godwin's ideal. "Unlike Smith, who regarded human selfishness as a given, Godwin regarded it as being promoted by the very system of rewards used to cope with it."[51] Structuring society to cope with selfishness, in other words, would, in the manner of a self-fulfilling prophecy, generate that very selfishness. Human character was the product of the social system, not nature. It followed that the system had to be radically transformed to achieve human perfection. In short, the constrained vision seeks to accommodate society to what it understands as the permanent features of human nature, while the unconstrained vision strives to change human "nature" by transforming the social system.

This opposition remains fundamental to many contemporary policy confrontations between the right and the left. It certainly affects the ongoing debate about private property. Whereas the heirs of Smith consider a system of private property rights as the best way to channel human selfishness, adherents to the unconstrained vision see it as the cause of that very selfishness. While the first view "supposes that there is a development from man's asociality to his property," the second "believes the development is from his property to his asociality."[52]

To be more specific, for the constrained vision human liberty necessarily entails giving scope to the ineradicable antisocial dimensions of human nature, and thus to competition and enmity. Indeed, "so strong is this propensity of mankind to fall into mutual animosities," says James Madison in *Federalist* No. 10, "that where no substantial occasion presents itself the most frivolous and fanciful distinctions have been sufficient to kindle their unfriendly passions and excite their most violent conflicts."[53] Since this tendency to "faction" cannot be overcome, it seems prudent to turn it into the least destructive channel, and this turns out to be the pursuit of property. If the "latent causes of faction," which are "sown in the nature of man," are denied this outlet, they will find others, including

> [a] zeal for different opinions concerning religion, concerning government, and many other points, as well of speculation as of practice; an attachment to different leaders ambitiously contending for pre-eminence and power; or to persons of other descriptions whose fortunes have been interesting to the human passions....[54]

History has shown these latter outlets for man's antisocial tendencies to be highly destructive, usually ending in civil strife or even outright civil war. Far better, then, according to proponents of the constrained vision, to tame and soften human competitiveness by diverting it into the pursuit of property. After all, those consumed by the accumulation of material things are unlikely to embrace the sacrifices necessary for religious crusades. Thus Madison considers "the protection of different and unequal faculties of acquiring property" to be "the first object of government."[55]

For the unconstrained vision, by contrast, it seems perverse and misguided to choose between different sources of faction—to choose the lesser evil, as it were—when the evil can be entirely overcome. Liberty need not entail freedom for the sources of faction, according to this view, because those sources are not "sown in the nature of man." For the unconstrained vision, it is possible to envision "a social state in which men would wish to benefit themselves only in ways that are beneficial or at least not harmful to others, [a state in which] men's perfect integration into the community would be indistinguishable from their perfect freedom to do as they please."[56] To achieve this state, one must overcome the social (as opposed to natural) source of selfishness, namely, private property.

Rather than being a prudent way of channelling natural selfishness, the system of private property is seen as the cause of selfishness, and thus as the main obstacle to the ideal integration of perfect liberty with perfect community.

This conflict about property is closely related to the clash between proponents of equality of opportunity and equality of result, around which we have organized this chapter. The constrained vision assumes that inequality is as natural as enmity. Thus Madison emphasizes equality of opportunity for "the *different* and *unequal* faculties of acquiring property," assuming that this will "immediately result" in "the possession of different degrees and kinds of property."[57] Believers in the unconstrained vision, on the other hand, are unwilling to tolerate the distortions of natural meritocracy stemming from socialization within an inegalitarian system. They see unacceptable injustice in a system of private property stemming from the fact that the talents of parents are not precisely reproduced in their children. "The children of the naturally gifted do not always inherit those gifts but nevertheless benefit from the status attained by their parents. Similarly, the gifted children of lower-class parents suffer many disadvantages." In short, "because reproduction is not cloning, the inequality generated by natural differences [will] be confounded with a conventional social inequality that does not correspond to the natural meritocracy."[58]

This distortion means that certain groups who are disproportionately concentrated at the lower reaches of the status or class hierarchy will tend to remain there, even if the distribution of strictly natural talents within these groups is the same as within more successful groups. Believers in the unconstrained vision consider it a sham to speak of formal equality of opportunity as long as the reality of group inequality persists. "To them, equality of opportunity means *equalized probabilities of achieving given results*."[59] And the test of when the probabilities have been equalized is the actual achievement of equal results, not necessarily in the sense of all individuals being equal, but in the sense of the formerly disadvantaged groups having equal shares of coveted positions and benefits.

Proponents of the constrained vision do not entirely disagree. They are quite aware that a complete correspondence between natural ability and status in the social and economic hierarchies cannot be maintained. They believe, however, that too much freedom must be sacrificed to achieve the perfection of natural meritocracy. For them, as long as mobility remains formally possible—as long as the truly gifted from whatever class can, with determined effort, find their natural level—the conventional distortion of the natural hierarchy has to be tolerated in order to maintain freedom itself.[60] For the constrained vision, the danger in the left's desire to equalize the probabilities of achieving given results[61]

> was spelled out in Plato's *Republic,* in which a perfectly just meritocracy was shown to require the rule of philosopher kings, supplemented by a "guardian" elite. To ensure that children would be placed in their natural rather than conventional classes, the natural preference of parents for their own children had to be overcome.[62] Ultimately this meant taking children from their parents at birth and raising them in common, taking every precaution to prevent those related by blood from recognizing each other.[63] In other words, the perfect achievement of the natural meritocracy requires extreme political inequality and the complete destruction of the private realm.[64]

There is, however, an important difference between Platonic communism and the contemporary left. Both share the conviction that the tendency to prefer one's own is the chief obstacle to justice, but in Plato's proposals this tendency is assumed to be permanent, requiring unending control and suppression by the guardian elite. The modern unconstrained vision, by contrast, denies that preference for one's own is natural, and that the attempt to overcome it will require the perennial suppression of freedom. If "man [is indeed] capable of directly feeling other people's needs as more important than his own, and therefore of consistently acting impartially, even when his own interests or those of his family were involved," as Godwin thought, then the contrary tendency to prefer one's own is the temporary manifestation of undesirable social systems, and will disappear with the institution of an appropriate social structure. Once the revolutionary transformation has occurred, liberty and equality will be in perfect harmony. To repeat: in this future condition "men's perfect integration into the community would be indistinguishable from their perfect freedom to do as they please." Thus the suppression of freedom by a guardian elite is necessary only to bring about the transition between the imperfect present and the ideal future. What seems unacceptable to modern partisans of freedom who believe that human nature, including its self-regarding dimension, is fixed, becomes harsh but necessary medicine to those who believe human imperfection can be cured. As Sowell puts it:

> Those with the unconstrained vision may indeed advocate more draconian impositions, for a transitional period, than would be accepted by those with the constrained vision. But the very willingness of some of those with the unconstrained vision to countenance such transitional methods is predicated precisely on the belief that this is only necessary transitionally, on the road to far more freedom and general well-being than exist currently.[65]

The problem, of course, is that however temporary it may be, the suppression of freedom remains a necessity for the transformatory left—and this returns us to our immediate question: why the unconstrained left favours the undemocratic elitism of judicial review. By definition, the majority of people, whose "natures" have been formed by the present system, are unlikely to overthrow that system. Indeed, granting them power, as representative democracy does, will simply reproduce the system. "If the point is to remake man by changing the social environment, then those who were molded by the old environment cannot be permitted the freedom and power to perpetuate it."[66] Thus the project of the contemporary left tempts it to promote the predominant influence of a vanguard elite, which has seen the future and knows how to attain it. The elitist rule of philosopher kings and guardians is as important to the egalitarian project of today's left as it was to Plato's communism. The main difference is that the modern left sees its own elitism as temporary, needed only during a transitional phase, after which the human traits that required suppression will have died away. This new "guardian elite," moreover, can be said to practise "democratic elitism," because its purpose is to bring about the conditions for a new, purer, more perfect democracy in the future—one based on real, substantive equality, rather than on the "charade" of formal equality among those who are really unequal.

Needless to say, believers in the constrained vision deny that the new "guardian elite" can be any less permanent than Plato's, because they deny that the preference for one's own can be overcome. Because those who attempt to do so are attempting the impossible, their efforts, and hence their elitist guardianship, will be unending. In effect, self-styled "equality seekers" will become "equality mandarins" with a vested interest in perpetuating the allegedly "transitional" order they administer. In this view, the true "charade" is the image of a more perfect future democracy; on the alter of this unattainable image, today's "democratic elitists" will have sacrificed the only realistic form of democracy: the representative, liberal democracy they abhor.

Whatever the objective merits of this debate, we are now in a better position to understand the left's temptation to embrace judicial review. Short of outright revolution, what branch of the existing government better suits the model of philosopher kings ruling with the aid of a guardian elite? Judicial review offers the vanguard elite the opportunity of instituting policies the less enlightened democratic majority, acting through its representatives, is unwilling to embrace.

■ THE TOCQUEVILLIAN LEFT

The transformatory left is not monolithically in favour of judicial review, however. It includes those who think it naive that the judiciary can be persuaded to accept and act upon the left's policy agenda. Some hold this view because the judiciary is composed mainly of older, white males of considerable means. These critics believe that the robed members of this highly unrepresentative and elitist stratum of society are unlikely to use their power in progressive ways. In support of this contention, some leftist critics adduce the historical record. In Chapter Eight we quoted Agresto's conclusion that the American Supreme Court's civil liberties record is "heavily weighted not with cases in which the Court deferred to the illiberality of the more political branches but with cases in which the Court, invoking the name of either the Constitution or of liberty, itself voided liberating and progressive as well as necessary legislation." In Canada, Alan Borovoy has made the same point. "Rarely," writes Borovoy, "has the U.S. Supreme Court struck down federal legislation that suppressed civil liberties."[67] Indeed, except for the era of the Warren Court, a "mere interlude in [the Supreme Court's] history," Borovoy considers the Court's influence to have been positively regressive, benefiting mainly the one minority that didn't deserve judicial protection: the rich.[68]

This "pessimistic" view is open to counter-argument. It might be suggested, for example, that the legal profession has changed, that it has become more open to women and disadvantaged minorities, and that this will eventually affect the composition of the bench. And in the meantime some gains might be made through a concerted effort to sensitize sitting judges to the plight of the oppressed.[69]

Although such counter-arguments give comfort to some leftist proponents of judicial activism, they do not persuade an influential group of intellectuals on the Canadian left who are mounting a wholesale assault on activist judicial review of the Charter of Rights, and even on the very idea of constitutionalized rights. This component of the left agrees with Tocqueville's conclusion that the legal mind is inherently conservative, regardless of the kinds of people who inhabit the legal profession. Its manifesto is Michael Mandel's 1989 book *The Charter of Rights and the Legalization of Politics in Canada.*

As others have done, Mandel points out that those on the left who expect great things from judicial activism have been too much bedazzled by the Warren Court era in the United States. Over the long term, he argues, judicial review has served conservative rather than liberal causes, and the twenty years between *Brown* v. *Board of Education* and *Roe* v. *Wade* were clearly an exception.[70] Nor does the exception show that the judicial arena is "an empty vessel into which *any* form of politics can be poured, conservative, liberal, right wing or left wing."[71] Mandel insists that, if equality of result is the goal, judicial politics is destined to be conservative politics. It is so destined by precisely the trait identified by Tocqueville, namely, an abstract and tradition-bound formalism.

Despite the intellectual victories of legal realism, even those inclined toward leftist judicial activism are forced by the institutional position of the courts to rely on an abstract and formalistic manner of reasoning. Because they lack democratic legitimacy, appointed judges can never admit that they are making policy on the basis of a utilitarian weighing of overall social costs and benefits. Instead, they must couch their arguments in terms of abstract "principles," which often bear little relation to the concrete social problems at stake. For example, the question of Sunday closing, which in the late 20th century turns mainly on secular struggles among such interests as unions, consumers, and small and large retailers, must ultimately be decided by the courts in terms of the "principle" of religious freedom.[72] Similarly, "one can talk about capital punishment in terms of whether it is the most efficient way of preventing murder [the utilitarian argument] or in terms of whether murderers deserve to die or whether victims have the right to retribution [the argument from 'principle']."[73] Mandel concedes that, since most issues can be looked at from either perspective, the courts have a great deal of freedom in choosing how to characterize them. But this choice will be closely linked to their inclination to make activist or restrained decisions. "If they are inclined to intervene, they can characterize the question as principle, if not, they can call it policy."[74] In short, activist decisions will almost always be couched in the abstract and formalistic language of "principle."

For Mandel, legal principles are not just abstract and formal; they are necessarily backward looking. The same reasons that compel courts "to characterize their interventions as principle and not policy in the first place"—i.e., the democratic illegitimacy of making policy in an appointed and politically independent institution—force them to "find" the required principles embedded in the traditions, practices, and institutional arrangements of the community. This is true even of such liberal proponents of judicial activism as Ronald Dworkin, who

> insists [that electorally unrepresentative judges] only enforce *institutional* rights, that is, those which can be extracted from *existing* institutions and *accepted* practices, including prior judicial decisions under the doctrine of *stare decisis*.... How are they to do this? They are to develop a theory which best *justifies* these institutions and practices and then they are to apply that theory to the question at hand.[75]

Clearly judges have much discretion in deciding which of the many and contradictory traditions are sufficiently "fundamental" to become constitutional principles, but the necessity of grounding principles in the past places serious limits on their creativity. True "radicality," says Mandel, "is ruled out by the very form of the argument." Not that courts cannot occasionally make a real "break with the past." "It just requires bending some important rules, and courts risk throwing over the whole game every time they do it. So they tend not to."[76] Radical departures by the courts will thus be rare exceptions to the general rule of "start[ing] from, tak[ing] for granted, and indeed *justify[ing]* basic social arrangements."[77] Far from being a useful vehicle for social transformation, Mandel sees judicial review as "a distinctive way of making things acceptable, a distinctive *form of legitimation*."[78]

Mandel agrees with Tocqueville's assessment of the essentially conservative character of the courts because he understands the truly radical departures that must be made to achieve equality of result. He dreams of redistributive policy based on a recognition of the determining power of the existing "relations of unequal social power."[79] He believes that, far from representing the inevitable outcome of freedom (understood as formal equality of opportunity), existing inequalities reproduce themselves in ways that are little affected by real merit. Liberal regimes may have rejected the overt, political enforcement of a status hierarchy,[80] but real power is more economic and social than political in any case. People are not "free" of this "power," and it "enforces" status just as surely as its more direct political predecessors.[81] From this perspective, it makes little sense to enforce contracts between economic unequals as though they had been "freely" entered into, or to punish allegedly "voluntary" crimes as though the criminals were free of the "relative compulsions of class or lack of property."[82] Existing contract and criminal law treat the symptoms rather than the cause of the disease. The real task is fundamentally to restructure entrenched relations of social and economic inequality. Only when substantive social and economic power are as equal as our formal political status will true freedom be possible.

The courts are an inadequate vehicle for achieving the kind of restructuring Mandel would prefer because there is nothing in the traditions of liberal democratic society that could support it. To repeat, the courts "must start from, take for granted, and indeed *justify* basic social arrangements." And existing arrangements are fundamentally "relations of unequal social power." The legal principles drawn from these arrangements are necessarily blind to the realities of unequal social and economic power. Indeed, their formal and abstract character consists precisely of their steadfast refusal to acknowledge these "power relations."[83] It is simply unrealistic, argues Mandel, to expect the courts to stop treating contracts as bargains between formally equal parties, or to stop incarcerating criminals because, being "compelled" by their social position to commit the crime, they really do not deserve the punishment. Because courts must blind themselves to the real problems, moreover, it is even more unrealistic to expect them to come up with the positive policies that might realistically address those problems. For Mandel, the formalistic legal mind described by Tocqueville remains very much in place and is unlikely to change. It will always be a bulwark of formal equality of opportunity and an impediment to the pursuit of equal results. Tocqueville likes this aspect of the legal mind and Mandel does not; otherwise their analyses are quite compatible.

Segments of the result-oriented left that were originally enamoured of the Charter have recently found themselves edging toward Mandel's analysis. Feminists are perhaps the best example. Canadian feminists played a leading role in the process of Charter-making, securing favourable clauses and wording in several important parts of the document.[84] With an eye to how the National Association for the Advancement of Colored People (NAACP) successfully used the United States courts in achieving desegregation, they quickly established the Legal Education and Action Fund (LEAF) to ensure that feminist arguments would be heard in court and that judicial review of the Charter would fulfil their policy expectations.[85] For the feminists, the Charter's "equality rights" section (section 15), which they played such a significant role in drafting, was designed to achieve "substantive equality of disadvantaged groups such as women," by which they mean "not simply equality in the form of law (formal equality), but equality in the actual conditions of women's lives."[86] From this perspective, "equality is *not* merely or even primarily a matter of same treatment, but rather a matter of addressing and overcoming the disadvantage of historically oppressed and excluded groups."[87]

An interesting example of what this means in practice concerns the employment of female prison guards in male prisons and vice versa. There are many more male than female prisoners and thus more employment opportunities for guards in male prisons. In order to remedy the historical disadvantage of women in the employment sphere, some feminists argue that women must be afforded the opportunity to work as guards in male prisons. Moreover, this opportunity cannot be limited to jobs that respect male privacy because, given the nature of prison life, few such jobs exist. Thus female guards must be permitted to be present during strip searches of male prisoners and to conduct cell surveillance.[88] The fact that male privacy must give way to the employment needs of women is justified as a necessary cost of the historical oppression of women by men; it is part of the cost men must pay to redress the balance. The same principle justifies the opposite result in the case of women's prisons. There the balance is redressed by preferring women's privacy interests to the principle of equal employment opportunities for men—that is, although women can perform duties that involve the invasion of male privacy, male guards cannot perform such duties in female prisons. Such a policy obviously violates any notion of abstract and formal equality, but it makes perfect sense if "equality rights" are conceived in terms of what is necessary to achieve substantive equality of result. Indeed, achieving such results requires formally *un*equal treatment. Thus a differential prison-guard policy is justified by the fact that it serves "to assist women inmates and women guards to overcome inequality."[89]

Feminists had hoped the courts would use section 15 of the Charter "proactively" to institute result-oriented policies where none existed. To their dismay, judges have often used notions of formal equality to undermine such policies when legislatures have established them. The prison-guard issue is a dramatic example. The differential policy described above had in fact been embodied in regulations. When these were challenged by male prisoners, the court upheld the regulation permitting women to search men, but in order to maintain formal equality, it struck down the

254 The Dimensions of Charter Politics

corresponding prohibition of men searching women. Feminists applauded the first conclusion, but deplored the second.[90] Although part of the victory they had won in the normal policy-making realm had been upheld, another part had been dismantled—and all because of the court's reliance on the traditional principle of formal equality. The court's dedication to the principle was made all the more obvious by the fact that it went out of its way to strike down the regulation applying to female prisons when not required by the factual context to do so. After all, the case concerned men who were challenging an invasion of their privacy; why compensate for their loss by imposing a similar loss on women prisoners when the case did not involve a male guard's complaint of reduced employment opportunities? (Here we find feminists, who often champion the oracular court, paying tribute to the more traditional adjudicative principle of sticking to the facts of the case.) Feminists wondered how the men could benefit from the loss of the women.[91] One answer is that they were simply being vindictive. A more plausible explanation is that the judgment satisfied a "formal" sense of fair play—i.e., fairness understood as formal equality. Whatever may have motivated the claimants' legal argument, it is surely the court's dedication to this sense that explains the outcome.

The notion of formal equality has also affected cases involving monetary benefits targeted for women. It is true, as noted earlier, that the Federal Court extended additional "paternity" benefits to men rather than simply striking the law down or reducing the amount available to women by dividing existing benefits among both parents, but this case is an exception. Indeed, the continuing reluctance of judges to order governments to spend money was displayed even in this case by the fact that the judge took the "unusual step of putting his judgment in abeyance pending appeal."[92] More common is a Nova Scotia case in which benefits available to single mothers but not to single fathers were simply struck down.[93] Not that this did any real damage. The amount of money necessary to implement additional, gender-neutral benefits was relatively small and the Nova Scotia government did so immediately.[94] Still, on a symbolic level the case contributed to the notion that section 15 is primarily a protection of formal equality. The same thing is implied when courts uphold gender-specific benefits as "reasonable limits" on the protected rights under section 1 of the Charter.[95] In such cases, the satisfaction feminists feel in seeing the law upheld is undermined by the more important fact that section 1 is required to defend infringements of *formal* equality.

Clearly the formalism of the legal mind identified by Tocqueville is still very much in evidence. This has led some feminists to ask whether the Charter they so eagerly welcomed represents "one step forward or two steps back."[96] "If formal equality becomes the prevailing definition of equality applied under section 15," they argue, "women stand to lose more than they can gain from the Charter."[97] They stand to lose because achieving equal results requires special, proactive policy designed to equalize historical disadvantages, and the idea of formal equality does nothing to encourage this. Result-oriented feminists believe that governments have not gone nearly far enough in providing special benefits for women. Far from forcing them to do so, the courts are using section 15 to call existing gender-specific benefits into question on the basis of the idea of formal equality. Where achieving formal equality by *adding* to existing benefits is expensive, the result is likely to be a new division of the existing pie, with a consequent reduction of benefits for women. As Gwen Brodsky and Shelagh Day point out, "formal equality that dictates the same treatment for everyone does not distinguish between equalizing up, by expanding benefits and protections, and equalizing down, by reducing benefits and protections, to eliminate legislative distinctions."[98] Given the reluctance of governments to increase expenditures, the result will often be to equalize down.

At a deeper level, truly effective "equalizing up," the kind of redistribution that would really achieve equality of result, is unlikely as long as one accepts a free market economy. Mandel uses the example of mandatory retirement in the universities, arguing that however the courts decide this issue, "somebody is going to lose—either the younger or older generation of faculty—*unless there is more public-sector money.*"[99] And the courts, using the Charter, can hardly be expected to achieve a real shift of money from the private to the public sectors:

> The point is that using the Charter to improve general living standards is something like printing more money to improve incomes. If anybody wins, it is going to be at somebody else's expense. General living standards cannot be improved through purely redistributive means, unless what is redistributed is *power*. But this means contradicting the logic of the marketplace. It means the expansion of the public sector and the contraction of the private. Otherwise, growth is strictly limited by profitability, with the lion's share going to the lions who always insist on being fed first. Any "trickling down" has to wait. To go beyond the narrow confines of profitabil-

ity and to generalize the benefits of this, the economy has to be politically redirected in the general interest. The Charter obviously has nothing to do with that. In fact, its mission is precisely the opposite. It interferes as little as possible with the logic of the market and profitability. Its redistributive effects are purely *lateral* ones among the limited pool of resources available to the mass of average wage-earners. It leaves the hoards of power and power itself untouched.[100]

The Charter leaves "private power" untouched because of another traditional and formal distinction: that between the public and private spheres. The Charter in its very form, and certainly as it has been interpreted, assumes that the only power of note, the only power against which citizens require constitutional protection, is governmental power[101]; the existence of what the result-oriented left considers the much more fundamental stratum of "private" social and economic "power" is not even acknowledged.[102]

■ CONCLUSION

Following in the footsteps of their American counterparts, many leftist legal intellectuals in Canada have enthusiastically embraced the judicialization of politics, hoping that an activist judiciary might aid in the pursuit of equal results. This judgment seems to belie Tocqueville's description of the legal mind as inherently conservative, and indeed lawyers and judges have been much democratized since Tocqueville wrote. Legal realism has won significant victories, and many of the procedural formalities that limited the scope of judicial policy-making have been weakened or abandoned. Nowadays, judges are much more likely to accept cases that would formerly have been considered nonjusticiable, and to order positive remedies that never would have occurred to their predecessors. In short, today's courts are much more hospitable to the left than were the courts of Tocqueville's day. On the other hand, the further one moves to the left on the political spectrum the less momentous (and hence less inviting) these changes are likely to appear. Those who are most radical in their dedication to equal results, and most clear-headed in their assessment of what it takes to achieve them, see courts and lawyers much as Tocqueville did: as dominated by an abstract, tradition-bound formalism that will weigh more heavily on the side of equal opportunity than on the side of equal results. In short, if one limits one's political vision to a moderate range on either side of centre, the courts have clearly moved to the left, and one will judge Tocqueville to have been mistaken; if, on the other hand, one widens one's gaze to take in the political extremes,[103] Tocqueville will appear to have been mistaken only about details, not about the crux of the matter. Those who, like Tocqueville, favour the regime of equal opportunity clearly have less to hope for from lawyers and judges than he did; perhaps they also have less to fear from them than first impressions might suggest.

PART THREE

Case Studies

CHAPTER TEN

■■■■■■

Abortion

The Supreme Court of Canada has decided three important abortion cases: *R. v. Morgentaler,*[1] *Borowski* v. *Canada (A.-G.),*[2] and *Tremblay* v. *Daigle.*[3] When studied together, these cases richly illustrate several important dimensions of Charter politics.

No set of cases better illustrates the growing involvement of interest groups in the judicial process. The Charter of Rights says nothing, implicitly or explicitly, about abortion. This omission was intentional.[4] Notwithstanding the Charter's silence, within seven years the Court had handed down three major abortion decisions. This gap between the constitution (the text of the Charter) and constitutional law (the words of the Supreme Court judges) reflects the efforts of pro-choice and pro-life interest groups who have used the Charter and the courts to try to change public policy. Just as governments "work" the federalism side of the Canadian constitution for whatever advantages they can derive, so a new breed of political interest groups are working the Charter, urging the judges to interpret Charter language in ways that further their policy objectives.

The abortion cases also illustrate the different judicial approaches to Charter interpretation and the different results they can produce. Since the Charter is silent on abortion, partisan attempts to persuade the Court to "find" a right to abortion or a right to life necessarily denigrate interpretivist judicial fidelity to original meaning and legislative intent, and instead invoke noninterpretivist approaches to interpreting the Charter, especially the creative use of "purposive" analysis. As a corollary to the purposive approach, both sides have inundated the Court with opposing theories of justice and with "social facts" about the operation of the abortion law and fetal development. The Supreme Court's own response to the partisan demands placed upon it shows it to be an active player rather than an impartial referee in the game of Charter politics.

■ MORGENTALER (1988)

On January 28, 1988, the Supreme Court of Canada declared that Canada's abortion law violated the Charter of Rights and was therefore invalid. Its decision culminated a twenty-year campaign of civil disobedience by Dr. Henry Morgentaler, the abortion activist from Montreal. The Court's decision in *Morgentaler* immediately became its most celebrated, most publicized, and most controversial Charter of Rights decision.

The Supreme Court's decision dramatizes just how much the Charter has changed Canadian politics. Twenty years ago, the federal government amended Canada's abortion law, section 251 of the Criminal Code, to allow significantly greater access to abortion services. During the long and controversial process leading to this change (1966–69), there was not a single attempt to use a court challenge to influence the process of abortion law reform. Interest-group use of litigation to do an "end run" around "responsible government" was viewed as "un-Canadian," an idiosyncrasy of American politics. From start to finish, the 1969 reform was entirely a government-parliamentary matter.

The 1969 abortion reform represented a political compromise. Legal abortions became more readily available than before, and doctors who performed them received legal protection. Yet the reform stopped short of decriminalizing abortion completely. Section 251 of the Criminal Code still treated abortion as a serious crime punishable by a maximum sentence of life imprisonment for the abortionist and two years for the woman. The only legal abortions were those performed under the exculpatory or "excusing" provisions of subsection 4, which defined a "legal" abortion as one performed in an accredited hospital after approval by the hospital's therapeutic abortion committee (TAC). Approval hinged on three doctors finding that the continuation of the pregnancy would be likely to endanger "the life or health" of the woman. The meaning of "health" was left to the judgment of the TAC. The Trudeau government touted its reform as broadening access to legal and safe hospital abortion services, while ensuring this new freedom was not "abused." Under the new law, the number of abortions per year rose from less than 20 000 prior to 1970 to about 67 000 by 1978. It remained at this level until 1988, the year of the *Morgentaler* decision; since then it has risen by 13 percent to over 79 000.[5]

By the mid-1970s, law reform by lawsuit was no longer unthinkable in Canada. Encouraged by the American Supreme Court's 1973 abortion decision, *Roe* v. *Wade*,[6] Henry Morgentaler, a then obscure Montreal doctor, set out on a one-man crusade of civil disobedience to challenge Canada's abortion law. Morgentaler was acquitted at trial by a jury, but then convicted by the Quebec Court of Appeal.[7] On appeal to the Supreme Court of Canada, Morgentaler drew upon the 1960 Bill of Rights to argue that Canada's abortion law violated the individual liberty and right to privacy of Canadian women.[8] Although essentially the same argument had been accepted by the American Supreme Court in *Roe* v. *Wade* one year earlier, it was rejected by the Supreme Court of Canada. After a brief recess during oral argument, the Court announced that the Bill of Rights argument was without merit and told the Crown that it need not even rebut the argument. In its written opinion nine months later, only one judge—Chief Justice Laskin—bothered to acknowledge the Bill of Rights argument. In distinguishing the *Morgentaler* case from *Roe,* the Chief Justice observed "how foreign to our constitutional traditions, to our constitutional law and to our conceptions of judicial review was any interference by a Court with the substantive content of legislation." This difference, Laskin explained, stemmed from the fact that the Canadian Bill of Rights was not constitutionally entrenched.

> It cannot be forgotten that it is a statutory instrument, illustrative of Parliament's primacy within the limits of its assigned legislative authority, and this is a relevant consideration in determining how far the language of the Canadian Bill of Rights should be taken in assessing the quality of federal enactments which are challenged under s. 1(a).[9]

On March 27, 1975, Henry Morgentaler was sent to prison for ten months.

In 1983, Morgentaler renewed his campaign of civil disobedience. With financial backing from the Canadian Abortion Rights Action League (CARAL), he opened abortion clinics in Toronto and Winnipeg. Once again he was acquitted by a jury, and once again he saw his acquittal overturned by a court of appeal. Eleven years after the Supreme Court had sent him to prison, Henry Morgentaler was back in the same court challenging the same law—only this time his arguments were based on the Charter of Rights, and this time he won. What had been unthinkable in the 1960s, unlikely in the 1970s, became a reality in 1980s.

While the constitutional status of the Charter of Rights appears to have erased the Court's previous doubts about the legitimacy of its power to review and nullify Parliament's laws, the 1988 *Morgentaler* decision cannot be explained by the Charter alone. Equally important were developments in Canadian society, especially among legal and judicial elites. The *Mor-*

gentaler decision reflects the emergence of feminism as a major force in Canadian politics. There was almost no feminist influence on the 1969 abortion law reform.[10] Although several pro-choice groups were allowed to intervene in the first *Morgentaler* case in 1975, their Bill of Rights arguments were ignored by all but the Chief Justice.

The social and political climate had changed dramatically by the time Morgentaler returned to the Supreme Court in 1986. *Morgentaler* was not the only defeat suffered by feminists under the 1960 Bill of Rights. Feminist groups worked successfully to obtain more favourable wording in the 1982 Charter of Rights and then helped to mobilize public support for its adoption.[11] Feminists subsequently organized LEAF—the Legal Education and Action Fund—a nation-wide organization to identify and litigate women's issues under the Charter. This development coincided with changes in the legal profession and the judiciary. In 1982 the first woman was appointed to the Supreme Court of Canada—Madam Justice Bertha Wilson, who went on to write the feminist perspective on abortion into her concurring opinion in the *Morgentaler* decision. Subsequently two more women—Madam Justice Claire L'Heureux-Dubé (1987) and Madam Justice Beverley McLachlin (1989)—were appointed to the Court. This change at the top of the legal profession had its counterpart at the bottom. In twenty years, the number of women in Canadian law schools has gone from less than 10 percent to almost half.

These changes within the legal world reflected similar changes in the larger political landscape of the 1980s. Feminists converted the legal defeats of the 1970s into political victories. In the 1974 case of *A.-G. Canada* v. *Lavell and Bedard,* the Supreme Court rejected a sex-discrimination challenge to a section of the Indian Act that deprived Indian women of their official Indian status if they married non-Indians.[12] No similar disability applied to Indian men who married non-Indian women. *Lavell and Bedard* became a *cause célèbre* among feminists, and by 1983 they persuaded Parliament to amend the Indian Act to end the disabilities that previously attached to Indian women. Feminists enjoyed similar success in persuading Parliament to reverse another Bill of Rights decision, *Bliss* v. *A.-G. Canada.*[13] In this 1979 decision, the Supreme Court had upheld the denial of regular unemployment insurance benefits to a woman who could not qualify for the more restricted maternity-leave benefits. After much protest and pressure, Parliament amended the Unemployment Insurance Act to cover all pregnancy-related unemployment.[14] Victories such as these testified to the new-found political influence of feminism in the 1980s.

Judges are not immune to these shifts in public opinion. The growth of feminist influence in political, educational, and legal elites was a necessary precondition for the *Morgentaler* decision. The Charter provided Morgentaler a new weapon, but its successful use was contingent upon a more receptive legal and political context.

Developments since January 1988 have made it increasingly apparent that the *Morgentaler* decision was a major political victory for the prochoice side of the abortion conflict. This was not initially obvious, as the Court's actual reasoning was relatively narrow and divided. Recall that in addition to a dissenting judgment, the five-judge majority produced three different opinions on why the law was invalid, with only Justice Wilson explicitly declaring a constitutional right to abortion. Together, these four opinions illustrate the full spectrum of Charter interpretation and its inescapable connection to lawmaking and public policy.

Madam Justice Wilson's solo judgment is one of the purest examples of judicial activism under the Charter. While the four other judges who voted to nullify the abortion law limited their decision to procedural violations of section 7, Wilson said this would be wasting Parliament's time. The government might spend months redrafting the procedural aspects of the abortion law only to be told in a subsequent case that it also violated a woman's substantive right to abortion. To address only the procedural issues, wrote Wilson, "begs the central issue in this case ... [Does section 7] confer on the pregnant woman the right to decide for herself whether or not to have an abortion?"[15]

Wilson was technically correct in this assertion, but she obviously did not share the concern of her four colleagues that the Court would be well advised *not* to confront Parliament on "the central issue." What they saw as a danger to be avoided, Wilson saw as an opportunity to be seized. For her, it was more important to use the *Morgentaler* case to declare a constitutional right to abortion for women than to finesse the "central issue" by limiting the judgment to procedural grounds.

As she proceeded to map out the contours of a woman's substantive right to liberty and security of the person, Wilson never once referred to legislative history or the framers' intent. Knowing full well that these sources of interpretive guidance would point in the opposite direction from the one she preferred to take, she chose simply to ignore them. While ignoring specific intent, however, Justice Wilson was happy to invoke "purposive analysis."

The purpose of section 7 turns out to be broad indeed. According to Justice Wilson, the rights to liberty and security of the person are intended to protect and promote "human dignity and worth." Her "purposive" interpretation of section 7 led her to conclude that "the right to liberty ... guarantees to every individual a degree of personal autonomy over important decisions intimately affecting their private lives." Does "this class of protected decisions" include "the decision of a woman to terminate her pregnancy?" "I have no doubt that it does," declared Wilson.[16]

Wilson goes on to give an equally broad interpretation to "security of the person," and finds that it too is violated. The "essence" of section 251, she proclaims, is to assert,

> that the woman's capacity to reproduce is not to be subject to her own control. It is to be subject to the control of the state. She may not choose whether to exercise her existing capacity or not to exercise it. This is ... a direct interference with her physical "person."... She is truly being treated as a means—a means to an end which she does not desire but over which she has no control. She is the passive recipient of a decision made by others as to whether her body is to be used to nurture a new life. Can there be anything that comports less with human dignity and self-respect? How can a woman in this position have any sense of security with respect to her person?[17]

These are bold words indeed. The American Supreme Court's ruling in *Roe v. Wade* seems timid and pale by comparison. Justice Wilson in effect reads almost the entire pro-choice perspective on abortion into five words of section 7, their legislative history notwithstanding. It would be difficult to find a clearer example of noninterpretivist judicial activism.

Justice Wilson's desire to use the *Morgentaler* case as an opportunity to influence any new abortion legislation by Parliament is also evident in her handling of the section 1 "reasonable limitations" issue. Wilson begins by identifying the purpose of section 251 as the protection of the fetus, which, predictably, she quickly describes as "a perfectly valid legislative objective." "The question," she continues, is

> at what point in the pregnancy does the protection of the fetus become such a pressing and substantial concern as to outweigh the fundamental right of the woman to decide whether or not to carry

the fetus to term? At what point does the state's interest in the protection of the fetus become "compelling" and justify state intervention in what is otherwise a matter of purely personal and private concern?[18]

Wilson's answer is "that the value to be placed on the fetus as potential life is directly related to the stage of its development during gestation." This "developmental view" of the fetus, she concludes,

> supports a permissive approach to abortion in the early stages of pregnancy and a restrictive approach in the later stages. In the early stages the woman's autonomy would be absolute; her decision ... not to carry the fetus to term would be conclusive. Her reasons for having an abortion would, however, be the proper subject of inquiry at the later stages of her pregnancy when the state's compelling interest in the protection of the fetus would justify it in prescribing conditions.[19]

Justice Wilson is admirably frank in admitting that this is only "my view," which raises the troublesome issue of why "her view" should be preferred to the collective view of Parliament. This problem is made more acute by her concession that "the fetus is potential life from the moment of conception,"[20] a position that supports a nondevelopmental view. Presumably it was to avoid this appearance of "judicial second-guessing" that the other four judges for the majority limited their decision to procedural grounds.

Justice Wilson might still have avoided the appearance of overt judicial lawmaking had she left her decision at this. Her vague terms of "early stages" and "later stages" left considerable room for Parliament to work. Perhaps conscious of how closely she was working the law–politics distinction, Wilson herself at one point declared that it is up to "the informed judgment" of Parliament to determine "the precise point in the development of the fetus at which the state's interest in its protection becomes 'compelling.'" In the end, however, she could not resist suggesting her own solution. "It seems to me," she concludes, "that it might fall somewhere in the second trimester."[21]

The casual fashion in which it is presented—almost as an afterthought—cannot disguise the very political purpose of this closing remark. As it was completely gratuitous to her section 1 analysis, it can only have been intended to influence subsequent deliberations in Parliament. Wilson is subtly suggesting that if Parliament enacts a new abortion law, this is what she would accept. Wilson commends this approach by noting more than once that it is essentially the "trimester" policy adopted by the American Court in *Roe*. Since about 90 percent of abortions in Canada are now performed in the first trimester, her recommendation, if followed, would represent a significant triumph for the pro-choice side of the abortion battle.

If Justice Wilson's opinion represents the activist end of the judicial spectrum, then the McIntyre–La Forest opinion represents the opposite end. McIntyre's decision is a model of judicial self-restraint. According to McIntyre, the Court should never have allowed itself to be drawn into the abortion controversy by the *Morgentaler* case. The abortion issue, he notes, turns on the respective rights of women and the unborn, none of whom are present in this case. The appellants are all doctors charged with conspiracy to violate the Criminal Code. None of the doctors can claim that they have been denied a therapeutic abortion. The Court's grappling with the section 7 issues has thus been on a purely "hypothetical basis," and should have been avoided.[22] In effect, McIntyre is once again chastising the majority for adopting an oracular rather than an adjudicative view of their function under the Charter. Since the rest of the Court did decide the case on these issues, McIntyre reluctantly concludes that he must address them also. Significantly, however, he prefaces his section 7 analysis with a lengthy discourse on the new political role of the Court under the Charter. For McIntyre, Charter interpretation cannot be divorced from its institutional context.

Although McIntyre agrees with Chief Justice Dickson's observation that the Court is now responsible for "ensuring that the legislative initiatives pursued by our Parliament and legislatures conform to the democratic values expressed in the Charter," he insists that "the courts must confine themselves to such democratic values as are clearly found and expressed in the Charter and refrain from imposing or creating other values not so based."[23] The responsibility of the Court, McIntrye continues, is "not to solve or seek to solve ... the abortion issue," but to determine whether section 251 violates any "clearly expressed" rights in the Charter. "If a particular interpretation enjoys no support, express or reasonably implied, from the Charter, then the Court is without power to clothe such an interpretation with constitutional status." "The Court must not," McIntyre warns, decide the *Morgentaler* case "on the basis of how many judges may favour 'pro-choice' or 'pro-life.'"[24]

While McIntyre's approach to Charter interpretation is the antithesis of Wilson's opinion, both rely heavily on American constitutional authorities. Unlike Wilson, however, McIntyre marshals lengthy quotations from American justices to demonstrate the dangers of judicial attempts to enact the judges' views of enlightened public policy in the name of constitutional interpretation. Drawing from Justice Harlan, McIntyre condemns the "current mistaken view of the Constitution and the constitutional function of this Court ... that every major social ill in this country can find its cure in some constitutional 'principle,' and that this Court should 'take the lead' in promoting reform when other branches of government fail to act."

> The Constitution is not a panacea for every blot upon the public welfare, nor should this Court, ordained as a judicial body, be thought of as a general haven for reform movements.... This Court ... does not serve its high purpose when it exceeds its authority, even to satisfy justified impatience with the slow workings of the political process. For when, in the name of constitutional interpretation, the Court adds something to the Constitution that was deliberately excluded from it, the Court in reality substitutes its view of what should be so for the amending process.[25]

With this warning against judicial amendment of constitutional meaning still ringing in his readers ears, McIntyre quickly dispenses with the Wilson view: "The proposition that women enjoy a constitutional right to have an abortion is devoid of support in the language of s. 7 of the Charter or any other section."[26] McIntyre notes that while other controversial rights are specifically mentioned, "the Charter is entirely silent on the point [of abortion]." Drawing on the legislative history ignored by his fellow judges, McIntrye emphasizes that this silence was no oversight. Parliamentary debate and the minutes of the Special Parliamentary Committee on the Constitution show that its framers deliberately excluded abortion from the Charter.[27]

As for the alleged procedural violations of section 7, McIntyre was sceptical of the evidence, which was drawn primarily from the Badgley and Powell reports, policy studies commissioned by the federal and Ontario governments. While conceding the Court has become more receptive to this kind of "extrinsic evidence" in constitutional cases, McIntrye observes that he would still "prefer to place principal reliance upon the evidence given under oath in court."[28] This preference for sworn testimony that can be tested by the heat of cross-examination is another characteristic of the adjudicative viewpoint. Of those who so testified, he notes, not one doctor or woman claimed to have ever had a TAC application for an abortion rejected. For McIntyre, this conflict between extrinsic evidence and sworn testimony made it "anything but clear" that the procedure mandated by section 251 made the section 251(4) defence "illusory."[29] Ironically, a report commissioned to assist possible legislative reform of the abortion law was now being used by courts to accomplish the same task. The majority's frank use of legislative facts indicates the legislative character of the Court's new role under the Charter.

On other procedural issues, McIntyre conceded that the defence provided by section 251(4) was a narrow one, but that the narrowness or breadth of the defence reflects Parliament's judgment of when "the disapprobation of society is not warranted." It is not for judges to "second-guess" Parliament's choices in these matters. As for the claim (accepted by three other justices) that the meaning of the word "health" in section 251(4) was so vague as to render it invalid, McIntyre notes that this claim was unanimously rejected by the Court in its 1975 *Morgentaler* decision. If the meaning of "health" was sufficiently clear in 1975, it was still acceptable in 1988.[30]

McIntyre concludes by emphasizing that he is expressing "no opinion" on the abortion issue. His decision is based exclusively on the fact that "no valid constitutional objection to s. 251 of the Criminal Code has been raised." "If there is to be a change in the abortion law," he continues, "it will be for Parliament to make."

> This is not because Parliament can claim all wisdom and knowledge but simply because Parliament is elected for that purpose in a free democracy and, in addition, has the facilities—the exposure to public opinion and information—as well as the political power to make effective its decisions....[31]

The core of the *Morgentaler* decision is found in the Dickson-Lamer and Beetz-Estey judgments. While there are important differences in reasoning between these two opinions, together they defined a middle ground between the Wilson and McIntyre positions. Unlike McIntyre, their "bottom line" was to strike down section 251. Unlike Wilson, however, they limited their rulings of invalidity to procedural violations.

Morgentaler's lawyer had invited the Court to interpret the section 7 right to liberty as creating "a wide ranging right to control one's own life and to promote one's individual autonomy ... [including] a right to privacy and a right to make unfettered decisions about one's own life." This, wrote Dickson, "is neither necessary nor wise.... I prefer to rest my conclusions on a narrower analysis." Dickson concluded that it "will be sufficient to investigate whether or not [section 251] meets the procedural standards of fundamental justice."[32]

Justice Wilson was right in claiming that the majority's reliance on procedural grounds amounted to ducking the issue. Yet in the adjudicative courtroom, "ducking the issue" is often a virtue rather than a vice. There is a well-established canon of construction that constitutional cases should be decided on the narrowest legal reasoning possible. This rule is based primarily on respect for Parliament, but it also embraces an element of judicial self-interest. Reflecting judicial respect for the duties of the legislative branch, and the desire to intrude as little as possible on those duties, it is also based on the perception that it can be dangerous for the Court to become prematurely or unnecessarily embroiled in volatile political issues. The Canadian justices—with the memory of American court-packing plans still fresh in their minds—were well aware of the high price the American Supreme Court was paying for its attempt to take the political lead on the abortion issue. For the Dickson-Lamer and Beetz-Estey opinions, both principle and prudence dictated avoiding Wilson's "central issue." They sought to minimize the Court's role in shaping Canada's abortion policy, while she sought to maximize it.

The two middle-ground opinions thus did not address the question of whether the Charter creates a right for women to decide for themselves whether to have an abortion. Provisionally accepting the authority of Parliament to prohibit nontherapeutic abortions, they focused on whether the defence allowed by section 251(4)—the certificate of approval from a TAC—restricted the section 7 right to "security of the person" in a manner inconsistent with "the principles of fundamental justice." That is, given Parliament's decision to allow a defence to the crime of abortion, was this defence in fact available in a timely and reasonable manner? Both the Dickson and Beetz opinions concluded that *in practice* it was not.

The key to this finding was extensive reliance by both justices on extrinsic evidence drawn mainly from the 1977 Badgley Report. The product of a royal commission established by the federal government in the wake of the 1976 *Morgentaler* decision, the Badgley Report found uneven access and delays to abortion services, attributing both to the haphazard implementation of the TAC requirements. Not only did these delays increase the threat to the health of pregnant women seeking abortions, the judges concluded, but the delays themselves were caused by the requirements of section 251.

Section 251 stipulated that abortions must be performed in "accredited" hospitals. Only larger hospitals that provided a certain minimum number of specified services were eligible for accreditation. Similarly, a hospital could offer abortions only if it had at least four doctors to authorize and perform them. The combined effect of these two requirements was that 58.5 percent of Canadian hospitals were ineligible to perform abortions. Furthermore, of the 559 general hospitals that were qualified, only 271, or 20 percent of the total, had chosen to create TACs, and most of these were in the larger metropolitan areas. Finally, the Badgley Committee reported considerable inconsistency in how different TACs applied the "threat to health" criteria. What qualified for abortion certificates in some hospitals was unacceptable in others. The problem, for Dickson, lay in Parliament's failure to define "health," thus leaving the TACs with an inadequate standard to determine when lawful abortions should be permitted. Some TACs interpreted "health" broadly to encompass mental and psychological health, while others limited it to only threats to physical health. The former definition made it relatively easy to get abortions, while the latter made it more difficult. This administrative inconsistency, declared Dickson, was "a serious procedural flaw."[33]

"The combined effect of all these problems with the procedure stipulated by s. 251," concluded Chief Justice Dickson, "is a failure to comply with the principles of fundamental justice." "One of the basic tenets of our system of criminal justice," he continued, "is that when Parliament creates a defence to a criminal charge, the defence should not be illusory or so difficult to attain as to be practically illusory."[34] This, both he and Justice Beetz concluded, was presently the case under the section 251 regime, which therefore violated section 7 of the Charter.

While the Dickson-Lamer and Beetz-Estey opinions agreed on this point, they were divided over the seriousness of the "procedural flaws" of section 251. Dickson defined "security of the person" very broadly as a right against "state interference with bodily integrity and serious state-imposed psychological stress." Section 251 infringed this right by "forcing a woman, by threat of criminal sanction, to carry a fetus to term unless she meets criteria entirely unrelated to her own priorities and aspirations."[35] This very broad definition of "security of the person" was almost identical to Justice Wilson's, and suggests that any third-party, TAC-style determination of a woman's decision to abort her pregnancy would be unacceptable.

Justice Beetz gave a narrower interpretation of "security of the person." He repeatedly stressed that it was the threat of criminal sanctions, not restrictions on access to abortion, that created the section 7 violation.

Unlike Dickson and Lamer, Beetz and Estey rejected the claim that "threat to health" was unconstitutionally vague. Indeed, they explicitly accepted the principle of limiting abortions to "therapeutic" reasons (reasons of health), and also the use of some sort of third-party determination to ensure "a reliable, independent and medically sound opinion in order to protect the state interest in the fetus."[36] This implied that a revised section 251 with a "streamlined" determination process would be acceptable. In sum, for Beetz and Estey, section 251 violated section 7 because it imposed "unnecessary rules [that] impose delays which result in additional risk to women's health."[37] The problem with section 251 was not what it tried to achieve, but how it went about it. Beetz and Estey would require some procedural retooling of section 251(4), but not as much as Dickson and Lamer.

A final point of importance in the Beetz-Estey opinion is its not-so-subtle criticism of Justice Wilson's *obiter dicta*. Like Wilson, these judges affirm that the state has a legitimate interest in protecting the fetus because it is "potential human life." They also agree with Wilson that this interest cannot justify a complete prohibition of abortion. The crucial question then becomes when and under what circumstances can the state prefer the interest of the mother to the interest of the fetus? Wilson, it will be recalled, endorsed the "developmental approach" adopted by the U.S. Supreme Court suggesting that this point was "somewhere in the second trimester," as the fetus becomes viable, or capable of living outside the womb. Beetz and Estey counter by quoting from a dissenting judgment by Justice Sandra Day O'Connor, the first woman ever to serve on the U.S. Supreme Court:

> The difficulty with this analysis is clear: potential life is no less potential in the first weeks of pregnancy than it is at viability or afterward.... The choice of viability as the point at which state interest in potential life becomes compelling is no less arbitrary than choosing any point before viability or any point afterward. Accordingly, I believe that the state's interest in protecting potential human life exists throughout the pregnancy.[38]

Justice Beetz's digression on this point is no less gratuitous than Justice Wilson's. Both are pure *obiter*. They are nonetheless important because they reveal the political calculations that sometimes underlie judicial opinion writing under the Charter. Both anticipate a response by Parliament to the Court's decision. Wilson tried to send one type of message to Parliament, Beetz and Estey responded with a different one.

To summarize, while five of seven justices held that the section 251 abortion law violated section 7 of the Charter, they disagreed on why. There was no single, unified decision of the Court. Only one justice out of seven declared a constitutional right to abortion. The other four members of the majority coalition found only procedural violations of the Charter, and were further divided on their seriousness. Four of the seven justices— Beetz and Estey, plus McIntyre and La Forest—a majority, seemed willing to accept a reformed version of the current law. Finally, all seven justices explicitly recognized the legitimate interest of the state in protecting the life of the unborn child. They disagreed—four different ways—on when and how. It was now up to the Mulroney government to decipher the meaning of the Court's 196-page ruling, and to decide what, if any, new abortion legislation to bring to Parliament.

■ BOROWSKI (1989)

The *Morgentaler* decision represented a double setback for the pro-life movement. Most obviously, Henry Morgentaler's victory meant that his abortion clinic in Toronto was now free to operate and indeed expand. The second blow was more subtle. The Supreme Court's nullification of section 251 threatened to put an end to Joe Borowski's pro-life challenge to the same law. When the Court declared section 251 invalid, it pulled the legal rug out from under Borowski's claim. How could he challenge the constitutionality of a statute that no longer existed? Borowski's case seemed to become "moot" with the invalidation of section 251.

Like Morgentaler, Borowski had been fighting Canada's abortion law for over a decade, trying to persuade the courts to declare section 251 invalid. Like Morgentaler, Borowski based his challenge on the new Charter of Rights. His legal argument was deceptively simple. Section 7 of the Charter declares that "everyone has the right to life, liberty and security of the person." Invoking the "purposive" approach to Charter interpretation, he argued that the unborn child is included in the concept "everyone." At trial Borowski had tried to substantiate this claim with testimony from medical experts about the human character of the unborn. The conclusion, argued Borowski, was inescapable: a law that allows the unborn to be killed violates the Charter. Borowski was asking the Supreme Court to declare section 251 invalid because it allowed abortions. In the process of his legal campaign against the abortion law, Borowski had become to Canada's pro-life movement what Henry Morgentaler was to the pro-choice camp: a hero, a symbol, an opportunity to win in the courts what they could not win in Parliament.

If the legal question seemed simple and narrow, its potential policy consequences were anything but. This explained the presence of lawyers representing three interveners. LEAF supported the Crown's position. Supporting Borowski were REAL Women, a conservative women's group, and the Interfaith Coalition, a diverse alliance of Catholic, Protestant, Jewish, Islamic, Hindu, Evangelical, and native Indian groups.

When Joe Borowski began his case back in 1978, the government had argued that he had no business being in the courts at all. Borowski's claim was alleged to lack the threshold legal requirement of standing: that there be an actual dispute between the government and a private citizen before any court can hear the case. Simple disapproval of government policy was not sufficient to engage the jurisdiction of the courts. It took Borowski three years and $150 thousand to defeat the government's claim. Even then, only a precedent-setting 1981 Supreme Court decision that dramatically expanded the law of standing allowed Borowski to begin his abortion challenge.[39]

The then Chief Justice, Bora Laskin, wrote a prescient dissent. He warned that if Borowski were granted standing, "other persons with an opposite point of view might seek to intervene and would be allowed to do so, [and] the result would be to set up a battle between parties who do not have a direct interest, to wage it in a judicial arena."[40] In October 1988, Joe Borowski, joined by three interest groups, was back in the Supreme Court to debate the merits of the abortion issue. Laskin's fears seemed realized. The courtroom could just as easily have been a parliamentary committee. Here was Charter politics in its purest form.

Because of the *Morgentaler* decision, however, it was far from clear that Joe Borowski was finally going to get his day in court. The government, supported by LEAF, vigorously argued that the Court's January decision invalidating section 251 left Borowski with no law to challenge. The case, they argued, was now moot and should be dismissed. The Court spent almost the entire first day of oral argument trying to decide whether to decide. The Chief Justice finally announced that the Court would reserve its decision on the issue of mootness, and hear Borowski's arguments on the merits. Joe Borowski would get his day in court.

As it turned out, this was all he got. Five months later, the Supreme Court announced its decision. It concluded that the *Borowski* case had indeed become moot, and refused to address the substantive issue of whether the unborn child is included in the concept of "person" and thus protected by section 7 of the Charter. To do so in the absence of any law, wrote Justice Sopinka for a unanimous court, would be like answering a "private reference," and could result in the appearance that the Court was trying to "pre-empt a possible decision of Parliament by dictating the form of legislation it should enact." Such unnecessary judicial pronouncements about the rights of the unborn would be "a marked departure from the traditional role of the Court."[41] Thus the Court decided not to decide.

From a political perspective, this second act of the Supreme Court's abortion drama was anticlimactic. From a legal perspective, the "nonresult" in *Borowski* was predictable. Six out of the seven judges who participated in the *Morgentaler* decision only nine months earlier had indicated their wish to avoid becoming embroiled in the substance of abortion policy. The *Borowski* decision simply reaffirmed the majority's sense of judicial prudence and self-restraint. Sensitive to the public's perception of fairness, they had given Joe Borowski his day in court, just as Henry Morgentaler had had his. But they refused to go further. In the wake of the *Morgentaler* decision, the ball was in Parliament's court, and the Court did not intend to act until there was a new abortion law. Justice Sopinka's opinion anticipated—correctly—that the abortion issue would return to the Court soon enough. What the justices did not anticipate was just how soon and how explosively.

▌ DAIGLE (1989)

Unlike the *Morgentaler* and *Borowski* cases, the Court's next encounter with abortion was by accident, not design. Neither Morgentaler nor Borowski was the isolated and powerless individual who, wronged by "the system," fought a long and lonely battle to the Supreme Court to vindicate his rights. Both were point-men for well-organized and well-financed national political movements trying to use the courts to change public policy. Morgentaler and Borowski came before the Supreme Court because they chose to. This was not the case with Chantal Daigle, whom fate dragged from the obscurity of private life across the judicial stage of abortion politics.

The *Daigle* case seemed to come from nowhere in the summer of 1989, bursting upon a political scene already simmering with abortion controversy. Despite its stated intention to do so, the Mulroney government had still not introduced new abortion legislation. This inaction gave rise to several surprising new developments in the abortion battle. The policy vacuum at the federal level opened the door for innovation and initiatives at the provincial level. While criminal regulation remained the exclusive jurisdiction of Parliament, the provinces had a variety of means to influence the availability of abortion services. By attaching conditions to public health-insurance funding of abortions and by permitting or prohibiting abortion clinics apart from hospitals, each province could influence the availability of abortion services. Predictably, within a year there were ten different provincial policies.

A second consequence of the policy vacuum was the appearance of a new kind of legal action—the "abortion injunction" case. While the players changed, the plot was always the same: a relationship goes sour, and the ex-lover/father goes to court seeking an injunction to stop his former partner from aborting their child. There had been such cases in Alberta[42] and Manitoba,[43] but no judge was willing to issue an injunction. Ending as quickly as they began, these cases had attracted only fleeting public attention. This changed on July 4, 1989, when an Ontario Supreme Court judge in Toronto granted Gregory Murphy a temporary injunction preventing his ex-girlfriend Barbara Dodd from having an abortion. While the injunction was overturned a week later, the fact that it had been issued at all, plus the fact that it occurred in Canada's media capital, made it headline news across the country for the next week. Pro-life and pro-choice forces rallied, marched, and shouted, right down to July 11, when Dodd received her abortion—for free—at the Morgentaler clinic in Toronto. Rather than fade away, the Dodd–Murphy saga reignited a week later when she called a press conference to announce that she regretted her choice of abortion and had acted under pressure from her family and pro-choice activists. The next week she was on the cover of *Maclean's*.[44]

As if this were not enough for one week, on July 5 the U.S. Supreme Court released its decision in the *Webster* case, upholding a Missouri law prohibiting public hospitals and other publicly funded facilities from performing or facilitating abortions.[45] *Webster* was widely interpreted as the first step toward overturning *Roe* v. *Wade* by a Supreme Court increasingly dominated by judges appointed by the conservative Republican president Ronald Reagan. Pro-choice Americans condemned the decision and sounded the alarm. While legally irrelevant in Canada, the *Webster* decision, coming on the heels of the Dodd–Murphy injunction, further stirred the pot.

On July 7, reports from Quebec brought the news that ex-boyfriend Jean-Guy Tremblay had persuaded a Quebec Superior Court judge to issue a preliminary injunction against an eighteen-week pregnant woman named Chantal Daigle. Pro-choice leaders once again protested what they denounced as unwarranted judicial interference in the private decisions of Canadian women. However, when the injunction against Barbara Dodd was set aside in Toronto several days later, they were confident that the Daigle affair would come to a similar, quick end.

To their shock and dismay, the opposite occurred. On July 17, Judge Viens of the Quebec Superior Court upheld the injunction, ruling that "a conceived child that is not yet born is a human being" protected under article 1 of the Quebec Charter of Human Rights.[46] Daigle immediately appealed this decision to the Quebec Court of Appeal, which, because of the urgency of the matter, heard it on July 20.[47] Pro-choice advocates were stunned again when, on July 26, a divided Court of Appeal upheld the injunction. With her pregnancy now in its twentieth week, Daigle filed a hasty appeal to the Supreme Court of Canada. In an unprecedented move, Chief Justice Dickson recalled the justices from their summer vacation to hear the application for leave to appeal on August 1. Leave was granted and a hearing date was set for August 8. Never before in the Court's history had a case moved from trial to the highest court in the land with such speed!

But what a difference a month had made. While the *Daigle* case had begun as a purely private dispute, it was now a *cause célèbre* for both sides of the abortion battle. Predictably, organizations from both camps requested intervener status for the August 8 Supreme Court hearing. Somewhat less predictably, given the critical lack of time to prepare or hear such arguments, the Supreme Court granted all requests. It then sought to contain the time problem by allowing each group only ten minutes of oral argument—barely enough time for most lawyers to clear their throats. A lineup of opposing groups and scrums of lawyers made the courtroom appear like a rugby tournament on the morning of August 8. Appearing on Daigle's behalf were the Canadian Abortion Rights Action League (CARAL), the Women's Legal Education and Action Fund (LEAF), and the Canadian Civil Liberties Association (CCLA). On the other side were the Campaign Life Coalition, Canadian Physicians for Life, L'Association des médecins du Québec pour le respect de la vie, and REAL Women of Canada.[48] Outside the Supreme Court building were hundreds of pro-choice and anti-abortion demonstrators waving placards, chanting slogans, and hurling the occasional insult at one another.

After suffering setbacks in both the *Morgentaler* and *Borowski* cases, the pro-life movement was ecstatic about *Daigle*. Not one but two courts had now accepted what the pro-life movement had been arguing for years: that the fetus is simply an unborn person, a human being, and is therefore entitled to the same protection of life as all other persons. The facts of the *Daigle* case also favoured the pro-life position. Daigle's pregnancy was voluntary. There were no extenuating circumstances such as rape or incest. She had stopped taking her birth control pills in February, and in the first four months of her pregnancy had made no attempts to terminate it. The pregnancy represented no health threats, either to her or her baby. Finally, she was already in the twentieth week (twenty-second by time of the Supreme Court's hearing) of her pregnancy. An abortion at this stage would destroy much more than the fingernail-sized embryo that Henry Morgentaler removes with his vacuum aspirator. There was only one reason for this abortion: Chantal Daigle no longer wanted to bear her child. This was a classic case of a "lifestyle abortion": the hardest to justify morally and the least accepted in the court of public opinion. Pro-life leaders hoped it would encounter similar difficulties in a court of law.

The advanced state of Daigle's pregnancy and her vague reasons for wanting an abortion made this a very unfavourable "test case" for the pro-choice groups. Intervening in the *Daigle* case violated LEAF's litigation strategy of seeking incremental change in favourable-fact circumstances. As Wayne MacKay, a constitutional law expert from Dalhousie University, observed: "I am not sure they want this to be their big case on the rights of the fetus."[49] While LEAF could hardly stand on the sidelines in such a case, its leaders must have been nervous about their involvement. From a tactical point of view, taking the *Daigle* case to the Supreme Court was like going for the home run instead of the drag bunt. Past experience indicated that the Supreme Court was not very likely to serve up home runs on the issue of abortion.

The legal issues in the *Daigle* case turned primarily on the Quebec Charter of Human Rights and Freedoms, but with clear implications for the Canadian Charter. Unlike section 7 of the Canadian Charter, section 1 of the Quebec Charter speaks of the "right to life" of every "être humain" or "human being" rather than "person." Section 2 declares: "Every human being whose life is in peril has a right to assistance."[50] A majority of the

Quebec Court of Appeal judges were willing to use the broader connotation of "human being" (compared to "person") to find legal protection for Chantal Daigle's unborn child.

Justice LeBel found the concept of "human being" to constitute a *prima facie* case for the fetus. "[I]t is difficult to deny that the fetus, especially once it reaches this stage of development, becomes part of human kind ... even if it has not yet reached the stage of life outside the body of the mother."[51] LeBel reinforced his finding by referring to the Quebec Civil Code's provision of various kinds of legal protection for the unborn. Section 18 of the Code declares that "every human being possesses juridical personality ... [and] has the full enjoyment of civil rights, except as otherwise expressly provided by law." Subsequent sections of the Code authorize the appointment of "curators" for "children conceived but not yet born," and allow them to be designated as lawful inheritors in wills.[52]

Justice Nichols found that the Quebec Civil Code by itself recognized the right to life of the unborn: "It would be paradoxical," he wrote, "if the legislator had wanted to protect the patrimonial rights of an unborn child but at the same time had remained indifferent to his right to life."[53] The third and final judge for the majority considered that the fetus has a "natural right" to be carried to term. Wrote Justice Bernier:

> The child conceived but not yet born, regardless of the term that is given to his civil status, constitutes a reality which must be taken into consideration. It is not an inanimate object, nor anyone's property, but a living human entity, distinct from that of the mother that carries it, which two human beings have given existence to ... and which ... is entitled to life and to the protection of those who conceived it.[54]

Justices Chouinard and Tourigny rejected the majority's interpretation of both the Quebec Charter and the Civil Code. There was no clear evidence that the term "human being" was intended to include the fetus. As for the rights of the "child conceived but not yet born" in the Civil Code, the dissenters noted that these rights can only be exercised by "the child who is born and viable." While not denying the existence of any rights for the fetus, the dissenting judges found that they were too vague and ill-defined to overrule "the fundamental right of the appellant to decide her health and security in complete freedom."[55]

On the morning of August 8, 1989, the Supreme Court convened to review the Quebec Court of Appeal's decision. Of immediate concern was whether the Court would uphold or overturn the injunction that had prevented Chantal Daigle from having an abortion. But behind the injunction question was a legal issue with practical consequences reaching far beyond the Daigle–Tremblay dispute: Is the fetus a "human being" and thus protected by the Quebec Charter of Rights? As the partisans of both sides demonstrated on the front steps of the court building, all nine Supreme Court justices, counsel for the two litigants, and the nine interveners began to sort out the conflicting answers given by the Quebec Court of Appeal. The justices listened passively all morning as opposing counsel presented their arguments. After breaking for lunch, the Court was set to resume when Daigle's lawyer, Daniel Bedard, approached the bench. He had just learned, he told the justices, that his client had had an abortion and so ended her twenty-two-week pregnancy.

The justices appeared shaken, and it was not clear what would happen next. Daigle's case suddenly seemed as moot as Borowski's. With Daigle's pregnancy terminated, the injunction no longer had any practical effect. One option was for the Court simply to dismiss the case as moot. Daigle was potentially subject to either civil or criminal contempt charges for disobeying the injunction, but this was a matter for the Quebec Court of Appeal to decide. Chief Justice Dickson asked Daigle's and Tremblay's lawyers if they wished to continue. Tremblay's lawyer opposed continuing, but not Bedard. The issues behind the injunction remained, he declared, and so posed the threat of similar injunctions against other women. The Court recessed briefly, and then announced that they would finish hearing the case. Less than two hours later, the Chief Justice announced that the Court had unanimously voted to overturn the injunction, and would issue its reasons at a later date.[56]

The next day front-page headlines blared news of the decision across Canada: "Court lifts injunction after Daigle abortion.... Pro-choice advocates support decision."[57] Canada's thirty-two-day mini-drama had come to a climactic end. The victory for the pro-choice side seemed as complete as the defeat of the high hopes of the pro-life movement. Chantal Daigle had become a national celebrity. Five months later, *Chatelaine* magazine named her "newsmaker of the year."[58] In the continuing policy vacuum created by the Mulroney government's inaction, the Supreme Court increasingly appeared to be the institution in charge of Canadian abortion policy.

Three months later, the Supreme Court released its written reasons for the *Daigle* decision in the form of a unanimous, unsigned "Judgment of the Court," a technique occasionally used in politically controversial cases to signal judicial solidarity in support of a decision and to enhance its authority. The decision focused primarily on the issue of whether the fetus has a right to life under Quebec law, and whether, as a corollary, the father has a right to protect it from an abortion. The Court answered both questions with an emphatic no.[59]

The key to this "difficult and controversial question," wrote the Court, was "whether a fetus was intended by the National Assembly of Quebec to be a person under s. 1."[60] "In our view," continued the Court,

> the Quebec Charter ... does not display any clear intention on the part of its framers to consider the status of a fetus ... this lack of an intention to deal with a fetus's status is ... a strong reason for not finding fetal rights under the Charter.... If the legislature had wished to grant fetuses the right to life, then it seems unlikely that it would have left the protection of this right to such happenstance.[61]

The attempts by Tremblay's lawyer and pro-life interveners to establish the "humanity" of the fetus through scientific evidence and ethical arguments were rejected as inappropriate. "The task of properly classifying a fetus in law and in science are different pursuits," the Court declared. The Court must properly restrict its reasons for decisions to purely legal reasons. "Decisions based upon broad social, political, moral and economic choices," the Court concluded, "are more appropriately left to the legislature."[62]

Tremblay's lawyer had also argued that proof that the fetus was protected by the Quebec Charter could be found in the "plain meaning" of its words. The adjective "human" denotes membership in the human race and the gerund "being" signifies "existing." Surely the fetus is a "human being" in the clear sense of these words. "This argument is not persuasive," wrote the Court.

> The meaning of the term "human being" is a highly controversial issue ... and it cannot be settled by linguistic fiat. A purely linguistic argument suffers from the same flaw as a purely scientific argument: it attempts to settle a legal debate by non-legal means.[63]

The claim that the fetus is also protected by the Civil Code was dispatched for similar reasons. Again the Court stressed the absence of any clear intention of the framers to this effect. As for the rights of the "child conceived but not yet born" explicitly found in the Civil Code, the Court took the same position as the dissenting judges in the Quebec Court of Appeal: that these rights can only be exercised by "the child who is born and viable."[64]

Tremblay's lawyer had also tried to use section 7 of the Canadian Charter of Rights to establish a right to life for the fetus—the same argument that Joe Borowksi had made. Again the Court ducked the question, this time by invoking a 1986 precedent, *Dolphin Delivery,*[65] which held that the Charter does not apply to civil disputes between private parties. *Dolphin Delivery* stands for the rule that for the Charter to apply, there must be some form of "state action." Tremblay could not point to any law or other form of government action that violated section 7. It was therefore "unnecessary" to decide the section 7 claim on behalf of the fetus, wrote the Court, and "unnecessary constitutional pronouncement should be avoided."[66]

At this point, the Supreme Court had decided all that was necessary to dispose of the *Daigle* appeal.[67] Rather than conclude, however, the Court launched into a new examination of the rights of the fetus under common law, as opposed to the civil law that is unique to Quebec. Why would the Court undertake to answer legal issues that were not pertinent to the case at hand? The Court did not try to conceal its oracular purpose. "It is useful," they wrote, "to do so ... to avoid the repetition of the appellant's experience in the common law provinces."[68]

The Court's historical survey of abortion legislation found that while "the fetus has always been protected to some extent in our law ... abortion has not generally been considered equivalent to murder." From this somewhat ambivalent record they concluded "that it could be argued that ... a fetus has not been viewed as having the rights of a person in the full sense."[69] Their survey of the case law of Canada and several other common law jurisdictions found that in similar and relevant cases, judges had usually—although not always—reached the conclusion that "a fetus is treated as a person [in law] only where it is necessary to do so in order to protect its interests *after it is born.*"[70] This brief but emphatic excursion into the common law made it clear that the Court did not want to see any more *Daigle*-like cases, and that it was not willing to wait for legislative action to clear up the legal ambiguity nourishing the abortion-injunction cases.

Unlike the *Morgentaler* and *Borowski* decisions, the release of *Daigle* was a political nonevent. The climax of the *Daigle* drama had been on August 8, when the Court invalidated the injunction that Daigle had already defied. When the Supreme Court released the reasons for its decision three months later, there was little public interest. This political obscurity notwithstanding, the *Daigle* decision says a great deal about the politics of the Charter.

From one perspective, the *Daigle* decision can be understood as an act of judicial self-restraint, in which the Court refused to become entangled in the abortion conflict. By invoking the "state action" doctrine of *Dolphin Delivery,* the Court once again dodged the issue of fetal rights under section 7 of the Charter, thereby leaving Ottawa a free hand in fashioning a new abortion law. True, the Court had ruled that the fetus was not protected by the Quebec Charter, but the Quebec Charter was only a statute. If the Quebec Assembly thought that the Supreme Court had misunderstood its "intended meaning" of "human being," then it could easily amend the act. In sum, the Court had quickly and narrowly dispatched the Tremblay–Daigle conflict, without encroaching upon the larger legislative question of a national abortion policy.

Yet upon a closer reading, there are strong undercurrents of judicial activism in *Daigle,* undercurrents that flow in a pro-choice direction. To begin with, the Court could be charged with violating its own maxim against unnecessary judicial pronouncements—and not once but twice. When the justices learned that Chantal Daigle had had her abortion, why did they persist in ruling on the issues involved rather than declaring the case moot—which it clearly was? Similarly, why did the Court expand the scope of its ruling to include the common law when this was not necessary for a Quebec appeal?

The Court had its reasons: "in order to resolve the important legal issue raised so that the situation of women in the position in which Ms. Daigle found herself could be clarified"[71]—and, they should have added, not repeated. This aspect of the justices' decision was clearly motivated by their sympathy with Daigle and, by extension, with other women who might find themselves in a similar situation. Those who share this sympathy no doubt approve of the Court's decision. But what about those who think that it is wrong to abort a perfectly healthy 22-week-old unborn child simply because the mother has changed her mind about her relationship with the father? From this perspective, it was bad enough that Daigle was allowed to abort her unborn child. To bend the Court's own rules to extend this option to others is hardly seen as defensible. Is this simply to say that a person's approval or disapproval of the results of the Court's decision colours one's approval of the means used to reach it? Perhaps. But this does not change the fact that for many this aspect of the *Daigle* decision encourages the suspicion that the Supreme Court is less than neutral on the abortion issue.

In fact, there were competing reasons—legal reasons—why the Court should have declared the case moot and avoided deciding the issue of fetal rights. At a time when other Charter cases were taking from three to five years from trial to final decision by the Supreme Court, Daigle traversed this entire path in exactly one month. Of course, there were special reasons for this. But why, after being advised of her abortion, did the Court persist in proceeding on such short notice and with such little input? Lawyers had only one day after leave was granted to file affidavits and then only one week to prepare their cases. Interveners (except for the federal government) were given only ten minutes of oral argument. As Peter Russell observed *before* the Court had granted leave: "It is very difficult to accommodate her [Daigle's] timetable and still do justice to the issues.... You do not want to produce it in a hothouse, emergency atmosphere. This opinion will be with us for centuries."[72] Once Daigle's pregnancy was terminated, so was the "emergency." Why did the Court deem it necessary to continue?

The suspicion of critics is reinforced by a second aspect of the *Daigle* decision: its very clear and very negative implications for a *Borowski*-like Charter challenge to any future federal abortion law. Technically speaking, *Daigle* has no direct impact on section 7 Charter claims on behalf of the fetus. The Court avoided addressing Charter issues because of the lack of any "state action." The focus of the Court's analysis of fetal rights was the Quebec Charter, not the Canadian Charter. Yet anyone familiar with *Borowski* would recognize fatal similarities between the two. The concept "human being" (the term used in the Quebec Charter) is inherently broader than "person" (the term used in the Canadian Charter), and thus more capable of a judicial construction that includes the fetus or unborn child. If pro-life advocates cannot persuade the Court that the fetus is a human being, especially when the particular fetus in question was 22 weeks old, then it is unlikely they could ever persuade the Court that the fetus, in the abstract, is a "person."

A future pro-life claim under section 7 of the Charter will also have to contend with the method of interpretation used in *Daigle*. Borowski's lawyer, Morris Schumiatcher, had urged the Court to adopt a "purposive" approach to Charter interpretation, and then bombarded the judges with scientific and medical evidence to show that the "persons" branch of the "living tree" now included the unborn. In *Daigle*, the justices ignored the "purposive" approach in favour of strict fidelity to the intent of the framers as they construed it. They also curtly rejected the use of scientific evidence as an illegitimate attempt "to settle a legal debate by non-legal means." Without a wholesale change of heart (or personnel) on the Canadian Supreme Court, it is hard to imagine any future pro-life Charter challenge surviving this *obiter*. Intentionally or not, the Supreme Court seems to have used the facts of *Daigle* to decide the issues of *Borowski*.

Joe Borowski had spent ten years and nearly half a million dollars to bring the issue of the rights of the unborn before the Supreme Court. He was told to try again if and when a new abortion law was enacted. Chantal Daigle had spent thirty days. At his initial trial in 1983, Borowski had assembled a panel of fifteen "expert witnesses" in genetics, prenatal and neonatal medicine who testified as to "the individuality, separateness and the uniqueness" of the human qualities and characteristics of the unborn. This testimonial evidence was brought to the Supreme Court, repeated by Borowski's lawyer Morris Schumiatcher, and challenged by pro-choice interveners. In *Daigle*, interveners had one day to file their factums, one week to prepare their oral arguments, and ten minutes to present them. The *Borowski* case was clearly moot. Although the Court stressed that mootness per se is no longer an absolute barrier to continuing, it applied the traditional concept of mootness to discontinue Borowski's case. Once Daigle had proceeded with her abortion, her case was equally moot. Why under these circumstances, sceptics wonder, did the Court persist in deciding the issue of fetal rights? Why did it treat Borowksi and Daigle so differently?

The Court's sharply contrasting approaches to Charter interpretation in the *Daigle* and *Morgentaler* cases also raise questions about judicial bias. Why did the Court adopt a narrow and legalistic approach to determine fetal rights, but a broad, purposive approach to decide abortion rights? In *Morgentaler* Chief Justice Dickson begins by declaring:

> The goal of Charter interpretation is to secure for all people "the full benefit of the Charter's protection." To attain that goal, this Court has held consistently that the proper technique for the interpretation of Charter provisions is to pursue a "purposive" analysis of the right guaranteed. A right recognized in the Charter is "to be understood ... in the light of the interests it was meant to protect."[73]

In order to discover the "interests [the Charter section] was meant to protect" the judges must of course identify the "underlying philosophy," which in turn allows the Court to add "implied" meaning. In practice, the invocation of a purposive interpretation almost always serves as a prelude to a widening of the scope of the right in question. Justice Wilson's "discovery" of an implied right to abortion and Chief Justice Dickson's very broad definition of security of the person both typify the results of a purposive approach.

By contrast, in *Daigle* there is no mention of a purposive approach. Instead, the Court is consumed by fidelity to the framers' intent. The Court was probably correct in *Daigle* when it reasoned that "if the legislature had wished to grant fetuses the right to life, then it seems unlikely that it would have left the protection of this right to such happenstance." But this was precisely Justice McIntyre's point in his *Morgentaler* dissent: "the Charter is entirely silent on the point of abortion," and the legislative history makes it clear that this omission was intentional. Why, one should ask, are the three plurality opinions in *Morgentaler* completely silent on the "intent of the framers."

Similar contrasts are evident in the Court's assessment of the relevance of nonlegal reasons in the two cases. In *Daigle,* the Court adopted a very narrow view of relevant information: "Decisions based upon broad social, political, moral and economic choices are more appropriately left to the legislature."[74] This position is difficult to square with the Court's behaviour in *Morgentaler,* where the majority opinions relied extensively on the "social facts" presented in the Badgley and Powell reports, research that had been commissioned by legislatures to serve legislative decision-making.

The Court's exclusion of "scientific" evidence in *Daigle* is hard to reconcile with the judicial discussions of fetal development, trimesters, and viability in *Morgentaler*. Indeed, after her emphasis on viability as the permissible point for state intervention to protect the fetus, one might have expected Justice Wilson to attach some significance to the advanced state of Chantal Daigle's pregnancy, with the "baby" on the threshold of viability. This was an important consideration in the majority judgments in the Quebec Court of Appeal.

In *Daigle,* the Court eschews any "philosophical and theological debates about whether the fetus is a person."[75] Yet in *Morgentaler* Justice Wilson quotes freely from John Stuart Mill's theory of liberty ("pursuing our own good in our own way ... so long as we do not attempt to deprive others of theirs")[76] in order to support her interpretation of the right to liberty in section 7. While the two other plurality opinions steer clear of any explicit use of philosophical argument, this is the exception, not the rule, in the Court's Charter jurisprudence. Indeed, the Court's frequent "purposive approach" to Charter interpretation typically drives the judges "beyond text" and into the realm of political and legal philosophy. Their Charter decisions are liberally sprinkled with excerpts from Mill, Tocqueville, Dworkin, Rawls, Hart, and others. As one critic observed: "If metaphysical arguments are or may be 'relevant,' why were they not considered? And if scientific arguments are not 'determinative,' they must by implication at least be relevant. Why were these ignored?"[77]

Questions such as these challenge the view that *Daigle,* like *Borowski,* was another example of the Supreme Court's self-restraint and deference to legislative handling of abortion policy. At the most explicit and obvious level, this view is accurate. But at a more subtle but still significant level, there is contradictory evidence. The *Daigle* majority uses the methods of the *Morgentaler* minority. Why did the Court exercise the techniques of judicial self-restraint when ruling on the rights of the unborn, but the tools of judicial activism when dealing with the rights of the mother? It is difficult to avoid the conclusion that the Court was playing Charter politics rather than declaring constitutional law.

■ CONCLUSION

Pro-life antipathy notwithstanding, the Supreme Court's three abortion decisions largely left Parliament with a free hand to craft a new abortion law. While the Court acquitted Morgentaler, told Borowski to go home, and reaffirmed the legality of Daigle's decision to abort, it avoided broad, sweeping pronouncements on either a woman's right to abortion or the fetus's right to life. The Canadian Court did not repeat the attempt by the American Supreme Court to construct a new national abortion policy in one bold stroke of the judicial pen. The ball was still in Parliament's court. In the wake of *Daigle,* the Mulroney government finally decided to act.

The abortion-injunction cases had embarrassed the Tory government. Prime Minister Mulroney, viewing them as a consequence of the post-*Morgentaler* policy vacuum, saw them as posing an issue of leadership.[78] Within a month of *Daigle,* Mulroney formed a caucus committee composed of both pro-life and pro-choice MPs and ordered them to reach a consensus. They reported back several weeks later with a compromise measure, which the government introduced in the House of Commons on November 3, 1989, as Bill C-43.

Had Bill C-43 passed, it would have made abortion an indictable offence unless "induced by or under the direction of a medical practitioner who is of the opinion that if the abortion were not induced, the health or life of the female person would be likely to be threatened." The bill went on to define "health" as including "physical, mental and psychological health." "Medical practitioner" was left to provincial definition, and was thus not limited to doctors. "Opinion" was defined as "an opinion formed using generally accepted standards of the medical profession." The maximum penalty for violating these restrictions was set at two years.

The imprint of the *Morgentaler* decision on Bill C-43 was clear. The government was proposing procedural but not substantive changes. It had ignored Wilson's solo position on a woman's liberty to decide abortion for herself, and instead had closely followed the reasoning of the Dickson-Lamer opinion. Bill C-43 would retain abortion in the Criminal Code, but throw out the old TAC mechanism, making abortion legally available upon the opinion of a single doctor of the pregnant woman's choice. "Health" was left undefined in the old abortion law, and thus subject to wide variations in interpretation—the target of Dickson's criticism. Bill C-43 made explicit that health was to be given the broader meaning of mental and psychological as well as physical health. Finally, Bill C-43 did not restrict abortions to accredited hospitals, a requirement that had restricted access and caused delays under the old law.

Bill C-43 was, as the government repeated constantly, a compromise measure. It said abortion was wrong in principle, but available in practice. It still treated abortion as a crime, but created a broader and more efficient exemption procedure than the old abortion law. As one legal expert put it: "It [was] anti-choice but it [was] not pro-life."[79] It was, in short, the kind of compromise solution Mary Ann Glendon argued is typical when the "legislative process is allowed to operate" in this controversial policy field: a muddy, middle-ground compromise "that is apt to be distasteful to pro-life and pro-choice activists alike," but that is acceptable to the majority.[80] In Canada, however, the legislative process did not operate in the manner observed by Glendon in most European regimes. Instead, the pro-life and pro-abortion extremes, which had dominated the earlier stage of court-room politics, continued to play a leading role in the legislative arena. Certainly neither extreme of the abortion conflict was prepared to accept the compromises of Bill C-43. The front-page headlines in *The Globe and Mail* announced the bill's frosty reception: "Abortion bill draws hail of criticism; Lack of accessibility, protection for fetus cited."[81]

Caught in the crossfire of these opposing criticisms, Bill C-43 was ultimately defeated. Although it was approved by a "free vote" in the House of Commons, 140–131, on May 22, 1990, both pro-life and pro-abortion MPs voted against it. This alliance of extremes against the middle failed largely because the "free vote" did not apply to the Cabinet, which maintained its solidarity and voted *en masse* in favour of the bill. A similar critical mass supporting the legislation did not exist in the Senate, however, and there the "curious alliance of pro- and anti-abortion forces" prevailed, amassing enough votes against the legislation to exactly balance those in favour (forty-three votes were cast on each side). Since a tie is considered a defeat under Senate rules, the legislation died. The government announced that it would make no further attempts to enact new abortion legislation.[82] In effect, the preferences of the pro-abortion extreme, temporarily implemented by the Supreme Court in *Morgentaler*, had become established public policy.

The failure in Canada of the kind of compromise common in Europe was no doubt attributable in part to the climate of polarized intransigence promoted by the black-and-white, rights-based quality of Charter litigation. From the day it was announced, Bill C-43 was attacked as a violation of the Charter. Liberal justice critic Robert Kaplan protested that Bill C-43 could not "meet the tests of the Constitution and the Charter" and urged the government to refer it to the courts before debate. NDP justice critic Dawn Black rose to declare that "there is a serious problem of access in this country, a problem the government has chosen to intensify."[83] Allan Hutchinson, a Charter expert from Toronto, wrote that Bill C-43 "provides an opening for the pro-choice supporters to air [this] whole issue of accessibility. The government has a constitutional obligation under the Charter to ensure that any legislative benefits are equally available."[84] Feminist Charter experts suggested that Bill C-43 also violated a woman's liberty under section 7 and was a form of "sex discrimination" prohibited by section 15.[85]

Not surprisingly, pro-life activists claimed that the bill violated the section 7 right to life of the unborn child—the issue the Court had declared moot in its *Borowski* decision. While the enactment of a law would solve the mootness problem, pro-life leaders were less sanguine about the prospect of judicial vindication of their claim. "We have wasted our time and thousands and thousands of dollars on Supreme Court cases," declared

Stephen Jalsevic, a director of Campaign Life Coalition. "The pro-abortion people seem to have far more influence on lawyers and courts and judges. I think [litigation] will be the last thing on our agenda."[86] Nevertheless, despite this preference for the legislative arena, pro-lifers were no more apt than their pro-abortion counterparts to relent on principle in favour of compromise. No doubt their tendency intransigently to stand on principle has many sources, but it probably was encouraged and strengthened by the polarizing nature of Charter politics.

Canadian abortion politics reveals two ways to use the Charter to influence public policy. The first is to challenge the validity of an existing law, as Morgentaler and Borowski did. The debate over Bill C-43 illustrates a second: to invoke the principles of the Charter (and the not-so-veiled threat of future litigation) to shape public policy *during* the legislative process.[87] When the first tactic succeeds in invalidating a legal restriction, in effect establishing a highly permissive policy, the second strategy may suffice to maintain that policy. As we suggested in Chapter Five, it may be easier to achieve a middle-ground compromise by moving from a more restrictive than from a less restrictive status quo. The fate of Bill C-43 certainly supports this hypothesis.

The Court's abortion decisions can be understood as legal battles in a larger political war. Politics, not the Charter, brought these cases to the Court. The resulting judicial pronouncements provided the winners with new resources with which to return to the larger political struggle. Although a legal loss does not necessarily mean political defeat,[88] success in the judicial arena is always desirable, and in this case at least it seems to have achieved the policy ends of one of the contending extremes, if not permanently, at least for the foreseeable future.

CHAPTER ELEVEN

Prisoners' Voting Rights

Section 3 of the Charter guarantees every citizen's right to vote. The core of this right is the nearly universal adult suffrage that has been achieved through successive waves of reform over the past century. These reforms overcame racial, sexual, and property qualifications on the right to vote, gradually enabling every adult citizen outside mental institutions or prisons to cast ballots in public elections. What these reforms achieved through ordinary legislation has been constitutionally entrenched by section 3. Precisely because this degree of suffrage represents a now-uncontroversial consensus, however, it is unlikely to arise for judicial determination. A government that reinstated racial or sexual qualifications for the right to vote would clearly be acting unconstitutionally, but it is inconceivable that any contemporary Canadian government would take such a regressive step. And in the unlikely event that such restrictions on the franchise were once again to become politically acceptable, the government that enacted them would hardly be deterred by judicial finger wagging about constitutional proprieties.

As with Charter jurisprudence generally, the questions that actually go to court under section 3 occur at some distance from the consensual core. These questions are of two kinds. First, does the broad language of section 3 invalidate some of the remaining restrictions on the franchise, such as the widespread disqualification of prisoners? Does it, in other words, entitle even more citizens to cast ballots than can do so now? Litigation challenging the prisoner disqualification is the subject of this chapter. Second, even if the franchise were broadened to include all citizens, would their section 3 right be fulfilled by the simple entitlement to mark and cast ballots, or does it further entitle them to substantively "fair and effective representation"? The latter question has been raised by cases challenging discrepancies of constituency size that enable voters in sparsely populated rural constituencies to cast more powerful votes than their counterparts in populous urban ridings. This question is addressed in the next chapter.

Unlike abortion, the issue of prisoners' voting rights has not attained great public prominence. One suspects that many people have strong feelings on this issue, but they have not been publicly mobilized as have the opposing extremes in the abortion controversy. Nor do as many existing political interests have the kind of obvious stake in the outcome of the prisoners'-voting-rights litigation that they have in the electoral districting cases discussed in Chapter Twelve. The somewhat more obscure prisoners'-rights cases are important for another reason: they provide a striking illustration of the courtroom politics of conflicting visions of social order and justice. In these cases we find libertarianism, which eschews the use of law to promote morality, clashing with moralism, which insists not only that morality is publicly relevant, but also that it requires legal support. This clash is occasioned especially by the question whether, for purposes of section 1 analysis, the disqualification should be understood as having the "compelling purpose" of promoting a "decent and responsible" citizenry. The cases also pose conflicting theories of punishment, turning on different assessments of the worth and relative weight of the retributive and rehabilitative dimensions of the penal system.

■ THE CASES

Regarding provincial laws, the issue of prisoners' voting rights was first raised soon after the Charter came into effect in *Re Reynolds and A.-G. B.C.*[1] The British Columbia Election Act declared that persons convicted of indictable offences were ineligible to vote in provincial elections while serving their sentence. The province applied the law to offenders on probation on the assumption that they were serving their sentence even though not in prison. Justice Macdonell found that the application of the law to probationers was unconstitutional. He came to a different conclusion about the disqualification of imprisoned criminals, however. Although the latter disqualification was not directly in issue, Justice Macdonell concluded in *obiter* that it survived Charter scrutiny. The case was pursued to the B.C. Court of Appeal where Chief Justice Nemetz, writing for the majority, upheld Macdonell's decision. In a dissenting opinion, Justice Craig argued that even the disqualification of probationers was justified as a reasonable limit under section 1.[2]

The provincial disqualification of imprisoned criminals was raised directly in the 1986 case of *Badger* v. *Manitoba,* which we discussed for other purposes in Chapter Five.[3] Recall that Justice Scollin invalidated the law because its blanket disqualification of all inmates was too broad to pass the proportionality component of the *Oakes* test. He did not, how-

Case Studies

ever, order the immediate enfranchisement of prisoners, concluding that "the only remedy to which the applicants are entitled is the declaration that the impugned law is invalid."

About two years later in *Grondin* v. *Ontario,* Justice Bowlby of the Ontario High Court invalidated a similar blanket disenfranchisement of all penal inmates in his province.[4] Although Bowlby accepted Justice Scollin's objections about the disproportionality of disqualifying *all* inmates, his own reasons went much further. Whereas Scollin thought a law limiting the disqualification to those incarcerated for more serious offences could be justified under section 1, Bowlby seemed to favour the enfranchisement of all prisoners because of the rehabilitative potential of the vote. "The harmful effect of disenfranchisement on the rehabilitation of convicted inmates is of such significance," he wrote, "that, in my view, disenfranchisement falls outside the parameters of s. 1 of the Charter."[5] There is no indication that Bowlby thought only the disenfranchisement of minor offenders was unreasonable under section 1, as Justice Scollin and others argued; indeed, the logic of his argument requires the disenfranchisement of all prisoners to be placed outside the bounds of section 1 justification— after all, serious offenders need rehabilitation as much as, if not more than, minor offenders.

At the federal level the issue of prisoners' voting rights was first raised in 1983 in *Re Jolivet.*[6] Justice Taylor of the British Columbia Supreme Court held that the federal disqualification of prisoners was justified as a "reasonable limit" under section 1 because, lacking freedom of association, assembly and discussion, and unencumbered access to the free flow of ideas and information, prisoners could not "make the free and democratic electoral choice contemplated by the Constitution."[7]

The issue of prisoners' voting rights in federal elections was not brought to a head, however, until the fall of 1988, just prior to that year's general elections. The two weeks before the November 21 election date saw three judicial decisions in two cases. The first was Justice Hirschfield's November 4 decision in Badger's federal case, which we encountered in Chapter Five.[8] Badger had filed his case barely two months earlier, on August 24, leaving little time to develop and consider the issues. Justice Hirschfield's order to enfranchise prisoners immediately placed the government under even tighter time constraints. Not surprisingly, the government appealed.

The decision in the second case, *Sauvé* v. *The Queen,*[9] was handed down by Madam Justice Van Camp of the Supreme Court of Ontario on November 7, between the trial and appeal decisions of *Badger.* Unlike

Badger, the *Sauvé* case had been in the works for some time. The action was commenced in 1984, and the intervening years had been spent in part developing expert testimony relevant to the issues. The hearing, held in mid-September, when an election was expected but had not yet been called, lasted four days,[10] with most of the time devoted to oral expert testimony in support of written submissions. (Although some of the written material developed for *Sauvé* was subsequently filed in *Badger,* Justice Hirschfield's tight schedule precluded the luxury of oral testimony.) Justice Van Camp agreed that the prisoner disqualification infringed section 3, but unlike Justice Hirschfield, she found no section 1 infirmities in the law at all. She was not even impressed by the argument that a blanket disqualification applying even to minor offenders failed the proportionality test. Justice Van Camp thus upheld the law in its entirety.

In the meantime, Badger's appeal was underway. With the elections drawing inexorably closer, this would be no leisurely appeal. Indeed, "the case was so rushed that counsel for the Attorney-General of Canada had his factum," along with other materials, couriered to the residences of the sitting judges on the afternoon of Sunday, November 13.[11] The Court of Appeal delivered its judgment on November 18, just three days before the election.

Justice Van Camp's *Sauvé* opinion clearly played a role in the *Badger* appeal. The judges of the Manitoba Court of Appeal were generally more persuaded by Van Camp's reasoning than by Hirschfield's opinion in the case before them.[12] Consequently, they overruled Hirschfield, and upheld the law. The decision was unanimous, although one of the three judges expressed some reservations about the blanket nature of the disqualification.[13] While the other two judges were clearly wholehearted in their acceptance of substantive justifications of the law, they were also obviously influenced by immediate practical considerations. As Chief Justice Monnin observed, if Hirschfield's judgment was upheld, inmates in Manitoba could vote in the federal election "while inmates in Ontario could not on the basis of Madam Justice Van Camp's decision."[14] Monnin concluded that "such a ridiculous situation in a federal state should not even be contemplated much less allowed to exist. Either all inmates in Canada vote next Monday or none do."[15] Since the Manitoba Court of Appeal exercised no jurisdiction in Ontario, the only way it could ensure uniformity was to side with Justice Van Camp and overrule Justice Hirschfield.

Badger requested leave to appeal to the Supreme Court of Canada, but was refused. This need not, however, be taken as indicating Supreme Court approval of the reasoning or outcome in either *Badger* or *Sauvé*. It may be that the Supreme Court wanted to await a better vehicle for presenting all of the issues. *Badger* had clearly been rushed, and lacked a full record of expert testimony. Nor had the judges in *Badger* been afforded the leisure to give full consideration to the issues. The Supreme Court might have preferred to wait for a case like *Sauvé*, with its more complete record. They might also have wanted to allow other courts—such as the Federal Court or the Ontario Court of Appeal in the expected appeal of *Sauvé*—to further develop the issues before making a final and authoritative determination.

In the absence of a Supreme Court appeal, a Federal Court case was particularly desirable. The Federal Court has jurisdiction over cases involving the powers of federal administrative bodies, including the country's chief electoral officer, who was clearly implicated in litigation concerning prisoners' voting rights. In *Badger* there was some discussion as to whether litigating the issue in the Federal Court might not be preferable to hearing it in the superior courts of general jurisdiction in various provinces. For Chief Justice Monnin, the prospect of the same federal law being subject to conflicting interpretations in different provinces demonstrated the value of leaving the matter to the Federal Court, whose judgments would apply across the country:

> On this issue we have an Ontario judge saying to the inmates "No, you can't vote" and a Manitoba judge saying "Yes, you can vote." If similar actions or motions had been launched in each of the 10 provinces, we would be faced with a very unsatisfactory state of affairs and perhaps an unusual tally of ayes and nays. There is merit to the proposition or theory that this matter should be heard and dealt with by the federal trial court and its appellate division since it obviously transcends provincial borders.[16]

We have seen that the decision of Monnin's court restored uniform application of the law, but this would not prevent cases being brought in other provinces, with the renewed potential in each case of undermining unified application. Short of an authoritative determination by the Supreme Court, the prospect of disparate interpretations could best be averted by bringing the issue to the Federal Court.

A Federal Court case was not long in coming. The action was commenced in 1988 by Walter Belczowski, then an inmate of the Bowden penitentiary in Alberta serving a sentence of life imprisonment for second-degree murder. Before the case could be heard, however, Belczowski was granted parole, and since the federal voting disqualification applied only while offenders were actually in prison, he was now entitled to vote. From the traditional adjudicative perspective, Belczowski's case would probably have been considered moot and would not have proceeded. In the era of the oracular court, however, it comes as no surprise that Belczowski was granted standing to continue the action. The only gesture to adjudicative propriety was the somewhat strained argument that Belczowski still had a live case because he *might* violate the conditions of his parole and find himself back in prison on voting day.[17]

The case was heard in Edmonton in late January 1991 before Justice Strayer of the Federal Court's trial division.[18] When Strayer handed down his decision about a month later, on February 28, he respectfully acknowledged that the disqualification had been upheld in both *Sauvé* and *Badger*. Although he was bound by neither precedent, he conceded the importance of considering the decisions of other courts. However, Strayer was inclined to discount the reasoning of both *Sauvé* and *Badger* because they "were taken on an urgent basis in the face of a pending federal election."[19] In fact, this characterization seems less applicable to *Sauvé* than it does to *Badger*. We have seen that neither the development of evidence for *Sauvé* nor its consideration during trial was rushed in any way. In fact, the consideration of oral expert testimony was much more extensive in *Sauvé* than in *Belczowski*. The practice of the Federal Court allowed less time for such testimony. Thus what had taken about three days in *Sauvé* was boiled down to one in *Belczowski*. It is true that Justice Van Camp deliberated in part during the election campaign, but she nevertheless took about one and a half times longer to reach a decision and deliver her reasons than did Justice Strayer in *Belczowski*.[20] Strayer certainly has a point about *Badger*, on the other hand. As we observed above, that case was surely rushed, and its conclusion seemed to be influenced by the urgent need to achieve a uniform application of the electoral law on election day three days hence. At any rate, having discounted *Sauvé* and *Badger*, Justice Strayer declared himself ready to consider the issue afresh.

Removing obstacles to a fresh consideration of an issue is often preliminary to deciding it differently, and it thus comes as no surprise that Justice Strayer declared the law unconstitutional. As we write, this is the most recent judicial pronouncement on the question. Unlike *Sauvé* or *Badger*, moreover, its effect is not territorially limited to a single province. Nevertheless, there is apparently some doubt whether this decision really restores the uniform application of law throughout the country. Can a decision of the Federal Court's trial division supplant the decision of the

Manitoba Court of Appeal, which enjoys higher status in the judicial hierarchy? If not, then the disqualification would remain in place in Manitoba, although *Belczowski* would give prisoners the right to vote everywhere else in the country. Since Sauvé has appealed to the Ontario Court of Appeal, the anomaly could be compounded if that court upholds Justice Van Camp. Presumably a Federal Court of Appeal decision, which could withstand contrary judgments by provincial courts of appeal, could ensure legal uniformity in this area, and indeed, an appeal of *Belczowski* to this court is pending.

Obviously the existing decisions do not dispose of the issue. Both the Federal and Ontario courts of appeal will have their say in *Belczowski* and *Sauvé* respectively, and in all likelihood the issue will find its way to the Supreme Court. In the meantime, however, the existing cases provide plenty of scope for reflection on this episode in Charter politics.

■ COMPELLING PURPOSE: THE ALTERNATIVES

Section 1 of the Charter quickly became the focal point of virtually all of the judgments rendered in these voting-rights cases. Only Justice Lyon of the Manitoba Court of Appeal defined the section 3 right to vote in a manner that excluded prisoners from its scope. He grounded this definitional limit, moreover, on a very traditional or interpretivist view of constitutional interpretation:

> In my opinion, the enactment of s. 3 of the Charter was intended to entrench and to constitutionalize the traditional and fundamental right to vote enjoyed and practiced by Canadian citizens subject to the reasonable statutory conditions and disqualifications then extant which attached to it. Thus, the right to vote in s. 3 should be read as reflecting that right as it had developed and was known in our country. I am satisfied that the framers of the Charter did not intend to create a new right, reflecting some unfamiliar, unconditional and abstract ideal which had never been enjoyed or accepted by the citizens of Canada. In these circumstances, it is clear that [the federal disqualification of prisoners], an integral part of the right to vote since Confederation, cannot be construed as being in breach of s. 3

of the Charter. With respect, I find that to hold otherwise, given the history and development of the right to vote in our country, requires a rigid, blinkered and literal interpretation of s. 3 which is unreasonable, unrealistic and unjustified.[21]

In the age of noninterpretivism Justice Lyon should have known that he was swimming against the tide. His colleague, Chief Justice Monnin, certainly knew it. Like Justice Lyon, Monnin was "inclined to say" that section 3 of the Charter could be "abridged" by Parliament in this respect "without s. 1 coming into play."[22] But Monnin recognized that "the majority of judgments delivered so far on the subject in various jurisdictions in Canada are of the opposite view and hold that [the disqualification] is clearly in breach of s. 3 of the Charter."[23] Monnin decided not to resist the trend. The trend, of course, is based on the modern rejection of "frozen concepts" in favour of a noninterpretivist vision of the "living tree." In his *Belczowski* opinion Justice Strayer made this plain in a pointed criticism of Justice Lyon.[24]

On the section 1 question it should come as no surprise that all of the opinions in these cases found that the prisoner disqualification passed the "compelling purpose" component of the *Oakes* test. As we indicated in Chapter Six, judges who wish to argue with legislatures have good reasons for disputing the means the latter have chosen to achieve their ends rather than the ends themselves. The judges differed significantly, however, in the ends they attributed to this legislation.

One side of the question was represented by the opinions of Justice Macdonell in *Reynolds* and Justice Taylor in *Jolivet*. These judges upheld the prisoner disqualification because they did not believe prisoners enjoyed the freedom of association, assembly, and discussion, or sufficient access to the free flow of information, to cast a meaningful vote. They did not think any other justification was possible. They agreed, for example, that "disenfranchisement of criminal offenders is not justifiable by any supposed need to protect society from the votes of 'unfit persons.' "[25] Justice Taylor thought this conclusion further implied that "any use of disenfranchisement for punitive purposes must be unconstitutional."[26] Punishment, in his view, was concerned with deterrence and rehabilitation, and the prisoner disqualification contributed to neither: "The prospect of loss of voting rights is hardly likely to operate as a deterrent to the commission of criminal offences, and disenfranchisement holds no hope of reforming offenders."[27]

Justices Taylor and Macdonell were clearly in the minority in resting their justification of the disqualification on the inability of prisoners "to cast a meaningful vote." No other judge involved in these cases thought the disqualification could be justified by restrictive prison conditions. In *Belczowski*, for example, Justice Strayer rejected the government's contention that since voting assumes the possibility of debating the issues with others, the prisoner disqualification "is a recognition that 'the conditions which … prevail in a penal institution, are inimical to such discussion and interplay.'"[28] Strayer noted that Belczowski "in his own testimony related how he was able to follow public events in prison through watching numerous public affairs programs on television and reading newspapers and magazines regularly available to inmates."[29] Nor do inmates lack all opportunity to discuss public matters among themselves. In addition, inmates can often avail themselves of educational opportunities, thus enhancing their capacity to deliberate thoughtfully on issues of public concern. Sauvé, for example, used his time in prison to acquire an undergraduate degree from Queen's University, and then enrolled in a graduate program. In fact, Sauvé's decision to pursue the right to vote stemmed directly from his growing interest in public affairs. It is difficult to argue that Sauvé or Belczowski are less informed than many voters outside the prison system. Indeed, as Justice Strayer suggests, if inability or unwillingness to participate fully in public life is the criterion, there are plenty of better candidates for disqualification than such prisoners:

> If one were to join this particular crusade advocated by Crown counsel, it would be necessary to disenfranchise the sick and the elderly who are confined to their homes or institutions, those in hospital prior to an election, probably those out of the country during election campaigns, the illiterate, those who live in remote parts of the country and, most of all, those hundreds of thousands who live in our midst and who, according to regular polls, take no interest whatever in politics.[30]

Even the government seemed to concede the weakness of the "prison conditions" justification for the disqualification, for although it put the argument to Justice Strayer in *Belczowski*, it called no evidence in its support.[31]

If Justices Macdonell and Taylor garnered little support among their judicial colleagues for their prison-conditions argument, Justice Taylor did no better with his corollary claim that "disenfranchisement for punitive purposes must be unconstitutional." Justice Strayer in *Belczowski* rejects this view, arguing that "sanctioning offenders" is in fact the *only* objective available to justify the disqualification.[32] Indeed, conceding that this objective is sufficiently compelling to justify some limitation of prisoners' right to vote, Justice Strayer invalidates the law mainly because its means are not proportional to this purpose.

Yet Taylor is surely right in thinking that disenfranchisement has little deterrent or rehabilitative value. If Strayer thinks the prisoner disqualification serves a punitive purpose, it must be because he thinks punishment extends beyond deterrence and rehabilitation to encompass the traditional function of retribution. In this Strayer is clearly right. If we punished mainly to deter, we would not bother punishing those who commit serious crimes of passion, such as many murders, which are notoriously difficult to deter. Similarly, we neither release serious criminals earlier than they would otherwise be eligible for parole because they have been quickly rehabilitated, nor keep petty criminals in prison beyond the sentence imposed on them because they appear not to have mended their ways. These qualifications on the principles of deterrence and rehabilitation stem from the retributive conviction that offenders should "pay" (and be "paid back") for their antisocial actions in approximate proportion to the seriousness of the offence. We have allowed considerations of deterrence or rehabilitation to mitigate this retributive principle, but not completely to overwhelm it. From the retributive perspective, disenfranchisement may be an ingredient in the overall loss of desirable things with which offenders "pay their debt" to society.

Although Justice Strayer took a broader view of punishment than Justice Taylor, other judges took a view that is broader still. In *Sauvé*, for example, Justice Van Camp argued that the disqualification served symbolically to reinforce the kind of morally responsible citizenry on which liberal democratic constitutionalism depends. She summarized her contention as follows:

> Parliament was justified in limiting the right to vote with the objective that a liberal democratic regime requires a decent and responsible citizenry. Such a regime requires that citizens obey voluntarily; the practical efficacy of laws relies on the willing acquiescence of those subject to them. The State has a role in preserving itself by the symbolic exclusion of criminals from the right to vote for the lawmakers. So also, the exclusion of the criminal from the right to vote reinforces the concept of a decent responsible citizenry essential for a liberal democracy.[33]

For Justice Van Camp, the voting disqualification is obviously more than simply a matter of direct punishment for offenders; it also serves a wider educative function for society as a whole. She believes that laws such as this have a legitimate role in promoting a certain kind of "public morality." Justice Scollin may have had something similar in mind when he wrote in Badger's provincial case that the prisoner disqualification has the legitimate objective "of preserving the currency of the franchise and both symbolically and practically stigmatizing those who deliberately breach their duty to society."[34] Certainly the grounds for a "public morality" interpretation of the disqualification's purpose had been presented to Justice Scollin in a brief prepared by Professor John Courtney.[35] Suggesting that the "small [and not very helpful] literature on the subject ... provides an important clue about how society has taken for granted (and, for the most part, likely widely accepted) the values implicit in the centuries-old practice of denying the vote to criminals," Courtney argues that to make these values explicit one must look for them where they "lie hidden in the historical development of the franchise."[36]

> It is true, after all, as Friedrich Hayek and others have reminded us, that many principles for which there is widespread support today are often taken for granted rather than explicitly stated, and that because their precise origins frequently have been lost with the passage of time the reasons for their existence must be inferred from developments covering many centuries. So it is with the exclusion of sentenced prisoners from the electoral franchise.[37]

In reviewing the relevant history, Courtney discerns a pattern of justifying franchise limitations in terms of restricting the vote to responsible citizens. He contends, for example, that the "responsible behaviour principle" lies "behind the [earlier] propertied class's monopoly on the ballot,"[38] and that the same principle explains the disenfranchisement of criminals. "It was only natural," he writes, "that the link between voting rights and responsible, non-criminal behaviour would have been established both in the law and in the public's mind."[39] Courtney notes, moreover, that as the franchise broadened in the 19th century, "the fundamental principle of voting as a *responsible* act remained unchallenged." In particular, with the "change away from the property qualification" came explicit disqualifications of convicted felons, as well as those engaged in bribery and corrupt electoral practices.[40] In short, tests for the desired responsibility based on status (who one was), such as the property test, came to be replaced by narrower tests based on behaviour (what one had done), such as the prisoner disqualification. The underlying purpose of associating voting with responsible behaviour, however, remained constant. Very similar arguments had been placed before Justice Van Camp (who was clearly persuaded) in *Sauvé* and Justice Strayer in *Belczowski*. These views appear to have influenced Justice Scollin's decision, although he does not express them as fully and clearly as did Justice Van Camp.

Justice Strayer, by contrast, explicitly rejected the "public morality" view of the disqualification in *Belczowski*. He was not impressed by the claim that there are unlikely to be clear statements of legislative purpose when the legitimacy of a policy is simply taken for granted—indeed, that the original Canadian legislation had occasioned virtually no debate at all[41]—and that purpose should thus be retrospectively inferred in the manner suggested by Courtney. For Strayer, such "restrospective rationalizations" would not suffice. In the absence of more immediate indications "as to the purpose of Parliament in adopting this legislation," he was "unable to see evidence of a legitimate objective of requiring a 'decent and responsible citizenry.'"[42] Strayer insisted that he had "only the words of the Act and judicial notice of community characteristics to guide" him,[43] and that these revealed only the narrower purpose of sanctioning criminals as an available justification of the legislation under the first branch of the *Oakes* test.

This disagreement between Justices Van Camp and Strayer constitutes the symbolic heart of the issue. Not that one's opinion on this matter necessarily determines the immediate outcome of the litigation. It may be possible, for example, to adopt Justice Van Camp's broader, "public morality" view of legislative purpose and still to find the legislative means disproportional to that purpose. Indeed, we have noted that Justice Scollin appears to have arrived at just such a conclusion. Thus if one is concerned primarily with the immediate issue of the law's validity, the disagreement about purpose may seem secondary to the proportionality issue. But we have seen that judicial reasoning often has significance far transcending the immediate issue it is used to resolve. Even when it does not determine the immediate outcome, judicial reasoning can enhance the status of the broader visions of justice it embodies, and judicial disagreements often reflect conflicting visions. In this case, the disagreement between Justices Van Camp and Strayer about legislative objectives can be understood as one episode in a wider struggle between competing visions of the appropriate functions of law in a liberal society. This struggle pits libertarians, who resist the legal inculcation of morality, against moralists, who insist that the moral foundations of liberal democracy need legal support. To appreciate the full significance of the litigation about prisoners' voting rights, we need to unearth the conflicting visions underlying it. In undertaking this task, we rely on the expert evidence provided to the courts (especially in *Sauvé, Badger,* and *Belczowski*), which provides a fuller statement of the conflicting visions than do the judgments themselves. (At this point we should again note our own participation in the development of this evidence. The Crown hired Morton to prepare section 1 evidence for Badger's provincial case and Knopff to do the same thing for the *Sauvé* litigation. Knopff also gave oral testimony in *Sauvé* and *Belczowski*, and his written submission was filed in Badger's federal case. Some of the following discussion reproduces and develops material found in Knopff's written evidence.)

Our discussion of the conflict of visions conveniently breaks down into four main questions: (1) Does liberal democratic constitutionalism require a decent and responsible citizenry? (2) if so, does the required responsibility simply flow from widespread agreement with the justice of the regime and its laws, or does it also depend on moral self-restraint? (3) if morality is involved, does it need legal support? and (4) if so, is the prisoner disqualification among the legitimate kinds of legal support?

■ CONSTITUTIONALISM AND A RESPONSIBLE CITIZENRY

It is important to recognize that the combatants in this conflict of visions do not disagree about all four of these questions; they accept the common premise that liberal democratic constitutionalism requires a decent responsible citizenry. To appreciate the nature of their disagreement, we must first understand this point of common departure.

The Police State Argument

The most obvious argument that liberal democracy requires a minimally moral citizenry is fairly simple. As Justice Van Camp suggests, a liberal democracy depends on voluntary law-abidingness on the part of most people. If obedience were wholly dependent on the fear of punishment, the coercive power of the state would have to expand to such an extent that it could no longer be considered liberal. Where law and interest do not coincide, fear of punishment and self-restraint are the two supports of law-abidingness. A liberal regime must depend more on the latter than the former. George Grant summarizes this perspective:

> [T]he free acceptance of a certain minimum of public order on the part of the citizens depends on what those citizens believe to be true about their lives. For example … if citizens come to believe that their immediate desires must be satisfied even if it involves breaking the law and will therefore break the law unless they are afraid of being caught, this inevitably brings an increase in police power, to an extent which cannot but be inimical to constitutional government…. The constitutional state then has an interest in limiting pluralism of belief: that limitation being what is necessary to a continuance of constitutional government.[44]

Justice Strayer did not quarrel with this point. "[A] liberal democracy," he wrote, "cannot be maintained where laws are not generally acceptable to most people because otherwise the police measures necessary for effective law enforcement would destroy individual rights and liberties."[45]

The Constitutionalism Argument

Liberal democratic constitutionalism requires self-restraint from its governors as well as from the governed. Indeed, constitutionalism is largely an exercise of self-restraint. True, governments are subject to binding constitutional law, but what makes that law effective? John Austin, the great 19th-century legal philosopher, defined law as the enforceable command of a sovereign governmental authority. According to this radically "positivist" definition, the idea of "constitutional law" seems a contradiction in terms. While it might make sense to conceive of the criminal law as commanded by the state in its legislative aspect, and enforced by the state in its judicial and executive aspects, constitutional law binds the state itself and is enforceable only by one branch of the state (the courts) against the other branches. But as Alexander Hamilton pointed out, the courts wield the power of neither sword nor purse. They can enforce nothing against the other branches that the latter (especially the executive) do not willingly accept.[46] Sir Ivor Jennings makes the same point:

> Force cannot be used against those who control the force. A Government cannot coerce itself, though a Government can coerce one of its members. The courts cannot control the Government. They can give verdicts or judgements against it, but they have no force at their disposal save that controlled by the Government itself.[47]

Constitutional law is in this respect indistinguishable from constitutional convention. Constitutional laws are formally embodied in legal documents that can become the basis of judgment by courts of law, while conventions are political understandings that cannot be enforced in court. In the decisive respect, however, both remain largely a matter of voluntary self-restraint on the part of office-holders.[48] In the words of Sir Ivor Jennings: "The constitution of a country, whatever it be, rests upon acquiescence. Constitutional laws and constitutional conventions are in substance the same."[49] The self-restrained rulers required to sustain constitutionalism, of course, are likely to emerge only from a general population imbued with moral self-restraint.

Law as Command vs. Law as Consent

Austin understood that constitutional law is unenforceable in the sense of his definition, which is why he denied it the status of "law" and relegated it to the realm of "positive morality" instead.[50] Yet, contrary to Austin, most modern observers consider entrenched constitutional documents to be law, a position that makes sense only if law is characterized not primarily by command and enforcement, as Austin thought, but by being substantially rooted in popular acceptance. Nowadays, most reputable legal theorists reject Austin's "command theory" of law in favour of some form of consensus theory.[51]

The command theory has been abandoned not merely to "save" the notion of "constitutional law," but also because it does not really fit other kinds of law either. Thus it has been suggested that even criminal law, which most obviously suits the Austinian model, is not well explained by it. Is criminal law effective mainly because it takes the form of enforceable command? We have already noted that if criminal law were not based on the prevailing sense of right and wrong, the liberal state would soon become a police state. As if this were not bad enough, one must ask how such a state could recruit a reliable police force from a population that does not accept the legal regime.[52] Visions of mercenary corruption spring to mind, but only to crowd out all images of an orderly and free democracy. W.R. Lederman draws the appropriate conclusion:

> Law is not primarily a matter of coercion and punishment, rather it is primarily a matter of setting standards for society and devising solutions for critical social problems that attract willing acceptance from most people because these standards and solutions offer some measure of the modern concept of substantial justice.[53]

■ RATIONAL AGREEMENT VS. MORAL HABIT

Justice Strayer is quite willing to agree with the argument up to this point. His *Belczowski* opinion explicitly concedes that "it is essential to a modern liberal democracy that the majority of people be 'decent and responsible' in the sense of accepting the existence of the state and the legitimacy of its legal system as well as obeying most of its positive laws...."[54] Yet Strayer appears to assume that correspondence between the legal regime and the "modern concept of substantive justice" is sufficient to maintain the required degree of law-abidingness. This assumption may also be implicit in the just-quoted statement by Lederman. Rational agreement with the justice of the legal regime, in this view, is assumed to be sufficient to secure the required degree of law-abidingness. If this is true, then there is little need to use law as an educative tool in the promotion of morality.

To proponents of the legal support of public morality, however, rational agreement with the justice of laws, though necessary, is not a sufficient condition for law-abidingness. Voluntary law-abidingness certainly depends to some extent on the correspondence between law and prevailing standards of justice, but for moralists this correspondence is not enough. Simply agreeing with the justice of a law, they insist, will often not suffice to induce obedience. The moral habit of self-restraint is also required, which is why early liberal theorists placed so much emphasis on morality.

According to this "moralist" argument, the necessity for moral self-restraint becomes apparent when we reflect on how common it is to accept the desirability of laws—or, more generally, the propriety of obeying even laws one does not wholeheartedly support—and nevertheless to be tempted by immediate interest to break the law. Even the thief must rationally concede both the justice of the laws that make his activity illegal and the desirability of most people obeying those laws. If too many people followed the thief's example, the order and security required to sustain the production of wealth would degenerate into the proverbial Hobbesian state of nature, a war of each against all in which there would be little incentive to produce anything worth stealing. Thus we must understand theft as the self-interested infringement of rules the thief rationally accepts as just. To use contemporary terminology, the thief has succumbed to the temptation to "free ride" on the law-abidingness he rationally supports for everyone else.

Free riding, of course, is a universal temptation. We all benefit from the order and security provided by effective laws, and we thus rationally support the idea of law-abidingness, especially if the laws correspond to our substantive sense of justice; yet, if only self-interest is consulted, we would each benefit even more if we could evade the cost of law-abidingness while everyone else paid it. The example of taxes comes readily to mind. Most people would prefer to avoid paying even taxes they consider just, although they almost invariably support the necessity of taxation in principle. Each individual would benefit most by evading taxes while everyone else paid them. The money saved is very significant to the individual, but an almost imperceptible fragment of overall tax revenues. Thus the isolated tax delinquent will continue to benefit from a virtually unchanged level of government services, while evading his personal share of the cost of those services. In effect, he has his cake and eats it too.

The difficulty is that everyone else is likely to reason the same way. Thus there is a tendency for free riding to become generalized to everyone's disadvantage. Effective government would decline, and the cost in increased instability would significantly outweigh what each individual saved through tax evasion. In short, if everyone pursues the best individual outcome (evade while others pay), the ironic result is for everyone to be worse off than if they had all paid. Paying along with everyone else might not be as good as evading while they all pay, but it is significantly better than no one paying, which is what happens if everyone succumbs to the temptation to have their cake and eat it too.

But why should this indicate the necessity of moral self-restraint in a liberal society? Surely individuals who can calculate the individual advantage of isolated evasion can also foresee the disastrous consequences of everyone succumbing to the same temptation. Might this rational calculation not be enough to induce everyone (or at least most people) voluntarily to pay their taxes? This seems to have been the view of such thinkers as Beccaria, the 18th-century founder of modern criminology. For Beccaria, the same self-interested calculation that tempted people to break the law would, when "enlightened," lead them to recognize the generalized disorder of the "state of nature" to which widespread disobedience would return them. This rational recognition would sustain the required degree of law-abidingness:

> The vigorous force of the laws, meanwhile, remains immovable, for no enlightened person can fail to approve of the clear and useful public compacts of mutual security when he compares the inconsiderable portion of useless liberty he himself has sacrificed [on leaving the state of nature] with the sum total of liberties sacrificed by other men, which, except for the laws, might have been turned against him. Any person of sensibility, glancing over a code of well-made laws and observing that he has lost only a baneful liberty to injure others, will feel constrained to bless the throne and its occupant.[55]

Not everyone accepts this view, however. Dostoevsky, for example, dismissed it as the product of infantile innocence:

> But these are all golden dreams. Oh, tell me, who was it first announced, who was it first proclaimed, that man only does nasty things because he does not know his own interests; and that if he were enlightened, if his eyes were open to his real normal interests, man would at once cease to do nasty things, would at once become good and noble because, being enlightened and understanding his real advantage, he would see his own advantage in the good and nothing else, and we all know that not one man can, consciously, act against his own interests, consequently, so to say, through necessity, he would begin doing good? Oh, the babe! Oh, the pure innocent child![56]

Dostoevsky's judgment finds some support in modern game theory. The problem of tax laws we have been exploring—indeed, the problem of law-abidingness as such—is a particular example of a more general phenomenon known to game theorists as "prisoner's dilemma." Prisoner's

Dilemma takes its name from the following hypothetical situation. Two accomplices in crime are taken into custody and interrogated separately by the police. Although the police have enough information to convict each of a minor offence carrying a penalty of one year's imprisonment, they are fairly certain, though they cannot yet prove beyond a reasonable doubt, that the suspects are also guilty of a more serious offence. Each prisoner is told that he will go free if he confesses and implicates his partner in the major crime; this will net the partner twenty years in prison. If both "squeal," they will each be sentenced to five years. If neither talks, of course, they will each get one year for the lesser offence. Each is aware that the same deal has been offered to the other, and they are unable to communicate with each other.

The strategic choices of each "player" are indicated in the following matrix. Each prisoner "cooperates" with the other if he remains silent; he "defects" if he squeals. The numerical values in each cell indicate the "pay-offs" or number of years in prison each player receives for the pair of strategic choices represented by that cell. Obviously zero is best and twenty is worst. The first number in each cell represents the pay-offs of prisoner A (the "row player"), while the second number represents the pay-offs of prisoner B (the "column player").

Figure 1

PRISONER B

	Cooperate	Defect
Cooperate	-1 -1	-20 0
Defect	0 -20	-5 -5

(PRISONER A)

Examining the matrix from A's perspective, we find that the best he can hope for from cooperation (remaining silent) is one year in prison if B also cooperates (the upper left cell). If B does cooperate, however, A would have done even better by defecting. He then would have gone scot-free while his partner languished in prison for twenty years (lower left). This is known as the "temptation pay-off." If A cooperates and B defects, on the other hand, A would get twenty years (the "sucker's pay-off") while B went free (upper right). In this case A would have done better by also defecting: instead of twenty years he would have been imprisoned for only five (lower right). No matter what B does, in other words, A is always better off defecting: A will get zero rather than one year if B cooperates, and five rather than twenty years if B defects. Examining the matrix from B's perspective shows that he is in the same position.

Thus it is individually rational for both players to defect. This, of course, will net them both five years in prison. For each player this is better than suffering the sucker's pay-off of twenty years, but it is clearly worse than the one year they each would have received had they cooperated. Clearly the "temptation pay-off" of going free is unlikely for either player unless his partner is irrational or stupid. Thus the best practicable solution is mutual cooperation. But this solution is prevented by the fear of being taken for a sucker and getting twenty years. In other words, what is collectively preferable (mutual cooperation) is individually irrational. The most likely result is mutual defection, with each player better off than a sucker but worse off than he could have been had both cooperated.

Our hypothetical taxpayer is like one of the "players" in "prisoner's dilemma." The major difference is that the taxpayer is playing not against a single opponent, but against all other taxpayers. As Figure 2 shows, if only rational calculations of individual self-interest are taken into account, the individual is always better off evading taxes. For the sake of simplicity we present only the individual's pay-offs. The pay-offs are arbitrary representations of the likely order of preference, with 10 representing the best and 0 the worst.

If everyone else pays their taxes, the individual can always obtain a greater pay-off through evasion. This is the temptation pay-off, and because isolated evasion is likely to go unnoticed, it is a substantial temptation. It is the most attractive alternative and is thus given the highest value. On the other hand, the individual is always worried about being played for a sucker if he pays while everyone else evades. This sucker's pay-off is even worse than the scenario in which no one pays, and is to be avoided at all cost, which is why it is given the lowest value. The pay-offs for mutual cooperation (everyone pays) and mutual defection (no one pays) rank between these two extremes, with the former of greater value than the latter.

Figure 2   EVERYONE ELSE

	Pay	Evade
Pay	**5**	**0**
Evade	**10**	**2**

INDIVIDUAL

The individual would like to achieve the temptation pay-off, but knows that everyone else is similarly tempted. Thus achieving the temptation pay-off is unlikely. This will not induce the individual to cooperate, however, because that would expose him to the risk of being played for a sucker. Experiencing the strength of the temptation to evade himself, he knows that it is not unlikely for cooperation to net him the sucker's pay-off. The only sure way to avoid being played for a sucker, of course, is evade himself. In short, no matter what the rest of the taxpaying population does, the individual taxpayer, like the prisoner in the archetypical game, is always better off evading. If everyone else pays, he can do better by evading; if everyone else evades, he would be a sucker to pay. Since all individuals are actually in the same situation, making the same calculations, generalized tax evasion is the predictable result, despite the fact that everyone finds this less desirable than generalized payment. Again, the matrix shows that while everyone prefers general cooperation to general evasion, the latter is the more likely outcome. What is collectively preferable is unlikely because it is individually irrational.

Prisoner's Dilemma shows that Dostoevsky was right: rational agreement on the collective superiority of one behavioural pattern to another is not enough to achieve the preferable pattern. This is why Thomas Hobbes considered general consent to rules of conduct a necessary but not sufficient condition for general obedience to these rules. The problem of tax evasion is, in this respect, simply a particular example of a more general phenomenon. Something in addition to widespread agreement on the justice of rules is required to achieve general obedience, or to overcome the problem of generalized free riding. The most obvious additional factor is punitive deterrence. Thus we do not rely on the general agreement in the necessity of taxes to ensure their payment; instead we enact tax laws with known penalties for disobedience. The penalties embodied in many other laws, such as those prohibiting theft or fraud, can be explained in the same way.

But in a liberal society punishment alone is unlikely to be enough because, as suggested above, a virtual police state would be necessary to ensure law-abidingness in a population whose obedience was secured mainly by the threat of punishment. The deterrent effect of punishment works to the extent that it is credible—i.e., to the extent that there is a reasonable chance of getting caught. In a society where only the threat of punishment restrains people, the prospect of getting caught varies directly with the size of policing resources. A relatively limited policing power will increase the temptation to free ride, and as more people give in to that temptation the prospects of any particular individual getting caught will decrease, thus further increasing the temptation to free ride. The predictable result is spiralling disobedience, which could be stemmed only by increasing the police power. The kind of limited police power preferred by liberal democrats can maintain a credible threat of punishment only if the pool of potential free riders is also relatively limited—that is, only if a substantial majority of the population obeys voluntarily. Yet, as we have seen, simple agreement with the justice of the laws is not enough to secure this voluntary obedience—even disobedient free riders often rationally concede the justice or necessity of the laws they disobey. Thus agreement must be supplemented with the habit of moral self-restraint. These considerations help us understand why many liberal theorists considered moral self-restraint to be a necessary foundation for liberal democratic regimes.

This liberal concern with public morality should not be misunderstood. Liberals clearly substitute freedom for virtue as the end or purpose of political life. The purpose of the political community is not, as it was for pre-modern regimes, to promote high virtue, but to secure the conditions of liberty and comfortable self-preservation. In Plato's *Laws* we find politics defined as the "art whose business it is to care for souls."[57] John Locke better expresses the modern liberal view. "The commonwealth," he says, is constituted solely for the "preservation and advancement of ... life, liberty, the integrity and freedom from pain of the body, and the possession of external things, such as estate, money, furniture, and so forth...."[58]

Nevertheless, although the two themes of liberty and public morality are different, many of the most influential theorists of liberalism saw no necessary opposition between them. Although virtue was no longer the *end* of political life, a minimal degree of morality remained an indispensable *means* to the more limited ends of the liberal state. In this view, a liberal regime is not interested in the production of saints, but it depends on at least a minimal degree of morality—enough to sustain the law-abidingness required to maintain order without an excessive resort to force. Even those liberal thinkers who most assiduously emphasized the substitution of institutional checks and balances for virtue as the guarantee of freedom rarely abandoned virtue altogether. Thus James Madison, the great theorist of the American system of checks and balances, conceded in *Federalist* No. 55 that

> as there is a degree of depravity in mankind which requires a certain degree of circumspection and distrust, so there are other qualities in human nature which justify a certain portion of esteem and confidence. Republican government presupposes the existence of these qualities in a higher degree than any other form. Were the pictures which have been drawn by the political jealousy of some among us faithful likenesses of the human character, the inference would be that there is not sufficient virtue among men for self-government; and that nothing less than the chains of despotism can restrain them from destroying and devouring one another.[59]

The cogency of the argument that liberal democracies require a foundation in public morality is shown by the fact that it was accepted even by John Stuart Mill, the acknowledged founder of radical "libertarianism." Mill's *On Liberty* established the libertarian thesis that law should be used only to prevent individuals from directly and palpably harming others, not to inculcate morality. This view did not lead him to depreciate the importance and necessity of morality, however. Indeed, Mill suggests that a minimal level of morality (i.e., basic self-restraint) is the basis of progress in an atmosphere of liberty, giving mankind "the capacity of being guided to their own improvement by conviction or persuasion" rather than by compulsion. "Liberty," said Mill, "has no application to any state of things anterior to the time when mankind have become capable of being improved by free and equal discussion"—i.e., anterior to the time when they are capable of governing their passions. Mill did not hesitate to distinguish between civilization and barbarism in these terms. "Despotism," he wrote, "is a legitimate mode of government in dealing with barbarians, provided the end be their improvement and the means justified by actually effecting that end."[60]

■ PRIVATE VS. PUBLIC PRODUCTION OF PUBLIC MORALITY

As the example of Mill shows, the considerable agreement on the necessity of public morality in a liberal democracy does not entail a similar agreement on the question of how to create and sustain this moral foundation. In rejecting the ancient emphasis on virtue as the end of political life, liberal democracy clearly rejected character formation as the central public preoccupation. For some liberal theorists, character formation became a completely illegitimate form of government activity; for others, some degree of the public promotion and even the legal "enforcement of morals" remained necessary and legitimate. Prominent in the former camp is John Stuart Mill, who argued that "the sole end for which mankind are warranted, individually or collectively, in interfering with the liberty of action of any of their number is self-protection.... His own good, either physical or moral, is not a sufficient warrant. He cannot rightfully be compelled to do or forbear because it will be better for him to do so, because it will make him happier, because, in the opinions of others, to do so would be wise or even right."[61] As we have seen, Mill thought that such liberty "has no application ... [until] mankind have attained the capacity of being guided to their own improvement by conviction or persuasion," but he immediately added that this point had "long since [been] reached in all nations with whom we need here concern ourselves"[62]—i.e., in the modern liberal democracies. Mill clearly placed great faith in the notion of progress and believed that once the moral foundations of civilization had been established there would be no backsliding.[63] Indeed, he thought that civilization had reached the point where people would break with prevailing morality not out of passion or interest, but mainly because they had been rationally persuaded that what seemed unorthodox was in fact a new and better way. Not only did such moral experimentation not need to be controlled, but Mill considered it the engine of further progress. Like Socrates and Christ the unorthodox were to be prized as pathbreakers.[64] Once civilization had been established, in other words, complete moral liberty would lead not to moral decline, but to moral improvement. Liberal democracy required public morality, but that morality did not require legal support—indeed, its improvement depended precisely on the absence of legal support. Public morality would be privately produced.

The opposite opinion is expressed by Lord Patrick Devlin, who argues that Mill "did not really grapple with the fact that along the paths that depart from traditional morals, pimps leading the weak astray far outnumber spiritual explorers at the head of the strong."[65] In this aphorism Devlin expresses his disagreement with the idea of inexorable progress. Mill was wrong, he suggests, to believe that the required moral foundation of liberal democracy was immune from the forces of barbarism after a certain point of historical progress. Departures from moral orthodoxy, Devlin believes, are at all times far more likely to be undertaken out of passionate self-interest than in the spirit of altruistic moral experimentation—and the former can hardly be expected to contribute to moral improvement.[66] In short, whereas Mill clearly fits within Sowell's "unconstrained" vision—inasmuch as he appears to think that human nature itself will be transformed by historical progress, so that the inclinations that formerly required legal control will decline—Devlin takes his bearings from the "constrained" vision's tendency to "see each new generation born [as] in effect an invasion of civilization by little barbarians, who must be civilized before it is too late."[67] The forces of barbarism, in the latter view, are permanent features of human nature, not historically contingent features that will fade with historical progress. Thus, if legal control of the forces leading to barbarism was ever justified, it is always justified. Devlin concludes that if one concedes the need for public morality (as *On Liberty* did), and if one doubts inevitable progress (as *On Liberty* did not), one cannot simplistically reject the legal "enforcement of morals."

Consistent with their vision of minimal morality as a means to liberty, liberal societies have certainly emphasized the private production of morality over its legal enforcement. For example, in former times established state religions were the vehicle of public morality. Liberal democracies, by contrast, favour the separation of church and state, thereby banishing religion to the private sphere. Indeed, liberalism was arguably born of the attempt to avoid the warlike divisiveness inherent in the theocratic principle, and its early theorists saw the separation of church and state (or public toleration) as a way of weakening and taming dangerous religious zealotry.[68] An atmosphere of religious freedom would promote the proliferation of sects, and where no one sect could easily dominate, all would acquire an interest in continued toleration. "A variety of sects," said Madison, "must secure the national councils against any danger" of religiously based "political factions."[69] However, this did not necessarily mean that religion was no longer expected to play a role in the formation of public morality in liberal democracies. Although liberalism was hostile to state-imposed religion, few of its theorists embraced the opposite extreme of state-imposed atheism. Rather, it was thought that a multiciplicity of sects, weaned from their destructive political ambitions, would continue to flourish in the private sphere, less zealous in orientation, but nevertheless contributing to the minimal level of public morality required in the liberal democratic context. Thus the same Thomas Jefferson who spoke of the "wall of separation" between church and state wrote that "the only firm basis" for "the liberties of a nation" is the "conviction in the minds of the people that these liberties are the gift of God," that "they are not to be violated without his wrath."[70] Jefferson's views in this respect vividly illustrate both the liberal belief in the importance of morality and the faith that the required morality is best produced privately.

Nevertheless, although liberal democracies have relied less than premodern regimes on the overtly public promotion of morality, public involvement has never been abandoned altogether. Public education, for example, has never been understood simply as a way of transmitting information, but has always been expected to help, more or less directly, in the inculcation of good citizenship.[71] Indeed, despite their dedication to the principle of religious freedom, liberal regimes have often encouraged religious instruction and practice in the schools. In the United States this was made possible by understanding the separation of church and state as preventing only the public preference of one church over all others, not the nondiscriminatory public support of religion as such.[72] This understanding was rejected by the Supreme Court in 1947 in favour of a more radical "wall of separation" between the two realms,[73] but American policy-makers still strive to find ways of aiding religious private schools and facilitating prayers and religious instruction in the public schools.[74] Canada has traditionally gone even further in this direction by providing a separate Catholic stream within the public educational system, a practice that is itself constitutionally protected.[75] As in the United States, however, religious practices and instruction within the secular stream of the public system are increasingly coming under attack.[76]

Public law in liberal societies has also retained the function of embodying and supporting essential moral principles. This is perhaps most obvious in the formerly common practice of legislating against so-called "victimless crimes." For example, liberal regimes in the past often legislated against consensual sexual practices thought to undermine the traditional

family, that small society in the midst of the larger one that was traditionally seen as the locus of the first education in social self-restraint and obedience to legitimate authority. Legislation against obscenity and gambling
reflected similar concerns. As in the case of the public support of religion,
however, the prohibition of "victimless crimes" is increasingly controversial
and under attack.

Less open to question in a liberal society is the legitimacy of punishment for crimes that palpably harm obvious victims. What is not always
appreciated is that punishments of this sort serve not only to deter crime,
but also to provide a kind of education in public morality, thereby diminishing the wellsprings of criminal inclination. The disenfranchisement of
prisoners is best justified by reference to this educational function of punishment.

Criminologists have long noted that punishments educate the public
as well as penalize the criminal. According to Johannes Andenaes, "punishment as a concrete expression of society's disapproval of an act helps to
form and to strengthen the public's moral code and thereby creates conscious and unconscious inhibitions against committing crimes."[77] We
noted above that Justice Strayer rejected the notion that the disenfranchisement of imprisoned criminals could be justified with respect to an educational purpose of this kind, though he agreed that the disenfranchisement
of at least some criminals might be justified as a component of their punishment. If Andenaes is right, Strayer's attempt to separate punishment
from symbolic education is like attempting to separate the convex from the
concave sides of a curved line. For Andenaes, the two functions are inseparable.

Or, rather, symbolic education is inseparable from punishment as long
as the latter retains a retributive aspect. To repeat, the punishment of
crimes is influenced by the principle of retribution as well as by those of
deterrence and rehabilitation. The retributive principle insists that offenders get what they deserve—i.e., that they be "paid back" for an offence in
proportion to its seriousness—even if their "just deserts" serve the purposes of neither deterrence nor rehabilitation. Thus the retributive principle argues against lopping off the hands of petty thieves, even if such a
punishment would be an effective deterrent, because it is disproportionate to the offence. Similarly, the retributive principle insists that serious
punishment be attached to serious crimes, even if those crimes are impossible to deter or the perpetrators are quickly rehabilitated. Thus we do not
subject murderers to lengthy imprisonment primarily because of the deterrent value of this punishment—after all, the more serious death penalty

was abolished in Canada partly because of the claim that it was not an effective deterrent; nor do we do so because murderers generally take a long time to rehabilitate—many murderers are one-time offenders who need little rehabilitation. We insist on long prison sentences, rather, because serious crimes *deserve* serious punishments. Perhaps the most dramatic example of this principle is the ongoing attempt in liberal democracies to bring Nazi war criminals to justice and punish them. Why should we do this? asks Walter Berns:

> To rehabilitate them? The very idea is absurd. To incapacitate them? But they present no present danger. To deter others from doing what they did? That is a hope too extravagant to be indulged.

For Berns, and, he supposes, for "everyone else who agrees that they should be punished," the answer "was clear: *to pay them back*."[78]

We value punishment, in other words, not simply because it causes fear in those who would otherwise be inclined to commit a like offence. For the majority of law-abiding citizens, punishment performs the quite different function of affirming their sense of the seriousness of the offence. In affirming that sense, moreover, the punishment also strengthens it. Punishment not only reflects a public standard, in other words, but contributes to the ongoing symbolic education of citizens in the appropriateness of that standard. The theory behind this holds that citizens take their moral cues at least in significant part from prevailing public standards, and that in a liberal society those standards are most authoritatively represented by the legal penalties attached to violating them.

The Supreme Court adopted an educative view of criminal law punishments in *R. v. Keegstra*.[79] This case addressed the constitutionality of the Criminal Code provision making it a punishable offence to "wilfully promote hatred against any identifiable group." Writing for the majority, Chief Justice Dickson upheld the law as a "reasonable limit" on the Charter's guarantee of freedom of expression. He did so in part because the law "serves to illustrate to the public the severe reprobation with which society holds messages of hate directed towards racial and religious groups."[80] For Dickson, "the existence of a particular criminal law, and the process of holding a trial when that law is used, is ... itself a form of expression" that is valuable not just for its immediate deterrent effect, but for the message it sends out to society at large. In this case "the message sent out is that hate propaganda is harmful to target group members and threatening to a harmonious society." Not only do "the many, many Canadians who belong to identifiable groups surely gain a great deal of comfort from the knowledge that the hate-monger is criminally prosecuted and his or her ideas rejected," but "equally, the community as a whole is reminded of the importance of diversity and multiculturalism in Canada, the value of equality and the worth and dignity of each human person being particularly emphasized."[81]

According to Walter Berns, the psychological mechanism that often underlies the educative dimension of criminal law punishments is anger. When someone commits a crime, and thus breaks important standards of public morality, law-abiding citizens who have internalized those standards experience anger. This anger, which varies in intensity with the perceived seriousness of the crime, is a natural and healthy concomitant of attachment to the rule or standard that has been violated. One would expect the anger to disappear only to the extent that commitment to the standard wanes. People will cease to be angry with thieves or killers, in other words, only to the extent that they lose the sense that theft and murder are serious moral offences. And who, asks Berns, would want to live in a community where citizens did not become angry at murderers? The anger experienced by law-abiding citizens expresses itself in the demand for retribution, and is satisfied by punishments designed not primarily to deter or rehabilitate (though they may incidentally fulfil those functions as well), but to pay the criminal back in approximate proportion to the seriousness of the offence.

Retributive punishments do more than simply reflect and satisfy public anger, however; more significantly they legitimate and justify that anger, and thus strengthen the law-abiding dispositions out of which the anger springs. As Mary Ann Glendon argues, although law cannot be too far out of touch with social consensus if it is to be respected and effective, it is not always simply an epiphenomenal reflection of such consensus. If law was effective only when it blindly followed social consensus, it would be "most effective where it is least needed," and would thus be "wholly marginal to the main disturbances of modern life."[82] In fact, "law itself often assists in the formation of a consensus, by influencing the way people interpret the world around them as well as by communicating that certain values have a privileged place in society."[83] Law, in short, is a way "of interpreting our culture to ourselves, of summing up our ideals *while at the same time reinforcing them.*"[84] When the criminal law exacts retribution, it performs the latter, "reinforcing" function by symbolically telling the community that it is right to experience anger, that the offence is indeed worthy of its anger.

Retribution confirms most citizens in the moral rightness of their own law-abidingness, communicating to them the "privileged place" this value has in society. In blaming the criminal, in other words, retributive punishments also praise law-abiding citizens. Praise and blame, of course, are among the chief tools of moral education, and retributive punishment is thus a symbolic education in important public standards. Ironically, punishments that, except in a police state, cannot possibly succeed in deterring everyone, may contribute to the moral education required to avoid a police state. Punishments perform this function to the extent that they embody the retributive principle.

How does the prisoner disqualification fit this theory? Criminal law exacts retribution by imposing pain on offenders, usually by depriving them of highly valuable things, such as freedom. Defenders of the prisoner disqualification consider it a reasonable component of this punitive deprivation. Moreover, it seems admirably suited to the retributive principle of proportionality between offence and punishment. What could be more appropriate than to deprive those who have demonstrated their disrespect for law of their normal share in the sovereign function of lawmaking, at least for the duration of their imprisonment. As Justice Van Camp observed, the prisoner disqualification raises the question "whether it is justifiable that the person who breaks the law should participate in the choice of those who make the law." This way of phrasing the question invites the negative answer Justice Van Camp gave.

If the prisoner disqualification does not deter crime directly, as Justice Taylor argued in *Re Jolivet,* it nevertheless symbolically underscores the important connection between law-abidingness and liberal democratic citizenship. By depriving offenders of something generally considered to be valuable, it teaches the importance of law-abidingness. At the same time, the disqualification symbolically teaches the inherent dignity and value of the franchise by making law-abidingness a precondition of its exercise. The wholesale enfranchisement of prisoners is likely to teach a radically different lesson about the value of the franchise.

Even John Stuart Mill showed some sympathy for this view in his only discussion of prisoner voting. Mill did not think that giving the vote to criminals would do much "direct" harm. Indeed, he admitted that "as far as the direct influence of their votes went, it would scarcely be worth while to exclude them." His concern was with the symbolic influence of prisoner voting on what he called the "moral character" of the franchise. "As an aid to the great object of giving a moral character to the exercise of the suffrage," he wrote, "it might be expedient that in the case of crimes evincing a high degree of insensibility to social obligation, the deprivation of this and other civic rights should form part of the sentence."[85]

■ PROPORTIONALITY

The debate about legitimate legislative objectives is in many respects the most theoretically interesting part of the prisoners'-voting-rights litigation, but it did not conclude the legal analysis. Once legislative objectives have been established, and assuming they are sufficiently compelling, the *Oakes* test requires judges to ask whether the legislative means are proportional to those ends. This question also generated significant controversy.

On one side we find Justice Van Camp, who, having accepted the broader, "public morality" reading of legislative purpose, did not find any disproportionality between the legislation and that purpose. In particular, she thought the disqualification had been crafted carefully enough to pass the "minimal impairment" branch of the proportionality test:

> Parliament has carefully considered the extent to which those con-
> victed should be disenfranchised. It has not removed the right to
> citizenship. It has not removed the right from all those who have
> been convicted. It has not provided that the disqualification is for
> all time. It has not made the return of the right dependent upon any
> subsequent decision. The return is automatic as soon as the person
> ceases to be an inmate. It has provided for the return of the vote
> before the sentence is completed, as soon as the prisoner has
> shown the requisite for a gradual return to society. The disqualifi-
> cation is in fact upon those who disqualify themselves.[86]

Justice Strayer disagreed. He did not, of course, accept the broader reading of legislative purpose, and thus did not have to ask whether the legislative means were proportional to that purpose. Nevertheless, he addressed the question for the sake of argument. Even if the law had the objective of promoting a decent and responsible citizenry, he wrote, its means were entirely "arbitrary," and thus failed the "rational connection" component of the proportionality test:

It is arbitrary in singling out one category of presumably indecent or irresponsible citizens to deny them a right which they otherwise clearly have under section 3. It is self-apparent that there are many indecent and irresponsible persons outside of prison who are entitled to vote and do vote; on rare occasions some even get elected to office. On the other hand there are many law-breakers who are never charged with offences, and a high percentage of those who are never imprisoned. Those who have been identified among the indecent and irresponsible by a sentence of imprisonment do not necessarily become decent and responsible upon release, although their voting rights automatically arise again under the *Canada Elections Act.*[87]

This argument for the disproportionality of the disqualification is not terribly convincing. After all, we do not refuse to imprison the criminals we catch because we cannot succeed in catching all, or even a majority of them. Nor do we forego punishment because the occasional undetected criminal might get elected to public office. Why, then, should it count against the prisoner disqualification that not everyone who deserves this punishment is actually subjected to it?

Furthermore, to the extent that a legal punishment serves symbolic and educational purposes, it is not clear why it must be comprehensively applied. The deterrent function of a punishment is certainly improved by catching and sentencing all, or at least most, of those who infringe the law, but why does the educational effect of punishment on the law-abiding part of the community require this? The educational "message sent out" by trials and punishments "when a law is used" need not be diminished by the fact that not all lawbreakers are caught.

An even deeper difficulty with Justice Strayer's argument comes to light when we ask what kind of law would not be arbitrary. By Strayer's criteria, a voting disqualification cannot be proportional to the purpose of promoting public morality unless it "catches" not only all lawbreakers, but also all lawbreakers who remain indecent and irresponsible after their sentence, as well as all indecent and irresponsible people who have not yet gotten around to breaking the law. In other words, having made the obvious point that immorality and criminality are not co-extensive, Strayer proceeds to suggest that if the object is to promote morality, it is arbitrary to focus only on lawbreakers. In a word, in punishing only a part of what it is meant to discourage, the law is "underinclusive." A proportional law would presumably disqualify the indecent and irresponsible part of the community comprehensively and directly, rather than focusing only on its overtly lawless component.

In fact, there are historical examples of the direct disqualification of immoral citizens. For example, the legislation of the New England states in the 17th century directly specified good character as the precondition for voting rights.[88] Thus Pennsylvania restricted the vote to "reputable citizens," who were "not convicted of ill-fame or of unsober or dishonest conversation."[89] Massachusetts disqualified those who were "under conviction of evil carriage against the government or the churches" or who were "vicious in life."[90] In Connecticut voters had to "be men of an honest and peaceable conversation,"[91] and Rhode Island required them to "acknowledge and [be] obedient to the civil magistrates."[92]

Such provisions avoid Justice Strayer's problem of underinclusiveness, but he would surely find them even more objectionable than the more limited disqualification of prisoners, and rightly so. In fact, these old New England laws are far more illiberal than the present prisoner disqualification. They are dangerously vague and open-ended, and grant too much discretionary power to their enforcers. They conjure up visions of roving morality inspectors issuing official seals of respectability. In a liberal society it is surely preferable to specify narrowly defined traits that can serve as reasonably accurate proxies or tests for the desired "good character." In the past, one of the tests was possession of "freehold property." It was assumed that the ability to acquire and maintain property was a reliable index of good character, and the vote was thus restricted to the propertied. These and similar tests have all been abandoned, in part because the connection between them and good character was too loose or too controversial. The only remaining test of this sort is the disqualification of those convicted of breaking the law. This is a fairly simple and reliable test because lawbreakers have demonstrated beyond all doubt their unwillingness to exercise the minimal self-restraint required in a liberal democratic society. Moreover, while it may be underinclusive in not reaching all immoral citizens, the prisoner disqualification does not suffer from the overinclusiveness of the former property requirement, which disqualified the moral poor. In this sense, too, the prisoner disqualification is more liberal, for a liberal society must prefer a punishment or legal deprivation that reaches only part of its target to one that overshoots its mark, hitting unintended targets as well.

In this connection, it should again be emphasized that a liberal regime uses law to promote not the high virtue aspired to by the former establishments of religion, but a floor of morality below which liberal democratic citizens should not be allowed to fall. The point is to establish a list not of "thou shalts," but of "thou shalt *nots*," reflecting the Hobbesian reformulation of the Golden Rule: "Do *not* that to another, which thou wouldest *not* have done to thyself."[93] This perspective also supports the contemporary preference for negative tests of morality, such as the disqualification of convicted criminals, to the positive requirement of good character evident in the old New England legislation. The legal establishment of such minimal morality is not so obviously akin to the establishment of an official church. The latter clearly undermines liberal democratic constitutionalism; the former is what liberal theorists consider to be its necessary foundation. In this view, those who violate the moral foundation have demonstrated that they are unfit to participate in the democratic formulation of public policy under the Rule of Law in a constitutional regime.

This minimalism accounts not only for the fact that liberal societies do not require positive demonstrations of morality before allowing those who have reached the age of maturity to begin voting, but also for the fact that they often return the right to vote upon release from prison without inquiring whether the released prisoner has become moral in the interim. Because liberal society prefers not to meddle in personal affairs, it simply assumes that upon reaching the age of maturity its citizens have acquired the degree of morality required to sustain the regime, and inquires no further in granting them the right to vote. Since only the minimal morality manifested by law-abidingness is required, there is no reason to deprive anyone of the vote until it is demonstrated that he or she has fallen below the line by breaking the law. Once the sentence has been served, society once again assumes the citizen will be law-abiding and returns the right to vote, at least until it is proven wrong in its generous assumption by the citizen's resumption of illegal behaviour. In sum, the prisoner disqualification is far from being the kind of arbitrary law Justice Strayer thinks it is. Indeed, of the kinds of voting disqualifications that might be imagined, the disqualification of prisoners best suits the liberal approach to legally promoting public morality.

Justice Strayer gives more plausible reasons for finding the law disproportional to the narrower purpose of "sanctioning criminals." Some of these reasons stem from the retributive function of punishment. We argued above that Justice Strayer accepted the legitimacy of retribution, at least implicitly, when he conceded that sanctioning criminals is a sufficiently compelling purpose to justify some degree of prisoner disqualification under section 1 of the Charter. To repeat, some kinds of punishments might be sufficiently compelling because of their deterrent or rehabilitative value, but it is difficult to believe that the prisoner disqualification contributes much to either of these purposes. The only punitive purpose that might explain the disqualification is retribution. But we have seen that the central principle of retribution is proportionality between the seriousness of the offence and the severity of the punishment. Thus if the loss of voting rights is understood as severe punishment, it should be reserved for serious offenders. Such an intuition appears to be involved in Justice Strayer's conclusion that the blanket disqualification of prisoners is not proportional to its punitive ends, that it does not respect the "minimal impairment" requirement. He notes that the disqualification "applies no matter what the seriousness of the crime may be for which the inmate is being punished. In the same vein, he is troubled by the fact that "someone in prison for two weeks for non-payment of parking fines could lose his vote for four years," while "someone sentenced to prison for five years for fraud or sexual assault and released on parole after three and one-half years might never miss the opportunity to vote."[94] Justice Strayer clearly prefers the laws of many foreign jurisdictions, which "limit the deprivation of the vote to those serving sentences for the most serious crimes." As compared to the "blunt instrument" of Canada's blanket disqualification, such jurisdictions display "a more sensitive regard for proportionality."[95]

Ironically, the "minimal impairment" arguments Strayer found compelling in relation to "sanctioning criminals" would have served him equally well in showing that the disqualification was disproportionate to the law's alleged "public morality" purpose, much better in fact than the "rational connection" arguments he actually employed to show that the law was completely arbitrary in relation to that purpose. After all, if we are right in thinking that the educative function of punishment is a function of its retributive dimension, that function would also depend on the proportionality essential to the retributive principle. Punishment is likely to fulfil its educational purpose, in other words, only so long as proportionality between offence and punishment is respected. Far from reinforcing the public in the virtue of law-abidingness, punishments that are either too light (e.g., a suspended sentence for murder) or too heavy (e.g., hanging for petty theft) to satisfy the prevailing sense of proportionality are likely to elicit disrespect for the law. Thus it would be plausible to argue that if disenfranchisement is to be understood as a serious punishment, it should be reserved for serious offences.

Against this conclusion, one might well claim that the seriousness of disenfranchisement as a punishment depends on its duration, and that any lawbreaking act that merits imprisonment also deserves disenfranchisement for the period of incarceration. Thus disenfranchisement remains proportional even for lesser offences because, like the sentence of imprisonment itself, it is imposed for much shorter periods of time. But this contention would not take care of offences that we clearly believe merit fines rather than imprisonment, but where incarceration may result through inability to pay. Should we look with equanimity on the difference between petty offenders who pay their fines and their counterparts who default and find themselves in jail on voting day? Nor does our counter-argument address Strayer's concern that the effective disenfranchisement of minor offenders might involve more loss of voting opportunities than some offenders sentenced to longer terms, depending on the timing of elections. In short, the blanket disqualification cannot avoid issues of proportionality even if it is understood as serving the broader purpose of promoting public morality.

This conclusion underlines once again the fact that the bottom-line outcome of the case need not turn on the debate about the "public morality" function of the disqualification. If the "arbitrariness" arguments Strayer actually used to suggest the disproportionality of the law to the "public morality" purpose were the only ones available, their weakness might indicate that a plausible invalidation of the law depended on rejecting that purpose. In fact, Strayer could easily have accepted the "public morality" purpose and still found the law unconstitutional on the basis of the same (more compelling) proportionality arguments he used vis-à-vis the narrower purpose of "sanctioning criminals." No doubt he would have done so had he felt compelled to undertake more than a passing consideration of proportionality to the public morality purpose. He was not forced to undertake a more thorough examination of this question, however, because he had already rejected the public morality purpose in its own right. He did not reject it because that seemed necessary to invalidate a law he didn't like, but because he found it a "dubious proposition to accept as a corollary" of the necessity of public morality "that legislators may impose tests of 'decency' and 'responsibility' on voters going beyond basic requirements of capacity (related to maturity and mental condition) to cast a meaningful vote."[96] In short, Strayer's opinion displays the contemporary libertarian reluctance to place law in the service of morality. This reluctance is also evident in his failure to perceive the moral education inherent in criminal punishment. Because it is not strictly necessary to the immediate outcome he wishes to achieve, Strayer's insistence on this libertarian perspective must be seen as part of the broader symbolic politics of vision. It gives additional legal weight to a vision, already well advanced in the Anglo-American legal culture, that rejects the educational or rhetorical dimensions of law. As Mary Ann Glendon notes: "The idea that law might be educational, either in purpose or technique, is not popular among us," at least as compared to the legal cultures of continental Europe.[97] Ironically, despite his reluctance to concede the educational dimension of law, Strayer cannot avoid sending a symbolic educational message. By enlisting the constitution in the battle against the older, educational view of law, his opinion clearly teaches an official preference for the libertarian vision and thus provides important symbolic ammunition for that vision's other causes.

Justice Strayer also gives symbolic support to those who favour rehabilitation over the other purposes of the penal system. We have seen that he must emphasize the retributive dimension of punishment in order to find that the law passes the "compelling purpose" part of the *Oakes* test—after all, the prisoner disqualification cannot be understood to contribute to rehabilitation and is unlikely to play a significant role in deterrence—but his acceptance of retribution is not terribly enthusiastic. He indicates his reservations about the retributive principle by calling it "vengeance," a term quite abhorrent to modern liberal sensibilities, evoking images of a barbaric past. Our penal system, he argues, has moved away from this older, now somewhat disreputable emphasis "in the direction of rehabilitation and the preparation of inmates for reentry into society." In our present system "the element of punishment is reduced in importance and the re-adjustment of the inmate to society is emphasized."[98]

Justice Strayer's view of the relative importance of retribution and rehabilitation in our penal system played a role in his assessment of the proportionality of the disqualification to the law's punitive purpose. Although punishment was a sufficiently compelling purpose to justify some denial of the right to vote, the strength of this justification "must depend in part on the importance of punishment by itself in the process." Since the importance of punishment has waned as rehabilitation has waxed, its ability to justify denial of the vote has diminished. This reduced justificatory power of the retributive component of punishment cannot sustain "an absolute interference" with the section 3 right to vote "throughout the term of imprisonment." This is especially so because the now more important rehabilitative principle might require the reintroduction of the right to vote prior to the sentence being completed. As Justice Strayer notes, the rehabilitative process generally "begins before inmates complete their sentences and may include vocational or academic training in prison or extramurally, temporary passes, day parole, full parole, or mandatory supervision."[99] Like Justice Bowlby in *Grondin*, Strayer suggests that voting during imprisonment might well form an important part of this rehabilitative process. He concludes that the blanket denial of the right to vote of all prisoners for the duration of their incarceration is too broad to be proportional to the relatively unimportant purpose of retributive punishment.

It should be noted that Justice Strayer's preference for rehabilitation over retribution is arrived at without any evidence concerning the rehabilitative effect of the vote. Certainly none was placed before him by expert witnesses. However this may be, Justice Strayer's rehabilitative arguments substantially augment the activism of his decision. While his earlier argument—that the disqualification went too far in disenfranchising even petty offenders—would have allowed new legislation disqualifying more serious criminals for the duration of their incarceration, he now implies that, to the extent that serious offenders deserve a rehabilitative effort, even they should have their vote returned to them sometime before their release.

This broader suggestion also seems particularly open to Monahan's charge of second-guessing legislative purposes. True, Strayer does not deny that the law has a retributive purpose, but he accords this purpose a lessened importance in the overall balance of penal objectives. He then finds a disqualification for the duration of incarceration (call it the "durational" disqualification) too broad to be proportional to this diminished purpose. But the reasoning could easily be reversed. One could with equal justification argue that the very existence of the durational disqualification indicates the continuing vigour of the retributive principle, that far from being an anomalous departure from the new balance between retribution and rehabilitation, it should count as evidence of the balance that actually exists. In this view, the durational disqualification reveals the limits of the rehabilitative trend, rather than being a holdover from more barbaric times that should be swept away by that trend. For the advocate of judicial restraint, in other words, Justice Strayer is attempting to extend a legislative trend further than legislators themselves are prepared to go. He tries to finesse this fact by attributing to the legislature the objective of extending the trend, so that his own intervention can be seen as simply helping the legislature draft legislation more "proportional" to *its* purpose, but he is really substituting *his own* preferred balance between retribution and rehabilitation for the balance actually chosen by the legislature.

We have already indicated that, whether they are applied to the law's public morality purpose or to the narrower purpose of "sanctioning criminals," Justice Strayer's other reasons for finding the disqualification disproportional are more compelling and less intrusive. There is something to be said, on the basis of the retributive principle itself, for limiting the disqualification to relatively serious offenders. If the point is to promote public morality, moreover, one might wish to associate the disqualification more explicitly with offences involving palpable immorality, as the Americans and the French have done. The French Electoral Code, for example, disqualifies (1) felons; (2) those sentenced to more than one month imprisonment for such misdemeanours as larceny, swindling, breach of trust, embezzlement, perjury, or a variety of other "moral offences"; (3) those "sentenced to more than three months' jailing without suspended sentence, or to a jail term of more than six months with suspended sentence for a misdemeanor" unless it is a misdemeanour "conviction for which is not subject to proof of their author's bad faith and which [is] punishable by fine only" (i.e., strict-liability regulatory offences). Those incarcerated for nonspecified reasons are not deprived of the right to vote. As in the case of many U.S. provisions, the French disqualifications clearly embody the view that those who have fallen below the minimal level of morality indicating responsible citizenship should not vote. Interestingly, the Code also emphasizes personal responsibility by disqualifying persons "convicted of personal bankruptcy."[100] A plausible argument could be made that such laws are more proportional to the public morality purpose of the law.

Furthermore, there remain the real problems of coherence stemming from the vagaries of election timing—the potential that the short-term prisoner might be deprived of more voting opportunities than a more serious criminal whose incarceration is completed between elections—and from the differential treatment of petty offenders depending on whether they pay their fines or go to jail in default. Again, one might wish to address these questions without challenging a major substantive purpose of the law.

Even here, however, advocates of judicial restraint, including those who would prefer a different law, might insist that these are essentially political decisions that should be left to the legislature. After all, in addition to the substantive purpose of any law, administrative convenience is a legitimate legislative objective, and a blanket disqualification of all prisoners for the duration of their incarceration certainly satisfies this criterion. Charter sceptics who think that questions occurring at the margins of the right to vote are generally open to reasonable disagreement might well wonder whether the admitted incoherencies in the blanket disqualification of prisoners are really so serious as to outweigh administrative convenience. After all, as the Supreme Court itself has pointed out, the constitution does not require perfection in legislative drafting. Even the analysis of alternative means under the "minimal impairment" test does not require legislatures to choose what judges might think is the very best alternative.[101] Some alternatives might be so bad as to require judicial intervention, but above a certain line between the worst and best alternatives legislatures must be free to make their own choices, even if judges think they could have made better ones. Why, our apostle of restraint might ask, should this be considered a matter that falls below rather than above the line? Why should it be a matter for judicial intervention rather than legislative discretion? This, of course (as we have had ample opportunity to observe), is one of the central questions of Charter politics.

■ CONCLUSION

In addition to affecting the immediate interests of the litigants, constitutional cases often involve much broader symbolic conflicts within the community at large. Does the law have a legitimate role to play in inculcating public morality? Is retribution the distasteful legacy of barbarous times, to be supplanted by rehabilitation whenever possible, or is it the cornerstone of a decent criminal justice system? These matters of ongoing debate within our society were at stake in the prisoners'-voting-rights cases. By placing the weight of the constitution on one side or the other in these debates, the judges in these cases were doing much more than deciding whether a Sauvé or Badger or Belczowski could vote in federal or provincial elections. To the extent that they are seen as oracles of the constitution, the judges were also contributing to the community's official definition of itself, privileging certain visions over others by according them official status, and thus giving the partisans of the favoured visions an edge in future battles with their foes. On both the immediate and broader symbolic issues, however, the outcome of this prisoners'-rights litigation remains in doubt. It must await the judgment of the chief oracle, the Supreme Court.

CHAPTER TWELVE

Fair and Effective Representation

Section 3 of the Charter raises questions concerning not only the possible extension of the franchise, but also the ability of the existing allocation of constituencies to achieve "fair and effective representation." Does section 3 simply guarantee the right to cast a ballot, or does it also require that voters cast equally powerful ballots? Does it, in other words, guarantee only the "equal right to vote" or also the "right to an equal vote"? The latter reading of section 3 calls into question the common Canadian practice of constructing electoral constituencies that vary substantially in size. Although there has been a trend toward more equal constituencies, it is not unusual even today to find some constituencies in Canadian jurisdictions that are twice the size (or more) than others. This enables voters in small constituencies to cast ballots that are considerably more powerful than those cast in large constituencies. To put it another way, the relatively small numbers of people in some localities enjoy the same level of representation as much larger numbers in other localities.

The justification for constituencies of varying population size is that the fair and effective representation of sparsely populated rural areas cannot be achieved under a strict system of "representation by population." This justification, however, is in tension with the deeply rooted liberal democratic norm that population should be the main basis of political representation. The latter norm was pithily formulated in 1964 by former U.S. Chief Justice Earl Warren when he wrote that "legislators represent people, not trees or acres."[1] From the perspective of this norm, apportioning constituencies to populations of varying size, thus overrepresenting less densely populated places, is known as "malapportionment." Because it remains an open question whether this kind of apportionment is really good or bad, we shall use the less loaded term of "variable apportionment." The U.S. Supreme Court, however, clearly came to see it as *mal*apportionment, and ruled that American constituencies must be constructed to give effect to the principle of "one person, one vote"—that is, constituencies must be virtually equal in size. This chapter examines litigation in British Columbia, Alberta, and Saskatchewan in which the claimants urged the Canadian judiciary to read a similar rule into section 3 of the Charter.

Questions of immense political significance were obviously at stake in this litigation. The issue of representation lies at the core of any discussion of liberal democracy. The rules determining how citizens are "represented" shape their legislatures and determine the character of their democracy. Unlike most constitutional "rights" cases, which challenge the output of the legislative process, the electoral-districting cases challenged the very structure of that process.

More mundane partisan interests were also at stake. The reapportionment litigation was fuelled not only by abstract liberal democratic principle, but also by considerations of partisan advantage. Proponents of the one-person-one-vote rule, in short, are often associated with opposition parties who see variable apportionment as a "gerrymander" favouring the governing party.

The term "gerrymander" was coined to describe an 1812 Massachusetts constituency designed to pack many supporters of the opposition Federalist Party into a single district, thus reducing the number of representatives they could elect. Since the Federalists did not all inhabit a conveniently focused locality, the district was twisted and elongated, rather resembling a salamander. The Federalists dubbed it a gerrymander in honour of Governor Elbridge Gerry, who signed the electoral map into law. A gerrymander is thus the drawing of electoral boundaries intentionally to advance the partisan interest of one party by reducing the effective voting strength of other parties.

There are several kinds of gerrymanders. As in the original example, gerrymanders may "pack" opposition supporters into a few seats, leaving the governing party in a majority position elsewhere. It is also possible, however, to "fragment" opposition supporters into nearly certain minority positions in contiguous districts. Ingenious location of constituency boundaries can achieve both kinds of gerrymanders even in a system in which all constituencies contain exactly equal populations.

Varying the size of constituencies can be yet another form of gerrymander. It takes on this appearance to the extent that overrepresented rural voters tend to vote for different parties than their underrepresented urban counterparts. If the NDP does better in the cities and the Conservatives in the countryside, not an uncommon occurrence in Canada, then the former party is likely to view the electoral overrepresentation of rural voters as a gerrymander in favour of the latter. Certainly the perception of variable apportionment as a partisan gerrymander was a driving force behind the "reapportionment" litigation in both Canada and the United States.

The U.S. Supreme Court ventured into the reapportionment waters in a trilogy of decisions in the early 1960s: *Baker* v. *Carr* (1962),[2] *Wesberry* v. *Sanders* (1964),[3] and *Reynolds* v. *Sims* (1964). Abandoning a hundred years of judicial restraint on this question, the Warren Court decided it had jurisdiction to hear claims of malapportionment in *Baker*. The trial court had refused to hear the case for the traditional reason that it was a non-justiciable "political question." According to the "political questions" doctrine, certain constitutional questions should be left to the sole discretion of legislatures because they are not fit for judicial resolution. In *Baker* the U.S. Court decided that apportionment should no longer be considered a "political question" and remitted the case back to the trial court, although it did not actually specify a precise standard by which to measure malapportionment and devise remedies. It took this step over the objections of advocates of judicial self-restraint, such as Justice Felix Frankfurter, who warned against judges entering the "political thicket" of apportioning constituencies, arguing that this was a matter best left within the nonjudicial realm of "political questions." In *Wesberry* and *Reynolds,* supplying the remedial standards that were missing from *Baker,* the Court imposed the one-person-one-vote rule on both the federal House of Representatives and all fifty state legislatures.

It is difficult to exaggerate the political significance of the American reapportionment decisions. Certainly Chief Justice Earl Warren recognized their importance when, upon his retirement in 1968, he called them the "most important" decisions of his fifteen-year tenure.[4] Warren was right. His Court's "reapportionment revolution" changed the balance of power between urban and rural areas in every state in the Union,[5] and is considered as one of the leading examples of the assertion of judicial power in American politics. The advent of the Charter in 1982 opened the door to a similar, judge-driven reapportionment revolution in Canada. Would the Canadian judiciary walk through that door?

∎ THE CASES

The idea of equalizing the power of votes across constituencies in Canadian jurisdictions received a degree of judicial support in *Dixon,* a 1989 British Columbia case.[6] The litigation had been launched in 1986 by Robert Dixon, a professor of philosophy. Dixon had the legal and financial backing of the British Columbia chapter of the Canadian Civil Liberties

Association—he was then its president—as well as the tacit support of the provincial New Democratic Party. Not surprisingly, the NDP disliked the current underrepresentation of urban areas of NDP voting strength and corresponding overrepresentation of rural regions, which usually supported the governing Social Credit Party.[7] The case was argued before Justice McLachlin (now on the Supreme Court of Canada).

Arguing that "more is intended [by section 3] than the bare right to place a ballot in a box,"[8] Justice McLachlin invalidated British Columbia's distribution of constituencies because the size discrepancies were deemed too large. She did not require fully equalized constituencies, however. Instead of a strict one-person-one-vote standard, she read section 3 of the Charter as requiring only the "relative equality of voting power."[9] This somewhat ambiguous standard represents an obvious compromise between the more extreme activism of "one person, one vote" and the completely hands-off, political-questions restraint recommended by Justice Frankfurter.

This middle-ground compromise poses a dilemma, however. "Relative equality of voting power" seems an inherently fluid or situational standard, difficult to define with any precision. How is a legislature to know how much inequality is too much? Failure to provide a more precise standard might make the judicial decision look subjective and arbitrary, and would leave legislatures in the dark as to what might be acceptable. Recognizing this, Justice McLachlin admits that "it is for the court to articulate an objective and manageable standard by which the legislature can be guided."[10] To "operationalize" the meaning of "relative voter equality," however, turns out to be equally problematic. In the absence of any clear textual support, it seems too obvious an act of judicial legislation to specify a maximum permissible range of deviation. Why, for example, should 25 percent be preferred to 15 or 35 percent? While a plausible argument could be made for each, there is certainly nothing in the Charter that authorizes judges to choose—and thus to impose—one over the other.

To extricate herself from this dilemma Justice McLachlin refused to specify a numerical standard directly, but indirectly endorsed one proposed by the recently completed report of a commission established to look into British Columbia's electoral system. The "Fisher Commission," as it was known, had recommended that constituencies be permitted to vary within a range of plus or minus 25 percent of the provincial average, the same standard applying to federal ridings within each province. While it was up to the legislature to choose a numerical standard, Justice McLachlin wrote,

> I may be so bold as to suggest it may be aided by the efforts of the
> Fisher Commission.... The maximum deviation from the electoral
> quota appears to be within a tolerable limit, given the vast and
> sparsely populated regions to be found in British Columbia, while
> the individual deviations in each riding appear to be justified by the
> proper application of geographic and regional considerations.[11]

This clever tactic allowed Justice McLachlin to "suggest" a sufficiently specific measurement of "relative voter equality" without appearing to impose
it on the government. She merely "endorsed" what the government's own
royal commission had already recommended.

Although Justice McLachlin's reasoning embodies an obvious compromise between activism and restraint, it justified an activist result. The proposed 25 percent rule was clearly a much more relaxed standard than the
American rule of one person, one vote. Nevertheless, British Columbia's
electoral system did not measure up. Thirty-two percent of the province's
constituencies exceeded the 25 percent limit. Nor did Justice McLachlin
think such extreme inequality was justified under section 1.[12]

The *Dixon* decision cast doubt on other provincial electoral systems,
though not on all of them. Manitoba certainly had little reason to be concerned, because it had reformed its legislation in 1988, placing a 10 percent deviation limit on all but the two northern divisions of the province.
Saskatchewan had also recently amended its legislation, though it had
actually expanded its deviation limit, moving from a 15 percent to a 25
percent limit for all but its two northern constituencies, which were
allowed to deviate from the average by up to 50 percent. Still
Saskatchewan might well have believed that its legislation fell within the
spirit of *Dixon*.

Other provinces could not afford to be so sanguine. In Alberta, for
example, the variation in the size of constituencies made British Columbia's system pale by comparison: fully 51 percent of Alberta's constituencies varied from the provincial average by more than 25 percent. The
Alberta government thus immediately launched a process of legislative
reform, which culminated late in 1990 in new legislation.[13] In an obvious
attempt to Charterproof the province's new constituencies, this legislation
established the now familiar 25 percent deviation limit for most constituencies.[14]

In fact, adherence to the 25 percent rule endorsed by *Dixon* did not
deter further Charter challenges to the electoral districting of either
Saskatchewan or Alberta. Saskatchewan's legislation[15] drew criticism

because it established a fixed allocation of seats for both urban and rural areas that was out of proportion to their respective shares of the provincial population. The urban centres received twenty-nine, or 43.9 percent, of the seats, slightly less than their 47.6 percent share of the province's population. Conversely, the thirty-seven seats allocated to rural Saskatchewan contained 52.4 percent of the population, but constituted 56 percent of the seats.[16] This meant that urban ridings would on average be larger than rural ridings, though, with the exception of the two "northern" districts, the difference could easily be accommodated within the overall 25 percent deviation limit.

The imbalance between urban and rural representation created the widespread impression that the Tory government was using electoral reform to consolidate its electoral powerbase in rural Saskatchewan. After all, 84 percent of existing Tory seats (thirty-two of thirty-eight) were based in rural districts, while 84 percent of the NDP's seats (twenty-one of twenty-five) came from urban ridings. The perception of partisan bias soon generated a Charter case. In 1989 a group of nine university professors and lawyers from Regina and Saskatoon formed a nonprofit corporation, "The Society for the Advancement of Voter Equality" (SAVE), "to carry and finance the legal case."[17] A parallel group calling itself "Equal Justice for All" also formed to intervene in the case. SAVE challenged the government to refer the act to the courts for a ruling, and when the government failed to respond, it launched its own Charter challenge in January 1989.[18] The government openly criticized both SAVE and Equal Justice for All as being "politically motivated" stalking-horses for the NDP.[19] While they denied this charge, both groups were in fact widely perceived as having the tacit support of the NDP,[20] which was reluctant to openly attack the act in its own name for fear of appearing "antirural." As one SAVE founder put it, in a province where the majority of voters still lived rurally, such a tactic would amount to "political suicide."[21] Faced with the inevitability of a lawsuit, the government referred the new act and the electoral boundary map directly to the Saskatchewan Court of Appeal for a ruling.[22]

Charter-based challenges of constituency apportionment had also been launched in Saskatchewan's neighbour to the west. Alberta's old legislation had employed the same kind of fixed urban–rural categorization of constituencies being challenged in Saskatchewan. In Alberta's case, forty-two seats had been allocated to the urban, and forty-one to the rural areas. This almost-equal division of seats, however, was superimposed on a much more urbanized population than Saskatchewan's (two-thirds of Albertans live in urban centres as opposed to just under half of

Saskatchewan's residents). Many more urban voters had to be packed into proportionally fewer seats in Alberta, which accounts for the huge differences in constituency size under the old legislation. With the process of legislative reform already underway, two lawsuits were nevertheless brought against the old act,[23] presumably to prevent the government's reformist intentions from faltering. When the new legislation was passed in December 1990, these legal challenges were dropped.

Alberta could have achieved more equal constituencies simply by increasing the number of urban seats and/or reducing the number of rural ones, leaving the basic urban–rural categorization intact. Instead, its new legislation significantly blurred the boundary between the old categories by providing for a new kind of "hybrid" district containing both urban and rural voters. The urban centres were guaranteed forty-three of the province's eighty-three constituencies, but the electoral boundaries commission—the body charged with designing the actual constituencies—was permitted (and in a few cases required) to blend adjacent urban and rural districts in creating the remaining forty ridings. These hybrid districts were one version of what the act called "multi-municipality" constituencies.[24] The more the commission included urban voters in such multi-municipality districts, the fewer urban voters would remain in the forty-three wholly urban ridings, and the smaller those ridings would be on average. The smaller the average size of wholly urban ridings, moreover, the larger the average size of the rest, and thus the greater the relative equality among constituencies generally. The degree of equality among Alberta constituencies, in short, would depend on the extent to which the electoral boundaries commission used its discretion to create new multi-municipality districts. In any case, the commission was required to stay within the overall 25 percent deviation limit.

Although the hybrid-district option opened the door to more equalized ridings, it was not welcomed by the government's partisan foes. Critics saw hybrid districts as a clever way of maintaining the disproportionate influence of rural voters, which, as in Saskatchewan, constituted the electoral powerbase of the ruling Progressive Conservative Party. They feared that in constructing the new hybrid districts small slices of the urban population would be incorporated into predominantly rural constituencies. The greater equality of constituency size facilitated by the multi-municipality option, in other words, might come at the cost of a continued dilution of the electoral influence of the urban vote. In mock honour of Alberta's premier, the critics spoke of "Getty fingers" reaching out to pull urban voters into the sphere of rural control. The term "Gettymander" was also employed.

Needless to say, determining the validity of a "Gettymandering" claim would have to await the drawing of an actual electoral map. After all, it was equally possible for the boundaries of hybrid districts to be drawn in a manner that "swamped" a minority of rural voters in a largely urban voter population. Even without a new electoral map, however, the Alberta government decided in February 1991 to clarify the legal situation by referring the legislation itself to the Court of Appeal for a ruling on its constitutionality. The cities of Calgary, Edmonton, Red Deer, Grande Prairie, and groups of NDP and Liberal members of the legislature received intervener status to argue against the legality of the new act, while the Alberta Association of Municipal Districts and Counties intervened in its support. The Alberta Court of Appeal scheduled argument for June 17, 1991.

The litigants opposing the new legislation in both Saskatchewan and Alberta sought a reading of section 3 that required greater equality of constituency size than the 25 percent deviation limit Justice McLachlin appeared to endorse in *Dixon*. After all, both the Alberta and Saskatchewan acts generally met this standard. These litigants must have been heartened when, on March 6, 1991, the Saskatchewan Court of Appeal unanimously struck down that province's new act.

The Saskatchewan judgment quoted extensively from Justice McLachlin's *Dixon* opinion, but escalated her definition of what section 3 required to "relative or *substantial* equality of voting power."[25] The addition of the adjective "substantial" seemed significant, since the same formulation had been used by the U.S. Supreme Court in *Reynolds* v. *Sims*.[26] Nevertheless, although the Court ruled that "the controlling and dominant consideration in drawing electoral constituency boundaries must be voter population,"[27] it did not require "absolute equality" because such "mathematical precision ... [is] a practical impossibility."[28] It is impossible, for example, because people move between the announcement of an election and voting day, thus upsetting even the best laid plans for equal constituencies. And the problem is compounded by the uncertain timing of elections in a parliamentary system. Since elections can occur at any time, the electoral map must be drawn well in advance, giving a mobile population even more time to undermine the planned equality of constituencies.[29] The Court of Appeal described such unavoidable limitations on equality as "inherent in a representative, parliamentary democracy," and distinguished them from "noninherent limitations" based on the attempt effectively to represent such nonpopulation-based interests as geographic region. Only inherent limits could be allowed to affect the definition of the section 3 right to vote. Noninherent limitations were necessarily a *prima facie* violation of that right, and would be allowed only if they could be "demonstrably justified" as "reasonable limits" under section 1.[30] The logic of this position necessarily called into question Saskatchewan's 25 percent deviation limit. Since the unavoidable "inherent" limitations would cause only minor departures from equality, Saskatchewan's generous 25 percent deviation limit must be understood as accommodating "noninherent" limitations, and an electoral map drawn to take advantage of that limit would be in *prima facie* violation of the Charter.

The most obvious noninherent limitation, of course, was the explicit division of the province into underrepresented urban and overrepresented rural categories. For the Court, this "arbitrary division of the province" placed avoidable limits on the degree of equality the Electoral Boundaries Commission could achieve. It "shackled" the commission, foreclosing it "from giving proper effect to the concept of equality of voting power."[31] The urban–rural categorization was thus *prima facie* unconstitutional, despite the fact that in itself it was responsible for only relatively small inequalities of constituency size. After all, the allocation of seats to urban Saskatchewan was only 3.7 percent (or about two and a half ridings) less than its share of the population warranted.

Much larger inequalities were attributable less to the legislation than to the way in which the Electoral Boundaries Commission exercised its discretion. The urban–rural categorization obviously did not require unequal constituencies *within* either of those categories, yet the commission created such inequalities. For example, Saskatoon Greystone, the largest urban constituency, had 12 567 voters as compared with only 7684 in the adjacent urban riding of Saskatoon Sutherland-University. Indeed, even the smallest rural constituency, Morse, had slightly more voters (7757) than Saskatoon Sutherland-University. Within the rural category, Cut Knife–Lloydminster, with 11 800 voters, was significantly larger than not only Morse, but also the adjacent constituency of Wilkie (8775 voters).[32] Since neither the legislation nor "inherent limitations" constrained the commission to create inequalities of such magnitude *within* the two major categories, it was probably trying to accommodate a variety of nonpopulation-based considerations. But according to the Court of Appeal's logic, substantial variations designed to accommodate "noninherent" limitations necessarily violate the Charter. The Court concluded that the legislation was invalid, "unless justified under section 1."[33]

The Court of Appeal's relegation of nonpopulation-based factors to the section 1 side of the interpretive equation is symbolically significant. In *Dixon* Justice McLachlin had incorporated a balance between population and nonpopulation considerations into the very definition of the section 3 right to vote. She thus confronted the dilemma of where precisely to strike the balance, but there was no question that some such balance was legitimate and would not violate the Charter. For the Saskatchewan Court of Appeal, by contrast, section 3 could not definitionally accommodate this kind of balance. Any attempt to dilute the principle of equal constituencies in the name of nonpopulation-based considerations was unconstitutional unless it could be justified under section 1. To be sure, it remained theoretically possible to justify such departures from strict equality, but only as external *limits* on a Charter right. Given the symbolic power of the language of rights, this way of justifying the balance would almost certainly detract from the perceived legitimacy of its nonpopulation side.

In fact, the Saskatchewan Court of Appeal did not justify the legislation, or the electoral map based on it, as "reasonable limits in a free and democratic society." It found that the legislation failed the first branch of the *Oakes* test because it did not have a purpose sufficiently compelling to justify the infringement of Charter rights. There was thus no need to proceed to the proportionality stage of section 1 analysis.[34] We have observed how unusual it is for a court to question the constitutional legitimacy of legislative purposes. That the Court did so in this case seems to reflect the depth of its feeling on the subject. The urban–rural categorization, it said, "creates a statutory stranglehold in the hands of non-urban voters and assumes that an arbitrary apportionment of rural and urban interests is required in representative democracy in Saskatchewan."[35] The Court made no such assumption. "Representative democratic government," it said, "should neither be, nor be seen to be, a fight between rural and urban interests."

> We have no evidence that members of the Legislature from "rural" areas are insensitive to concerns and community interests of urban or northern people. Likewise we have no evidence that "urban" members of the Legislative Assembly are insensitive to concerns and community interests of rural or northern people.[36]

Nor did the Court find any "evidence to justify" the act's 25 percent deviation limit under section 1.[37]

The Court of Appeal did not wish to "foreclose reasonable consideration of valid geographic, regional and other relevant matters in drawing constituency boundaries,"[38] but in a hint at "minimal impairment" analysis, it insisted that these factors could "be nurtured by other, non-infringing and equally effective methods."

> For example, Members of the Legislative Assembly who represent larger geographic areas might be provided with additional travel allowances, support staff and "up-to-date" communication services.[39]

This judgment was a clear victory for the Canadian proponents of "one person, one vote." If the shift from *Dixon* to the Saskatchewan Court of Appeal decision indicated a trend, Canada's judiciary seemed to be following in the activist footsteps of the Warren Court. Everything, of course, would depend on the ultimate judgment of the Supreme Court of Canada.

A Supreme Court case was not long in coming. The Court of Appeal's decision had precipitated a crisis for Saskatchewan Premier Grant Devine, whose Tory government was nearing the end of its five-year term. Faced with the prospect of having to call elections within five months under now-invalid legislation, the government requested an expedited appeal to the Supreme Court of Canada. Acknowledging the urgency of Saskatchewan's position, the Supreme Court granted leave to appeal on March 17, 1991, and set argument for April 29 and 30. Meanwhile, on the political front the Tories tried to turn the decision to their advantage by blaming it on the the NDP, claiming that the NDP was "trying to destroy the rural vote." Opposition leader Roy Romanow called the charge "absolutely despicable."[40]

Plans for the June hearing of Alberta's reference case were thrown into disarray by the Saskatchewan decision and its expedited appeal to the Supreme Court. Given the likelihood of the Supreme Court's ruling pre-empting whatever the Alberta Court of Appeal might decide, the Alberta government and most other interested parties scurried to file petitions requesting intervener status in the Supreme Court case, all of which were granted. For its part, the Alberta Court of Appeal announced that it would postpone the hearing of its own reference until after the Supreme Court had decided the Saskatchewan appeal.

Although the parties to the Alberta litigation were allowed to intervene in the Supreme Court's hearing of the Saskatchewan case, they had some trouble introducing the "social fact" evidence they had developed for their own case. In Chapter Eight we discussed the difficulties courts have in obtaining and assessing the social facts relevant to major policy decisions. To address this problem litigants often hire "experts" to prepare relevant background studies, and sometimes to give oral testimony about their findings. The authors, for example, played this role in some of the prisoners'-voting-rights cases examined in the previous chapter. In the Alberta apportionment case (in which the authors were also involved), there was a veritable stampede to hire expert consultants: nine different academics were retained by six different parties to the suit.[41] In this respect, some court cases have come to resemble royal commissions, whose stock in trade is to solicit and assess "expert" studies. Royal commissions, however, are not restricted by the procedural rules and time constraints that govern lawsuits. All of the reports commissioned for the Alberta case (except ours) were prepared on less than a month's notice. When the parties who commissioned these reports rushed to intervene in the expedited appeal of the Saskatchewan case, there was little time for additional research. Moreover, even the evidence already developed could not readily be used in the Supreme Court because of rules prohibiting the introduction of new evidentiary material not already considered by the court below. In principle this appeared to preclude any use in the Saskatchewan case of the research commissioned for the Alberta reference. In the end, the Alberta government found a loophole that allowed it to append its commissioned report to its factum, as did the City of Edmonton.[42] The Supreme Court thus decided its first electoral-districting case without the benefit of a considerable body of relevant research. It also decided in a hurry, handing down its written decision five weeks after the oral hearing—five times more quickly than its normal six-month "gestation" period. This case provides a dramatic illustration of the policy-making difficulties posed by the judicial context.

The parties to the Alberta case were not the only interveners before the Supreme Court. In addition to the Attorney General for Saskatchewan and his court-appointed opponent,[43] Roger Carter (the former dean of the province's law school), fourteen other parties were present to "lobby" the Court on this issue. Supporting Saskatchewan's stand against a strictly egalitarian interpretation of section 3 were the governments of Canada, five provinces (Quebec, British Columbia, Prince Edward Island, Alberta, Newfoundland), and both territories, as well as the Alberta Association of

Municipal Districts and Counties. In support of the one-person-one-vote orientation of the Saskatchewan Court of Appeal opinion were the British Columbia Civil Liberties Association, a group of private citizens from Yellowknife, Saskatchewan's Equal Justice for All, and the Alberta cities of Edmonton and Grande Prairie. The swarm of interveners who descended upon the Supreme Court on April 29 indicated the potential significance of the case. All of the parties awaited the Court's judgment with bated breath.

■ TO AMERICANIZE OR NOT TO AMERICANIZE?

The Supreme Court was faced with a stark choice: whether to adopt or reject the American rule of one-person-one-vote. Canadian proponents of this rule have relied heavily on the American example for the proposition that in a liberal democracy it is "intolerable that any one citizen could exercise more voting power than any other."[44] In fact, there are several problems with this comparison. First, the scope and magnitude of the variable apportionment prompting judicial intervention in the United States in the 1960s did not exist in the Canada of 1991. In *Colegrove* v. *Green* (1946),[45] the discrepancy between the largest and the smallest congressional districts in Illinois was 914 053 to 112 116. In *Reynolds* v. *Sims,* the case that initiated the American Court's entry into the reapportionment of state legislatures, the ratio between voter populations was as high as forty-six to one in the state Senate and sixteen to one in the lower house.[46] When the Court decided *Baker* v. *Carr* in 1963, "disparities between largest and smallest districts of ten to one or higher were common in most states for both congressional and state legislative districts."[47] In Tennessee, the source of *Baker,* districts for the lower house of the state legislature ranged from 42 298 to 2340. The Tennessee legislature had not authorized a reapportionment since 1901![48]

The qualitative counterpart to this quantitative inequality was a strong consensus that rurally based legislators had a stranglehold on the legislatures of the nation; that they would not willingly relinquish this power; and that until they did, "the staggering problems of metropolitan America"[49]—transportation, public health and housing, race relations, and education—could not be dealt with. A decade and a half of political lobbying and organizing had gotten reformers nowhere. In the words of C. Herman Pritchett, then president of the American Political Science Association, "the

Supreme Court was justified in taking the lead on reapportionment in state legislatures because no other channels of protest were open."[50]

In sharp contrast to this American experience, Canadian legislatures had taken the lead in addressing the reapportionment issue. In 1964, the very year that the U.S. Supreme Court was forcing American states to deal with the malapportionment problem, Parliament passed legislation preventing federal constituencies in each province from deviating from the provincial average by more than 25 percent. The 1964 reforms also turned the boundary adjustment process over to independent commissions, thus putting an end to the hitherto common occurrence of overtly partisan gerrymanders.[51] Most of the provinces soon followed suit.[52] Only Nova Scotia, New Brunswick, and Prince Edward Island now lack legislated deviation limits, and only Prince Edward Island is without an independent commission. Moreover, there is no evidence that voter inequality in any province is so pronounced as to impair the responsiveness of the government to changes in public opinion. To the contrary, the last decade of provincial elections has witnessed changes of government in seven of the ten provinces, a reliable indicator of a healthy and fair electoral system.[53] Indeed, as the Supreme Court was preparing to deliver its judgment in the Saskatchewan appeal, a poll indicated that the opposition NDP was poised to crush the Devine Conservatives, with or without the government's new electoral boundary map.[54] Obvious "malapportionment" of the kind faced by the United States in the 1960s does not exist in contemporary Canada. The argument for judicial intervention is thus less compelling.

Such an argument would not, of course, satisfy the committed partisan of "one person, one vote," for whom the point is to overcome variable apportionment altogether, not merely the kind of extreme malapportionment that functions as a blatant gerrymander. From this perspective the achievement of virtually equal constituencies is the ideal for any self-respecting liberal democracy, and the United States remains an attractive model of the achievement of this ideal. For such a person, the Warren Court's intervention in apportionment issues is justified not because it was necessary to overcome the worst excesses, but because it achieved the ideal. By analogy, the absence of similar excesses in Canada does not excuse the Canadian judiciary from its obligation to achieve the same ideal.

The problem with this view is that the U.S. Supreme Court itself seems to have required the closest possible approximation of strict mathematical equality for constituencies less because it believed that it was inherently correct than because it was the only available standard that was "judicially manageable" and thus avoided the perception of overt judicial policy-making. Facing the same dilemma that confronted Justice McLachlin in *Dixon,* the U.S. Court began with a similar reluctance to impose strict equality, but ultimately found itself driven toward that standard.

The Court's ambivalence about the one-person-one-vote principle is evident in the fact that it did not initially mandate precise mathematical equality for either congressional or state districts, but only that districts be "as nearly of equal population as is practicable."[55] Since it is quite "practicable" to achieve almost complete equality,[56] the Court's failure to insist upon it suggested that there were some nonpopulation-based considerations that might legitimately be weighed against the one-person-one-vote principle. Indeed, the Court explicitly conceded the existence of such criteria, including maintaining the integrity of political subdivisions and providing for compact districts of contiguous territory.[57] What the Court did not specify was how much departure from the equal-population rule such criteria might justify.[58]

The Court's failure to articulate a precise objective standard stemmed from the judges' reluctance to interfere with what they recognized as *normally* a legislative choice.[59] In these initial reapportionment cases, however, the malapportionment was so gross as to overcome the judges' reluctance. They intervened to strike down the extreme malapportionments before them, but without giving a precise rule for doing so. In effect, the Court said: "The constitution requires a relative degree of voter equality; how much we are not sure, but certainly more than this." They thus postponed the central issue: How much equality is enough?[60]

This question could only be postponed, not avoided. In fact, however, there was no answer short of strict mathematical equality that would not appear to be the arbitrary imposition of a judicial policy choice. If it is legitimate to balance some nonpopulation-based considerations against the principle of one person, one vote, in other words, why should that balancing be permitted only within a 5 percent deviation range as opposed to a 10 percent range? Indeed, why not a 15 percent, or for that matter a 25 percent range? At some point an obviously unjustifiable extreme is reached, but short of that extreme, what constitutional magic is there in any of these figures? None, of course, which is why the judicial imposition of any one of them would appear as nothing more than the blatant second-guessing of legislative choices. Having started down the road of correcting malapportionment, the only principled stopping place for the Court was a standard of virtually absolute equality. This, of course, would mean abandoning the notion that nonpopulation-based considerations could legitimately be weighed in the balance; indeed, there would be no balance, just a single overriding rule. By the same token, of course, there could be no policy balances to second-guess, only a rule to enforce.

It comes as no surprise, therefore, that in subsequent cases the Supreme Court set increasingly strict standards of equality for congressional districting. In its 1969 decision of *Kirkpatrick* v. *Preisler,* the Court struck down a Missouri reapportionment plan that allowed a maximum 6 percent deviation from the average. Justice Brennan said the constitution "requires a State to make a good-faith effort to achieve precise mathematical equality,"[61] and discounted the legitimacy of the countervailing legislative goals identified by Chief Justice Warren in *Reynolds.*[62] The threshold set in *Kirkpatrick* was further lowered in the 1973 case of *White* v. *Weiser,*[63] which invalidated a Texas plan allowing 5 percent variation, and was lowered yet again in 1983 with a decision invalidating a congressional districting plan for New Jersey with less than 1 percent deviation![64]

By this point any pretence that nonpopulation-based factors had a legitimate role to play had been abandoned, and with it any necessity of second-guessing legislative policy choices. A truly "manageable" judicial standard had been achieved! If the need for such a standard, rather than the intrinsic merit of mathematically equal constituencies, is the main explanation for its adoption in the United States, however, then the American example offers less obvious support for the Canadian partisan of one person, one vote. The U.S. Court seemed impelled toward this standard once it had entered the field to rectify extreme injustices. (For the opponent of one person, one vote, this is a classic example of "hard cases making bad law.") In Canada, by contrast, no similar extremes exist to propel the Court onto the same road.

The American analogy is further weakened by the fact that even the U.S. Court has been selective in its application of the one-person-one-vote rule. It has applied it strictly to national House of Representatives constituencies, but more leniently to state legislatures. This is important for assessing the relevance of American experience for Canada because, in crucial respects, Canadian legislatures are more like American state legislatures than the House of Representatives. The factors they share in common, moreover, are precisely those that account for the U.S. Court's more lenient approach to apportionment issues at the state level.

The U.S. Court could afford to apply the one-person-one-vote rule strictly to the House of Representatives because nonpopulation-based representation in the national government is embodied in the Senate. Indeed, a balance between representation by population and representation by place is explicitly built into the national constitution, where seats in the House of Representatives have always been apportioned more or less (much more since the Court's reapportionment decisions) according to population, while in the Senate every state enjoys two senators no matter how small its population. In 1787, it was only after the so-called "Connecticut Compromise" established this equal representation of the states in the Senate that the American Founders were free to establish a pure population standard for the House of Representatives. One hundred and seventy-five years later the Supreme Court could afford to require House districts to adhere strictly to the one-person-one-vote rule because the Senate already satisfied the demand for effective and equal representation of regional interest irrespective of population.

Until the 1960s this was also true of the states. Forty-nine of the fifty states had followed the federal model in adopting bicameral solutions to their own problems of legislative representation. Most state governments consisted of a lower house based on "rep. by pop.," and a Senate where counties enjoyed more equal representation. In its 1964 ruling in *Reynolds* v. *Sims,* the Supreme Court ended this practice for the states by requiring the equal-population rule for both houses of bicameral state legislatures.[65] Nevertheless, while the Court was tightening its equality criteria for congressional districting, it gave somewhat more latitude to state legislatures.

Such a double standard was hinted at from the start. In *Reynolds* v. *Sims,* the Court stated that somewhat "more flexibility may ... be constitutionally permissible with respect to state legislative apportionment than in congressional districting."[66] In its 1973 decision of *Mahan* v. *Howell,*[67] the Court "held that the rigid standards enunciated in *Kirkpatrick* were inapplicable to problems concerning state legislative apportionment."[68] A decade later *Karcher* v. *Dagett* reaffirmed strict equality for congressional districts, while *Brown* v. *Thompson,* released the same day, held that "in state legislative districts, population disparities of up to 10% were *de minimis* and did not require justification by the state."[69]

The explanation for the Court's double standard is not difficult to discern. The Court appears to concede that in a fair system of representation nonpopulation-based considerations must play some role, and that the federal and state governments cannot use the same strategies to give weight to these considerations. With "places" already represented in the federal

Senate—where Wyoming, with fewer people than Calgary, has the same number of senators as California, a state with more people than all of Canada—it is hardly unreasonable to demand strict equality of population for House of Representatives constituencies. State legislatures, which now must apportion seats according to population for both chambers, are not comparable. States can balance nonpopulation-based considerations against the one-person-one-vote principle only by varying the size of their constituencies.

Canadian legislatures, both federal and provincial, are like U.S. state legislatures in this respect. They, too, must simultaneously represent "places and people" in the same legislative chamber. This is most obviously true of the unicameral provincial legislatures, but it is true even of the federal Parliament, despite its bicameral structure. To be sure, regional representation was one of the intended functions of the Canadian Senate, but as an appointed, patronage-based body the Senate enjoys little legitimacy in a democratic age, and is thus not able to play this role effectively. As John Courtney has observed, the absence of an effective Senate in Canada "has had the effect of transferring part of the *federal* representational task to the House of Commons."[70] Thus, as we noted in Chapter Four, the principle of "rep. by pop." in the House of Commons has been compromised several times over the years to protect slow-growth provinces from a proportional decline in their complement of MPs. As a result, two-thirds of the provinces now enjoy "special protection of a non-population kind" in the House of Commons.[71]

■ CANADIAN TRADITION

In *Dixon* Justice McLachlin wrote that "the rights and freedoms guaranteed by the Charter must be defined against the wider historical and philosophic tradition of Canadian society."[72] If the American analogy provides little support for adopting a strict one-person-one-vote rule in Canada, Canadian tradition seems to provide still less. Indeed, from the beginning, the Canadian tradition appears to have been based on a conscious attempt to balance population and nonpopulation factors in the allocation of constituencies. As already noted, the Senate was originally intended to play an important part in achieving this balance at the federal level. Thus George Brown declared during the Confederation debates:

> The very essence of our compact is that the union shall be federal and not legislative. Our Lower Canada friends have agreed to give us representation by population in the Lower House, on the express condition that they shall have equality in the Upper House. On no other condition could we have advanced a step.[73]

Nor was representation by population an inviolable principle even in the House of Commons. As John A. Macdonald said of the 1872 readjustment of constituency boundaries:

> [I]t will be found that,… while the principle of population was considered to a very great extent, other considerations were also held to have weight; so that different interests, classes and localities should be fairly represented, that the principle of number should not be the only one.[74]

We have seen, moreover, that as the Senate declined as a politically salient institution, the attempt to balance population and nonpopulation factors increasingly shifted to the House of Commons.

The seminal 1964 reforms to the federal electoral districting policy took a step toward greater equality of House of Commons constituencies by instructing the newly authorized independent commissions to design electoral divisions "as nearly as may be" to the average constituency population for their respective provinces.[75] But the commissions were also instructed to take into consideration "the community of interest or community of identity in or the historical pattern of an electoral district … and a manageable geographic size for districts in sparsely populated, rural or northern regions."[76] To accommodate the latter considerations, constituencies were allowed to deviate from the provincial average by as much as plus or minus 25 percent. The legitimacy of balancing population and non-population factors was still very much alive.

The lack of any momentum toward a strict one-person-one-vote rule was evident in the debates about the 1964 reforms. The 25 percent rule reflected a compromise between advocates of a stricter rule and those who favoured still greater flexibility. Predictably, the debate cut across party lines and reflected the urban and rural character of the members' constituencies. Significantly, however, there were virtually no advocates of a strict one-person-one-vote rule, despite the then recent U.S. Supreme Court decision embracing that principle.[77] More than twenty years later observers such as John Courtney could still characterize the 25 percent rule as a thoughtful compromise "befitting a geographically large, sparsely populated and federally structured country with a multitude of competing interests."[78] Canadian tradition, in short, seems to offer little comfort to the proponent of one person, one vote.

Yet the reader of Chapter Five will remember that insofar as tradition is a touchstone for interpretation, the courts have emphasized its "evolving" rather than its static nature. Tradition must been seen as a "living tree" rather than a set of "frozen concepts." Courts can thus argue that a tradition embodies a progressive trend that better expresses the "purpose" of a Charter right than many of the tradition's actual manifestations. Indeed, the ideal toward which the trend points can be used by creative judges to sweep away the less progressive remnants of earlier times. Is there any reason to believe that Canadian electoral tradition is evolving toward the rule of one person, one vote? There are indications that the Saskatchewan Court of Appeal thought so.

The Saskatchewan Court conceded that the "purposive approach" to Charter interpretation "includes an examination of the traditions of Canadian society," but insisted that "we must not, in looking to the past, re-introduce the sterility of interpretation developed in the Canadian Bill of Rights."[79] The Court was referring, of course, to the infamous interpretive approach under which legal provisions become "frozen in time to the moment of adoption with little or no possibility of growth, development and adjustment to changing societal needs."[80] The Court obviously thought that the kind of "malapportionment" represented by the Saskatchewan legislation was ready to join such previous restrictions of "fundamental democratic values" as racial and sexual restrictions of the franchise on the scrap heap of history. Indeed, it portrayed its invalidation of Saskatchewan's malapportionment as the logical extension of the earlier repudiation of explicit franchise restrictions.[81]

The Court seemed particularly impressed by the trend toward greater equality in the size of federal constituencies within provinces. It observed, for instance, that the Federal Electoral Boundaries Commission for Saskatchewan had managed to design federal ridings for that province that deviated from the provincial average by less than plus or minus 5 percent. Using this achievement as a standard, the Court concluded that Saskatchewan's 25 percent rule was too generous. The Court, in other words, saw the Saskatchewan law as out of step with an emerging trend toward the one-person-one-vote principle.

This comparison is flawed in two important respects. First, it ignores the difference between the federal task of dividing Saskatchewan into fourteen electoral divisions for purposes of voting on national policy issues and the task of dividing the same province into sixty-six constituencies for more local purposes. Second, and more important, the Court's comparison is of the "apples-and-oranges" variety: it compared the provincial *de jure* deviation limit with the federal de facto deviation. In fact, the federal commission was working with the same *de jure* 25 percent limit. Furthermore, the actual average deviation of constituencies created by the Saskatchewan commission was 11 percent. The difference between the two de facto achievements, in short, was only 6 percent, not the much more dramatic 20 percent suggested by the Court's comparison of the actual federal apportionment with the provincial *de jure* limit.

The Court also ignored[1] the fact that although federal ridings have indeed been tending toward greater equality within each province, there remains considerable inequality among the provinces. Indeed, the federal 25 percent rule itself applies only *within* each province; there is no maximum deviation rule for the allocation of federal ridings *among* provinces.[82] Thus the average voter population in the four federal ridings in Prince Edward Island is 30 627, while the averages for Ontario, Quebec, British Columbia, and Alberta are all over 85 000. The average voter population in the three federal ridings in the northern territories is less than 23 000. Of the 295 federal ridings represented in House of Commons, almost a quarter deviate more than 20 percent from the average.[83] The average deviation for all federal constituencies, moreover, is 14.4 percent.[84] This is not new or atypical. Systematic studies show that voter inequality is consistently greater for the House of Commons collectively than for the federal ridings within each province.[85]

It should also be noted that the federal 25 percent rule is not absolute even within the provinces. Amendments made in 1986 allow a commission to exceed the 25 percent deviation from the intraprovincial average in "extraordinary circumstances." Some provinces immediately took advantage of this exception. In 1987 the Newfoundland commission created one constituency that was 61 percent less than the provincial norm and another that was 29 percent above. Since both the amendments and the changes they authorized took place after 1982, Parliament presumably judged that they did not compromise or violate the section 3 right to vote.[86]

If the Saskatchewan Court wished to compare provincial and federal jurisdictions, in other words, the most accurate comparison would have been between the actual electoral divisions in a given province and all 295 federal constituencies, not just the federal constituencies within the same province. This comparison would have shown that the de facto average deviation achieved under the impugned act for the sixty-six Saskatchewan constituencies (11 percent) was actually *less* than the comparable federal figure of 14.4 percent. The Court's difficulty with statistical issues was compounded by the fact that it ignored evidence submitted by the Saskatchewan attorney general showing that the province's new electoral redistribution placed it third among the ten provinces in maximizing voter equality.[87] It would be one thing if the Court had not received this data, but to receive it and then simply to ignore it altogether seems irresponsible. Once again we confront an illustration of judicial ineptitude in dealing with social-fact evidence.

In sum, on a more careful comparison with both the federal jurisdiction and the other provinces, Saskatchewan would not have been out of line with established Canadian traditions. A more comprehensive look at the evidence would not have suggested a clear trend away from the tradition of balancing population and nonpopulation factors in the construction of Canadian electoral systems.

Indeed, the legitimacy of balancing the two kinds of factors was reaffirmed in the Constitution Act, 1982. The constitutional amending formula entrenched by that act confirms the importance of regional communities of interest and the legitimacy of nonegalitarian distributions of voting power in the Canadian state. Formal changes to the written constitution under the general amending formula (section 38) are hardly a matter of "one person, one vote" and majority rule. Rather, constitutional amendment requires the very undemocratic process of gaining the consent of Parliament plus two-thirds of the provincial governments of provinces with more than 50 percent of the total population. As Professor Kilgour has shown, this formula represents

> a compromise between two competing and irreconcilable principles: that each *province* should have equal voice, and that each *voter* should have equal voice.[88]

Kilgour proceeds to demonstrate that since each province, regardless of population, has one vote in this process, the smaller (less populous) provinces are favoured and voter inequality is significant. A subsequent study mathematically demonstrated that voters in Prince Edward Island have more than six times more "amending power" than voters in Ontario. Similarly, voters in Quebec have less than half the "amending power" of voters in Newfoundland, Nova Scotia, or New Brunswick.[89] The relevant point here is that the constitutional amending formula, adopted at the same time as section 3 of the Charter, allocates political power according to a variety of criteria, of which voter equality is one, but not the most important.

In sum, while "rep. by pop." has always been a guiding principle of Canadian practice, it has never been consistently followed or considered absolutely binding. Both federal and provincial practice have sought to balance "rep. by pop." with representation of places. Provincial legislation directing electoral boundaries commissions to take into account such non-population factors as "communities of interest" falls squarely within this Canadian tradition.

■ THE SUPREME COURT DECIDES

Clearly the legitimacy of balancing nonpopulation-based considerations against the principle of "rep. by pop." is well established in Canadian practice and argument. Nor does the American example with a strict one-person-one-vote standard provide compelling reasons for Canada to adopt such a rule. Evidence concerning both these matters was included in the presentations of the governments involved in the Saskatchewan appeal *Carter* v. *Saskatchewan (A.-G.)*. One after another these governments warned the Court that a decision affirming the Saskatchewan Court of Appeal could render almost every legislative assembly in Canada, including the House of Commons, unconstitutional.

These arguments had their intended effect. On June 6, 1991, the Supreme Court, by a vote of six to three, decided *Carter*,[90] allowing the appeal and reinstating the Saskatchewan act and boundary map. The majority judgment was written by Justice McLachlin, the same judge who had decided *Dixon* in 1989.

McLachlin identified two major alternatives to the interpretation of section 3. The first starts "from the premise that the purpose of the section is to guarantee equality of voting power,"[91] and logically ends with the view that nonessential (or noninherent) deviations from this ideal are suspect. This is the position of the Saskatchewan Court of Appeal. As we have seen, this position cannot incorporate a balance between population and nonpopulation factors into the very definition of the section 3 right to vote. If the latter factors are to be permitted to influence the construction of unequal constituencies, they must first clear the section 1 hurdle.

Justice McLachlin's second alternative, the one she adopts, starts "from the premise that the purpose of s. 3 is to guarantee effective representation." Those who take this second view, she writes, "see the right to vote as comprising many factors, of which equality is but one."[92] This does not mean that equality is relatively unimportant in light of the "many" other factors that must be considered. Indeed, Justice McLachlin considers "parity of voting power" the "first" condition of effective representation, and refers to it as being "of prime importance."[93] Nevertheless, fair and effective representation often requires bringing other considerations to bear. "[T]o insist on voter parity," she argues, "might deprive citizens with distinct interests of an effective voice in the legislative process as well as of effective assistance from their representatives in their 'ombudsman' role."[94] The "distinct interests" of those inhabiting "vast, sparsely populated territories" are only one example of "community interests" that would not be effectively represented in a system of strict equality. Justice McLachlin also refers to "minority representation"[95] and "cultural and group identity"[96] as concerns that must be accommodated to achieve "effective and fair representation conducive to good government."[97] This second interpretive alternative, in short, permits a balance between equality and what the Saskatchewan Court called noninherent limitations on equality to be built into the very definition of section 3. Given such a definition, nonminimal deviations from strict equality would not necessarily violate section 3, and thus might not have to be justified under section 1. In view of this, Justice McLachlin reaffirms her conclusion in *Dixon* that section 3 requires only "*relative* parity of voting power."[98] And she takes care to emphasize that this standard is intended to accommodate more than the unavoidable departures from equality described by the Saskatchewan Court as "inherent limitations": "such relative parity as may be possible of achievement may prove undesirable because it has the effect of detracting from the primary goal of effective representation."[99]

Justice McLachlin used interpretivist rhetoric to support this relatively restrained reading of section 3. Not only did she appeal extensively to Canadian tradition, invoking the authority, for example, of John A. Macdonald, but she combined her reading of tradition with an appeal to the interpretivist touchstone of founding intention:

> [T]here is little in the history or philosophy of Canadian democracy that suggests that the framers of the Charter in enacting s. 3 had as their ultimate goal the attainment of voter parity. That purpose would have represented a rejection of the existing system of elec-

toral representation in this country. The circumstances leading to the adoption of the Charter negate any intention to reject existing democratic institutions.... The framers of the Charter had two distinct electoral models before them—the "one-person-one-vote" model espoused by the United States Supreme Court ... and the less radical, more pragmatic approach which had developed in England and in this country through the centuries and which was actually in place. In the absence of any supportive evidence to the contrary ... it would be wrong to infer that in enshrining the right to vote in our written constitution the intention was to adopt the American model. On the contrary, we should assume that the goal was to recognize the right affirmed in this country since the time of our first Prime Minister, Sir John A. Macdonald, to effective representation in a system which gives due weight to voter parity but admits other considerations where necessary.[100]

The concurring opinion of Justice Sopinka was equally emphatic about founding intention: "[I]n using the simple words in s. 3 that 'every citizen ... has the right to vote ...', the framers did not intend to invent or give birth to a right not previously enjoyed by the citizens of Canada."[101]

Turning to the Saskatchewan electoral map, Justice McLachlin found that it did not infringe section 3 as she had defined it. The urban–rural categorization did not concern her because the over- and underrepresentation it caused was "relatively small" and consistent with similar deviations under the previous legislation, which did not impose a similar categorization on the commission.[102] Furthermore, McLachlin was impressed by evidence suggesting "that not only are rural ridings harder to serve because of difficulty in transport and communications, but that rural voters make greater demands on their elected representatives, whether because of the absence of alternative resources to be found in urban centres or for other reasons." She concluded that "the goal of effective representation may justify somewhat lower voter populations in rural areas."[103]

As for inequalities not caused by the urban–rural categorization, Justice McLachlin thought they could generally be justified by such legitimate considerations as "natural community dividing lines," such as rivers and municipal boundaries. In some cases, discrepancies were also justified by projections of differential population growth. Thus a seat might be allocated to a locality with relatively few voters in the expectation that the constituency would experience relatively high population growth.[104] For these reasons, among others, Justice McLachlin found no violations of section 3 that required section 1 justification.

Justice Cory, who was joined by Chief Justice Lamer and Justice L'Heureux-Dubé, wrote a dissenting opinion. The disagreement was not about how to read section 3, but about how to apply that reading to the facts of the case. Thus Cory agreed that "relative" equality of votes was the proper standard, and approvingly quoted Justice McLachlin's formulation that deviations from equality are permissible when they "can be justified on the ground that they contribute to the better government of the populace as a whole, giving due weight to regional issues within the populace and geographic factors within the territory governed." But while Justice Cory thought it was legitimate for an electoral boundaries commission to "consider such factors as geography, demography and communities of interest," he insisted that "any body charged with creating an electoral map should commence with the proposition that, to the extent that it is reasonable and feasible, the voter population of each constituency should be approximately equal." The legislatively required overrepresentation of rural areas and underrepresentation of urban centres prevented the commission from starting from this assumption and was thus unconstitutional. "[N]o explanation has been given," wrote Justice Cory, "as to why the balancing of the relevant factors could not, as it was previously, be left to the commission rather than being mandated by the legislature. The province has failed to justify the need to shackle the Commission with the mandatory rural–urban allocation and the confinement of urban boundaries to municipal limits." In Justice Cory's view, this "shackling" of the commission produced greater inequality than necessary.

As Justice Sopinka put it, Cory appears to be "of the view that once an independent boundaries commission was established, it was incumbent upon the Saskatchewan legislature to ensure that the commission was able to fulfill its mandate freely without unnecessary interference such as [the urban–rural categorization]."[105] Justice Sopinka could not agree:

> It was not necessary for the Saskatchewan legislature to create an independent commission, and, had it simply legislated the impugned boundaries, the process itself would not have been subject to judicial scrutiny. Having chosen to delegate the task to the commission, there is no reason why the legislature should be prohibited from laying down tight guidelines delineating the powers to be conferred on the commission.[106]

Justice Sopinka was not suggesting that legislatures could do what they wanted. Indeed, he explicitly says that an urban–rural categorization could be structured so as to produce variations "so extreme as to amount to a breach of the right to vote." In his view, however, that had not happened in this case.

While the disagreements among the judges in this case are important, they should not blind us to the broad underlying agreement. The judges unanimously agreed that it was legitimate to balance population and non-population considerations in constructing the kind of "fair and effective representation" required by section 3. None of the judges accepted the Saskatchewan Court of Appeal's view that section 3 requires strict equality of constituencies, subject only to limits "inherent" in a parliamentary system.

∎ FAIR AND EFFECTIVE REPRESENTATION VS. EQUAL CONSTITUENCIES

The Court was surely on solid ground in concluding that fair and effective representation is not guaranteed by a regime of virtually equal constituencies. In fact, this conclusion was implicitly conceded by those critics of Alberta's new multi-municipality districts who worried that they would "dilute" the influence of urban voters by "swamping" them in predominantly rural constituencies. This "urban dilution" argument logically implies that nonpopulation-based considerations should be factored into a fair electoral system. Upon careful inspection, the fear that hybrid districts will dilute urban influence reflects the conviction that certain important communities of interest will not be effectively represented. The "urban dilution" objection to hybrid districts is that mixing, say, parts of Calgary with a large rural area adjacent to the city will "dilute" Calgary's electoral influence. But the "dilution" objection clearly implies that what is at stake is not just the votes of isolated individuals, but the collective interests of the communities in which these voters live. As long as the number of voters in each division is roughly equal—something that can be achieved through the creation of hybrid districts—there can be no "dilution" of *individuals'* votes. The "dilution" objection refers to a collective urban interest that deserves to be "represented fairly" in the legislature. But if there are identifiable urban community interests, then there are also identifiable rural community interests that cannot be ignored either.

To make the same point negatively, someone claiming that voter equality is the *only* relevant criterion cannot logically object to slicing up and mixing urban and rural "communities." By emphasizing the counting of *individual* heads, such a strict "rep. by pop." egalitarian has logically implied that "communities" do not exist. To lament the "dilution" of urban votes in constituencies of equal (or "relatively equal") size, on the other hand, is implicitly to concede that communities of interests do exist and that unqualified "rep. by pop." egalitarianism is not the only relevant standard. (If population were the *only* standard, how could one object to "hybrid" constituencies that met the standard of population equality?) Those who make the "dilution" objection on behalf of urban interests are able to fudge this contradiction because the community interest they support coincides relatively easily with the "equal population" standard—i.e., constituencies of equal size can easily be drawn in a manner that benefits urban interests. Nevertheless, it remains the case that "urban dilution" objectors are interested not merely in constituencies of equal size, but more important, in the kinds of voters (or community interests) encompassed by those constituencies. Having conceded that a just system of representation must balance the simple counting of heads against considerations of community interest, the "dilution" objectors cannot logically deny the benefits of such balancing to other community interests, including those whose fair representation cannot so easily be accommodated in a system of equal constituencies (e.g., rural interests). In sum, the "dilution" objection implicitly concedes that nations, provinces, cities, and villages are all communities whose collective interest should be factored into a fair and effective system of representation.

Alberta's "urban dilution" objectors were concerned with where the boundaries between more equal constituencies were located. They worried especially that the boundaries would be gerrymandered to favour the rural strengths of the Conservative Party. Experience in the United States confirms the claim that constituencies of equal size can be effectively gerrymandered, and that equal size is thus no guarantee of fair and effective representation. Indeed, by 1969 the American Court's single-minded pursuit of mathematical equality of population in congressional districts "had paradoxically encouraged the potential for widespread gerrymandering."[107] In the pursuit of equality, map-makers were now free to disregard county and municipal boundary lines. The result, observed one expert, was that "[i]n state after state, grotesquely shaped districts completely ignoring local subdivision lines or communities of interest are justified by politicians and approved by judges with the solemn chant, 'one person, one vote.'"[108] As one New York state legislator candidly admitted, "[t]he Supreme Court is making it easier to gerrymander than before."[109]

Not only did this kind of "political gerrymandering" become easier in the United States, but the advent of the computer made it frighteningly more effective. Computer technology allows the "fine tuning" of electoral boundaries in a manner that simultaneously maintains voter equality while creating partisan advantage. This "new degree of sophistication [in] boundary manipulation ... [has] made it more durable than the 'crude guess work' methods of before."[110] In the past, respect for traditional local boundaries and identities restricted such gerrymandering. These restraints have now been swept aside in the name of mathematical equality.

The most famous and effective of the political gerrymanders occurred in California after the 1980 census. In 1981 the Democratic-controlled state government used computer technology to draw a new congressional districting map[111] that increased the Democrats' partisan advantage over the Republicans from 22–21 to 28–17 after the 1982 elections, but in which none of the forty-five districts varied from the average by more than sixty-seven people.[112] The effect of this type of political gerrymander on the right to vote is very destructive. As Gordon Baker observes: "A mathematically equal vote which is politically worthless because of gerrymandering" is no better than a vote diluted by malapportionment.[113]

Not only does the new political gerrymander have a pernicious effect on "fair and meaningful representation," but it is even more resistant to detection and remedy than "malapportionment." Almost anyone can determine if electoral districts have unequal populations. Proving a systematic pattern of political gerrymander is a very different matter. Mountains of electoral data, tables, charts, and maps, subject to conflicting statistical analyses by "experts" hired by both sides, have been thrust upon the courts. While this new stage in the reapportionment wars represents a growth industry for American political scientists,[114] its implications for the courts are not auspicious.

This kind of gerrymandering persists in the United States because the drawing of electoral maps remains under the direct and immediate control of elected legislators. It is much less likely in Canada because map drawing has been largely turned over to independent commissions. The decreased likelihood of such blatant gerrymandering in Canada is beside the present point, however, which is simply that Justice McLachlin was correct in concluding that fair and effective representation is not guaranteed by equal constituencies alone. Fair and effective representation seems to require giving "deserving" groups or "communities of interest" (including but not limited to political parties) an appropriate degree of electoral influence. This goal can be undermined intentionally through explicit gerrymandering, or inadvertently through independent commissions paying too much attention to a standard of population equality.

In the United States the broader notion of "fair and effective" representation has been used not only to oppose intentional gerrymandering *against* some interests, but also to favour "affirmative gerrymandering" to benefit certain groups, especially blacks. In a system of judicially mandated equality of constituencies, such as exists in the United States (especially in the House of Representatives), affirmative gerrymandering takes the form of careful line-drawing to increase the electoral influence of specified interests. It can also, of course, take the form of varying the size of constituencies. The Supreme Court of Canada seems to have recognized the legitimacy of using variable apportionment as an "affirmative gerrymander" benefiting rural dwellers. Its choice of words suggests, moreover, that it would look with similar favour on "affirmative gerrymanders" in favour of "minorities" based on "cultural and group identity." Constructing smaller than usual constituencies, and carefully locating their boundaries, in order to enhance the electoral influence of sparsely populated Indian reserves springs to mind. Such an affirmative gerrymander would address the claim of native advocates that "the scattered nature of native population marginalizes them in the political process even more than their small share of the population would warrant."[115]

In terms of the symbolic politics of status, Justice McLachlin's judgment might thus be seen as augmenting the status of rural dwellers and certain unspecified "cultural minorities" vis-à-vis the urban majority. It would not be surprising to see this case exploited as a resource by section 15 minorities seeking affirmative gerrymandering on their behalf. The case does not explicitly require such gerrymanders, of course, but it may contribute to a symbolic climate supportive of them. In this sense, it could form an important backdrop to lobbying directed at legislatures.

■ ACTIVISM OR RESTRAINT?

Although Justice McLachlin's judgment provides some resources to those who wish to act in the legislative realm, it does not at first glance offer much hope for future judicial activism in the realm of electoral districting. Certainly the Supreme Court dashed the hopes of those who wanted Canada to adopt an American-style one-person-one-vote standard. The Court upheld legislation under which some constituencies could easily be two-thirds larger than others, and which in special cases permitted even larger discrepancies. As compared to the Warren Court in the 1960s, Canada's Supreme Court appeared to have chosen the route of judicial restraint in the matter of electoral districting. But appearances can be deceiving. Although Justice McLachlin's judgment is not an activist one in its immediate context, neither is it an example of unalloyed restraint. Future judicial intervention in electoral districting remains a distinct possibility.

Significantly, the Canadian Court did not reject the one-person-one-vote principle because, as Justice Frankfurter had suggested, the matter of apportioning constituencies was a "political question" beyond the legitimate scope of judicial intervention. Nor was this unexpected. The concept of nonjusticiable "political questions" is inherently uncongenial to the fundamental premises of the modern oracular judiciary, which, as we have seen, Canada's Supreme Court has generally embraced. According to the political questions doctrine, there are certain areas of constitutional law where the courts lack not only the final say, but any say at all. In these areas the legislature does not merely share interpretive authority with the courts (difficult enough for judicial oracularists to comprehend), but exercises *exclusive* interpretive authority (utterly inconceivable to the oracular mind). It comes as no surprise, therefore, to learn that Canada's Supreme Court has decisively turned its back on the idea of political questions beyond judicial purview.

The leading case is *Operation Dismantle,*[116] in which it was claimed that the federal government's policy of permitting American cruise-missile testing in Canadian airspace increased the likelihood of war and thus threatened the life and security of Canadian citizens contrary to section 7 of the Charter. The government's argument that cabinet decisions relating to foreign policy were political questions, unreviewable by the courts, was scornfully rejected by Justice Wilson. "Difficulties of evidence of proof" or issues involving "weighty matters of state," Wilson argued, do not "absolve the Court from making a certain kind of decision if it can be established on other grounds that it has a duty to do so. I think we should focus our attention on whether the courts *should* or *must* rather than on whether they *can* deal with such matters." She concludes:

> The question before us is not whether the government's defence policy is sound but whether or not it violates the appellants' rights under s. 7 of the Charter of Rights.... This is a totally different question.

Wilson's sharp separation of the policy question (Is it wise?) from the legal question (Is it constitutional?) is, of course, a perfect example of the legalism discussed in Chapter Six, and is subject to the criticisms outlined there. Charter sceptics, such as Patrick Monahan, do not believe it is possible to maintain the distinction between the two types of questions.[117] However that may be, Justice Wilson's pronouncement on the political questions doctrine has not been seriously challenged by other Supreme Court justices. Certainly none of them took up Justice Frankfurter's cause in the Saskatchewan electoral-districting case.

The Supreme Court's rejection of the one-person-one-vote principle, in short, did not entail an explicit disavowal of judicial authority in the matter of electoral districting. Thus, despite her interpretivist appeals to tradition and founding intention, Justice McLachlin also invoked the concept of the "living tree" to caution against "the specious argument that historical anomalies and abuses can be used to justify continued anomalies and abuses, or to suggest that the right to vote should not be interpreted broadly and remedially as befits Charter rights."[118] Her definition of the right to vote gave generous leeway to the use of nonpopulation considerations in constructing electoral maps, and she found no constitutional imperfections in Saskatchewan's act, but she nevertheless insisted that "[d]epartures from the Canadian ideal of effective representation may exist," and that "[w]here they do, they will be found to violate s. 3 of the Charter."[119]

What kinds of violations did Justice McLachlin have in mind? One possibility is the more extreme variation in constituency size that she invalidated in *Dixon.* Nothing in McLachlin's Supreme Court opinion indicates a repudiation of *Dixon;* indeed, she several times quotes her earlier opinion with approval. One may reasonably conclude that the B.C. legislation at stake in *Dixon,* or the more extreme inequalities embodied in Alberta's pre-1990 electoral map, would still violate section 3. Justice McLachlin did not repeat her indirect endorsement of the 25 percent rule in her Supreme

Court opinion, but she upheld legislation explicitly adopting that rule, indicating that it remains a good rule of thumb. As long as electoral maps remain within that limit they would seem to be relatively safe from the kind of extreme malapportionment challenge successfully brought against British Columbia. In fact, straying beyond that range is now possible only in Nova Scotia, New Brunswick, and Prince Edward Island, the only provinces that lack legislated deviation limits. It is also theoretically possible to challenge some of the substantial *inter*provincial discrepancies in federal constituencies, though the Court would almost certainly consider these justified by the exigencies of federalism.

The 25 percent rule seems to be a good rule of thumb, but should probably not be considered an inflexible rule. Certainly the Court avoided articulating any such rule, and Justice McLachlin's reasoning suggests that discrepancies in excess of 25 percent from the average might be justified in certain cases. Her judgment posed no challenge to Saskatchewan's northern constituencies, for example, which are allowed to vary by as much as 50 percent. In addition, her opinion might be read as leaving room for variations of more than 25 percent if they are justified as affirmative gerrymanders in favour of certain minorities. Smaller constituencies for natives, for example, might be looked upon with favour. Discrepancies going beyond the 25 percent rule might need explicit justification, however, while discrepancies within that limit are probably immune from charges of extreme malapportionment, such as those successfully brought against British Columbia in *Dixon*.

Although staying within the 25 percent rule would seem to be adequate protection against a charge of malapportionment, it does not preclude another kind of challenge. Had such a deviation limit been enough to "Charterproof" electoral legislation, Justice McLachlin would not have bothered to inquire further into Saskatchewan's electoral map. She found that the size discrepancies embodied in that map were justified by legitimate factors, but by that very fact implied that similar size discrepancies, even within the 25 percent deviation limit, might sometimes be illegitimate. They might be illegitimate, for instance, if they were introduced for purposes of partisan gerrymandering rather than to accommodate such considerations as regional representation, natural boundaries, or anticipated population growth. Indeed, even constituencies of equal size might be found to undermine "fair and effective representation" if it could be shown that they were gerrymandered in this way. Again, however, we must note that such partisan gerrymandering is unlikely when electoral maps are drawn by independent commissions. Only Prince Edward Island currently lacks a commission.

The most intriguing prospect for judicial intervention and activism emerges out of Justice McLachlin's solicitude for cultural minorities. We have noted that her opinion seems to permit affirmative gerrymanders in favour of such minorities although it does not *explicitly* require them. Might it *implicitly* require certain affirmative gerrymanders? The Court read section 3 as guaranteeing "fair and effective" representation, and conceded that affirmative gerrymanders, such as Saskatchewan's overrepresentation of rural dwellers, are sometimes necessary to achieving this goal. In suggesting that fair and effective representation might be promoted by similar affirmative gerrymanders in favour of cultural minorities, the Court not only gave such groups an important symbolic weapon to use in lobbying legislatures, but also invited them to seek judicial redress should their legislative lobbying prove unsuccessful. A cultural minority dissatisfied with its level of electoral influence now has every reason to launch a court case claiming that its section 3 right to fair and effective representation is not being fulfilled. Having left the door open to such claims, it remains to be seen whether the Court will be hospitable to them if and when they walk through the door.

Suppose a racial minority claimed that its interests were not fairly and effectively represented because the existing electoral map prevented it from electing its own members in proportion to its share of the overall population. In Halifax, for example, a black neighbourhood has complained that it is unable to elect a black member because it is divided between two ridings.[120] The Court would no doubt find it relatively easy to intervene if it were persuaded that such reduction of a minority's electoral influence was the product of a deliberate racist gerrymander. But what if, as is more likely nowadays, the group's low level of electoral success was the inadvertent result of constructing constituencies with an eye to other, nonracial criteria. For example, a racial concentration might be fragmented into minority positions within two adjacent constituencies by a natural boundary. Or an electoral boundaries commission that focused on increasing the equality of constituencies might reduce the number of seats allocated to sparsely populated areas dominated by the racial group. Would the Court invalidate such schemes and require new, affirmative gerrymanders in favour of the group? We cannot confidently predict, but the same reasoning underlying the Court's posture of restraint toward

Saskatchewan's overrepresentation of rural dwellers leaves the door open to such activism. At the very least, the Court has insisted on a supervisory role in the pursuit of fair and effective representation.

■ POLITICAL QUESTIONS AND JUDICIALLY MANAGEABLE STANDARDS

If Justice McLachlin was correct in concluding that equal constituencies could not guarantee fair and effective representation, was she equally correct in insisting on continued judicial involvement in the achievement of fair and effective representation? Would she have done better to adopt the more extreme restraint of Justice Frankfurter's "political questions" orientation?

While fair and effective representation obviously involves giving "deserving" groups an appropriate level of electoral influence, the key question is which groups are "deserving." Nor is it possible in a single-member, first-past-the-post constituency system such as ours to represent all groups in proportion to their actual strength. Because the candidate with the "most" votes (not necessarily a majority) wins the seat, all opposing votes are, in a sense, "wasted." So are votes cast for the winner in excess of what is required to win. If a party or political interest is consistently overrepresented among the "wasted" votes—as may happen if its supporters are in the minority in many constituencies (thus losing them all), or packed into a few constituencies in greater numbers than necessary to win (thus electing fewer members than possible)—it will be underrepresented (sometimes dramatically so) in electoral seats. The influence of any particular party or group can be improved through careful apportionment and boundary adjustment, but only at the cost of diminishing the influence of some other group. The NDP's electoral influence might be improved, for example, by constructing wholly urban constituencies in proportion to the urban share of the population, but only at the cost of less effective representation of rural interests. Drawing constituency boundaries to be fair to existing political parties, moreover, might disadvantage emergent political movements. Respecting historical and natural boundaries might dilute the influence of certain racial or ethnic groups. The list of trade-offs could easily be expanded. The point is that under our system of single-member constituencies there is no neutral set of constituency boundaries. Every electoral map will be somebody's gerrymander.

Perhaps a system of proportional representation could more nearly represent all interests in proportion to their actual strength, but no one pretends that section 3 of the Charter requires such a dramatic reform. As long as the existing system remains in place, the pursuit of fair and effective representation will involve painful choices of who is sufficiently "deserving." Since there are many competing claims for the privilege of representation—ethnic, regional, economic, demographic, to name just the traditional contenders—the choice is a constitutional choice in the most fundamental sense of "Who governs?" It thus affects the very nature of the regime. In modern democracies, one normally expects this constitutive act to be performed by either the people directly or their delegates. When it is performed by unelected, unaccountable judges in the absence of any clear constitutional rule the implication is that the legislatures themselves are unfit to make this choice. This implication is somewhat ironic. As Ward Elliott has observed about the American Court's reapportionment revolution:

> [It] tended to extend equality in form while debasing it in substance.
> It granted equal access to representative institutions, in a sense, but
> it also treated the institutions as though they were unfit to decide
> the main questions.[121]

For these reasons, the American courts refused for over a century to become embroiled in voting-rights cases alleging gerrymandering or malapportionment. Speaking for the majority in 1946, Justice Frankfurter described this issue as having "a peculiarly political nature and therefore not meet for judicial determination."[122] Like the clause guaranteeing the states "a republican form of government" in article 4 of the American constitution, Frankfurter explained, demands for fair and equitable representation are "not enforceable by courts because they clearly fall outside the conditions and purposes that circumscribe judicial action."[123] The electoral-districting issue, Frankfurter observed, "concerns matters that bring the courts into immediate and active relations with party contests."[124] "The courts," he concluded, "ought not to enter this political thicket."[125]

Sixteen years later, in *Baker* v. *Carr,* the American Supreme Court entered the political thicket, assuming jurisdiction over apportionment matters, but without actually fashioning a precise remedial standard. Now Frankfurter wrote in dissent. The apportionment issue, he protested, was "a wholly different matter from denial of the franchise to individuals because of race, color, religion or sex,"[126] over which the courts legitimately exercised jurisdiction. "What is actually asked of the Court," he continued, "is to choose among competing bases of representation—ultimately, really among competing theories of political philosophy."[127] There was no judicially manageable standard by which to determine these questions. The majority's decision to ignore this difference "presages the futility of judicial intervention in the essentially political conflict of forces by which the relation between population and representation has time out of mind been and now is determined."[128]

The majority in *Baker* was not frightened off by Frankfurter's invocation of the "political questions" doctrine. Referring to the Court's experience since *Brown* v. *Board of Education*,[129] the Court's 1954 school desegregation ruling, Justice Brennan confidently asserted that there was no problem of "judicially manageable standards" or illegitimate judicial "policy determinations": "judicial standards under the Equal Protection Clause are well developed and familiar."[130] Not only was Frankfurter not persuaded by this analogy, but he taunted Brennan and the majority that their failure to fashion a specific remedy "implies a sorry confession of judicial impotence."[131] How could the majority rule that a right had been violated, if they could not say what enforcement of that right meant in practice?

While Frankfurter clearly lost this battle, it remains to be seen whether he also lost the war. We have seen that the U.S. Court ultimately did specify the judicially manageable standard of virtually equal constituencies, but that this did not guarantee fair and effective representation—indeed, that it might actually have made political gerrymandering easier. In view of this, the Court has been pressured to go beyond the simple rule of population equality and accept cases turning on a broader concept of fair and effective representation. A sharply divided Court finally did so in the 1986 case *Davis* v. *Bandemer*. The disagreement among the judges aptly captures what is at stake when judges accept a supervisory role in the achievement of fair and effective representation broadly conceived.

Bandemer came out of Indiana, and was based on facts similar to those in the California gerrymander described above, only this time it was a Republican-dominated legislature that had "packed" and "fragmented" the opposition Democrats. While the population deviation between state legislative districts was less than 1.2 percent, the results of the 1982 state elections strongly suggested that the new electoral map unfairly disadvantaged the Democrats. In the House elections, Democratic candidates won 51.9 percent of the state-wide vote, but only 43 percent of the seats. In two counties, they received 46.6 percent of the votes, but won only three of twenty-one seats. This, argued the Democrats, denied them the equal protection of the laws.

For the first time, a majority of six judges ruled that the claim of political gerrymander was justiciable. The other three, led by Justice O'Connor, insisted that the case raised a "political question" not fit for judicial resolution. The six judges who were prepared to accept jurisdiction, however, divided among themselves about the actual electoral map in question. Four, speaking through Justice White, upheld the Indiana map, while two, led by Justice Powell, voted to strike it down. The four "moderates" thus combined with the three advocates of "political questions" restraint to make seven votes in favour of the legislation. This drove Powell and his colleague into dissent on the bottom-line question, although they agreed with the White plurality on the question of justiciability.

The issues at stake are most clearly set out in the Powell and O'Connor opinions. *Reynolds* v. *Sims,* declared Powell, "recognized that equal protection encompasses a guarantee of equal *representation,* requiring a state to seek to achieve through redistricting 'fair and effective representation' for all citizens." "The concept of representation," he continued, "necessarily applies to groups: groups of voters elect representatives, individual voters do not."[132] The group being unfairly represented in the immediate case, of course, was a political party, but Powell elsewhere defines the targets of justiciable gerrymanders as "politically weak segments of the community," including "racial, ethnic, religious, economic or political" groups.[133] Like Justice McLachlin's Canadian judgment, Powell's opinion opens the door to litigation by all such groups. Indeed, its relevance to Canada lies primarily in its openness to claims by racial, ethnic, religious, and economic groups, for as we have seen, openly partisan gerrymanders in favour of political parties are less likely here because of the map-drawing role of independent commissions.

Unlike Justice McLachlin, however, Powell was unable to persuade a majority of the Court to join his opinion. Justice O'Connor was particularly troubled by implications of an activist decision in this case:

> If members of the major political parties are protected by the Equal Protection Clause from dilution of their voting strength, then members of every identifiable group that possesses distinctive interests and tends to vote on the basis of those interests should be able to bring similar claims.[134]

The result would be an endless stream of litigation from parties and groups claiming that they were denied "fair representation" in the political process. The federal courts would be left in the position of trying "to reconcile the competing claims of political, religious, ethnic, racial, occupational, and socio-economic groups."[135] Not only does the Court have no criteria by which to order such claims, O'Connor declares, but there is "not a shred of evidence to suggest that the Framers of the Constitution intended the judicial power to encompass the making of such fundamental choices about how this Nation is to be governed."[136] The claim, O'Connor concludes, presents a nonjusticiable "political question" and should not even be considered by the Court.

Had Justice O'Connor been on Canada's Supreme Court she might have made this argument even more strongly. In the United States she could still take comfort from the Supreme Court's longstanding rule that a claim of unconstitutional discrimination can succeed only if the discrimination is shown to be intentional.[137] This would at least place some limits on the scope of gerrymandering litigation, for it would require groups claiming constitutionally unfair and ineffective representation to show that the electoral map was consciously designed to dilute their political influence. In Canada, by contrast, the Supreme Court has decided that to sustain a *prima facie* case of unconstitutional discrimination there need be no discriminatory intention; it suffices to show a "discriminatory effect."[138] This rule, combined with an open-door policy to groups complaining of unfair and ineffective representation, would draw the Canadian court even more thoroughly into the political thicket than its American counterpart.

Coming back to *Bandemer*, Justice White's four-judge plurality tried to steer a middle course between the Powell and O'Connor wings of the Court. Like Powell, White wanted to bring the gerrymandering issue within judicial jurisdiction. Like O'Connor, on the other hand, White did not want to "invite attack on all or almost all reapportionment statutes," which, he feared, "would too much embroil the judiciary in second-guessing what has consistently been referred to as a political task for the legislature." He thus rejected the claim, accepted by Powell, that a party's seat totals should more or less reflect its vote totals. "[S]uch a low threshold for legal action,"[139] he warned, would bring about the endless litigation and judicial second-guessing he wished to avoid.

In place of a "proportionality" test, White's plurality opinion declares that unconstitutional discrimination occurs "only when the electoral system is arranged in a manner that will consistently degrade a voter's or group of voters' influence on the political process as a whole."[140] The meaning of this alternative criterion is hardly clear. One commentator described it as an example of "flagrant imprecision."[141] What is clear is that Justice White and his supporters were not eager to encourage a new round of litigation by establishing a low threshold of evidentiary proof. If the facts of the Indiana case are not sufficient to sustain a successful challenge, it will take a dramatic gerrymander indeed to do so.

White's opinion seems too "muddy" to stand the test of time, but it helps to expose the real alternatives. There is really no point in assuming jurisdiction if the Court cannot find the Indiana gerrymander unconstitutional. It might as well have sided with the "political questions" perspective of the O'Connor group. Only with a lower "threshold of legal action," such as that employed by Powell, does it make sense to accept jurisdiction. A lower threshold, however, risks endless litigation and political second-guessing of the most fundamental political choices.

These are also the main alternatives for the Canadian Court. Although Justice McLachlin's opinion provides considerable hope for those who would like the Court to take the path suggested in the United States by Justice Powell, this opinion is unlikely to be the last word. A single swallow does not a summer make, and a single judicial opinion (even a Supreme Court majority opinion) does not necessarily set a long-term course. The Court's opinion was written to sustain an affirmative gerrymander in favour of rural dwellers. In the course of justifying this affirmative gerrymander, the Court suggested that similar gerrymanders in favour of cultural minorities might also be necessary to achieve the constitutional goal of fair and effective representation. This suggestion may well stimulate further litigation by such minorities. But invalidating electoral maps that do not effectively represent minorities—and thus, by implication, requiring new affirmative gerrymanders in favour of these minorities—is very different from upholding an existing affirmative gerrymander. The Court has clearly opened the door to minorities seeking electoral reform in their favour; whether it will allow such claims to proceed much beyond the threshold remains an open question. If not, it will have taken the "political questions" approach to the problem of minority representation in practice, if not in theory. If the Court proves to be inhospitable to the minority claims it appears to have invited, it might still play a role in the field of electoral districting. It might be spurred into action, for example, if extreme malapportionment or a blatant gerrymander were to arise in a jurisdiction without a deviation limit or an electoral boundaries commission. Given the generous leeway established in the Saskatchewan case, however, this role is likely to be quite limited, especially in comparison to the American Court's role in apportionment politics. If, on the other hand, the Court gives a warm welcome to minorities alleging unfair and ineffective representation, it risks being drawn into the very heart of the "political thicket."

■ CONCLUSION

The Supreme Court's rejection of the one-person-one-vote principle in *Carter* did not entail an explicit disavowal of judicial authority in the matter of electoral districting. Nor did the Court accept the view that the section 3 right to vote was satisfied by the simple entitlement to cast a ballot, regardless of the fairness or effectiveness of the resulting representation. Indeed, the Court was quite explicit in affirming that section 3 was designed to promote "fair and effective" representation, not just to affirm the existing right to mark and cast a ballot. The Court rejected the one-person-one-vote principle mainly because it did not think it would ensure fair and effective representation. Indeed, in upholding Saskatchewan's electoral districting, the Court suggested that fair and effective representation for rural interests may actually require some departure from strict population equality.

Even if this were not the case—i.e., even if rural interests deserved no special protection and constituencies of equal size were thus desirable in principle—the achievement of equal constituencies would not guarantee fair and effective representation. American experience with equal constituencies shows that fair and effective representation is affected by a host of factors that work independently of variation in the size of constituencies. Indeed, strict adherence to the one-person-one-vote rule in the United States has arguably enhanced threats to fair and effective representation in the form of political gerrymanders. Thus right-to-vote litigation in the United States did not cease as equal constituencies were achieved. Nor is further litigation in Canada foreclosed because our Court has not mandated equal constituencies. In affirming a judicial interest in fair and effective representation even as it rejected a strict one-person-one-vote rule, Canada's Supreme Court has closed only one door to judicial activism, leaving others open. The Court's decision in the Saskatchewan case, in other words, ends one chapter in this area of Charter politics—a very short chapter as compared to its American counterpart—but it may not have concluded the book. As in the United States, the one-person-one-vote jurisprudence may be only the first installment in a continuing story.

CHAPTER THIRTEEN

A Note on the Charter and National Integration

The Charter was intended to exercise a nationalizing influence on Canadian politics. It was expected to do so in part by restricting provincial policy-making power. We conclude this book by considering more precisely the factors that promote or inhibit this national-unity function of judicial decisions, and by briefly assessing the actual impact of judicial review on national integration.

The extent to which judicial review of the Charter will contribute to national unity is not a foregone conclusion. It is affected by, among other things, the balance between judicial activism and judicial restraint. An activist decision overturning a provincial policy on Charter grounds necessarily invalidates the identical policies of other provinces, or denies them the previously available option of enacting such a policy. Such a decision sets at least a negative standard—a standard of what may *not* be done—which applies uniformly throughout the country. A restrained decision, on the other hand, leaves intact the decisions of governments. In provincial areas of jurisdiction, therefore, judicial restraint in applying the Charter leaves more scope for provincial variability in policy formulation. Thus, although the unifying and standardizing potential inherent in the transfer of policy-making power from legislatures to courts is readily apparent, how far it is pushed depends greatly on the judges themselves.

In Chapter Five we argued that the degree of activism or restraint displayed by a judgment depends not only on the bottom-line result of the case, but also on the reasoning used to arrive at that result. This distinction must also be taken into account in assessing the effect of judicial review on federalism. It is not a simple matter of activist decisions that unify or nationalize and restrained decisions that do not. In light of the distinction between the outcome of a decision and its justifying reasons, it is better to think of a continuum between two extremes and to judge the unifying potential of a decision by where it falls on the continuum.

To illustrate, consider again the Supreme Court's review in *Edwards Books* of Ontario's Retail Business Holidays Act.[1] To recapitulate, the case turned on the question whether the religious freedom of Saturday-sabbatarian retailers was infringed because of the competitive disadvantages they suffered. Actually the legislature had made some attempt to accommodate Saturday sabbatarians by including a so-called Saturday exemption in the act. This exemption allowed stores to open on Sunday if they had closed the preceding Saturday. To avoid requiring retailers to pass a religious-sincerity test in order to take advantage of this exemption, Ontario formulated it in religiously neutral terms, making it available regardless of religious affiliation. On the other hand, to prevent the exemption from undermining the rule, it was limited to relatively small stores. Larger stores, even if owned by Saturday sabbatarians, still had to close on Sunday.

This act was upheld in its entirety by six of the seven judges involved. As far as the bottom-line result is concerned, this was certainly a restrained decision. But there were several degrees of restraint in the reasoning employed to reach this result. At the most restrained end of the continuum were Justices Beetz and McIntyre, who found no infringement of the Charter because they thought the economic disadvantage suffered by Saturday sabbatarians was caused by their religious conscience, not by the law. Had this been the majority view, section 2 of the Charter would have placed virtually no limits on provincial legislative authority over secular pause-day legislation.

The other four judges who upheld the law found that it violated section 2 of the Charter, but that it was a "reasonable limit" under section 1. In addressing the section 1 question, these judges agreed that the purpose of the law was sufficiently compelling to justify some infringement of religious freedom, but divided on the necessity of judging whether the legislature could have chosen less oppressive means to achieve this purpose. Justice Dickson, writing for Chouinard and Le Dain, compared Ontario's Saturday exemption to such alternatives as New Brunswick's similar, but religiously targeted exemption, which used religious sincerity rather than size as the limiting test. Justice Dickson weighed the comparative costs and benefits of these alternatives and concluded that Ontario's policy was justified.

Justice La Forest objected to this weighing of alternative means. This was a policy area, he argued, in which "there is no perfect scenario in which the rights of all can be equally protected."[2] No matter what the legislature did, somebody would lose. If there was no law at all, Saturday sabbatarians would still suffer competitive disadvantages vis-à-vis their nonreligious competitors, though they would now share that misfortune with their Sunday-observing counterparts. If the legislature chose to act, the best balancing of competing interests would depend entirely on local circumstances, which legislatures were best equipped to judge. In such cases, it was sufficient for section 1 purposes to determine whether the infringement of religious freedom served a compelling purpose. If it did, the question of means should be left to the legislature. What kind of exemption should be enacted, and indeed whether there should be any exemption at all, was not a question to be determined by the courts.

Next to the Beetz-McIntyre opinion, Justice La Forest's opinion was obviously the most restrained and thus the least restrictive of provincial policy-making authority. Although he found a violation of religious freedom, Justice La Forest upheld the law under section 1. More important, because he saw this as essentially a matter for political or policy judgment, he applied section 1 so as to preserve virtually unhindered legislative freedom. As long as the provincial legislation is enacted for the secular purpose of promoting a common day of rest, the legislature is free to decide how to accomplish this end. Since this is a matter of provincial jurisdiction, it follows that no significant limits are placed on the variability of provincial policies by La Forest's judgment.

Justice Dickson's opinion also represented judicial restraint inasmuch as it upheld the law. But Dickson did not concede that legislatures are entirely free in formulating secular pause-day legislation. Unlike Justice La Forest, he thought it proper for the courts to judge whether the legislature had pursued its legitimate purposes in ways that infringed the Charter right as little as possible. Whereas Justice La Forest was prepared to abandon the proportionality side of the *Oakes* test in this policy area, Justice Dickson insisted on applying it. Nevertheless, as we noted in Chapter Three, Dickson softened the minimal impairment test somewhat, reformulating his statement in *Oakes* that legislation should infringe the Charter "as little as possible," so that it now read "as little as is *reasonably* possible." Under this less stringent test Ontario's legislation emerged unscathed from Dickson's proportionality assessment. Perhaps it did not represent the "least drastic means" in some absolute sense, but its infringement was "reasonable." This meant that Ontario's legislation would not be constitutionally undermined by the mere fact that some other province had found a less intrusive way of achieving the same end.[3] Limiting the "Saturday exemption" to stores under a specified size, for example, would not be open to challenge simply because another province enacted a larger size limit, thereby making the exemption more broadly available. Along the continuum from least to most restrictive means, provinces were thus free to vary up to the point represented by Ontario. By adopting a somewhat more restrained approach to the minimal impairment test, in other words, Justice Dickson preserved room for the kind of policy variation federalism is designed to protect.

But what of provincial policies that are more restrictive than Ontario's? Quebec, for example, also has a religiously neutral Saturday exemption for "small stores," but the size limit is considerably smaller than Ontario's, and the exemption is thus not as readily invoked. Under Justice Dickson's judgment the existence of less restrictive policies cannot undermine the legitimacy of Ontario's legislation, but might Ontario's policy become a minimum standard applicable against more restrictive policies? Might it represent the outer limit on the minimal-impairment continuum? This is precisely what concerned Justice La Forest, who worried that Quebec's more restrictive version of the Saturday exemption might be found wanting in light of the more liberal standards of the Ontario law.[4]

Justice Dickson's opinion does not explicitly establish Ontario's law as the outer limit of restrictiveness; it remains possible that even more restrictive policies might be upheld under his approach. Nevertheless, his approach implies that there must be some outer limit. If there is to be any point to his comparative assessment of legislative means, in other words, it must be capable of failing some policy alternatives. Thus, although it led to a restrained result in the Ontario case, Justice Dickson's opinion holds out the promise of more activist decisions in the future. Certainly it implies a narrower range of permissible variance among provincial pause-day policies than do the Beetz-McIntyre or La Forest opinions. For example, Dickson insisted that some kind of exemption for Saturday sabbatarians was constitutionally required while La Forest, like Beetz and McIntyre, would have upheld even legislation that lacked such an exemption. This underscores the importance of distinguishing between the result in a case and the reasoning on which it is based. A result that indicates restraint may be based on more or less restrained reasoning. The more the reasoning tends toward the activist end of the continuum, the greater its tendency to restrict policy diversity.

For the same reason, one should not overstate the tendency of cases with an activist result to restrict legislative freedom. Much depends on how broadly or narrowly the courts frame the reasons for such a decision. As we have seen, Justice Wilson's judgment in *Morgentaler* would restrict legislative policy discretion much more than the Beetz-Estey judgment, and somewhat more than the Dickson-Lamer opinion, although all three have the same activist result of striking down the law under consideration.[5]

Morgentaler, of course, involved a federal law and does not therefore speak directly to the question of restrictions on provincial policy variation stemming from the judicial invalidation of a provincial policy. The same principles apply, however. The more narrowly the courts frame the invalidation of a provincial law, the less they impede provincial policy initiatives, and hence the more they leave room for policy diversity among the provinces.

Both Peter Hogg and Katherine Swinton have suggested that, in *Edwards Books,* Justices Dickson and La Forest gave a restrained twist to the *Oakes* test (though to different degrees) precisely because they appreciated the value of diversity in a federal system and did not want the Charter to undermine it.[6] Such judicial respect for federal diversity has also been evident in cases turning on the validity not of provincial laws, but of the differential provincial application of federal laws. Although the Criminal Code and the Young Offenders Act are federal acts, they are administered and enforced in part by the provinces, who are permitted some leeway in how they carry out these functions. For example, there is some variation among provinces in whether those accused of certain crimes are entitled to choose trial by judge alone or must be tried by judge and jury.[7] Similarly, provincial prosecutors may exercise their discretion differently, thus leading to variation in the application of Criminal Code provisions.[8] Under the Young Offenders Act provinces are authorized to establish "alternative measures" to judicial proceedings for dealing with young offenders, but not all provinces have done so.[9] Such variation in the provincial administration of federal law has been challenged as violating "either the guarantee of equality in section 15 of the Charter or the implicit value of equality in many of the other Charter rights."[10] The Court has turned back these challenges, arguing, for example, that variation in prosecutorial practices "may be inevitable and, indeed, desirable, in a country where a federal statute is administered by local authorities,"[11] or that "differential application of federal law can be a legitimate means of forwarding the values of a federal system."[12]

In sum, Canada's Supreme Court judges are obviously sensitive, to varying degrees, to the value of federal diversity, and have incorporated this value into their Charter jurisprudence. It has led them to sustain the differential application of federal laws, and has encouraged less activist reasoning in cases challenging provincial legislation. The unifying potential of the Charter is obviously not being pushed to its logical extreme.

Nevertheless, the unifying impact of judicial review of the Charter remains significant. One indication of this emerges from an examination of cases actually invalidating provincial policies. To repeat, such invalidations represent bottom-line activism, and thus have some standardizing effect, but this effect is moderated to the extent that the reasons for invalidating are narrowly framed. In fact, narrowly framed invalidations appear to occur less often at the provincial than at the federal level. Between 1982 and 1988, appeal courts nullified thirty-two federal and thirty-one provincial statutes.[13] Eighty-eight percent (twenty-eight of thirty-two) of the federal statutes and only 42 percent (thirteen of thirty-one) of the provincial statutes were nullified on procedural grounds. The remaining 58 percent of the provincial statutes were invalidated on broader, substantive grounds. Moreover, although the total number of invalidations is about equal, appeal courts have struck down provincial statutes at a much higher rate than federal statutes.[14] And we have seen that even when a law is upheld, the judicial reasoning may exercise a standardizing influence.

The same pattern is evident if one looks only at Supreme Court decisions. In its first one hundred Charter cases, the Court struck down eleven provincial and eight federal statutes. Seven of the eight nullifications of federal statutes were procedural in character, and half were based on the legal-rights provisions of the Charter. By contrast, nine of the eleven nullifications of provincial statutes were substantive in character.[15] The difference is illustrated by the fact that *Morgentaler* left considerable room for a new, more carefully drafted criminal prohibition of abortion, while the very essence of Quebec's language-of-education policy was struck down in the *Protestant School Boards* case.[16] Moreover, the invalidated provincial statutes tended to be more recently enacted, and more integral parts of the current policy agendas of the governments were involved. With the important exception of abortion, the federal legislation overturned by the Court has not involved major policy concerns. By contrast, seven of the nine substantive provincial invalidations were based directly or indirectly on French–English minority language and education issues—a perennial source of conflict in Canadian politics. These findings suggest that the Charter may indeed be standardizing provincial policy to some extent.

Five provinces have lost legislation to Charter challenges: Quebec, British Columbia, Alberta, Saskatchewan, and Manitoba. Of the five, Quebec has clearly been most affected. The Quebec Protestant School Board successfully challenged the education provisions of Bill 101. At the time the Charter was adopted, René Lévesque bitterly denounced section 23, which was clearly intended to strike down the education policy embedded in Bill 101. "No self-respecting Quebec government," he declared, "could ever abandon the smallest fraction of this fundamental right to protect the only French island in the English-speaking sea of the North American continent."[17] Because section 23 is excluded from the scope of the section 33 legislative override, Quebec had no alternative but to accept the Court's decision.

Three years later, the Supreme Court struck down another section of Bill 101—the "French-only" public signs requirements. This provision prohibited the use of English in commercial signs (billboards, storefront advertising, and the like). Quebec anglophones, especially the 650 000 living in Montreal, considered it oppressive and humiliating, and challenged it as a violation of the Charter right to freedom of expression. Quebec nationalists considered the French-only rule essential to preserving the "French face" of Montreal, and harshly denounced the Supreme Court's decision. The Liberal government of Robert Bourassa—contrary to promises it had made to anglophone voters in the 1985 election—gave in to nationalist sentiment and invoked the section 33 legislative override to reinstate the French-only public signs policy. This override of the Supreme Court's decision infuriated many people in English Canada and contributed to the subsequent defeat of the Meech Lake Accord.

In one sense, Quebec presents the clearest example of the counter-majoritarian character of judicial review, where the Court uses the Charter to protect the rights of a local minority against the local majority. From a different perspective, however, the same decisions, particularly in conjunction with the language-rights cases from Alberta, Manitoba, and Saskatchewan, show how the Charter, through the Supreme Court, can serve as a vehicle for imposing majority rule rather than restricting it. The catch is that the will of a *national* political majority is being imposed on what is deemed to be the perverse and unacceptable behaviour of regional majorities in Quebec or the West.

This is consistent with American experience, where some commentators argue that rather than being a restraint on Congress and the president, the American Supreme Court has more often participated actively in ruling national coalitions,[18] especially when it comes to curbing state or local policies that are offensive to the ruling national coalition. This interpretation is supported by persuasive evidence. The U.S. Supreme Court has declared unconstitutional seven times more state laws (970) than federal laws (135). Between 1984 and 1989, while the Supreme Court of Canada was striking down eleven provincial and eight federal statutes under the Charter, eighteen state statutes and only two federal statutes were declared invalid for violating the American Bill of Rights. If a similar trend develops under the Charter—and there is early evidence to suggest that it might—then the previously decentralized character of Canadian federalism may be slowly eroded.

Judicial policy-making under the Charter may contribute to national unity in yet another sense. In the past, judicial review of the constitution probably exacerbated the tendency of most political issues to transform themselves into issues of federalism. If questions of rights and freedoms became the subject of constitutional review under the BNA Act, they had to be cast in the language and categories of federalism. Questions of freedom of religion or speech, for example, were decided in terms of which level of government had jurisdiction to infringe them.[19] Under the Charter the same issues can be formulated directly as civil liberties issues dividing Canadians from each other on policy rather than regional lines—in terms of their support or opposition to Sunday-closing laws or censorship, for example, rather than in terms of their views on centralization or decentralization. The Charter may bypass "governments and [speak] directly to Canadians as bearers of rights."[20]

But the same Canadians who have these rights in common, regardless of where they live, are divided by their interpretation. This highlights an ironic aspect of the unifying role of the Charter. When the politics of Sunday closing or hate literature (or almost anything else) goes to court, it remains controversial and divisive politics. As Sanford Levinson argues, one can speak of a constitution "as a common symbol guarantee[ing] meaningful national political unity" only so long as one ignores the reality of constitutional interpretation. Constitutions unify political regimes, Levinson argues, in the same sense that holy books unify religions. Holy books are certainly the cornerstones of religious identity, but they are equally the basis of religious schism because they are notoriously open to conflicting interpretations. Since the meaning of constitutions is similarly controversial, Levinson believes they are as likely "to serve as the source of fragmentation and *dis*-integration" as they are to promote unity or integration.[21] The Charter is certainly an opportunity for schismatic interpretation. In this sense, the Charter does not promote unity by overcoming divisions among Canadians; it is more accurate to say that it encourages national rather than regional divisions. If judicial review under the Charter contributes to national unity, it does so in the sense of stimulating ideological divisions that transcend regional boundaries rather than symbolically emphasizing what all Canadians have in common.

It is not even clear that the Charter will always subordinate regional to national divisions. The prolonged and bitter debate over the "distinct society" clause in the Meech Lake Accord, for example, reflected the Charter's disproportionate impact on Quebec, and underscored an important cleavage between francophone Quebec and the rest of Canada concerning the value of the Charter. The Quebec government hoped that the distinct society clause would mitigate the impact of the Charter on Quebec's attempts to protect and promote the use of the French language. For the same reason, many English Canadians, especially those within Quebec, were strongly opposed to the distinct society clause, and thus to the entire accord. As far as the tensions between Quebec and the rest of Canada are concerned, the Charter seems to be fuelling rather than dousing the fire.

The Charter's ability to exercise a nationalizing influence needs to be qualified in yet another sense. On reflection, it turns out that judicial review can sometimes actually stimulate policy activity, and hence variation, at the provincial level rather than impeding it. Once again the *Morgentaler* case provides a useful illustration. That case struck down a federal law. Yet because the majority of the Court framed the constitutional constraint narrowly—in terms of procedural problems rather than in terms of a positive right to abortion—it left substantial room for legislative experimentation with regulatory substitutes.[22] Some of the available substitutes lie within provincial jurisdiction, and for some time the provinces were more active than the federal government in responding to *Morgentaler*. Only the federal government, of course, could enact a new criminal prohibition of abortion, because criminal law is a federal matter, but provinces that wished to preserve the pre-*Morgentaler* environment with respect to abortion could use their health-insurance programs as a lever of influence. Soon after *Morgentaler*, for example, Alberta sought to preserve significant elements of the invalidated federal policy by refusing to pay for abortions that did not meet some of that policy's standards. Under the invalidated federal law, abortions had to be approved by a therapeutic abortion committee (TAC) in an accredited hospital. Alberta abandoned the requirement of TAC approval, but decided to pay for an abortion only if the performing physician sought a second opinion. Like the old federal law, Alberta also insisted that abortions be performed in an accredited hospital rather than in a free-standing clinic. Again, the main difference in the two policies was the provincial reliance on monetary rather than penal sanctions. Alberta also "continued the practice established [under the federal law] of leaving the issue of whether a hospital would perform abortions to the discretion of individual hospital boards."[23]

Other provinces responded to the policy vacuum created by *Morgentaler* in a variety of ways. All provinces decided to pay for abortions in accredited hospitals, but only British Columbia, Ontario, and Quebec were willing to pay for abortions performed in free-standing clinics. The latter three provinces placed few other restrictions on funding, although British Columbia announced that it would spend $20 million on a program to discourage abortion. Some of the provinces that would fund only hospital abortions also imposed other qualifications. Prince Edward Island, for example, funded abortions only if a health-insurance committee of five doctors considered it medically necessary. In New Brunswick, two doctors had to be satisfied that the same "medical necessity" standard had been met. Thus the invalidation of a federal law prompted a variety of provincial policies.[24]

The provincial response to *Morgentaler* shows that a narrowly framed judicial invalidation of a *federal* law, which permits a wide range of regulatory substitutes, can actually stimulate legislative activity at the *provincial* level. This leads to the replacement of a national law by several provincial policies, which is likely to mean more rather than less policy variation. We have seen that the unifying or standardizing potential of judicial review under the Charter depends on how broadly or narrowly the courts choose to frame a constitutional constraint, and that courts have tended to impose broader constitutional constraints on the provinces to the detriment of provincial policy diversity. Yet we must also acknowledge that in some cases a narrowly framed constraint, far from restricting policy diversity, might actually stimulate it.

Another qualification on the Charter's ability to standardize provincial policy is found in section 33, the legislative override. The override certainly allows provinces to protect their policy preferences from Charter review, though it should be recalled that it can override only sections 2 and 7 to 15 of the Charter. Thus, when the Supreme Court struck down Quebec's controversial "French-only" signs law because it violated the section 2 right to freedom of expression,[25] the province was able to use section 33 to reinstate the policy. By contrast, Quebec could not override the Court's invalidation of Bill 101's language-of-education provisions[26] because that ruling was based on section 23, which is not subject to the section 33 override. Quebec, in fact, is the only province thus far to use section 33 extensively. As part of its protest against patriating the constitution (including the new Charter) without its consent in 1982, the Parti Québécois government immediately enacted a blanket override applying to all existing legislation and thereafter inserted a notwithstanding clause in all new legislation. When the Liberals under Robert Bourassa defeated the PQ in 1985, they discontinued this practice. Outside of Quebec, only Saskatchewan has used section 33. It did so to immunize strike-ending, back-to-work legislation from Charter review.[27] Ironically, this turned out to be unnecessary because the Supreme Court was soon to rule that the "freedom of association" clause of section 2 did not embrace the right to strike.[28]

To summarize, the role of the Charter in national integration is highly nuanced and somewhat ironic. In its attempt to lay the constitutional groundwork for national unity, the Trudeau government did not want to rely on a policy of institutional reform that would domesticate regional conflict by better reflecting it in the central institutions of government.[29] To repeat Jennifer Smith's observation: this way of promoting national unity "risks an identifiable national discourse by promoting a self-consciously regional one. It unavoidably promotes while it accepts and placates regionalism, in which case the remedy exacerbates, not cures, the political ill."[30] The Trudeau government promoted the Charter as an alternative strategy. Instead of bringing regional divisions into the central institutions of government, it hoped the Charter would transcend these divisions by promoting a common and inclusive Canadian identity, symbolically bypassing governments and emphasizing the relations between the state as such and the people. The government may also have hoped that the Charter would promote national unity by transferring policy-making authority from a federally divided legislative to a unified judicial process, thereby replacing some of the policy diversity that flows from federalism with national, rights-based standards. We have seen, however, that this unifying effect of the Charter depends on the mix of judicial activism and self-restraint in the courts. There is evidence suggesting that appeal courts have been more activist, and thus standardizing, in their invalidation of provincial statutes. On the other hand, we also noted that some invalidations of *federal* laws may actually stimulate *provincial* diversity.

Symbolically the Charter may indeed promote nonregionalized identities. It is not clear, however, that it will promote a single all-encompassing Canadian identity. Ironically, the Charter often unifies by dividing, by promoting particularized identities and divisions, which unify because they are nonregional, but which are divisive nonetheless. In this sense, the Charter's impact is more like the policy of unifying by bringing regional conflict to the centre than like the clear-cut alternative to that policy envisaged by Trudeau.

APPENDIX

Constitution Act, 1982
Schedule B to Canada Act 1982 (U.K.)

■ PART I
Canadian Charter of Rights and Freedoms

Whereas Canada is founded upon principles that recognize the supremacy of God and the rule of law:

Guarantee of Rights and Freedoms

Rights and freedoms in Canada

1. The **Canadian Charter of Rights and Freedoms** guarantees the rights and freedoms set out in it subject only to such reasonable limits prescribed by law as can be demonstrably justified in a free and democratic society.

Fundamental Freedoms

Fundamental freedoms

2. Everyone has the following fundamental freedoms:
- **(a)** freedom of conscience and religion;
- **(b)** freedom of thought, belief, opinion and expression, including freedom of the press and other media of communication;
- **(c)** freedom of peaceful assembly; and
- **(d)** freedom of association.

Democratic Rights

Democratic rights of citizens

3. Every citizen of Canada has the right to vote in an election of members of the House of Commons or of a legislative assembly and to be qualified for membership therein.

Maximum duration of legislative bodies

4. **(1)** No House of Commons and no legislative assembly shall continue for longer than five years from the date fixed for the return of the writs at a general election of its members.

Continuation in special circumstances

(2) In time of real or apprehended war, invasion or insurrection, a

House of Commons may be continued by Parliament and a legislative assembly may be continued by the legislature beyond five years if such continuation is not opposed by the votes of more than one-third of the members of the House of Commons or the legislative assembly, as the case may be.

Annual sitting of legislative bodies

5. There shall be a sitting of Parliament and of each legislature at least once every twelve months.

Mobility Rights

Mobility of citizens

6. (1) Every citizen of Canada has the right to enter, remain in and leave Canada.

Rights to move and gain livelihood

(2) Every citizen of Canada and every person who has the status of a permanent resident of Canada has the right

(a) to move to and take up residence in any province; and

(b) to pursue the gaining of a livelihood in any province.

Limitation

(3) The rights specified in subsection (2) are subject to

(a) any laws or practices of general application in force in a province other than those that discriminate among persons primarily on the basis of province of present or previous residence; and

(b) any laws providing for reasonable residency requirements as a qualification for the receipt of publicly provided social services.

Affirmative action programs

(4) Subsections (2) and (3) do not preclude any law, program or activity that has as its object the amelioration in a province of conditions of individuals in that province who are socially or economically disadvantaged if the rate of employment in that province is below the rate of employment in Canada.

Legal Rights

Life, liberty and security of person

7. Everyone has the right to life, liberty and security of the person and the right not to be deprived thereof except in accordance with the principles of fundamental justice.

Search or seizure

8. Everyone has the right to be secure against unreasonable search or seizure.

Detention or imprisonment

9. Everyone has the right not to be arbitrarily detained or imprisoned.

Arrest or detention

10. Everyone has the right on arrest or detention
  (a) to be informed promptly of the reasons therefor;
  (b) to retain and instruct counsel without delay and to be informed of that right; and
  (c) to have the validity of the detention determined by way of *habeas corpus* and to be released if the detention is not lawful.

Proceedings in criminal and penal matters

11. Any person charged with an offence has the right
  (a) to be informed without unreasonable delay of the specific offence;
  (b) to be tried within a reasonable time;
  (c) not to be compelled to be a witness in proceedings against that person in respect of the offence;
  (d) to be presumed innocent until proven guilty according to law in a fair and public hearing by an independent and impartial tribunal;
  (e) not to be denied reasonable bail without just cause;
  (f) except in the case of an offence under military law tried before a military tribunal, to the benefit of trial by jury where the maximum punishment for the offence is imprisonment for five years or a more severe punishment;
  (g) not to be found guilty on account of any act or omission unless, at the time of the act or omission, it constituted an offence under Canadian or international law or was criminal according to the general principles of law recognized by the community of nations;
  (h) if finally acquitted of the offence, not to be tried for it again and, if finally found guilty and punished for the offence, not to be tried or punished for it again; and
  (i) if found guilty of the offence and if the punishment for the offence has been varied between the time of commission and the time of sentencing, to the benefit of the lesser punishment.

Treatment or punishment

12. Everyone has the right not to be subjected to any cruel and unusual treatment or punishment.

Self-crimination

13. A witness who testifies in any proceedings has the right not to have any incriminating evidence so given used to incriminate that witness in any other proceedings, except in a prosecution for perjury or for the giving of contradictory evidence.

Interpreter **14.** A party or witness in any proceedings who does not understand or speak the language in which the proceedings are conducted or who is deaf has the right to the assistance of an interpreter.

Equality Rights

Equality before and under law and equal protection and benefit of law **15. (1)** Every individual is equal before and under the law and has the right to the equal protection and equal benefit of the law without discrimination and, in particular, without discrimination based on race, national or ethnic origin, colour, religion, sex, age or mental or physical disability.

Affirmative action programs **(2)** Subsection (1) does not preclude any law, program or activity that has as its object the amelioration of conditions of disadvantaged individuals or groups including those that are disadvantaged because of race, national or ethnic origin, colour, religion, sex, age or mental or physical disability.

Official Languages of Canada

Official languages of Canada **16. (1)** English and French are the official languages of Canada and have equality of status and equal rights and privileges as to their use in all institutions of the Parliament and government of Canada.

Official languages of New Brunswick **(2)** English and French are the official languages of New Brunswick and have equality of status and equal rights and privileges as to their use in all institutions of the legislature and government of New Brunswick.

Advancement of status and use **(3)** Nothing in this Charter limits the authority of Parliament or a legislature to advance the equality of status or use of English and French.

Proceedings of Parliament **17. (1)** Everyone has the right to use English or French in any debates and other proceedings of Parliament.

Proceedings of New Brunswick legislature **(2)** Everyone has the right to use English or French in any debates and other proceedings of the legislature of New Brunswick.

Parliamentary statutes and records **18. (1)** The statutes, records and journals of Parliament shall be printed and published in English and French and both language versions are equally authoritative.

New Brunswick statutes and records

(2) The statutes, records and journals of the legislature of New Brunswick shall be printed and published in English and French and both language versions are equally authoritative.

Proceedings in courts established by Parliament

19. (1) Either English or French may be used by any person in, or in any pleading in or process issuing from, any court established by Parliament.

Proceedings in New Brunswick courts

(2) Either English or French may be used by any person in, or any pleading in or process issuing from, any court of New Brunswick.

Communications by public with federal institutions

20. (1) Any member of the public in Canada has the right to communicate with, and to receive available services from, any head or central office of an institution of the Parliament or government of Canada in English or French, and has the same right with respect to any other office of any such institution where

(a) there is a significant demand for communications with and services from that office in such language; or

(b) due to the nature of the office, it is reasonable that communications with and services from that office be available in both English and French.

Communications by public with New Brunswick institutions

(2) Any member of the public in New Brunswick has the right to communicate with, and to receive available services from, any office of an institution of the legislature or government of New Brunswick in English or French.

Continuation of existing constitutional provisions

21. Nothing in sections 16 to 20 abrogates or derogates from any right, privilege or obligation with respect to the English and French languages, or either of them, that exists or is continued by virtue of any other provision of the Constitution of Canada.

Rights and privileges preserved

22. Nothing in sections 16 to 20 abrogates or derogates from any legal or customary right or privilege acquired or enjoyed either before or after the coming into force of this Charter with respect to any language that is not English or French.

Minority Language Educational Rights

Language of instruction

23. (1) Citizens of Canada

(a) whose first language learned and still understood is that of the English or French linguistic minority population of the province in which they reside, or

(b) who have received their primary school instruction in Canada in English or French and reside in a province where the language in which they received that instruction is the language of the English or French linguistic minority population of the province,

have the right to receive primary and secondary school instruction in that language in that province.

Continuity of
language
instruction

(2) Citizens of Canada of whom any child has received or is receiving primary or secondary school instruction in English or French in Canada, have the right to have all their children receive primary and secondary school instruction in the same language.

Application
where numbers
warrant

(3) The right of citizens of Canada under subsections (1) and (2) to have their children receive primary and secondary school instruction in the language of the English or French linguistic minority population of a province

(a) applies wherever in the province the number of children of citizens who have such a right is sufficient to warrant the provision to them out of public funds of minority language instruction; and

(b) includes, where the number of those children so warrants, the right to have them receive that instruction in minority language educational facilities provided out of public funds.

Enforcement

Enforcement of
guaranteed
rights and
freedoms

24. (1) Anyone whose rights or freedoms, as guaranteed by this Charter, have been infringed or denied may apply to a court of competent jurisdiction to obtain such remedy as the court considers appropriate and just in the circumstances.

Exclusion of
evidence
bringing
administration
of justice into
disrepute

(2) Where, in proceedings under subsection (1), a court concludes that evidence was obtained in a manner that infringed or denied any rights or freedoms guaranteed by this Charter, the evidence shall be excluded if it is established that, having regard to all the circumstances, the admission of it in the proceedings would bring the administration of justice into disrepute.

General

Aboriginal rights and freedoms not affected by Charter

25. The guarantee in this Charter of certain rights and freedoms shall not be construed so as to abrogate or derogate from any aboriginal, treaty or other rights or freedoms that pertain to the aboriginal peoples of Canada including

(a) any rights or freedoms that have been recognized by the Royal Proclamation of October 7, 1763; and

(b) any rights or freedoms that now exist by way of land claims agreements or may be so acquired.

[Note: Originally section 25(b) read as follows: "any rights or freedoms that may be acquired by the aboriginal peoples of Canada by way of land claims settlement." The present wording was substituted by the Constitution Amendment Proclamation, 1983.]

Other rights and freedoms not affected by Charter

26. The guarantee in this Charter of certain rights and freedoms shall not be construed as denying the existence of any other rights or freedoms that exist in Canada.

Multicultural heritage

27. This Charter shall be interpreted in a manner consistent with the preservation and enhancement of the multicultural heritage of Canadians.

Rights and freedoms guaranteed equally to both sexes

28. Notwithstanding anything in this Charter, the rights and freedoms referred to in it are guaranteed equally to male and female persons.

Rights respecting certain schools preserved

29. Nothing in this Charter abrogates or derogates from any rights or privileges guaranteed by or under the Constitution of Canada in respect of denominational, separate or dissentient schools.

Application to territories and territorial authorities

30. A reference in this Charter to a province or to the legislative assembly or legislature of a province shall be deemed to include a reference to the Yukon Territory and the Northwest Territories, or to the appropriate legislative authority thereof, as the case may be.

Legislative powers not extended

31. Nothing in this Charter extends the legislative powers of any body or authority.

Application of Charter

Application of Charter

32. (1) This Charter applies

(a) to the Parliament and government of Canada in respect of all matters within the authority of Parliament including all matters relating to the Yukon and Northwest Territories; and

(b) to the legislature and government of each province in respect of all matters within the authority of the legislature of each province.

Exception

(2) Notwithstanding subsection (1), section 15 shall not have effect until three years after this section comes into force.

Exception where express declaration

33. (1) Parliament or the legislature of a province may expressly declare in an Act of Parliament or of the legislature, as the case may be, that the Act or a provision thereof shall operate notwithstanding a provision included in section 2 or sections 7 to 15 of this Charter.

Operation of exception

(2) An Act or a provision of an Act in respect of which a declaration made under this section is in effect shall have such operation as it would have but for the provision of this Charter referred to in the declaration.

Five year limitation

(3) A declaration made under subsection (1) shall cease to have effect five years after it comes into force or on such earlier date as may be specified in the declaration.

Re-enactment

(4) Parliament or the legislature of a province may re-enact a declaration made under subsection (1).

Five year limitation

(5) Subsection (3) applies in respect of a re-enactment made under subsection (4).

Citation

Citation

34. This Part may be cited as the **Canadian Charter of Rights and Freedoms**.

▌PART II
Rights of the Aboriginal Peoples of Canada

Recognition of existing aboriginal and treaty rights

35. (1) The existing aboriginal and treaty rights of the aboriginal peoples of Canada are hereby recognized and affirmed.

Definition of "aboriginal peoples of Canada"

(2) In this Act, "aboriginal peoples of Canada" includes the Indian, Inuit and Metis peoples of Canada.

Land claims agreements

(3) For greater certainty, in subsection (1) "treaty rights" includes rights that now exist by way of land claims agreements or may be so acquired.

Aboriginal and treaty rights are guaranteed equally to both sexes

(4) Notwithstanding any other provision of this Act, the aboriginal and treaty rights referred to in subsection (1) are guaranteed equally to male and female persons.

[Note: sections 35(3) and (4) were added by the Constitution Amendment Proclamation, 1983.]

Commitment to participation in constitutional conferences

35.1 The government of Canada and the provincial governments are committed to the principle that, before any amendment is made to Class 24 of section 91 of the "**Constitution Act, 1867**," to section 25 of this Act or to this Part,

(a) a constitutional conference that includes in its agenda an item relating to the proposed amendment, composed of the Prime Minister of Canada and the first ministers of the provinces, will be convened by the Prime Minister of Canada; and

(b) The Prime Minister of Canada will invite representatives of the aboriginal peoples of Canada to participate in the discussions on that item.

[Note: Section 35.1 was added by the Constitution Amendment Proclamation, 1983.]

■ PART III
Equalization and Regional Disparities

Commitment to promote equal opportunities

36. (1) Without altering the legislative authority of Parliament or of the provincial legislatures, or the rights of any of them with respect to the exercise of their legislative authority, Parliament and the legislatures, together with the government of Canada and the provincial governments, are committed to

(a) promoting equal opportunities for the well-being of Canadians;

(b) furthering economic development to reduce disparity in opportunities; and

(c) providing essential public services of reasonable quality to all Canadians.

Commitment
respecting
public services

(2) Parliament and the government of Canada are committed to the principle of making equalization payments to ensure that provincial governments have sufficient revenues to provide reasonably comparable levels of public services at reasonably comparable levels of taxation.

■ PART IV
Constitutional Conference

Constitutional
conference

37. (1) A constitutional conference composed of the Prime Minister of Canada and the first ministers of the provinces shall be convened by the Prime Minister of Canada within one year after this Part comes into force.

Participation
of aboriginal
peoples

(2) The conference convened under subsection (1) shall have included in its agenda an item respecting constitutional matters that directly affect the aboriginal peoples of Canada, including the identification and definition of the rights of those peoples to be included in the Constitution of Canada, and the Prime Minister of Canada shall invite representatives of those peoples to participate in the discussions on that item.

Participation
of territories

(3) The Prime Minister of Canada shall invite elected representatives of the governments of the Yukon Territory and the Northwest Territories to participate in the discussions on any item on the agenda of the conference convened under subsection (1) that, in the opinion of the Prime Minister, directly affects the Yukon Territory and the Northwest Territories.

[Note: Part IV was repealed effective April 17, 1983, by section 54 of this Act.]

■ PART IV.1
Constitutional Conferences

Constitutional
conferences

37.1 (1) In addition to the conference convened in March 1983, at least two constitutional conferences composed of the Prime Minister of Canada and the first ministers of the provinces shall be convened by the Prime Minister of Canada, the first three years after April 17, 1982 and the second within five years after that date.

Participation of aboriginal peoples

(2) Each conference convened under subsection (1) shall have included in its agenda constitutional matters that directly affect the aboriginal peoples of Canada, and the Prime Minister of Canada shall invite representatives of those peoples to participate in the discussions on those matters.

Participation of territories

(3) The Prime Minister of Canada shall invite elected representatives of the governments of the Yukon Territory and the Northwest Territories to participate in the discussions on any item on the agenda of a conference convened under subsection (1) that, in the opinion of the Prime Minister, directly affects the Yukon Territory and the Northwest Territories.

Subsection 35(1) not affected

(4) Nothing in this section shall be construed so as to derogate from subsection 35(1).

[Note: Part IV.1 was added by the Constitution Amendment Proclamation, 1983. By the same proclamation, it was repealed effective April 18, 1987. See section 54.1 of this Act.]

▮ PART V
Procedure for Amending Constitution of Canada

General procedure for amending Constitution of Canada

38. (1) An amendment to the Constitution of Canada may be made by proclamation issued by the Governor General under the Great Seal of Canada where so authorized by

    (a) resolutions of the Senate and House of Commons; and

    (b) resolutions of the legislative assemblies of at least two-thirds of the provinces that have, in the aggregate, according to the then latest general census, at least fifty per cent of the population of all the provinces.

Majority of members

(2) An amendment made under subsection (1) that derogates from the legislative powers, the proprietary rights or any other rights or privileges of the legislature or government of a province shall require a resolution supported by a majority of the members of each of the Senate, the House of Commons and the legislative assemblies required under subsection (1).

Expression of dissent

(3) An amendment referred to in subsection (2) shall not have effect in a province the legislative assembly of which has expressed its dissent thereto by resolution supported by a majority of its members prior to the issue of the proclamation to which the amendment relates unless that legislative assembly, subsequently, by resolution supported by a majority of its members, revokes its dissent and authorizes the amendment.

Revocation of dissent

(4) A resolution of dissent made for the purposes of subsection (3) may be revoked at any time before or after the issue of the proclamation to which it relates.

Restriction on proclamation

39. (1) A proclamation shall not be issued under subsection 38(1) before the expiration of one year from the adoption of the resolution initiating the amendment procedure thereunder, unless the legislative assembly of each province has previously adopted a resolution of assent or dissent.

Idem

(2) A proclamation shall not be issued under subsection 38(1) after the expiration of three years from the adoption of the resolution initiating the amendment procedure thereunder.

Compensation

40. Where an amendment is made under subsection 38(1) that transfers provincial legislative powers relating to education or other cultural matters from provincial legislatures to Parliament, Canada shall provide reasonable compensation to any province to which the amendment does not apply.

Amendment by unanimous consent

41. An amendment to the Constitution of Canada in relation to the following matters may be made by proclamation issued by the Governor General under the Great Seal of Canada only where authorized by resolutions of the Senate and House of Commons and of the legislative assembly of each province:

(a) the office of the Queen, the Governor General and the Lieutenant Governor of a province;

(b) the right of a province to a number of members in the House of Commons not less than the number of Senators by which the province is entitled to be represented at the time this Part comes into force;

(c) subject to section 43, the use of the English or French language;

(**d**) the composition of the Supreme Court of Canada; and

(**e**) an amendment to this Part.

Amendment by general procedure

42. (**1**) An amendment to the Constitution of Canada in relation to the following matters may be made only in accordance with subsection 38(1):

(**a**) the principle of proportionate representation of the provinces in the House of Commons prescribed by the Constitution of Canada;

(**b**) the powers of the Senate and the methods of selecting Senators;

(**c**) the number of members by which a province is entitled to be represented in the Senate and the residence qualifications of Senators;

(**d**) subject to paragraph 41(d), the Supreme Court of Canada;

(**e**) the extension of existing provinces into the territories; and

(**f**) notwithstanding any other law or practice, the establishment of new provinces.

Exception

(**2**) Subsections 38(2) to (4) do not apply in respect of amendments in relation to matters referred to in subsection (1).

Amendment of provisions relating to some but not all provinces

43. An amendment to the Constitution of Canada in relation to any provision that applies to one or more, but not all, provinces, including

(**a**) any alteration to boundaries between provinces, and

(**b**) any amendment to any provision that relates to the use of the English or French language within a province,

may be made by proclamation issued by the Governor General under the Great Seal of Canada only where so authorized by resolutions of the Senate and House of Commons and of the legislative assembly of each province to which the amendment applies.

Amendments by Parliament

44. Subject to sections 41 and 42, Parliament may exclusively make laws amending the Constitution of Canada in relation to the executive government of Canada or the Senate and House of Commons.

Amendment by provincial legislatures

45. Subject to section 41, the legislature of each province may exclusively make laws amending the constitution of the province.

Initiation of amendment procedures

46. (**1**) The procedures for amendment under sections 38, 41, 42, and 43 may be initiated either by the Senate or the House of Commons or by the legislative assembly of a province.

Revocation of authorization

(2) A resolution of assent made for the purposes of this Part may be revoked at any time before the issue of a proclamation authorized by it.

Amendments without Senate resolution

47. (1) An amendment to the Constitution of Canada made by proclamation under section 38, 41, 42 or 43 may be made without a resolution of the Senate authorizing the issue of the proclamation if, within one hundred and eighty days after the adoption by the House of Commons of a resolution authorizing its issue, the Senate has not adopted such a resolution and if, at any time after the expiration of that period, the House of Commons again adopts the resolution.

Computation of period

(2) Any period when Parliament is prorogued or dissolved shall not be counted in computing the one hundred and eighty day period referred to in subsection (1).

Advice to issue proclamation

48. The Queen's Privy Council for Canada shall advise the Governor General to issue a proclamation under this Part forthwith on the adoption of the resolutions required for an amendment made by proclamation under this Part.

Constitutional conference

49. A constitutional conference composed of the Prime Minister of Canada and the first ministers of the provinces shall be convened by the Prime Minister of Canada within fifteen years after this Part comes into force to review the provisions of this Part.

■ PART VI
Amendment to the Constitution Act, 1867

[NOTE: We omit Part VI, which in sections 50 and 51 gave the provinces additional authority over "non-renewable natural resources, forestry resources and electrical energy."]

■ PART VII
General

Primacy of Constitution of Canada

52. (1) The Constitution of Canada is the supreme law of Canada, and any law that is inconsistent with the provisions of the Constitution is, to the extent of the inconsistency, of no force or effect.

Constitution of Canada

(2) The Constitution of Canada includes
  (a) the **Canada Act, 1982**, including this Act;
  (b) the Acts and orders referred to in the schedule; and
  (c) any amendment to any Act or order referred to in paragraph (a) or (b).

Amendments to Constitution of Canada

(3) Amendments to the Constitution of Canada shall be made only in accordance with the authority contained in the Constitution of Canada.

Repeals and new names

53. **(1)** The enactments referred to in Column I of the schedule are hereby repealed or amended to the extent indicated in Column II thereof and, unless repealed, shall continue as law in Canada under the names set out in Column III thereof.

Consequential amendments

(2) Every enactment, except the **Canada Act 1982**, that refers to an enactment referred to in the schedule by the name in Column I thereof is hereby amended by substituting for that name the corresponding name in Column III thereof, and any British North America Act not referred to in the schedule may be cited as the **Constitution Act** followed by the year and number, if any, of its enactment.

Repeal and consequential amendments

54. Part IV is repealed on the day that is one year after this Part comes into force and this section may be repealed and this Act re-numbered, consequentially upon the repeal of Part IV and this section, by proclamation issued by the Governor General under the Great Seal of Canada.

Repeal of Part IV.1 and this section

54.1 Part IV.1 and this section are repealed on April 18, 1987.

[Note: Section 54.1 was added by the Constitution Amendment Proclamation, 1983.]

French version of Constitution of Canada

55. A French version of the portions of the Constitution of Canada referred to in the schedule shall be prepared by the Minister of Justice of Canada as expeditiously as possible and, when any portion thereof sufficient to warrant action being taken has been so prepared, it shall be put forward for enactment by proclamation issued by the Governor General under the Great Seal of Canada pursuant to the procedure then applicable to an amendment of the same provisions of the Constitution of Canada.

English and French versions of certain constitutional texts

56. Where any portion of the Constitution of Canada has been or is enacted in English and French or where a French version of any portion of the Constitution is enacted pursuant to section 55, the English and French versions of that portion of the Constitution are equally authoritative.

English and French versions of this Act

57. The English and French versions of this Act are equally authoritative.

Commencement

58. Subject to section 59, this Act shall come into force on a day to be fixed by proclamation issued by the Queen or the Governor General under the Great Seal of Canada.

Commencement of paragraph 23(1)(a) in respect of Quebec

59. (1) Paragraph 23(1)(a) shall come into force in respect of Quebec on a day to be fixed by proclamation issued by the Queen or the Governor General under the Great Seal of Canada.

Authorization of Quebec

(2) A proclamation under subsection (1) shall be issued only where authorized by the legislative assembly or government of Quebec.

Repeal of this section

(3) This section may be repealed on the day paragraph 23(1)(a) comes into force in respect of Quebec and this Act amended and renumbered, consequentially upon the repeal of this section, by proclamation issued by the Queen or the Governor General under the Great Seal of Canada.

Short title and citation

60. This Act may be cited as the **Constitution Act, 1982,** and the Constitution Acts 1867 to 1975 (No. 2) and this Act may be cited together as the **Constitution Acts, 1867 to 1982.**

References

61. A reference to the **"Constitution Acts, 1867 to 1982"** shall be deemed to include a reference to the **"Constitution Amendment Proclamation, 1983."**

[Note: Section 61 was added by the Constitution Amendment Proclamation, 1983.]

NOTES

Chapter One

1 This term was first used by Peter H. Russell, "The First Three Years in Charterland," *Canadian Public Administration* 28 (1985).
2 The latter issue arose in *Jack and Charlie* v. *The Queen*, [1985] 2 S.C.R. 332.
3 Peter H. Russell, "The Political Purposes of the Canadian Charter of Rights and Freedoms," *Canadian Bar Review* 61 (1983); Rainer Knopff and F.L. Morton, "Nation Building and the Canadian Charter of Rights and Freedoms," in Alan Cairns and Cynthia Williams, eds., *Constitutionalism, Citizenship and Society in Canada* (Toronto: University of Toronto Press, 1985).
4 Alan C. Cairns, "Citizens (Outsiders) and Governments (Insiders) in Constitution-Making: The Case of Meech Lake," *Canadian Public Policy* 14: supplement (1988).
5 Richard Simeon, "Meech Lake and Shifting Conceptions of Federalism," *Canadian Public Policy* 14: supplement (1988), 10.
6 Russell, "The Political Purposes of the Canadian Charter," 51–52.
7 *Morgentaler* v. *The Queen*, [1976] 1 S.C.R. 616.
8 *R.* v. *Morgentaler*, [1988] 1 S.C.R. 30.
9 *Robertson and Rosetanni* v. *The Queen*, [1963] 1 S.C.R. 651.

Chapter Two

1 So central was the Charter to Trudeau's political agenda that Stephen Clarkson and Christina McCall have called it his "magnificent obsession." *Trudeau and our Times, Volume I: The Magnificent Obsession* (Toronto: McClelland and Stewart, 1990).
2 Pierre Trudeau, "A Constitutional Declaration of Rights" (an address to the Canadian Bar Association, Sept. 4, 1967), in Trudeau, *Federalism and the French Canadians* (Toronto: Macmillan, 1968).
3 See Donald V. Smiley, *Canada in Question: Federalism in the Eighties*, 3rd. ed. (Toronto: McGraw-Hill Ryerson, 1980), 76–77.
4 Ibid., 77–78.
5 Ibid., 79–83.
6 See Trudeau, *Federalism and the French Canadians*.
7 Peter H. Russell, Rainer Knopff, and Ted Morton, *Federalism and the Charter: Leading Constitutional Decisions—A New Edition* (Ottawa: Carleton University Press, 1989), 706.
8 This assumption is open to challenge. See Eugene Forsey, "The Courts and the Conventions of the Constitution," *University of New Brunswick Law Journal* 33 (1984).
9 Russell, Knopff, and Morton, *Federalism and the Charter*, 706.
10 Ibid., 706–10. See also Rainer Knopff, "Legal Theory and the Patriation Debate," *Queen's Law Journal* 7 (1981).

11   Peter W. Hogg, *Canada Act 1982 Annotated* (Toronto: Carswell, 1982), 1.
12   Section 23 of the Charter.
13   And were successfully challenged in *Ford* v. *A.-G. Quebec*, [1988] 2 S.C.R. 712.
14   David Milne, *The Canadian Constitution* (Toronto: Lorimer, 1991), 107–8.
15   Russell, Knopff, and Morton, *Federalism and the Charter*, 707.
16   Peter H. Russell, "Bold Statescraft, Questionable Jurisprudence," in Keith Banting and Richard Simeon, eds., *And No One Cheered: Federalism, Democracy and the Constitution Act* (Toronto: Methuen, 1983). See also Knopff, "Legal Theory and the Patriation Debate."
17   Russell, Knopff, and Morton, *Federalism and the Charter*, 19.
18   Ibid.
19   *The Queen* v. *Drybones*, [1970] S.C.R. 282.
20   For the pronounced judicial restraint more characteristic of the Court's Bill of Rights jurisprudence, see   *Robertson and Rosetanni* v. *The Queen*, [1963] 1 S.C.R. 651; *Attorney General of Canada* v. *Lavell and Bedard*, [1974] 1 S.C.R. 1349; and *Hogan* v. *The Queen*, [1975] 2 S.C.R. 574.
21   See *Lowry and Lepper* v. *The Queen* (1972), 26 D.L.R. (3d) 224; and *Brownridge* v. *The Queen*, [1972] S.C.R. 926.
22   F.L Morton, Peter H. Russell, and Michael J. Withey, "The Supreme Court's First One Hundred Charter of Rights Decisions: A Statistical Analysis," *Osgoode Hall Law Journal* (forthcoming).
23   See *R.* v. *Therens*, [1985] 1 S.C.R. 613, overruling *Chromiak* v. *The Queen*, [1980] 1 S.C.R. 471; and *R.* v. *Big M Drug Mart Ltd.*, [1985] 1 S.C.R. 295, overruling *Robertson and Rosetanni*.
24   *Therens.*
25   *R.* v. *Manninen*, [1987] 1 S.C.R. 1233.
26   *R.* v. *Hebert*, [1990] 2 S.C.R. 151.
27   *Clarkson* v. *The Queen*, [1986] 1 S.C.R. 383.
28   *R.* v. *Brydges*, [1990] 1 S.C.R. 190.
29   *Hamill* v. *The Queen* (1987), 38 D.L.R. (4th) 611.
30   *R.* v. *Simmons*, [1988] 2 S.C.R. 495.
31   *Hunter* v. *Southam Inc.*, [1984] 2 S.C.R. 145.
32   *R.* v. *Collins*, [1987] 1 S.C.R. 265. See the more extensive discussion of the exclusionary rule in Chapter Three.
33   Robert Harvie and Hamar Foster, "Ties That Bind? The Supreme Court of Canada, American Jurisprudence, and the Revision of Canadian Criminal Law Under the Charter," *Osgoode Hall Law Journal* 28:4 (1990).
34   *Illinois* v. *Perkins*, 110 S.Ct. 2394 (1990); *Hebert.*
35   *R.* v. *Morgentaler*, [1988] 1 S.C.R. 30.
36   *Singh et al.* v. *Minister of Employment and Immigration*, [1985] 1 S.C.R. 177.
37   Ibid., 218.
38   Ibid., 213.
39   Ibid., 218.
40   Ibid., 220.
41   Michael Mandel, *The Charter of Rights and the Legalization of Politics in Canada* (Toronto: Wall and Thompson, 1989), 175.
42   Ibid.
43   Ibid.
44   "Committee wants refugee amnesty," *Calgary Herald*, Nov. 30, 1990, B12.
45   *R.* v. *Big M Drug Mart*, [1985] 1 S.C.R. 295.
46   *R.* v. *Edwards Books and Art Ltd.*, [1986] 2 S.C.R. 713.

47 "Ontario Won't Amend Sunday Shopping Bill," *Globe and Mail*, Feb. 2, 1989, A8.

48 Bill 64, announced on May 2, 1985, the same day as the *Big M Drug Mart* decision, repealed the Alberta Lord's Day Act and amended sections 241 to 246 of the Municipal Government Act to give municipalities full responsibility for regulating Sunday closing. Bill 64 was assented to on June 5. See the Municipal Government Amendment Act, S.A. 1985, c. 43, ss. 31, 42.

49 See Ronald J. MacDonald, "The Law and Politics of Sunday Closing in Alberta," M.A. Thesis, University of Calgary, 1989.

50 *National Citizens' Coalition Inc. and Brown* v. *Canada (A.-G.)* (1984), 5 W.W.R. 436.

51 *Dixon* v. *A.-G. British Columbia* (1989), 59 D.L.R. (4th) 247.

52 *Saskatchewan* v. *Carter*, (unreported at time of writing) decision rendered June 6, 1991.

53 *Wilson* v. *Medical Services Commission of British Columbia* (1988), 30 B.C.L.R. (2d) 1.

54 "Ministers Announce Extension of Court Challenges Program," Government of Canada news release, Sept. 25, 1985, S-09/85-35.

55 *Operation Dismantle Inc.* v. *The Queen*, [1985] 1 S.C.R. 441.

56 *A.-G. Quebec* v. *Quebec Association of Protestant School Boards*, [1984] 2 S.C.R. 66.

57 *Mahé* v. *Alberta*, [1990] 1 S.C.R. 342.

58 See F.L. Morton, *Morgentaler v. Borowski: Abortion, The Charter, and The Courts* (Toronto: McClelland and Stewart) (forthcoming).

59 Ibid.

60 *Borowski* v. *Canada (Attorney-General)*, [1989] 1 S.C.R. 342.

61 Elizabeth Atcheson, Mary Eberts, and Beth Symes, *Women and Legal Action—Precedents, Resources and Strategies for the Future* (Ottawa: Queen's Printer, 1984), 163.

62 F.L. Morton, "The Political Impact of the Canadian Charter of Rights and Freedoms," *Canadian Journal of Political Science* 20 (1987), 42.

63 *Tremblay* v. *Daigle*, [1989] 2 S.C.R. 30.

64 *Blainey* v. *Ontario Hockey Association* (1986), 54 O.R. (2d) 513.

65 *Suzanne Cowan (a.k.a. Suzanne Bertrand)* v. *The Commissioner of the Yukon Territory*, May 15, 1984, judgment without reasons (Y.T.S.C., registry #153.85); *Catherine Paul and David Wright* v. *The Registrar General, Vital Statistics Act and The Minister of Consumer and Commercial Relations*, Dec. 9, 1985, judgment without written reasons (Ont. S.C., Toronto registry #2618/85).

66 *Schachter* v. *Canada*, [1988] 3 F.C. 515 (F.C.A.). See Mary Eberts, Gwen Brodsky, and Susan Joanis, *Litigation Works, A Report on LEAF Litigation Year Two* (Agincourt: Carswell Legal Publications, 1987).

67 See pp. 7, 10, 13 of the Factum of Women's Legal Education and Action Fund (LEAF) for *Andrews* v. *Law Society of British Columbia*, [1989] 1 S.C.R. 143.

68 Because the Constitution Act, 1982, was adopted without the consent of Quebec, Premier Lévesque and many other political leaders in Quebec viewed it as unconstitutional. Lévesque's argument was subsequently heard and rejected by the Supreme Court of Canada in *Re: Objection to a Resolution to Amend The Constitution* (Quebec Veto Reference), [1982] 2 S.C.R. 793. See Roy Romanow, John Whyte, and Howard Leeson, *Canada Notwithstanding: The Making of the Constitution, 1976–1982* (Toronto: Carswell/Methuen, 1984), ch. 8.

69 Lévesque's pre-emptive and "blanket" application of the override was especially controversial, since it shattered the expectation that section 33 would
only be used retroactively and in a case-by-case fashion in response to a judicial decision nullifying a statute. In *Ford*, the Supreme Court affirmed that
general and prospective overrides are permissible.

70 The Devine government claimed that it was protecting its "back-to-work"
legislation from an earlier Charter precedent that overturned a similar law.

71 See Howard Leeson, "Devine's Bill 144: 'setting aside the basic law of the
land,'" *Regina Leader Post*, Feb. 4, 1986, A6 and *Ottawa Citizen*, Feb. 8, 1986.

72 See Dale Eisler, *Regina Leader Post*, Jan. 23, 1986, A4.

73 The decisions of provincial courts of appeal in provincial reference cases may
be appealed as of right to the Supreme Court of Canada.

74 Early examples are discussed in Gerald Rubin, "The Nature, Use and Effect of
Reference Cases in Canadian Constitutional Law," in W.R. Lederman, ed., *The
Courts and the Canadian Constitution* (Toronto: McClelland and Stewart,
1964), 226. Much of the abuse and ensuing controversy over the constitutional reference was caused by its ambiguous relationship to the federal government's disallowance power. On this see Jennifer Smith, "The Origins of
Judicial Review in Canada," *Canadian Journal of Political Science* 16 (1983).
In both instances the source of the problem is the difficulty of making a hard
and lasting distinction between "policy issues" and "legal issues." For an
explanation of how this dilemma led to the demise of the disallowance
power, see Robert C. Vipond, "Constitutional Politics and the Legacy of the
Provincial Rights Movement in Canada," *Canadian Journal of Political Science* 18 (1985), 282–84.

75 The potential for abuse is heightened by the ability of a government, directly
or indirectly, to refer the legislation of a second government to its own court
of appeal. In the most notorious modern case—*A.-G. Manitoba* v. *Manitoba
Egg and Poultry Association* (The Chicken and Egg Reference), [1971] S.C.R.
689—the Manitoba government persuaded its own Court of Appeal to declare
an Ontario marketing policy unconstitutional. This case is analyzed by Paul
Weiler, *In The Last Resort: A Critical Study of the Supreme Court of Canada*
(Toronto: Methuen, 1974), 156–64.

76 Joe Borowski came from this rural, Catholic, Saskatchewan society, and later
was an NDP cabinet minister in Manitoba until he resigned in protest of public funding of abortions in 1972.

77 Bill 53, also styled as the "Freedom of Informed Choice (Abortions) Act," had
two basic provisions. The first was a consent requirement for husbands of
married women and the parents of minors. The second was a requirement
that women desiring an abortion must first be read descriptions of the probable age, physical characteristics, and abilities of the unborn child; the abortion procedure and its medical risks; and a list of public and private agencies
available to assist the woman to carry the child to term.

78 See Neil Scott, "PC caucus has agreed to pass abortion bill: MLA," *Regina
Leader Post*, June 11, 1985, A4; Murray Mandryk, "Abortion bill set aside until
court rules—MLAs unanimous," *Regina Leader Post*, June 12, 1985, A1.

79 *Reference re The Freedom of Informed Choice (Abortions) Act* (1986), 44 S.R.
104. The Court of Appeal ruled that Bill 53 trenched upon the federal government's Criminal Code jurisdiction and so was *ultra vires*. The Charter issue
was not reached.

80 *Reference re Education Act of Ontario and Minority Language Education
Rights* (1984), 10 D.L.R. (4th) 491.

81 See Peter H. Russell, "The First Three Years in Charterland," *Canadian Public Administration* 28 (1985), 382–83.

82 Section 93 of the British North America Act protects the "rights and privileges" possessed by denominational schools at the time of Confederation and guarantees the same education rights to the Protestant minority in Quebec as those possessed by Catholic minorities outside of Quebec. This mutual guarantee of publicly funded separate school systems between the French Catholics in Quebec and the English Protestants in Ontario was one of the compromises that made Confederation possible.

83 Orland French, "Volatile issue is ticking," *Globe and Mail*, March 29, 1985, 7.

84 John Cruikshank and Robert Matas, "Miller accuses archbishop of reopening religious wounds," *Globe and Mail*, April 26, 1985, 1.

85 *Reference re Bill 30, An Act to Amend The Education Act*, [1987] 1 S.C.R. 1148.

Chapter Three

1 Donald V. Smiley, *Canada in Question: Federalism in the Eighties*, 3rd ed. (Toronto: McGraw-Hill Ryerson, 1980), 76.

2 Roy Romanow, John Whyte, and Howard Leeson, *Canada Notwithstanding: The Making of the Constitution, 1976–1982* (Toronto: Carswell/Methuen, 1984), 243.

3 Peter W. Hogg, *Canada Act 1982 Annotated* (Toronto: Carswell, 1982) 13.

4 Ibid.

5 Christopher Manfredi, "The Use of United States Decisions by the Supreme Court of Canada Under the Charter of Rights and Freedoms," *Canadian Journal of Political Science* 23:3 (1990), 508.

6 *Re Ontario Film and Video Appreciation Society and Ontario Board of Censors* (1983), 41 O.R. (2d) 583.

7 See Bob Woodward and Scott Armstrong, *The Brethren: Inside the Supreme Court* (New York: Avon Books, 1979), 227–41; Ralph Rossum and G. Alan Tarr, *American Constitutional Law* (New York: St. Martin's Press, 1991), 360.

8 Woodward and Armstrong, *The Brethren*, 290–300.

9 They discriminate not just against the "rich" in some absolute sense, but against anyone who is "better off" than you are, and against you too, to the extent that you are better off than someone else.

10 G. Gunther, "Foreword: In Search of Evolving Doctrine on a Changing Court; A Model for a Newer Equal Protection," *Harvard Law Review* 86 (1972), 8.

11 See Rainer Knopff, *Human Rights and Social Technology: The New War on Discrimination* (Ottawa: Carleton University Press, 1989), 150–57.

12 Cf. Dale Gibson, *The Law of the Charter: Equality Rights* (Toronto: Carswell, 1990), 265.

13 Ibid., 262.

14 David Beatty, *Talking Heads and the Supremes: The Canadian Production of Constitutional Law* (Toronto: Carswell, 1990), 113.

15 Ibid., vii; see also 114.

16 *Reference re Public Service Employee Relations Act* (Alberta Labour Reference), [1987] 1 S.C.R. 313.

17 *R. v. Jones*, [1986] 2 S.C.R. 284.

18 Ibid., 313–15.

19 Ibid. This was the decision of Justice La Forest, writing for himself and Chief Justice Dickson, with Justice Lamer concurring in a separate opinion. Justice McIntyre, writing for himself and Justices Beetz and Le Dain, agreed with Justice Wilson that there was no section 2(a) violation.

20 Peter H. Russell, "Canada's Charter of Rights and Freedoms: A Political Report," *Public Law* (Autumn 1988), 396.

21 Paul A. Bender, "Justifications for Limiting Constitutionally Guaranteed Rights and Freedoms: Some Remarks about the Proper Role of Section One of the Canadian Charter," *Manitoba Law Journal* 13:4 (1983), 674.

22 Ibid.

23 *R. v. Oakes*, [1986] 1 S.C.R. 103.

24 Ian Greene, *The Charter of Rights* (Toronto: Lorimer, 1989), 55.

25 This approach was taken by Justice Strayer in *Belczowski* v. *The Queen*, (unreported at time of writing) decision rendered Feb. 28, 1991, Court No. T-1182-88 draft judgment 6: "The existence of section 1 removes any lingering doubt that one might have as to giving section 3 its plain and obvious meaning. A contrast can be made with the United States Constitution, whose First Amendment provides that Congress shall make no law 'abridging the freedom of speech.' The U.S. Constitution has no provision comparable to section 1 of the Charter. It has therefore been thought necessary for the U.S. courts to read qualifications into broad guarantees such as the First Amendment guarantee of freedom of speech, giving lesser protection to 'commercial speech.' This approach was expressly rejected by the Supreme Court of Canada.... "

26 Cf. Hogg, *Canada Act 1982 Annotated*, 13: "It is even possible that a limitation clause could strengthen the enumerated guarantees. Section 1 of the Charter would have this effect if it were interpreted as imposing a requirement of justification which is more difficult for the government to discharge than the requirement which would have been implied by the courts in the absence of a limitation clause."

27 *Andrews* v. *Law Society of British Columbia*, [1989] 1 S.C.R. 143 (S.C.C.) 184.

28 Ibid.

29 *Rocket* v. *Royal College of Dental Surgeons of Ontario*, [1990] 2 S.C.R. 232 (S.C.C.) 246.

30 Peter W. Hogg, "Federalism Fights The Charter of Rights," in David P. Shugarman and Reg Whitaker, eds., *Federalism and Political Community* (Peterborough: Broadview Press, 1989), 257–60. See also Katherine E. Swinton, *The Supreme Court and Canadian Federalism: The Laskin-Dickson Years* (Toronto: Carswell, 1990), 347.

31 *R. v. Edwards Books and Art Ltd.*, [1986] 2 S.C.R. 713 (S.C.C.) 772.

32 Ibid., 781–82.

33 *United States of America* v. *Cotroni*, [1989] 1 S.C.R. 1469 (S.C.C.) 1481.

34 *Ford* v. *Quebec (A.-G.)*, [1988] 2 S.C.R. 712; *Irwin Toy Ltd.* v. *Quebec (A.-G.)*, [1989] 1 S.C.R. 927.

35 *Reference re Ss. 193 and 195.1(1)(c) of the Criminal Code (Man.)* (Prostitution Reference), [1990] 1 S.C.R. 1123.

36 *R. v. Keegstra* (1990), 117 N.R. 1.

37 *Irwin Toy*, 976.

38 *Rocket*, 247.

39 *Rocket*, 247; *Irwin Toy*, 976.

40 *Rocket*, 247.

41 Ibid.

42 *Prostitution Reference*, 1136.
43 *Keegstra*, 67.
44 Ibid., 72.
45 *Rocket*, 246–47.
46 *R.* v. *Wray*, [1971] 1 S.C.R. 272; *Hogan* v. *The Queen*, [1975] 2 S.C.R. 574.
47 *R.* v. *Manninen*, [1987] 1 S.C.R. 1233.
48 Ibid., 1238.
49 Ibid.
50 Ibid., 1246.
51 *R.* v. *Therens*, [1985] 1 S.C.R. 613.
52 See *Mapp* v. *Ohio*, 367 U.S. 643 (1961), where the Supreme Court of Ohio upheld earlier decisions stating that "the purpose of the exclusionary rule is to deter—to compel respect for the constitutional guaranty in the only effectively available way—by removing the incentive to disregard it." See also *United States* v. *Calandra*, 414 U.S. 338, 347 (1974): "The purpose of the exclusionary rule is not to redress the injury to the privacy of the victim ... instead, the rule's prime purpose is to deter future unlawful police conduct and thereby effectuate the guarantee of the Fourth Amendment against unreasonable search and seizures.... "
53 In *Therens*, 622, Justice Estey said: "To do otherwise than reject this evidence on the facts and circumstances in this appeal would be to invite police officers to disregard Charter rights of the citizen and to do so with an assurance of impunity."
54 *R.* v. *Collins*, [1987] 1 S.C.R. 265 (S.C.C.) 280–81.
55 Emphasis added.
56 Dale Gibson, *The Law of the Charter: General Principles* (Calgary: Carswell, 1986), 236–47.
57 *Collins*, 282–83.
58 *Collins*, 284; *R.* v. *Jacoy*, [1988] 2 S.C.R. 548 (S.C.C.) 558.
59 *Collins*, 284.
60 *Collins*, 284; *Jacoy*, 559.
61 See *Collins*; *Clarkson* v. *The Queen*, [1986] 1 S.C.R. 383.
62 *R.* v. *Ross*, [1989] 1 S.C.R. 3 (S.C.C.) 16.
63 *Therens*.
64 This was the issue in *Ross*. Cf. the search-and-seizure cases *R.* v. *Dyment*, [1988] 2 S.C.R. 417 (blood samples/medical records), and *R.* v. *Wong et al.* (1990), 120 N.R. 34 (videotapes).
65 Robert Harvie and Hamar Foster, "Ties That Bind? The Supreme Court of Canada, American Jurisprudence, and the Revision of Canadian Criminal Law Under the Charter," *Osgoode Hall Law Journal* 28:4 (1990), 747.
66 *Dyment; Ross; R.* v. *Pohoretsky*, [1987] 1 S.C.R. 945.
67 Peter Russell, "On Standing Up For Notwithstanding," in Mark Charlton and Paul Barker, eds., *Contemporary Political Issues* (Scarborough: Nelson, 1991), 73.
68 *Jacoy*, 559.
69 *R.* v. *Duarte*, [1990] 1 S.C.R. 30.
70 Ibid., 59.
71 Ibid., 60.
72 *Jacoy*, 559.
73 *Collins*, 286; *Jacoy*, 559.
74 *Ross*, 16.

75 F.L. Morton, Peter H. Russell, and Michael J. Withey, "The Supreme Court's First One Hundred Charter of Rights Decisions: A Statistical Analysis," *Osgoode Hall Law Journal* (forthcoming).

76 See Andrew Heard, "The Charter of Rights in the Supreme Court of Canada: The Importance of Which Judge Hears an Appeal," *Canadian Journal of Political Science* 24:2 (1991).

77 Jeffrey A. Segal and Harold J. Spaeth, "Decisional Trends on the Warren and Burger Courts: Results from the Supreme Court Data Base Project," *Judicature* 73:2 (1989), 103–7.

Chapter Four

1 Peter H. Russell, "Overcoming Legal Formalism: The Treatment of the Constitution, the Courts and Judicial Behaviour in Canadian Political Science," *Canadian Journal of Law and Society* 1 (1986), 6.

2 For example, W.P.M. Kennedy explained that his purpose in writing *The Constitution of Canada* was "to challenge the Austinian doctrine of sovereignty by showing how Canada's emergence as an independent but loyal Dominion demonstrates that sovereignty need not be absolute." Ibid.

3 Ibid., 9.

4 Quoted in ibid.

5 Quoted in Donald Smiley, *Canada in Question: Federalism in the Eighties,* 3rd ed. (Toronto: McGraw-Hill Ryerson, 1980), 37. Smiley had said much the same thing in 1962 in his article "The Rowell-Sirois Report and Provincial Autonomy," *Canadian Journal of Political Science and Economics* 28 (1962), 59: "The federal aspects of the Canadian constitution, using the latter term in the broadest sense, have come to be less what the courts say they are than what the federal and provincial cabinets and bureaucracies in a continuous series of formal and informal relations determine them to be."

6 *Brown* v. *Board of Education (No. 1),* 347 U.S. 483 (1954); *Brown* v. *Board of Education (No. 2),* 349 U.S. 294 (1955).

7 *Swann* v. *Charlotte-Mecklenberg Board of Education,* 402 U.S. 1 (1971).

8 *Keyes* v. *School District No. 1, Denver,* 413 U.S. 189 (1973).

9 *Engel* v. *Vitale,* 370 U.S. 421 (1962); *School District of Abington* v. *Schemp,* 374 U.S. 203 (1963).

10 *West Virginia State Board of Education* v. *Barnette,* 319 U.S. 624 (1943).

11 *Roe* v. *Wade,* 410 U.S. 113 (1973).

12 *Mapp* v. *Ohio,* 367 U.S. 643 (1961).

13 *Baker* v. *Carr,* 369 U.S. 186 (1962); *Reynolds* v. *Sims,* 377 U.S. 533 (1964).

14 See, for example, *Reference re Alberta Statutes,* [1938] 2 S.C.R. 100, and *Switzman* v. *Elbling,* [1957] 1 S.C.R. 285.

15 *Boucher* v. *The King,* [1951] 1 S.C.R. 265; *Saumur* v. *Quebec,* [1953] 2 S.C.R. 299; *Birks and Sons (Montreal) Ltd.* v. *Montreal,* [1955] 1 S.C.R. 799; *Chaput* v. *Romain,* [1955] S.C.R. 834; *Switzman; Roncarelli* v. *Duplessis,* [1959] 1 S.C.R. 121.

16 See *Morgan* v. *Attorney General of P.E.I.,* [1976] 2 S.C.R. 349 and *Attorney General of Canada and Dupond* v. *Montreal,* [1978] 2 S.C.R. 770.

17 Cynthia Williams, "The Changing Nature of Citizen Rights," in Alan Cairns and Cynthia Williams, eds., *Constitutionalism, Citizenship and Society in Canada* (Toronto: University of Toronto Press, 1985).

18 See *The Queen* v. *Drybones*, [1970] S.C.R. 282.

19 Peter H. Russell, "The Effect of a Charter of Rights on the Policy-Making Role of Canadian Courts," *Canadian Public Administration* 25:1 (1982).

20 Russell, "Overcoming Legal Formalism," 9.

21 *Garcia* v. *San Antonio Metropolitan Transit Authority*, 469 U.S. 528.

22 Peter H. Russell, Rainer Knopff, and F.L. Morton, *Federalism and the Charter: Leading Constitutional Decisions* (Ottawa: Carleton University Press, 1989), 8: "Whereas the *Supreme Court Reports* for the first half of the 1970s contain only nine decisions on the division of powers, the *Reports* for the last five years of the decade record thirty-six decisions on constitutional issues—a fourfold increase. The trend continued into the 1980s. Forty-two constitutional decisions are reported for the four-year period from 1980 to 1983—the period preceding the Court's first decision on the Charter."

23 See Peter H. Russell, "The Supreme Court and Federal-Provincial Relations: The Political Use of Legal Resources," *Canadian Public Policy* 11 (1985).

24 Cf. Robert C. Vipond, *Liberty and Community: Canadian Federalism and the Failure of the Canadian Constitution* (Albany, N.Y.: State University of New York Press, 1991), 8.

25 Eric A. Nordlinger, *On the Autonomy of the Democratic State* (Cambridge, Mass.: Harvard University Press, 1981); Peter B. Evans, Dietrich Rueschemeyer, and Theda Skocpol, *Bringing the State Back In* (Cambridge: Cambridge University Press, 1985).

26 Alan C. Cairns, "The Judicial Committee and Its Critics," *Canadian Journal of Political Science* 4:3 (1971), 319.

27 Ibid., 319–27. Also see Edwin R. Black and Alan C. Cairns, "A Different Perspective on Canadian Federalism," in J. Peter Meekison, ed., *Canadian Federalism: Myth or Reality*, 3rd ed. (Toronto: Methuen, 1977).

28 Cairns, "The Judicial Committee and Its Critics," 322.

29 Ibid., 319.

30 Black and Cairns, "A Different Perspective," 31: "Economic and social factors respond to political forces just as political forces respond to them."

31 Alan C. Cairns, "The Governments and Societies of Canadian Federalism," *Canadian Journal of Political Science* 10:4 (1977).

32 Quoted in ibid., 696.

33 Alan C. Cairns, "The Embedded State," in Keith Banting, ed., *State and Society: Canada in Comparative Perspective* (Toronto: University of Toronto Press, 1986), 55.

34 Ibid.

35 Ibid., 56, 70.

36 Ibid., 60.

37 Ibid., 61.

38 Cairns, "Governments and Societies," 699.

39 See generally Cairns, "The Embedded State."

40 Black and Cairns, "A New Perspective," 33.

41 Cairns, "The Embedded State," 57.

42 Russell, "The Supreme Court and Federal-Provincial Relations," 165.

43 Ibid.

44 Ibid.

45 Patrick Monahan, *Politics and the Constitution: The Charter, Federalism and the Supreme Court of Canada* (Toronto: Carswell/Methuen, 1987), 161.
46 Russell, "The Supreme Court and Federal-Provincial Relations," 165.
47 Ibid. More recently the Supreme Court of Canada may have given anticombines legislation a new home in the federal trade and commerce power. See *Attorney General of Canada* v. *Canadian National Transportation*, [1983] 2 S.C.R. 206.
48 Ibid.
49 *A.-G. Manitoba et al.* v. *A.-G. Canada et al.*, [1981] 1 S.C.R. 753.
50 Ibid., 166.
51 Ibid.
52 Cairns, "The Embedded State," 62.
53 Pierre Elliott Trudeau, *Federalism and the French Canadians* (Toronto: Macmillan, 1968), 32–33.
54 Jennifer Smith, "Intrastate Federalism and Confederation," in Stephen Brooks, ed., *Political Thought in Canada: Contemporary Perspectives* (Toronto: Irwin, 1984), 273.
55 Hugh R. Innis, ed., *Bilingualism and Biculturalism: An Abridged Version of the Royal Commission Report* (Toronto: McClelland and Stewart, 1973), 4.
56 Task Force on National Unity, *A Future Together* (Ottawa: Minister of Supply and Services Canada, 1979), 15–16: "It was indeed the very definition of the country in dualistic terms both in the mandate and outlook of the B & B Commission, which helped to stimulate the assertiveness of these ethnic groups...."
57 See Rainer Knopff, "Language and Culture in the Canadian Debate: The Battle of the White Papers," *Canadian Review of Studies in Nationalism* 6:1 (1979).
58 To date multiculturalism has occupied a branch of the Secretary of State, though the Multiculturalism Act of 1988 promised the establishment of an independent department.
59 Reg Whitaker, "Democracy and the Canadian Constitution," in Keith Banting and Richard Simeon, eds., *And No One Cheered: Federalism, Democracy and the Constitution Act* (Toronto: Methuen, 1983), 246–47.
60 Ibid., 250.
61 Pierre Elliott Trudeau, *A Time for Action* (Ottawa: Minister of Supply and Services Canada, 1978), 8.
62 Pierre Elliott Trudeau, *The Constitution and the People of Canada* (Ottawa: Minister of Supply and Services Canada, 1969), 14.
63 Roy Romanow, John Whyte, and Howard Leeson, *Canada Notwithstanding: The Making of the Constitution, 1976–1982* (Toronto: Carswell/Methuen, 1984), 216–17.
64 See Rainer Knopff and F.L. Morton, "Nation-Building and the Canadian Charter of Rights and Freedoms," in Alan Cairns and Cynthia Williams, eds., *Constitutionalism, Citizenship and Society in Canada* (Toronto: University of Toronto Press, 1985), 146–50.
65 Alan C. Cairns, "Citizens (Outsiders) and Governments (Insiders) in Constitution-Making: The Case of Meech Lake," *Canadian Public Policy* 14: supplement (1988), 122.
66 Ibid., 143, n.1.
67 Ibid., 122.
68 Strictly speaking section 35 of the Constitution Act, 1982, is outside the Charter, but it is closely related and is obviously relevant in this context.
69 See Knopff and Morton, "Nation-Building and the Charter," 150–57.

70 Cairns, "The Embedded State," 71.

71 Ibid.

72 Richard Simeon, "Meech Lake and Shifting Conceptions of Canadian Federalism," *Canadian Public Policy* 14: supplement (1988), 20.

73 Cairns, "The Embedded State," 73.

74 Garth Stevenson, *Unfulfilled Union: Canadian Federalism and National Unity*, rev. ed. (Toronto: Gage, 1982), 122–23.

75 Alan C. Cairns, "The Canadian Constitutional Experiment: Constitution, Community and Identity," Killam lecture, Dalhousie University, November 24, 1983 (Revised Draft January 30, 1984), 29–30.

76 Roger Gibbins et al., eds., *Meech Lake and Canada: Perspectives from the West* (Edmonton: Academic Printing and Publishing, 1988), 5.

77 *Reference re Objection to a Resolution to Amend the Constitution* (Quebec Veto Reference), [1982] 2 S.C.R. 793.

78 Simeon, "Meech Lake and Shifting Conceptions of Canadian Federalism," 9.

79 Emphasis added.

80 Cf. Cairns, "Citizens (Outsiders) and Governments (Insiders)."

81 Peter W. Hogg, *Canada Act 1982 Annotated* (Toronto: Carswell, 1982), 52.

82 Romanow, Whyte, and Leeson, *Canada Notwithstanding*, 253–55.

83 Cairns, "Citizens (Outsiders) and Governments (Insiders)," 129.

84 Trudeau saw dualism as best expressed in a policy of coast-to-coast official bilingualism. It is also possible to see dualism as geographically bounded, with Quebec the jurisdictional expression of French Canada and the rest of the country representing English Canada. From the perspective of third-force Canadians, both forms of dualism give primacy to French–English relations in Canada.

85 Cairns, "Citizens (Outsiders) and Governments (Insiders)," 130.

86 Ibid., 132–34, 136.

87 The Fédération des femmes du Québec took the opposite position.

88 Cairns, "Citizens (Outsiders) and Governments (Insiders)," 130–32, 136.

89 Ibid., 137.

90 See F.L. Morton, "How not to amend the Constitution," *Canadian Parliamentary Review* 12:4 (1989–90).

91 Simeon, "Meech Lake and Shifting Conceptions of Federalism," 14.

92 See John Courtney, "Parliament and Representation: The Unfinished Agenda of Electoral Redistributions," *Canadian Journal of Political Science* 21:4 (1988).

93 Ibid., 686.

94 Ibid.

95 Ibid., 687.

96 Ibid., 689.

97 Gad Horowitz, "Creative Politics, Mosaics and Identity," *Canadian Dimension* 3 (1965), reprinted in R. Schultz, O.M. Kruhlak, and J.C. Terry, eds., *The Canadian Political Process*, 3rd ed. (Toronto: Holt, Rinehart and Winston, 1975), 75.

98 John Porter, *The Vertical Mosaic* (Toronto: University of Toronto Press, 1965), 369.

99 Neil Nevitte and Roger Gibbins, *New Elites in Old States* (Toronto, London, and New York: Oxford University Press, 1990), 17.

100 This is true not only in Canada, but in the Anglo-American democracies generally. See ibid., 17–19.

101 John Stuart Mill, *On Liberty*, edited, with an introduction, by Currin V. Shields (Indianapolis: Bobbs-Merrill, 1956).

102 One of the best expressions of this view is Harry Clor, *Obscenity and Public Morality: Censorship in a Liberal Society* (Chicago: University of Chicago Press, 1969).

103 Varda Burstyn, ed., *Women Against Censorship* (Vancouver: Douglas and McIntyre, 1985).

104 Alec Stone, Review of Donald P. Kommers, "The Constitutional Jurisprudence of the Federal Republic of Germany" and Louis Favoreu, "La politique saisie par le droit," *Comparative Political Studies* (October 1990), 410.

105 *Andrews* v. *Law Society of British Columbia*, [1989] 1 S.C.R. 143.

106 See LEAF's factum in *Andrews*, 2: "LEAF takes no position on the constitutional validity of the citizenship requirements in section 42 of the *Barristers and Solicitors Act....* LEAF restricts its arguments to the question of what approach should be taken by this Court in analysing section 15 of the *Canadian Charter of Rights and Freedoms* and in determining its relationship to section 1 of the *Charter.*" On the intervention of the Advocacy Resource Centre for the Handicapped (ARCH), which represented the Coalition of Provincial Organizations of the Handicapped (COPOH), see *Canadian Human Rights Advocate* 3:8 (1987), 11: "COPOH takes no position on the outcome of the appeal, but rather, wants to ensure that an interpretation of Section 15 favourable to disabled persons is made by the Supreme Court of Canada."

107 See LEAF's *Andrews* factum, 18–20.

108 Ibid., passim.

109 See Michael Mandel, *The Charter of Rights and the Legalization of Politics in Canada* (Toronto: Wall and Thompson, 1989), 222–34.

110 See LEAF's *Andrews* factum, 14–20, especially the following at 20: "It is accordingly submitted that limits should be imposed in providing access to the equality guarantees on the basis of the non-enumerated grounds. Aside from process claims discussed below, only claims based on non-enumerated grounds *which are proxies for enumerated grounds* [as, for example, 'small people' are proxies for 'women'] or akin to enumerated grounds should be permitted." Emphasis added. See also Rainer Knopff, *Human Rights and Social Technology: The New War on Discrimination* (Ottawa: Carleton University Press), 28, 153–54, 157–59.

111 See Peter H. Russell, "The Anti-Inflation Case: The Anatomy of a Constitutional Decision," *Canadian Public Administration* 20 (1977).

Chapter Five

1 Peter H. Russell, Rainer Knopff, and Ted Morton, eds., *Federalism and the Charter: Leading Constitutional Decisions—A New Edition* (Ottawa: Carleton University Press, 1989), 19.

2 *R.* v. *Morgentaler*, [1988] 1 S.C.R. 30.

3 *Reference re Public Service Employee Relations Act* (Alberta Labour Reference), [1987] 1 S.C.R. 313. This instance of judicial policy-making (denying labour strikes constitutional protection) by exercising judicial self-restraint proves that both activism and restraint may be regarded—and not only by cynics—as two-edged swords. See also Chapter Seven.

4 Nor, as Ely points out, with interpretivism and noninterpretivism (discussed below), which Ely, sees as categories cutting across each other "virtually at right angles." John Hart Ely, *Democracy and Distrust: A Theory of Judicial Review* (Cambridge, Mass.: Harvard University Press, 1980), 1.

5 *Brown* v. *Board of Education*, 347 U.S. 483 (1954).

6 *Green* v. *County School Board*, 391 U.S. 430 (1968).

7 *Swann* v. *Charlotte-Mecklenburg Board of Education*, 402 U.S. 1 (1971).

8 Donald L. Horowitz, *The Courts and Social Policy* (Washington, D.C.: The Brookings Institution, 1977), 4.

9 Michael Mandel, *The Charter of Rights and the Legalization of Politics in Canada* (Toronto: Wall and Thompson, 1989), 265.

10 *Schachter* v. *Canada (C.A.)*, [1990] 2 F.C. 129.

11 *Mahé* v. *Alberta*, [1990] 1 S.C.R. 342.

12 *Badger* v. *A.-G. Canada* (1989), 55 M.R. (2d) 211 (Man. Q.B.).

13 Ibid., 215.

14 Ibid., 213, quoting Justice Scollin in *Badger* v. *A.-G. Manitoba* (1986), 51 C.R. (3d) 163 (Man. Q.B.) 171.

15 *Badger* v. *A.-G. Canada*, 214 (Man. Q.B.).

16 *Badger* v. *A.-G. Canada* (1989), 55 M.R. (2d) 198 (Man. C.A.).

17 *Badger* v. *A.-G. Manitoba*, (Man. Q.B.).

18 Ibid., 173.

19 *Badger* v. *A.-G. Canada*, 203 (Man C.A.).

20 *Badger* v. *A.-G. Manitoba*, 173 (Man. Q.B.).

21 Ibid.

22 Ibid.

23 Constance E. Robinson, "Sunday Closing and the Charter of Rights," M.A. Thesis, University of Calgary, 1988, 81.

24 Ibid.

25 Ibid., 82.

26 Ibid., 83.

27 Mandel, *The Charter of Rights*, 233.

28 Ibid.

29 *Katz* v. *U.S.*, 389 U.S. 347 (1967).

30 *R.* v. *Wong et al.* (1990), 120 N.R. 34.

31 *Attorney General of Quebec* v. *Blaikie*, [1979] 2 S.C.R. 1016 (S.C.C.) 1029. In *Mercure* v. *Attorney General for Saskatchewan*, [1988] 1 S.C.R. 234, Justice La Forest distinguishes between proper and improper uses of the "living-tree" analogy. It was properly used to extend the provisions of section 133 to cover modern administrative agencies at the federal level and in Quebec ("mere appendages" of the governments specified by the section); it would be improperly used to extend it to cover "quasi-separate areas possessing democratic institutions for their governance" (i.e., the Northwest Territories, to which section 133 did not explicitly apply).

32 See Walter Berns, *The First Amendment and the Future of American Democracy* (New York: Basic Books, 1976), ch. 1.

33 It is also possible, of course, for understandings of rights to become narrower, but those who advocate judicially updating the meaning of rights do not have this kind of change in mind. In this sense, the "living-tree" analogy suits their purpose perfectly. As living trees, rights cannot shrink, they can only grow.

34 See Katherine Swinton, *The Supreme Court and Canadian Federalism: The Laskin-Dickson Years* (Toronto: Carswell, 1990), 328.

35 Alexander M. Bickel, *The Morality of Consent* (New Haven: Yale University Press, 1975), 120.

36 *Dubois* v. *The Queen,* [1985] 2 S.C.R. 350.

37 Ibid., 384.

38 *Lochner* v. *New York,* 198 U.S. 45 (1905). In fact, a "substantive" reading of the fifth amendment's due process clause had already been used by the U.S. Supreme Court (against Congress) in 1857 to uphold slavery in the new territories: *Dred Scott* v. *Sandford,* 19 Howard 393 (1857).

39 *Adkins* v. *Children's Hospital,* 261 U.S. 525 (1923).

40 *Attorney General of Canada* v. *Attorney General of Ontario* (Employment and Social Insurance Act Reference), [1937] A.C. 355; *Attorney General of British Columbia* v. *Attorney General of Canada* (Natural Products Marketing Act Reference), [1937] A.C. 377; *Attorney General of Canada* v. *Attorney General of Ontario* (Labour Conventions Case), [1937] A.C. 327.

41 See G.P. Browne, *The Judicial Committee and the British North America Act* (Toronto: University of Toronto Press, 1967).

42 Lord Haldane, "The Work of the Empire of the Judicial Committee of the Privy Council," *Cambridge Law Journal* 1 (1923), 150.

43 *West Coast Hotel* v. *Parrish,* 300 U.S. 379 (1937).

44 *Roe* v. *Wade,* 410 U.S. 113 (1973).

45 Ely, *Democracy and Distrust,* 1.

46 *Griswold* v. *Connecticut,* 381 U.S. 479 (1965).

47 Ronald Dworkin, *A Matter of Principle* (Cambridge, Mass.: Harvard University Press, 1985), 57.

48 Christopher Wolfe, *The Rise of Modern Judicial Review: From Constitutional Interpretation to Judge-Made Law* (New York: Basic Books, 1986), 323.

49 Ibid., 325.

50 Ibid., 325–26.

51 Ibid., 327.

52 Ibid., Part II (chs. 5–8), and 325–26.

53 Ibid., 326.

54 Cf. Christopher Manfredi, "The Use of United States Decisions by the Supreme Court of Canada Under the Charter of Rights and Freedoms," *Canadian Journal of Political Science* 23:30 (1990), 513.

55 See F.L. Morton and Rainer Knopff, "Permanence and Change in a Written Constitution: The 'Living Tree' Doctrine and the Charter of Rights" (1990), 1 S.C.L.R. (2d).

56 See Allan Bloom, ed., *Confronting the Constitution* (Washington, D.C.: The AEI Press, 1990), 4–5. Cf. Sanford Levinson, *Constitutional Faith* (Princeton, N.J.: Princeton University Press, 1988), 176–77.

57 James W. Tuttleton, "Authority in English Studies," *Academic Questions* 2:4 (1989), 85.

58 Quoted in ibid.

59 Quoted in Levinson, *Constitutional Faith,* 177.

60 Ibid., 86.

61 Bloom, *Confronting the Constitution,* 5.

62 Dinesh D'Souza, "Illiberal Education," *The Atlantic* (March 1991), 72.

63 Cf. Swinton, *The Supreme Court and Canadian Federalism,* 329.

64 Ronald Dworkin, *Taking Rights Seriously* (Cambridge, Mass.: Harvard University Press, 1977), 135–36.

65 Robert Bork, *The Tempting of America: The Political Seduction of the Law* (New York: Free Press, 1990), 213.

66 Dworkin, *Taking Rights Seriously*, 136.
67 Ibid., 134.
68 Ibid.
69 Ibid.
70 Ibid., 137.
71 Ibid., 135.
72 Bork, *The Tempting of America*, 123.
73 Ibid., 171.
74 Ibid.
75 Ibid., 171
76 Quoted in ibid., 162.
77 Ibid.
78 Quoted in ibid., emphasis added.
79 Ibid., 77.
80 E.g., Raoul Berger, *Government by Judiciary* (Cambridge, Mass.: Harvard University Press, 1977), ch. 7.
81 Richard Morgan, *Disabling America: The Rights Industry in Our Time* (New York: Basic Books, 1984), 166.
82 Bork, *The Tempting of America*, 76.
83 Ibid., 82.
84 Ibid.
85 Morgan, *Disabling America*, 167, emphasis added.
86 Bork, *The Tempting of America*, 78.
87 The following account draws heavily from Cairns, "The Judicial Committee and Its Critics."
88 Pierre Elliott Trudeau, *Federalism and the French Canadians* (Toronto: Macmillan, 1968), 198.
89 Manfredi, "The Use of United States Decisions."
90 *Law Society of Upper Canada* v. *Skapinker*, [1984] 1 S.C.R. 357.
91 Peter H. Russell, "Canada's Charter of Rights and Freedoms: A Political Report," *Public Law* (Autumn 1988), 389.
92 *Reference re s.94(2) of the British Columbia Motor Vehicle Act*, [1985] 2 S.C.R. 486 (S.C.C.) 509.
93 Patrick Monahan, *Politics and the Constitution: The Charter, Federalism and the Supreme Court of Canada* (Toronto: Carswell/Methuen, 1987), 76.
94 *R.* v. *Big M Drug Mart*, [1985] 1 S.C.R. 295.
95 *Robertson and Rosentanni* v. *The Queen*, [1963] S.C.R. 651.
96 See especially *Big M Drug Mart*.
97 Russell, "Canada's Charter of Rights and Freedoms: A Political Report," 395. Cf. Manfredi, "The Use of United States Decisions," 515.
98 *Reference re Public Service Employees Relations Act*.
99 Ibid., 394.
100 *Morgentaler*.
101 This statement is found on the dust jacket of Bork's *The Tempting of America*.
102 *Reference re s.94(2) of the British Columbia Motor Vehicle Act*.
103 Ibid.
104 *Morgentaler*, 161–62.
105 Bork, *The Tempting of America*, 3.
106 Ironically, the very success of the educational tactic might signal its obsolescence. If feminists succeed in persuading enough judges to take more open stands favouring the feminist side of major moral issues, other judges, urged on by other interests, may be impelled to take the opposite stands. Once

judges (and potential judges) have become accustomed to engaging directly in major substantive controversies, however, post-appointment education may no longer be an effective tactic.

107 Russell, "Canada's Charter of Rights and Freedoms: A Political Report," 399.

Chapter Six

1 The French system of separation of powers, as introduced by the Revolution of 1789, involves an even stricter separation as to functions and personnel, especially with regard to the "ordinary courts," which are totally prohibited from interfering with either legislative or executive/administrative action.

2 *Reference re s.94(2) of the British Columbia Motor Vehicle Act,* [1985] 2 S.C.R. 486 (S.C.C.) 497. American judges, of course, tirelessly repeat the same refrain; see, for example, *Lochner* v. *New York,* 198 U.S. 45 (1905).

3 *Reference re s.94(2) of the British Columbia Motor Vehicle Act,* 497.

4 Martin Diamond, "The Dependence of Fact Upon Value," *Interpretation* 2:3 (1972).

5 Andrew Petter and Allan C. Hutchinson, "Rights in Conflict: The Dilemma of Charter Legitimacy," *U.B.C. Law Review* 23:3 (1989), 535.

6 See John Agresto, *The Supreme Court and Constitutional Democracy* (Ithaca, N.Y.: Cornell University Press, 1984), 25; and Katherine Swinton, *The Supreme Court and Canadian Federalism: The Laskin-Dickson Years* (Toronto: Carswell, 1990), 326, 328, 330.

7 Barry L. Strayer, *The Canadian Constitution and the Courts: The Function and Scope of Judicial Review,* 2nd ed. (Toronto: Butterworths, 1983), 54.

8 Peter H. Russell, "The Political Purposes of the Canadian Charter of Rights and Freedoms," (1983) 61 *Canadian Bar Review,* 43–44.

9 Rainer Knopff, "The Triumph of Liberalism in Canada: Laurier on Representation and Party Government," *The Journal of Canadian Studies* (forthcoming).

10 Russell, "Political Purposes," 44.

11 *Dred Scott* v. *Sandford,* 19 Howard 393 (1857).

12 Rainer Knopff, "Quebec's 'Holy War' as 'Regime Politics': Reflections on the Guibord Case," *Canadian Journal of Political Science* 12:2 (1979).

13 A. Alan Borovoy, *When Freedoms Collide: The Case for our Civil Liberties* (Toronto: Lester & Orpen Dennys, 1988), 202–3.

14 Russell, "Political Purposes," 44.

15 *Jack and Charlie* v. *The Queen,* [1985] 2 S.C.R. 332.

16 *R.* v. *Edwards Books and Art Ltd.,* [1986] 2 S.C.R. 713.

17 *Dubois* v. *The Queen,* [1985] 2 S.C.R. 350.

18 In *Braunfield* v. *Brown,* 366 U.S. 599 (1961), the Supreme Court upheld the Pennsylvania Sunday-closing law; the law imposed a substantial burden on Orthodox Jews, but it met the requirements of (1) furthering an important state aim, which (2) could not be achieved by less restrictive means. This approach is also seen in *Sherbert* v. *Verner,* 374 U.S. 398 (1963) where the Supreme Court declared invalid a South Carolina unemployment compensation regulation. The regulation violated the freedom of religion of the claimant Seventh Day Adventist as it required her to be available for employment on her Sabbath if she was to be eligible for benefits. In Canada the leading case is *Edwards Books.*

19 John Locke, *A Letter Concerning Toleration,* quoted in Clifford L. Pannam, "Travelling Section 116 with a U.S. Road Map" *Melbourne University Law Review* 4 (June 1963), 62.

20 Petter and Hutchinson, "Rights in Conflict," 537.

21 Agresto, *The Supreme Court,* 109.

22 Paul C. Weiler, "Rights and Judges in a Democracy: A New Canadian Version," *Journal of Law Reform* 18:1 (1984), 83.

23 Patrick Monahan, *Politics and the Constitution: The Charter, Federalism and the Supreme Court of Canada* (Toronto: Carswell/Methuen, 1987), 53.

24 Ibid.

25 Ibid., 67.

26 Ibid., 68–71.

27 Ibid., 69.

28 Ibid., 70

29 David Beatty, *Talking Heads and the Supremes: The Canadian Production of Constitutional Law* (Toronto: Carswell, 1990), 105.

30 Ibid., 75, 111.

31 Ibid., 31, 114.

32 Ibid., 115.

33 Ibid., 106.

34 *Reference re Ss. 193 and 195.1(1)(c) of the Criminal Code (Man.)* (Prostitution Reference), [1990] 1 S.C.R. 1123.

35 Criminal Code, R.S.C. 1970, c. C-34, s. 195.1(1).

36 Ibid., s. 195.1(2).

37 *Prostitution Reference,* 1215.

38 Ibid., 1207.

39 Ibid., 1210.

40 Ibid., 1214.

41 Ibid.

42 Ibid., 1137.

43 Ibid., 1136.

44 Ibid., 1137.

45 Ibid., 1194.

46 Ibid.

47 *Globe and Mail,* June 23, 1990, A3; *Calgary Herald,* Nov. 30, 1989, B12; see generally *Report of the Auditor General of Canada to the House of Commons* (Ottawa: Supply and Services Canada, 1990), 347–51.

48 See the decision of Madam Justice Wilson in *Singh et al.* v. *Minister of Employment and Immigration,* [1985] S.C.R. 177.

49 In response to the *Singh* decision, for example, the government revised the refugee claimant process to provide an oral hearing, but then made it much more difficult to enter the country in order to exercise this right.

50 Monahan, *Politics and the Constitution,* 53.

51 Petter and Hutchinson, "Rights in Conflict," 537.

52 Peter Russell, "The Supreme Court and the Charter: A Question of Legitimacy," in David P. Shugarman and Reg Whitaker, eds., *Federalism and Political Community* (Peterborough: Broadview Press, 1989), 232.

53 See Donald V. Smiley, "The Case Against the Canadian Charter of Rights," *Canadian Journal of Political Science* 2 (1969), and *The Canadian Charter of Rights and Freedoms, 1981* (Toronto: Ontario Economic Council, 1981). For Alan Blakeney's views, see Canadian Intergovernmental Secretariat, *Federal-Provincial Conference of First Ministers on the Constitution* (Ottawa: Sept. 8–13, 1980), 493.

54 Although the Australian constitution has no full-blown bill of rights, it contains four provisions of the kind often found in such bills, including a freedom of religion guarantee modelled on the first amendment of the U.S. constitution. These provisions only apply to the Commonwealth, not to the states.

55 That is, matters within state jurisdiction and thus not covered by the existing provision.

56 See, for example, the speech of Senator Durack, Senate *Debates,* May 24, 1988, 2815.

57 Senate *Debates,* May 23, 1988, 269.

58 Ibid., 2693.

59 Patrick Monahan, *Politics and the Constitution,* 62.

60 While unanimity was achieved in 85 percent of Charter cases in 1984 and 1985, it has subsequently dropped to the 60 percent range. See F.L. Morton, Peter H. Russell, Michael J. Withey, "The Supreme Court's First One Hundred Charter of Rights Decisions: A Statistical Analysis," *Osgoode Hall Law Journal* (forthcoming).

61 *Edwards Books,* 770.

62 Ibid., 795.

63 Ibid., 797.

64 Ibid.

65 Ibid., 806.

66 Ibid., 801.

67 Ibid., 802.

68 Ibid., 783.

69 Canadian Intergovernmental Secretariat, *Federal-Provincial Conference of First Ministers on the Constitution.*

70 John McMillan, Gareth Evans, and Haddon Storey, *Australia's Constitution: Time For Change?* (Sydney: Allen & Unwin, 1983), 335.

Chapter Seven

1 Cf. Louis Fisher, *Constitutional Dialogues: Interpretation as Political Process* (Princeton N.J.: Princeton University Press, 1988), ch. 7.

2 Sanford Levinson, *Constitutional Faith* (Princeton, N.J.: Princeton University Press, 1988), ch. 1.

3 See ibid., 92, 122–23.

4 *Marbury* v. *Madison* 5 U.S. (1 Cranch) 137, 180 (1803).

5 *Eakin* v. *Raub,* 12 S & R 330, 353 (Pa. 1825).

6 Ibid.

7 Ibid., 354.

8 Christopher P. Manfredi, "Adjudication, Policy-Making and the Supreme Court of Canada: Lessons From the Experience of the United States," *Canadian Journal of Political Science* 22:2 (1989), 316.

9 Alexander Hamilton, James Madison, John Jay, *The Federalist Papers,* Clinton Rossiter, ed. (New York: New American Library, 1961), 465–66.
10 Ibid.
11 *Marbury,* 179.
12 Manfredi, "Adjudication, Policy-Making and the Supreme Court of Canada," 316.
13 Ibid., 316.
14 *Brown* v. *Board of Education,* 347 U.S. 483 (1954).
15 *McCulloch* v. *Maryland,* 17 U.S. 316 (1819).
16 John Agresto, *The Supreme Court and Constitutional Democracy* (Ithaca, N.Y.: Cornell University Press, 1984), 85; Levinson, *Constitutional Faith,* 38.
17 Quoted in Agresto, *The Supreme Court,* 85.
18 Quoted in Levinson, *Constitutional Faith,* 48–49. Emphasis in Levinson's text.
19 Ibid., 49.
20 *Dred Scott* v. *Sanford,* 19 Howard 393 (1857).
21 Agresto, *The Supreme Court,* 89–90.
22 Ibid., 89.
23 For a modern statement of the same view see Fisher, *Constitutional Dialogues,* 232.
24 Agresto, *The Supreme Court,* 91–92.
25 Levinson, *Constitutional Faith,* 39.
26 Quoted in ibid.
27 *R.* v. *Maier* (1989), 64 A.L.R. 383 (Alta. Q.B.).
28 "Seat-belt legislation is unconstitutional, Alberta judge decides," *Globe and Mail,* Feb. 3, 1989, A1–A2.
29 *R.* v. *Maier* (1989), 101 A.R. 126 (Alta. C.A.).
30 Alexis de Tocqueville, *Democracy in America,* ed. J.P. Mayer, trans. George Lawrence (Garden City, N.Y.: Anchor, 1969), 103.
31 *Schachter* v. *Canada,* [1988] 3 F.C. 515.
32 Kenneth P. Swan, "Intervention and Amicus Curiae Status in Charter Litigation," in Gerald A. Beaudoin ed., *Charter Cases, 1986–87: Proceedings of the October 1986 Colloquium of The Canadian Bar Association in Montreal* (Cowansville, Quebec: Les Éditions Yvon Blais, 1987), 95.
33 Tocqueville, *Democracy in America,* 103.
34 Ibid.
35 *Minister of Justice of Canada et al.* v. *Borowski,* [1981] 2 S.C.R. 575 (S.C.C.) 578–79.
36 Ibid., 579
37 Ibid., 598, emphasis added.
38 Ibid., 597.
39 Ibid.
40 Ibid., 580.
41 *Thorson* v. *A.G. Canada,* [1975] 1 SC.R. 138.
42 Ibid., 580.
43 Ibid., 585.
44 Swan, "Intervention and Amicus Curiae Status," 95.
45 *Borowski* v. *Canada (A.-G.),* [1989] 1 S.C.R. 342.
46 *R.* v. *Mercure,* [1988] 1 S.C.R. 234.
47 *Law Society of Upper Canada* v. *Skapinker,* [1984] 1 S.C.R. 357.
48 *Borowski,* (1989) 360.
49 Ibid., 360–61.
50 Ibid., 362.

51 Cf. Donald L. Horowitz, *The Courts and Social Policy* (Washington, D.C.: The Brookings Institution, 1977), 8: "That some cases might forever escape judicial scrutiny because of the doctrine that a moot case is not a case at all would have struck even bold judges of a few decades ago as entirely natural."

52 In some areas of law the Supreme Court's tendency to indulge in this practice is strengthened by a decline in the number of cases it hears. Thus former Justice Bertha Wilson has argued that "if we are only going to bring up one or two tort cases or one or two property cases in a year, then we should make the most of the opportunity by adopting a more expansive approach to our decision-making role." Quoted in Carl Baar and Ellen Baar, "Diagnostic Adjudication in Appellate Courts: The Supreme Court of Canada and the Charter of Rights," *Osgoode Hall Law Journal* 27:1 (1989), 9–10.

53 *R* v. *Big M Drug Mart*, [1985] 1 S.C.R. 295 (S.C.C.) 312.

54 Cf. Michael Mandel, *The Charter of Rights and the Legalization of Politics in Canada* (Toronto: Wall and Thompson, 1989), 55.

55 *R.* v. *Smith (Edward Dewey)*, [1987] 1 S.C.R. 1045.

56 Ibid., 1053.

57 Ibid., 1083.

58 Ibid.

59 Ibid.

60 Ibid.

61 Horowitz, *The Courts and Social Policy*, 32.

62 Mandel, *The Charter of Rights and the Legalization of Politics*, 225.

63 Horowitz, *The Courts and Social Policy*, 9.

64 *Muskrat* v. *United States*, 219 U.S. 345 (1911).

65 *A.-G. Ontario* v. *A.-G. Canada* (Validity of References Case) (1912), 3 D.L.R. 509.

66 Ibid., 512.

67 This term was used in *Borowski*, (1989) 365.

68 *B.C.G.E.U.* v. *British Columbia (A.-G.)*, [1988] 2 S.C.R. 214.

69 Mandel, *The Charter of Rights and the Legalization of Politics*, 205.

70 *B.C.G.E.U.*, 229.

71 Ibid., 252.

72 The full quote, attributed to American Justice Charles Evan Hughes, reads: "We are under a constitution, but the Constitution is what the Judges say it is." See Paul Weiler, *In the Last Resort: A Critical Study of the Supreme Court of Canada* (Toronto: Carswell/Metheun, 1974), 155. A splendid American example of open judicial identification of the constitution with its judicial interpretation is *Cooper* v. *Aaron*, 358 U.S. 1 (1958): "[T]he interpretation of the Fourteenth Amendment enunciated by this Court ... is the supreme law of the land...."

73 Quoted in Fisher, *Constitutional Dialogues*, 244.

74 *R.W.D.S.U.* v. *Dolphin Delivery Ltd.*, [1986] 2 S.C.R. 573 (S.C.C.) 600.

75 For an argument that, contrary to *Dolphin Delivery*, the courts are subject to the Charter, see Peter W. Hogg, "The Dolphin Delivery Case: The Application of the Charter to Private Action," *Saskatchewan Law Review* 51:2 (1987).

76 *Reference re s.94(2) of the British Columbia Motor Vehicle Act*, [1985] 2 S.C.R. 486.

77 Mandel, *The Charter of Rights and the Legalization of Politics*, 152–53.

78 Ibid., 153.

79 Ibid.

80 *R.* v. *Vaillancourt*, [1987] 2 S.C.R. 636.

81 Ibid., 663.
82 Mandel, *The Charter of Rights and the Legalization of Politics,* 154.
83 *R.* v. *Lyons,* [1987] 2 S.C.R. 309.
84 Ibid., 157.
85 Ibid.
86 Swan, "Intervention and Amicus Curiae Status," 95. Cf. Baar and Baar, "Diagnostic Adjudication," 20, 23, 25.
87 Swan, "Intervention and Amicus Curiae Status," 102–3; Submissions to the Supreme Court of Canada, Re Interventions in Public Interest Litigation, From Canadian Civil Liberties Association per A. Alan Borovoy (General Counsel), July 17, 1984; J. Welch, "Charter Litigation in the Supreme Court of Canada: A Role For Interest Groups as Interveners," *University of Toronto Faculty of Law Review* 43 (1985).
88 Stephen Bindman, "Door opens: Supreme Court lets groups intervene in cases," *Ottawa Citizen,* March 9, 1991.
89 As we observed in Chapter Four, this occurred in the *Andrews* case, where LEAF could not rely on Andrews to press its favoured interpretation. See Chapter Four, note 106 and accompanying text.

Chapter Eight

1 *R.* v. *Morgentaler,* [1988] 1 S.C.R. 30.
2 For example, section 33 of the Canadian Charter of Rights allows legislatures to override certain sections of the Charter for renewable five-year periods by including an explicit "notwithstanding" clause in the relevant legislation.
3 Quoted in Herbert Storing, "The Constitution and the Bill of Rights," in M. Judd Harmon, ed., *Essays on the Constitution of the United States* (Port Washington, N.Y.: Kennikat Press, 1978), 42.
4 Quoted in Sir Robert Menzies, *Central Power in the Australian Commonwealth* (London: Cassell, 1967), 53.
5 Ibid., 54.
6 James Bryce, *Studies in History and Jurisprudence* (Oxford: Clarendon Press, 1901), 503.
7 Quoted in John Uhr, "Parliament and Public Administration," in John Nethercote, ed., *Parliament and Bureaucracy* (Sydney: Hale and Iremonger, 1982), 32.
8 Senate *Debates,* May 26, 1988, 3061.
9 Senate *Debates,* May 25, 1988, 2900, emphasis added.
10 Senate *Debates,* May 26, 1988, 2963.
11 Ibid., 3062.
12 Roger Gibbins, "Beyond Quebec: The Need for Structural Reform," A Presentation to the Institute for Political Involvement, University of Toronto, Feb. 6, 1991, 5. Ironically, in the United States the opposite case is sometimes made. According to some American observers, their system suffers from too many checks and balances, and would be improved by shifting in the direction of parliamentary responsible cabinet government. See Sanford Levinson, *Constitutional Faith* (Princeton, N.J.: Princeton University Press, 1988), 190.
13 Gibbins, "Beyond Quebec."

14 Christopher P. Manfredi, "Adjudication, Policy-Making and the Supreme Court of Canada: Lessons From the Experience of the United States," *Canadian Journal of Political Science* 22:2 (1989), 318.
15 Storing, "The Constitution and the Bill of Rights," 41.
16 See F.L. Morton, "Judicial Review in France: A Comparative Analysis," *The American Journal of Comparative Law* 36 (1988).
17 Quoted in John Agresto, *The Supreme Court and Constitutional Democracy* (Ithaca, N.Y.: Cornell University Press, 1984), 33.
18 Alexander Hamilton, James Madison, and John Jay, *The Federalist Papers* (New York: New American Library, 1961), 384.
19 Agresto, *The Supreme Court,* 31.
20 Ibid., 27.
21 Ibid., 33.
22 Paul Weiler, "Rights and Judges in a Democracy: A New Canadian Version," *Journal of Law Reform* 18:1 (1984), 70.
23 Donald L. Horowitz, *The Courts and Social Policy* (Washington, D.C.: The Brookings Institution, 1977), 45.
24 Ibid.
25 Ibid., ch. 6.
26 Ibid., 38.
27 See Richard Morgan, *Disabling America: The "Rights Industry" in Our Time* (New York: Basic Books, 1984), ch. 4; Thomas Sowell, *Knowledge and Decisions* (New York: Basic Books, 1980), 272.
28 Horowitz concludes that the evidence on whether the difficulty of conviction under the exclusionary rule promotes better police behaviour or its opposite is inconclusive, but that preliminary indications suggest that it does some of both, with more scrupulous behaviour probably outweighing a "displacement effect" in the opposite direction. He points out, however, that there is great variation among local police forces and among different kinds of police units. See *The Courts and Social Policy,* ch. 6.
29 *R.* v. *Therens,* [1985] 1 S.C.R. 613.
30 Ibid., 621–22.
31 *Chromiak* v. *The Queen,* [1980] 1 S.C.R. 471.
32 This is the wording of section 10(b) of the Charter. The Bill of Rights gives the right to counsel to anyone "who has been arrested or detained."
33 *Miranda* v. *Arizona,* 384 U.S. 439 (1966).
34 Robert Harvie and Hamar Foster, "Ties That Bind? The Supreme Court of Canada, American Jurisprudence, and the Revision of Canadian Criminal Law Under the Charter," *Osgoode Hall Law Journal* 28:4 (1990), 755.
35 See generally ibid., 751–55.
36 *R.* v. *Duarte,* [1990] 1 S.C.R. 30.
37 "Attitudes Towards Civil Liberties and the Canadian Charter of Rights: A survey research project conducted for Paul Sniderman, Joe Fletcher, Peter Russell, and Philip Tetlock."
38 Of senior lawyers, 68.6 percent favoured exclusion.
39 Sixty-six percent of English Canadians and 71 percent of French Canadians favoured admitting the evidence. Of these, 65 percent of English Canadians and 81 percent of French Canadians indicated that they would be angry if the evidence were excluded.
40 *R.* v. *Edwards Books and Art Ltd.,* [1986] 2 S.C.R. 713 (S.C.C.) 774.
41 Ibid.

42 Ibid., 779.

43 Ibid., 780.

44 Ibid., 779.

45 Ibid., 800.

46 Horowitz, *The Courts and Social Policy*, 41.

47 Ibid., 33.

48 Sowell, *Knowledge and Decisions*, 273; cf. Horowitz, *The Courts and Social Policy*, 32.

49 Horowitz, *The Courts and Social Policy*, 44.

50 Morgan, *Disabling America*, 113–14.

51 Ibid., ch. 5 passim.

52 Ibid., 117.

53 Ibid., 107.

54 *R. v. Askov*, [1990] 2 S.C.R. 1199.

55 Ibid., 1239.

56 Ibid.

57 Ibid., 1240.

58 Donn Downey, "Courts catching up on backlog of cases created by Askov," *Globe and Mail*, July 11, 1991, A10. Cf. Don Brillinger, "Ont. C.A. puts brakes on 'Draconian' result of S.C.C. *Askov* ruling," *Lawyers Weekly*, June 14, 1991, 13.

59 Stephen Bindman, "Justice shocked by ruling's impact," *Calgary Herald*, July 16, 1991, A8.

60 Downey, "Courts catching up."

61 *R. v. Bennett*, unreported decision of the Ontario Court of Appeal.

62 Ibid.

63 Ibid.

64 This evidence was not more centrally located in the evidence and factums because no one had anticipated the Court asking what standard might be appropriate to the run of cases.

65 They could have asked for reargument on an appropriate standard.

66 *R. v. Bennett*.

67 We cannot resist pointing out the dilemma posed by this argument. If it is true that the undesirable results of *Askov* were due to its widespread (in fact, almost universal) misinterpretation, one is surely left to wonder about the quality of the Court's opinion writing. Either the Court's opinion was very badly crafted, or the judges simply made a mistake and the attempt to blame it on the misinterpretation of others is a face-saving excuse. Not an attractive set of alternatives.

68 Bindman, "Justice shocked by ruling's impact."

69 Comments by Peter Russell, reported in "Review of Askov ruling sought," *Globe and Mail*, July 19, 1991, A4. Russell opposed the idea of off-the-bench clarifications of judicial decisions. For a defence of Justice Cory's action, see Allan Hutchinson, "Taking off the robes and speaking out," *Globe and Mail*, July 25, 1991, A15.

70 "Review of Askov ruling sought," A4.

71 Ibid.

72 See, for example, sections 11(b) and (d) of the Canadian Charter of Rights and Freedoms.

73 Horowitz, *The Courts and Social Policy*, 34, 38.

74 Sowell, *Knowledge and Decisions*, 275–80.

75 Ibid., 276.

76 Morgan, *Disabling America,* 76–79.
77 Sowell, *Knowledge and Decisions,* 277.
78 Peter Russell, "The effect of a Charter of Rights on the policy-making role of Canadian courts," *Canadian Public Administration* 25:1 (1982) 32.
79 T.C. Pocklington, "Some Drawbacks of the Politics of Constitutional Rights," *Constitutional Forum* 2:2 (1991), 43.
80 Horowitz, *The Courts and Social Policy,* 22–23.
81 Ibid., 44.
82 See Mary Ann Glendon, *Abortion and Divorce in Western Law* (Cambridge, Mass.: Harvard University Press, 1987), ch. 1.
83 Ibid.
84 Leslie A. Pal, "Abortion: New legislation and broader debate," *The Financial Post,* Nov. 8, 1989, 10. Glendon, *Abortion and Divorce,* 24. On how rights rhetoric has polarized abortion politics in the United States while the absence of such rhetoric has moderated abortion politics in Europe, see Glendon, *Abortion and Divorce,* 38–39.
85 Pal, "Abortion"; Glendon, *Abortion and Divorce,* 25.
86 Glendon, *Abortion and Divorce,* 40.
87 Pal, "Abortion." This passage is summarizing Glendon's book.
88 Glendon, *Abortion and Divorce,* 41.
89 Ibid., 2.
90 Cf. Carl Baar and Ellen Baar, "Diagnostic Adjudication in Appellate Courts: The Supreme Court of Canada and the Charter of Rights," *Osgoode Hall Law Journal* 27:1 (1989), 3–4.
91 Agresto, *The Supreme Court,* 112.
92 Ibid., 114.
93 Ibid., 115.
94 Ibid., 105.
95 Ibid., 119.
96 Ibid., 134.
97 Russell, "The effect of a Charter of Rights," 32.
98 Peter H. Russell, "On Standing Up For Notwithstanding," in Mark Charlton and Paul Barker, eds., *Contemporary Political Issues* (Scarborough: Nelson, 1991).
99 Ibid., 73.
100 Weiler, "Rights and Judges," 83.
101 Russell, "On Standing Up For Nothwithstanding," 73–74.
102 Ibid., 76.
103 Weiler, "Rights and Judges," 84.
104 Russell, "On Standing Up For Nothwithstanding," 74.
105 Ibid., 74–77.
106 Ibid., 75.
107 Ibid., 74.
108 Ibid., 76.
109 Ibid., 77. And see Weiler, "Rights and Judges"; Peter H. Russell and Paul Weiler, "Don't scrap override clause—it's a very Canadian solution," *Toronto Star,* June 4, 1989, B3.
110 Quoted in Robert C. Vipond, *Liberty and Community: Canadian Federalism and the Failure of the Constitution* (Albany: State University of New York Press, 1991), 193.
111 *RWDSU* v. *Dolphin Delivery Ltd.,* [1986] 2 S.C.R. 573 (S.C.C.) 600.
112 Stephen Bindman, "Door opens: Supreme Court lets groups intervene in cases," *Ottawa Citizen,* March 9, 1991, B8.

113 Quoted in Louis Fisher, *Constitutional Dialogues: Interpretation as Political Process* (Princeton, N.J.: Princeton University Press, 1988), 244.
114 Gibbins, "Beyond Quebec: The Need for Structural Reform," 4.
115 Cf. Horowitz, *The Courts and Social Policy*, 18, 24.

Chapter Nine

1 The term "conservative" is being used here in its modern sense. By the standards of his own day Tocqueville was hardly conservative.
2 Alexis de Tocqueville, *Democracy in America*, ed. J.P. Mayer, trans. George Lawrence (Garden City, N.Y.: Anchor, 1969), 100–101.
3 Ibid., 270.
4 Ibid.
5 The tendency of lawyers to play a leading political role is shown by the fact that "for five hundred years [they] have taken part in all the movements of political society in Europe." Ibid., 264.
6 Ibid., 266.
7 Ibid., 269, 270.
8 Ibid., 270.
9 Ibid., 266.
10 Ibid.
11 Ibid., 264.
12 Ibid., 430.
13 Ibid., 431.
14 Ibid., 430.
15 Ibid., emphasis added.
16 Ibid., 447.
17 Ibid., 472–73.
18 Ibid., 459.
19 "If Pascal had had nothing in view beyond some great gain, or even if he had been stimulated by the love of fame alone, I cannot conceive that he would have been able, as able he was, to rally all the powers of his mind to discover the most hidden secrets of the Creator. When I see him, if one may put it so, tearing his soul free from the cares of this life so as to stake the whole of it on this quest, and prematurely breaking the ties which bound him to the flesh, so that he died of old age before he was forty, I stand amazed, and understand that no ordinary cause was at work in such an extraordinary effort. The future will show whether such rare, creative passions come to birth and grow as easily in democracies as in aristocratic communities. For myself, I confess that I can hardly believe it." Ibid., 461–62.
20 Ibid., 57.
21 See Clifford Orwin, "Welfare and the New Dignity," *The Public Interest* 71 (1983), 89. Tocqueville points to another reason for such policy, namely, that in order for a regime of private property to be respected there must be no proletarians, who, being altogether without property and unable to imagine getting any, have no stake in defending the system. Even the poor will respect the system if they have some share in its benefits and if they can realistically imagine improving their status within it. *Democracy,* 238.

22 Orwin, "Welfare," 89.
23 Tocqueville, *Democracy,* 544.
24 Ibid., 464, 476–77.
25 Ibid., 264.
26 Ibid., 267.
27 Ibid., 264.
28 Ibid., 266.
29 Ibid.
30 Ibid. According to this view, any attempt to incorporate more explicit aristocratic forms into a regime without the hereditary landed wealth on which aristocracy depends is bound to fail. The Canadian Senate, which was supposed to represent the propertied class, even though the latter was no longer hereditary, is an example of such failure. For further analysis of the difficulty in adapting aristocratic forms—in this case hereditary titles without a foundation in hereditary landed wealth—see Goldwin Smith, *Canada and the Canadian Question* (Toronto: University of Toronto Press, 1971), 124: "Baronetcies, the fashion of creating which has of late been revived, are open to the further objection which was urged with decisive force against the creation of an hereditary peerage in a country where there are no entailed estates. We may someday have a baronet blacking shoes. To make a Canadian politician a baronet is to tempt and almost to constrain him to use his political opportunities for the purpose of accumulating a fortune to bequeath to his son." For this reason, Smith thought that the attempt to introduce hereditary chivalric titles into democratic Canada could feed "nothing but flunkeyism."
31 Tocqueville, *Democracy,* 270.
32 Ibid., 263. Later Tocqueville lists the judicial power as one of "three factors [that] seem to contribute more than all others to the maintenance of a democratic republic in the New World." The other two are federalism and communal institutions. Of the courts, Tocqueville says they "correct the aberrations of democracy" and "though they can never stop the movements of the majority, they do succeed in checking and directing them." 286–87.
33 Ibid., 269.
34 See F.L. Morton, "Judicial Activism in the Context of Popular Sovereignty: The French Experience," in Kenneth M. Holland, ed., *Judicial Activism in a Comparative Perspective* (New York: St. Martin's, 1991), ch. 9.
35 R.F. Adie and P.G. Thomas, *Canadian Public Administration: Problematical Perspectives,* 2nd ed. (Scarborough: Prentice-Hall, 1987). Quoted in Christian Jaekl, "The 'New' Judicial Ascendency: Are Legislators Abdicating Their Responsibilities?" unpublished manuscript.
36 J.A.G. Griffith, *The Politics of the Judiciary,* 3rd ed. (London: Fontana Press, 1985). Quoted in Jaekl, "The 'New' Judicial Ascendency."
37 See Richard Morgan, *Disabling America: The 'Rights Industry' in our Time* (New York: Basic Books, 1984).
38 Tocqueville, *Democracy,* 265.
39 Ibid.
40 Ibid., 265.
41 Ibid., 103.
42 *B.C.G.E.U.* v. *A.-G. B.C.*
43 Tocqueville, *Democracy,* 103.
44 Thomas Sowell, *A Conflict of Visions: Ideological Origins of Political Struggles* (New York: William Morrow, 1987).

45 Quoted in ibid., 20.
46 Ibid., 21.
47 Ibid., 23.
48 Quoted in ibid., 24.
49 Ibid.
50 Quoted in ibid.
51 Ibid.
52 Joseph Cropsey, "Conservatism and Liberalism," in his *Political Philosophy and the Issues of Politics* (Chicago: University of Chicago Press, 1977), 122.
53 Alexander Hamilton, James Madison, and John Jay, *The Federalist Papers* (New York: New American Library, 1961), 79.
54 Ibid.
55 Ibid., 78.
56 Cropsey, "Conservatism and Liberalism," 124–25.
57 Hamilton, Madison, and Jay, *The Federalist Papers*, 78.
58 Rainer Knopff, *Human Rights and Social Technology: The New War on Discrimination* (Ottawa: Carleton University Press, 1989), 18.
59 Sowell, *A Conflict of Visions,* 123. Emphasis in original.
60 Morgan, *Disabling America,* 139.
61 The following quote, complete with footnotes, is from Knopff, *Human Rights and Social Technology,* 18.
62 Plato, *The Republic,* 415(b).
63 Ibid., 460(c) & (d).
64 Cf. Yves Simon, *The Philosophy of Democratic Society* (Chicago: University of Chicago Press, 1951), 222–30.
65 Sowell, *Knowledge and Decisions,* 102.
66 Knopff, *Human Rights and Social Technology,* 21–22.
67 A. Alan Borovoy, *When Freedoms Collide: The Case for our Civil Liberties* (Toronto: Lester & Orpen Dennys, 1988), 203.
68 Ibid., 203–5.
69 See Sheilah Martin and Kathleen E. Mahoney, *Equality and Judicial Neutrality* (Toronto: Carswell, 1987).
70 Michael Mandel, *The Charter of Rights and the Legalization of Politics in Canada* (Toronto: Wall and Thompson, 1989), 49. See also Borovoy, *When Freedoms Collide,* ch. 10.
71 Mandel, *The Charter of Rights and the Legalization of Politics,* 55.
72 Ibid., 222–34.
73 Ibid., 55.
74 Ibid.
75 Quoted in ibid., 56, emphasis in original.
76 Ibid., 57.
77 Ibid.
78 Ibid., 52, emphasis in original.
79 Ibid., 57.
80 However, the provision of legal (even constitutional) status to groups defined by religious, racial, ethnic, sexual, and similar traits seems to be drawing liberal regimes back in the direction of an official status hierarchy.
81 For a critique of the idea that private property and economic interests are equivalent to governmental power see Sowell, *Knowledge and Decisions,* passim.

82 Mandel, *The Charter of Rights and the Legalization of Politics*, 58.

83 Ibid., 57.

84 Knopff, *Human Rights and Social Technology*, 41–44.

85 See M. Elizabeth Atcheson, Mary Eberts, and Beth Symes (with Jennifer Stoddart), *Women and Legal Action: Precedents, Resources and Strategies for the Future* (Ottawa: Canadian Advisory Council on the Status of Women, 1984).

86 Gwen Brodsky and Shelagh Day, *Canadian Charter Equality Rights for Women: One Step Forward or Two Steps Back?* (Ottawa: Canadian Advisory Council on the Status of Women, 1989), 29.

87 Ibid., 30.

88 Ibid., 58.

89 Ibid., 84.

90 Ibid., 58, 83–84.

91 Ibid., 58.

92 Mandel, *The Charter of Rights and the Legalization of Politics*, 265.

93 Brodsky and Day, *Equality Rights for Women*, 57.

94 Mandel, *The Charter of Rights and the Legalization of Politics*, 263–64.

95 Brodsky and Day, *Equality Rights for Women*, 57.

96 Note the subtitle to ibid. See note 86 above.

97 Ibid., 38.

98 Ibid., 87.

99 Mandel, *The Charter of Rights and the Legalization of Politics*, 267, emphasis added.

100 Ibid. Although expansion of the state at the expense of the private sphere is usually undertaken in the name of redistribution, the evidence shows "that the actual 'redistribution' of money and power from the public to the government vastly exceeds any 'redistribution' from one income class to another." Sowell, *Knowledge and Decisions*, 329.

101 *R.W.D.S.U.* v. *Dolphin Delivery Ltd.*, [1986] 2 S.C.R. 573. For critiques of the notion that governmental power is the primary danger to liberty, see Mandel, *The Charter of Rights and the Legalization of Politics;* Patrick Monahan, *Politics and the Constitution: The Charter, Federalism and the Supreme Court* (Toronto: Carswell/Methuen, 1987); and Andrew Petter, "Canada's Charter Flight: Soaring Backwards into the Future," *Journal of Law and Society* 16:2 (1989). Of course, the libertarian assumption that government is the only serious danger to civil liberties can also be criticized from a more conservative perspective. See Walter Berns, *Freedom, Virtue and the First Amendment* (New York: Greenwood, 1969), 158–60, 175.

102 Glasbeek and Mandel use the U.S. Court's approach to abortion to illustrate this point. On the one hand, the Court has prevented the state from officially prohibiting abortions during much of the pregnancy; on the other hand, it refuses to do anything about the unequal access to this new constitutional "freedom of choice" caused by economic indigency. The latter falls within the private sphere; it is not a matter of official governmental power. See Harry J. Glasbeek and Michael Mandel, "The Legalization of Politics in Advanced Capitalism: The Canadian Charter of Rights and Freedoms," *Socialist Studies* 2 (1984), 108–9.

103 What Tocqueville might have called "great party" extremes. See *Democracy*, 174–78.

Chapter Ten

1 *R.* v. *Morgentaler*, [1988] 1 S.C.R. 30.
2 *Borowski* v. *Canada (Attorney-General)*, [1989] 1 S.C.R. 342.
3 *Tremblay* v. *Daigle,* [1989] 2 S.C.R. 530.
4 The Trudeau government resisted pressure from both sides to deal with abortion in the Charter.
5 "Abortions rise to highest level ever," *Globe and Mail,* April 4, 1991, A4.
6 *Roe* v. *Wade,* 410 U.S. 113 (1973).
7 *R.* v. *Morgentaler,* [1974] C.A. 129 (Que. C.A.).
8 *Morgentaler* v. *The Queen,* [1976] 1 S.C.R. 616 (S.C.C.).
9 Ibid., 632.
10 The primary agents of the 1969 reform were the Canadian Medical Association and the Canadian Bar Association and the then minister of justice, Pierre Elliott Trudeau. See Alphonse de Valk, *Morality and Law in Canadian Politics: The Abortion Controversy* (Montreal: Palm Publishing, 1974).
11 See R. Knopff and F.L. Morton, "Nation Building and the Canadian Charter of Rights and Freedoms," in Alan Cairns and C. Williams, eds., *Constitutionalism, Citizenship, and Society in Canada* (Toronto: University of Toronto Press, 1986), 133–82. Also see Sandra Burt, "Women's Issues and the Women's Movement in Canada Since 1970," in Alan Cairns and C. Williams, eds. *The Politics of Gender, Ethnicity and Language in Canada* (Toronto: University of Toronto Press, 1986), 111–70.
12 *A.-G. Canada* v. *Lavell and Bedard,* [1974] 1 S.C.R. 1349.
13 *Bliss* v. *A.-G. Canada,* [1979] 1 S.C.R. 183.
14 See Leslie A. Pal and F.L. Morton, "Bliss v. Attorney-General of Canada: From Legal Defeat to Political Victory," *Osgoode Hall Law Journal* 24:1 (Spring 1986), 141–60.
15 *Morgentaler,* (1988) 163.
16 Ibid., 171.
17 Ibid., 173–74.
18 Ibid., 181.
19 Ibid., 182–83.
20 Ibid.
21 Ibid., 183.
22 Ibid., 133. To make the same point differently, if section 251 punished only the doctor who performed the abortion and not the woman/patient, this would be an open and shut case of criminal conspiracy, with no need or reason to explore the issue of a woman's right to an abortion.
23 Ibid., 137–38.
24 Ibid., 138–39.
25 Ibid., 141.
26 Ibid., 143.
27 Ibid., 143–46.
28 Ibid., 149.
29 Ibid., 151.
30 Ibid., 152–54.
31 Ibid., 157–58.
32 Ibid., 53.
33 Ibid., 69.
34 Ibid., 70.
35 Ibid., 56.

36 Ibid., 110.
37 Ibid., 121–22.
38 Ibid., 113.
39 *Minister of Justice et al.* v. *Borowski,* [1981] 2 S.C.R. 575 (S.C.C.).
40 *Borowski,* (1981) 587.
41 *Borowski,* (1989) 365.
42 *Mock* v. *Brandanburg* (1989), 61 A.L.R. (2d) 235.
43 *Diamond* v. *Hirsch,* unreported decision of Man. Q.B., rendered July 6, 1989.
44 *Maclean's,* July 31, 1989.
45 *Webster* v. *Reproductive Health Services,* 109 S.Ct. 3040 (1989).
46 *Tremblay* v. *Daigle,* [1989] R.J.Q. 1980 (Que. S.C.).
47 *Daigle* v. *Tremblay* (1989), 59 D.L.R. (4th) 609 (Que. C.A.).
48 The attorneys general of Canada and Quebec also sought and received intervener status, but did not argue the issue of the right to life of the unborn. Rather they focused on the federalism issue raised by the injunction: Does the issuance of an injunction that is based on provincial laws prohibiting an abortion, which is a matter of federal criminal jurisdiction, violate the federal division of powers? In the end, the Supreme Court did not address this issue.
49 Quoted in Robert D. Nadeau, "The Anatomy of Evasion: A Critique of Daigle," in Ian Gentles, ed., *A Time to Choose Life: Women, Abortion and Human Rights* (Toronto: Stoddart, 1990), 188.
50 The preamble and sections 1 and 2 of the Quebec Charter read as follows:
Whereas every human being possesses intrinsic rights and freedoms designed to ensure his protection and development;
Whereas all human beings are equal in worth and dignity, and are entitled to equal protection of the law;
1. Every human being has a right to life, and to personal security, inviolability and freedoms....
2. Every human being whose life is in peril has a right to assistance.
Every person must come to the aid of anyone whose life is in peril, either personally or calling for aid, by giving him the necessary and immediate physical assistance....
51 *Daigle,* (Que. C.A.) 632.
52 Articles 338, 345, 608, 771, 838, 945, and 2543 of the Civil Code.
53 *Daigle,* (Que. C.A.) 617.
54 Ibid., 613.
55 Ibid., 620.
56 *Daigle,* (S.C.C.) 538–39.
57 "Court lifts injunction after Daigle abortion.... Pro-choice advocates support decision," *Globe and Mail,* Aug. 9, 1989, A1.
58 *Chatelaine,* January 1990.
59 Since the Court answered this first question in the negative, it did not need to address the other two issues: Is an injunction the proper remedy in this case? Does the injunction encroach upon federal criminal law jurisdiction?
60 *Daigle,* (S.C.C.) 553.
61 Ibid., 555.
62 Ibid., 553.
63 Ibid., 553–54.
64 Ibid., 560.
65 *R.W.D.S.U.* v. *Dolphin Delivery,* [1986] 2 S.C.R. 573.
66 *Daigle,* (S.C.C.), 571.

67 The corollary issue of "father's rights" depended heavily on the existence of a prior finding of the "right to life" of the fetus. Once the latter was denied by the Court, the "father's rights" argument was quickly and easily dispatched.
68 *Daigle,* (S.C.C.) 565.
69 Ibid., 567.
70 Ibid., 563. Several abortion-injunction cases very similar to *Daigle* had been decided against the father/husband. The Court's version of the *Montreal Tramways* case was considered the controlling precedent in the area of tort law. The outcomes of cases under provincial child welfare legislation, however, were evenly divided between "mother's rights" and "fetal rights"—cases in which children's aid societies sought court orders to intervene to protect unborn children from the effects of the drug or alcohol abuse of their mothers. See *Montreal Tramways* v. *Léveillé,* [1933] S.C.R. 456.
71 *Daigle,* (S.C.C.) 571.
72 Quoted in Nadeau, "The Anatomy of Evasion," 188.
73 *Mortentaler,* (1988) 51–52.
74 *Daigle,* (S.C.C.) 553.
75 Ibid., 552.
76 *Morgentaler,* (1988) 166–67.
77 Nadeau, "The Anatomy of Evasion," 191.
78 Graham Fraser, "Mulroney sought compromise from Tory caucus on new bill," *Globe and Mail,* Nov. 4, 1989, A8.
79 Professor Bernard Dickens, quoted in Kirk Makin, "New law could face years of court challenges, Ottawa warned," *Globe and Mail,* Nov. 4, 1989, A8.
80 Mary Ann Glendon, *Abortion and Divorce in Western Law* (Cambridge, Mass.: Harvard University Press, 1987), 40.
81 "Abortion bill draws hail of criticism; Lack of accessibility, protection for fetus cited," *Globe and Mail,* Nov. 4, 1989, A1.
82 L.A. Pal, "How Ottawa Dithers: The Conservatives and Abortion Policy," in Frances Abele, ed., *How Ottawa Spends* (Ottawa: Carleton University Press, 1991), 296.
83 "Ministers in abortion debate appeal for calm, compromise," *Globe and Mail,* Nov. 8, 1989, A5.
84 Cf. Allan Hutchinson, "Challenging the abortion law," *Globe and Mail,* Nov. 13, 1989, A7.
85 Cf. Sheilah L. Martin, "The New Abortion Legislation," in *Constitutional Forum* 1:2 (Winter 1990), 5–7.
86 Quoted in Makin, "New law could face years of court challenges."
87 Mary Eberts, "The Use of Litigation Under the Canadian Charter of Rights and Freedoms as a Strategy for Achieving Change," in Neil Nevitte and Allan Kornberg, eds., *Minorities and The Canadian State* (Oakville, Ont.: Mosaic Press, 1985), 53.
88 Recall the ability of feminists to convert legal defeats under the 1960 Bill of Rights into political victories, discussed at the outset of this chapter.

Chapter Eleven

1 *Re Reynolds and A.-G. B.C.* (1982), 143 D.L.R. (3d) 365 (B.C.S.C.).
2 *Re Reynolds and A.-G. B.C.* (1984), 11 D.L.R. (4th) 380 (B.C.C.A.); leave to appeal to S.C.C. granted Oct. 22, 1984 (1984), 11 D.L.R. (4th) 380, and abandoned Feb. 16, 1988.

3 *Badger* v. *A.-G. Manitoba* (1986), 51 C.R. (3d) 163 (Man. Q.B.); appeal re: remedies dismissed (1986), 32 D.L.R. (4th) 310 (Man. C.A.); appeal on merits abandoned (1990), 57 C.C.C. (3d) 436 (Man. C.A.).
4 *Grondin* v. *Ontario (A.-G.)* (1988), 65 O.R. (2d) 427.
5 Ibid., 432.
6 *Re Jolivet and Barker and The Queen* (1983), 1 D.L.R. (4th) 604.
7 Ibid., 608.
8 *Badger* v. *A.-G. Canada* (1989), 55 M.R. (2d) 211 (Man. Q.B.).
9 *Sauvé* v. *The Queen* (1988), 66 O.R. (2d) 234.
10 The hearing ran from September 12 through September 15, and the election was called on October 1.
11 *Badger* v. *A.-G. Canada* (1989), 55 M.R. (2d) 198 (Man. C.A.) 201; leave to appeal dismissed, [1989] 1 S.C.R. v.
12 Ibid., see generally Justice Monnin at 203–5 and Justice Philp at 207–8.
13 Ibid., Justice Philp at 207 and 208.
14 Ibid., 200.
15 Ibid.
16 Ibid., 202. Chief Justice Monnin's reasoning in this context is very similar to some of the original justifications for establishing a Federal Court. See Peter H. Russell, *The Judiciary in Canada: The Third Branch of Government* (Toronto: McGraw-Hill Ryerson, 1987), 313.
17 *Belczowski* v. *The Queen*, (unreported at time of writing) decision rendered Feb. 28, 1991, Court No. T-1182-88, draft judgment, 3.
18 While the Federal Court is based in Ottawa, its judges travel around the country to hear cases.
19 *Belczowski*, 4.
20 Justice Van Camp took fifty-three days while Justice Strayer took only thirty-five. Nor did Justice Strayer note that *Jolivet*, which was also against him, was not decided in a rush.
21 *Badger* v. *A.-G. Canada*, 209–10 (Man. C.A.).
22 Ibid., 202.
23 Ibid.
24 "It appears to me that this view of Charter rights is based on the 'frozen concept' interpretation applied to the Canadian Bill of Rights. It is my understanding that the Supreme Court of Canada has rejected this concept as a guide to the interpretation of the Charter," *Belczowski*, 7.
25 *Re Jolivet*, 606.
26 Ibid.
27 Ibid.
28 *Belczowski*, 17.
29 Ibid.
30 Ibid., 20.
31 Ibid., 17.
32 Ibid., 19.
33 *Sauvé*, 238.
34 *Badger* v. *A.-G. Manitoba*, 170 (Man. Q.B.).
35 John C. Courtney, "Prisoners and the Right to Vote," a brief prepared for *Badger* v. *A.-G. Manitoba*.
36 Ibid., 2.
37 Ibid.
38 Ibid., 3–4.
39 Ibid., 4.

40 Ibid.

41 House of Commons *Debates,* April 28, 1898, columns 4461–69. These columns cover the debate on section 6, subsection 4, which disqualified criminals, lunatics, and paupers. Not a word was said on the first of these.

42 *Belczowski,* 16.

43 Ibid.

44 George Grant, *Technology and Empire: Perspectives on North America* (Toronto: Anansi, 1969), 48. See also Alexander M. Bickel, *The Morality of Consent* (New Haven: Yale University Press, 1975), 106–7.

45 *Belczowski,* 15.

46 Alexander Hamilton, James Madison, and John Jay, *The Federalist Papers* (New York: New American Library, 1961), 465.

47 I. Jennings, *The Law and the Constitution,* 5th ed. (London: University of London Press, 1959), 343.

48 See W.R. Lederman, *Continuing Canadian Constitutional Dilemmas* (Toronto: Butterworths, 1981), 193–94; L. Fuller, "Positivism and Fidelity to Law— A Reply to Professor Hart," in J. Feinberg and H. Gross, eds., *Law in Philosophical Perspective* (Belmont: Wadsworth, 1977), 71.

49 Jennings, *The Law and the Constitution,* 346.

50 J. Austin, *Lectures on Jurisprudence,* R. Campbell, ed. (London: J. Murray, 1904), 105–6.

51 This seems to be true of Kelsen's Grundnorm and Hart's rule of recognition. See Fuller, "Positivism and Fidelity to Law," 71.

52 See H.L.A. Hart, *The Concept of Law* (Oxford: Clarendon Press, 1961), 23; Jennings, *The Law and the Constitution,* 344.

53 Lederman, *Continuing Canadian Constitutional Dilemmas,* 7.

54 *Belczowski,* 16.

55 Quoted in Walter Berns, *For Capital Punishment: Crime and the Morality of the Death Penalty* (New York: Basic Books, 1979), 132.

56 Quoted in ibid.

57 Plato, *The Laws,* 650b.

58 John Locke, *A Letter Concerning Toleration* (The Hague: Martinus Nijhoff, 1963), 14–17, quoted in Thomas L. Pangle, "Executive Energy and Popular Spirit in Lockean Constitutionalism," *Presidential Studies Quarterly* 17:2 (1987), 257.

59 Hamilton, *The Federalist Papers,* 346.

60 John Stuart Mill, *On Liberty,* Currin V. Shields, ed. (Indianapolis: Bobbs-Merrill, 1956), 14.

61 Ibid., 13.

62 Ibid., 14.

63 Hilail Gildin, "Mill's On Liberty," in Joseph Cropsey, ed., *Ancients and Moderns: Essays on the Tradition of Political Philosophy, in Honour of Leo Strauss* (New York: Basic Books, 1964).

64 Mill, *On Liberty,* ch. 2.

65 Patrick Devlin, *The Enforcement of Morals* (London: Oxford University Press, 1965), 108.

66 Ibid., 107–8.

67 Thomas Sowell, *A Conflict of Visions* (New York: William Morrow, 1987), 150.

68 See Walter Berns, *The First Amendment and the Future of American Democracy* (New York: Basic Books, 1977), chs. 1 and 2.

69 Hamilton, Madison, and Jay, *The Federalist Papers,* 84.

70 Thomas Jefferson, *Notes on the State of Virginia* (New York: Harper and Row, 1964), 156.
71 Wayne MacKay and Gordon Krinke, "Education as a Basic Human Right: A Response to Special Education and the Charter," 2 *Canadian Journal of Law and Society* (1987), 85–86.
72 Berns, *The First Amendment,* ch. 1.
73 *Everson* v. *Board of Education,* 330 U.S. 1 (1947).
74 See Ralph Rossum and G. Alan Tarr, *American Constitutional Law* (New York: St. Martin's Press, 1991), 413–15; Richard E. Morgan, *Disabling America, The "Rights Industry" in Our Time* (New York: Basic Books, 1984), ch. 2.
75 *Reference re Bill 30, An Act to Amend the Education Act,* [1987] 1 S.C.R. 1148.
76 See *Zylberberg* v. *Sudbury Board of Education* (1989), 52 D.L.R. (4th) 577; *Corporation of the Canadian Civil Liberties Association* v. *Ontario (Minister of Education)* (1990), 65 D.L.R. (4th) 1 (Ont. C.A.); *Russow* v. *B.C. (A.-G.)* (1989), 62 D.L.R. (4th) 98.
77 Quoted in Berns, *For Capital Punishment,* 143–44. On the educational function of criminal law, see also Mary Ann Glendon, *Abortion and Divorce in Western Law* (Cambridge, Mass.: Harvard University Press, 1987), 29–30.
78 Berns, *For Capital Punishment,* 8.
79 *R.* v. *Keegstra* (1990), 117 N.R. 1.
80 Ibid., 75.
81 Ibid.
82 Glendon, *Abortion and Divorce,* 58. The second part of this quotation is itself Glendon's quotation of Clifford Geertz, *Local Knowledge: Further Essays in Interpretive Anthropology* (New York: Basic Books, 1983), 217.
83 Glendon, *Abortion and Divorce,* 59.
84 Ibid., 111.
85 J.S. Mill, "Thoughts on Parliamentary Reform," in *Essays on Politics and Society,* vol. XIX of *The Collected Works of John Stuart Mill* (Toronto: University of Toronto Press, 1977), 322.
86 *Sauvé,* 240.
87 *Belczowski,* 16–17.
88 This point was first brought to our attention by Courtney, "Prisoners and the Right to Vote," 5.
89 Albert E. McKinley, *The Suffrage Franchise in the Thirteen Colonies in America* (New York, 1905), 275.
90 Ibid., 324.
91 Ibid., 388.
92 Ibid., 448.
93 Thomas Hobbes, *Leviathan,* C.B. Macpherson, ed. (Harmondsworth: Penguin, 1968), 214, emphasis added.
94 *Belczowski,* 21–22.
95 Ibid., 22–23.
96 Ibid., 16.
97 Glendon, *Abortion and Divorce,* 7.
98 *Belczowski,* 22.
99 Ibid.
100 Electoral Code, article L 5.
101 *R.* v. *Edwards Books and Art Ltd.,* [1986] 2 S.C.R. 713 (S.C.C.) 781–83, 794–95; *Irwin Toy Ltd.* v. *Quebec (A.-G.),* [1989] 1 S.C.R. 927; *Reference re Public Service Employee Relations Act,* [1985] 2 W.W.R. 289 (Alta. C.A.); appeal dismissed [1987] 1 S.C.R. 313; *McKinney* v. *University of Guelph* (1990), 118 N.R. 1.

Chapter Twelve

1 *Reynolds* v. *Sims*, 377 U.S. 533, 562 (1964).
2 *Baker* v. *Carr*, 369 U.S. 186 (1962).
3 *Wesberry* v. *Sanders*, 376 U.S. 1 (1964).
4 Earl Warren, *The Memoirs of Earl Warren* (Garden City, N.Y.: Doubleday, 1977), 306–8.
5 See Robert G. Dixon, Jr., *Democratic Representation: Reapportionment in Law and Practice* (New York: Oxford University Press, 1968).
6 *Dixon* v. *B.C. (A.-G.)*, [1989] 4 W.W.R. 393.
7 For a more detailed account of electoral redistribution in British Columbia, see Norman J. Ruff, "The Cat and Mouse Politics of Redistribution: Fair and Effective Representation in British Columbia," *BC Studies* 87 (1990).
8 *Dixon*, 403.
9 Ibid., 413.
10 Ibid., 431.
11 Ibid., 431–32.
12 Ibid., 420.
13 Electoral Boundaries Commission Act, S.A. 1990, c. E-4.01.
14 An exception from this rule is made for up to four divisions, which will be allowed to have as much as 50 percent less population than the average. To qualify for this exception, certain specified criteria must be met [s.17(2)]. This limited exception for divisions under the normal 25 percent lower limit is not replicated for divisions at the other end of the size continuum: no constituency is allowed to exceed the 25 percent upper limit.
15 Electoral Boundaries Commission Act, S.S. 1986–87–88, c. E-6.1.
16 For convenience we are including the two "northern" districts in the "rural" category. Section 14 of the Saskatchewan Electoral Boundaries Commission Act actually divided the province into "urban," "rural," and "northern" segments.
17 From the recruitment letter of "The Society for the Advancement of Voter Equality Inc." No date.
18 "Professors to test riding boundaries law," *Saskatoon Star Phoenix*, Jan. 10, 1990, A3; "Group to challenge legality of changes," *Regina Leader Post*, Jan. 9, 1990, A4.
19 Ibid.
20 Murray Mandryk, the legislative bureau chief for the *Regina Leader Post*, wrote that because it would be politically "unwise for the NDP to be zealous in the promotion of one-person, one-vote," it has instead "relied on nine user-friendly academics to carry the ball for them." May 18, 1990, A4.
21 Ron Fritz, "Boundary revision challenge could succeed, law professor says," *Saskatoon Star Phoenix*, Aug. 26, 1988, A3.
22 *Reference re Saskatchewan Electoral Boundaries*, (unreported at time of writing) Sask. C.A., decision rendered March 6, 1991, file no. 639, draft judgment.
23 See "Voter imbalance sparks legal fight," *Calgary Herald*, Nov. 1, 1990, B1; "Province hit with second lawsuit," *Calgary Herald*, Nov. 3, 1990, B3; and "Redrawing the electoral map," *Alberta Report*, Sept. 17, 1990, 6.
24 Electoral Boundaries Commission Act, S.A. 1990, s. 12(a).
25 *Saskatchewan Reference*, 41. Emphasis added.
26 *Reynolds* v. *Sims*, 579.
27 *Saskatchewan Reference*, 23.

28 Ibid., 21.
29 Ibid.
30 Ibid., 24.
31 Ibid., 30.
32 Ibid., 38–39.
33 Ibid., 40.
34 Ibid., 47–48.
35 Ibid., 46.
36 Ibid., 48.
37 Ibid., 51.
38 Ibid., 49.
39 Ibid., 50.
40 "Tory accusations NDP trying to destroy rural vote 'despicable,'" *Saskatoon Star Phoenix,* March 9, 1991, A11.
41 The authors prepared a report for the Edmonton lawfirm of Field and Field, Perraton Masuch, who represented the Alberta government. Barry Cooper (Pol. Sci.) and David Bercuson (History) of the University of Calgary prepared a study for the City of Calgary. Allan Tupper (Pol. Sci.) of the University of Alberta did the same for the City of Edmonton. Keith Archer (Pol. Sci.) and Sheilah Martin (Law) of the University of Calgary were retained by the New Democratic Party. Peter McCormick (Pol. Sci.) of the University of Lethbridge prepared a study for the Liberal Party, while Roger Gibbins (Pol. Sci.) of the University of Calgary provided advice for the Alberta Association of Municipal Districts and Counties. By our rough estimate, between January and May 1991, consulting costs alone for the Alberta case were at least $50 thousand. (One can be assured that legal fees were at least double this figure.) If nothing else, this explains why the "People's Package" is so popular with lawyers and academics!
42 While new evidence cannot be introduced, "published authorities" can be.
43 As there is no real opponent in a reference case, courts will appoint one to ensure opposing interests and arguments are adequately presented and considered.
44 David J. Bercuson and Barry Cooper, "Maintaining a tyranny of the minority," *Globe and Mail,* June 18, 1991, A16.
45 *Colegrove* v. *Green,* 328 U.S. 549 (1946).
46 Laurence Tribe, *American Constitutional Law,* 2nd ed. (Mineola, N.Y.: The Foundation Press, 1988), 1065.
47 Robert G. Dixon, "Fair Criteria and Procedures for Establishing Legislative Districts," in Bernard Grofman, Arend Lijphart, Robert B. McKay, and Howard A. Scarrow, eds., *Representation and Redistricting Issues* (Lexington, Mass.: Lexington Books, 1982), 12.
48 See *Baker* v. *Carr.*
49 Dixon, "Fair Criteria and Procedures," 7–19.
50 Herman Pritchett, "Representation and the Rule of Equality," in Robert A. Goldwin, ed., *Representation and Misrepresentation* (Chicago: Rand McNally, 1966), 19.
51 John C. Courtney, "Theories Masquerading as Principles: Canadian Electoral Boundary Commissions and the Australian Model," in John C. Courtney, ed., *The Canadian House of Commons: Essays in Honour of Norman Ward* (Calgary: University of Calgary Press, 1985), 135.

52   See Ruff, "The Cat and Mouse Politics of Redistribution"; R.K. Carty, "The Electoral Boundary Revolution in Canada," *American Review of Canadian Studies* 15 (1985).
53   The majority opinion in *Davis* v. *Bandemer*, 478 U.S. 109, 133 (1986), defined an unconstitutional gerrymander as "continued frustration of the will of the majority of the voters or effective denial to a minority of voters of a fair chance to influence the political process." Commentators have interpreted this to mean "long-run and fundamental political disadvantage," a test that presumably every Canadian province would pass.
54   David Roberts, "Electoral Waterloo predicted for Saskatchewan Premier: Tories trailing NDP by 44 percentage points, poll shows," *Globe and Mail*, June 6, 1991.
55   *Reynolds* v. *Sims*, 577.
56   Tribe, *American Constitutional Law*, 1069.
57   However, it also identified certain other objectives as impermissible, including "history ... economic or other sorts of group interests ... keeping districts a manageable size ... and balancing urban and rural interests in the state legislature." See ibid., 1072.
58   Ibid., 1069.
59   Ibid.
60   In a certain sense the majority's failure to give a precise rule vindicates Frankfurter's dissent. Notice that Justice McLachlin did almost the same thing in *Dixon*.
61   *Kirkpatrick* v. *Preisler*, 394 U.S. 526, 530–31 (1969).
62   Ibid.
63   *White* v. *Weiser*, 412 U.S. 783 (1973).
64   *Karcher* v. *Daggett*, 462 U.S. 725 (1983).
65   This was made explicit in *Maryland Committee for Fair Representation* v. *Tawes*, 377 U.S. 656 (1964).
66   *Reynolds* v. *Sims*, 578.
67   *Mahan* v. *Howell*, 410 U.S. 315 (1973).
68   Tribe, *American Constitutional Law*, 1070.
69   Ibid., 1071; *Brown* v. *Thompson*, 103 S.Ct. 2690 (1983).
70   Courtney, "Federalism and Representation: Voter Equality and Electoral Reapportionment in Canada and The United States," A Presentation to the Conference on Comparative Federalism: Changing Theory and Practice in the Adaptive Canadian and American Federal Systems, at Nelson A. Rockefeller Center for the Social Sciences (Hanover, New Hampshire: Dartmouth College, Feb. 6, 1991), 17.
71   John Courtney, "Parliament and Representation: The Unfinished Agenda of Electoral Redistributions," *Canadian Journal of Political Science* 21:4 (1988).
72   *Dixon*, 404.
73   Quoted in R. MacGregor Dawson, *The Government of Canada*, 4th ed. Revised by Norman Ward (Toronto: University of Toronto Press, 1963), 304.
74   *Dixon*, 410.
75   Electoral Boundaries Readjustment Act, 13 Eliz. II, c. 31, s. 13(a).
76   Elections Canada, *Representation in the Federal Parliament* (Ottawa: Minister of Supply and Services, 1986), 12.
77   Courtney, "Theories Masquerading as Principles," 136.
78   Ibid.
79   *Saskatchewan Reference*, 15.

80 *Reference re s. 94(2) of the B.C. Motor Vehicle Act,* [1985] 2 S.C.R. 486 (S.C.C.) 509.

81 *Saskatchewan Reference,* 11–12.

82 Electoral Boundaries Readjustment Act, R.S.C. 1985, c. E-2. The 25 percent rule applies to *provinces only* [section 15(2)]. All that is said of the Yukon Territory is that it has one electoral district (section 30). Section 15 applies to the provinces and the Northwest Territories, which has two electoral districts. Subsection (1) requires the commissions to divide electoral districts and create boundaries on the basis of population, corresponding as "nearly as may be" to the electoral boundaries. This general rule may be departed from where required or deemed desirable by the "geographical sizes and shapes of the electoral districts," or by any "special consideration or diversity of interest of the inhabitants." Provincial commissions may also account for other special geographical considerations, including a sparse or dense population and accessibility of the region, whereas the Northwest Territories commission may instead consider the ease of transportation and communication within the electoral district.

83 Ibid.

84 This calculation is based on the statistics presented in Table 4 of the Revised Appendices of the "Report of the Chief Electoral Officer: Thirty-Fourth General Election, 1988." We here use the "true" average, which is the total population of Canada divided by 295, or 85 794. This is smaller than the "official" quotient of 87 005, which is calculated using a divider of 279, as specified by the amalgam formula.

85 See Tables 17 and 19 in Courtney, "Theories Masquerading as Principles," 163, 165.

86 Courtney, "Parliament and Representation," 680–81.

87 This evidence was based on a statistical measurement known as the GINI index, which is widely used by Canadian social scientists. When opposing lawyers asked permission to call an "expert witness" to explain the GINI index, the Court refused, saying that such explanation was not necessary. The Court obviously took this approach not because it was satisfied with its understanding of the GINI index, but because it intended to ignore the evidence altogether.

88 Marc Kilgour, "A Formal Analysis of the Amending Formula of Canada's Constitution Act, 1982," *Canadian Journal of Political Science* 16 (1983), 769.

89 Terrence J. Levesque and James W. Moore, "Citizen and Provincial Power Under Alternative Amending Formulae: An Extension of Kilgour's Analysis," *Canadian Journal of Political Science* 17 (1984), 163.

90 *Carter* v. *Saskatchewan (A.-G.),* S.C.C., decision rendered June 6, 1991, unreported at time of writing, draft judgment.

91 *Carter,* draft judgment of McLachlin J., 8.

92 Ibid., 9.

93 Ibid., 10–11.

94 Ibid., 16.

95 Ibid., 11.

96 Ibid., 16.

97 Ibid., 9–10.

98 Ibid., 10.

99 Ibid., 11.

100 Ibid., 12–13.

101 Ibid., draft judgment of Sopinka J., 1–2.

102 Ibid., draft judgment of McLachlin J., 21.

103 Ibid., 24.

104 Ibid.

105 Ibid., draft judgment of Sopinka J., 2.

106 Ibid., 3.

107 Gordon Baker, "What ever happened to the Reapportionment Revolution in the U.S.," in Bernard Grofman and Arend Lijphart, eds., *Electoral Laws and Their Political Consequences* (New York: Agathon Press, 1986), 269.

108 Ibid., 271.

109 Ibid., 270.

110 Ibid., 271.

111 While the number of seats in the House of Representatives assigned to each state is determined by Congress, the actual electoral boundaries are drawn by the governments of each state. Thus whichever political party controls a state's legislative process after each decennial census (1980, 1990, etc.) can carve the state's congressional districts in a way that maximizes their electoral strength.

112 For a graphic analysis of the California gerrymander, see Leroy Hardy and Alan Heslop, *The Westside Story: A Murder in Four Acts* (Claremont, Calif.: The Rose Institute of State and Local Government, 1990).

113 Baker, "The Reapportionment Revolution," 272.

114 See "Political Gerrymandering: *Badham* v. *Eu*, Political Science Goes to Court." *P.S.* 18:3 (1985). This "mini-symposium" recounts the participation of four political scientists as expert witnesses in a case challenging the California congressional districting plan described above. Predictably, the "experts" were evenly divided between the two sides!

115 "Inside Job: Native MPs demand guaranteed representation," *Alberta Report*, May 27, 1991, 11.

116 *Operation Dismantle Inc.* v. *The Queen*, [1985] 1 S.C.R. 441.

117 Patrick Monahan, *Politics and the Constitution* (Toronto: Carswell/Methuen, 1987), 52–53.

118 *Carter*, 15.

119 Ibid.

120 "Border war over built-in favouritism," *Alberta Report*, June 24, 1991, 10.

121 Cf. Ward E.Y. Elliot, *The Rise of Guardian Democracy: The Supreme Court's Role in Voting Rights Disputes, 1845–1969* (Boston: Harvard University Press, 1974), 2. It is significant that Australians, voting in national referendums in 1988, rejected a proposed constitutional amendment entrenching the principle of "one vote, one value" in part because "the citizens of each State political community should have the right to choose their own electoral system." See Campbell Sharman, "The Referendum Results and Their Context," in Brian Galligan and J.R. Nethercote eds., *The Constitutional Commission and the 1988 Referendums* (Canberra: Centre for Research on Federal Financial Relations, 1989), 112.

122 *Colegrove* v. *Green*, 552.

123 Ibid., 556.

124 Ibid., 553.

125 Ibid., 556.

126 *Baker* v. *Carr*, 267.

127 Ibid., 300.

128 Ibid., 267.

129 *Brown* v. *Board of Education*, 347 U.S. 537 (1896).

130 Ibid., 226.
131 Ibid., 269–70.
132 *Davis* v. *Bandemer*, 166–67.
133 Ibid., 164.
134 Ibid., 147.
135 Ibid.
136 Ibid., 145.
137 *Washington* v. *Davis*, 426 U.S. 229, 248 (1976).
138 *Andrews* v. *Law Society of British Columbia*, [1989] 1 S.C.R. 143 (S.C.C.) 174.
139 *Davis* v. *Bandemer*, 133.
140 Ibid., 132.
141 Frank Sorauf, review of *Political Gerrymandering and the Courts*, by Bernard Grofman, ed., *The Law and Politics Book Review* 1:1 (1991).

Chapter Thirteen

1 *R.* v. *Edwards Books and Art Ltd.*, [1986] 2 S.C.R. 713.
2 Ibid., 795.
3 This would be the effect of David Beatty's insistence that in section 1 analysis virtually all of the action falls under the minimal impairment test, and that this test should be stringently applied. This approach would clearly make the least intrusive provincial legislation in any policy area the standard for the rest of the provinces. See the discussion of Beatty's views in Chapter Three. Cf. Katherine Swinton, *The Supreme Court and Canadian Federalism: The Laskin-Dickson Years* (Toronto: Carswell, 1990), 341 n. 62.
4 *Edwards Books*, 801.
5 See Ian T. Urquhart, "Federalism, Ideology, and Charter Review: Alberta's Response to Morgentaler," *Canadian Journal of Law and Society* 4 (1989), 159–60.
6 Peter Hogg, "Federalism Fights the Charter of Rights," in David P. Shugarman and Reg Whitaker, eds., *Federalism and Political Community: Essays in Honour of Donald Smiley* (Peterborough: Broadview Press, 1989), 257–60; Swinton, *The Supreme Court and Canadian Federalism*, 342–48. Hogg's suggestion in this regard is somewhat more implicit than Swinton's.
7 *R.* v. *Turpin*, [1989] 1 S.C.R. 1296.
8 *R.* v. *Lyons*, [1987] 2 S.C.R. 309.
9 *R.* v. *S.(S.) (Sheldon S)*, [1990] 2 S.C.R. 254.
10 Swinton, *The Supreme Court and Canadian Federalism*, 343.
11 *Lyons*, 349.
12 *Sheldon S.*, 289.
13 F.L. Morton, G. Solomon, I. McNish, and D.W. Poulton, "Judicial Nullification of Statutes under the Charter of Rights and Freedoms, 1982–1988," *Alberta Law Review* 28:2 (1990). It should be noted that only about one-third of all Charter cases during this period involved challenges to statutes. The other two-thirds concerned official conduct in the enforcement of legislation—e.g., police conduct in enforcing the criminal law.
14 There have been 256 challenges to federal statutes and only 119 to provincial statutes. The success ratio for challenges is thus 26 percent for provincial and 12.5 percent for federal statutes. Ibid.

15 F.L. Morton, Peter H. Russell, and Michael J. Withey, "The Supreme Court's First One Hundred Charter of Rights Decisions: A Statistical Analysis," *Osgoode Hall Law Journal* (forthcoming).

16 *A.-G. Quebec* v. *Quebec Association of Protestant School Boards*, [1984] 2 S.C.R. 66.

17 René Lévesque, quoted in 26 *Journal des Débats* 4 (Nov. 9, 1981).

18 See Robert A. Dahl, "Decision-Making in a Democracy: The Supreme Court as a National Policy-Maker," *Journal of Public Law* 6 (1957).

19 See for example, *Reference re Alberta Statutes*, [1938] 2 S.C.R. 100, and *Switzman* v. *Elbling*, [1957] 2 S.C.R. 285.

20 Alan C. Cairns, "Citizens (Outsiders) and Governments (Insiders) in Constitution-Making: The Case of Meech Lake," *Canadian Public Policy* 14 (1988), S122.

21 Sanford Levinson, *Constitutional Faith* (Princeton, N.J.: Princeton University Press, 1988), 17. Cf. Hogg, "Federalism Fights the Charter," 249–50.

22 See Ian T. Urquhart, "Federalism, Ideology, and Charter Review: Alberta's Response to Morgentaler," *Canadian Journal of Law and Society* 4 (1989).

23 Ibid., 161–62.

24 This information is reported by Christine Rideout in her honours thesis for the Department of Political Science, University of Calgary, 1990.

25 *Quebec* v. *Ford*, [1988] 2 S.C.R. 712.

26 *Quebec Association of Protestant School Boards*.

27 See F.L. Morton, "The Political Impact of the Canadian Charter of Rights and Freedoms," *Canadian Journal of Political Science* 20:1 (1987), 46–47.

28 *Reference re Public Service Employee Relations Act* (The Alberta Labour Reference), [1987] 1 S.C.R. 313.

29 See the discussion of this point in Chapter Four.

30 Jennifer Smith, "Intrastate Federalism and Confederation," in Stephen Brooks, ed., *Political Thought in Canada: Contemporary Perspectives* (Toronto: Irwin, 1984), 273.

INDEX

activism (*see* judicial review)

Adkins v. *Children's Hospital*, 414

Advisory Council on the Status of Women, 87

affirmative action, 93 (*see also* discrimination)

A.-G. Manitoba et al. v. *A.-G. Canada et al.* (1981, Patriation Case), 17–18, 72, 188

A.-G. Manitoba v. *Manitoba Egg and Poultry Association* (Chicken and Egg Reference), 404

A.-G. Ontario v. *A.-G. Canada* (1912, Validity of References Case), 188, 420

A.-G. Quebec v. *Quebec Association of Protestant School Boards*, 27–28, 379

Agresto, John, 151, 206, 207, 226–29, 249

Alberta Labour Reference (see *Ref. re Public Service Employee Relations Act*)

Alberta Press Case (see *Ref. re Alberta Statutes*)

amendment (*see* constitutional amendment)

Andenaes, Johannes, 318

Andrews v. *Law Society of British Columbia*, 29, 406, 421, 440

appointments (*see* judicial appointments)

Attorney General of British Columbia v. *Attorney General of Canada* (1934, Natural Products Marketing Act Reference), 414

Attorney General of Canada and Dupond v. *Montreal*, 408

Attorney General of Canada v. *Attorney General of Ontario* (1935, Employment and Social Insurance Act Reference), 414

Attorney General of Canada v. *Attorney General of Ontario* (1937, Labour Conventions Case), 414

Attorney General of Canada v. *Canadian National Transportation*, 410

Attorney General of Canada v. *Lavell and Bedard*, 402, 429

Attorney General of Quebec v. *Blaikie*, 413

Austin, John, 305, 306

Australia, 138, 161–62, 165, 199, 201–3, 204

Baar, Carl, 217, 218, 424

Baar, Ellen, 424

Badger v. *Canada*, 103–6, 294–99

Badger v. *Manitoba*, 104–6, 293–94, 304

Badgley Report, 271, 272, 287

Baker, Gordon, 360

Baker v. *Carr*, 334, 344, 367, 368

B.C.G.E.U. v. *British Columbia*, 189, 241

Beatty, David, 42–43, 45, 132–33, 155–56, 158–59, 440

Beccaria, Cesare, 309

Belczowski v. *The Queen*, 296–304, 307, 322–31

Bender, Paul, 44–46

Bennett, R.B., 63

Berns, Walter, 319–20

biculturalism, 75, 197, 201, 203

bilingualism, 75, 88

Bill C-55 (refugee determination), 24

Bill C-43 (abortion), 22, 289, 290, 291

Bill 53 (abortion), 404

Bill of Rights: Canada (*see* Canadian Bill of Rights and Charter of Rights); Quebec (*see* Quebec); United States (*see* United States Constitution)

Bill 101 (language), 27, 379, 380, 383

Bindman, Stephen, 423, 424

Birks and Sons (Montreal) Ltd. v. *Montreal*, 408

Black, Dawn, 290

Clarkson v. *The Queen*, 402, 407
class dealignment, 92, 93
Colegrove v. *Green*, 344, 439
Constitution Act, 1982, 13, 18, 29, 36, 85, 86, 89, 140, 163, 232, 334, 353, 383: **section 35**, 80; **section 52**, 36–37, 178 (*see also* Charter of Rights and Freedoms)
constitutional amendment, 13–18, 76, 83–85, 86, 89, 94, 108, 123, 139, 140, 141, 144, 150, 151, 162, 168, 203, 228, 269, 284, 353, 354
conventions, 17, 72, 138, 142
Cooper v. *Aaron*, 420
Corry, J.A., 64
Corwin, Edward S., 190
Cotroni (see *United States of America* v. *Cotroni*)
Court Challenges Program, 27, 29, 275, 379
court party, 58, 79, 123
Courtney, John, 92, 302, 303, 351
Cowan, Suzanne (a.k.a. Suzanne Bertrand) v. *The Commission of the Yukon Territory*, 403

Dahl, Robert, 206, 207
Daigle v. *Tremblay*, 8, 29, 261, 279–88
Davis v. *Bandemer*, 368–71
Davis, William, 31, 32
Day, Shelagh, 255
deconstructionism (*see* interpretation)
desegregation, 64, 127, 128, 368
determinism: legal, 67–68, 69; sociological, 68–69
deterrence, 52, 299, 301, 313, 318, 319, 323, 328
Devine, Grant, 30, 342
Devlin, Lord Patrick, 316
Diamond v. *Hirsch*, 430
Diefenbaker, John, 19, 65, 130
discrimination, 41, 42, 87, 88, 127, 164: reverse, 93; systemic, 41 (*see also* affirmative action)
Dixon, Robert, 334
Dixon, Sir Owen, 199, 201

Dixon v. *A.-G. British Columbia*, 334–36, 339, 342, 346, 349, 354, 355, 363, 364
Dodd, Barbara, 277, 278
Dolphin Delivery (see *R.W.D.S.U.* v. *Dolphin Delivery*)
Dostoevsky, Fyodor, 309, 312
Dred Scott v. *Sandford*, 176–77
Drybones (see *Queen, The* v. *Drybones*)
dualism, 86–89
Dubois v. *The Queen*, 111–12 129, 130, 132, 148
due process, 112, 114, 120, 130, 145, 216, 220: procedural, 114, 130, 135, 379; substantive, 113–16, 125, 130, 135, 136, 295, 307, 308, 330, 379
Duplessis, Maurice, 70
Dworkin, Ronald, 115, 119–25, 145, 149, 251, 288

Eakin v. *Raub*, 172
electoral boundaries: Alberta, 25, 92, 332, 336–39, 343, 359; British Columbia, 25, 332, 335, 336, 364; Canada, 333, 345, 353; New Brunswick, 345, 354, 364; Nova Scotia, 345, 354, 364, 365; Prince Edward Island, 345, 353, 354, 364, 365; Saskatchewan, 25, 332, 336, 337, 340–42, 345, 351–53, 356, 357, 364, 366, 371, 372
Elliott, Ward, 367
Ely, John Hart, 124, 153
Engel v. *Vitale*, 408
Equal Justice for All, 344
equality, 126, 127, 147, 167, 178: formal opportunity vs. substantive results, 93, 150, 234–57 (*see also* affirmative action; discrimination)
Everson v. *Board of Education*, 434
evidence: emanating from the accused vs. real, 53–56; historical/adjudicative facts vs. legislative/social facts, 208–21, 343; participant surveillance, 55
exclusionary rule, 21, 36, 50–57, 58, 64, 100, 112, 209, 210, 211, 212